Encyclopedia of Interest Groups and Lobbyists in the United States

Volume One

Encyclopedia of
INTEREST GROUPS
★ ★ ★ ★ ★ and ★ ★ ★ ★ ★
LOBBYISTS
in the United States

Volume One

IMMANUEL NESS
Brooklyn College, City University of New York

S SHARPE REFERENCE
an imprint of M.E. Sharpe, Inc.

SHARPE REFERENCE

Sharpe Reference is an imprint of M.E. Sharpe INC.

M.E. Sharpe INC.
80 Business Park Drive
Armonk, NY 10504

© 2000 by M.E. Sharpe INC.

All rights reserved.

No part of this publication may be reproduced, stored in a retrieval system or transmitted in any form or by any means, electronic, mechanical, photocopying, recording, or otherwise, without the prior permission of the copyright holders.

Library of Congress Cataloging-in-Publication Data

Ness, Immanuel
Encyclopedia of interest groups and lobbyists in the United States / Immanuel Ness
p. cm.
Includes bibliographical references and index.
Summary: Provides information about a variety of organizations, arranged alphabetically within such groupings as Agriculture, Environment, Health and Medical, Labor, and Political, Religious and Ideological.
ISBN 0-7656-8022-X (set : alk. paper)
1. Pressure groups—United States—Encyclopedias. 2. Lobbyists—United States—Encyclopedias. [1. Pressure groups—Encyclopedias. 2. Lobbyists—Encyclopedias.] I. Title.
JK1118.N47 2000
324'.4'097303—dc21
99-048849

Printed and bound in the United States of America

The paper used in this publication meets the minimum requirements of American National Standard for Information Sciences—Permanence of Paper for Printed Library Materials
ANSI Z 39.48.1984.

BM (c) 10 9 8 7 6 5 4 3 2 1

Vice President and Director of Sharpe Reference: Evelyn M. Fazio
Vice President and Production Director: Carmen P. Chetti
Senior Reference Editor: Andrew Gyory
Senior Production Editor: Angela Piliouras
Editorial Coordinator: Aud Thiessen
Editorial Assistant: Esther Clark
Fact Checker: Jeff Jenson
In-house Typesetter: W. Bryan Lammers

CONTENTS

Contributors xi
Abbreviations and Acronyms xiii
Introduction xvii

VOLUME ONE

PART I. INTEREST GROUPS

Section 1. Banking, Finance, Insurance, and Real Estate

Introduction 3
American Bankers Association 8
America's Community Bankers 12
American Council of Life Insurance 15
American Financial Services Association 18
American Institute of Certified
    Public Accountants 21
Credit Union National Association 24
Independent Community Bankers
    of America 27
Independent Insurance Agents of America ... 30
Investment Company Institute 33
Mortgage Bankers Association of America 36
National Association of Independent
    Insurers 39
National Association of Insurance
    Commissioners 42
National Association of Life Underwriters 45
National Association of Professional
    Insurance Agents 49
National Association of Realtors 52
National Venture Capital Association 55
Securities Industry Association 58

Section 2. Service, Trade, and Professional

Introduction 62
American Bar Association 67
American Gaming Association 70
American Hotel and Motel Association 73
American Library Association 75
American Association of Advertising
    Agencies 78
Association of Trial Lawyers of America 80
Food Marketing Institute 83
Fraternal Order of Police 86
National Association of Convenience
    Stores 89
National Association of Retired Federal
    Employees 92
National Association of Social Workers 95
National Automobile Dealers Association...... 99
National Beer Wholesalers Association 102
National Federation of Independent
    Business 105
National Funeral Directors Association 108
National Restaurant Association 111
Petroleum Marketers Association
    of America 114
United States Chamber of Commerce 117

Section 3. Media, Entertainment, and Information

Introduction 120
Accuracy in Media 125
American Council on Education 127
Association of American Publishers 130

Fairness and Accuracy in Reporting 133
Magazine Publishers of America 135
Motion Picture Association of America 138
National Association of Broadcasters 142
National Cable Television Association 146
Newspaper Association of America 150
Recording Industry Association of
 America 153
Software and Information Industry
 Association 157

Section 4. Health and Medical

Introduction 159
American Academy of Ophthalmology 164
American Cancer Society 167
American Chiropractic Association 169
American College of Emergency
 Physicians 172
American Dietetic Association 175
American Federation for AIDS Research 178
American Healthcare Association 181
American Heart Association 184
American Hospital Association 186
American Medical Association 189
American Nurses Association 193
American Occupational Therapy
 Association 196
American Psychiatric Association................... 199
American Society of Anesthesiologists 202
Blue Cross and Blue Shield Association........ 205

Section 5. Agriculture

Introduction 209
American Farm Bureau Federation 215
American Agriculture Movement 218
American Meat Institute 220
American Sugarbeet Growers Association ... 223
International Dairy Foods Association 226
National Association of Wheat Growers....... 229
National Cattlemen's Beef Association 231
National Chicken Council 234
National Cotton Council of America 237
National Council of Farmer Cooperatives 240
National Farmers Organization 242
National Farmers Union 244
National Grange 247
National Pork Producers Council 249

Organic Trade Association 252
United Egg Association 254

Section 6. Environment

Introduction 256
Environmental Defense Fund 262
Friends of the Earth 265
Greenpeace 269
Izaak Walton League 272
League of Conservation Voters 275
National Audubon Society 278
National Wildlife Federation........................... 281
Rainforest Action Network 284
Sierra Club 287
Wise Use Movement 291

Section 7. Industry, Construction, and Transport

Introduction 294
Aerospace Industries Association 298
Air Transport Association 300
American Forest and Paper Association 304
American Furniture Manufacturers
 Association 307
American Textile Manufacturers Institute 309
American Trucking Associations 312
Associated Builders and Contractors 315
Business Roundtable 318
Chemical Manufacturers Association............ 321
Distilled Spirits Council of the
 United States 323
Edison Electric Institute 326
National Association of Home Builders 329
National Association of Manufacturers 332
National Mining Association 335
Nuclear Energy Institute 338
Pharmaceutical Research and
 Manufacturers of America 341
Printing Industries of America 343
Semiconductor Industry Association 346
Technology Network....................................... 348

VOLUME TWO

Section 8. Labor

Introduction 350
Airline Pilots Association 356

American Federation of Labor–Congress
of Industrial Organizations 359
American Federation of State, County, and
Municipal Employees 363
American Federation of Teachers 366
American Postal Workers Union 369
Communications Workers of America 372
Hotel Employees and Restaurant
Employees International Union 375
International Association of
Fire Fighters 378
International Association of Machinists and
Aerospace Workers 381
International Brotherhood of
Electrical Workers 384
International Brotherhood of
Teamsters 387
International Union of
Operating Engineers 390
Laborers' International Union of
North America 393
National Education Association 396
Seafarers International Union of
North America 399
Service Employees International
Union 401
Transport Workers Union of America 404
Union of Needletrades, Industrial,
and Textile Employees 407
United Automobile Workers 410
United Food and Commercial
Workers International Union 413
United Steelworkers of America 416
United Transportation Union 419

Section 9. Civil and Human Rights

Introduction 422
ACORN (Association of Community
Organizations for Reform Now) 430
American Civil Liberties Union 433
Anti-Defamation League 435
Freedom House 438
Human Rights Watch 441
League of Women Voters of the United
States 444
Legal Services Corporation 447
National Coalition for the Homeless 450
National Lawyers Guild 452

Section 10. Political, Religious, and Ideological

Introduction 454
American Conservative Union 460
American Enterprise Institute 463
Americans for Democratic Action 466
Americans for Tax Reform 469
Brookings Institution 472
Cato Institute 475
Center for Public Integrity 477
Center for Responsive Politics 479
Christian Coalition 481
Citizens for a Sound Economy 483
Common Cause 485
Economic Policy Institute 487
Heritage Foundation 490
Hudson Institute 492
John Birch Society 494
National Council of the Churches
of Christ 496
National Taxpayers Union 498
Public Citizen 500
United States Catholic Conference 502
U.S. Public Interest Research Group 504

Section 11. Single Issue

Introduction 506
Americans United for the Separation of
Church and State 513
Citizens Flag Alliance 516
Council for a Livable World 518
Handgun Control, Inc. 521
Mothers Against Drunk Driving 524
National Abortion and Reproductive
Rights Action League 526
National Committee to Preserve
Social Security and Medicare 529
National Rifle Association 532
National Right to Life Committee 536
People for the Ethical Treatment
of Animals 539
Planned Parenthood Federation
of America 542
Union of Concerned Scientists 545
U.S. English 547
U.S. Term Limits 550
Zero Population Growth 553

Section 12. Identity

Introduction 555
American Association of Retired Persons 561
American Indian Movement 564
American Legion 567
Congress of Racial Equality 569
Emily's List 572
Human Rights Campaign 575
National Association for the Advancement
    of Colored People 578
National Gay and Lesbian Task Force 581
National Organization for Women 583

Section 13. Foreign

Introduction 586
China 591
Cuban Exiles 594
European Union 597
Israel 600
Japan 603
Mexico 606
Nigeria 609
Russia 611
Taiwan 614
Turkey 616

PART II. POLITICAL ACTION COMMITTEES AND LOBBYISTS: TABLES AND FIGURES

Section 1. Political Action Committees

Introduction 621
Top Agriculture PACs 627
Top Livestock/Poultry PACs 628
Top Dairy PACs 629
Top Tobacco PACs 629
Top Forestry and Paper PACs 629
Top Business PACs 630
Top Food and Beverage PACs 631
Top Retail PACs 632
Top Miscellaneous Services PACs 632
Top Gambling/Recreation/Tourism
    PACs 632
Top Miscellaneous Business PACs 633
Top Construction PACs 633
Top Building Equipment/Materials
    PACs 634

Top Engineering/Architecture PACs 635
Top Contractors and Builders PACs 635
Top Defense PACs 636
Top Electronics/Communications PACs 638
Top Electronic/Computer
    Manufacturing PACs 639
Top Telephone PACs 639
Top TV/Music/Movies PACs 639
Top Telecommunications PACs 640
Top Printing and Publishing PACs 640
Top Energy/Resource PACs 641
Top Oil and Gas PACs 643
Top Mining PACs 644
Top Electric Utility PACs 645
Top Nuclear/Misc. Energy PACs 645
Top Waste Management/Environmental
    Service PACs 645
Top Finance, Insurance, and
    Real Estate PACs 646
Top Commercial Bank PACs 647
Top Savings and Loan/
    Credit Union PACs 648
Top Finance/Credit Company PACs 649
Top Security and Investment PACs 650
Top Insurance PACs 651
Top Accounting PACs 652
Top Real Estate PACs 652
Top Health PACs 653
Top Health Professional PACs 655
Top Hospital/Nursing Home PACs 656
Top Pharmaceutical and Health Product
    PACs 656
Top Democratic/Liberal PACs 657
Top Republican/Conservative PACs 658
Top Women's Issue PACs 659
Top Miscellaneous Human Rights/Identity
    Groups PACs 660
Top Law Firm PACs 661
Top Lobbyist Firm PACs 661
Top Manufacturing PACs 662
Top Chemical Manufacturing PACs 663
Top Steel PACs 663
Top Textile PACs 664
Top Miscellaneous Manufacturing PACs 664
Top Single-Issue PACs 665
Top Pro-Israel PACs 666
Top Environment PACs 667
Top Gun and Gun Control PACs 667
Top Pro-Choice and Pro-Life PACs 667

Top Miscellaneous Single-Issue
    PACs 667
Top Transport PACs 668
Top Air Transport PACs 669
Top Automobile PACs 670
Top Trucking PACs 670
Top Railroad PACs 670
Top Sea Transport PACs 670
Top Union PACs 671
Top Industrial Union PACs 672
Top Transport Union PACs 673
Top Building Trade Union PACs 674
Top Public Sector Union PACs 674
Top Miscellaneous Union PACs 675
Top Soft-Money Donors, 1997-98
    Election Cycle 676

Section 2. Lobbyists

Introduction 678
Top Banking, Security, and Investment
    Companies Lobbying Expenditures 684
Top Business Associations Lobbying
    Expenditures 685
Top Computer Companies Lobbying
    Expenditures 686
Top Entertainment/Media Institutions
    Lobbying Expenditures 687
Top Government Agencies Lobbying
    Expenditures 688
Top Health Professional Associations
    Lobbying Expenditures 688
Top Insurance Companies Lobbying
    Expenditures 689
Top Oil and Gas Companies Lobbying
    Expenditures 690
Top Pharmaceutical/Health Product
    Companies Lobbying Expenditures 691
Top Single Issue/Identity Groups
    Lobbying Expenditures 692
Top Tobacco Companies Lobbying
    Expenditures 693
Top Corporations/Associations Lobbying
    Expenditures 694
Top Industries—Lobbying
    Expenditures 697
Top Telephone/Utilities Lobbying
    Expenditures 699
Top Transportation Companies
    Lobbying Expenditures 700
Top Lobbying Firms 701
Top Clients of Top Lobbying
    Firms 703

Contact Information 705

Glossary 719

Bibliography 725

Index 739

CONTRIBUTORS

Banking, Finance, Insurance, and Real Estate
Loree Bykerk, University of Nebraska, Omaha

Service, Trade, and Professional
Daniel Ness, Columbia University
Miriam Jiménez-Hernández

Media, Entertainment, and Information
Julie M. Walsh, St. Joseph's College, New York

Health and Medical
Immanuel Ness, Brooklyn College
James Ciment, New School University

Agriculture
Andrew D. McNitt, Eastern Illinois University
Melinda Mueller, Eastern Illinois University
James Seroka, Auburn University

Environment
Frank Codispoti, Austin State University

Industry, Construction, and Transport
James Ciment, New School University
Vivian Wagner

Labor
Immanuel Ness, Brooklyn College
James Ciment, New School University

Civil and Human Rights
Brian Smentkowski, Southwest Missouri State University
Kathryn Beth Adkins, Southwest Missouri State University
Theresa Haug, Southwest Missouri State University

Political, Religious, and Ideological
Raymond B. Wrabley, Jr., University of Pittsburgh, at Johnstown

Single Issue
Glenn Daigon

Identity
Michael Levy, Southwest Missouri State University

Foreign
Allyson Ford, Columbia University

Political Action Committees
Gary Mucciaroni, Temple University

Lobbyists
Gary Mucciaroni, Temple University

ABBREVIATIONS AND ACRONYMS

AAAA	American Association of Advertising Agencies
AAM	American Agriculture Movement
AAOP	American Academy of Ophthalmology
AAP	Association of American Publishers
AARP	American Association of Retired Persons
ABA	American Bankers Association
ABC	American Builders and Contractors; see America's Community Bankers
ACA	American Chiropractic Association
ACE	American Council on Education
ACEP	American College of Emergency Physicians
ACLI	American Council of Life Insurance
ACS	American Cancer Society
ACU	American Conservative Union
ADA	Americans for Democratic Action; American Dietetic Association
AEI	American Enterprise Institute
AF&PA	American Forest and Paper Association
AFCA	American Financial Services Association
AFL-CIO	American Federation of Labor—Congress of Industrial Organizations
AFMA	American Furniture Manufacturers Association
AFSCME	American Federation of State, County, and Municipal Employees
AFT	American Federation of Teachers
AGA	American Gaming Association
AHA	American Heart Association; American Hospital Association
AHCA	American Healthcare Association
AHMA	American Hotel and Motel Association
AIA	Aerospace Industries Association
AICPA	American Institute of Certified Public Accountants
AIM	Accuracy in Media; American Indian Movement
ALPA	Airline Pilots Association
AMA	American Medical Association
AmFAR	American Federation for AIDS Research
AMI	American Meat Institute
ANA	American Nurses Association
AOTA	American Occupational Therapy Association
APA	American Psychiatric Association
API	American Petroleum Institute
APWU	American Postal Workers Union
ASA	American Society of Anesthesiologists
ASGA	American Sugarbeet Growers Association
ATA	Air Transport Association; American Trucking Associations
ATMI	American Textile Manufacturers Institute
ATR	Americans for Tax Reform
AU	Americans United for Separation of Church and State
BCBSA	Blue Cross and Blue Shield Association

xiii

CFA	Citizens Flag Alliance	IMF	International Monetary Fund
CLW	Council for a Livable World	IRA	Individual Retirement Accounts
CMA	Chemical Manufacturers Association	IUOE	International Union of Operating Engineers
CORE	Congress of Racial Equality		
CPA	Certified Public Accountant	JBS	John Birch Society
CPI	Center for Public Integrity	LCW	League of Conservation Voters
CPR	Center for Responsive Politics	LIUNA	Laborers' International Union of North America
CSE	Citizens for a Sound Economy		
CUNA	Credit Union National Association	MADD	Mothers Against Drunk Driving
CWA	Communications Workers of America	MBAA	Mortgage Bankers Association of America
DISCUS	Distilled Spirits Council of the United States	MPA	Magazine Publishers of America
		MPAA	Motion Picture Association of America
DoD	Department of Defense		
DRI	Dietary Reference Intakes	NAA	Newspaper Association of America
EDF	Environmental Defense Fund	NAACP	National Association for the Advancement of Colored People
EEI	Edison Electric Institute		
EPA	Environmental Protection Agency	NAB	National Association of Broadcasters
EPI	Economic Policy Institute	NAFTA	North American Free Trade Agreement
FAIR	Fairness and Accuracy in Reporting		
FCC	Federal Communications Commission	NAHB	National Association of Home Builders
FDA	Food and Drug Administration	NAIC	National Association of Insurance Commissioners
FTC	Federal Trade Commission		
HCFA	Healthcare Financing Administration	NAII	National Association of Independent Insurers
HCI	Handgun Control, Inc.		
HERE	Hotel Employees and Restaurant Employees International Union	NALU	National Association of Life Underwriters
HHS	Department of Health and Human Services	NAM	National Association of Manufacturers
		NAPIA	National Association of Professional Insurance Agents
HIAA	Health Insurance Association of America		
		NAR	National Association of Realtors
HMO	Health maintenance organization	NARAL	National Abortion and Reproduction Action League
HRC	Human Rights Campaign		
IAFF	International Association of Fire Fighters	NAWG	National Association of Wheat Growers
IAMAW	International Association of Machinists and Aerospace Workers	NCBA	National Cattlemen's Beef Association
IBEW	International Brotherhood of Electrical Workers	NCC	National Council of Churches of Christ; National Chicken Council (formerly National Broiler Council)
IBT	International Brotherhood of Teamsters		
ICBA	Independent Community Bankers of America	NCCA	National Cotton Council of America
		NCFC	National Council of Farmer Cooperatives
ICI	Investment Company Institute		
IDFA	International Dairy Foods Association	NCPSSM	National Committee to Preserve Social Security and Medicare
IIAA	Independent Insurance Agents of America	NCTA	National Cable Television Association
		NEA	National Education Association

ABBREVIATIONS AND ACRONYMS

NEH	National Endowment for the Humanities	SEIU	Service Employees International Union
NEI	Nuclear Energy Institute	SIA	Semiconductor Industry of America; Securities Industry Association
NFO	National Farmers Organization		
NFU	National Farmers Union	SIIA	Software and Information Industry Association
NGLTF	National Gay and Lesbian Task Force		
		SIU	Seafarers International Union of North America
NLRA	National Labor Relations Act		
NMA	National Mining Association	TechNet	Technology Network
NOW	National Organization for Women	TI	Tobacco Institute
NPPC	National Pork Producers Council	TWUA	Transport Workers Union of America
NRA	National Rifle Association		
NRLC	National Right to Life Committee	UAW	United Automobile, Aerospace, and Agricultural Implement Workers of America
NTU	National Taxpayers Union		
NVCA	National Venture Capital Association		
		UCS	Union of Concern Scientists
OCC	Office of the Controller of the Currency	UEA	United Egg Association
		UFCW	United Food and Commercial Workers Union
OTA	Organic Trade Association		
PAC	Political Action Committee	UNITE	Union of Needletrades, Industrial, and Textile Employees
PETA	People for the Ethnical Treatment of Animals		
		US PIRG	U.S. Public Interest Research Group
PhRMA	Pharmaceutical Research and Manufacturers of America		
		USCC	United States Catholic Conference
PIA	Printing Industries of America		
PMA	Petroleum Marketers Association	USDA	United States Department of Agriculture
PPFA	Planned Parenthood Federation of America		
		USTL	US Term Limits
PPO	Preferred Provider Organization	USWA	United Steelworkers of America
RDA	Recommended Dietary Allowances	UTU	United Transportation Union
RIAA	Recording Industry Association of America	WIPO	World Intellectual Property Organization
SEC	Securities and Exchange Commission	WTO	World Trade Organization
		ZPG	Zero Population Growth

INTRODUCTION

Interest groups and lobbyists play a central role in the American political system. With thousands of staffers and hundreds of millions of dollars at their command, these groups and individuals influence elections, shape government agendas, and help draft legislation. Some interest groups represent huge industries or people in a specific field or business; others are labor unions representing workers in particular trades. Still other interest groups are devoted to a single issue or cause. Interest groups represent both small and large constituencies and help to educate the public on many issues.

While interest groups engage in numerous, diverse activities—from public relations to providing industry databases for members—their political functions essentially include one or both of the following: donating money to candidates' campaigns, and hiring lobbyists to influence the course of legislation of concern to the members of the interest group. Lobbyists, who are either on the payroll of a given interest group or who work for a professional lobbying firm, then try to educate lawmakers to the views of the interest group the lobbyists represent. Often, lobbyists' efforts go beyond education to applying pressure on legislators through public relations and advertising campaigns, such as the (in)famous "Harry and Louise" ads that sunk President Bill Clinton's universal healthcare insurance plan in 1994. Whatever their many functions, interest groups have become so ubiquitous that it is impossible to understand modern American politics without understanding the enormous power these groups wield in shaping the national political debate.

The phenomenon of interest group politics is nothing new. In the 1830s, the great French political theorist Alexis de Tocqueville noted the propensity of Americans to form associations to effect social, political, and economic change. Such groups included abolitionists, who fought to end slavery, as well as other groups who sought to outlaw dueling, capital punishment, and the consumption of alcohol. The growth of the federal government in the twentieth century, however, sparked the rise of modern, Washington-based interest groups. Progressive Era legislation in the early 1900s and the New Deal in the 1930s created new regulatory agencies that expanded the federal bureaucracy and spurred development of business-oriented interest groups. The ferment of the 1960s led to broader social programs and triggered the formation of numerous groups dedicated to environmental, civil rights, humanitarian, educational, and economic goals. These various groups supported candidates, advocated specific laws and regulations, and pressured members of Congress and government officials to pass them.

As interest groups exerted more influence, Congress attempted to reel them in by enacting legislation limiting the size of individual contributions to candidates. Ironically, campaign reforms passed in the wake of the Watergate scandal actually helped to enhance their power. Legislation banning large, direct contributions from individuals to candidates and office holders in the 1970s prodded interest groups to establish political action committees (PACs). These PACs were able to pool donations by individuals and present them to candidates as one huge contribution, thereby enhancing the influence of the donors—and the PACs themselves.

Since the 1970s, PAC money from interest groups has played an increasingly important role in congressional elections. As the supply of campaign money has risen so has the demand. The exploding costs of running for office—and especially of placing political advertisements on television—have made many candidates reliant on PAC and interest-group support. Over the past quarter-century, the role of interest groups and money, now exponentially enhanced by "soft-money" loopholes, has stirred controversy. Soft money is money contributed to political parties—rather than directly to candidates—for partisan or issue advocacy. By focusing on specific issues supported by a candidate, advertisements paid for by soft money can be extremely influential, and there are no limits on soft-money contributions. Poll after poll has shown that a majority of Americans want fundamental campaign reform to rein in the power of interest groups over elections and the legislative process. Conversely, congressional resistance to such legislation has revealed the dependency of many office holders on interest groups and their money.

CHALLENGES TO AMERICAN DEMOCRACY

The tight relationship between members of Congress and interest groups, which shower them with hundreds of millions of dollars and lobby them for specific legislation, has bred cynicism among the electorate and cast doubt on the credibility of the American political process. The nation's democratic system—rooted in the principle of one person, one vote—becomes muddied when powerful interest groups that represent a narrow issue, a single profession, or a small minority of the people play a decisive role in electing candidates and influencing policy. Only the very wealthy can afford to make substantial special-interest contributions, and these contributions are often critical in helping candidates win office.

The all-consuming influence of special-interest money has a secondary effect on elections and the political process: it limits the pool of congressional candidates by dissuading qualified people who cannot raise huge funds from running for office. Consequently, the very wealthy, who can dip into their personal fortunes, often dominate political campaigns and force their opponents to rely on support from special interests. Because money is so central, both the Republican and Democratic parties have sought to recruit wealthy individuals capable of financing their own races. The influence of money can also jeopardize the job security of independent-minded government officials who challenge the interests of big contributors. Members of Congress who oppose the demands of powerful donors on the basis of principle or the best interests of the majority of Americans who cannot contribute large sums of money sometimes face strong challenges from opponents who are backed by the very contributors seeking to protect special privileges. Thus, many legislators vote in support of the established political and economic interests of their contributors.

Advocates of unlimited contributions to politicians from interest groups and PACs argue that restricting such donations would violate the First Amendment to the United States Constitution. In 1976, the Supreme Court ruled in *Buckley v. Valeo* that financial contributions to political campaigns were a form of freedom of speech and thus constitutionally protected. Some limits could be imposed on contributions from donors, but no limits could be placed on the amount of money candidates could spend on their own campaigns. This ruling imposed major obstacles to efforts to regulate spending and, despite growing public outrage, Congress has failed to pass significant campaign finance reform.

Both the Supreme Court decision and the ongoing resistance from Congress to pass meaningful reform have created a climate where money flows freely, greasing the political process. In recent years this flow of money has become a flood. During the 1996 elections, contributions to congressional races reached nearly $800 million, and spending for federal campaigns—including the presidential race—topped $2.1 billion, a sum expected to double in the early twenty-first century.

According to the Center for Responsive Politics, a watchdog agency that tracks political spending (and is, in effect, an interest group itself), the average cost of a seat in the House of Representatives in 1996 was $674,000. A Senate seat cost $4.7 million. Much of this massive amount of money came from a tiny sliver of the American people. The Center for Responsive Politics found that less than .1 percent of Americans contributed 40 percent of all money raised in the 1996 congressional elections.

Soft money continues to play a major role in political campaigns. Under *Buckley v. Valeo*, the Supreme Court ruled that no restrictions could be placed on soft money intended for issue advertisements. Thus, while the Federal Election Commission (FEC) closely monitors and restricts campaign contributions to specific campaigns, it does not limit the amount of money that individuals and special-interest groups can contribute to parties for issue advertisements. Parties frequently use soft money to pay for advertisements criticizing opponents and issues associated with them, thereby circumventing the rigorous FEC regulations on direct contributions to candidates. This gives interest groups and their PACs enormous influence on a wide range of issues, from gun ownership and tobacco price supports to school vouchers and offshore oil drilling, to name a few. In an October 18, 1999, article in the *Nation*, journalist Robert Dreyfuss reported that soft-money contributions tripled from $86 million in 1992 to $262 million in 1996 and are expected to rise to between $500 million and $750 million in 2000.

INFLUENCE ON POLICY

Although interest groups and rich contributors cannot dictate how members of Congress will vote, their large donations provide them access to people in office and the opportunity to directly present their positions. In many cases, this access—along with the implicit threat of withdrawing future support—translates into votes. Powerful interest groups and affluent contributors can thus shape public policy in ways that favor big business, large corporations, and wealthier Americans. To critics of the existing system—formerly on the political left, but of late increasingly mainstream—the results are plain to see: the United States has greater income inequality, higher poverty rates, and more persons without adequate healthcare than other industrialized countries where campaigns cost far less. These critics argue that special-interest groups have kept the minimum wage down, trimmed social programs, and prevented adequate regulation of business activities. In the 1990s, they claim, interest groups representing powerful insurance companies helped kill the Clinton administration's plans for universal healthcare coverage. Thus, through contributions and special interest groups, wealthy Americans wield a disproportionate share of power in Washington, D.C., and enjoy access denied to many poor and working-class Americans.

Not all interest groups represent the rich, of course. Many focus on specific issues that have little do with economics. If well-organized and efficiently operated, they too can shape public policy, often against the interests of a majority of a politician's constituents. On the issue of gun control, for example, polls have consistently shown Americans in favor of certain measures, but gunowners' groups have lobbied Congress to prevent passage of meaningful legislation. By threatening to remove financial support, interest groups can sway politicians and influence policy.

Whatever criticisms Americans may level at the role interest groups play in the political process, these groups do perform important and beneficial services. Many of the groups examined in this encyclopedia offer research and data-collection facilities to their member companies, allowing them to share trade information and new business strategies. In many cases, interest groups set and, to a degree, enforce industry standards. Sometimes this is done to thwart potentially more stringent government regulations as, for example, was the case with the movie rating system established by the Motion Picture Association of America.

Trade associations and other interest groups can also have a positive effect on the legislative and regulatory process. They act as a collective voice for a multitude of companies in a given industry—making the needs of that industry clearer to lawmakers and administrators—and can educate both legislative and executive branch officials on the needs of their trades and businesses. This can be a crucial function, particularly for newer industries that are largely unknown or older industries undergoing technological transformation. Indeed, as business and industry become more complex, trade associations and other interest groups become a critical source of information for government officials. In some cases, members of interest groups have even been used to draw up legislation involving highly technical issues. Of course, this often means that the legislation is written in such a way that favors one particular industry over another, or over the interests of the environment or the public at large.

Defenders of interest groups argue that rather than posing a threat to democracy such groups actually fulfill some of America's earliest and most enduring political ideals. In *Federalist Paper Number 10*, written in 1787–88 to promote ratification of the Constitution, James Madison argued that the diversity of interests in the new republic would prove the best defense against tyranny. Since no single interest group would be large or powerful enough to achieve a governing majority on its own, compromise among groups would be inevitable and vital, thereby assuring a multiplicity of voices in government. And indeed, as a glance at this encyclopedia's table of contents indicates, there is a multiplicity of voices among the many interest groups in Washington, D.C., today. Labor unions, environmental groups, civil and human rights organizations, single-issue proponents, even foreign governments—all vie for the ear of legislators and all compete to place their own stamp on new laws, policies, and regulations. In the final analysis, of course, it would be naïve to think that all voices are heard equally in the nation's capital. Business and industry groups, by the sheer number of lobbyists employed, campaign funds contributed, and influence exerted, outstrip all other interest groups combined, with the possible exception of organized labor. Interest groups and lobbyists of all persuasions will likely shape the American political system for years to come.

HOW TO USE THIS ENCYCLOPEDIA

The *Encyclopedia of Interest Groups and Lobbyists in the United States* is divided into two parts. Part I includes entries on 197 specific interest groups. These interest groups are divided into 13 sections: 1) Banking, Finance, Insurance, and Real Estate; 2) Service, Trade, and Professional; 3) Media, Entertainment, and Information; 4) Health and Medical; 5) Agriculture; 6) Environment; 7) Industry, Construction, and Transport; 8) Labor; 9) Civil and Human Rights; 10) Political, Religious, and Ideological; 11) Single Issue; 12) Identity; and 13) Foreign. Every section begins with an introductory essay outlining general themes and issues.

Entries in each section of Part I are listed alphabetically. Each entry itself is divided into four subsections: an introduction, which describes the interest group as it exists today; history, which explains the group's origins and development; activities: current and future, which describes the group's present and prospective legislative and political agenda; and financial facts, which covers the interest group's overall expenses and political donations. Many entries for organizations that contribute to political campaigns include graphs that trace those donations over several recent election cycles.

Part II of the encyclopedia consists largely of tables and figures. These tables and figures are divided into two sections. Section 1 covers donations for 1997 and 1998 from political action committees representing corporations, trade associations, unions, and other interest groups. Section 2 covers lobbying expenses of all of these groups, along with other firms and their clients. All tables are organized by descending order of donated money or lobbying expenses, and both sections begin with introductory essays highlighting critical issues.

The encyclopedia also contains ancillary materials. These include contact information for every organization listed in Part I (name, address, phone number, and, where available, fax number and web site); a list of acronyms and abbreviations; a glossary of terms; a bibliography of books and articles devoted to lobbying and political donations generally, as well as materials on specific interest groups and industries; and an index.

The goal of this encyclopedia is to provide readers with vital information on all the major interest groups and lobbyists active in the United States today. This material will give readers a fuller understanding of the many organizations shaping public policy and the electoral system—organizations that often escape public scrutiny. By understanding the origins of these various groups and recognizing their impact on the political process, citizens will better comprehend the forces influencing federal legislation, the functions of our government, and American life today.

PART I
INTEREST GROUPS

SECTION ONE
BANKING, FINANCE, INSURANCE, AND REAL ESTATE

The interests of banking, finance, insurance, and real estate organizations affect virtually every aspect of today's material existence. Whether you are born into wealth or poverty, whether you experience upward or downward mobility, your career options, the taxes you pay, your housing, your workplace, the car you drive, how you invest, the retirement you experience, and the estate you leave all come within the influence of these organizations. Although the American Bankers Association, for example, is not an everyday term in most households, the resources it and other groups in this sector are able to wield make them politically important. Members of these organizations have the same professional and economic interests. All of the organizations in this sector are resource rich. The smallest of their budgets is $4 million a year. Although money is not everything, it is a flexible resource that allows an organization to buy at least some of what it may not have otherwise—for example, a skilled lobbyist, if none of its members has a relationship with an important member of Congress.

The current-issue agenda of groups in this sector is a long one, but financial services restructuring is clearly at the top of the list. Major changes have already taken place over the past two decades, but pending legislation has the potential to foster more dramatic, rapid alterations in how Americans save, spend, borrow, invest, insure, and conduct other financial transactions.

Finance, insurance, and real estate interest groups use all the lobbying tactics known to scholars and observers. They are strongest in direct types of lobbying activities, where their lobbyists and members work directly with legislative and executive decision makers and their staffs. Because of the positions these groups occupy in the economy, their expertise, input, and cooperation are critical to successful policy-making. While these groups use grassroots techniques, they typically interact with their members and employees rather than with the public. They do, however, use advertising and the mass media to bolster their public standing.

These organizations focus on all three branches of government at both the national and state levels. The focus of this encyclopedia is at the national level, but a careful student must also be aware of state and local policy decisions on many of these issues.

AREAS OF INTEREST

Finance, insurance, and real estate interests have been influential in American politics since before the nation's founding. Thomas Jefferson warned that banks are more dangerous than standing armies, while Alexander Hamilton promoted cooperation with financial interests. The debate has continued. In modern times, the health of this sector has been regarded as critical to a sound economy and political stability. Instability, scandal, or failures have led to governmental efforts to impose reforms in order to restore political order, foster prosperity, protect consumers, and promote the public interest.

Individualism and materialism remain powerful forces at the end of the twentieth century. Americans, to borrow a phrase from historian Richard Hofstadter, are all "expectant capitalists"—demonstrating a faith in the continued expansion of prosperity that is almost utopian. The generation that remembers the Great Depression is no longer influential. Today's hero is the billionaire who invents a new technology and uses his wealth for mansions around the world, or the college student who makes millions trading stocks on the Internet on a daily basis and retires at age 19 to play at her computer.

The economic context at the turn of the century assumes continued growth, restrained inflation, and continuing development of new technologies. Recent successes persuade some that the old law that what goes up must come down no longer applies. Low unemployment rates bring more goods within the reach of the upwardly mobile; thus poverty is regarded as a matter of personal responsibility. There is widespread faith in the outcomes of competition and the allocation of a free-market economy. Any cloud on the horizon takes the shape of the pending retirement of baby boomers. There is little attention to wages lagging behind while profits are soaring; any mention of extraordinarily high executive salaries as compared with average wages is quickly labeled "class warfare."

The late 1990s political context in which finance, insurance, and real estate interests operate has been very nearly ideal for them. Most voices support free trade and praise democracy combined with capitalism as the successful model for the entire world. The collapse of the former Soviet Union is openly used to illustrate that higher powers do indeed smile on the American model.

Few seriously question whether the rules of the game are fair; the focus is on the successful players who are vocal and seem to be larger than life. The possibility of redistributing wealth to those who have fallen out of the capitalist competition is not even a consideration. The current focus is on which subsector can claim a larger share of an expanding pie; government scurries to catch up with changes already made by specific industries but faces barriers thrown up by their refusal to compromise or be harnessed.

TYPES OF ORGANIZATIONS

Most members of the interest groups in the finance, insurance, and real estate sector are institutions such as banks or insurance companies. Having institutions or organizations as members offers numerous benefits, including greater financial resources, expertise supported by corporate positions, and relative permanence. The main disadvantage is that the members tend to vary more in size than is possible among individuals. For example, Prudential Insurance and Woodmen Accident and Life may both be members of the American Council of Life Insurance, but they are so different in size as to have significantly different perspectives on many issues. In fact, the staff of the organization spends substantial resources interpreting issues in order to forge a consensus.

Some of the organizations in this sector only have individuals as members. Members of these groups have the same profession, such as accountants, insurance agents, or real estate agents. For these groups, difference in size is not an obstacle, but they may have different subspecialties, which create similar internal divisions. Individual membership groups do not have the same access to financial resources that financial, insurance, and real estate institutional groups enjoy, but neither do they have to penetrate organization structures to motivate individuals to be politically active.

Measured in financial terms, these organizations are very well supported. Not all of them release budget figures, but the average budget of the 12 organizations from which data are available is over $36 million annually. The range of budget figures is from the $4 million American Financial Services Association annual budget to the $145 million American Institute of Certified Public Accountants (AICPA).

Data on staff size are available from all the organizations profiled and are another valid measure of the resources that the group can bring to bear on issues. The average staff size of the 17 groups is 193 persons; the largest staff is employed by the AICPA, with 700, and the smallest is nine, employed by the National Venture Capital Association. Volunteer support from well-placed persons with institutional support and expertise is also of tremendous importance for some of these organizations. While it is difficult to develop data on volunteer resources, one of the groups noted an effort including over 1,000 volunteers from member companies, another an effort by 3,400 volunteers spending 21,000 hours.

CURRENT ISSUES

The most important legislative issue in finance, insurance, and real estate in the late twentieth century is the restructuring of the financial services industry, which includes commercial and savings banks, mutual funds, insurance companies, and the securities industry. This issue has been brought to the agenda by the aggressive efforts of banks to break down traditional barriers between types of financial service providers. The main target is the 1933 Glass-Steagall Act, which, in an effort to promote soundness and confidence, required separate financial underpinnings for banks, insurers, savings and loan associations, credit unions, and securities companies, with so-called fire walls between them. The intent was to prevent the sort of massive collapse of financial institutions that characterized the Great Depression. The merger of Citicorp with Travelers Group in April 1998 sparked government efforts to overturn Glass-Steagall, which were successful in October 1999.

Spurred by technological changes in moving funds to the best investment, the various businesses began over the last several decades to compete for market share. Large banks started offering insurance, selling securities and stocks, and providing other financial services. Their efforts have been facilitated by the Office of the Comptroller of the Currency (OCC), the courts, and Congress. Interests other than banks have not had similar regulatory support to counter competition and have been seeking legislation to give them the same opportunities. However, they are hampered by being unable to reach satisfactory compromises that would serve to protect all their interests.

Finance, insurance, and real estate interests are perennially attentive to the tax code and how their segment of capital is defined and treated. During the 1980s and 1990s, they weighed in on proposals to revise the treatment of capital gains, mortgage interest deductions, value of life insurance, employee benefits, benefits bought by the self-employed, and the deductibility of consumer interest.

Revision of bankruptcy laws is also on the legislative agenda for finance, insurance, and real estate groups. With more debtors filing for bankruptcy, lenders and creditor interests want to make it harder for debtors to write their debts off entirely. There is also competition among types of credit holders to obtain more favorable standing relative to repayment criteria.

A number of the consumer protection provisions passed in the 1960s and 1970s are under attack by these interest groups. Requirements for fuller information disclosure on interest rates, terms for saving and borrowing, and specified procedures for closing a real estate mortgage are attacked as cumbersome and confusing. Community reinvestment requirements imposed on banks, demanding that their lending patterns undergo scrutiny and meet standards of local stewardship, are also challenged as burdensome and antimarket.

Environmental laws governing liability for toxic and hazardous waste sites are on the legislative lists of real estate development interests. Their argument is that if liability could be limited legislatively, large areas that are now unused could become available for development. Proposals to reform America's healthcare system draw attention from insurance interests, as do vehicle and driving safety.

Although these interests generally portray themselves as favoring less government, in some areas they advocate on behalf of government protection. For example, they want to protect deposit insurance, federally subsidized insurance for crops, and federal support for mortgage lending. It has been accepted for two decades that major players in the industry are too big to be allowed to fail, so smaller players often voice these concerns and expect government support if necessary.

Regulatory relief has been a rallying cry for American business for more than two decades. However, the current focus on financial services restructuring makes clear that most businesses are comfortable with known relationships and are eager only to have their competitors' relationships altered. For example, insurers want expanded financial services functions to be structured as holding companies regulated by the Federal Reserve, whereas banks want them to be structured as subsidiaries, regulated by the U.S. Treasury and the OCC. Holding companies are entities that control subsidiaries but do not generally participate directly in their operations. This same issue displays how federal and state regulators compete to determine who will oversee insurance sold by banks.

Many issues relevant to these groups have already been acted upon by Congress. Most recently, the federal government provided protection against year 2000 liability lawsuits for businesses that made good faith efforts to resolve known computer problems.

Other major policy questions that concern these interests are on the agenda but unresolved. Funding the impending wave of baby boomer retirements calls for revamping Social Security and improving savings rates and pensions. The possibility of partial privatization of Social Security holds the promise of dramatic expansion of the pool of capital available to be managed by this business sector.

A number of increasingly important issues have the potential to affect these interests. All of these organizations and their members are increasingly reliant upon technology but are only beginning to deal with resulting client privacy concerns. Growing interest in selling their products and services via the Internet raises the issue of whether and how Internet commerce will be taxed. And finally, the efforts by these groups to compete in the global economy also require that they come to grips with demands and institutions outside the United States.

Although an increasing share of Americans hold equity investments, own real estate, and anticipate retiring in the next decade, public opinion does not appear to be very attentive to critical but complicated issues in this sector. A very positive climate of confidence, growth, and well-being characterizes the present era. Consumer questions tend to focus on automated teller machine charges, home equity loans, and the availability of credit cards. Troublesome questions about speculative financial instruments, the growth of conglomerates, and the increasing detachment of financial institutions from communities are seldom raised.

ACTIVITIES: CURRENT AND FUTURE

Lobbying by contributing to campaigns for federal office is the norm for organizations in this sector. Only the National Association of Insurance Commissioners has no political action committee (PAC). The other organizations have active PACs, as do many of their institutional members; there is evidence that their individual members are also active contributors. A scan of these PAC contributions from 1987 through 1998 reveals interesting patterns. Standing consistently head and shoulders above the rest is the National Association of Realtors PAC, with contributions ranging from $1.9 million to $3.1 million per election cycle. The American Bankers Association, the American Institute of Certified Public Accountants, and the National Association of Life Underwriters are also major contributors, with amounts over $1 million per election cycle. The American Financial Services Association and the Securities Industry Association are smaller PACs in this sector.

Data from the past decade also display interesting partisan activity because of the change from Democratic to Republican majorities in Congress. From 1987 through 1992, contributions leaned slightly toward Democratic recipients, with only two exceptions. The Investment Company Institute consistently was the most generous to Democratic candidates, giving approximately 80 percent of its contributions to them. On the other side, the National Association of Independent Insurers (NAII) gave most (about 80 percent) of its funds to Republicans.

In the 1993–1994 election cycle, before the Republicans gained a majority, contributions still leaned toward the Democrats, but their share narrowed noticeably. However, since the 1995–1996 election cycle, every one of these PACs has been squarely in the Republican column. And they are more generous to Republicans, even with their narrow majority, than they were previously to the Democrats. This reflects a perceived preference on the part of this sector for Republican Party principles and the ability of Republicans to persuade business interests to discontinue support for the opposition. The NAII continues to stand out as most partisan, now giving 95 percent of its total contributions to Republicans. More cautiously, the Mortgage Bankers Association of America calculates the numbers of Republicans and Democrats in Congress to determine how much to contribute to each party.

Effective lobbying requires much more active political influence than making campaign contributions. All of the organizations in the finance, insurance, and real estate sector have sufficient resources to monitor policy activity and access decision makers in order to present their case. Due to their expertise, they are frequently called upon to help craft legislation and present testimony; they also enjoy the support of loyal defenders on Capitol Hill. Every member of Congress receives telephone calls, letters, telegrams, and personal visits from his or her accountant, banker, broker, insurance agent, and realtor. Inviting members of important governmental committees and agencies to speak at organization meetings promotes familiarity and provides a forum for communication for key decision makers.

These organizations also wield the critical resources of data and expertise; they are able to claim the status of experts in their fields, so their arguments and presentations have a high level of validity. The few critics who question whether self-interest influences their arguments more than is healthy for the public interest tend not to have the same status in policy circles as industry lobbyists.

The activities and resources of these interest groups extend to lobbying the executive branch of government as well. Representatives are provided regular access through serving on agency advisory committees. This allows them to have input and knowledge of forthcoming regulations. Institutionalized access is provided by the Treasury Department, Internal Revenue Service, Federal Reserve, Securities and Exchange Commission, Home Loan Bank System, Department of Housing and Urban Development, Small Business Administration, and many other agencies.

The data and expertise wielded by these groups even help to shape the language of regulations, and their representatives are sometimes invited to negotiate the content. Their staffs give feedback to the agencies by means of commenting on proposed regulations and testifying at regulatory hearings. One organization has even sponsored a mass demonstration to influence the outcome of regulatory hearings. And if these methods do not succeed, they sue.

Lobbying the courts includes bringing test cases and filing *amicus curiae* (friend of the court) briefs. A prominent judicial strategy for these organizations, in response to losing some expensive class-action cases, is now more subtle. Their legal teams are trying to counter class action suits by persuading the courts to decertify the class (thereby depriving it of legal standing), limit redress to actual damages, and limit attorneys' fees.

These organizations also engage in efforts to lobby the public. Many provide consumer education through information brochures or web site service and product directories. Some groups sponsor educational programs for elementary and secondary students; others reach into higher education by funding fellowships for college professors and research through cooperating foundations. However, most of their educational focus is on their own organizations—these groups devote substantial resources to technical, managerial, and political advocacy training for their members.

For their own members, decision makers, and the attentive public, they promote their interests by developing a framework in which to explain their issues, set out their arguments in attractive ways, and communicate them persuasively. These associations craft appealing stories, buy advertising campaigns, and help their members do the same. All maintain regular contact with the media, provide articulate spokespersons for their points of view, and provide frequent press releases. They also sponsor the education of specialized journalists; for example, the American Bankers Association offers fellowships for financial reporters, and the Securities Industry Association sponsors sabbaticals for financial editors and correspondents.

Interest groups in the finance, insurance, and real estate sector generally do not organize beyond their own members, employees, and retirees. In fact, many are wary of the mixed public regard for insurance agents, bill collectors, tax accountants, and the like. However, these groups do organize formal grassroots networks, including training of grassroots managers, teaching employees how to write letters to their senators and representatives, and encouraging them to take part in campaigns. Their highest-profile grassroots efforts are their "fly ins," in which hundreds of members are flown to Washington to storm Capitol Hill.

LOREE BYKERK

Bibliography

Center for Responsive Politics web site: www.crp.org

Maney, Ardith, and Loree Bykerk. *Consumer Politics: Protecting Public Interests on Capitol Hill.* Westport, CT: Greenwood Press, 1994.

Pertschuk, Michael. *Revolt Against Regulation: The Rise and Pause of the Consumer Movement.* Berkeley: University of California Press, 1982.

Phillips, Kevin. *Arrogant Capital: Washington, Wall Street, and the Frustration of American Politics.* Boston: Little, Brown, 1994.

West, Darrell M., and Burdett A. Loomis. *The Sound of Money: How Political Interests Get What They Want.* New York: W.W. Norton, 1999.

Wolpe, Bruce C., and Bertram J. Levine. *Lobbying Congress: How the System Works.* 2d ed. Washington, DC: Congressional Quarterly, 1996.

Zuckerman, Edward, ed. *The Almanac of Federal PACs, 1998–99.* Arlington, VA: Amward, 1998.

AMERICAN BANKERS ASSOCIATION

The American Bankers Association (ABA) represents the commercial banks and trust companies that dominate the financial services industry. Its mission is to protect and enhance the role of commercial banks as the preeminent providers of financial services. The combined assets of its members account for over 90 percent of the assets of the banking industry in the United States. The ABA positions itself as spokesperson for the banking industry, and its 8,000 members include the full range of banks. Although the majority of its members are small banks, with less than $500 million in assets, the ABA is regarded as the policy voice for larger banks.

Because the ABA stakes out such a wide policy territory, many issues become part of its interest agenda. Efforts to reshape financial services since the late 1970s have kept the organization highly visible in national policy circles. This is particularly true because technological and product developments in banking have been the driving force in financial services restructuring. Thus the organization supports the expansion of the banks into handling insurance and securities, through either subsidiaries or bank holding companies. At the same time, however, the ABA opposes the expansion of commercial, nonbanking companies such as General Electric and Archer Daniels Midland into the business of banking. The ABA targets merchant banking as a particular threat, pointing out that the largest finance company in the country is a subsidiary of General Electric, rather than a "real" banking firm.

By contrast, the ABA is generally opposed to legislation or regulations that impose costs or limitations on banks. In this vein, the organization opposes community reinvestment requirements that mandate investing money in the neighborhoods in which their offices are located. The ABA also opposes their disclosure standards on credit card charges and truth-in-savings and truth-in-lending requirements. It argues that these individual laws accumulate into a burden on banks' efforts to compete with other financial services businesses not subject to what the organization perceives as the same onerous rules. The ABA also opposes limits on the liability of consumers who lose their credit and automated teller machine cards.

In seeking relief from requirements of the Community Reinvestment Act, the ABA has supported giving banks that generally have a satisfactory rating a safe harbor, so that regulators could not deny or delay merger or branch opening applications due to protests by community groups demanding greater local investment. Banks with assets of less than $250 million would be allowed to self-certify that they are obeying the community reinvestment standards; banks with less than $100 million in assets would be exempt from the law.

HISTORY

Founded in 1875, the ABA is the oldest of the financial services trade associations. Whether banking services should be regulated and by whom have been issues since the founding of the Bank of the United States at the urging of Alexander Hamilton during President George Washington's administration. The Depression era witnessed major federal intervention with the passage of the Glass-Steagall Act in 1933 to create so-called fire walls between banking, insurance, and securities for the protection of each. Those fire walls have been under attack since the 1970s, with banks and their regulators leading the charge. Large banks have taken the lead in expanding into securities and insurance, and their regulators cheered them on. For example, in 1986, the Office of the Comptroller of the Currency issued a letter allowing nationwide sales of insurance by banks. The following year the Federal Reserve Board issued an opinion allowing bank holding companies to set up subsidiaries to

**American Bankers Association
Political Action Committee Contributions**

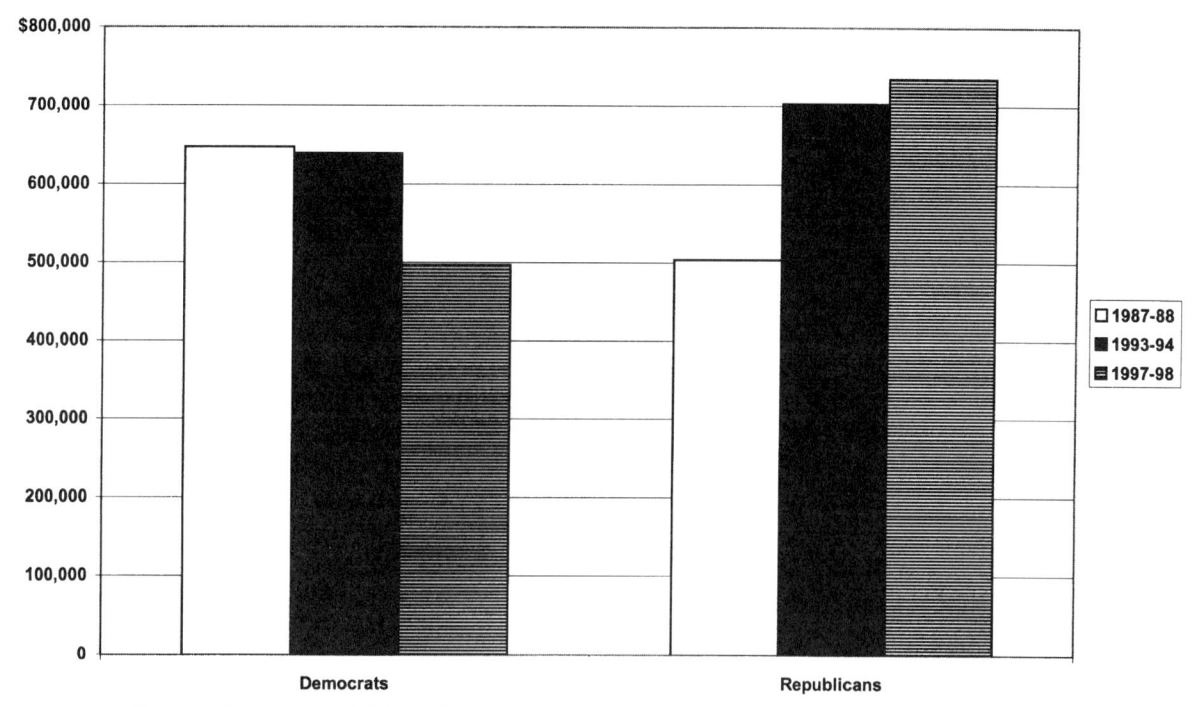

Data derived from official studies available from the Federal Election Commission, Washington, DC, 1987–1998.

sell insurance. These were followed by 1994 legislation permitting banks to set up branch offices nationwide.

The ABA has a reputation for significant success in pursuing its demands regardless of which political party is in power. It has successfully opposed life-line rates (low-cost basic services) for low-income and elderly customers, lining up against the American Association of Retired Persons. If the bankers can be said to have failures, it is in their inability to roll back the consumer reforms legislated in the early 1970s. While some aspects of the truth-in-lending, truth-in-savings, and community reinvestment requirements have been eased, the core standards of the legislation still remain.

ACTIVITIES: CURRENT AND FUTURE

Edward L. Yingling, executive director of government relations, is the lead figure for the ABA's lobbying presence in Washington. He is often quoted as the voice of banking by both the specialized and the general media. The diverse membership of the ABA sometimes means that the organization must be very restrained in its lobbying position. For example, when the administration of President George Bush proposed major financial services overhaul legislation in 1991, the ABA was able to give general support but unable to take a stand on such key issues as interstate branching because of division among its members. However, when it is able to forge a position, its staff and members have excellent access to members of Congress and their staffs. The ABA is frequently invited to present testimony to congressional subcommittees and committees on proposals related to banking.

A key lobbying issue for the ABA in the 1990s is how Congress will contribute to assuring that banks will be a "one-stop" financial services firm for most customers. The ABA argues that consumers want to use their banks for savings and investments, allowing them to create a customized financial plan and to track all their finances on one monthly statement. In October 1999, the ABA's effort to overturn the provisions of the 1933 Glass-Steagall Act separating financial services proved successful. In addition, the group argues that lifting regulatory barriers will facilitate more competition and more efficient provision of services. A related aspect of this approach is the ABA demand that Congress eliminate the federal thrift charter. The ABA's position is that the thrift charter is the primary route for competitors such as Wal-Mart to expand merchant banking. Hence, it advocates legislation to eliminate the charter altogether.

Critics of the ABA position are concerned that deregulation will lead to consolidation and higher customer costs rather than competition and lower fees. They also argue that banks may let customers believe that all their investments, rather than just their checking and savings accounts, are guaranteed by the Federal Deposit Insurance Corporation. In addition, critical observers note that banks are well positioned to impose tying agreements on customers—for example, requiring that prospective homebuyers purchase home or life insurance from them if they want their application for a mortgage loan approved.

ABA staff monitors regulatory agencies, maintains liaisons with regulatory staff, and frequently comments on proposed regulations. ABA members and staff serve on numerous executive branch advisory committees for the Department of the Treasury, Office of the Comptroller of the Currency, Federal Deposit Insurance Corporation, Federal Reserve, and Office of Thrift Supervision. ABA staff, in addition, serve as the secretariat of the International Monetary Conference and the Financial Institutions Committee for the American National Standards Institute.

Besides lobbying Congress and the executive branch, the ABA conducts litigation on behalf of the commercial banking industry. It acts as a plaintiff directly and also intervenes as a friend of the court on a wide range of banking issues. For example, the ABA and four North Carolina banks sued the National Credit Union Administration for its decision to allow nonaffiliated employee groups to join the AT&T credit union. And although it won in the courts, Congress altered legislative language to protect credit union expansion.

The ABA staff numbers over 400 individuals. The General Convention, the annual membership meeting, has the power to set policy for the organization. Each member, regardless of size, has one vote in the General Convention. Members have access to a wide range of services including an extensive library with toll-free telephone reference access, fingerprint processing in conjunction with the Federal Bureau of Investigation, and discounts on income-producing projects through the Corporation for American Banking. The ABA's most impressive organizational development is American Financial Skylink, its own subscription satellite telecommunications network.

The American Institute of Banking, the largest industry-sponsored adult education program in the world, is managed by the ABA. Approximately 120,000 persons take courses each year through local chapters and study groups on such topics as bank operations, consumer credit, and trust management. Education programs for senior bank executives, the Stonier Graduate School of Banking, and 24 other specialized banking schools are managed by the ABA. It prides itself on being a leader in introducing new educational technology such as computer-based tutorial programs and simulations. It also sponsors the ABA Educational Foundation and the Personal Economics Program, which is aimed at educating schoolchildren about banking, economics, and personal finance. Fellowships supporting academicians and financial journalists are also part of the ABA's efforts to shape ideas about banking.

The ABA aids its members directly and indirectly in their relations with the media. The national staff selects and trains individual bankers to do media tours of the country. The association conducts national advertising programs and provides support for other special advertising programs. It publishes a weekly newspaper that circulates not only to ABA members but also to members of Congress. It publishes a general monthly publication, *ABA Banking Journal,* and a number of monthly or quarterly journals devoted to specialized topics such as agricultural lending, consumer credit delinquency, security and fraud prevention, employee benefits, and regulatory compliance.

Future concerns for the ABA include both organizational and larger policy issues. Organizationally, the ABA must cope with a membership base increasingly divided between enormous international megabanks and small banks trying to find a survival niche. The financial services environment will continue to be shaped by rapid, technological changes, development of new and different products and services, privacy considerations, and the perennial question of whether to regulate.

FINANCIAL FACTS

The ABA's annual budget is more than $67 million and it wields the largest political action committee (PAC) in the banking industry. Forty-eight state bankers association PACs are affiliated with the ABA PAC, aptly named BankPac.

LOREE BYKERK

Bibliography

Bykerk, Loree, and Ardith Maney. *U.S. Consumer Interest Groups: Institutional Profiles.* Westport, CT: Greenwood Press, 1995.

The Encyclopedia of Associations. 34th ed. Detroit: Gale, 1999.

Hosansky, David. "Paralyzed Congress on Sidelines in Financial Services Evolution." *Congressional Quarterly Weekly Report,* September 27, 1997.

Nitschke, Lori. "GOP Touts 'One Stop Shopping' as Key Benefit of Overhaul Bill." *Congressional Quarterly Weekly Report,* March 21, 1998.

Taylor, Andrew. "Disputes Over Regulatory Relief May Put Bill on Crash Course." *Congressional Quarterly Weekly Report,* June 24, 1995.

Zuckerman, Edward, ed. *The Almanac of Federal PACs, 1998–99.* Arlington, VA: Amward, 1998.

AMERICA'S COMMUNITY BANKERS

America's Community Bankers (ACB) is a trade association for savings and loan associations, mutual savings banks, cooperative banks, and other types of financial institutions that are not commercial banks or credit unions. The organization describes its members as progressive community banks and positions itself to speak for an industry with more than $1 trillion in assets and over 250,000 employees. The ACB has 2,100 members from all 50 states, Puerto Rico, the Virgin Islands, and Guam.

The ACB's interests include any policy that affects savings, lending, credit, or housing. The organization emphasizes that savings and loan institutions are vital to economic stability and growth. Most of the investments made by its members are in residential real estate loans, but they also invest in commercial loans, student and consumer loans, and the credit card business. Members provide trust services and insurance as well.

In light of the low savings rate in the United States compared with other countries, the ACB supports policies to promote savings. Increased savings would aggregate funds for valuable purposes such as home ownership, higher education, retirement support, business investment, and the creation of jobs. The organization thus has an interest in continued federal insurance of savings deposits as a means to protect and promote saving.

Dramatic changes in the structure of financial services since the 1970s have made the savings and loan business highly unstable. It was allowed to become more speculative in the early 1980s in order to compete with other savings sectors, but quickly ran into financial and political trouble. Fraud, deregulation, expanding economic conditions, the executive branch, and Congress are responsible for a share of blame for the savings and loan fiasco. Scholars and observers are still debating how so many thrifts collapsed, losing many depositors' funds, costing billions in deposit insurance, and necessitating a massive federal restructuring. Whether there is any longer a legitimate specific niche for what used to be called the "thrift" industry has become an open question. Commercial banking interests want Congress to repeal the federal thrift charter as repayment for their contributions to bailing out the savings and loan business; the availability of the thrift charter to nonbanks also represents an opening for "merchant banking," which commercial banks oppose.

Along with the rest of the real estate finance industry, the ACB has a keen interest in maintaining the tax deductibility of mortgage interest payments. Thus, anytime reform of the tax code is proposed, the ACB rallies to defend the favored treatment of mortgage interest as a principal support of the American dream of home ownership.

HISTORY

America's Community Bankers was originally called the Savings and Community Bankers of America (it changed its name in 1994). The organization was created in 1992 by a merger of the United States League of Savings Institutions and the National Council of Community Bankers. The league dated from 1892; the council, formerly the National Council of Savings Institutions, was formed by a 1983 merger of the National Savings and Loan League and the National Association of Mutual Savings Banks. The 1992 merger and the name change were part of an effort to improve the image of the industry in the wake of the savings and loan scandals and government bailout in the early 1990s.

Considering the thrift industry's mercurial past, it is difficult to sort achievements from debacles. Persuading policy-makers to deregulate was regarded as a great victory at the time, but in hindsight it turned out to be disastrous. It may yet prove to be the death knell of this segment of the financial services industry.

**America's Community Bankers
Political Action Committee Contributions**

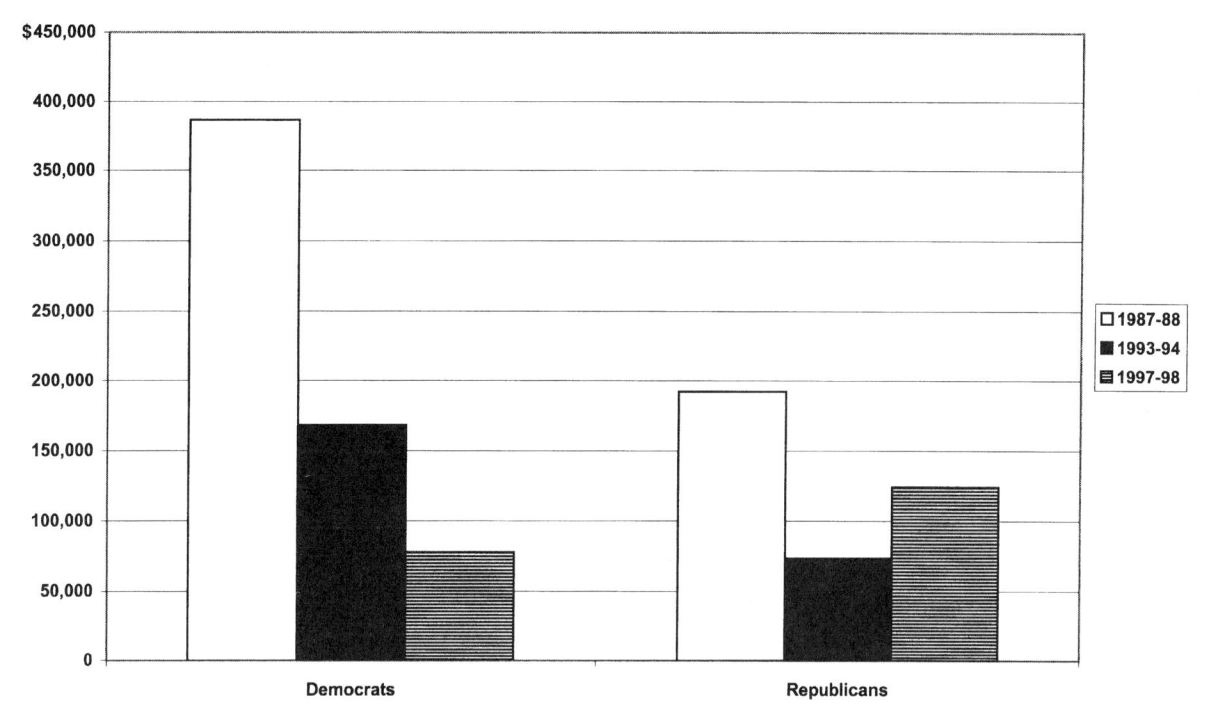

[Bar chart showing PAC contributions to Democrats and Republicans for 1987-88, 1993-94, and 1997-98. Democrats: ~$385,000 (1987-88), ~$170,000 (1993-94), ~$75,000 (1997-98). Republicans: ~$190,000 (1987-88), ~$75,000 (1993-94), ~$125,000 (1997-98).]

Data derived from official studies available from the Federal Election Commission, Washington, DC, 1987–1998.

ACTIVITIES: CURRENT AND FUTURE

The effort to gain regulatory relief is the principal current lobbying topic on which the ACB shares a position with other financial institutions. This includes eased truth-in-lending requirements and more streamlined real estate settlement procedures. In addition, the ACB seeks protection from the class-action suits that borrowers have successfully brought against lenders who provided inaccurate information about mortgage loans. Relatively recent efforts to provide legislative protection for the privacy of customer data are also of concern to the ACB. At present, no federal legislation forbids the sale of customer data or requires even the disclosure to customers that data about them will be or have been sold. Proposals for such protection are strongly opposed by the ACB and other financial service providers.

Current proposals to reform bankruptcy law have also brought the ACB to Capitol Hill. Here the concern of mortgage lenders is that their position in bankruptcy settlements not be disadvantaged by comparison to other claimants on the remaining resources of debtors filing for bankruptcy.

During the repeated efforts to restructure financial services in the United States, the ACB has taken various positions. In the early 1990s its position was to support the idea of a dual banking system. By the late 1990s, it was overwhelmed by the rate of change among the bigger players, who were becoming even bigger through buyouts—purchasing a controlling number of shares in a company—and mergers. Hence, the ACB has begun to focus more on keeping credit unions out of its business arena, treating them as possible buyout candidates for multiline financial services holding companies or even commercial conglomerates.

The ACB monitors hundreds of proposed laws and regulations each year to decide how they will affect the organization's members. The staff provides technical expertise and information to its members and to policymakers. Executives of member financial institutions are encouraged to contact members of Congress through letters, telephone calls, and personal visits. ACB staff and members also provide testimony at congressional committee and subcommittee hearings, submit letters and comments, and maintain ongoing contact with regulators. The Federal Home Loan Bank System, the Office of Thrift Supervision, and the Federal Deposit Insurance Corporation are the executive agencies with which the ACB maintains particularly attentive liaison.

The ACB has a Washington, D.C., staff of 120 persons. Paul Schosberg, its president, came to the organization from the New York League of Savings Institutions and previously served as chief of staff for two members of Congress from New York. The association has five for-profit subsidiaries providing investment products, credit card services, financial forms, real estate auction programs, and insurance endorsements. The Center for Financial Studies is its education affiliate. The center conducts a variety of courses to prepare managers for wider responsibilities and also sponsors the National School of Banking, a graduate-level program for high-potential managers. Additionally, the ACB holds special seminars for directors and trustees of member institutions.

Members also have access to services supporting their needs in economic forecasting, business development, public relations, marketing, and the like. Publications for members include guides on fiduciary responsibilities, legislation, regulations, and compliance procedures. Periodic publications keep members updated on topics such as developments in policy circles, changes in marketing techniques, changes in the economy, and the housing market.

Outreach programs that the ACB supports serve both to burnish the industry's image and to advocate for its members' basic interests. Members are encouraged to sponsor in-school savings programs for children, employment training for hopeful future homeowners and borrowers, and workshops on the financial needs of retirees.

Organizationally, the ACB has remained remarkably stable considering the name change and efforts to shed its past. The future, however, is clouded by the possible demise of the federal thrift charter. Even if one assumes basic survival, restructuring, privacy issues, and other consumer provisions will continue to prove challenging to the industry.

FINANCIAL FACTS

The organization's political action committee (PAC) is now called the America's Community Bankers Community Campaign Committee. Before 1994, it was the Savings and Community Bankers of America Community Campaign Committee and, before that, the U.S. League of Savings Association Political Elections Committee. Most notable here is the sharp decline in funds raised after the savings and loan scandal became public. The industry was on its knees financially and politically, and contributions were neither forthcoming nor so highly sought. Also striking is the swing of contributions from Democrats to Republicans after the GOP gained control of Congress. Even in 1993–1994, when some business money began to migrate to Republican candidates, 69 percent of the ACB's contributions went to Democrats and only 30 percent to Republicans. However, by the 1997–1998 election cycle, nearly 63 percent of the organization's contributions went to Republican candidates for Congress.

LOREE BYKERK

Bibliography

Bykerk, Loree, and Ardith Maney. *U.S. Consumer Interest Groups: Institutional Profiles*. Westport, CT: Greenwood Press, 1995.

The Encyclopedia of Associations. 34th ed. Detroit: Gale, 1999.

Maney, Ardith, and Loree Bykerk. *Consumer Politics: Protecting Public Interests on Capitol Hill*. Westport, CT: Greenwood Press, 1994.

Meier, Kenneth J. *Regulation: Politics, Bureaucracy, and Economics*. New York: St. Martin's Press, 1985.

Zuckerman, Edward, ed. *The Almanac of Federal PACs, 1998–99*. Arlington, VA: Amward, 1998.

AMERICAN COUNCIL OF LIFE INSURANCE

The American Council of Life Insurance (ACLI) is the umbrella trade association for life insurance companies doing business in the United States. It represents their interests in legislative, executive, and judicial forums at federal and state levels of government and with the National Association of Insurance Commissioners (NAIC). Its member companies are responsible for more than 90 percent of the life insurance in the United States. Among its 557 members are giants of the industry such as Prudential and John Hancock, but also numerous small, regional companies. Both mutual and stock insurance companies are members of the ACLI. (Mutual insurance companies are owned by policyholders, while stock insurance companies are owned by investors.) This makes it difficult for the organization to forge agreement on tax provisions that, in differentiating the two types of companies, tend to favor one or the other.

Because life insurance companies typically also sell annuities, disability coverage, and health insurance, the range of interests that the ACLI represents is broad. The structure of financial services and proposals for reform were high on the organization's agenda during the 1990s. These proposed reforms are the most recent variant of periodic challenges to the McCarran-Ferguson Act, which assigned the regulation of insurance to state governments. The ACLI has long defended the act, and both the states and the insurance industry have a long-standing commitment to the relationship.

HISTORY

The ACLI was founded in 1976 with the merger of the American Life Insurance Association and the Institute of Life Insurance. Its history has been marked by overt conflicts between large and small companies, and between mutual and stock companies.

Federal taxation, such as corporate taxation, is a perennial concern, as is protecting the tax exemption granted to life and health insurance coverage conferred as employee benefits and the tax treatment of the value of life insurance. In addition, occasional proposals to legislate underwriting—by outlawing the use of gender, sexual preference, and genetic information, for example—have become significant concerns for the organization.

ACTIVITIES: CURRENT AND FUTURE

The foremost issue on the ACLI's lobbying agenda is financial services restructuring. In order to participate actively on this issue, the organization has taken the position of endorsing reform legislation permitting insurers and banks to affiliate as long as it is through a holding company and subject to functional regulation. The ACLI argues that acceptable reform legislation should define insurance by reference to the federal tax code, thus blocking the Office of the Comptroller of the Currency (OCC) from authorizing new insurance powers for national banks or to preempt state regulation. In addition, it seeks a dispute resolution mechanism between banking and insurance regulators that would not defer to the OCC. The ACLI is also working in the states on restructuring, combining efforts with the NAIC over several years to stimulate greater state involvement.

Other important issues being lobbied by the ACLI include retirement policy, proposals to revise Social Security, and private pension policy. The ACLI is trying to expand awareness among legislators, the media, and the public of the insurance industry's role in retirement security. Its position is to promote expanding the private retirement system with tax incentives to encourage long-term savings. In addition, it is working to incorporate long-term care and disability income insurance as part of the solutions discussed in retirement security policy. Because the insurance industry is the only institution allowed to sell these products, this linkage would

**American Council of Life Insurance
Political Action Committee Contributions**

[Bar chart showing PAC contributions to Democrats and Republicans for 1987-88, 1993-94, and 1997-98. Democrats: approximately $152,000 (1987-88), $278,000 (1993-94), $130,000 (1997-98). Republicans: approximately $141,000 (1987-88), $318,000 (1993-94), $365,000 (1997-98).]

Data derived from official studies available from the Federal Election Commission, Washington, DC, 1987–1998.

advantage insurance companies in the market for retirement and financial services products.

Tort reform is another issue on which the ACLI has been active in recent years. It funded a study by the Rand Corporation on the punitive damage awards in financial injury cases in order to bolster its argument that these awards are out of hand and need to be limited. The research findings were widely publicized and helped support federal and state legislative initiatives promoted by the ACLI.

In almost every budget cycle, legislators target some aspect of insurance as a possible source of taxation. The value of employee benefits, the accrued value of life insurance policies, premiums, the investment income of companies, and other items have all been part of budget proposals in recent years. When the industry is not split along mutual–stock company lines, the ACLI is able to mount aggressive campaigns against increased tax burdens.

The leading issue on the ACLI's agenda at the turn of the twenty-first century is genetic testing in life insurance underwriting. Federal and state policy-makers are struggling to distinguish between beneficial and detrimental uses of information gained from advancing genetic technology. The ACLI is working to differentiate between routine medical test information and genetic testing, and to defend the use of genetic information in life insurance underwriting, although some states have already prohibited its use in underwriting long-term care and disability income insurance.

On the international scene, the ACLI has worked to assure U.S. companies a level playing field when operating abroad. International trade agreements such as the North American Free Trade Agreement have led the ACLI to support fast-track negotiating powers for the president and to conduct negotiations with the Office of the U.S. Trade Representative and the World Trade Organization.

The ACLI's grassroots lobbying efforts are formally organized as the Insurance Industry's Citizen Action Network (ICAN). More than 200,000 volunteers from 350 member companies in all 50 states are part of ICAN. The network keeps informed on issues through a newsletter and mobilized by special action alerts to hold district meetings with candidates and office holders, to write letters, and to make telephone calls to legislators. Phone banks and toll-free telegrams are also used on high-profile issues.

The ACLI's legal staff assists member companies with inquiries and litigation support. It also develops and files *amicus curiae* (friend of the court) briefs and test cases. In a recent year it filed more than 35 such briefs on topics including bank regulatory decisions, punitive damages, pensions, fraud, and disability insurance. In class-action cases against insurance interests, the ACLI has sought decertification of the class that is acting as plaintiff, thereby depriving it of legal standing.

Carroll A. Campbell Jr., the ACLI's president, is a former governor of South Carolina, and a former Republican member of Congress. The organization's staff numbers approximately 200 people but it mobilizes substantial volunteer assistance from member companies. In developing policy positions, the ACLI utilizes the expertise of member company CEOs organized in steering committees to oversee proposals developed by volunteer task forces of member company staff experts. More than 1,000 volunteer experts support ACLI policy development in this way every year. The ACLI's board of directors makes the final policy decisions, which are implemented with the support of legislative strategy groups composed of member company government relations specialists.

On the state level, the ACLI acts as a clearinghouse, monitor, and expert on developing legislation and regulations. Member services include providing information and analysis of state activities. For example, in a recent year its state relations department received more than 20,000 proposals for state legislation for analysis. Other state issues include accounting practices, disclosure requirements, solvency regulations, and taxation. Although the ACLI does not provide introductory education found through some trade associations, it sponsors specialized meetings and seminars for industry executives, creating information-sharing forums for member company personnel such as chief investment officers, political action directors, attorneys, and pension officers. Chief executives of smaller companies are brought together in the Forum 500, an annual meeting, always held in Washington, D.C., that facilitates interaction among member representatives and national policy-makers.

The ACLI devotes substantial resources to public relations and advocacy. For example, on the retirement security issue previously discussed, it conducted research on baby boom generation concerns about long-term care and financing a lengthy retirement. The results were publicized in a research report that became part of an information packet delivered to every member of Congress; a press conference and a satellite media tour helped spread the news nationwide.

In addition, the ACLI encourages member companies to engage in and claim credit for community service activities. It publishes an annual report on the industry's community involvement for public officials and the media. The ACLI staff is a frequent source of media information and fields inquiries on every aspect of the insurance business.

The future of the ACLI remains somewhat uncertain because of the wave of large-scale consolidations among insurers—including international mergers—and the increasing competition among financial service providers. On the other hand, the approaching retirement of 75 million baby boomers promises a wealth of opportunities in the industry. But federal government and private-sector policy and actions will influence both the organization and future prosperity of the life insurance industry.

FINANCIAL FACTS

The ACLI has a budget of over $40 million annually. It has a relatively successful political action committee (PAC), and many of its members—among them Principal Financial Group, New York Life Insurance, and Equitable—have their own sizable PACs as well. ACLI's contribution pattern is typical of trade associations in that it maintains ties on both sides of the aisle no matter who is in the majority, but contributes more to winners than to losers. Nevertheless, the ACLI's contribution pattern reflects an affinity for Republican candidates, being much more generous to their narrow majority than it was to the Democrats' wider majority before the 1994 elections.

LOREE BYKERK

Bibliography

Bykerk, Loree "Business Power in Washington: The Insurance Exception." *Policy Studies Review* 11, no. 3/4 (1992): 259–279.

———. "Gender in Insurance: Organized Interests and the Displacement of Conflicts." *Policy Studies Journal* 17, no. 2 (1988): 261–276.

The Encyclopedia of Associations. 34th ed. Detroit: Gale, 1999.

Pertschuk, Michael. *Revolt Against Regulation: The Rise and Pause of the Consumer Movement.* Berkeley: University of California Press, 1982.

Zuckerman, Edward, ed. *The Almanac of Federal PACs, 1998–99.* Arlington, VA: Amward, 1998.

AMERICAN FINANCIAL SERVICES ASSOCIATION

The American Financial Services Association (AFSA) is the national trade association for market-funded providers of financial services to consumers and small businesses. Over 500 member companies engage in direct credit lending to consumers, providing unsecured personal loans, automobile loans, home equity loans, and credit cards through specialized bank institutions. Among the members of AFSA are Beneficial Corporation, GE Capital Corporation, American Express, General Motors Acceptance Corporation, Household Finance, and TRW Information Services.

The mission of AFSA is to assure a strong and healthy consumer lending industry committed to providing quality and cost-effective service, promoting a financial system that enhances competitiveness, and supporting responsible delivery and use of credit and credit-related products. Thus, the organization is concerned with the tax status of interest paid, interest rates, credit disclosure requirements, collection processes, information privacy, credit ratings, bankruptcy provisions, and the structure of financial services.

HISTORY

AFSA was founded with 41 members in 1916 as the National Consumer Finance Association. In 1971, the organization absorbed the American Industrial Bankers Association, and, in 1983, took its present name. It has been consistently in the niche of consumer credit but has expanded in scope as the whole area of consumer credit has developed new services and instruments.

Interest payments on consumer credit could be deducted from taxable income until tax code reforms in the early 1990s, a change that represented a major loss for AFSA. Consumer legislation requiring uniform calculations and detailed disclosure of interest rates and allowing consumers a grace period to back out of a home equity loan also was not in the interest of AFSA members. Consumer advocates also sought and won more stringent laws protecting borrowers against the tactics of collection agencies. On the other hand, proposed consumer-friendly legislation to allow borrowers to correct inaccurate credit rating data has been defeated repeatedly by AFSA and related interests.

ACTIVITIES: CURRENT AND FUTURE

Issues on which the organization is active include revision of the Real Estate Settlement Procedures Act and the Truth in Lending Act. Real estate settlement procedures in the former legislation require that borrowers be provided with copies of financial forms upon closing a mortgage loan, including a second mortgage or home equity loan, and that borrowers have the right to rescind a loan within three days if they change their minds. The legislation also allows borrowers to recover damages from lenders who provide inaccurate loan information. The Truth in Lending Act requires lenders to provide simple and accurate information about the credit costs of loans so that borrowers can comparison shop.

AFSA is lobbying to remove home equity loans from the provisions pertaining to real estate, or at least to allow for more flexibility in the information required to be disclosed. In addition, the organization seeks legislation to make it more difficult for borrowers to bring class-action suits against lenders, to limit redress to actual damages, and to restrain attorneys' fees.

AFSA argues that truth-in-lending requirements are burdensome to lenders—particularly the small businesses conducted by independent credit companies—and that the information is confusing rather than helpful to potential borrowers. AFSA argues that simplification

**American Financial Services Association
Political Action Committee Contributions**

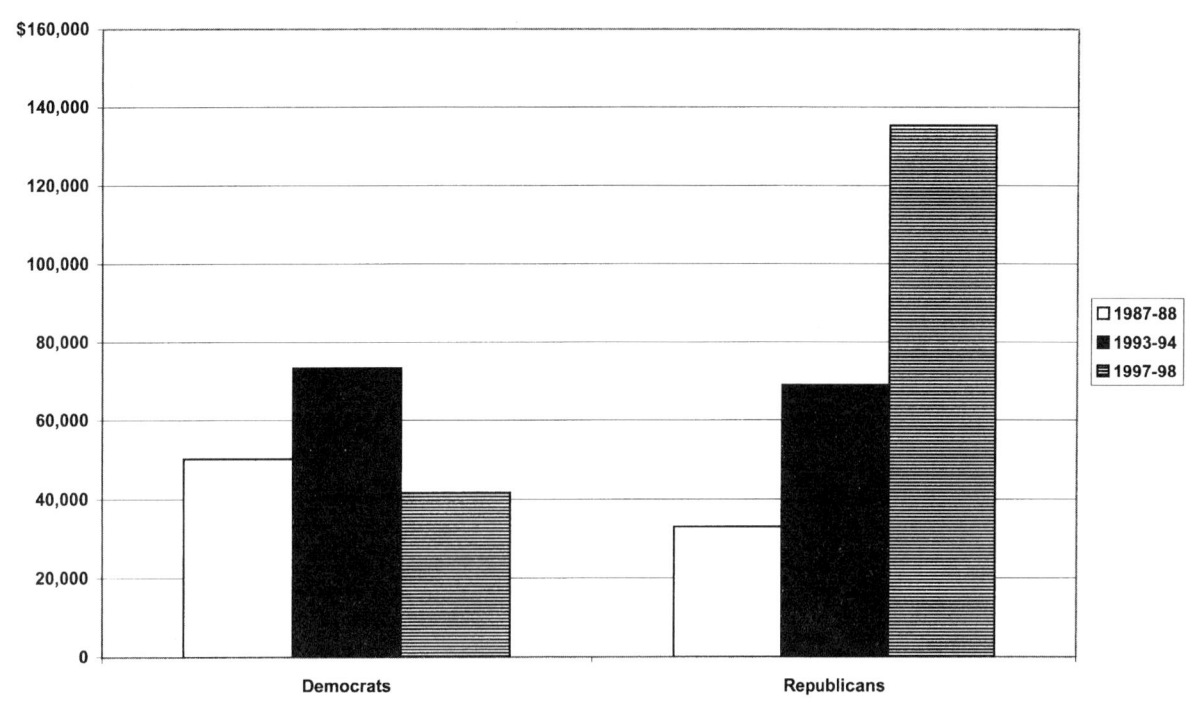

Data derived from official studies available from the Federal Election Commission, Washington, DC, 1987–1998.

or greater flexibility would make the legislation more acceptable.

Recent tax reform proposals have threatened the deductibility of interest paid on home mortgage loans, including home equity loans. AFSA has lobbied against such changes, arguing that deductibility encourages home ownership, improvements, and maintenance, all of which are good for the overall economy and integral to the American dream.

Interest rates charged on credit card debt and the ease with which multiple cards are available to consumers—even those who have sought bankruptcy protection—periodically are on the national agenda. Although lenders are required to disclose the interest on unpaid credit card balances, studies indicate that consumers are not effectively informed of the cost of this credit before they get into financial trouble. AFSA's position is that credit cards are an integral tool in the American economy, and those who use them must become more careful consumers. The association also works to protect the recovery position of credit card lenders in proposals to reform bankruptcy laws and regulations.

AFSA activates grassroots involvement through its congressional action program, communicating with members who in turn contact their senators and representatives. The organization maintains relationships with regulatory agencies, particularly those related to lending and housing, and also monitors state legislative and regulatory action. The AFSA also takes part in major litigation affecting the industry by filing *amicus curiae* (friend of the court) briefs.

AFSA has a staff of 30 and is governed by a 56-member board of directors; the board includes a representative of the National Home Equity Mortgage Association. In addition to an annual meeting and product expositions, the association sponsors conferences, seminars, and a management development program at the University of North Carolina. AFSA collects statistical data and provides periodical publications for members.

Independent operators—those not owned by large conglomerates—have a special section within the organization, created in 1983. The section has its own newsletter, annual conference, and educational materials. Among the education materials are personnel training videos, a data processing guide, and an administrators' guide. The independents' section even has its own philanthropic project, the Children's Miracle Network (fund-raising for children's hospitals) and its own golf and tennis tournaments.

AFSA serves as the industry's voice to the public and informs the media about developments and issues that arise. Industry leaders frequently serve as the organization's spokespersons for opportune media appearances. The affiliated education foundation is part of a coalition promoting personal financial literacy; its strategy is to encourage curriculum enrichment so that students who graduate from high school will have financial management skills. Such skills include balancing a checkbook and understanding the basic relationships between earning, spending, saving, and investing.

Looking ahead, the probable churning of ownership of financial services providers will make the consumer credit niche occupied by AFSA members more difficult to protect. Independent companies not already part of a large corporation will face significant competition from bigger players and may well become buyout targets. Although the home equity loan and credit card businesses may be attractive to bigger competitors, the personal loans for which this sector is known are unlikely to be sought out by other businesses and are likely to remain in place as long as they are profitable.

FINANCIAL FACTS

The organization has an annual operating budget of more than $4 million. In 1997–1998 AFSA's political action committee (PAC) contributed 24 percent of its funds to Democrats and 76 percent to Republicans—a reversal of the PAC's contributions in the 1987–1988 election cycle, when it contributed 60 percent to Democrats and 40 percent to Republicans. The group swung to the Republicans in 1991–1992 but then back to the Democrats in 1993–1994, when the Republicans captured the majority in Congress. In recent election cycles, the PAC devoted a heavy share of contributions to Republicans, perhaps to make up for previous election cycles when it leaned in the wrong direction.

LOREE BYKERK

Bibliography

Bykerk, Loree, and Ardith Maney. *U.S. Consumer Interest Groups: Institutional Profiles*. Westport, CT: Greenwood Press, 1995.

The Encyclopedia of Associations. 34th ed. Detroit: Gale, 1999.

Zuckerman, Edward, ed. *The Almanac of Federal PACs, 1998–99*. Arlington, VA: Amward, 1998.

AMERICAN INSTITUTE OF CERTIFIED PUBLIC ACCOUNTANTS

The American Institute of Certified Public Accountants (AICPA) is the professional association of accountants certified by the states and territories to practice accounting. Its central mission is to establish auditing and reporting standards and to control access to the profession. Preparing and grading the national Uniform Certified Public Accounting Examination for the state and territorial licensing boards is the principal means of controlling access to the profession. The exam tests for knowledge of accounting theory, accounting practice, auditing, and business law.

Membership in AICPA is approximately 332,000 individuals, accounting for about 75 percent of the country's certified public accountants. The largest share of the membership (44 percent) is employed in business and industry, followed by 40 percent employed in public accounting. The organization is sensitive to the racial and gender composition of the profession and has developed programs to recruit and mentor minorities and women. The organization collaborates with the National Association of Black Accountants and the American Association of Hispanic CPAs to involve minority members in AICPA activities and offer them mentoring. Minority high school students receive grants for college preparatory programs. An executive committee surveys public accounting firms' family-related policies in an effort to promote flexible work arrangements.

Maintenance of accounting as a significant profession is the core interest of AICPA—involving not only continued attention to its education and examination requirements, but also an effective code of professional conduct—and an arena of recognized, required functions. Thus, any business practice or government requirement touching upon accounting standards, auditing requirements, taxation, or financial records comes within AICPA's purview.

HISTORY

AICPA was founded in 1887 with the initial mission of elevating accounting to the status of a distinct profession. In most respects the organization has succeeded in that goal. The challenge now is to protect its niche as finance, reporting, and information change at an unprecedented rate. AICPA is seeking to extend the profession's role into the burgeoning commerce of the World Wide Web. AICPA has launched what it describes as a family of assurance services, labeled WebTrust, intended to extend certified public accountants' (CPA) domain to electronic commerce. CPAs trained and licensed by AICPA will review the business practices of a company conducting commerce over the Internet. Companies that pass the review may be awarded a WebTrust seal to display on their web sites.

ACTIVITIES: CURRENT AND FUTURE

The highest-profile issue for AICPA in recent years is reform of the Internal Revenue Service (IRS). After a number of years of effort, the 105th Congress passed legislation to restructure the IRS. AICPA lobbied for an improved IRS management structure, better taxpayer service, stability and simplification of the tax law, and strengthened taxpayer rights. In addition, the organization also gained an extension of taxpayer confidentiality to include tax advice from CPAs in noncriminal proceedings, a complexity-analysis procedure for pending tax legislation, a prohibition on "lifestyle audits," an oversight board for the IRS, and a fixed five-year term for the IRS commissioner.

Maintaining the principle of professional self-regulation is an important political issue for AICPA,

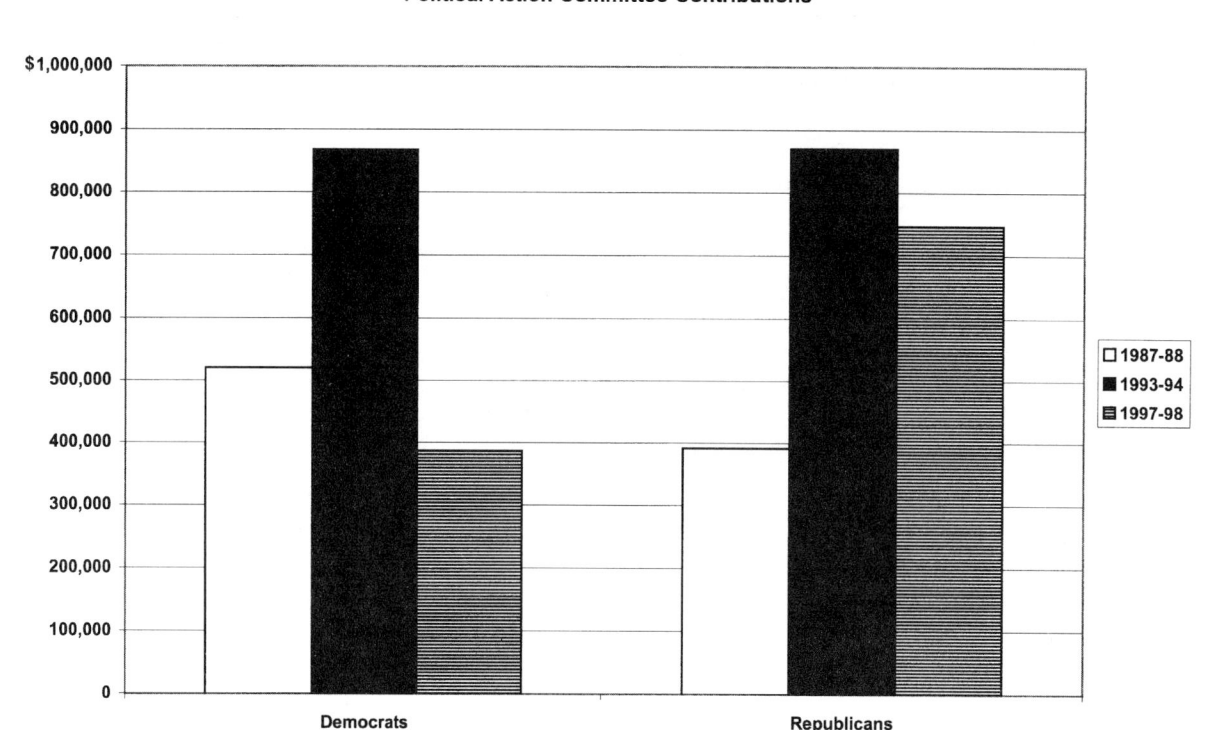

American Institute of Certified Public Accountants
Political Action Committee Contributions

Year	Democrats	Republicans
1987–88	~520,000	~390,000
1993–94	~870,000	~870,000
1997–98	~385,000	~745,000

Data derived from official studies available from the Federal Election Commission, Washington, DC, 1987–1998.

which succeeded in lobbying against legislative proposals in both houses of Congress that would have altered the private-sector standard-setting process used by the Financial Accounting Standards Board to establish generally accepted accounting principles. This effort included legislative lobbying and working with executive branch officials as well.

On the executive side, the Securities and Exchange Commission (SEC) was persuaded to formally recognize the Independence Standards Board as the standard-setting body designated to develop independence requirements and offer guidance to auditors of publicly held companies. The SEC chairman praised the organization for defeating the legislation and called for closer cooperation between the CPA profession and the commission. Among other recent successes with the SEC, AICPA persuaded the commission to issue disclosure guidelines for investors on assessment and remediation efforts for "year 2000" (Y2K) problems by U.S. public companies.

AICPA has also successfully sought shelter from investor class-action lawsuits by appealing to Congress. Working in coalition with the National Venture Capital Association, the American Electronics Association, the Securities Industry Association, and high-technology companies, AICPA persuaded Congress to pass the Private Securities Litigation Reform Act of 1995. This legislation created a safe harbor provision for forward-looking statements, limitations on joint and several liability interpretations, a ban on the use of "professional plaintiffs," and limits on attorneys' fees. Even in the wake of this legislation, CPAs faced increased liability exposure by plaintiffs bringing suits in state courts. The coalition went back to Congress and gained corrective legislation providing that class-action securities suits involving more than 50 people can be removed to federal court where the protective legislation applies.

Congress also responded to AICPA lobbying aimed at extending CPAs' practice arena into the credit union business. The National Credit Union Administration had ruled that credit unions' financial information could be audited by nonlicensed practitioners; AICPA argued that this violated state accountancy laws and was not in the public interest. AICPA took its case to Congress and won legislation requiring large credit unions to use licensed professional auditors.

AICPA works with the National Association of State Boards of Accountancy to influence practice standards set by the states. A powerful means of forging uniformity among the states is the model Uniform Accountancy Act, which the professional associations recently revised to facilitate electronic practice and other alternative practice settings.

Although the organization is headquartered in New York City, it also supports a Washington, D.C., office for federal affairs. A staff of over 700 is employed by AICPA. In addition, the group draws upon volunteer resources from its members. A recent strategic planning process drew approximately 3,400 members—including managing partners, chief financial officers, government regulators, and accounting professors—who devoted more than 21,000 hours. Members ask to serve on AICPA committees in such numbers that some are deferred; a page on the organization's web site now allows those members to contribute their input electronically via virtual committee.

AICPA offers and promotes continuing education for its members and persuades states to require continued training. Most states have adopted a 150-hour continuing professional education requirement promoted by the organization. AICPA also seeks to influence accounting education in colleges and universities; efforts allied with the American Accounting Association are aimed at enhancing faculty development in higher education.

AICPA's publications include the monthly *CPA Client Bulletin*, which provides practical information on taxes, business management techniques, government regulations, and personal financial planning. Other publications cover continuing education programs, conferences, practice management, tax issues, and legislative and regulatory developments.

The organization also offers members software tailored to specific tasks and an interactive web site, which is of particular value to tax and accounting practitioners, who use it almost as much as they use the web site of the Internal Revenue Service. Other tax-related member services include a tax information phone service and a 24-hour fax hotline.

AICPA was active in addressing public concern about the Y2K problem, issuing a study clarifying the auditor's role and providing guidance on communication with clients and employers. A special resource page on its web site was intended to provide assurance to a public anxious about Y2K. AICPA's advocacy role extends to participating in the debate over reforming Social Security. AICPA initiated a comprehensive study of proposed reforms to analyze how they will affect the overall economy and Americans' finances.

AICPA is engaged in a multiyear image-enhancement campaign, including print and radio advertisements promoting the importance of having CPAs in strategic decision-making roles in senior management. The campaign is also attempting to burnish the profession's image and encourage people to become CPAs. A series of advertisements featuring entertainment and sports celebrities accompanied by their CPAs is intended to send the message that CPAs are important to the stars' financial well-being; the tagline is "Be a star in business—be a CPA."

As international commerce rapidly expands, AICPA intends to participate in setting international rules on accounting standards—including rules for financial instruments through the International Accounting Standards Committee. The institute has a senior staff position in international affairs and is a member of the international auditing practices committee of the International Federation of Accountants.

FINANCIAL FACTS

The organization's annual operating expenses exceed $145 million. Membership dues support 40 percent of operating revenue; sales of publications and software comprise 27 percent and investment income 9 percent of operating revenue. The organization's political action committee (PAC) is called the AICPA's Effective Legislation Committee. Inspection of the PAC's contribution pattern indicates a swing toward the GOP following the 1995 Republican takeover of Congress. In the 1993–1994 election cycle, the PAC had divided its contributions evenly among Democrats and Republicans. By the 1997–1998 election cycle, 66 percent of the Effective Legislation Committee's contributions went to Republicans.

LOREE BYKERK

Bibliography

Annual Report, 1997–1998: A Future in the Making. New York: American Institute of Certified Public Accountants, 1998.

The Encyclopedia of Associations. 34th ed. Detroit: Gale, 1999.

Zuckerman, Edward, ed. *The Almanac of Federal PACs, 1998–99*. Arlington, VA: Amward, 1998.

CREDIT UNION NATIONAL ASSOCIATION

The Credit Union National Association (CUNA) is a federated trade association representing 11,500 local credit unions, affiliated with the CUNA through their state credit union leagues. Credit unions are not-for-profit, member-owned cooperatives providing savings accounts (called "share" accounts) and low-interest personal, vehicle, and mortgage loans to members. Credit unions may also offer checking account, credit card, direct deposit, payroll deduction, and automated teller machine services.

More than 90 percent of America's credit unions representing 74 million consumers are affiliated with CUNA. U.S. credit unions have more than $280 billion in savings, $200 billion in loans outstanding, and $320 billion in assets. Credit union deposits are insured up to $100,000 by the National Credit Union Share Insurance Fund, administered by the National Credit Union Administration (NCUA), an agency of the federal government.

HISTORY

CUNA was founded in 1934, although the first credit union in America was established in 1908 and is still operating. Credit unions have consistently occupied a respectable if unglamorous niche in the financial services industry.

CUNA's mission is to promote credit union membership, use of services, and organization of new credit unions. It works to monitor and change laws and regulations governing credit unions, and to serve as the public voice of credit union interests in national policy. Credit unions try to cultivate the image as the financial institution through which working people of modest means save and borrow for basic purposes such as buying a car or a house.

Longstanding areas of interest for CUNA include the structure of financial services, governance of credit unions at state and national levels, savings rates, availability of credit, and consumer protections such as truth-in-lending legislation. In recent years, interest rates, home equity loans, real estate settlement regulations, definition of membership eligibility, and the year 2000 issue have also become important areas of activity.

ACTIVITIES: CURRENT AND FUTURE

Association members are encouraged to be politically active through an annual conference on legislative and regulatory issues, a weekly newsletter devoted to political affairs, and a political action handbook. The most important issue facing CUNA is the attack by banks, led by the American Bankers Association, on the client base of credit unions. The bankers have filed over 20 lawsuits challenging the credit union industry definition of membership eligibility. The dispute centers on how closely associated persons must be to comprise an eligible collectivity to form a credit union membership.

Traditionally, credit unions were formed among people working for the same employer, belonging to the same association, or living in the same community. Efforts by credit unions and their regulators to maintain or expand their position in the fiercely competitive financial services arena have been challenged by banks. The many questions raised in the litigation include the following: What defines a local community? What is reasonable proximity or a single common bond? Should family and household members be included in calculating the membership of a group? And may credit unions merge? Although CUNA lost the protracted judicial struggle leading all the way to the Supreme Court, it persuaded Congress to effectively overturn the Court's ruling. Congress passed the Credit Union Membership Access Act in August 1998 with strong bipartisan support. However, bankers' suits have continued, now against the NCUA regulations interpreting the new statute.

Along with other financial institutions, CUNA lobbies Congress for regulatory relief. It supports amending the truth-in-lending requirements relating to variable rate and periodic payment disclosures, arguing that changes would be in the interest of lenders and borrowers. However, cooperative relationships between CUNA and banking interests have been damaged by the series of lawsuits over membership definition.

Credit union interests are represented on Capitol Hill by both CUNA staff and well-positioned members. For example, the president of an Amarillo, Texas, credit union testified before the Senate Banking, Housing, and Urban Affairs Committee on proposed bankruptcy legislation. Citing data from his own credit union, he argued that consumers with ability to repay all or some of their debts should be required to file for Chapter 13 bankruptcy as opposed to Chapter 7, which erases all of their debts. In support of this argument for borrower responsibility, he explained that most credit unions counsel their members who are in financial difficulty or refer them to a specialized counseling service.

In 1999, CUNA had a staff of 185; its president and chief Washington, D.C., spokesperson, Daniel A. Mica, was a former Democratic congressman from Florida. CUNA staff and members have regular contact with executive agencies by serving on advisory committees and councils. For example, CUNA has members on the Federal Reserve's Thrift Institutions Advisory Council and on the Internal Revenue Service's Information Reporting Program Advisory Committee. CUNA also worked with the Federal Reserve, Treasury Department, and National Credit Union Administration on the year 2000 liquidity and liability protection. However, CUNA has lobbied for a special credit union advisory council to the Federal Reserve, arguing that credit unions need improved access to the Federal Reserve than they currently have in order to protect their specific business interests.

Although CUNA generally has a close, positive relationship with its regulatory agency, it does occasionally go around the agency with an appeal to Congress. For example, CUNA is currently lobbying Congress to support a more expansive definition—compared to NCUA rules—of credit union powers to make business loans to members. CUNA argues that the NCUA's interpretation of the Credit Union Membership Access Act is not what Congress intended in regard to credit union flexibility to make member business loans.

CUNA works to develop new services, including new payment systems, and assists in training credit union officials and employees. It compiles statistics on the industry for use by its members and for policy-makers and the media. Among its most widely circulated publications is *Everybody's Money,* a quarterly magazine used as a promotional piece and to educate members. Credit union directors, managers, and staff also receive specialized publications including a weekly newsletter on legislative and regulatory issues and association activities. CUNA holds an annual governmental affairs conference in addition to its annual symposium, an educational convention with exhibits.

CUNA is affiliated with CUNA Mutual Group, an insurance company providing services to its members, and with the Defense Credit Union Council, which serves military personnel and civilian employees of the Department of Defense. It is also affiliated with the National Federation of Community Development Credit Unions and the World Council of Credit Unions.

The association provides education and training conferences and seminars on such topics as electronic funds transfer and data management. An executive development program at Stanford University is its most prestigious educational offering.

CUNA members draw upon association support for advocacy and public relations efforts. Staff develop image and advocacy campaigns, work to build positive relations with individuals in the media and supply the media with materials reflecting the credit union perspective on issues. For example, an editorial essay by Daniel Mica on the bankers' harassing lawsuits appeared in prominent newspapers.

Although the recent attack by the banking industry is still a potential threat, it is likely that CUNA and its members can continue to survive and even prosper in their niche. On the other hand, the risk remains that in an era of dramatic change, credit unions may get trampled in the stampede when increasingly larger financial services conglomerates are racing ahead of ineffectual efforts to legislate or regulate.

FINANCIAL FACTS

CUNA's annual operating budget is approximately $27 million. The organization's political action committee (PAC), the Credit Union Legislative Action Council, indicates a pattern of protecting access to the majority party but not cutting off relations with the minority. In the 1993–1994 election cycle, 59 percent of the PAC's contributions went to Democrats. By the 1997–1998 election cycle, 57 percent of the PAC's contributions went to Republicans.

LOREE BYKERK

Bibliography

The Encyclopedia of Associations. 34th ed. Detroit: Gale, 1999.

Meier, Kenneth J. *Regulation: Politics, Bureaucracy, and Economics.* New York: St. Martin's Press, 1985.

Zuckerman, Edward, ed. *The Almanac of Federal PACs, 1998–99.* Arlington, VA: Amward, 1998.

INDEPENDENT COMMUNITY BANKERS OF AMERICA

The Independent Community Bankers of America (ICBA) represents small and mid-sized community banks, portrayed as "Main Street" banks. Its membership numbers about 5,500, down from over 6,000 in the early 1990s. The organization's mission is to protect and promote the position of smaller banks in the financial services industry. Small community banks are represented as essential building blocks of the towns and rural areas they serve. They are locally owned, locally operated, and set their own policies. The very survival of community banks has been threatened over the last two decades by dramatic changes in financial services, particularly the trend toward concentration of banking and credit.

Recent issues affecting ICBA include maintaining deposit insurance at existing levels, recapitalizing the bank insurance fund, and rolling back consumer regulations that it regards as too costly. Requirements for truth-in-savings disclosure, truth-in-lending disclosure, and community reinvestment reporting are particular targets of ICBA's pleas for regulatory relief. ICBA is also involved in agriculture legislation, including provisions for crop insurance, commodity supports, and rural housing mortgage loans, and generally supports programs necessary to the survival of small-town and rural economies. At the same time, ICBA tries to prevent federal agencies from lending directly to customers who would otherwise be served by local banks.

Credit union infringement on ICBA member customer territory has been a lively issue during the 1990s. ICBA documented credit union expansion to a wider member base and has fought in the courts, the Congress, and with regulators to roll back the credit union business. The banks' issue with credit union competition is that the latter enjoy taxation and deposit insurance advantages not shared by banks. Technology, electronic transactions, privacy, and personal bankruptcy legislation are also on the group's issues agenda.

HISTORY

ICBA was founded in 1930 by 25 local bankers in response to attempts by major bank holding companies to acquire banks throughout Minnesota and neighboring states. Its essential mission has been consistent since its founding. Formerly known as the Independent Bankers Association of America, the ICBA adopted its present name in 1999.

Community banks were generally opposed to the deregulatory movement for financial services in the late 1970s and early 1980s. Proposals by President George Bush to overhaul federal legislation were regarded by ICBA as leading to consolidation of the nation's financial services on Wall Street at the expense of Main Street. Smaller banks wanted continued barriers between banking and commerce and restrictions on branch banking.

ACTIVITIES: CURRENT AND FUTURE

ICBA uses a multitude of lobbying tactics to influence public policy. For example, individual members are encouraged to form personal relationships with their members of Congress and to communicate their interests frequently. ICBA occasionally uses "fly-in campaigns" to bring members to Washington to meet with their congressional delegations on high-profile issues. For example, 300 member bankers went to Capitol Hill, at a cost of $1 million, during the 1998 credit union battle over expanded eligibility for credit union membership. Although the Georgia delegation met with House Speaker Newt Gingrich (R-GA), he was unswayed from his support of the credit union position on pending legislation.

Members and staff provide testimony before con-

**Independent Community Bankers of America
Political Action Committee Contributions**

[Bar chart showing PAC contributions to Democrats and Republicans for 1987-88, 1993-94, and 1997-98. Democrats: ~$115,000 (1987-88), ~$215,000 (1993-94), ~$210,000 (1997-98). Republicans: ~$62,000 (1987-88), ~$152,000 (1993-94), ~$252,000 (1997-98).]

Data derived from official studies available from the Federal Election Commission, Washington, DC, 1987–1998.

gressional committees as they did before the Senate Banking Committee on automated teller machine (ATM) fees. ICBA testified that Congress should allow market forces to determine whether ATM fees would be imposed and how much those fees would be.

The organization and its members have close relationships with executive branch and regulatory agencies. The ICBA board executive committee meets periodically with the full board of governors of the Federal Reserve System, and ICBA members serve on the Federal Reserve's Federal Advisory Council and on the Kansas City Federal Reserve Board. It has similar ongoing relationships with the Financial Accounting Standards Board, the Internal Revenue Service (IRS), the Small Business Administration, and others.

ICBA uses judicial tactics as well, by bringing test cases and acting as a friend of the court. For example, it filed suit against the Farm Credit System for expanding into general financing to nonfarmers and rural businesses and later appealed the lower-court ruling allowing the expansion. ICBA also participated in the Supreme Court case on defining credit union membership eligibility.

The organization is governed by a 90-member board of directors, led by a six-member executive committee. The Washington, D.C., office has the largest staff and is responsible for legislative and regulatory issues as well as information services. A Sauk Centre, Minnesota, office manages educational programs, meetings, membership recruiting, and accounting services, and a western regional office is located in Newport Beach, California. State independent banking associations join the national association on grassroots efforts; they are affiliated with ICBA but function independently.

ICBA runs the Community Banking Network, which offers members a variety of products and services. These include Visa and MasterCard credit cards, travelers checks, property and casualty insurance, credit life reinsurance, mortgage loans, provision of bank supplies, mutual funds, annuities, retirement plans, and discount brokerage services.

Member education is a significant function of the organization. Approximately 2,000 members a year use some of ICBA's seminars to learn about compliance issues, to become certified in various specialties, and the like. Educational newsletters to members cover such topics as IRS positions and legislative developments. Members receive a monthly journal, *The Independent*

Banker: The National Voice of America's Independent Bankers, the *Washington Weekly Report* newsletter, and special bulletins on developing issues. *The ICBA Compliance Deskbook and Compliance Bulletin* updates provide in-depth information on the regulations with which banks must comply; disclosure forms and model compliance action plans are included.

An annual convention and Techworld (the organization's high-tech product and service exhibition) provides not only workshops and displays but also an audience for useful and important speakers. For example, the 1998 meeting in Hawaii brought Federal Reserve Chairman Alan Greenspan, Comptroller of the Currency Eugene Ludwig, Federal Deposit Insurance Corporation Chairman Andrew "Skip" Hove, and Deputy Treasury Secretary (and future Secretary) Lawrence Summers to the ICBA podium.

ICBA helps members get the community banking message to their customers and to the media with press releases, posters, advertising, CDs, and videos. Community bank preparedness on potential year 2000 problems was the topic of one recent advocacy campaign. The year 2000 controversy gained significant public attention in the late 1990s as many experts predicted that computer technology would cease to operate with the changing of the millennium—leading to financial chaos and technical disaster. ICBA staff also prepare news releases, hold press conferences, engage in one-on-one conversations with journalists around the country, and occasionally appear on major national news shows.

Looking into the future, ICBA as an organization will continue to face the challenges of financial services restructuring and the trends favoring larger, even international service providers. Although the potential membership pool may dwindle, the organization may be buoyed by its provision of profitable services, which allow its remaining members to compete more effectively than they could without those services. Privacy concerns, particularly relating to electronic data, will continue to be an issue, as will the supportive role of the federal government in the rural economy.

FINANCIAL FACTS

ICBA has a staff of 50 and an annual budget of approximately $14 million; its Community Banking Network subsidiaries have revenues of over $61 million annually and assets of more than $115 million. Notable in the organization's contribution pattern is the inverse relationship between 1987–1988 and 1995–1996: ICBA's political action committee (PAC) switched its one-third to two-thirds ratio in favor of the majority Republican Party candidates, but moved to a more balanced contribution pattern in the next election cycle.

LOREE BYKERK

Bibliography

Annual Report. Washington, DC: Independent Bankers Association of America, 1999.

Bykerk, Loree, and Ardith Maney. *U.S. Consumer Interest Groups: Institutional Profiles.* Westport, CT: Greenwood Press, 1995.

Cranford, John R. "Marketplace Forces Hold Key to Future Bank Legislation." *Congressional Quarterly Weekly Report,* January 4, 1992.

Taylor, Andrew. "Bill on Interstate Branching Sails Through Senate Panel: What Opponents Seek." *Congressional Quarterly Weekly Report,* February 26, 1994.

Zuckerman, Edward, ed. *The Almanac of Federal PACs, 1998–99.* Arlington, VA: Amward, 1998.

INDEPENDENT INSURANCE AGENTS OF AMERICA

The Independent Insurance Agents of America (IIAA) represents insurance sales agents who sell all types of insurance and represent multiple insurance companies. Members are small-business owners who handle auto, home, business, life, and health insurance. The organization is structured as a federation of 50 state and 1,200 local associations, with 34,000 individual members.

The IIAA's interests include aspects of insurance and of small, independent business owners. Thus, it is generally concerned with the structure of financial services and with regulatory burdens as well as with the impact of taxation on insurance, regulation of insurance, and product liability standards. More specifically, in the past few decades, it has been concerned with keeping banks out of the insurance business and with protecting the McCarran-Ferguson Act, under which insurance is regulated by the states.

HISTORY

The organization traces its roots to 1896, when two fire insurance agents happened to meet in Denver and began to discuss how agents could sell their customers products from more than one insurance company. Their meeting led to the founding of the National Association of Local Fire Insurance Agents, which later became the National Association of Insurance Agents. The group's current name was adopted in 1975.

ACTIVITIES: CURRENT AND FUTURE

The IIAA is regarded as a lobby force in Washington, D.C. Its lobbyists are well known on Capitol Hill, and the agents are expected to have a place at the table on any legislative proposals affecting their interests. For more than the last decade, the principal issue on the agenda has been financial services restructuring. The IIAA's position is to protect the sector available to insurance agents from being further usurped by banks or other forms of banking organization. It points out that banks already have been allowed to expand into the insurance business by their regulators and the courts; insurers have not been allowed similar access to the banking business. Thus Congress, in order to keep the playing field at all level, must at least protect agents' niche from further incursions in any restructuring legislation. The IIAA argues that, at a minimum, banks should be allowed to sell insurance only through affiliates that are regulated by state insurance commissioners.

Although insurers and agents do not have a federal regulatory agency and, in fact, want to protect the relationships they have with state regulators, they do have strong ties with members of Congress. Republican leaders, including House Majority Leader Richard Armey of Texas and House Rules Committee Chairman David Dreier of California, are staunch agent supporters. Former House Speaker Newt Gingrich (R-GA) was consistently willing to take the agents' position against banks and securities firms. But the real source of the IIAA's power is that every congressional district has insurance agents and they are often well-known, articulate, persuasive individuals who are an integral part of the hometown, Main Street business community.

The IIAA's agenda extends beyond financial services reform. It has promoted legislation to address federal natural disaster response and with grassroots support moved a bill out of committee for the first time in 1998. It also is involved in aspects of the multiple health-care reform proposals that have been considered by Congress during the 1990s. Its specific interest is to protect the position of agents—which it has succeeded in doing, for example, by blocking provisions that would allow patients to sue their health plans over coverage decisions.

**Independent Insurance Agents of America
Political Action Committee Contributions**

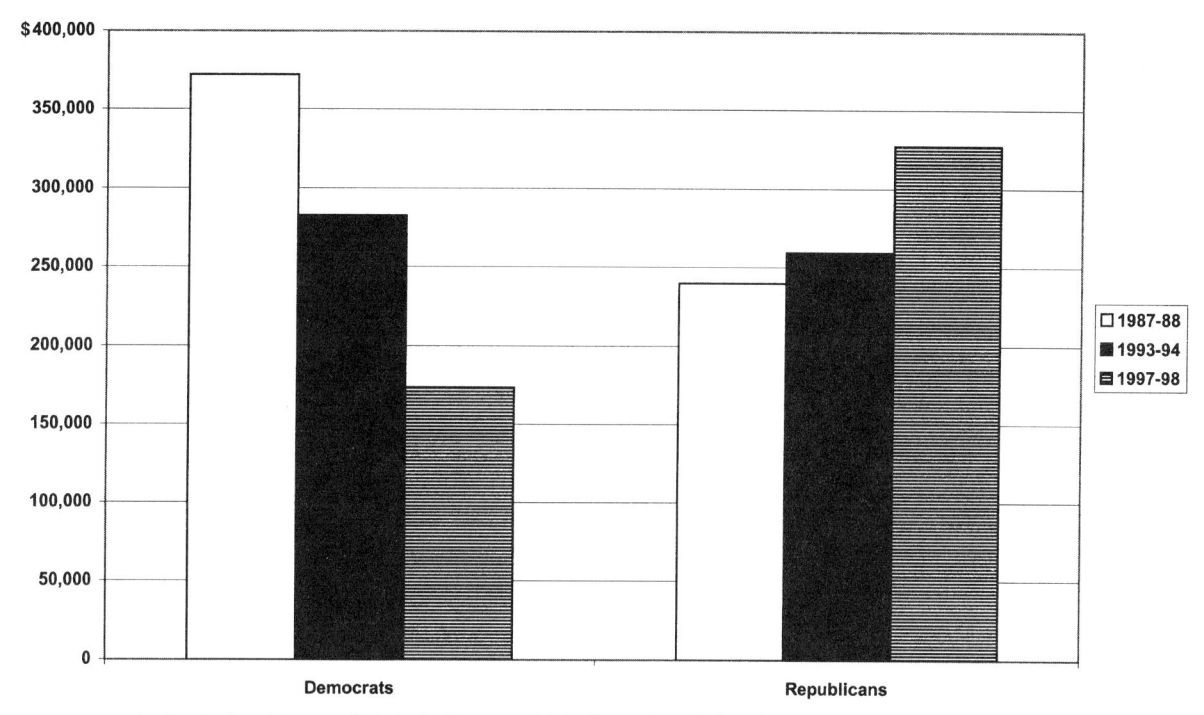

Data derived from official studies available from the Federal Election Commission, Washington, DC, 1987–1998.

Because of the wide range of policies sold by independent agents, the IIAA also is involved in agriculture legislation and auto issues. With respect to automobile coverage, it has dealt with agent liability and licensing issues and worked to protect insurer sharing of accident and repair data. It worked with the Republican leadership on auto issues and on crop insurance; on the latter its effort was to secure long-term funding for crop insurance support.

Not only does the IIAA lobby in Washington, D.C., it also is active in state politics. Among the issues on the states' agendas are financial services reform, agent licensing, and electronic commerce. The IIAA promotes model legislation on issues in which it is supporting state action; it has been successful in persuading states to enact its model provisions on financial services restructuring.

The IIAA works with the National Association of Insurance Commissioners (NAIC), most recently cooperating on streamlining the agent licensing process and working toward interstate reciprocity. It is also working on natural disaster issues, auto insurance, and healthcare reform at the state level.

In addition to direct state lobbying and cooperating with the NAIC, the IIAA also supports lobbying in the states through a grant program. State organization efforts such as improving government affairs operations or promoting legislation such as graduated drivers license laws receive grants from the national group.

The IIAA is able to draw on substantial volunteer expertise from its members. Membership committees are organized into commercial lines, personal lines, education, government affairs, technical conference, and young agents. Through its staff of 68, education, public relations, and other services are made available to members.

Benefits available to IIAA members include technical and sales courses; new agents get special attention, but continuing development for established agents is encouraged as well. A conference for young agents features sessions on legislative initiatives, media training, and leadership. Educational workshops and seminars focus on sales skills, sales management, and customer service. Courses may lead to recognition or certification in specialized areas, such as accreditation for customer service representatives. Among the other widely distributed member services is a series of best practices manuals; recent topics include management succession and producer compensation.

Through the IIAA, members have access to employment practices liability insurance coverage, errors and omissions coverage, including year 2000 coverage (which would protect policyholders from ramifications of computer and other technological failure with the turning of the year 2000), and retirement programs, including Individual Retirement Accounts (IRAs) and 401(k) plans. Employee benefit plans including disability, dental, and long-term care coverage, and personal insurance for members covering motorcycles, snowmobiles, and jet skis are also available. Members' legal inquiries on such issues as their contracts with insurance companies, antitrust issues, and others are fielded by IIAA staff.

Member publications include the monthly *Independent Agent,* handbooks and periodicals focusing on management topics, and the bimonthly *Actiongram.* The web site is also used for rapid-response grassroots action notices. An annual convention with exhibits draws about 3,000 attendees; speakers include high-profile political figures. An annual Legislative Conference is held to focus members on lobbying.

The IIAA sponsors a program serving both education and public relations functions in what it calls InVEST. Videos and other teaching materials on business and insurance skills are provided for high school and community college students. Leading the list of the IIAA's public image events is its 31-year sponsorship of the Insurance Youth Golf Classic, the largest golf tournament of its type.

The organization also works cooperatively with its members on a media program including consumer guides, brochures, and national broadcast and print media advertisements. Broadcast and cable network spots for a recent campaign were purchased on CNN Headline News and the Weather Channel to reach more than 239 million households. Agents are recruited to participate in on-camera media training conducted by the IIAA communications staff. In addition, a joint venture with a national advertising agency to support state associations, local boards, and individual members in advertising their agencies is under way. The IIAA also boasts an award-winning web site at www.independentagent.com, where consumers can find more than 26,000 agency listings.

The IIAA has expanded its range of services dramatically over time and is now poised to expand into the savings bank business. It is launching InsurBanc, a federal bank thrift, which will provide deposit and loan services to member agents and provide them with financial products and services to offer their customers.

The expansion of technology is the IIAA's major concern for the future. Electronic product and service availability poses both risks and opportunities for the independent agent, and the organization is attempting to help its members weigh the balance in a positive direction. Its goal is to help agents control their own destiny in an environment of electronic commerce. However, in the nearer term, the threat of continued expansion by banks into insurance is the highest concern.

FINANCIAL FACTS

The IIAA is regarded as a significant player in Washington, D.C., circles, in part because of its generous campaign support. Over the last decade, contributions to Republicans have increased markedly. In the 1993–1994 election cycle, nearly half of the organization's contributions went to Republicans. After the Republicans gained control over Congress, contributions to Republicans increased to a level more generous than they had been to the previous Democratic majority, a pattern reflecting close ties to House leadership.

In response to the serious issues facing the organization, it has made some changes in administering its political action committee (PAC). The IIAA began in 1998 to solicit contributions earlier in the year and also began accepting contributions by credit card to facilitate added contributions in a more convenient process.

LOREE BYKERK

Bibliography

The Encyclopedia of Associations. 34th ed. Detroit: Gale, 1999.
Hosansky, David. "Taxes, Regulations Sought by Business Lobbyists." *Congressional Quarterly Weekly Report,* April 18, 1998.
"IIAA—A Year in Review." *Independent Insurance Agent* (December 1998).
Taylor, Andrew. "Glass-Steagall Rewrite Stalls as Industry Foes Do Battle." *Congressional Quarterly Weekly Report,* March 2, 1996.
Zuckerman, Edward, ed. *The Almanac of Federal PACs, 1998–99.* Arlington, VA: Amward, 1998.

INVESTMENT COMPANY INSTITUTE

The Investment Company Institute (ICI) is the national trade association for mutual fund and closed-end investment companies registered under the Investment Company Act of 1940. A mutual fund company is required to repurchase stocks from shareholders when they demand it, whereas a closed-end company is not. Investment advisors and underwriters to these companies, unit investment trust sponsors, and interested others may also join the organization. Its membership represents 7,521 mutual funds, 447 closed-end funds, and 10 sponsors of unit investment trusts. Its mutual fund members represent more than 73 million individual shareholders and manage more than $5.7 trillion in investments.

The ICI presents itself as spokesperson for its members and their shareholders in matters related to legislation, regulation, taxation, public information, economic and policy research, business operations, and statistics. It endeavors to enhance public understanding of the investment company business, to serve the public interest by encouraging high ethical standards in the industry, and to promote the interests of shareholders. Areas of interest for this organization include savings rates and incentives, investment choices, the structure of the financial services industry, communication with investors, the overall health of the economy, and oversight of investment advisor conduct.

Within the financial services industry, the ICI is distinguished by the mutual fund safeguards of the 1940 Investment Company Act. That legislation provided investor protections including full and fair disclosure, strict limits on borrowing, prohibition of affiliated transactions, and oversight by independent directors. These standards are credited with keeping mutual funds out of the crises and debacles affecting other pooled investments such as those in real estate and hedge funds. As a result, much wider shares of the population have relied upon mutual funds for the sort of professionally managed diversified portfolio that was previously available only to a few.

HISTORY

The ICI was founded with the passage of the Investment Company Act of 1940 as the National Association of Investment Companies. In 1973 it absorbed the Association of Mutual Fund Plan Sponsors; in 1961 it took its present name. In 1987 it absorbed the Association of Publicly Traded Investment Funds.

The mutual fund industry has grown since 1940 from $400 million to over $5.5 trillion. As compared with other sectors of the financial services industry, it has been relatively free of scandal, a record attributed by the Securities and Exchange Commission (SEC) to the effective watchdog function served by independent directors of the funds. Both the SEC and the ICI have an interest in protecting that record and periodically revisit the standards and procedures required of the funds.

Important historic benchmarks of cooperation between the industry and its regulators include revision of rules on advertising fund performance, making prospectuses more understandable, and presenting fees in tabular format. These disclosure reforms are credited with encouraging shareholders to move to lower-cost funds and bringing down the cost of investing in mutual funds.

ACTIVITIES: CURRENT AND FUTURE

Funding of Americans' retirement is a major arena of activity for the ICI at the present time. This includes work on Social Security reform and on pension legislation. The ICI participated in the White House Conference on Social Security, convened by President Bill Clinton in December 1998. The ICI's position stressed that the long-term health of Social Security must be ensured, and its status as a universal system must be

**Investment Company Institute
Political Action Committee Contributions**

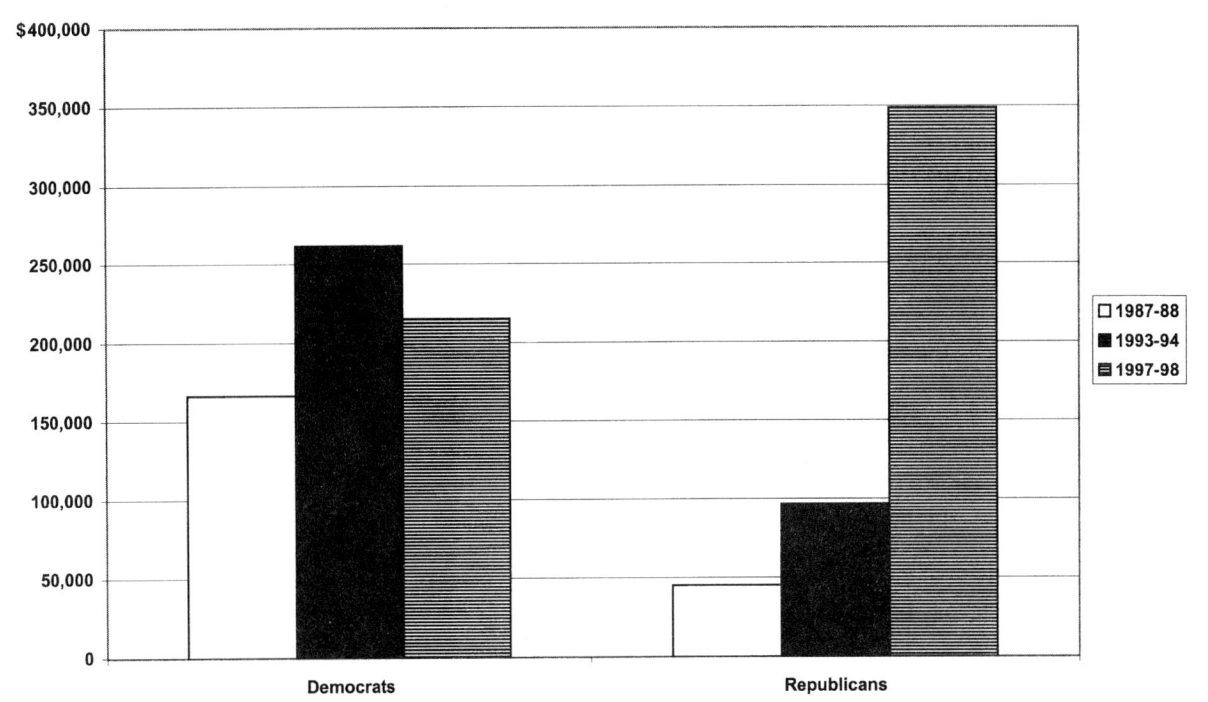

Data derived from official studies available from the Federal Election Commission, Washington, DC, 1987–1998.

maintained. Together, these will continue to assure a modicum of income security to Americans who do not have employer-sponsored programs or individual savings.

The ICI is cautious on privatizing Social Security. If Congress chooses to proceed with individual accounts, the ICI maintains that investor protections similar to those in securities laws must be put in place. In addition, a significant public education campaign must be conducted to explain investment principles, markets, risks, and product disclosure. If individual accounts are created, they initially should be invested in government-sponsored funds to provide for a transition period, after which individuals should be allowed to elect other investment options that meet their own objectives. If such choices were not allowed, government-managed investment pools would become so large as to have significant, possibly unintended impacts on private markets.

In the area of pensions, the ICI is particularly focused on proposals aimed at expanding defined contribution pension plans and making them more portable. It supports raising the limits on contributions, permitting after-tax contributions, permitting catch-up contributions for workers aged 50 and older, and giving small employers tax credits for setting up plans. It is also in support of allowing employees to move pension assets from one type of plan to another when they change jobs. In addition, the ICI is promoting legislation restoring simple, universal Individual Retirement Accounts (IRAs) that would allow anyone to set aside a tax-exempt sum annually, arguing that complex reforms have had the unintended consequence of dampening savings rates among middle- to lower-income workers. Its testimony before the House Ways and Means Subcommittee on Oversight also urged Congress to raise the $2,000 limit on contributions to IRAs.

Whether there is sufficient price competition in the mutual fund industry to protect consumers is an issue that comes before Congress and regulators periodically. Both Republican and Democratic members of the House Commerce Subcommittee on Finance and Hazardous Materials made opening statements characterizing their September 1998 hearings as a checkup for a healthy patient. At the time, the ICI president Matthew P. Fink testified that competition in the industry is healthy and working in the interests of investors. He described funds as competing in price, performance, investment philosophy, experience, specialized expertise, and service.

The ICI works cooperatively with the SEC by creating and serving on advisory groups studying regulatory issues. For example, the ICI's board chairman presently serves on an advisory group established to review practice standards for fund directors; the group was created to self-study and self-regulate pursuant to SEC suggestions that a review was in order. Work is also under way on disclosure of the impact of taxes on fund performance and on advertising rules. Guidelines issued by the SEC in 1998 requiring prospectuses to be written in plain English were the result of substantial prior joint study and feedback over a year-long comment period.

The organization's close working relationship with the SEC are further revealed by the ICI testimony supporting an increased level of SEC funding for fiscal year 2000. The ICI's statement defended an increase to support the commission's responsibilities in enforcing plain-English requirements in prospectuses, in monitoring progress toward year 2000 compliance and disclosure, and in public education.

The ICI has also worked with state regulators to sort out which investment advisors must register with their states and which with the SEC. Changes in these arrangements were mandated by the National Securities Markets Improvement Act of 1996.

The ICI maintains a staff of 150, who monitor policy developments and provide member services, such as access to a reference library, an online member network, and various publications including a service directory, a fact book, and monthly industry data and trends. The ICI also makes available to members brochures and videos for consumer education. The general membership meeting is held annually in Washington, D.C., and includes product and service exhibits.

The ICI and its members are the high-status, high-integrity players in the financial services sector; they are keenly aware of that status and intend to protect it. They are well positioned to grow with private retirement savings and even more so with partial privatization of Social Security. By the same token, dramatic growth in the latter would also raise issues of investor understanding, telemarketing contacts, and the privacy of investor data.

FINANCIAL FACTS

The organization has an annual budget of more than $30 million. Even more valuable are the high-status volunteers it is able to mobilize; presidents of prominent mutual funds and their staffs have excellent access to policy-makers in Washington and other capitals. The ICI has its own political action committee (PAC), and many of its members—such as Dean Witter Reynolds Financial Group, J.P Morgan and Company, Merrill Lynch Asset Management, Paine Webber, and Scudder Kemper Investments—also sponsor PACs. Inspection of the ICI's PAC contribution data over the last decade shows an effort to maintain ties with the minority Democrats, with even more generosity bestowed on them than had been bestowed on Republicans when they were the minority party in Congress. In the 1993–1994 election cycle, 73 percent of the ICI's contributions went to Democrats and 27 percent went to Republicans. In the 1997–1998 election cycle—two years after Republicans had taken control over Congress—38 percent of the organization's contributions went to Democrats while 62 percent went to Republicans.

LOREE BYKERK

Bibliography

The Encyclopedia of Associations. 34th ed. Detroit: Gale, 1999.
Zuckerman, Edward, ed. *The Almanac of Federal PACs, 1998–99.* Arlington, VA: Amward, 1998.

MORTGAGE BANKERS ASSOCIATION OF AMERICA

The Mortgage Bankers Association of America (MBAA) is a trade association representing the real estate finance industry. This includes mortgage bankers, mortgage brokers, commercial banks, credit unions, savings and loan associations, savings banks, and life insurance companies. Mortgage bankers make, sell, and service mortgages secured by residential or commercial real estate. They serve as middlemen, arranging and making loans using short-term funding and then selling these loans to other lenders and investors, both within the U.S. secondary markets and abroad.

Buyers of mortgages include commercial banks, thrifts, life insurance companies, pension funds, and the secondary market agencies—the Federal National Mortgage Association (Fannie Mae) and the Federal Home Loan Mortgage Corporation (Freddie Mac), which purchase primarily conventional mortgage loans. The Government National Mortgage Association (Ginnie Mae) purchases government loans. All three are federal agencies created to provide liquidity to the mortgage market and affordable housing to home buyers and renters. Mortgage bankers also make use of federal and state government programs such as the U.S. Federal Housing Administration residential mortgage insurance program and the Department of Veterans Affairs (VA) home loan guarantee program. The VA program allows mortgage lenders to offer long-term, low down-payment mortgage financing to eligible veterans.

Three thousand companies involved in the mortgage banking business are members of the MBAA. The organization bases its status on the role of home and property ownership in the American political economy. It positions itself as representing an industry it describes as the engine that generates the capital to build and own homes, apartments, offices, hotels, shops—most of our physical surroundings. The real estate finance industry is the largest segment of the capital markets of the United States.

The MBAA's objectives are to achieve the lowest cost of credit for home buyers and other real estate borrowers and to maintain a stable, efficient, and assured source of mortgage credit. It works to create an environment suitable for an efficient and profitable real estate finance industry, and to ensure that federal legislation and regulation provide for safety, soundness, and consumer protection without undue burdens and costs being imposed on the industry.

HISTORY

The MBAA was founded in 1914. The favored income tax status granted to those who pay interest on home mortgages has been its continuous core concern. The long-term success in protecting that status accrues not only to the MBAA but also to the deep-seated American attachment to the goal of home ownership. The development and continuation of government-financed mortgage loan guaranties and support for the secondary market in mortgages represent significant success for mortgage bankers. Restrictions on the dollar amount of mortgages that federal agencies will guaranty, caps on the interest that may be deducted on multiple-home mortgages, and consumer protection laws constitute more disappointing outcomes for organized lender interests.

As an organization, the MBAA is engaged in a strategic planning process that appears to be leading it in the direction of dividing more distinctly between residential and commercial housing. This looming split could challenge the MBAA's mission of promoting the American dream of home ownership. It could also threaten the group's reliance on conservative Republicans who continue to favor both tax reform and the rolling back of consumer protection provisions.

**Mortgage Bankers Association of America
Political Action Committee Contributions**

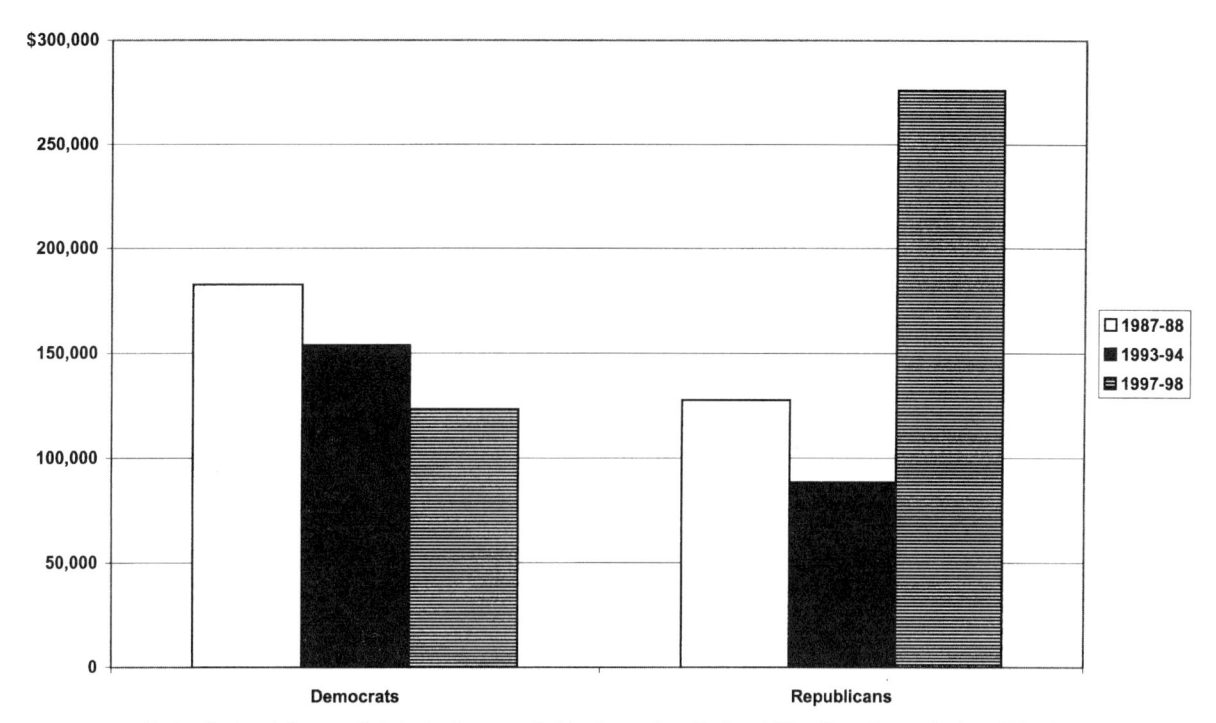

Data derived from official studies available from the Federal Election Commission, Washington, DC, 1987–1998.

ACTIVITIES: CURRENT AND FUTURE

A major concern of the MBAA is to protect the mortgage interest deduction each time there is any discussion of revising the federal tax code. Its position is that the interest paid on mortgages should continue to be deductible in full and should include mortgages on second homes and refinanced mortgages. Thus, each time a major revision of the tax system is proposed, particularly one calling for some version of a national sales tax, the MBAA swings into action along with the rest of the housing finance lobby.

The mortgage bankers advocate creating and maintaining a level playing field among the various types of housing finance providers. Thus, they participate in the legislative and regulatory fray over restructuring financial services. They generally support financial services reform and modernization; their position is that a fully competitive marketplace would be preferable to one with outdated and unfair barriers to some segments.

Reform of the 1968 Truth in Lending Act and the Real Estate Settlement Procedures Act are high on the MBAA agenda. The Truth in Lending Act requires lenders to provide simple and accurate information about loans so that borrowers can comparison shop. It also allows borrowers to recover damages from lenders who provide inaccurate loan information. The Real Estate Settlement Procedures Act requires that information and paperwork copies be given to borrowers when they close a mortgage loan and gives consumers the right to rescind a loan within three days. The requirements also extend to closing a second mortgage loan.

The MBAA regards these requirements as burdensome and confusing to consumers and is particularly concerned about class-action suits brought against lenders for what the MBAA regards as overly technical interpretations of the legislation. The MBAA advocates reforms including changing the information provided to consumers, an arbitration process, limiting redress to actual damages, and limiting attorneys' fees in class actions. It also advocates federal preemption of state laws in order to create standard requirements and procedures across the country.

Lobbying on these consumer protection rollbacks displays a wide array of tactics. The MBAA encourages grassroots input from its members as a means to influence legislators, including electronic letters on its web site that may be personalized but still convey the content of the group's position. The organization works with members of Congress, their staffs, and in coalitions with other industry groups to craft legislative and regulatory language. It provides testimony for congressional committees and subcommittees on housing finance proposals.

The MBAA works with the Department of Housing and Urban Development and the Federal Reserve, as it has done in trying to change truth-in-lending and real estate settlement procedures. In general, it maintains liaison with the Federal Home Loan Mortgage Corporation, the Federal National Mortgage Association, the Government National Mortgage Association, and the Veterans Home Loan Guarantee Board.

The MBAA staff numbers 135; they work with member committees in more than 20 functional areas, including affordable housing, residential loan production, commercial mortgage and asset management, loan administration, and regulatory compliance. The staff is responsible for research and publication of a quarterly newsletter reporting delinquency and foreclosure rates by state, by region, and nationally. An annual report of costs and revenues associated with originating and servicing loans for one- to four-unit residential complexes is also published by the MBAA. Mortgage banking statistics are also published in a monthly magazine, *Mortgage Banking: The Magazine of Real Estate Finance*. *Real Estate Finance Today*, a biweekly newsletter, reports events relating to legislative and regulatory issues. The MBAA's web site provides daily updates of statistics, issues, and news of interest to members.

Education services for MBAA members include clinics on all aspects of the mortgage finance business. The association sponsors the School of Mortgage Banking and makes correspondence courses available to its members. Conferences on special topics, such as international real estate, are held periodically, in addition to an annual convention featuring exhibits.

As previously discussed, the MBAA's public relations image relies heavily on the American dream of home ownership. The organization's message is that mortgage bankers provide most of the mortgages for low- to middle-income home buyers—the young couples buying their first, modest bungalow. Their role in commercial real estate, foreclosures, and the secondary market are not part of the featured portrait.

One specific ambition that the MBAA will continue to pursue is gaining access to the Federal Home Loan Bank system. Thus, it is part of a growing movement to revisit and revise that entire system.

FINANCIAL FACTS

Mortgage bankers' political preferences lean toward the Republican Party, which most believe to be more in line with their interests in private enterprise and profits. However, because Democrats largely controlled Congress from 1955 to 1994, they received the majority of contributions. This began shifting in favor of Republicans even before the party regained control of the House and Senate, but Democrats subsequently won back many of those contributions. Republicans have not yet gained the share of funds previously contributed to Democrats.

LOREE BYKERK

Bibliography

Birnbaum, Jeffrey H., and Alan S. Murray. *Showdown at Gucci Gulch: Lawmakers, Lobbyists, and the Unlikely Triumph of Tax Reform*. New York: Vintage Books, 1988.

The Encyclopedia of Associations. 34th ed. Detroit: Gale, 1999.

Taylor, Andrew. "Disputes Over Regulatory Relief May Put Bill on Crash Course." *Congressional Quarterly Weekly Report*, June 24, 1995.

Zuckerman, Edward, ed. *The Almanac of Federal PACs, 1998–99*. Arlington, VA: Amward, 1998.

NATIONAL ASSOCIATION OF INDEPENDENT INSURERS

The National Association of Independent Insurers (NAII) is a trade association of independent property and casualty insurance companies; its members write automobile, homeowners, business, workers' compensation, and surplus lines insurance coverage. (Surplus lines brokers provide insurance in states where coverage is not available through licensed insurers.) It is the largest full-service property and casualty company trade association, representing 619 members whose market share includes almost one-third of the total premium volume. Allstate, GEICO, SAFECO, and USAA are among the NAII's more prominent insurance company members.

The interests of the NAII include the overall structure of financial services at the national level and protecting the regulation of insurance by the states rather than the national government. The NAII presents itself as an aggressive, tenacious defender of state regulation of a competitive marketplace and an opponent of federal intrusion. It also is involved on shorter-term issues such as liability judgments by the courts; it has supported federal legislative proposals to establish limits on damage awards in product liability cases. Federal support for flood insurance, transportation infrastructure, and vehicle safety are also issues that bring the NAII and its members into national politics.

HISTORY

The NAII was founded in 1945 to represent an aggressive group of companies in a rapidly expanding insurance field. It has been involved in vehicle safety since the issue gained attention in the 1970s. It has supported efforts to require safety equipment such as airbags in automobiles, to revise state laws on driver's license availability, and to reduce drunken and drugged driving. The NAII is one of the organizations that has successfully promoted the Graduated Driver's License law aimed at reducing teen auto accidents and fatalities. It has also supported administrative revocation of drivers' licenses and lowering the legal blood alcohol concentration standard for convicting persons of drunken driving.

ACTIVITIES: CURRENT AND FUTURE

The association describes itself as an aggressive, proactive leader on issues; its staff numbers 180. NAII member companies are domiciled in 48 states. They are well connected politically, and the organization works to mobilize executives, employees, agents, and retirees. Its Washington, D.C., lobbyists bring members together with lawmakers at social gatherings, policy discussions, meetings with new legislators, and at fund-raising events.

The most serious current issue for the NAII is financial services restructuring legislation at the national level. It is working in coalition with the Independent Insurance Agents of America, the National Association of Life Underwriters, and the National Association of Insurance Commissioners to keep banks out of the insurance business. This industry coalition is vehemently opposed to the direction set by federal bank regulators, who have allowed banks to move into selling insurance.

The restructuring legislation passed by the House of Representatives in 1999 would, in the eyes of this insurance coalition, continue to give banks a decided competitive advantage. Rather than requiring insurance business conducted by banks to be regulated by state insurance commissioners, as the coalition prefers, the bill allows existing state insurance regulations to be preempted by federal regulators if they impact banks differently than they impact insurers. In addition, insurance companies pay into guarantee funds in each state to cover insurance company insolvencies; they fear banks will take advantage of the fact that these funds are in-

**National Association of Independent Insurers
Political Action Committee Contributions**

[Bar chart showing PAC contributions for 1987-88, 1993-94, and 1997-98. Democrats received approximately $52,000 (1987-88), $30,000 (1993-94), and $17,000 (1997-98). Republicans received approximately $193,000 (1987-88), $242,000 (1993-94), and $243,000 (1997-98).]

Data derived from official studies available from the Federal Election Commission, Washington, DC, 1987–1998.

sured by the Federal Deposit Insurance Corporation, backed ultimately by the federal government.

The insurance coalition, however, has succeeded in persuading the House to adopt one of its demands: the requirements of the Community Reinvestment Act have not been extended to insurers, which was a demand of the banking coalition, especially smaller banks and savings and loan associations who argue they are disadvantaged by its application.

Another federal issue currently receiving NAII attention is reform of Superfund, the Environmental Protection Agency (EPA) fund to clean up toxic waste sites nationwide. The NAII is supportive of reforming Superfund in the direction of minimizing litigation, hastening hazardous waste cleanup without new taxes, and eliminating retroactive joint and several liability. A proposed tax on insurance premiums to add revenue to Superfund does not get support from the NAII. The association is one of the supporters of the proposed Brownfields Redevelopment and Superfund Transformation Act, which would, they argue, effectively codify many of the reforms already administered by the EPA.

The NAII is engaged in two other federal legislative initiatives. The first is federal support for homeowners insurance in areas affected by natural disasters such as floods or hurricanes. A bipartisan bill to provide federal reinsurance for state disaster insurance programs and for private property casualty insurers is applauded by the NAII. The association was successful in having language included in the legislation that allows small and regional property-casualty companies to compete more effectively in the auction mechanism used for U.S. Treasury reinsurance contracts.

Clinton administration initiatives on transportation infrastructure and safety also are supported by the NAII. The association worked for the 1998 Transportation Equity Act, which addresses commercial vehicle safety issues caused by the North American Free Trade Agreement. The NAII's particular concerns are commercial vehicles crossing the border with heavier loads, less effective brakes, and drivers who have logged more miles without sleep than federal law allows. The Department of Transportation, with NAII input, is currently considering additional proposals on railroad, airline, and highway safety.

On state issues, the NAII devotes national staff, maintains regional offices in Atlanta and Sacramento, and also retains local counsel, including former state legislators and former insurance commissioners, in every state. Because of its substantial market share, it can claim to be a significant player in industry coalitions. The NAII is active on many state issues simultaneously. Among current topics are the use of credit history information in underwriting, the use of aftermarket parts in repairing cars (those items needed to maintain the vehicle), and whether an insurer may recommend an auto repair shop to its policyholders.

The organization has a formal, computerized grassroots network. Managers in member companies act as intermediaries, receiving onsite training from the national staff and a manager's handbook. Individual volunteers are matched with office holders, encouraged to send targeted messages that may be computer generated, and prompted by Action Alerts to make other contacts. Political training seminars coach managers and volunteers on how to contact legislators, get involved in campaigns, and maximize the impact of campaign contributions. An additional focused newsletter keeps activists informed about issues and gives them policy and position background.

The NAII claims to devote more resources than any other association to working with the National Association of Insurance Commissioners. It attends their meetings, works with them in coalitions, and provides a specialized publication, *NAIC Reporter*. The NAII also lobbies the courts, acting as *amicus curiae* (friend of the court) or a direct party in state and federal courts. For example, it filed an *amicus curiae* brief in a 1998 case on workers' compensation before the Supreme Court.

NAII services include the Independent Statistical Service that provides data services used by companies to comply with state reporting requirements. Members may access reference materials and publications through a fax-on-demand service and an extensive web site. Direct public relations services are part of the NAII's membership benefits. Using its position in the industry, it is able to assemble data to shape compelling evidence in support of its arguments.

The future of the NAII will be shaped by the direction of federal financial services restructuring and federal bank deregulation. As this is written, it appears likely that banking interests will win more of their demands than will insurance interests. Property and casualty insurers have a great deal to lose if banks and other businesses move into selling insurance on automobiles and homes. Business insurance may be similarly usurped by commercial bank subsidiaries or affiliates. Thus, the only fairly certain element on the horizon is continued change and turmoil.

FINANCIAL FACTS

The NAII has an annual budget in excess of $20 million and is also able to draw upon substantial volunteer expertise from member companies. It maintains offices in suburban Chicago, Atlanta, Sacramento, and Washington, D.C. The NAII political action committee (PAC) was the first PAC established by a property and casualty association, and it is the largest. Unlike most trade association PACs, the NAII PAC barely supported the Democrats when they were in the majority, and maintains negligible financial ties with them when they are in the minority. In the 1993–1994 election cycle, only 11 percent of the PAC's contributions went to Democrats. In the 1997–1998 election cycle, Democratic contributions dropped to 6 percent of all contributions. Whether the enthusiasm for the Republican majority withstands the outcome of financial services restructuring will be interesting to observe.

LOREE BYKERK

Bibliography

The Encyclopedia of Associations. 34th ed. Detroit: Gale, 1999.

Meier, Kenneth J. *The Political Economy of Regulation: The Case of Insurance*. Albany: State University of New York Press, 1988.

Olson, Walter, ed. *New Directions in Liability Law*. Vol. 37 of *Proceedings of the Academy of Political Science*. New York: Academy of Political Science, 1988.

Rosenthal, Alan. *The Third House: Lobbyists and Lobbying in the States*. Washington, DC: CQ Press, 1993.

Zuckerman, Edward, ed. *The Almanac of Federal PACs, 1998–99*. Arlington, VA: Amward, 1998.

NATIONAL ASSOCIATION OF INSURANCE COMMISSIONERS

The National Association of Insurance Commissioners (NAIC) is an association of the chief insurance regulatory officials of states, U.S. territories, and the District of Columbia. Its mission is to assist state insurance regulators in serving the public interest; promoting the reliability, solvency, and financial solidity of insurers; promoting competitive markets; and facilitating the fair and equitable treatment of consumers.

The NAIC operates in two ways. First, it provides a forum in which insurance regulators can discuss common issues and work cooperatively on regulatory matters. Second, it extends its influence to the legislative process by endorsing model laws and regulations, which it encourages all states to adopt. These models are usually preceded by a lengthy study process, a report that is widely circulated, and formal adoption by the assembled members.

The primary interest of the NAIC is to maintain and protect regulation of insurance by state officials as assigned by the federal McCarran-Ferguson Act of 1947. In recent years the federal government has encroached on this domain through policies related to retirement security, healthcare, consumer protections, disability protections, and others. During the 1990s, the greatest incursion into insurance regulation has come from federal banking regulators, particularly the Office of the Comptroller of the Currency (OCC).

The basic response of the NAIC to threatened encroachment is to demonstrate to federal decision makers that state regulation is effective, efficient, responsible, and in the public interest. When this strategy is ineffective in dissuading federal action, the NAIC attempts to build collaborative relationships with the new intruders so as to protect as much of their domain as possible.

HISTORY

The NAIC was founded in 1871 and is the oldest association of state officials. Until 1936, it was called the National Convention of Insurance Commissioners. It has served to upgrade and professionalize the regulation of insurance by state officials and their staffs. At the same time, the organization is inherently political, which is evident from the intense lobbying attention insurance companies and trade associations devote to its members and their deliberations. The intensity with which the regulators and the regulated defend the status quo suggests to some critics that perhaps the results are not as much in the public interest as would be beneficial.

ACTIVITIES: CURRENT AND FUTURE

Even though it is an association of public officials, the NAIC's lobbying activities look very much like those of other interest organizations. Their efforts on financial services restructuring provide the most extensive current example. NAIC members and staff have worked closely with members of House and Senate committees and their staffs; they have provided testimony, crafted legislative language, and fostered a coalition to lobby members. Among the allies they have mustered are the National Conference of State Legislatures, the North American Securities Administrators Association, and the National Governors' Association. The NAIC was part of the negotiations among banks, agents, and insurers who were attempting to arrive at an acceptable restructuring compromise. They persuaded individual insurance commissioners to contact their members of Congress, and the association wrote a formal letter to members as well.

The position of the NAIC is that modernization of financial services is a worthy goal but it must not be accomplished at the expense of insurance consumers. They seek to protect the ability of state officials to supervise the solvency of insurance providers, address market conduct problems, and review the soundness of affiliations among service providers. They object to the superior status granted federal regulators and the codification of bank expansion into insurance reflected in some of the legislative proposals.

The NAIC advocates requiring insurance activities of financial services conglomerates to be conducted through holding company affiliates rather than subsidiaries. The holding company structure provides more solvency protections for insurance policyholders and allows state insurance regulators to more effectively monitor for solvency. Although no legislation has been passed, the NAIC appears to be preparing for any eventuality by arranging meetings between state insurance regulators and their banking counterparts at the Federal Reserve Board, the Office of Thrift Supervision, the OCC, and the Conference of State Banking Supervisors.

Although other issues are less important than financial services restructuring, the organization is active on many additional fronts. An NAIC subcommittee is studying the use of credit reports in underwriting setting rates. After a task force study, an official report on the topic was adopted in 1997; the following year the subcommittee held extensive public hearings on the impact of using credit reports on the availability, affordability, and accessibility of insurance to urban consumers.

Initiatives on healthcare in President Bill Clinton's administration have included NAIC representation in an advisory capacity as exemplified by the 1997 Advisory Commission on Consumer Protection and Quality in the Healthcare Industry. One of the commission's recommendations was for development of a consumer bill of rights, including an external grievance review process. The NAIC produced a white paper on the issue to highlight achievements by the states and proceeded to develop model legislation. The model then became both the subject of intense interest from congressional members and staff and a resource for subsequent legislative considerations.

On other health issues, the NAIC works to educate executive agency officials, comment on proposed regulations, and shape the debate in various other ways. It has been part of groups created to negotiate regulations, such as the Healthcare Financing Administration, which worked to negotiate regulations on the role of provider-sponsored organizations in Medicare. Concern about discrimination against victims of domestic violence has spurred the NAIC to adopt model legislation against unfair treatment in health, life, disability, property, and casualty insurance.

On the international scene, the NAIC is currently involved with two principal issues—trade agreements and settlement of Holocaust victim claims. The NAIC's international committee works with the Department of Commerce and the Office of the U.S. Trade Representative on developments relating to insurance, such as the data privacy directive from the European Union and the bilateral trade agreement with Japan. The NAIC was influential in establishing the International Holocaust Commission, and its members currently serve on the commission along with insurance supervisors from Germany and Italy and representatives of survivor groups.

The NAIC maintains three office locations. It is headquartered in Kansas City; it has an office for its federal relations, international relations, financial analysis, and federal counsel functions in Washington, D.C.; it maintains a securities valuation office in the World Trade Center in New York City.

Its staff of 320 coordinates volunteer input from members and their staffs and also provides expertise in financial, actuarial, legal, computer, and economic areas. The staff conducts research, monitors federal government activity, creates publications, and maintains state-of-the-art database services, including a computer network linking all insurance departments.

An affiliate, the Insurance Regulatory Information Network, was created by the NAIC to set up a national network of data about insurance agents and brokers in order to make the licensing process more effective and efficient. In addition, the NAIC is attempting to streamline the regulatory process by taking increased advantage of electronic options for functions such as policy and statement filing and to facilitate the marketing of insurance over the Internet without sacrificing consumer privacy protections.

Another affiliate, the Education and Research Foundation, supports education for insurance regulators and their staffs. It has funded the development of an introductory text on insurance regulation for new regulatory staff members. It also has developed training programs and handbooks for market conduct examiners and for financial analysts, and supports an annual educational program held at Drake University in Iowa.

The NAIC develops consumer information publications such as its *Shoppers Guide to Long-Term Care*

Insurance and funds public service announcements on insurance issues. In addition, it encourages consumer participation in its deliberations by funding their expenses to attend NAIC meetings.

The main potential problems for the NAIC's future are likely to arise from financial services restructuring and trends toward globalization. The organization is moving to cope with these changes both domestically and abroad. NAIC members participate in the International Association of Insurance Supervisors, the Organization of Economic Cooperation and Development, and the Joint Forum on Financial Conglomerates in order to be involved in international developments; however, events may move with greater momentum than their established networks are able to handle. International financial services conglomerates threaten to rapidly make the NAIC and its members marginal players.

FINANCIAL FACTS

As an association of 55 public officials, the NAIC does not have a political action committee (PAC). However, it is not unusual for insurance commissioners to be politically ambitious and to use their position as a steppingstone to higher office. As a result, they undoubtedly are contributors as individuals. Perhaps more important, as state officials they enjoy both a level of respect and access in national policy debates that many private interests can only observe with envy. The association's operating budget is more than $40 million annually; database fees, subscriptions, and publications sales make up their largest revenue sources.

LOREE BYKERK

Bibliography

Bykerk, Loree, and Ardith Maney. *U.S. Consumer Interest Groups: Institutional Profiles.* Westport, CT: Greenwood Press, 1995.

The Encyclopedia of Associations. 34th ed. Detroit: Gale, 1999.

Grant, H. Roger. *Insurance Reform: Consumer Action in the Progressive Era.* Ames: Iowa State University Press, 1979.

Issues 1999. Kansas City, MO: National Association of Insurance Commissioners, 1999.

NAIC: Performing in the Public Interest. Kansas City, MO: National Association of Insurance Commissioners, 1999.

NATIONAL ASSOCIATION OF LIFE UNDERWRITERS

The National Association of Life Underwriters (NALU) is a federation of 50 state and 950 local associations of life and health insurance sales professionals. Life insurance agents, general agents, and managers comprise most of the 100,000 members. Independent insurance agents, general managers of life insurance companies, and other life and health insurance professionals may be associate members.

NALU's mission is to improve the business climate and to enhance the professional skills and promote the ethical conduct of life and health insurance agents. Financial services restructuring, healthcare reform, taxation, and federal regulation of insurance are primary issues for NALU. The entry of banks into insurance sales, with the support of the Treasury Department's Office of the Comptroller of the Currency (OCC), poses a serious threat to the business base of insurance agents. Proposals for healthcare reform that reduce the potential consumer demand for private insurance services and products are also anathema to this group. Efforts to alter the tax status of life insurance products, annuities, and employee insurance benefits also have posed recent challenges for NALU. On the other hand, tax proposals to make health insurance costs wholly deductible for self-employed persons are welcomed because they expand the market for insurance sales to professionals such as physicians, engineers, and lawyers.

The most persistent area of interest for NALU is protecting the 1947 McCarran-Ferguson Act, which provides that the business of insurance is to be regulated by the states. Insurance interests have invested years of effort in building relationships with state legislators, executives, and regulators, and they want to preserve that base. Thus, occasional proposals for federal intervention raise alarm bells for NALU and other insurance lobbies.

HISTORY

The organization was founded in 1890 and has consistently served the same constituency since that time. Although insurance agents do not enjoy high public regard, the association has helped, over time, to upgrade their practices and their image. A serious concern for NALU is declining membership numbers. Declining renewals and fewer new members have meant a drop from 120,000 to 100,000 in just the past few years. Efforts to reverse the decline are under way, including a new company relations program in which insurance companies provide endorsements and information about new agents to NALU and in turn to its local associations.

ACTIVITIES: CURRENT AND FUTURE

Challenges in most of its major policy areas have confronted NALU in the last several years; proposals from President Bill Clinton's administration and from Congress have required their response. White House budget proposals have included taxes on annuities, on the value of life insurance policies (referred to as the "inside build-up"), and on employer-provided life insurance by including them in individual assets or income. In coalition with the American Council of Life Insurance (ACLI) and the Association for Advanced Life Underwriting (AALU), NALU worked to defeat these changes during congressional deliberations. A grassroots campaign, including agent visits to members of the House of Representatives and Senate tax-writing committees, resulted in an Internal Revenue Service restructuring bill that did not include new taxes on insurance.

**National Association of Life Underwriters
Political Action Committee Contributions**

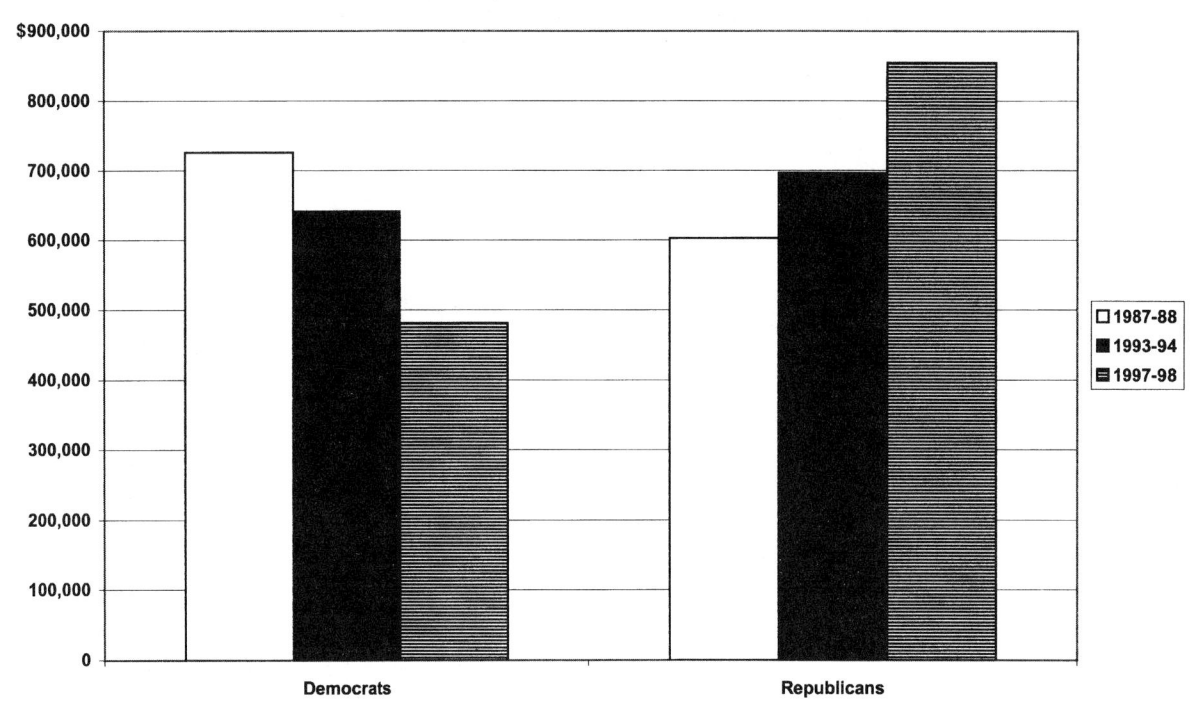

Data derived from official studies available from the Federal Election Commission, Washington, DC, 1987–1998.

NALU lobbying on financial services restructuring has proved challenging because not all the organizations representing insurance agents pursue the same strategy. NALU's position is that federal legislation is necessary to level the playing field in the financial services marketplace. It wants clarification of the states' authority to regulate the insurance activities of national banks and protections against banks' attempts to leverage their relationship with customers. When the Republicans gained control of Congress, NALU became better positioned on this issue. House Republican leaders invited NALU to negotiate with bank interests to arrive at language they could support. As a result, the bill passed by the House required that bank insurance agents be licensed and subject to state insurance regulation. It also gave the states equal footing with federal regulators on preemption issues through a new "equal deference" standard. NALU testified in support of the bill before the Senate Banking Committee, but in spite of its urging, the issue is still unresolved.

Healthcare reform issues brought NALU to Capitol Hill often in the 1990s. Recent debates over patient treatment by managed care plans gave rise to a proposal to establish federal healthcare ombudsmen. This function was regarded by NALU as usurping the responsibilities of insurance agents, and NALU worked with the Association of Health Insurance Agents to kill the proposal in the House.

NALU's grassroots efforts are formally organized as the Life Underwriters Political Involvement Committee (LUPIC). Federal congressional district and Senate coordinators lead groups of member constituents in meeting with their representatives and senators on NALU issues. Key members are flown to Washington, D.C., to meet with their representatives face-to-face on important issues, and thousands of members write letters and faxes conveying the same concerns. The LUPIC has direct contact with 529 members of Congress in this way, a 99 percent coverage rate. Timely information on the latest legislative developments is available to NALU members on their web site, which also provides background information and discussion points for letters or other contacts with policy makers.

Because of the significance of state regulation of the

insurance business, NALU supports its state chapters on local legislative and regulatory activity. Prominent topics at the state level parallel those at the national level, with banking reform currently the most prominent. NALU has drafted model legislation that would impose conditions under which banks may sell insurance, which about half the states have adopted in some form. The model bill prohibits credit tie-ins and coercion, provides safeguards against misleading consumers as to what products are insured by the Federal Deposit Insurance Corporation, forbids the use of confidential customer information for cross-marketing purposes without the customer's knowledge or consent, and prohibits discrimination against nonaffiliated insurance agents or brokers.

NALU represents insurance agents at meetings of the National Association of Insurance Commissioners (NAIC) and provides expertise to NAIC committees working to develop model legislation or regulations. NALU then also promotes adoption of the NAIC models by the states. For example, NALU has been promoting state adoption of an NAIC model regulation on how life insurance should be presented for sales purposes. The model addresses issues of disclosure, assumptions, and consumer understanding. NALU also is working on reciprocal agent licensing agreements and on a model regulation for governing replacement of policies.

Membership in NALU gives insurance agents access to education on topics such as sales and client services. NALU coordinates with the Life Underwriting Training Council in basic training leading to certification. Continuing education seminars are provided directly by NALU on topics such as Social Security, equity-indexed annuities, long-term care, and legal and ethical business practices. Seminars for agents selling property and casualty lines of insurance in addition to life and health are developed and offered cooperatively with the Independent Insurance Agents of America (IIAA). The two organizations, both organized as federations, also encourage cooperation and participation in education and training programs by their state associations.

Publications for members include a monthly magazine, *Life Association News,* which contains sales ideas, product and marketing trends, and news coverage. Access to information from NALU documents is available to members around the clock by using its automated fax-on-demand service. An annual convention with exhibits draws approximately 3,000 members.

NALU's public relations program seeks to project a positive image of insurance agents. It provides interviews for national publications such as the *Wall Street Journal,* circulates a consumer column, places supplements on life insurance in local newspapers, and contributes to op-ed columns. NALU is a contributor to the Life and Health Insurance Foundation for Education (LIFE); NALU's Washington headquarters houses LIFE's staff. LIFE is devoted to raising consumer awareness of the benefits of insurance and the value of agents. It designs and funds programs such as a multimedia presentation for high school students, a nationwide radio program with public service announcements about insurance, and a web site with information about different types of insurance.

The future holds serious challenges for NALU on two fronts. The most immediate concern is the aggressive encroachment by banks into the business of insurance. The role played by insurance agents may well be usurped by bank employees or even by computer software. (Rather than using agents, customers could directly enter application information via the Internet or telephone lines.) The other threat comes from continuing broad changes in healthcare services and how those services are paid for. Although national public-supported healthcare was beaten back in the early 1990s, incremental changes in funding and organization continue to make the agent's position fluid and vulnerable.

FINANCIAL FACTS

NALU has a staff of 110 to 125 persons and an operating budget of more than $15 million annually. More than half of its revenue is derived from member dues; revenue is also derived from advertising and subscriptions to its monthly magazine.

According to NALU's annual report, its political action committee (PAC) is the largest in the industry. It has an unusual mode of operation in that it shares half of the funds it raises with state life underwriters' associations for state races, whereas the other half goes to national candidates. NALU PAC was one of the few that switched more funds to Republican candidates in the 1993–1994 election cycle, giving them 52 percent of its contributions. Republicans swept Congress in 1994, and since then, NALU has given the party an increasingly larger share. By the 1997–1998 election cycle, Republicans received 64 percent of NALU's political contributions.

LOREE BYKERK

Bibliography

The Encyclopedia of Associations. 34th ed. Detroit: Gale, 1999.

Hrebenar, Ronald J., and Clive S. Thomas, eds. *Interest Group Politics in the American West.* Salt Lake City: University of Utah Press, 1987.

———. *Interest Group Politics in the Northeastern States.* University Park: Pennsylvania State University Press, 1993.

Zuckerman, Edward, ed. *The Almanac of Federal PACs, 1998–99.* Arlington, VA: Amward, 1998.

NATIONAL ASSOCIATION OF PROFESSIONAL INSURANCE AGENTS

The National Association of Professional Insurance Agents (NAPIA) is a trade association representing independent insurance agents and their employees who sell and service all kinds of insurance but specialize in coverage for autos, homes, and businesses. National membership numbers about 180,000, and there are 46 state and regional chapters. Their mission is not only to represent agents but also to provide education and business support and to compile statistics and research on insurance.

NAPIA is interested in issues affecting the health of property and casualty insurance as a business, regulation of insurance, auto safety issues, and environmental legislation and regulation. In general, it supports the McCarran-Ferguson Act, under which insurance is regulated by the states rather than by the federal government. It encourages enhanced auto safety features such as seat belts, child safety seats, and airbags, and it is generally in favor of state laws making the use of these features mandatory.

On environmental issues, NAPIA takes a more conservative position because of the impact on property and liability insurance rates of strict environmental protection standards. It also argues that insurers should not be taxed to fund liability relief. Trial attorneys are often their opponents on aspects of auto safety and environmental protection standards. The insurance agents argue that exorbitant attorneys' fees and damages awards do not serve to protect consumers but merely reward attorneys and raise everyone's insurance rates.

HISTORY

The association was founded in 1931 as the National Association of Mutual Insurance Agents and took its current name in 1976. It has worked over time to support the state governance of insurance and has allied with the National Association of Insurance Commissioners and the National Governors Association in that cause. In spite of periodic assaults, the principles of the McCarran-Ferguson Act are still in place.

ACTIVITIES: CURRENT AND FUTURE

Federal intervention in restructuring financial services is one of the crucial issues for NAPIA at the present time, as it was for much of the 1990s. NAPIA maintains that the Office of the Comptroller of the Currency (OCC) has overstepped its bounds in giving banks permission to sell insurance. Since the OCC's decision has been endorsed by the Supreme Court, NAPIA's position is that it is not seeking an advantage over bank-affiliated insurance agents but neither should an advantage be granted to banks. The strategy, then, is to lobby for inclusion in any restructuring legislation of language to ensure that the state insurance regulators have jurisdiction over insurance activities of banks. NAPIA argues that state insurance regulators are in a better position to enforce consumer protections against probable bank abuses.

House Resolution No. 10, considered in 1999, attempted to address the concern for state regulation by establishing 13 safe harbor provisions within which states could impose consumer protections. However, states could not impose standards more restrictive or burdensome than the federal provisions. NAPIA opposed this approach as inadequate and also wanted a requirement that banks separate their banking activities from their insurance activities.

NAPIA has provided expert testimony to House and Senate committees repeatedly on financial services restructuring proposals. Coalitions with other insurance agents groups and support of the position taken by the National Association of Insurance Commissioners strengthen their stand. However, they do want legislation to even the playing field, and that has not occurred.

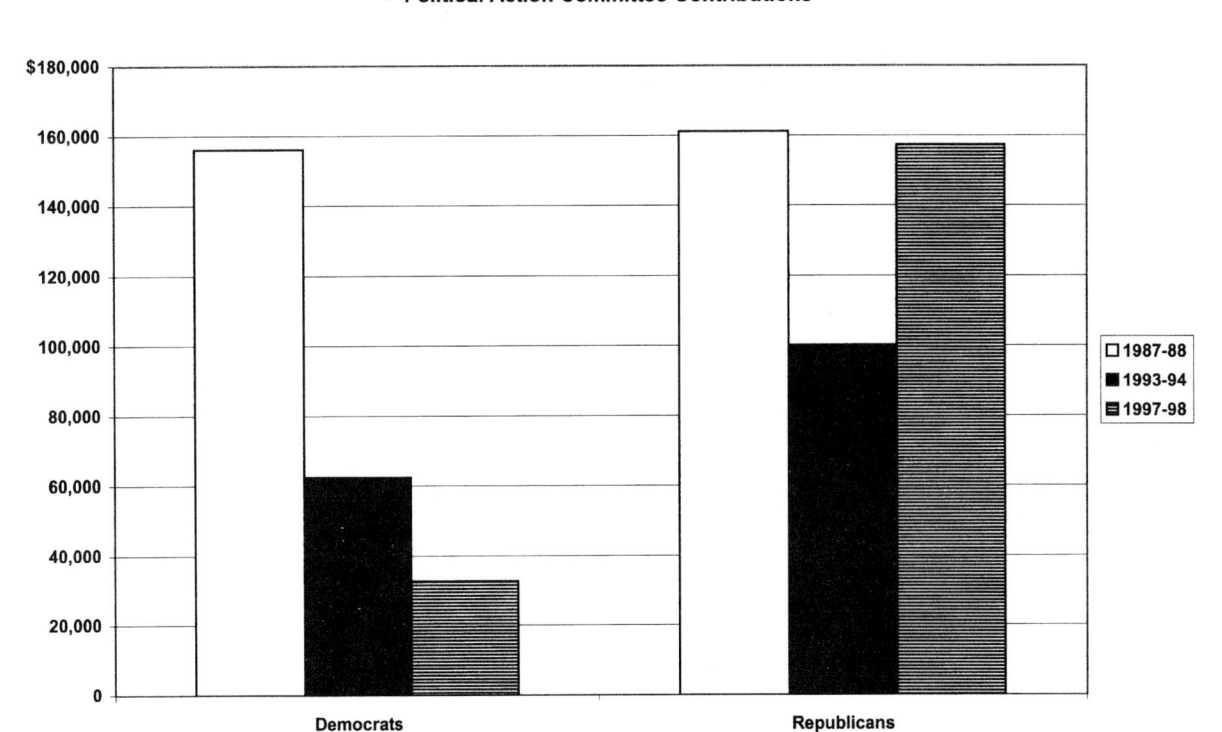

**National Association of Professional Insurance Agents
Political Action Committee Contributions**

Data derived from official studies available from the Federal Election Commission, Washington, DC, 1987–1998.

In coalition with other insurance agents organizations, NAPIA has fought bank expansion into insurance in the courts as well as in Congress. The agents financed and filed a lawsuit against the OCC's ruling that banks could sell crop insurance to farmers in conjunction with providing loans. The federal district court decision overturned the OCC ruling on the grounds that the National Bank Act limits national bank sales of insurance to offices located in towns with populations of less than 5,000 people. However, the OCC is expected to appeal the ruling.

Another issue that has come before national policy makers periodically is auto insurance reform. A recent version considered by Congress was the proposed Auto Choice Reform Act sponsored by Senators John McCain (R-AZ), Mitch McConnell (R-KY), Daniel Patrick Moynihan (D-NY), and Joseph Lieberman (D-CT). The bill was designed to lower the cost of auto insurance and reduce frivolous lawsuits by offering consumers a choice among policies with different levels of coverage for tort liability. In testimony before the Senate Commerce Committee, NAPIA applauded the goals but opposed the means on the grounds that the states must govern insurance standards. The insurance agents also could not accept that the bill included no provisions to protect agents from liability for errors and omissions when selling the policies. In addition, NAPIA is concerned that the rhetoric about rates may stimulate pressure for mandatory rate reductions.

The highest-profile lobbying that NAPIA conducts is its annual federal legislative conference, held every year since 1983. Prominent members of Congress address the conference about pending issues and prospects for action on them. NAPIA government affairs staff also provides background briefings for attendees. Thus prepared, the agents spend two days on Capitol Hill meeting with members of Congress and their staffs.

The legislative conference also provides a forum in which members of Congress can cultivate NAPIA support, as Representative Rick Hill (R-MT) did in 1999 by announcing that he would introduce legislation allowing insurers to establish tax-deferred reserves to pay disaster-related claims. NAPIA was invited to work with the representative and his staff to develop legislative language.

NAPIA has a staff of 60, who function in the areas of research, government relations, education, and marketing and advertising. An annual national conference with exhibits is available to members. Insurance for agents and their businesses is available, as are discounted products and services to support the agencies. Publications for members include a monthly magazine, *Professional Agent,* and a monthly action newsletter.

NAPIA sponsors more than 200 educational programs and seminars each year on a wide range of topics related to property and casualty insurance. Training is available for relatively new agency employees, new agents, and new and experienced managers of agencies of various sizes. Advanced technology, retraining costs, and dealing with diversity are some recent seminar topics. A relatively new development in this area is a series of television programs produced jointly by NAPIA and the Insurance Broadcast System, a satellite television network for the industry. Program topics include pending legislation, dealing with year 2000 problems, marketing in minority communities, workers' compensation insurance, and relations between companies and agencies.

NAPIA supports the public relations efforts of its members by developing advertising ideas and materials. It develops arguments articulating the organization's stands so that the public interest rather than their private interest appears foremost. It also works directly with the media, providing op-ed pieces on topics in the news. For example, during recent publicity on the dangers of airbags, it editorialized about the National Highway Traffic Safety Administration proposal to require an on/off switch for airbags.

It is difficult for NAPIA and other groups representing insurance agents to predict the future beyond the looming role of banks as insurance sellers. Now added to this is the challenge posed by the entry of retail giants such as Wal-Mart into banking, and thus into insurance. Compared to these threats to their existence, everything else on the horizon is minor.

FINANCIAL FACTS

The annual operating budget of NAPIA is about $5 million. Membership dues are the most significant part of its revenue base. Its political action committee (PAC), called PIA PAC, is one of the few trade association contributors that consistently follow ideological preferences for Republicans rather than maintaining access to the winners. It gave more to Republican candidates even when the Democratic Party was in control of Congress. In the 1993–1994 election cycle, the PAC increased the share of its contributions to Republicans, after which the GOP gained the majority. The PAC increased the Republicans' share even more significantly in the next election. By the 1997–1998 election cycle, Republicans in Congress received 83 percent of the organization's contributions.

LOREE BYKERK

Bibliography

Bykerk, Loree G. "Gender in Insurance: Organized Interests and the Displacement of Conflicts." *Policy Studies Journal* 17, no. 2 (1982): 261–276.

The Encyclopedia of Associations. 34th ed. Detroit: Gale, 1999.

Meier, Kenneth J. *The Political Economy of Regulation: The Case of Insurance.* Albany: State University of New York Press, 1988.

Rosenthal, Alan. *The Third House: Lobbyists and Lobbying in the States.* Washington, DC: CQ Press, 1993.

Zuckerman, Edward, ed. *The Almanac of Federal PACs, 1998–99.* Arlington, VA: Amward, 1998.

NATIONAL ASSOCIATION OF REALTORS

The National Association of Realtors (NAR) is the largest national trade association of professional realtors, and claims to be the world's largest trade association. It is organized as a federation, with 1,700 local and 54 state and territorial associations as members, along with 730,000 individual members. Membership in a local association automatically extends to the state and then to the national association. It represents realtors, brokers, agents, and realtor-associates and positions itself as the voice of private real property ownership. Its mission is to preserve the free enterprise system and the right to own, use, and dispose of real property.

NAR's interests at all levels of government are to protect the real estate industry from what it regards as cumbersome legislation and undue regulation; it seeks changes that support a realtor's ability to conduct business. The association dedicates itself to promoting the significance of home ownership, asserting that owning a home is one of the building blocks of a great nation and that realtors work to promote that end. Real estate plays a critical role in the economy, contributing more than $1.4 trillion annually, and an important role in the tax codes at local, state, and national levels. Thus, the NAR interest agenda includes property rights, taxation, lending, credit, financial services generally, insurance, liability, and information management.

HISTORY

The association was founded in 1908 as the National Association of Real Estate Exchanges by representatives of real estate boards from 13 states. In 1915 it became the National Association of Real Estate Boards and in 1973 took its present name. A strict code of ethics was adopted in 1913; the purpose of the code of ethics is to distinguish its adherents for their professionalism, integrity, and competence.

Protection of tax deductibility for mortgage interest is perennially a priority issue for NAR, which was part of the coalition credited with protecting that benefit during work on the 1986 Tax Reform Act. Other recent victories include extending to two years the deadline for taxpayers to roll over their profits from the sale of a house through purchase of another home of equal or greater value to thereby avoid paying capital gains taxes. NAR also supported the tax law change that allows persons 55 or older to shield $125,000 in profits from the sale of a home from capital gains taxes.

ACTIVITIES: CURRENT AND FUTURE

NAR's government affairs group monitors federal issues and promotes the group's positions with the legislative and executive branches of government. A wide array of current issues are on its agenda. On financial services restructuring, NAR advocates maintaining banking and commerce as separate functions and keeping real estate activities off-limits for bank holding companies and bank subsidiaries. It also supports restricting savings and loan holding companies in order to keep commercial firms out of banking; the argument is that mixing banking and commercial business exposes the financial system to higher risks and threatens its stability.

Proposals to reform the Real Estate Settlement Procedures Act are high on NAR's congressional lobbying agenda. The group's testimony before a Senate committee advocated one-stop shopping and was able to generate over 2,000 contacts to Senate offices in a five-day period. Although not so clearly related to the real estate mission, the grassroots membership of NAR made over 4,000 Capitol Hill contacts in opposition to a proposal by President Bill Clinton's administration to tax trade association income. NAR argued that the effect would be to raise membership dues and make it

**National Association of Realtors
Political Action Committee Contributions**

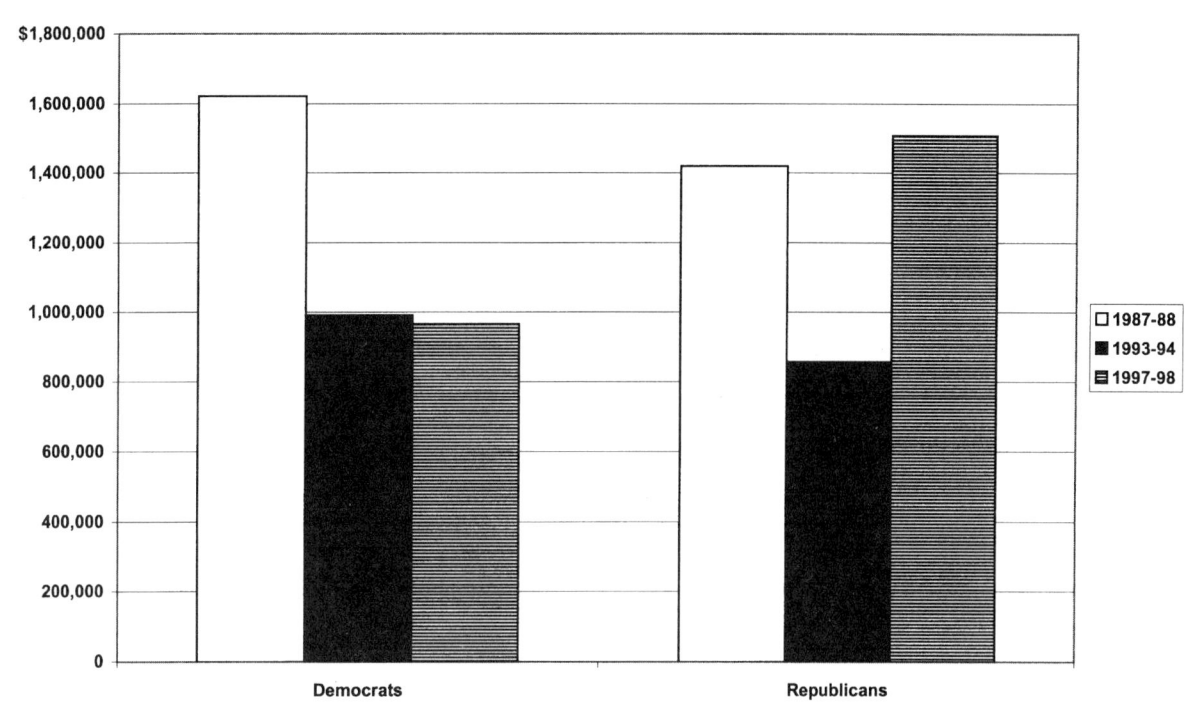

Data derived from official studies available from the Federal Election Commission, Washington, DC, 1987–1998.

more difficult to provide the level of services needed by members.

Two tax code issues are currently on the Washington, D.C., agenda. NAR is among those interest groups promoting revision of the time period for depreciation of capital improvements to commercial property. Rather than the current 39-year amortization period, NAR wants an 8- to 15-year amortization. It argues that such a change would provide an incentive to keep downtown commercial, office, and retail space more modern and competitive with suburban space, thus keeping these areas more economically viable. A tandem issue is the capital gains tax rate, which NAR contends should be as low as possible and structured so that it is effectively the same on sales of real estate as on sales of securities and other assets.

Property listings are a valuable part of realtors' business, and NAR advocates protection of this database from use by unauthorized parties who may sell it or use it for other purposes. NAR is seeking legislation to maintain electronic listings and consumer access to those listings, but to protect them from piracy by other parties. At the same time, NAR supports proposed legislation that would prohibit the Federal Communications Commission from imposing Internet access fees. The argument here is that if telephone service companies are allowed to charge time fees to Internet service providers, it would dampen the use of electronic real estate listing services by both realtors and consumers.

Also on NAR's wish list for Congress is the proposed Recycle America's Land Act, which would provide liability relief for property owners and promote redevelopment of abandoned or underutilized industrial sites thought to be contaminated by toxic wastes (also called brownfields).

NAR's PAC not only contributes to campaigns but also encourages members to volunteer, educates voters on issues related to property ownership, and encourages members to visit, call, write, and e-mail elected officials. A user-friendly web site function provides members ready access to their members of the House and Senate with messages on the topics that NAR is lobbying.

NAR maintains close ties with numerous executive branch agencies. Commercial real estate interests are currently involved with a Treasury Department study of depreciation of nonresidential real estate ordered by 1998 legislation. The Federal Reserve, the Department of Housing and Urban Development, the Federal Housing Authority, and other lenders and guarantors receive a special NAR liaison because of their impact on housing and finance. NAR also engages in legal advocacy through a special legal action committee that provides funds for test cases and participation in suits with *amicus curiae* (friend of the court) briefs.

NAR has a staff of 450, organized in divisions for communication, economics and research, education, forecasting, government affairs, legal affairs, and research. In addition, NAR has developed nine affiliates to facilitate specialized expertise, communication among members, and recognition for achievement. Affiliates are devoted to real estate counseling, commercial investment real estate, brokerage management, land sales, residential sales, industrial and office sales, national marketing, international issues, and women in real estate.

An annual convention and exposition features educational forums and trade demonstrations of innovative products and services. Meetings are held in Washington, D.C., and members receive detailed issue briefings before visiting their congressional delegations in large numbers.

NAR's publications include biweekly and monthly releases that provide news affecting the industry. Members may also access information about legislation, legal developments, marketing, and association events through the organization's website. Publications supported by the organization's research group focus on market conditions and trends. A group buying program for products and services provides travel, insurance, and retirement planning. In addition, specialized research from an extensive library may be requested by members.

Public relations campaigns for the industry are designed and funded by NAR. The organization launched a major new campaign in 1998 to educate the American public about the roles that real estate professionals play in transactions. Major broadcast and cable network prime-time slots were used for this effort.

Ongoing consideration of the tax base and the structure of the tax system will continue to keep NAR on the alert. The association has moved into electronic commerce and will also continue to be part of the effort to keep Internet transactions free of taxation. NAR helped win the 1998 Internet Tax Freedom Act moratorium, which may be a harbinger of future success.

FINANCIAL FACTS

The organization's political action committee (PAC) has been prominent among trade association political actors since the 1970s. After the Republicans won a majority in Congress in 1994, the PAC increased the share of its contributions to the party. From the 1993–1994 to the 1997–1998 election cycle, the share of the PAC's political contributions to the Democrats fell from 53 to 39 percent.

LOREE BYKERK

Bibliography

Birnbaum, Jeffrey H., and Alan S. Murray. *Showdown at Gucci Gulch: Lawmakers, Lobbyists, and the Unlikely Triumph of Tax Reform*. New York: Vintage Books, 1988.

Bykerk, Loree, and Ardith Maney. *U.S. Consumer Interest Groups: Institutional Profiles*. Westport, CT: Greenwood Press, 1995.

The Encyclopedia of Associations. 34th ed. Detroit: Gale, 1999.

Zuckerman, Edward, ed. *The Almanac of Federal PACs, 1998–99*. Arlington, VA: Amward, 1998.

NATIONAL VENTURE CAPITAL ASSOCIATION

The National Venture Capital Association (NVCA) is a trade organization of corporate financiers, venture capital groups, and individual venture capitalists whose business is investing private capital in young growth companies. Members of this group lend funds to launch new, relatively untried business ventures. These investments are high risk in that they have potential for either very high returns or complete failure. The goals of the NVCA are to foster greater understanding and appreciation for the role of venture capital in the U.S. economy, to stimulate the free flow of capital for investment, and to enhance the communication of ideas regarding investment capital in government, education, and the business community.

The organization argues that venture capital has nurtured economic growth, particularly in high-technology industries, resulting in job creation and international competitiveness. Microsoft, Genentech, Federal Express, and Intel are cited as examples of the results of contributions of venture capital to the economy. However, the role of venture capital and entrepreneurs is insufficiently appreciated, often overlooked or even hampered by public policy, problems that the NVCA seeks to correct.

Although the public image of a venture capitalist tends to focus on the individual investor, the NVCA is careful to dispel this image. According to the organization, over half of venture capital investments come from institutional public and private pension funds; the remainder comes from endowments, foundations, banks, insurance companies, and individuals. The norm is for these investors to allocate only 2 to 3 percent of their portfolios to venture funds in order to diversify their holdings.

The typical organizational form of venture capital investment is a limited partnership seeking a high rate of return after an investment period of five to seven years. The fund manager is a full partner and assumes a seat on the board of the enterprise in which funds are invested in order to be involved in management decisions on strategy, marketing, and planning. The fund reaps its profit when the new venture is acquired, merges, or goes public with a stock offering.

Among the NVCA's 230 members are some familiar names that illustrate the more institutional nature portrayed by the organization; these include Fidelity Ventures, Hewlett-Packard Company, and Norwest Venture Capital. The organization's interests focus on the treatment of investment vehicles in taxation, government regulation, trade policy, and technology issues.

HISTORY

The NVCA was created in 1973, and it in turn created the American Entrepreneurs for Economic Growth (AEEG) in 1992. This organization has both contributed to and taken advantage of the era; its interests and its message harmonized with the economy and ideology of the 1980s and 1990s. The entrepreneur is the new American hero, although the hero is supposed to look more like Bill Gates (founder and president of Microsoft) than Fidelity Ventures Fund or a public pension fund.

ACTIVITIES: CURRENT AND FUTURE

NVCA members and staff testify before congressional committees and work with various agencies of the executive branch. The association often works in coalition with other groups, such as the AEEG, to bring individual entrepreneurs into the advocacy arena. The AEEG does not have a political action committee (PAC) and maintains that it is a nonpartisan organization. Since its founding in 1992, it has grown to be the largest national

**National Venture Capital Association
Political Action Committee Contributions**

[Bar chart showing PAC contributions to Democrats and Republicans for 1987-88, 1993-94, and 1997-98. Democrats: ~$150,000 (1987-88), ~$130,000 (1993-94), ~$90,000 (1997-98). Republicans: ~$110,000 (1987-88), ~$90,000 (1993-94), ~$310,000 (1997-98).]

Data derived from official studies available from the Federal Election Commission, Washington, DC, 1987–1998.

organization of entrepreneurs that focuses on public policy.

As part of the Capital Gains Coalition, the NVCA played a role in the 1997 passage of a broad-based reduction in the capital gains tax. The legislation represented the largest tax victory ever for the venture capital and entrepreneurial communities, and the NVCA had worked on it for several years with testimony, PAC contributions, and grassroots activities. The NVCA has also been successful in persuading Congress to extend the tax deduction of the full market value for contributions of publicly traded stock to private foundations. The organization is attempting to follow this up with additional reductions in capital gains taxes and with tax credits for employee information-technology education.

Because of the high-risk nature of venture capital investments, the NVCA has also become involved in product liability issues. It successfully promoted the Biomaterials Access Assurance Act of 1998—legislation designed to protect the suppliers of raw materials to medical device companies from product liability lawsuits. The NVCA argued that the legislation would alleviate a shortage of raw materials and component parts for medical devices by relieving companies who do not design, test, or sell the devices from liability arising from the devices themselves.

The NVCA and AEEG are actively involved in securities litigation at both federal and state levels. They provided testimony, signed letters, and circulated petitions as part of the coalition to curb class-action securities lawsuits that were often targeted at high-technology companies. The legislation became law in spite of a presidential veto; it had the distinction of being the first veto override to occur during the administration of Bill Clinton. After federal legislation was passed, a California ballot proposition would have expanded the opportunity to file securities suits under state law. As part of the steering committee of Taxpayers Against Frivolous Lawsuits, the NVCA helped raise over $40 million to defeat the proposition by an overwhelming margin.

California was also the site of a tactic not usually found in the lobbying arsenal of financial trade associations. The Financial Accounting Standards Board (FASB), a federal agency, proposed to value stock options on corporate profit and loss statements. Over a several-year period, NVCA and AEEG members lobbied Congress, the Securities and Exchange Commission, and the FASB, and even persuaded the Senate to pass a resolution denouncing the proposal. While the FASB held a public hearing on its proposal in San Jose, the NVCA staged a 1960s-style rally across the street with over 4,000 employees from Silicon Valley companies protesting the threat to their stock options. The parties did reach a favorable compromise, but the FASB has since raised aspects of the issue in proposed regulations.

Intellectual property and international trade present somewhat more difficult issues for venture capital interests. Here the NVCA seeks increased and vigorous protection for their inventions, products, and ideas both domestically and internationally. Specifically, the NVCA is lobbying for a longer effective patent term for biotechnology companies and for a more favorable trade policy toward U.S. encryption technology products. At the same time the NVCA has avidly promoted legislation to increase the number of visas available for highly skilled foreign workers. It also urges Congress and the president to increase funds for basic scientific research and to ensure that research results are transferred for development and marketing through partnerships with entrepreneurs.

The NVCA has a staff of only nine persons; however, it augments its capabilities by allying with the Ewing Marion Kauffman Foundation, which underwrites research on topics of mutual interest. Members have discounted access to publications resulting from this research and also to management liability insurance programs. In addition, the NVCA is attempting to launch a data collection survey and database that captures all venture capital and private equity data. If successful, the database would serve members by providing access to industry statistics and would also enable the NVCA to better represent the industry in public policy venues. This effort is also underwritten by the Center for Entrepreneurial Leadership of the Ewing Marion Kauffman Foundation.

The NVCA sponsors educational programs for its members including seminars on topics such as hiring and compensating senior executives and a three-day "graduate program" at Emory University in Atlanta. It provides networking opportunities through a series of regional luncheons sponsored by accounting firms including Ernst & Young and PricewaterhouseCoopers. As long as small emerging ventures continue to create jobs and enjoy success in a booming economy, the NVCA's agenda is likely to succeed. Their demands for tax shelters and other inducements along with their self-portrait as risk-taking entrepreneurs sounds as American as the national anthem.

FINANCIAL FACTS

Political contributions of the organization's PAC, called VenturePAC, reflect political considerations. In 1987–1988, 58 percent of the organization's political contributions went to Democrats, who held a majority in Congress; however, the PAC shifted contributions following the Republican congressional victory in November 1994. The pattern evidenced here shows a dramatic swing toward the Republicans in 1995–1996, but ironically, not one foreseen in 1993–1994 contributions, when 59 percent of VenturePAC's contributions still went to Democrats. By the 1997–1998 election cycle, Republicans received 78 percent of the organization's contributions.

LOREE BYKERK

Bibliography

The Encyclopedia of Associations. 34th ed. Detroit: Gale, 1999.

Olson, Walter, ed. *New Directions in Liability Law.* Vol. 37 of *Proceedings of the Academy of Political Science.* New York: Academy of Political Science, 1988.

Pertschuk, Michael. *Revolt Against Regulation: The Rise and Pause of the Consumer Movement.* Berkeley: University of California Press, 1982.

Zuckerman, Edward, ed. *The Almanac of Federal PACs, 1998–99.* Arlington, VA: Amward, 1998.

SECURITIES INDUSTRY ASSOCIATION

The Securities Industry Association (SIA) is a trade association representing investment banks, broker-dealers, and mutual fund companies active in all markets and all phases of corporate and public finance. In the United States, SIA members account for about 90 percent, or $100 billion, of securities firms' revenue and 350,000 jobs. They manage the accounts of more than 50 million investors directly and tens of millions indirectly through corporate, savings, and pension plans.

The SIA has 775 members, for whom its mission is to foster an effective capital-raising and investment process, to present their views to legislators and regulators at state and federal levels of government, to provide a forum for addressing industry issues, and to be a catalyst for creative ideas.

Because of its position as a general association for the securities business, the SIA has a long list of policy interests, many of which have become more pertinent in recent years due to expanding technology and more widespread investing by Americans. Trading volume on U.S. stock markets is now 350 times what it was a decade ago; Internet transactions grew 700-fold in just four years. Thus, the role of securities firms as the intermediaries between investors and markets is changing rapidly.

Perennial issues for the SIA include tax policy, savings and investment incentives, the structure of financial services, and government oversight of market transactions. The securities industry has suffered in the last few years as a result of banks expanding into its business. Regulators have allowed banks to own securities firms as subsidiaries, stimulating a wave of acquisitions enabling banks to offer brokerage services along with deposit and lending services. Banks now lead-manage about 20 percent of the value of corporate bonds underwritten and 15 percent of the stock underwritten. By contrast, in 1990 their share of bond underwriting was about 1 percent and they did not underwrite stock. Hence, the securities industry is keenly interested in recovering its position among financial service providers.

HISTORY

The SIA was established in 1972 through the merger of the Association of Stock Exchange Firms, founded in 1913, and the Investment Bankers Association of America, founded in 1912. In recent years, the organization has faced a more rapidly changing environment characterized by accelerating technological developments, competition among financial service providers, and fluid legislative and regulatory guidelines.

CURRENT ACTIVITIES

The SIA has been lobbying for years to expand savings incentives for Americans. In 1997, it helped persuade Congress to raise the income eligibility levels for Individual Retirement Accounts (IRAs) and make them available for non-wage-earning spouses. The SIA advocates raising the maximum contribution limits for IRAs to $4,000 and indexing the limit to reflect cost-of-living increases; it also seeks to index the contribution limit to 401(k) pension plans in which employees set aside pre-tax income for retirement and to allow for "catch up" contributions for those years when individuals did not make their full contributions. In addition, the SIA wants Congress to eliminate the income test that determines whether IRA contributions are tax deductible. The association also lobbies on the capital gains tax issue and did succeed in getting the rate lowered in 1997 and getting the required holding period for securities restored to 12 months in 1998.

On financial services restructuring, the SIA believes that outdated federal laws impair the global competi-

**Securities Industry Association
Political Action Committee Contributions**

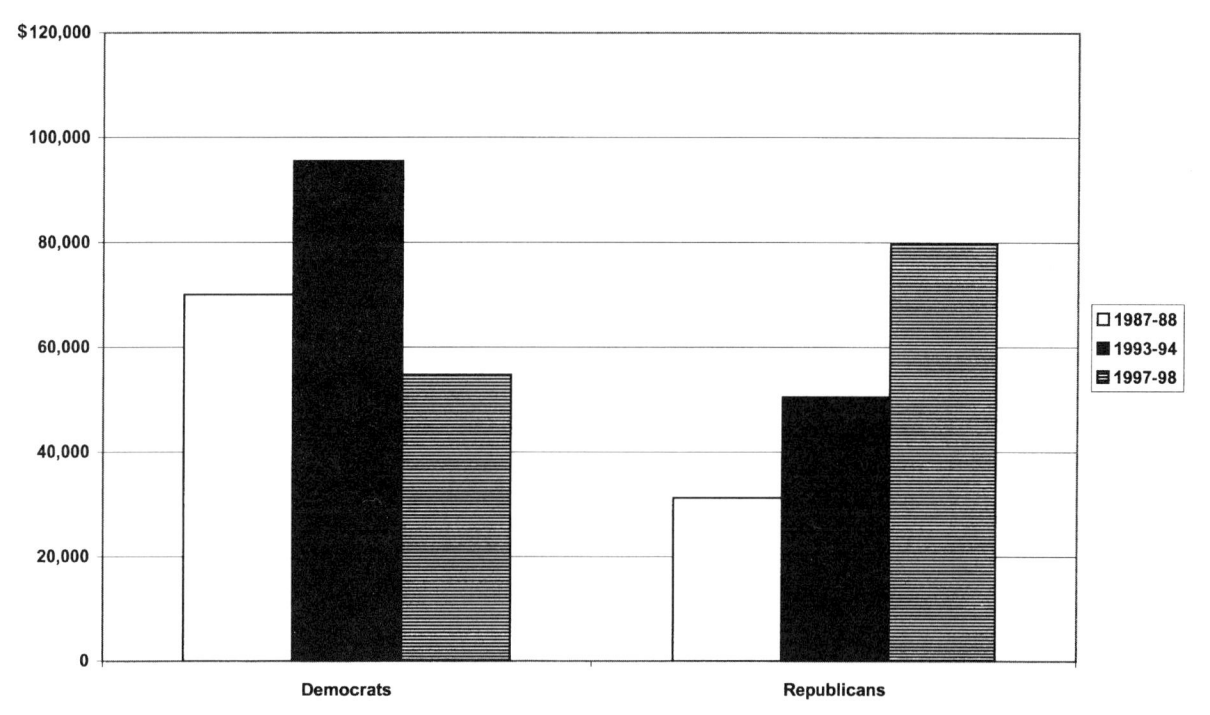

Data derived from official studies available from the Federal Election Commission, Washington, DC, 1987–1998.

tiveness of financial services firms, drive up costs, and threaten future growth. It argues that modernization of the 1933 Glass-Steagall Act, which restricted a company's ability to provide overlapping financial services, should allow brokerages to have the same ability that banks have to affiliate freely with other financial service providers. Reform should also align regulation functionally so that one federal agency applies the same set of rules to the same financial activity. Thus, brokerages would be allowed to own banks and, the SIA argues, generate more competition, which would lower costs for consumers.

Support for financial services legislation along these lines has been generated from the SIA's grassroots; thousands of employees of member firms contacted their representatives in Washington, D.C., promoting passage of legislation on the House floor. When the Senate took up the bill, a group of CEOs from member firms flew to Washington to meet individually with key senators, and another group from the SIA's grassroots network flew in for the Senate committee markup and passage.

Working with accountants and high-tech companies, the SIA persuaded Congress to make it more difficult for investors to bring class-action lawsuits against securities firms. In 1995 and 1998, Congress imposed uniform national standards for securities litigation, required that plaintiffs show specific evidence of misconduct, capped lawyers' fees, and created a safe harbor for companies to furnish investors with forecasts about future performance.

The SIA was also part of the lobbying force against taxing Internet commerce. It supported passage of the Internet Tax Freedom Act, which provides for a moratorium on Internet taxes and sets a policy against state or local interference with Internet commerce.

The growing significance of foreign markets draws the SIA to take positions intended to expand and protect their members' multinational and foreign businesses. The SIA is among the voices urging normalization of trade relations with China; it points out that China is poised to invest $1 trillion in transportation, communications, and energy over the next decade.

Relations with the European Union have brought client privacy issues onto the agenda. The SIA contends that existing U.S. laws and regulations provide adequate safeguards, and it provided the administration of President Bill Clinton with a report on industry practices making that point. Also in the interest of protecting client information, the SIA is promoting efforts to allow U.S. securities firms to export encryption products for protecting data they send worldwide. The SIA was able to persuade the Department of Commerce to allow securities firms to be included in guidelines allowing such exports.

In the regulatory arena, the SIA generally supports relying as far as possible on self-regulation. Its work with the Federal Reserve and the Securities and Exchange Commission (SEC) promotes revision of investor margin requirements so firms can maximize their use of capital without incurring imprudent levels of risk. The SIA is also working with the SEC on streamlining the process by which securities issuers access capital markets, including digital-age standards for prospectus delivery. A recent success with the SEC was the issuance of a new limited regulatory structure for over-the-counter derivatives dealers (dubbed "broker-dealer lite") to allow firms to compete with unregistered or overseas entities.

Preparing for transition to the year 2000 has brought forth an enormous cooperative effort within the securities industry, facilitated by a series of SIA forums and committees. The SIA obtained approval from the U.S. Department of Justice to allow members to share computer testing results and information on methods to correct problems without fear of antitrust litigation. The association also worked with Congress, the Clinton administration, and the business community to enact the Year 2000 Disclosure Act, to reduce liability concerns that may inhibit businesses from disclosing and sharing year 2000 information.

Joint purchasing of telecommunications services is available to SIA members. A contract with Sprint, used by 175 firms, saves them $25 million annually on a service volume of more than $75 million; it also generates revenue for the SIA that has amounted to over $5 million in seven years. Other service contracts are with Bell Atlantic, AT&T, and Teleport.

In pursuit of its education goals, the association offers members the Securities Industry Institute, branch management leadership training, and a professional conduct program. The institute draws professors from the prestigious Wharton School and provides industry professionals week-long seminars for three consecutive years on topics including management skills, information technology, market trends, and regulatory policy. The SIA's values statement demonstrates an awareness that member firms and employees have a responsibility to issuers and to investors and that the public's trust and confidence rest upon their integrity.

The SIA conducts programs to increase industry support for diversity in the workplace and the marketplace. It contends that demographic trends require employers to adapt to a labor market increasingly populated by minorities. It also emphasizes that women and minorities are a growing source of, and market for, investment capital. In furtherance of these goals, the Reverend Jesse Jackson was brought to address the association's annual meeting and a special conference that also featured speeches by President Clinton, Treasury Secretary Robert Rubin, regulators, and industry leaders. The SIA also worked with SEC Chairman Arthur Levitt to conduct meetings on diversity with CEOs in Los Angeles and Minneapolis.

The association provides poll data on a variety of topics for members' use. The SIA conducts 15 surveys annually to supply data for firms' use in planning their budgets, benchmarking branch production, and developing compensation policies. It also conducts consumer polls and focus groups to help member firms understand their clientele and improve their service offerings.

In addition to an annual meeting, the SIA sponsors multiple specialized conferences each year in various regions and on topics such as technology management and estate planning. Besides an extensive web site, members also may use reference material and data reports and receive periodic publications as well. There are six different periodicals related to legislation and regulation, including *Legislative Alerts* and *Legal Alert*.

The SIA supports member firms' advocacy efforts by developing client education programs and campaigns to persuade Americans to save more. This includes development of the Stock Market Game for use in the classroom to acquaint young people with how investing works.

Relationships between the securities industry and the media are enhanced by an annual two-day program in which reporters and editors are brought to visit firms' trading floors, computer operations centers, the stock market, and self-regulatory organizations. The SIA also supports a fellowship program allowing senior business correspondents and editors to spend a year's sabbatical studying at Columbia University. These ties are maintained at such events as a recent day-long conference on how the media covers Wall Street, held at the Columbia School of Journalism.

Looking ahead, the association is working to coordinate numerous consumer service upgrades for the securities industry. Among these are a program to shorten the clearing and settlement process from three days to one, having cut it from five to three days in 1995. The SIA is also coordinating efforts of broker-dealers, stock and futures markets, clearing and settlement organizations, and other industry utilities to shift equity pricing from fractions to decimals in the year 2000. It is also planning to address the impact of the Internet on the securities industry and to strengthen the industry's international capability.

FINANCIAL FACTS

The SIA has annual revenues exceeding $27 million. Member dues and investment income contribute 64 percent of that, and proceeds from member services, conferences, and publications comprise the remainder. The organization employs a staff of 107. Among the members are several large corporations that sponsor their own political action committees (PACs), including Goldman Sachs, Morgan Stanley, and Prudential Securities. The SIA's PAC did not anticipate the Republican takeover of Congress with its 1993–1994 contributions. In 1993–1994, 65 percent of the PAC's contributions still went to Democrats, who had maintained a majority in Congress. By the 1997–1998 election cycle, nearly 60 percent of the SIA PAC's contributions went to Republicans. Still, it is interesting to note that the securities industry is more generous to Democrats than are many financial services PACs.

LOREE BYKERK

Bibliography

Annual Report: Preparing for the Millennium. New York: Securities Industry Association, 1999.

The Encyclopedia of Associations. 34th ed. Detroit: Gale, 1999.

Phillips, Kevin. *Arrogant Capital: Washington, Wall Street, and the Frustration of American Politics.* Boston: Little, Brown, 1994.

Zuckerman, Edward, ed. *The Almanac of Federal PACs, 1998–99.* Arlington, VA: Amward, 1998.

SECTION TWO
SERVICE, TRADE, AND PROFESSIONAL

Of all the types of political interest groups, it is perhaps most difficult to find common themes in the ones that represent service, trade, and professional organizations. Their missions vary widely, as do their ideologies and organizational structure, their penchant for a particular political party, and the people whom they represent. Furthermore, although most service interest groups mentioned here have created their own political action committees (PACs) within the last few decades, some do not officially maintain PACs and may only influence government indirectly—that is, through various forms of media rather than lobbying before members of Congress. Their methods or strategies as lobbyists also vary greatly. Some lobby quietly; their lobbyists will bring their individual PAC's issues before Congress without including their interest group's members. Others lobby loudly by encouraging members to jam the phone lines and use the Internet so that they can communicate directly with congressional leaders.

The associations or federations mentioned in this section represent individuals with remarkably different political views and personal interests. Small-business–related interest groups—the National Federation of Independent Business (NFIB), for example—oppose legislation involving antitrust laws, increases in the minimum wage, and the increase of excise taxes on various products relating to member businesses. A handful of organizations, like the Fraternal Order of Police (FOP) and the National Beer Wholesalers Association (NBWA), have embraced ideological interest groups on the right, including the National Rifle Association (NRA), which has supported amendments that would soften gun-control laws. Other associations of this type have radically different views: the National Association of Social Workers (NASW)—in contrast to, say, the NFIB—favors minimum-wage increases and supports all types of legislation that not only furthers social workers' interests and social-science–related research but also benefits each individual's social, psychological, and physical well-being rather than serving the monetary interests of business owners or chief executive officers. Likewise, the Association of Trial Lawyers of America (ATLA) represents workers, not wholesale or retail business owners and operators, as many of the other service interest groups do. In particular, ATLA represents plaintiffs—generally employees—who are involved in workers' compensation lawsuits, and it has consistently lobbied in opposition to federal legislation that would establish a national ceiling on damages or that would enable states to preempt product liability laws.

These interest groups represent members of organizations that include business and law offices; law enforcement agencies; food and beverage, convenience, and chain-store operations; federal and social work agencies; and funeral homes, to name a few. Perhaps most noteworthy are the business PACs, the NFIB in particular, for they were seminal players in the Republican Party takeover of Congress in the 1994 elections, using both soft and hard money to advance their cause.

AREAS OF INTEREST

Like most other interest groups, service-related businesses and organizations have been a staple of American society since colonial times. Business regulation was then common, as British authorities regulated the trade of goods and services; colonies themselves, however, were still allowed to supervise and regulate business within their own borders.

The move to centralize civil institutions, such as law enforcement, came at a time when similar institutions were in the process of being organized into large bureaucratic systems. These include centralized school systems as well as centralized municipal services, firefighting agencies, and hospital emergency services. However, centralization did not mean that workers were satisfied with wages and benefits. The oldest interest group discussed in this section, the National Funeral Directors Association (NFDA), was established in 1882, five years before Congress passed the Interstate Commerce Act, which deprived the individual states of the power to control and regulate railroads. In 1890 Congress passed antitrust legislation—the Sherman Antitrust Act—for the purpose of mollifying farmers and small-business owners when it appeared that huge corporations would overwhelm and possibly bankrupt small "Main Street" businesses.

In 1914, in reaction to small-business owners and as part of President Woodrow Wilson's progressive program to regulate big business, the Federal Trade Commission (FTC) was established. It consisted of a five-member watchdog team of commissioners who had power to control competition by defining "unfair trade practices." It also issued cease and desist orders, which varied depending on who were members of the commission. One service and service interest group that seemed to benefit from this piece of legislation was petroleum wholesaling and the Petroleum Marketers Association (PMAA). Founded in 1909 as the Independent Petroleum Marketers Association, the PMAA wanted to limit the power of the Standard Oil Company, which seemed to monopolize the petroleum industry and overpower small petroleum wholesalers and retailers.

Issues related to tax increases and the fear of being monopolized by corporations and big business were prevalent since the need for services arose. To be sure, one of the reasons for establishing service interest groups was to ensure the existence of a voice for all individuals involved in serving the public, whether they were small-business owners or federal employees.

Other factors contributing to the creation of some interest groups were issues related to the sale of alcoholic beverages. As a result of the end of Prohibition, the NBWA was established as a means of giving wholesalers the power to regulate beer and malt beverage sales and to prevent breweries from oversupplying retailers.

More recently a number of laws were passed to enable interest groups to contribute directly to political candidates or use soft money as a means of influencing members and the public at large to endorse particular candidates who would serve on the interest group's behalf.

CURRENT CONTEXT

Despite the dramatic differences in lobbying style, mission, or general structure of each of the interest groups mentioned here, some stand out as being highly influential in political campaigning in the 1990s. The NFIB, for example, with the financial assistance of the National Restaurant Association, the NBWA, and ideological groups like the NRA and the Christian Coalition, strongly endorses the GOP and has been extremely influential in the dramatic changes that have occurred in both houses of Congress. Working in collaboration, these groups participated in The Coalition—Americans Working for Real Change, a strong antilabor and antiunion group that helped to counteract the efforts of the AFL-CIO, a powerful trade union federation that has favored Democratic candidates. Some claim that Lane Kirkland, president of the AFL-CIO, retired from his post in 1995 partially due to age but also as a result of the Republican takeover of Congress.

Another feature that makes the NFIB so powerful is its enormous membership—over 600,000 individuals. The NFIB encourages its members to flood telephone and Internet lines so that congressional representatives act immediately on the issues they vehemently oppose. In fact, the NBWA has gone so far as to encourage its members—mostly beer wholesale distributing company owners—to invite their employees to make toll-free calls as a means of lobbying members of Congress and presenting them with an increased head count.

In contrast, a large number of interest groups have been hit hard since the GOP assumed the majority in Congress. Some of these include those representing organized labor, such as the AFL-CIO, and several environmental organizations, like Greenpeace and the Sierra Club. The new GOP majority was quick to move on modifying pending environmental legislation and even questioned existing environmental laws. Similarly, the agendas of a few service interest groups have been frustrated by the GOP majority. The NASW as well as the National Association of Retired Federal Employees (NARFE), lobbying in support of the patient's bill of rights, sponsored by Tom Daschle (D-SD), failed in their endeavor after the Republican Congress turned down the measure and replaced it with its own version of healthcare.

TYPES OF ORGANIZATIONS

As stated earlier, service interest groups differ widely in terms of their interests, political philosophies, and organizational makeup. However, one similarity is that each of the organizations provides services—as varying as they may seem—to either members themselves (the NFIB or the PMAA, for example) or individuals served by memberships (as is the case with the NASW or the ATLA).

There really is no central theme that unites all service, trade, and professional interest groups. The majority attempt to further the interests of small-business owners and operators, although a few of them, for example the NBWA, have attempted to strengthen a few select businesses through advocating federal laws limiting the sale of alcohol through the mail, telephone, and Internet. The owners and operators can also be involved in wholesale or retail business. Such groups include the Food Marketing Institute (FMI), the National Association of Convenience Stores (NACS), the National Automobile Dealers Association (NADA), the NBWA, the NFIB, the NFDA, the PMAA and, perhaps most supportive in small-business politics, the U.S. Chamber of Commerce—the largest federation and organization among those listed here that regulate and foster small-business interests.

On the flip side, however, are service associations and related organizations that serve and benefit workers and their families rather than owners and management. Two groups, ATLA and the NASW, not only represent the rights and interests of lawyers and social workers but also the people whom they serve and counsel. Some groups, like NARFE, actually serve the interests of the workers themselves.

With the exception of four interest groups in this section—the American Bar Association (ABA), the American Library Association (ALA), the Fraternal Order of Police (FOP), and the U.S. Chamber of Commerce—the remaining 11 interest groups have established PACs as a means of sponsoring political candidates who will advance their goals and objectives. The four that do not specifically use PACs as a means of conducting their lobbying activities have addressed their political penchants through other types of media. The FOP, for example, has used both national and syndicated networks to its advantage by influencing network personnel to be sympathetic to its interests. Moreover, these associations have used soft money as a means of endorsing politicians who support group interests.

Other associations, like the FMI, make use of tax-exempt satellite associations as a means of furthering their interests. The FMI, for example, established the Food Marketing Institute Foundation as a means of carrying out much of its lobbying activities. Although the association formed the Food Marketing Institute Political Action Committee (FOODPAC), the FMI uses the Food Marketing Institute Foundation (FMIF) for lobbying politicians. Since it is filed under the Internal Revenue Service tax code Section 501(c)(3), the FMIF can lobby Congress and support particular candidates and issues while being tax-exempt at the same time. Also, federal tax laws, as well as federal election laws, have permitted certain interest groups to establish tax-exempt subsidiary or related groups as a means of influencing memberships, the public, and politicians themselves, through education and educational programs relating to political candidates and their issues. In recent years, however, these laws have allowed the PACs of these groups to use their money directly for the purposes of a particular candidate's election or defeat. The passing of these laws has been no doubt a financial boon for a number of interest groups, not only those representing service, trade, or professional personnel but also ideological groups, like the Progress and Freedom Foundation or Americans for Tax Reform, which fall under 501(c)(3) status.

CURRENT ISSUES

Current issues among service interest groups not only vary greatly but may be in diametric opposition to one another. On the one hand, there are interest groups that focus nearly all their attention on small businesses and their interests, while others devote considerable time to both member interests and issues relating to the people they serve. In general, small-business interest groups, as well as ideological service groups, like the FOP, have endorsed GOP candidates running for both legislative and executive offices, while groups representing individual members, mostly workers or individuals represented by these workers, have endorsed Democratic candidates.

The major issues and concerns for interest groups of small- and medium-sized businesses have always focused on the possibilities of tax increases or laws requiring the increase of wages for employees of these businesses. For the most part, these businesses are particularly wary of increases in excise taxes on various merchandise. Both the NBWA and NACS have lobbied Congress to repeal the Special Occupational Tax (SOT). The SOT was established in the 1860s as a means of generating funds for the Civil War by taxing businesses that sold alcohol. These interest groups, however, claim that there is little reason to require the SOT in the 1990s and accuse the defenders of this legislation of being against the sale of alcoholic beverages altogether.

Small-business interest groups also fear that a raise in the minimum wage will force a number of businesses to lay off employees. They argue that rather than aiding entry-level or unskilled employees, minimum-wage increase legislation, backed mostly by Democrats, only cuts down on the hiring of such employees because businesses will be unwilling to pay higher hourly wages. In contrast, the NASW strongly approves of federal legislation supporting minimum-wage increases for the purpose of relieving workers and their families of financial burdens that place them well below the poverty level. Furthermore, the NASW argues that increases in the minimum wage enhance the opportunities of entry-level employees rather than frustrate them.

This is not to say that all small-business–related groups support GOP candidates exclusively. The NACS, for example, has opposed the Hyde Amendment (H.R. 1501), which would hold convenience store owners and operators accountable for damage relating to the sale of "violent" or "sexually explicit material." Opposition to this amendment has received bipartisan support. In addition, the concerns of some interest groups, the Business Roundtable in particular, seem to diverge greatly from most of the other business-related interest groups. To illustrate, the Business Roundtable opposes a Republican healthcare package sponsored by Charles Norwood (R-GA), which, they argue, would make business owners and employers liable in state courts for the health benefits they would grant employees.

In addition, some small-business service interest groups—like a number of the interest groups representing media and the information and entertainment industries—are deeply concerned with issues relating to copyright, particularly regarding the playing of music. Two organizations representing the rights of composers, the American Society of Composers, Authors and Publishers and Broadcast Music Incorporated, have filed numerous lawsuits over the years against small-business members of the NFDA and the National Restaurant Association who have been accused of copyright infringement. Businesses that do not obtain permission to perform music that does not fall under public domain can receive stiff penalties if found guilty of violating copyright law. Part of the NFDA's and the National Restaurant Association's lobbying efforts, then, have focused on supporting amendments to copyright infringement laws. The National Restaurant Association firmly opposes the tenets of the Copyright Damages Improvement Act, which requires that restaurateurs and other food-service owners and operators obtain permission for every musical composition performed at their establishments.

Apart from business-related and worker-related interest associations and federations, some service interest groups have agendas that relate to the promotion of services. One such group is the ALA, whose lobbying efforts focus on furthering literacy in low-income urban and rural areas, opposing legislation on censorship or banning of certain books, and recruiting individuals from groups that have been oppressed historically, particularly people of color, women, and people with disabilities.

TYPES OF ACTIVITIES

As mentioned above, service interest groups engage in a number of forms of lobbying. Some have opened toll-free phone lines and have made Internet access available for members to communicate their issues or group interests with PAC administrators and lobbyists, or even senators and representatives themselves. Very few service interest groups, however, resort to this method exclusively. (Interest groups that solely exploit their large memberships and bury politicians in phone calls, Internet e-mails, and faxes are usually political, ideological, and religious groups.) Instead, they will adopt this so-called outsider method of lobbying in tandem with insider approaches, such as meeting with congressional leaders privately as a means of lobbying. Interest groups and PACs like the NFIB, the NBWA, or even NARFE fall into this category. In reaction to President Bill Clinton's plan to increase taxes on beer and alcohol sales as a means of reducing the federal deficit, the NBWA, for example, sent out more than 13,000 faxes to its members, urging them to contact members of Congress and even White House personnel to express their opposition to the plan.

Interest groups like the NFIB and the PMAA garner support from members as a way of influencing legislation that encourages competition and that prevents large corporations from monopolizing particular industries. In contrast, a number of corporate and trade associations lobby quietly before Congress, rather than focusing specifically on members.

While some interest groups' war chests have remained large, like NADA's over $1 million allocation for political contributions during the past decade, a number of other groups' allocations for legislative and executive candidates have grown exponentially. The NBWA's political contributions increased more than threefold—from under $400,000 in 1987 to more than $1.3 million in 1996. The NFIB, too, increased its funds more than threefold, from approximately $300,000 in 1987 to $1.1 million in the 1996 election cycle. Most of the groups that increased their war chests significantly were major GOP benefactors. The NBWA and the NFIB, in particular, are claimed by a number of advocates to have been responsible for the 104th Congress's Republican majority. On the other hand, some groups' political contribution allocations diminished over the years. Such had been the case for NARFE, whose political contributions, favoring Democratic candidates, amounted to nearly $2 million in 1988, while in the 1996 election year, total contributions amounted to only $1.2 million.

DANIEL NESS

Bibliography

Anderson, Brian, and Burdett A. Loomis. "Taking Organization Seriously: The Structure of Interest Group Influence." In *Interest Group Politics,* 5th ed., edited by Allan J. Cigler and Burdett A. Loomis. Washington, DC: Congressional Quarterly Press, 1998.

Biersack, Robert, Paul S. Herrnson, and Clyde Wilcox, eds. *After the Revolution: PACs, Lobbies, and the Republican Congress.* Boston: Allyn & Bacon, 1999.

Drew, Elizabeth. *Whatever It Takes: The Real Struggle for Political Power in America.* New York: Viking, 1997.

Herrnson, Paul S. *Congressional Elections: Campaigning at Home and in Washington,* 2d ed. Washington, DC: Congressional Quarterly Press, 1998.

Herrnson, Paul S., Ronald G. Shaiko, and Clyde Wilcox, eds. *The Interest Group Connection: Electioneering, Lobbying, and Policymaking in Washington.* Chatham, NJ: Chatham House, 1998.

Shaiko, Ronald G., and Marc A. Wallace. "From Wall Street to Main Street: The National Federation of Independent Business and the New Republican Majority." In *After the Revolution: PACs, Lobbies, and the Republican Congress,* edited by Robert Biersack, Paul S. Herrnson, and Clyde Wilcox. Boston: Allyn & Bacon, 1999.

Tyack, David. *The One Best System: A History of American Urban Education.* Cambridge: Harvard University Press, 1974.

Wilson, Graham, K. *Interest Groups.* Cambridge, MA: Basil Blackwell, 1990.

Zuckerman, Edward, ed. *The Almanac of Federal PACs, 1998–1999.* Arlington, VA: Amward, 1998.

AMERICAN BAR ASSOCIATION

A center and voice of the legal profession in the United States, the American Bar Association (ABA) represents practitioners in specialized areas of the law, geographic interests of some state and local bars, and those of law-related associations. It has around 400,000 members, including practicing lawyers, judges, and court administrators, public service nonpracticing lawyers, legal professionals working for firms and corporations, and law professors and students. The ABA represents nearly one-half of all lawyers in the country and is currently the world's largest voluntary professional association.

The ABA's mission is "to be the national representative of the legal profession, serving the public and the profession by promoting justice, professional excellence and respect for the law." The association is concerned with such goals as the achievement of high standards of professionalism, competence, and ethical conduct; the independence of the legal profession and the judiciary; the full and equal participation in the profession by minorities and women; and—more broadly—the improvement of the American system of justice and the promotion of the rule of law in the world. However, its influence goes beyond the legal profession itself; through its 24 sections and four divisions, the ABA touches virtually all aspects of the law. Its agenda includes serving the needs of a changing society, promoting meaningful access to legal services, and increasing public understanding of law.

HISTORY

In the last part of the nineteenth century, professional lawyers and professional politicians had become differentiated groups within the American state. After the Jacksonian era, lawyers were not the surrogate aristocracy that the French observer Alexis de Tocqueville had seen in the early 1830s, but they would continue to be a highly influential elite in a system of government where the judicial branch has the power of judicial review and, subsequently, the capacity to determine whether the actions of other branches comply with or oppose the U.S. Constitution.

The initiative to create a national bar came from Simeon Eben Baldwin, a lawyer who proposed it to the Connecticut Bar Association. Once the idea was accepted, Baldwin worked in the search for 14 well-reputed lawyers to sponsor a meeting in Saratoga Springs, New York, and took upon himself the task of sending personal invitations to a number of colleagues across the country. The call attracted responses from nearly 100 lawyers from 21 states, who approved the creation of the new association, along with a constitution to govern it, in August 1898.

The ABA was originally established for the "advancement of the science of jurisprudence, the promotion of the administration of justice and a uniformity of legislation throughout the country"; some committees to seek these aims were formed, along with others dealing with questions such as patents and bankruptcy. The interest in professionalization and training, however, was a priority for the ABA since its early years.

At the time, apprenticeship was the most frequent method of professional qualification and was at the same time an informal mechanism to regulate the entry and characteristics of new practitioners. Since the 1880s economic, demographic, and social change caused a gradual shift from apprenticeship to formal education in the legal profession. The process took four decades to be completed, and the ABA played a fundamental role in shaping its development.

The ABA established requirements for prelegal education and criteria for admissions, as well as for duration of programs. The ABA was also instrumental in the organization of the Association of American Law Schools (1900) and promoted a variety of standards to qualify and approve institutions and universities offering legal instruction. In addition, a written test—the bar examination—after completion of courses was institutionalized. Within 50 years state and local authorities would accept this centrally administered test.

The ABA's proposals resulted in the homogenization

of the standards of professional qualification and the demise of less demanding schools. As a consequence of this as well as the Depression and the Second World War, part-time law schools, in particular, disappeared by the 1950s. But critics maintain that the association's actions may have limited the entry of new practitioners and discouraged certain ethnic groups from entering the profession. Three requirements in particular—citizenship, residence, and "good character"—restricted the access of immigrants and political radicals. (All three were eventually struck down or considered as unconstitutional by the Supreme Court during the 1970s and 1980s.) Especially during the first 40 years, ABA membership was very exclusive and grew slowly; it was not until 1965 that the association reached a membership of 100,000.

An early area of concern for the ABA was the question of legal ethics. When the association was established, no ethical regulations existed regarding responsibility toward clients, courts, and opponents, other than the lawyers' consciences. The ABA can claim credit for being the first bar to adopt an ethical code—in 1908; in subsequent years local and state bars became increasingly involved in this issue. Critics still express concerns to the extent to which enforcement actually occurs in the legal profession; violations do not always receive sanctions and can actually help to advance clients' interests. However, the ABA has revised its original code, trying to adapt it to new situations. The last modifications were approved in 1982 and have become a basis for several other local and state regulations of professional conduct.

In 1937 the ABA opposed the attempt made by President Franklin D. Roosevelt to pack the Supreme Court's membership in order to overcome judicial opposition to his legislative plan. In the end, a majority of the Supreme Court accepted Roosevelt's proposals, but the mobilization undertaken by the ABA reinforced its public recognition as a salient voice of the legal profession. In the association itself, this was a time of change: a new constitution was adopted in 1936 to integrate into the bar's agenda a wider range of social, political, and economic concerns. Efforts were also made to recruit young lawyers.

Traditionally, the ABA has been very influential in the selection of judges at the state and federal level. In 1936 a special committee was created to work on these issues, but it was not until 1952 that the executive branch first invited the association to review qualifications of candidates. This practice persists up to the present time. Regarding nominations to the Supreme Court, on the other hand, there is no fixed pattern, and variations occur across administrations.

The legal profession today is quite diversified, and bar enrollment necessarily reflects this situation. Lawyers perform a variety of activities, not only in the judicial field but also as teachers, corporate lawyers, sole practitioners, and public officials. The ABA's leadership has been dominated by older practitioners—graduates of elite schools and law firm partners—as opposed to younger or sole practitioners, and has been seen as conservative compared to other bar associations. No monolithic voice can exist here. The ABA is only loosely linked to other organizations: state and local bars are mostly autonomous and are more likely to mobilize their particular interests at their respective levels of action. Still, the ABA plays a fundamental role as a setter of standards in the legal profession; it is a preeminent voice, and its opinions and influence cannot be underestimated.

ACTIVITIES: CURRENT AND FUTURE

The ABA's center in Chicago, Illinois, is a complex organization that extends its work to units in other states. The "Office of Washington" is of particular relevance because its staff works continuously on the status of bills, regulations, and policies. This information is then sent twice a month to state and local bar associations by way of *The Washington Summary*. A monthly publication, *The Washington Letter,* provides deeper analytical perspectives on those issues affecting the legal profession.

The Governmental Affairs Office (GAO), also located in Washington, works for the successful representation of the ABA's perspectives before the U.S. executive, legislative, and judicial branches. Between 1997 and 1998, for instance, lobbying activities were performed for over 100 issues, testimonies were presented at 28 congressional hearings, and 150 letters were sent to legislative committees and executive offices. More recently, GAO has launched new programs to track legislative activity at the state level.

The American Bar Endowment is a fund-raising organization providing support for education, research, and public-service activities, and it also supports the ABA Fund for Justice and Education, which deals with projects and awards for young lawyers. The American Bar Foundation is a think tank related to the ABA.

The ABA publishes the *American Bar Association Jour-*

nal, a general-interest magazine, more than 50 periodicals, and approximately 100 single titles per year on a variety of topics of professional and public concern. ABA members receive benefits that go from electronic information resources to insurance programs and investment advice. Beyond this, the ABA has expanded its agenda to include a number of programs addressing public concerns, such as child abuse, legal service, the high cost of justice, domestic violence, juvenile trial, problems of the elderly, fair trial, and free press.

FINANCIAL FACTS

The ABA's administrative staff includes 750 employees, working with an annual budget of $65 million. In 1997 and 1998, the ABA's lobbying expenditures reached $1,180,000 and $1,280,000, respectively, according to the Center for Responsive Politics; but the association does not make contributions to political campaigns and has no political action committee.

MIRIAM JIMÉNEZ-HERNÁNDEZ

Bibliography

Abel, Richard. *American Lawyers.* New York: Oxford University Press, 1989.

American Bar Association, Division of Media Relations and Public Affairs. "Overview." Washington, DC, July 1998.

———. "Profile" (January 1999). Washington, DC, 1998.

"The American Bar Association. One Hundred Years of Service." *The American Bar Association Journal* 64 (July 1978).

American Bar Association: www.abanet.org

AMERICAN GAMING ASSOCIATION

Located in Washington, D.C., the American Gaming Association (AGA) represents members of the gaming and entertainment industry and those who assist in the industry's success. The AGA has approximately 110 members, with casino and equipment manufacturers comprising only 25 percent of the total. Its remaining members consist of suppliers, vendors, and others servicing the gaming industry. The AGA is primarily interested in providing aggressive national representation for the industry and its related businesses via lobbying activities. Additionally, the AGA provides information to its members for purposes of improving the public image of the gaming industry. This latter goal is apparent in the selection of the name "gaming," as its connotation is more benign than that of "gambling."

HISTORY

The AGA has a very brief history, as it was founded in 1995. The instigating factor behind its creation was President Bill Clinton's proposal in 1994 to tax gambling at 4 percent to help pay for welfare reform. Deeming its interests threatened, the gambling industry joined forces and founded the AGA. Its political mission, if not already obvious, was underscored by its selection of President and Chief Executive Officer Frank J. Fahrenkopf Jr., who is a former chairman of the Republican National Committee. The AGA met with immediate success in its political efforts, as Clinton dropped the proposed gambling tax. The formation of a gaming trade association was not surprising at this time, given the sudden emergence and growth of the industry. As late as 1988, only two states had casinos. By the mid 1990s, gambling was on its way to becoming one of the nation's favorite forms of entertainment, with casinos in 27 states. *Mother Jones* magazine reported in 1997 that the revenue from gambling in the previous five-year period exceeded the revenue from movies, spectator sports, theme parks, cruise ships, and recorded music combined. Surely, an industry with such exorbitant growth rates would find itself in need of national representation.

Such representation was particularly necessary in this industry because of the many legal restrictions on gambling and the numerous opponents of its expansion. In fact, coalitions of clergy, elected officials, and community groups have waged successful campaigns to keep casinos out of Florida, Ohio, and New York. However, the AGA has had much to celebrate in its brief history, as it has defended against smoking bans in casinos and hotels, bankruptcy reforms that would preclude gaming-related debts from consideration, advertising restrictions, and the repeal of the wagering loss deduction that enables individuals to pay taxes on net, as opposed to gross, winnings from gambling. What is more, it helped to defeat two southern Republican governors, who opposed forms of gambling, in the 1998 elections.

ACTIVITIES: CURRENT AND FUTURE

The AGA utilizes an "insider" strategy, donating to campaigns and hiring lobbyists to influence governmental policy. Capitalizing on the financial resources of its members, the AGA has arranged tours of casinos for legislators and thereby built the foundation for friendly relationships. In addition, it has employed a Republican pollster to conduct surveys and political research. Currently, there are several issues in the legislative arena that have prompted the AGA to engage in these lobbying activities. For example, the AGA has closely monitored the legal status of Internet gambling in an effort to ensure that laws do not prohibit the industry's use of the medium for marketing purposes. Of

**American Gaming Association
Political Action Committee Contributions**

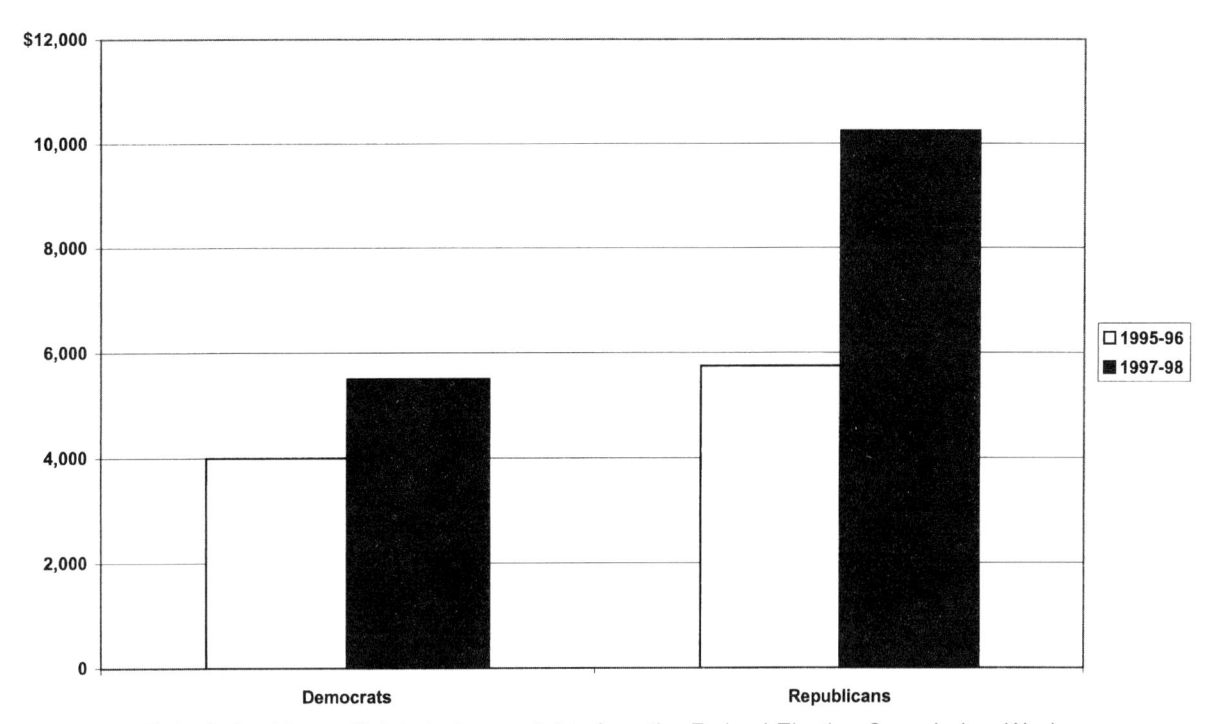

Data derived from official studies available from the Federal Election Commission, Washington, DC, 1995–1998.

more significance, the AGA, together with its individual members, is working to dilute the consequences of the National Gambling Impact Study Commission, which Congress charged to conduct a two-year study of gambling's political, social, and economic effects. The report, which is expected to be negative, was issued in 1999.

Closely related to its lobbying activities, the AGA additionally seeks to enhance the public image of the gaming industry. To this end, the AGA attempts to arm its members with information and statistics that can offset the industry's negative image. As is well known, the gambling industry is often blamed for increased crime, suicide, divorce, and bankruptcy. To offset these negative associations, the AGA runs a national information clearinghouse with data about the industry, publishes biweekly reports about the "good work" of the industry, and disseminates information about responsible gaming. Clearly, an improved public image for the industry would be an asset in any of the AGA's lobbying efforts. In addition to its political activities, the AGA offers its members promotional opportunities, a benefit that would surely be coveted by vendors and others serving the industry. As do most trade associations, the AGA also enables its members to network with others in the gaming industry via several sponsored events. For example, the AGA holds an Annual Meeting and Board of Directors' Reception, independent conferences and seminars, and task force meetings on newly emerging and important issues.

Despite occasional victories by community groups opposed to gambling, then, the future of the industry appears bright, and for the time being, the AGA's future seems secure as well. As the entertainment industry continues to consolidate in the current legal environment of deregulation, casinos, with their ability to make staggering profits, will be well placed to dominate the industry. For example, they will be in a superb economic position to purchase theme parks and movie studios. Indeed, Las Vegas is currently home to 11 of the 12 largest hotels in the world, with more such facilities in the works. The line between gambling and other forms of entertainment is likely to blur, as mega-hotels combine theme parks for children with casinos for their parents. In light of this potential, the AGA and its members will surely remain interested in any legislation aimed at the increasing concentration of ownership in the media industry. The future development of the Internet and the possibility of online gambling are issues that the AGA will continue to monitor closely as well. If approved and regulated by the state and federal governments, online gambling would move from offshore companies to the large casinos, which consumers would trust. Clearly, the financial stakes for the industry are enormous. The Internet is, of course, part of the larger information-entertainment industry and as a result, surely has the potential to be colonized by the lucrative gaming industry. The AGA has not taken a stand on Indian gambling because its members are divided, but it might be forced to confront this issue in the near future as well. Some of the AGA's members have contracts to manage the Indian casinos, while others claim that the tax-free status of these competitors is threatening. However these and other specific issues are resolved, the AGA's future is bound to grow more secure as the gambling industry becomes an increasingly significant economic and political force.

FINANCIAL FACTS

Indicative of its political interests, the AGA has its own political action committee (PAC). In its first election cycle in 1995–1996, the AGA's PAC had receipts of $23,600 and expenditures of $22,363. Its contributions in the last two election cycles were:

	Total	Democrat	%	Republican	%
1995–96	$ 9,750	4,000	41	5,750	59
1997–98	$15,750	5,500	35	10,250	65

Additionally, the AGA contributed $70,100 and $50,800 in soft money in the 1995–1996 and 1997–1998 election cycles, respectively. In 1997–1998, it gave $30,300 or 60 percent to the Democrats and the remainder to Republicans, but it had been close to evenly divided in its partisan giving in 1995–1996. Because the AGA speaks on behalf of casinos, it undoubdly benefits from their contributions as well. In 1997–1998, the gambling industry contributed $1.2 million to political candidates and $3.1 million in soft money to political parties. The AGA itself paid $760,000 to lobbyists in the calendar year 1997 alone. Despite relatively small PAC contributions, then, the AGA and its members clearly have invested much money in their effort to gain influence on Capitol Hill.

JULIE M. WALSH

Bibliography

American Gaming Association: www.americangaming.org
Center for Responsive Politics: www.crp.org
Koughan, Martin. "Easy Money." *Mother Jones,* July/August 1997. www.motherjones.com
Ota, Alan K. "Casinos Look to Improve Their Odds on Capitol Hill." *Congressional Quarterly* (January 23, 1999): 191–195.
Zuckerman, Edward, ed. *The Almanac of Federal PACs, 1998–1999.* Arlington, VA: Amward, 1998.

AMERICAN HOTEL AND MOTEL ASSOCIATION

The American Hotel and Motel Association (AHMA), located in Washington, D.C., has approximately 12,000 members in its national association, which is a federation of 70 state and city lodging associations in the United States and 33 foreign countries. It is the leading trade association for the $75.4 billion lodging industry in the United States. Its members consist primarily of lodging properties and businesses that supply goods and services to the lodging industry, though individual memberships are offered to members of the military, college faculties, and students planning a career in the hospitality industry. The AHMA represents the lodging industry at both the national and state levels, monitoring legislation that would impact the profitability of the industry and lobbying on the industry's behalf.

HISTORY

The AHMA traces its origins to 1910, when it was founded in Chicago. Before assuming its current name in 1962, the organization was called the American Hotel Protective Association and later, the American Hotel Association. Throughout its history, the AHMA has been able to win exemptions from the minimum wage and hour laws as well as tax deductions for meals and entertainment expenses. Increasingly, the interests of its most prominent and powerful members are merging with the American Gaming Association and the entertainment industries since the larger hotels are now invested in casinos and theme parks. In fact, Las Vegas currently houses 11 of the 12 largest hotels in the world.

ACTIVITIES: CURRENT AND FUTURE

The AHMA's government affairs department, which is responsible for overseeing lobbying efforts in Washington, D.C., relies upon "insider" strategies to foster a favorable business climate for the lodging industry. At its annual legislative action summit, the AHMA arranges appointments with senators and representatives for those members in attendance and provides instruction on the art of effective lobbying. It also briefs members about important issues affecting the industry. At the 1999 summit, the AHMA highlighted the importance of keeping the minimum wage at its present level, retaining the 50 percent deductibility of business meals, and preventing healthcare reforms that would increase or require employer contributions. In addition to the annual summit, the government affairs department prepares briefs analyzing the effects of proposed pieces of legislation on the industry and provides status reports about such legislation. Although state associations are charged with lobbying at the state and local level, the AHMA serves as an information center on these matters. In so doing, it enables members to share information and possibly work together on similar issues.

The AHMA does not limit its activities to lobbying, but instead provides many other services to members. For example, it operates an information center and publishes a lodging trade magazine. With more than 20 committees that enable members to participate in the organization and to address critical issues facing the industry, the AHMA additionally provides networking opportunities to its members. One of these committees, Copyright Music, negotiates with music licensing organizations about fee schedules at the behest of members who purchase musical entertainment. On this issue, its interests are at odds with others in the entertainment industry, such as recording companies.

In the future, the AHMA is thus likely to expand upon its traditional agenda of labor, tax, travel, and fire safety issues to include gambling and perhaps even copyright issues.

FINANCIAL FACTS

The AHMA has a staff of 65 in its national office and a budget of $7 million. Additionally, the AHMA has two

**American Hotel and Motel Association
Political Action Committee Contributions**

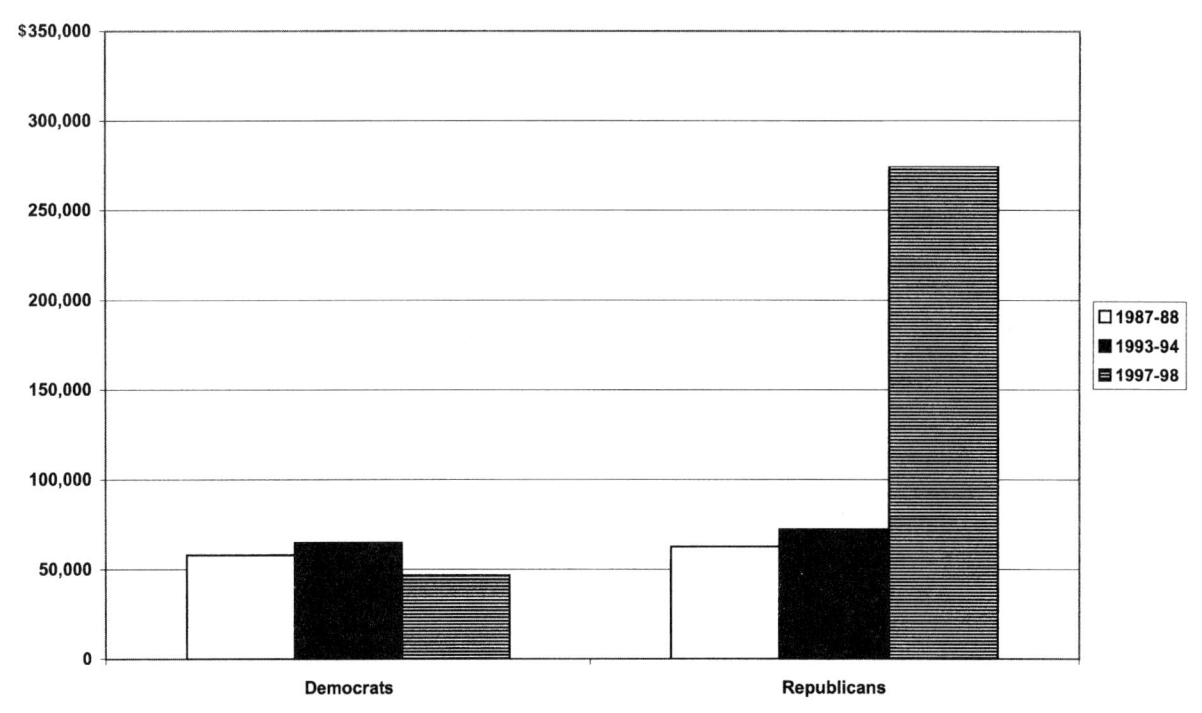

□ 1987-88
■ 1993-94
▤ 1997-98

Data derived from official studies available from the Federal Election Commission, Washington, DC, 1987–1998.

affiliate organizations, the Educational Institute, which is a source of training and educational materials for the lodging industry, and the American Hotel Foundation, which maintains the financial resources to support education and research within the lodging and other related industries. Like other trade associations, the AHMA has a political action committee (PAC). In the 1995–1996 election cycle, its PAC had receipts of $191,376 and expenditures of $196,011. Its contributions for the last two election cycles were:

	Total	Democrat	%	Republican	%
1995–96	$179,800	51,600	29	128,200	71
1997–98	$315,577	46,750	15	268,827	85

Prior to the Republican takeover of Congress in 1995, the AHMA was more balanced in its partisan contributions, even donating slightly greater dollar amounts to the Democrats in the 1989–1990 and 1991–1992 election cycles. Such a pattern is indicative of the PAC's pragmatic orientation. The AHMA's political budget is not limited to PAC contributions, but also includes lobbying expenditures and soft money contributions. Indeed, in 1997, the AHMA paid $160,000 to lobbyists. In the 1997–1998 election cycle, it contributed $48,000 to the Democrats and $96,738 to the Republicans in soft money. These amounts represented dramatic increases from the 1995–1996 cycle when the AHMA contributed $6,400 and $1,500 in soft money to the Democrats and Republicans, respectively.

JULIE M. WALSH

Bibliography

American Hotel and Motel Association: www.ahma.com
Center for Responsive Politics: www.crp.org
Zuckerman, Edward, ed. and compiler. *The Almanac of Federal PACs, 1998–1999.* Arlington, VA: Amward, 1998.

AMERICAN LIBRARY ASSOCIATION

The American Library Association (ALA) was established in 1876, with the main purpose of promoting librarians' interests. Today, more than a century later, the ALA is a complex organization with a wide agenda, working to improve its members' resources and welfare and extending its activities to questions as important as the defense of intellectual freedom in the United States.

The ALA is interested in state, public, school, academic, and special libraries, and supports the creation of methods to improve library systems and standards of service. The ALA also works for free access to library services and everyone's right to information, and promotes popular understanding and public acceptance of the value of these services and of librarianship in general.

The association has helped to establish libraries on Indian reservations, in hospitals and prisons, and in locations overseas, and has collaborated with executive agencies such as the U.S. Information Agency in the implementation of particular projects. Nowadays, the ALA has relations with over 70 other library associations (in the United States and at the international level) and works with several organizations in the fields of education, research, cultural development, recreation, and public service.

With 57,000 members (including librarians, trustees, publishers, supporters, and friends), the ALA is the world's oldest and largest national library association.

HISTORY

The ALA's origins are usually traced to a convention of librarians held in 1853. The idea of creating a permanent association was first stated there, but it was two decades later that the final impulse for such an initiative took place.

Melvil Dewey, creator of the Dewey decimal system and one of the most influential persons in the history of librarianship in the United States, was among a small group of librarians who worked intensely to attract interest and support for a conference to be held on the occasion of the nation's centennial celebration. The conference took place in Philadelphia, Pennsylvania, in October 1876, gathering 103 librarians from different states. The resolution to establish the ALA was approved during the final day of sessions.

The ALA's founders were a quite homogeneous group. These librarians were mostly Anglo-Saxon men who wanted to facilitate communication among themselves in order to identify and solve their common professional problems. Soon after the ALA was established, however, its members embraced some degree of social responsibility, when they recognized as part of their mission to get "the best reading, for the largest number, at the least cost." (Originally suggested by Dewey, this became the association's motto in 1879.)

During the first three decades of the association's existence, several discussions were centered on technical preoccupations of librarianship and the organization of the annual conferences. Then, gradually, the ALA created general indexes, maintained a periodical publication (*The Library Journal*), and established relations with librarians overseas. In 1899 the association was able to exert some influence on the appointment of the head of the Library of Congress.

In 1917 the ALA had reached a level of stability that allowed it to develop a wider set of activities. When the United States entered the First World War, the ALA's membership decided to work to supply books and services for soldiers at home and abroad. Two fund-raising campaigns were developed in order to acquire publications ranging from foreign language dictionaries and manuals to strategy and military affairs books. With some financial support form Andrew Carnegie and working in combination with organizations such as the Red Cross and the Young Men's Christian Association, the ALA was able to establish temporary libraries in several military stations. Such libraries continued working even when the war was over and then were gradually transferred to local administrations.

With these actions, the ALA achieved some national visibility for the first time in its history.

The Path to Intellectual Freedom

Between 1939 and 1969 the ALA was in a process of transformation that eventually led it to embrace the defense of intellectual freedom in the United States as a mission. When the ALA was created, its mostly homogeneous membership had taken for granted that librarians had jurisdiction and autonomy regarding book selection. In the following years, however, changes at the political level in the United States caused different waves of censorship, which eventually reached librarians and their jobs.

The advance of fascism in Europe and the nonaggression pact signed between Germany and the Soviet Union in 1939 were events that increased concerns about internal security in the United States. A variety of governmental and nongovernmental actors tried to restrict or ban the circulation of publications considered subversive or propagandistic on both leftist and rightist grounds. Then, the ALA sought to define the role of libraries in democratic systems and approved a bill of rights stating the association's commitment to providing the public with free access to information and different ideas.

Later, in the years from 1948 to 1953, librarians reacted against book burning, the imposition of loyalty oaths, material labeling, and directives to control and withdraw publications in libraries overseas, which were imposed during the wave of anticommunist censorship that characterized the years of McCarthyism. The ALA modified its bill of rights and made different efforts to assure wide distribution of *The Freedom to Read,* a statement meant to provide guidance to librarians and to the public in general. (This statement was endorsed by organizations such as the American Bar Association.)

The association's bill of rights was modified once again in the decade of the 1960s to promote free access to libraries and to contribute to the elimination of forms of racial segregation.

Not all actions were effective or immediately influential, and the ALA had to go from the formulation of statements to attempts to influence public opinion. It gradually developed more concrete activities such as the formulation of principles of intellectual freedom. Today the ALA's activities include participation in processes of arbitration and investigation, lobbying, and programs to support librarians who were affected by or lost their jobs in controversies involving intellectual freedom.

ACTIVITIES: CURRENT AND FUTURE

The ALA is headquartered in Chicago, Illinois, and maintains a research center and 10 offices addressing issues regarding international relations, library outreach services, and public programs, among others. The ALA currently has a staff of 275 persons and a member council composed of 175 persons governs it. In addition to this, 11 membership divisions deal with specific kinds of library services.

Currently the ALA identifies five main action areas: 1) the provision of services for diverse populations; 2) education and continuous learning for librarians; 3) equity of access to libraries; 4) intellectual freedom, including reading, search for information, and speech; and 5) twenty-first-century literacy, ensuring that children and adults develop the skills to participate in a global economy.

The association maintains an office in Washington, D.C., which plays a very important role in supporting the ALA's agenda. The office gathers and analyzes information regarding bills and coordinates coalitions to sponsor and support legislative initiatives. It also maintains communication with members of Congress and executive agencies, and publishes a newsletter.

Three units in particular develop activities regarding intellectual freedom: the ALA's Office for Intellectual Freedom, the Freedom to Read Foundation, and the Intellectual Freedom Roundtable. They deal with questions of communication, information, education, grassroots involvement, awards, and fund-raising. The ALA's publications on this subject—now complemented by Internet resources—have chronicled the challenges to intellectual freedom in the United States in a continuous way since the decade of the 1950s.

In addition to periodical publications such as the *ALA Bulletin,* the association produces books for librarians and researchers. The ALA also has a rich web site containing news, information, and a variety of resources regarding librarianship, education, and funding opportunities. The association's commitment to favor the access of information has faced some problems. In 1999, for instance, the ALA has been criticized by conservative moralists (such as talk-show host Laura

Schlesinger) for having included a Columbia University–sponsored web site in a reference guide for teenagers. The involved service ("Go Ask Alice") responds to questions in areas regarding health, sex, emotional health, and nutrition. This incident was about to have adverse repercussions on a grant that the private firm Toys "R" Us was going to give the ALA's Fund for America's Libraries, to be used for children's reading rooms.

FINANCIAL FACTS

The ALA has an annual budget of $31,597,153, 80 percent of which is generated by conferences and grants from other organizations. According to the Federal Election Commission, the ALA spent $279,394 in lobbying activities in 1997 and $321,426 in 1998; the main areas of interest are education, media, and budget.

MIRIAM JIMÉNEZ-HERNÁNDEZ

Bibliography

American Library Association: www.ala.org

The American Library Association, Public Information Office, "Fact Sheet." Chicago, 1999.

Robbins, Louise. *Censorship and the American Library. The American Library Association's Response to Threats to Intellectual Freedom, 1939–1969.* Westport, CT: Greenwood Press, 1996.

Thomison, Dennis. *A History of the American Library Association 1876–1972.* Chicago: American Library Association, 1978.

Wingand, Wayne A. *The Politics of an Emerging Profession. The American Library Association 1876–1917.* New York: Greenwood Press, 1986.

AMERICAN ASSOCIATION OF ADVERTISING AGENCIES

With offices in New York and Washington, D.C., the American Association of Advertising Agencies (AAAA) is the national trade association of the advertising agency business. Advertising, of course, is the major source of revenue for news providers and much of the entertainment industry. Advertisers are themselves seeking to convey information as well, albeit of a very biased nature. Ownership is highly concentrated in this industry, with seven or eight firms dominating the global market. The AAAA has approximately 600 members, who together account for 75 percent of all agency-produced advertising in the United States. Given that statistic, the AAAA clearly counts the dominant agencies among its members. As the industry's voice in Washington and state capitals, the AAAA takes an interest in any legislation that affects the industry, such as restrictions on advertising and tax issues.

HISTORY

Partly in response to growing concerns about false advertising and resultant demands for consumer protection, the AAAA was founded in 1917. Soon thereafter, in 1924, it published its code of Standards of Practice, which asked members not to produce false advertising. Because the AAAA did not have any means to enforce the code effectively, this effort at self-regulation did not solve the problem. However, the industry did not come under the scope of federal regulation until 1938 when the Wheeler-Lea Amendment to the earlier Federal Trade Commission (FTC) Act was passed. This amendment enabled the FTC to prohibit false or misleading advertising. It was not until the 1960s, though, that the advertising industry incurred a series of major legislative defeats. Between 1960 and 1972, Congress passed more than 25 laws regulating the industry. For example, the Cigarette Labeling Act of 1966 and the Public Health Smoking Act of 1970 regulated the advertising of cigarettes. Other laws protected children from harmful toys by prohibiting their advertisement, while still others protected consumers.

In response to this legislative surge, the AAAA coalesced with other organizations in an effort to prevent further regulations. The industry has been reasonably successful in this effort, even winning a relaxation of restrictions in some areas, such as medical advertising.

ACTIVITIES: CURRENT AND FUTURE

In its quest to protect the interests of advertising agencies from governmental regulation, the AAAA relies primarily upon "insider" tactics. It is a founding member of the State Advertising Coalition, which is a state lobbying group for the advertising industry. The AAAA enters into coalitions at the national level to further the interests of advertisers as well. Additionally, the AAAA seeks access to lawmakers through financial contributions to campaigns and based on its ability to provide information and expertise about the industry. Currently, the AAAA is working to preserve the full deductibility of advertising as a business expense, to prevent additional restrictions on alcohol and tobacco advertising, and to ease restrictions on auto-lease and airline advertising.

Like other trade associations, the AAAA hosts conferences and publishes a quarterly magazine for purposes of contributing to the professional development of its members. As an advocate of the industry, it promotes the value of advertising by way of various initiatives. The AAAA is also a founding member of the Advertising Council, which exists to conduct public service campaigns. With the help of the Advertising Council and others, the AAAA was instrumental in the creation of the Partnership for a Drug-Free America. Clearly, public service campaigns function not only to educate the citizenry, but also to improve the image of the in-

**American Association of Advertising Agencies
Political Action Committee Contributions**

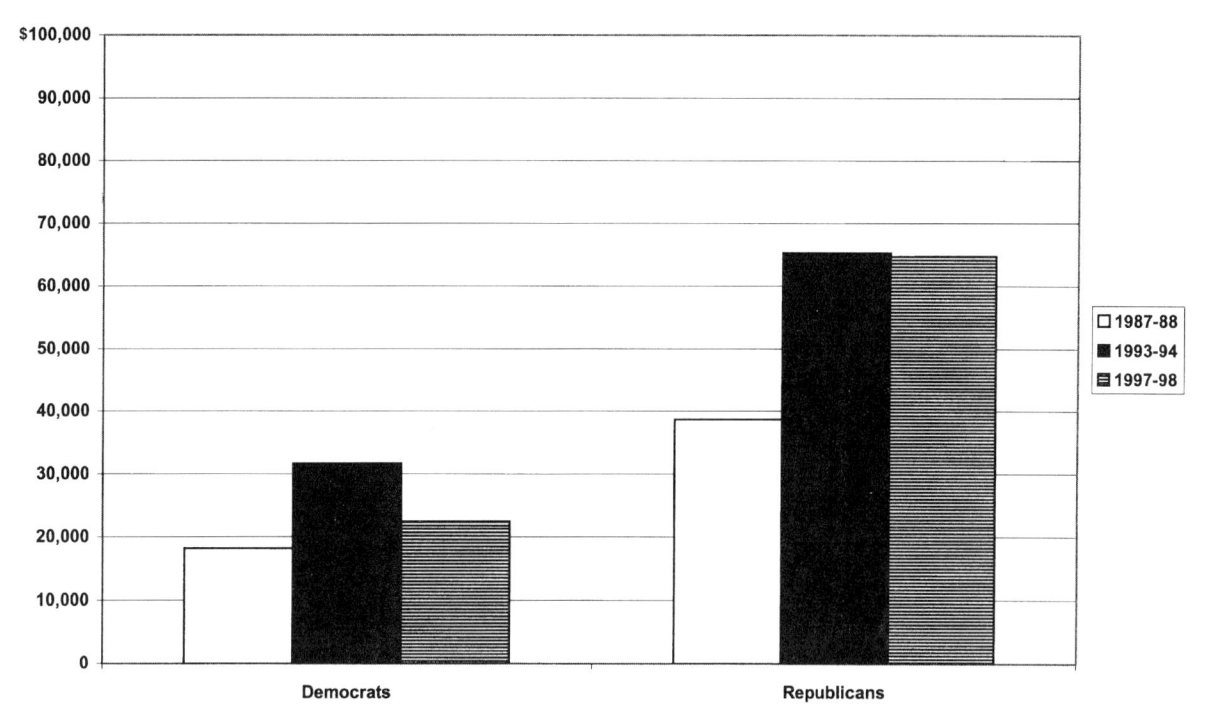

Data derived from official studies available from the Federal Election Commission, Washington, DC, 1987–1998.

dustry. A favorable image, in turn, helps to decrease the likelihood of regulatory legislation. In the future, the AAAA will continue to fight against regulation and will monitor legislation affecting the commercial development of the Internet.

FINANCIAL FACTS

Directed by a board comprised of chief executives from member agencies, the AAAA has a budget of $8 million and a staff of 90 individuals. The AAAA has a related political action committee (PAC), called Professionals in Advertising. The treasurer of this PAC, Harold A. Shoup, is the chief Washington lobbyist for the AAAA, and its members include the top executives of the major advertising agencies. In 1995–1996, this PAC had receipts of $144,750 and expenditures of $129,456. Its contributions for the past two election cycles were:

	Total	Democrat	%	Republican	%
1995–96	$111,750	34,750	31	77,000	69
1997–98	$86,899	22,499	26	64,400	74

Additionally, the AAAA contributed $1,500 and $21,300 in soft money to the Republican Party in the 1995–1996 and 1997–1998 election cycles, respectively. The AAAA paid a total of $296,000 to lobbyists in the 1997 calendar year.

JULIE M. WALSH

Bibliography

American Advertising Association: www.aaaa.org

Center for Responsive Politics: www.crp.org

Miracle, Gordon E., and Terence Nevett. *Voluntary Regulation of Advertising: A Comparative Analysis of the United Kingdom and the United States.* Lexington, MA: Lexington Books, D.C. Heath, 1987.

Zuckerman, Edward, ed. *The Almanac of Federal PACs, 1998–1999.* Arlington, VA: Amward, 1998.

ASSOCIATION OF TRIAL LAWYERS OF AMERICA

For 50 years the Association of Trial Lawyers of America (ATLA) has worked to promote justice and adequate compensation for injured persons, to safeguard victims' rights (such as the right to trial by jury), and to disclose information of critical importance to public health. ATLA has also sought to inform lawyers, to educate the general public, and, more broadly, to influence the modernization of the civil justice system in an age of technological development.

Established in 1946 as the National Association of Claimant's Compensation Attorneys (NACCA), it was the first bar association devoted to the defense of workers' compensation in the United States. In 1960, when the association admitted all personal injury lawyers, it was renamed the National Association of Claimant's Council of America. Four years later its membership was opened to those lawyers working in fields of admiralty, railroad, and tort practice, and it then became the American Trial Lawyers Association. The final change of name occurred in 1972, when ATLA added commercial litigation and environmental law sections. The association has continued to expand its membership to include lawyers working on family law, labor law, and military law.

ATLA is the world's largest trial association, with about 60,000 members worldwide, and has a network of U.S. and Canadian affiliates participating in diverse areas of trial advocacy. Its international membership extends to England, France, Sweden, Germany, Australia, and Japan.

HISTORY

ATLA was an initiative of Ben Marcus, a workers' compensation plaintiffs' attorney, and Samuel Horovitz, a labor lawyer. They were alike in their preoccupation with the incidence of 2 million victims of industrial accidents and the number of trials in which injured claimants were badly prepared or stood alone—while their employers were much better represented by skillful and resourceful insurers, doctors, and investigators. They were clear about the need for more legal knowledge to serve clients successfully and the need to achieve adequate plaintiff representation.

Gathering nine additional sympathetic colleagues, the two lawyers created the NACCA, with Ben Marcus appointed as president. All members committed themselves to extend and strengthen the incipient association and to encourage mutual cooperation and communication among members. Their recruitment efforts included trips, conferences, publications, and the establishment of local branches. These initiatives proved to be fruitful: within the first 10 years the association had already extended its activities to 44 state branches and affiliates and its membership had jumped to approximately 5,000 members.

Judicial activities have been a fundamental part of the association's program, ranging from position statements to the submission of *amicus curiae* (friend of the court) briefs. In civil trials, ATLA has long supported the preservation of the jury system to render verdicts rather than authorizing judges to determine guilt or innocence. Jurors may work less quickly and efficiently, ATLA members argue, but their common, everyday experiences enable them to identify more closely with plaintiffs and understand the value of losses and injuries in the real world.

ATLA has often differed from other bar associations, such as the Defense Research Institute (representing lawyers working in personal injury cases on behalf of firms and corporations) and the American Bar Association, on several issues regarding legal ethics, damages, and tort liability. More serious disagreements have occurred with respect to business organizations. Since the 1980s, for instance, ATLA has been actively opposed to the campaign led by insurance, manufacturing, and health industries seeking tort reform in Congress. More recently, in 1998, the U.S. Chamber of Commerce

**Association of Trial Lawyers of America
Political Action Committee Contributions**

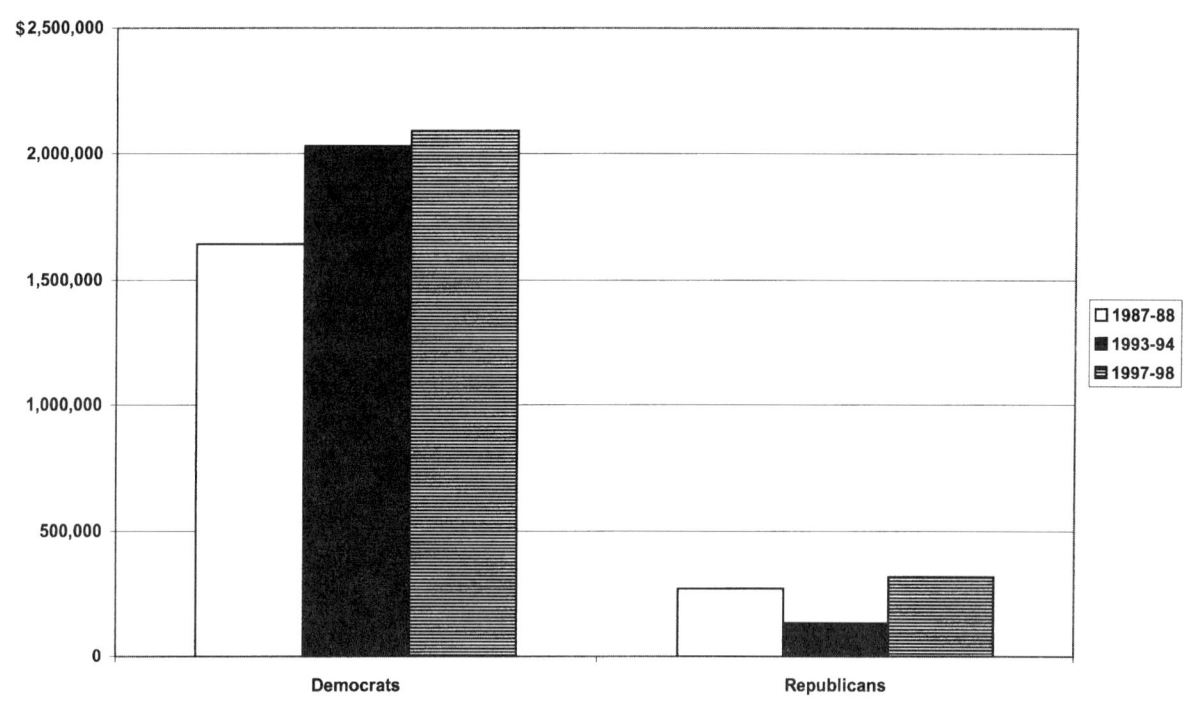

Data derived from official studies available from the Federal Election Commission, Washington, DC, 1987–1998.

started efforts to fund a campaign meant to target the legal procedures available in cases of product liability lawsuits, class-action litigation, and contingency fees. Through lobbying and advertisements, the objective was to portray trial lawyers as frivolous in their suits, causing the rise of the cost of goods and preventing manufacturers from introducing new products to the market. (Trial lawyers today work on cases ranging from toy defects to medical malpractice.)

Education and professional learning have been given central importance since the association's early years. A law journal was conceived as ATLA's main communication vehicle in 1948. It was a semiannual publication with a first printing of 1,600 copies; it included articles and reviews of leading law journals, and was a law digest reporting all cases of workers' compensation; railroad, admiralty, and tort law; and analyzing and commenting on the most relevant cases. One of ATLA's founding members, Samuel Horovitz, was the first person responsible for the publication. The second editor was Roscoe Pound, a former dean of the Harvard Law School and a very prestigious jurist. The journal became a respectable source cited by courts and requested by law libraries and was the starting point for more expansive publication efforts and the subsequent creation of a think tank.

ACTIVITIES: CURRENT AND FUTURE

In 1972 ATLA's headquarters were relocated from Boston, Massachusetts, to Washington, D.C.; there the association maintains a staff of 160, including 30 attorneys.

Since the first years of the association, its representatives realized that the provision of tools and information for successful trials solved only one part of the problem of injured persons. In their view favorable verdicts did not always result in fair compensation due to failure to account for inflation indexes or new conditions derived from social and economic changes. The conclusion was that "the law must be stable, and yet it cannot stand still."

ATLA has performed several legislative activities, including participation in debates, advocacy for the progressive development of the law, lobbying, and support for the political campaigns of candidates to the Senate and the House of Representatives.

The association's concern with the administration of justice to injured persons and the achievement of fair compensations and awards for accident victims has persisted in its agenda, but several other issues, such as medical malpractice and consumer affairs (e.g., product liability, premises liability) have also been pursued. In these cases the Civil Justice Foundation, created in 1986, builds coalitions between trial lawyers and grassroots organizations. The foundation has awarded grants of more than $700,000 to groups developing proposals and activities on behalf of injured consumers.

ATLA also has a think tank dating from 1956, the Roscoe Pound Foundation. Its mission is to stimulate the flow of ideas among lawyers, jurists, scholars, and consumer advocates, and it conducts appropriate research on legal issues and related scientific and medical information. The foundation today organizes forums for state and court judges and restricted roundtables for the analysis of particular problems. The Roscoe Pound Foundation also publishes the *Civil Justice Digest*, a quarterly, as well as several research papers and reports. Through its program of continuing education, ATLA organizes seminars and activities for paralegals and law students. More ambitiously, its National Board of Trial Advocacy develops activities to train and certify trial lawyers.

The association's library holds about 20,000 volumes, including books, periodical publications, articles, and a database of electronic resources, which are available to members only. ATLA publishes the monthly *TRIAL* magazine, *ATLA Law Reporter* (a research aid for lawyers), and a newsletter.

FINANCIAL FACTS

In lobbying activities ATLA spent a total of $2,128,339 in 1997 and $2,184,929 in 1998. In political campaigns ATLA's political action committee (PAC) is a successful fund-raiser, having received $5,380,418 in the 1996 election cycle and $3,976,180 in 1998. It favors Democrats over Republicans and is one of the three PACs spending the largest amounts in contributions to political candidates.

ATLA has a yearly budget of $19.4 million; its resources come mainly from individual contributions and membership. The association is governed by a board of representatives from the 50 states, the District of Columbia, and Puerto Rico; some international members are also included.

MIRIAM JIMÉNEZ-HERNÁNDEZ

Bibliography

Abel, Richard. *American Lawyers*. New York: Oxford University Press, 1989.

American Trial Lawyers Association: www.atlanet.org

American Trial Lawyers Association. "ATLA: The First Fifty Years." *TRIAL* 32, no. 7 (July 1996): 23–53.

———. "Chronicles: An Historical Trilogy." *TRIAL* 32, no. 7 (July 1996): 43–63.

———. "Rumor and Reflection." *The NACCA Journal* 18 (November 1957): 25–38.

American Trial Lawyers Association, Media Relations. "Fact Sheet." Washington, D.C.

Horovitz, Samuel B. "NACCA and Its Objectives." *The NACCA Journal* 10 (November 1952): 18–42.

FOOD MARKETING INSTITUTE

The Food Marketing Institute (FMI) is a trade organization serving more than 1,500 member companies. According to the FMI, this membership also includes more than 200 members from 60 countries. These companies operate approximately 21,000 food stores and supermarkets, whose posted sales exceeded the $220 billion mark in 1996, more than half of all grocery-related sales in the United States. Similar to other food-related political action committees (PACs) and interest groups, like the National Association of Convenience Stores (NACS), the National Beer Wholesalers Association (NBWA), and the National Restaurant Association, the FMI lobbies against antitrust laws and tax increases on beer and soft drinks. A number of members of the FMI are PAC-sponsoring organizations, mostly large supermarket chains including Safeway, Stop and Shop, Shop Rite, Winn-Dixie, and Kroger. FMI members also include large department and convenience store chains including Walmart and Kmart. In addition to large chains and franchises, FMI membership includes organizations that represent local grocers. The FMI also represents approximately 30 state wholesale and retail food organizations, also referred to as the FMI Association Council. Some of these organizations include the California Grocers Association, Gulf Coast Retailers, Pennsylvania Food Merchants Association, and the Texas Food Industry Association. An organization that represents both local grocers and is also a member of the FMI Association Council is the National Korean-American Grocers Foundation.

In general, members are those individuals or groups who own or operate businesses that are responsible for acquiring food and food-related merchandise from farmers and producers and making them available for consumers. FMI members can include both wholesale and retail business owners. According to the institute, part of their mission includes the coordination of programs in research and education related to the food industry. The headquarters of the FMI, as well as the Food Marketing Institute PAC (FOODPAC), is located in Washington, D.C. In addition to its headquarters the FMI also maintains five regional branches, located in Newport Beach, California; Moab, Utah; Edmond, Oklahoma; Atlanta, Georgia; and Libertyville, Illinois. FMI leadership is made up of a board of directors, who are owners of both wholesale and retail food distributors and supermarkets.

HISTORY

The FMI was formed in 1977 as the result of a merger between the National Association of Food Chains in Washington, D.C., and the Super Market Institute in Chicago. Among the original goals of the institute were to establish a national status for food retailers and wholesalers, and to advance research and promote services related to food safety. In 1996 the FMI created a new satellite foundation, the Food Marketing Institute Foundation (FMIF), whose primary purpose is to guarantee "quality and efficiency" in the food marketing business through charities, educational programs, and scientific investigations relating to food quality and food service. This goal, however, is similar to the FMI's mission, namely, maintenance and efficiency of food service from producer to consumer. According to the FMI, the FMIF is a tax-exempt organization that is filed under Section 501(c)(3)—a specific Internal Revenue Service tax code that indicates a nonprofit business's tax-exempt status.

ACTIVITIES: CURRENT AND FUTURE

The FMI's major lobbying activities include opposition to antitrust laws relating to the sale of beer and other alcoholic beverages, retail pricing laws, legislation on

**Food Marketing Institute
Political Action Committee Contributions**

Data derived from official studies available from the Federal Election Commission, Washington, DC, 1987–1998.

consumer packaging, legislation requiring certain types of containers for particular beverages, the sale of pharmaceuticals, legislation on federal consumer packaging, and support for amendments relating to the Food, Drug and Cosmetic Act and the Employees Retirement Income Security Act. The FMI claims to provide a large number of services for members, including food marketing research, education, industry relations, and public affairs. Based on their efforts to support amendments related to tax increases for store owners, minimum wage legislation, and laws related to recycling, FMI lobbyists tend to favor Republican Party members of Congress.

The research department of the FMI publishes five journals, newsletters, or reports—*Annual Financial Review, Facts About Store Development, The Food Marketing Industry Speaks, Operations Review,* and *Trends: Consumer Attitudes and the Supermarket.* This department is responsible for providing data related to food marketing and safety for members, the government, and the food marketing industry in general. The FMI asserts that the Food Information Service, which is affiliated with the research department, is the world's largest and most comprehensive library on food marketing, food distribution, and retail and wholesale services.

National and regional conferences and seminars are the FMI's primary vehicles for promoting educational programs. In addition to publishing guidebooks and training materials, the institute claims to "instill [an] awareness" of the social and economic environment of the food industry. It also claims to hold more than 50 annual conferences relating to a large range of food safety and service issues. Each May the FMI holds its annual International Supermarket Industry Convention and holds additional conventions, dealing with topics of concern to the food industry and technology.

Although claiming not to be involved in lobbying activity, the FMIF focuses on issues that relate to consumer education. The most current FMIF undertaking is to attempt to educate consumers on issues concerning the handling of food. In its Safeguarding Our Last Link campaign, the FMIF has been trying to raise more than $10 million for educating its "last link"—the consumer—on "safe food-handling practices." Fight BAC™, another FMIF program aimed at educating the general public about food-borne illness, was created in collaboration with the federal government, the food industry, and several consumer groups.

Ethical practice, when considering the rights of the

employees or consumers, may not be adopted by all FMI members. Several businesses and organizations affiliated with the FMI, for example, have been involved frequently in illegal labor practices, such as paying workers below the legal minimum wage and possibly firing those wanting to form unions. Grocers who are involved in these disputes over employee exploitation often complain that their establishments would go out of business if they were to keep to the minimum wage and reduce the number of hours for all employees.

FINANCIAL FACTS

Since 1988, FMI contributions to GOP candidates have exceeded contributions given to the Democrats. In the 1987–1988 election cycle, $169,468, or 56 percent of all contributions, which amounted to $304,581, were granted to Republicans running for office. However, in subsequent election years, GOP contributions were approximately double the amount of Democrat contributions. By the 1995–1996 election cycle the gap widened, again in favor of the GOP, whose FMI contributions amounted to $376,453, approximately 85 percent of the total political contributions during those election years. The total amount of contributions to the Democrats in 1995 and 1996 ($68,750) was less than half the amount given in the previous two-year election cycle ($142,554). This dramatic increase in contributions favoring the GOP is most likely due to the Republican takeover of Congress in the previous election cycle.

DANIEL NESS

Bibliography

Biersack, Robert, and Paul S. Herrnson. "Introduction." In *After the Revolution: PACs, Lobbies, and the Republican Congress,* edited by Robert Biersack, Paul S. Herrnson, and Clyde Wilcox. Boston: Allyn & Bacon, 1999.

Food Marketing Institute: www.fmi.org

Zuckerman, Edward, ed. *The Almanac of Federal PACs, 1998–1999.* Arlington, VA: Amward, 1998.

FRATERNAL ORDER OF POLICE

The Fraternal Order of Police (FOP) is an organization that represents approximately 277,000 law enforcement personnel. With almost 2,000 local lodges nationwide, the FOP is considered to be the largest police organization in the country. The Grand Lodge of the FOP is located in Warwick, Rhode Island. One of the FOP's slogans, Police Representing Police, is indicative of its belief that no one knows the dangers of a police officer better than a fellow officer and that the FOP "knows police officers best." Although it maintains a nonpartisan and nonprofit status, the FOP has often rubbed shoulders with Republican Party politicians, many of whom favor capital punishment laws and support legislation that eliminates controls or bans on guns and other types of assault weapons, particularly for off-duty law enforcement officers. Although not considered a political action committee (PAC) in that it does not claim to siphon off funds allocated for membership benefits and educational purposes to contribute directly to the campaigns of political candidates running for office, the FOP's sheer size in terms of its membership and its involvement in Washington politics is considerable indeed, and thus is deemed worthy of mention as a potentially influential political interest group. Another factor that distinguishes the FOP from other political interest groups is its ability to sway the media in favor of the interests and beliefs of police and law enforcement personnel.

HISTORY

There are a number of parallels between the bureaucratization of the American urban police force and that of other urban service agencies or institutions. By the middle of the nineteenth century, fire fighting, medical treatment, public works (such as road maintenance and plumbing), and education were systematized by specialized and impersonal agencies that accomplished the same work that individual households did decades earlier. The organization of police forces was a reaction on the part of urban business leaders, who wanted to quell riots, frequent skirmishes, and the rise in thefts, arson, and homicides within urban areas that local marshals, wards, constables, and night watchmen were unable to do by themselves.

From then until the years preceding the First World War, police officers often worked 12-hour shifts every day of the year. This allegedly caused much grievance among police officers throughout the country, so much so that two officers in Pittsburgh—Martin Toole and Delbert Nagle—formed the Fort Pitt Lodge No. 1 with 21 other officers and held the first meeting of the FOP on May 14, 1915. Since anti-union sentiment was at a peak at the time, Toole and Nagle designated the original group as Fort Pitt rather than the Fraternal Order or any similar title whose description implied unionization. From 1915 to the late sixties or seventies, the FOP served as a medium for voicing personal grievances of police officers, particularly those relating to wages, benefits, and the length of individual shifts. Thereafter, however, the FOP's agendas seemed to have become entrenched in more impersonal issues, such as amending gun-control laws and allowing law enforcement officers to carry concealed firearms outside their jurisdictions. These and other similar themes have been central to the FOP's lobbying efforts in Washington, where, to this day, it has played a major role in supporting certain members of Congress (mostly Republican) who have addressed and advocated the same issues.

ACTIVITIES: CURRENT AND FUTURE

Some of the FOP's key lobbying themes include an amendment (H.R. 59) to the Lautenberg Law, law enforcement officers' rights to due process, the right for law enforcement officers to carry concealed firearms (H.R. 218), public safety officers' collective bargaining rights (H.R. 1093), and mandatory participation in retirement programs other than Social Security.

The Lautenberg Law (also known as the Domestic Violence Offender Gun Ban), which was passed in 1996, prohibits any individual, including on-duty law enforcement and military personnel, from possessing firearms if they have been convicted of being a suspect in a domestic violence incident. The FOP vehemently opposes the Lautenberg Law, arguing that even individuals that are charged with a misdemeanor charge of domestic violence "lose their Constitutional rights if they are prohibited from owning firearms." Furthermore, it argues that an individual's misdemeanor charge of domestic violence "carries with it the loss of the Constitutional right to keep and bear arms." Taking the issue further, in January 1997 a lawsuit was filed, *Fraternal Order of Police v. United States*, in which the FOP challenged the "unconstitutionality" of the Lautenberg Law. The major argument was that law enforcement officers who were charged with a nondomestic felony crime were granted the privilege of bearing arms, while those charged with domestic violence misdemeanors were stripped of this privilege. Accordingly, the FOP strongly supports amendments to the Lautenberg Law, particularly H.R. 59, which has been sponsored by Representative Bob Barr (R-GA) and supported by the National Rifle Association and other significant ultraconservative or GOP-supporting PACs.

A second major theme in the FOP's political agenda is its staunch support for legislation that protects law enforcement officers' rights to due process. Claiming that a large number of jurisdictions nationwide do not protect the due process rights of law enforcement personnel, the FOP contends that officers are often dismissed from duty without explanation. In addition, it argues that a police officer's dismissal without warning diminishes that individual's chances of assuming subsequent posts in the law enforcement or public safety professions. The FOP is currently lobbying Congress to pass legislation that allows off-duty officers to engage in political activity, ensures that officers are notified of their dismissal and the allegations against them, ensures them the right to have counsel during an investigation, and would grant them seven other "basic rights."

A third high-priority theme in the FOP's lobbying efforts in Washington concerns its support for the Concealed Carry Law for Law Enforcement Officers (H.R. 218). This law would permit off-duty or retired law enforcement officers to carry concealed firearms outside their state or local jurisdictions. The FOP believes that a police officer or law enforcement official, either on or off duty, should be allowed to carry firearms in the event that "there is a threat to peace or to public safety." In addition, this law would exempt what the FOP considers "qualified officers" from local or state statutes that currently prohibit the carrying of concealed firearms by off-duty or retired officers.

One of the few themes that the FOP is currently pursuing vigorously that remotely resembles the issues raised when the order was forming earlier in the century is that of police officers' and other public safety employees' right to bargain collectively. Two members of Congress, Dale Kildee (D-MI) and Bob Ney (R-OH), introduced the Public Safety Employer-Employee Cooperation Act, which would provide firefighters and law enforcement employees with collective bargaining privileges. Ironically, the law would prohibit strikes, lockouts, or the involvement of the National Labor Relations Board, and instead would utilize the procedures set forth by the Federal Labor Relations Authority as a means of settling disputes. However, the law would permit officers the right to form or join unions, guarantee them the right to bargain collectively, and exclude top-ranking or supervisory officials from joining a bargaining unit, while including midranking officials.

A fifth theme that has recently surfaced in the FOP's present lobbying agenda concerns the order's position on Social Security benefits. First, the FOP vehemently opposes any mandatory participation in Social Security for law enforcement and public safety employees. Second, the FOP is currently lobbying Congress to pass legislation that would eliminate the Windfall Elimination Provision, enacted in 1983—a law that they believe is responsible for the lowering of Social Security benefits of retired officers who assume second careers. In addition, the order is lobbying Congress to pass legislation that would increase the benefits of surviving spouses of law enforcement personnel.

Finally, for the past decade or so, the FOP seems to have been extremely successful in gaining sympathy from several forms of media, most notably large networks like ABC/Disney, that have televised cases involving the murder of police officers, even at the expense of possibly falsely incriminating innocent defendants. One of the most controversial cases within the past two decades involves Mumia Abu-Jamal, who is currently on death row for the murder of Daniel Faulkner, a Philadelphia police officer who died of a gunshot wound to the chest in 1982. Despite conflicting evidence supporting Abu-Jamal's innocence, the FOP has been continuously hurling invectives at the defendant's supporters and has egged on the hastening of legislation in favor of capital punishment for all individuals convicted of murdering law enforcement officers. Furthermore, there is dispute concerning the judge, Albert Sabo, who presided over Abu-Jamal's case in 1982. Sabo, an FOP member, has put more people on death row—mostly African-American and Latino—than any other judge in U.S. history. In addition, prosecutors in the case placed more emphasis on Abu-Jamal's affiliation with the Black Panther Party, which they portrayed as a "hate group," than on Faulkner's murder. Although Abu-Jamal's supporters have demanded his release and called for a new trial, the FOP gained the sympathy of ABC/Disney, which, in effect, presented a one-sided version of the Faulkner murder in favor of the FOP.

FINANCIAL FACTS

Unlike most of the other service groups discussed in this section, the FOP is a nonprofit, nonpartisan organization, and most FOP lodges dissuade their members from participating in any type of union activity. A large number of lodges even prohibit union participation of their members. The FOP is a registered 501(c)(3) organization, meaning that it is a civic, tax-exempt group. Moreover, the order contributes less than $5,000 annually to any single political party. Despite its claim of nonpartisanship and not-for-profit status, the FOP has often siphoned off its income from membership dues, individual donations, or fund-raising activities for the purpose of educating individuals about the issues of political candidates, helping certain political candidates raise money, and even contributing funds to federal candidates themselves, even though nonprofit groups of this sort are prohibited from doing so.

DANIEL NESS

Bibliography

Biersack, Robert, and Paul S. Herrnson. "Introduction." In *After the Revolution: PACs, Lobbies, and the Republican Congress,* edited by Robert Biersack, Paul S. Herrnson, and Clyde Wilcox. Boston: Allyn & Bacon, 1999.

Fraternal Order of Police: www.grandlodgefop.org

Owens, James. "Mumia Abu-Jamal: The ABC Hatchet Job." *Covert Action Quarterly* 67 (Spring/Summer 1999).

Tyack, David. *The One Best System: A History of American Urban Education.* Cambridge: Harvard University Press, 1974.

NATIONAL ASSOCIATION OF CONVENIENCE STORES

The National Association of Convenience Stores (NACS) is a trade association with over 3,300 retail members. These individuals operate nearly 64,200 stores throughout the world, approximately 1,200 of which are associate members of the NACS. Unlike the Petroleum Marketers Association of America (PMAA), which caters to independent marketers, commissioned distributors, and retailers specializing in gasoline, heating, and diesel fuel, the NACS represents the convenience-store proprietor who sells gasoline and other petroleum products. In fact, gasoline sales at convenience stores accounted for 54 percent of all petroleum sales in the United States. The NACS claims that total convenience-store sales in 1998 exceeded $164 billion, a $12 billion increase from 1996. But this figure is suspect given the recent drop in tobacco sales in the United States—tobacco sales alone accounted for approximately 25 percent of convenience-store revenue. The NACS headquarters—along with its political action committee (PAC), the National Association of Convenience Stores PAC, or NACSPAC—is located in Alexandria, Virginia.

Although a good deal of NACS members' responsibilities, as well as the sale of certain products, overlap with those of business owners who belong to other interest groups, the NACS differs from other groups in a few important ways. One is that it primarily represents retail store owners and operators, while a number of other interest groups exclusively represent owners and operators of wholesale enterprises. A second major difference is that NACS members own or operate 19 to 20 stores each, on average, whereas members of other interest groups generally own one or two establishments with usually under 50 employees. In addition, the NACS claims that approximately 70 percent of all convenience stores are owned by members who manage single-store operations or stores which are part of a chain of 10 stores or less.

HISTORY

The NACS was established in 1961. At that time, convenience-store retailers sold merchandise running the gamut from candy and gum, frozen treats (like ice cream and flavored ices), and snacks and soft drink beverages to newspapers, cigarettes, and small toys and souvenirs. For nearly 40 years the NACS has used annual conventions and trade shows as events for attracting members. Over the years it has also run educational and public affairs programs as a means of promoting its interests in the national arena and in its Washington lobbying efforts. According to the association, the definition of convenience store today is a retail establishment that sells gasoline and related petroleum products, most types of fast foods, groceries (including most types of dairy products), cigarettes and other tobacco-related products (such as cigars and pipe tobacco), alcoholic beverages (including beer and wine coolers), soft drinks, snacks, newspapers, magazines, comic books, and other non–food-related items, which may include pharmaceuticals, over-the-counter medications, videocassettes, and toys. Since the 1980s convenience stores have also served as a popular venue for gambling, namely for the sale of tickets related to in-state and interstate lotteries.

ACTIVITIES: CURRENT AND FUTURE

Like other interest groups backing the Republican Party, the NACS opposes legislation that requires tax increases or new taxes of any kind. One proposal that the NACS is bringing to Congress is the repeal of an old alcohol tax, namely, the Special Occupational Tax (SOT). The SOT was established in the 1860s as a means of generating revenue during the Civil War. Prior to 1987 beer retailers were required to pay $24 in

**National Association of Convenience Stores
Political Action Committee Contributions**

Data derived from official studies available from the Federal Election Commission, Washington, DC, 1987–1998.

SOT per store. After the passage of a 1987 law, the SOT increased more than tenfold to $250 per store. Currently the NACSPAC and other similar PACs, like the National Restaurant Association PAC and the National Beer Wholesalers Association (NBWA) PAC, are urging the elimination of SOT on the grounds that defenders of the tax would like to banish the sale of alcohol in stores. A measure that is in favor of the elimination of the tax (H.R. 2735) is evidently receiving bipartisan support.

The NACS is a member of a coalition—Americans Against Unfair Family Taxation—that is pushing for the elimination of the estate tax that is taken upon the death of a business owner and was included in the Senate and House proposal for a nearly $800 billion tax cut. Other PACs in the coalition include the Food Marketing Institute PAC, the National Beer Wholesalers Association PAC, and the Petroleum Marketers Association of America PAC.

While the NACS has supported the GOP to a large extent, not all of its issues run parallel with Republican politics. To illustrate, the NACS is in firm opposition to the Hyde amendment (H.R. 1501, Protecting Children from the Culture of Violence), which would make it a felony punishable up to five years for a retailer or convenience-store employee to knowingly sell "explicit" and "violent" material to minors. According to Marc Katz, NACS vice president for government relations, this would place an extraordinary burden on retailers, expecting them to closely monitor any sale or rental of a picture, photograph, video, book, magazine, or audio material that, according to proponents of Representative Henry Hyde's (R-IL) amendment, "contain[s] explicit sexual material or explicit violent material." Another similar amendment, proposed by Representatives Bart Stupak (D-MI) and Zack Wamp (R-TN), would fine convenience stores and other similar establishments $10,000 for selling or renting "violent and sexually explicit" videos that are not labeled as such. One of the NACS's lobbying agendas, then, is to urge members of both houses of Congress to reject the Hyde amendment and other similar amendments that would force retailers and other store personnel to police the sale or rental of various merchandise to minors.

In contrast to their opposition to the Hyde bill, NACS leaders strongly support the regulation of sales of tobacco products to minors. In their program entitled No Ifs, Ands or Butts: Tobacco's Not for Kids, NACS chairman Fred Higgins and other NACS leaders proposed benchmarks that they hope would greatly curb or eliminate the sale of cigarettes and other tobacco products to individuals under 18 years of age. Some of these benchmarks include employee training, universal carding—which means that retailers would be required to ask for the identification of individuals who appear younger than 25 years of age and who wish to purchase tobacco products—and penalties against employees who sell tobacco products to minors. Ironically, however, the NACS is fearful of any amendment that would reduce the sale of tobacco products. In particular, the association is opposed to the Food and Drug Administration's (FDA) full control over the sale of tobacco production and claims itself to be the only trade association to be filing a lawsuit against the FDA. The U.S. Supreme Court began oral arguments in the fall of 1999.

In the past few years NACS lobbyists have also supported legislation that would prevent convenience-store owners and retailers from being liable for damages in civil cases. In particular, the NACS supports the Small Business Lawsuit Protection Act, sponsored by Senators Spencer Abraham (R-MI) and Joseph Lieberman (D-CT). A related law, the Small Business Liability Reform Act of 1999, has two parts: Small Business Lawsuit Abuse Protection and Product Seller Fair Treatment. Lawsuit Abuse Protection would limit small-business exposure to joint liabilities in noneconomic situations and also would put a cap on punitive damages—a $250,000 upper limit in penalties. Product Seller Fair Treatment would penalize the local distributors or retailers only if they were directly responsible for any injury or harm inflicted upon customers.

The NACS also rejects minimum-wage increases based on its belief that such legislation would cut the number of first-time or entry-level positions. NACS personnel also cite a study by the accounting firm Ernst and Young that posits that increases in the minimum wage can result in the loss of jobs for 6 percent of the nation's entry-level workforce, and that the convenience-store industry can expect "to lose 25,000 jobs if [a] proposed wage hike is enacted." NACS leaders also claim that first-time job opportunities "teach responsibility" and serve as a stepping stone to higher paying occupations. However, a large percentage of entry-level and first-time employees represent a segment of the population whose opportunities have diminished due to the imposition of a "glass ceiling"—an obstacle sometimes encountered by women and people of color that limits their professional advancement. Passing amendments on the minimum wage, then, is a major theme for most conservative PACs like the NACS.

FINANCIAL FACTS

The NACS has supported the GOP ticket for a number of reasons. For one, Republicans generally support a repeal of tax increases on alcohol products. Given that the convenience store is a major alcoholic beverage supplier, the NACS, in addition to other interest groups, like the NBWA and the National Restaurant Association, supports a repeal of the SOT. Most Republicans also reject any legislation in favor of increasing the minimum wage.

The NACS's contributions to political elections have been consistently pro-GOP. In every election cycle over the past decade, NACS contributions, which grew from $79,550 in the 1987–1988 election cycle to $370,939 in the 1995–1996 election cycle, favored Republican candidates over Democrats running for office. Throughout these years the NACS's contributions to the Democrats seem to have remained fairly steady at around one-fourth the amount given to GOP candidates. In 1987–1988 the NACS contributed $57,700, or about three-fourths of its finances for political elections (which totaled $79,550), to GOP candidates. In the 1996 election year the gap widened in favor of the GOP, whose contributions from the NACS exceeded $299,900—or more than four-fifths of its total political contributions for that year.

DANIEL NESS

Bibliography

C-Store Central-NACS Industry: www.cstorecentral.com

National Association of Convenience Stores: www.nacsnet.org

Zuckerman, Edward, ed. *The Almanac of Federal PACs, 1998–1999*. Arlington, VA: Amward, 1998.

NATIONAL ASSOCIATION OF RETIRED FEDERAL EMPLOYEES

The National Association of Retired Federal Employees (NARFE) is a membership organization with more than a half a million members, who are both current and retired federal employees. NARFE's raison d'être is to lobby Congress as well as executive branches of government to ensure the payment of civil service retirement annuities and the granting of other benefits for the more than 2 million retired federal employees. Moreover, NARFE has made attempts to use various forms of media to encourage public recognition and appreciation of government service. NARFE has also created a partnership with the Office of Personnel Management, a center that shares information with NARFE members and others about retirement benefits.

Membership in NARFE is open only to those individuals who are former federal employees and who have no right to a deferred retirement annuity, current federal employees who have been working in their present position for at least five years, or former members of Congress. NARFE members are either past or current employees of a wide array of different government services; the majority are represented by the Civil Service Retirement System and the Federal Employment Retirement System. Other federal agencies that represent NARFE members include the Central Intelligence Agency Retirement System, the Federal Judiciary Retirement System, the Foreign Service Retirement System, the Tennessee Valley Authority Retirement System, and about 40 other federal government agency retirement programs. In addition to the 1,710 local NARFE chapters throughout the United States, there are 50 state NARFE federations, a federation in the District of Columbia, as well as federations in Panama, the Philippines, and Puerto Rico. NARFE headquarters, along with the National Association of Retired Federal Employees political action committee (NARFEPAC), is located in Alexandria, Virginia. NARFE's monthly magazine, *Retirement Life,* attempts to keep members informed of issues that may affect their federal retirement annuities and matters concerning health and other benefits.

HISTORY

NARFE was established in 1921 by 14 federal workers. After the First World War automation eroded the control of production by skilled workers, thus limiting the power of unions and other labor organizations. The creation of NARFE was due in part to the deterioration of workers' rights as well as to unfair and despotic corporate and federal practices. Since its founding, it has been the only interest group in the country that is specifically geared to protecting the interests of federal employees, especially in terms of retirement benefits and pensions. NARFE leaders have lobbied Congress not only to support federal retirement legislation but to oppose any laws that would remotely affect benefit packages for both federal employees and employees who belong to related organizations.

ACTIVITIES: CURRENT AND FUTURE

In general NARFE ensures the entitlement of benefits and pensions for retired federal employees. The association will endorse and contribute to any candidate who supports and advances its interests. More Democrats than Republicans have recognized and followed through in carrying out a large number of NARFE's goals.

NARFE's leadership is determined during each of its biennial national conventions. Between conventions the association is governed by four national officers—president, vice president, secretary, and treasurer. These officers, along with ten national field vice presidents,

**National Association of Retired Federal Employees
Political Action Committee Contributions**

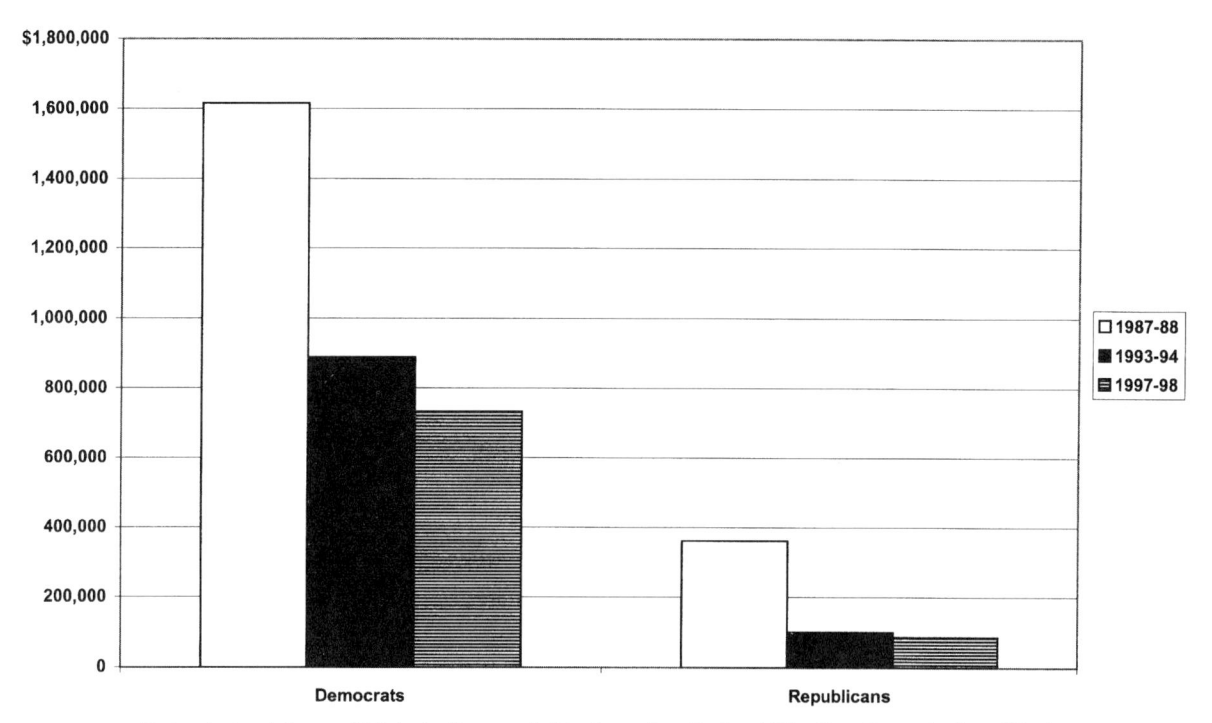

[Bar chart showing PAC contributions for 1987-88, 1993-94, and 1997-98 to Democrats and Republicans. Democrats: approximately $1,620,000 (1987-88), $890,000 (1993-94), $730,000 (1997-98). Republicans: approximately $360,000 (1987-88), $100,000 (1993-94), $80,000 (1997-98).]

Data derived from official studies available from the Federal Election Commission, Washington, DC, 1987–1998.

represent different geographic areas. NARFE maintains a staff of approximately 70 employees to support the elected officials. The major offices of the association are Legislative, Membership, Budget and Finance; Retirement Benefits; Public Relations; Office Operations; and the office that publishes *Retirement Life,* the official publication for NARFE members.

In addition to legislative representation in all levels of government, NARFE membership includes the services of its Office of Personnel Management; health, life, and auto insurance; travel services; and NARFENET, which allows members to obtain relatively easy access to the Internet.

NARFE's impact on the passing of various forms of legislation is mostly a result of its employment of "outside" lobbying strategies. "Inside" strategies are mostly lobbying tactics that refer to an organization's or PAC's ability to lobby before Congress quietly, or without including members or creating grassroots campaigns. "Outside" tactics, on the other hand, are used by interest groups and their PACs as a means of fostering a growing, supportive, and involved membership to lobby Congress and to participate in grassroots efforts that support their issues. Although NARFE has used both types of tactics as part of its lobbying activity, it is one of the few Democrat-supporting interest groups that profits by using its membership (more than 500,000) for political and lobbying purposes.

The provision of health insurance and other healthcare benefits, NARFE claims, is one of the essential and valuable benefits for federal employees and annuitants. NARFE's steadfast support for the patient's bill of rights is another significant factor contributing to its overwhelming endorsement of Democrats for Congress. This legislation, introduced by Senate Democratic Leader Tom Daschle (D-SD), would guarantee patients access to emergency services, medical specialists, and a fair appeals process when healthcare providers deny healthcare to patients. This bill would also hold health maintenance organizations (HMOs) accountable for decisions that would ultimately harm the patient. The Republican Party (GOP) has vehemently opposed this measure and has adopted its own version of healthcare that benefits only a select number of constituents.

NARFE has also tried to encourage the passing of laws supporting the cost of living adjustments (COLAs), which protect federal annuities from inflation. As a token of political debate, COLAs have been used by

NARFE's adversaries as a means of propaganda in allegedly misleading the public in perceiving federal employees as having generous incomes and large retirement packages. NARFE lobbyists have been using the media as vehicles for changing public perception of federal employees—in particular, workers who struggle for fair wages and adequate retirement benefits. NARFE has also been an opponent of source taxing—the taxing of a federal retiree who relocates to another state.

NARFE's mission benefits not only current and retired federal employees. Another agenda related to their central mission is the raising of funds for research in various diseases. In recent years much of the funds that were generated for this purpose went to research into Alzheimer's disease and other related debilitating illnesses.

FINANCIAL FACTS

Based on several forms of legislation over the past decade, like the patient's bill of rights backed by most Democrats, it is not surprising that NARFE's election contributions have been allocated primarily to Democratic challengers and incumbents. Along with the National Association of Social Workers and the Association of Trial Lawyers of America, NARFE has consistently endorsed and contributed to Democratic candidates running for office. Of the $1,243,350 in political contributions in 1996, 83 percent was contributed to the Democrats ($1,035,950), while NARFE's contributions to GOP candidates totaled $205,400. For the past decade NARFE's financial support for GOP candidates was always below 24.5 percent of its political election contributions, while Democratic candidates running for office always received at least 75 percent of NARFE's political election contributions.

DANIEL NESS

Bibliography

Biersack, Robert, and Paul S. Herrnson. "Introduction." In *After the Revolution: PACs, Lobbies, and the Republican Congress,* edited by Robert Biersack, Paul S. Herrnson, and Clyde Wilcox. Boston: Allyn & Bacon, 1999.

National Association of Retired Federal Employees: www.narfe.org

Zuckerman, Edward, ed. *The Almanac of Federal PACs, 1998–1999.* Arlington, VA: Amward, 1998.

NATIONAL ASSOCIATION OF SOCIAL WORKERS

The National Association of Social Workers (NASW) is a professional association of more than 155,000 certified or registered social workers. Most members have earned college degrees, anywhere from the baccalaureate to a master's degree or doctorate. The NASW's leaders lobby both houses of Congress to push for legislation that promotes and fosters all types of social services, including welfare and various income maintenance programs. In addition, they seek to pressure Congress to ensure that antidiscrimination laws are strictly enforced. As the largest membership organization of social workers in the world, the NASW is involved in all aspects of social services, including in-school social work services, on-the-job counseling, and work with senior citizens.

Unlike most of the other interest groups in this section, the NASW is highly concerned with issues dealing with the social, physical, and psychological well-being of all people, specifically aimed toward empowering those who are oppressed, vulnerable, or living in poverty. One of the key elements that distinguishes the NASW from other service interest groups is its strong belief that education and prevention are more valuable and efficient methods for solving social and psychological problems that face society than forms of punishment, like incarceration or probation. In particular, the NASW advocates programs that seek to find long-term solutions to the various existing social or economic barriers. The NASW has 56 chapters, with at least one chapter in each of the 50 states. Two of the more populous states, New York and California, have two chapters each, and there are three additional chapters—an international chapter, a Virgin Islands chapter, and another in Puerto Rico. The NASW's headquarters, along with its political action committee (PAC)—the National Association of Social Workers Political Action for Candidates Election (PACE)—is located in Washington, D.C.

HISTORY

The NASW was founded in 1955, after the merging of seven social worker organizations. Its initial lobbying efforts were geared to influence legislation that would help create or sustain programs relating to the mental health of all individuals. Moreover, the NASW has always been deeply concerned with issues relating to poverty as well as other factors leading to a number of different mental health concerns. Another NASW agenda in its early years was to convince the general public that social work is an indispensable profession, due both to the many ways in which it applies methods in psychology and other social sciences to counseling and therapy as well as to the fact that it seeks lasting solutions to various societal problems. As a result, the NASW has sought candidates who are concerned not with prosecuting and incarcerating individuals, but with rehabilitating or educating them.

ACTIVITIES: CURRENT AND FUTURE

As it states in the preamble of the NASW's Code of Ethics, "The primary mission of the social work profession is to enhance human well-being and help meet the basic human needs of all people, with particular attention to the needs and empowerment of people who are vulnerable, oppressed, and living in poverty." The NASW's important lobbying agendas, then, are to support and encourage legislation that fosters the social and psychological well-being of the individual within the context of society. Members of the NASW are concerned with sustaining programs for individuals of all ages, ranging from infant and daycare centers to retirement programs and geriatric care. In particular, the NASW's leaders lobby Congress on issues supporting

**National Association of Social Workers
Political Action Committee Contributions**

Data derived from official studies available from the Federal Election Commission, Washington, DC, 1987–1998.

Head Start programs, social services in the public schools, increases in the minimum wage, on-the-job counseling and therapy programs, benefits for retired employees, and programs for the elderly. They oppose issues relating to the use of educational vouchers, juvenile crime bills that sanction punishment by incarceration, and other forms of legislation that would cut funding for social services.

The well-being of children in general and ongoing funding for institutions of primary and secondary education have always been critical and sensitive issues for the association's lobbyists. Central concerns in this area include cuts in spending on various social services within the public schools, the rise in school violence in the 1990s (most likely in reaction to recent incidences in suburban schools), and other legislation that would pose dangers to children. The NASW supports legislation that will enhance the social and academic potential of all students, particularly students whose families fall well below the poverty level or who are at risk for other reasons. One such form of legislation is the Elementary and Secondary Education Act (ESEA), which has cited social workers and their services in contributing to the success in school programs throughout the country. The NASW has determined its priorities concerning the reauthorization of ESEA. The association maintains that its contributions fall under four titles of ESEA. These titles include Helping Disadvantaged Children Meet High Standards (Title I); the Dwight D. Eisenhower Professional Development Program (Title II); Safe and Drug-Free Schools and Communities (Title IV); and Programs of National Significance: Elementary School Counseling Demonstration Program (Title X).

Under Title I NASW members seek to use preventive measures as a means of helping students graduate each level of schooling. Some of these measures include helping students avoid teen pregnancy and develop self-discipline, helping parents play a greater role in their children's education, and enabling teachers to enhance their students' education, including the reporting of child abuse, drug abuse, or neglect. Under Title II social workers would have the responsibility of providing resources and other professional development activities for teachers as a means of enhancing student outcomes. Under Title IV social workers are in a unique position in helping school personnel and students either prevent or cope with acts of violence as well as providing them with methods to reduce or eliminate the abuse of drugs and alcohol. Under Title X the NASW has cited several sources that confirm that the implementation of conflict resolution, negotiation, and decision-making skills as early as elementary school will greatly reduce the chances of acts of violence in the future.

In response to its core belief that education and prevention should prevail over punishment and incarceration as ways to overcome various social dilemmas, the NASW has consistently condemned the Violent and Repeat Juvenile Offender Act of 1999, sponsored by Senate Majority Leader Trent Lott (R–MS). According to the NASW, the passing of this legislation undermines the disproportionate number of minority youth who are involved in juvenile crime and who are often incarcerated and tried as adults. The NASW has argued its case by referring to a study in California that demonstrated that minors of color were more likely to receive harsher punishment and stiffer sentences than white offenders who committed the same type of crime. Moreover, nothing in the bill alludes to measures of prevention, nor does it make firearms less accessible to children. According to the NASW, then, the juvenile crime bill is a harmful form of legislation that will pose great dangers to children of all ages.

In support of strengthening the institution of public schools, the NASW, like the American Federation of Teachers, is a strong opponent of educational vouchers, a topic that has become among the most controversial issues in the area of education. Both Cleveland and Milwaukee are in the process of adopting plans for public school students to obtain vouchers as a means of attending private schools of their choice, including parochial schools. In addition, the state of Florida has passed legislation that would provide educational vouchers to any child attending a "failing" public school. Voucher plans are also under way in New York City, where donated funds in the amount of $12 million have been allocated toward the use of vouchers for students to attend Catholic schools. Opponents have argued that the implementation of educational vouchers would strip state and federal funding of public schools, thus creating stronger ties between religious schools and local, state, and federal governments and possibly violating the constitutional separation between church and state. The provision of school vouchers is essentially a reaction, on the part of Republican Party politicians in particular, to failing public schools—mostly in urban areas—whose status as failing is based almost entirely on students' low achievement on standardized tests. The NASW opposes the concept of educational vouchers because it gives the erroneous impression that student failure in school is based solely on test scores and not on one's economic or social circumstances. Opponents of educational vouchers, then, do not necessarily hold public school administrators accountable; instead, they put the blame on severe socioeconomic conditions of students and their families and the lack of federal funding of public, particularly urban, schools.

Unlike the majority of the other service interest groups in this section, the NASW strongly supports the Fair Minimum Wage Act of 1999, sponsored by Senator Edward Kennedy (D-MA) and Representative David Bonior (D-MI). The NASW supports an increase of the minimum wage—from $5.15 to $5.65—because, as the Fair Labor Standards Act of 1938 stated, the minimum wage was enacted to provide a "minimum standard of living necessary for health, efficiency, and general well-being for workers." Under the current minimum wage, a full-time worker earns $10,712 per year. With a family of three—worker, spouse, and one child—this amounts to more than $3,000 below the poverty level. So, in addition to the population of unemployed, there is an increasing number of workers receiving minimum wage pay and their families who are attending soup kitchens, food pantries, and shelters for the homeless. Unlike the opponents of minimum wage increases, the NASW argues that moderate increases in the minimum wage, for the most part, do not lead to the loss of entry-level or first-time positions. The NASW has cited studies undertaken by the U.S. Department of Labor that show an increase in the number of teenagers, women, African Americans, and other people of color employed in entry-level positions between September 1996 and January 1998.

In summary, the NASW's election strategy for candidates running for Congress includes several elements. First, one of its most important strategies in the years ahead is to mobilize its membership by creating close ties between members and regional chapters as well as a strong link between the chapters and NASW headquarters. Another important endeavor is to support any incumbent or challenger social workers running for Congress. The NASW also plans to allocate, at the very least, $200,000 toward candidate contributions for each election cycle. In addition, the NASW decided to limit PACE contributions to 100 candidates who will be the strongest defenders of the goals of social workers. Finally, NASW leaders are seeking to form coalitions that will work toward restoring Democratic control of Congress.

FINANCIAL FACTS

With the exception of the National Association of Retired Federal Employees and the Association of Trial Lawyers of America, the NASW is one of the few organizations in this section on service interest groups that has given its overwhelming support—including financial contributions—to the Democratic Party. This is not surprising, given that the GOP has generally failed to support mental health programs or programs for the poor in previous years. Of the 18 candidates running for U.S. Senate and endorsed by the NASW (with an allocation of $93,500) in the 1998 elections, 14 won seats. In addition, with $128,500 allocated for House candidates, 58 of the 82 NASW-sponsored candidates were elected to the House of Representatives.

In the 1995–1996 election cycle, $168,550, which was 98.5 percent of the NASW's $171,550 financial contributions, helped support Democratic candidates while only $2,500 was given to GOP candidates. In fact, of all the service interest groups mentioned in this section, the NASW has contributed the least to the GOP—less than 2 percent in the 1996 elections. This overwhelmingly Democratic support is not surprising, given that Democrats, much more than the Republicans, have worked to promote most types of social service reforms. Although the NASW's revenue has increased steadily over the years—from a little more than $200,000 in the 1988 elections to more than $1 million by 1996—contributions to elections remained fairly stable, anywhere between $178,746 in 1992 and $122,490 in 1998. Contributions to the GOP during these years always remained extremely low—below the 2.5 percent mark—and will most likely remain that way in future election cycles.

DANIEL NESS

Bibliography

Biersack, Robert, and Paul S. Herrnson. "Introduction." In *After the Revolution: PACs, Lobbies, and the Republican Congress,* edited by Robert Biersack, Paul S. Herrnson, and Clyde Wilcox. Boston: Allyn & Bacon, 1999.

National Association of Social Workers: www.naswdc.org

Zuckerman, Edward, ed. *The Almanac of Federal PACs, 1998–1999.* Arlington, VA: Amward, 1998.

NATIONAL AUTOMOBILE DEALERS ASSOCIATION

The National Automobile Dealers Association (NADA) is a trade organization with more than 19,000 members. Nearly all these individuals are franchised auto dealers of both foreign and domestic automobiles and trucks; the more than 40,000 franchises specialize in both domestic and imported new cars and light, medium, and heavy-duty trucks. Of particular concern to NADA is legislation that would affect the sale of both domestic and foreign vehicles, excise taxes, particularly on luxury automobiles, laws on international trade, federal and state laws that pertain to highway and vehicle safety (such as the inclusion of airbags or the restriction of certain vehicles on various roadways), and legislation that may regulate environmental factors like fuel emissions and fuel consumption. NADA is also an ardent lobbying association especially in times of international crises, when the federal government may seek measures to impose a tax on the sale of various vehicles. The home of NADA headquarters, in addition to its political action committee (PAC)—Dealers Election Action Committee of the National Automobile Dealers Association—is located in McLean, Virginia, one of the outlying suburbs of Washington, D.C.

In addition to lobbying for NADA, some of the association's representatives, like those of a handful of other trade associations, also serve on the board of directors of the American Society of Association Executives, a conservative interest group consisting of approximately 22,000 members, whose PAC largely lobbies on issues relating to federal tax legislation affecting deductibility of trade associations' lobbying expenses, the imposing of taxes on unrelated business income, and restrictions on the inclusion of members in lobbying efforts on behalf of trade associations.

NADA has a number of membership benefits, including a $3.4 billion trust fund, entitled the National Automobile Dealership Retirement Trust, which provides dealers and a number of their employees with pension and retirement plans. In addition, the National Automobile Dealership Insurance Trust (NADIT) provides the families of dealers and their employees with group insurance plans. NADIT assets total more than $2.7 billion.

HISTORY

NADA was established in 1917 by a group of about 30 automobile dealers in Chicago in reaction to a 5 percent tax increase in the factory price of all vehicles. This tax increase was most likely the result of federal legislation that used tax revenue for war expenses during the First World War. According to NADA, early members argued that Congress did not consider automobiles as a worthy form of transportation, and they supposedly attempted to convince Congress to "change their views" about the private use of automobiles. The dealers from various localities collaborated and formed an association in Washington, D.C., whose primary agenda was to sway Congress into viewing automobiles not as luxurious commodities, but as mass consumer goods, which could make a vital and strong contribution to the economy.

Another important task for early NADA dealers was to increase its membership. In attempting to do this, they sent invitations to nearly 100 auto manufacturers. By 1919, two years after its formation, the first federal legislation sponsored by NADA had been passed—the National Motor Vehicle Theft Law. This bill made it a federal offense for someone to steal an automobile and transport it across state lines.

By 1928 NADA membership dues were changed from a fixed amount to a sliding scale, depending upon a dealership's gross sales in the previous year. However, an increasing number of members of NADA were unable to afford the dues even on a sliding scale. By 1932 the association had nearly folded as a result of the Depression, and NADA leaders searched for ways to keep the association afloat financially, including moving the headquarters to a location where the rent was not to exceed $50 per month. By 1935, after trimming back several benefits, like cutting the number of issues of the NADA newsletter, the association was once again able to survive and even increase its membership. NADA headquarters moved from St. Louis, Missouri to Detroit, Michigan in 1936 and to Washington, D.C. in 1941.

Issues during the early 1940s included the rationing of gasoline during the Second World War and a freeze on auto manufacturing and delivery. According to the March 1942 Census Bureau Report, of all the common types of businesses, automobile and truck dealerships suffered the most during the war years or during political and international crises. In the same year President Roosevelt allowed a large percentage of NADA dealerships to sell the government their cars and trucks—vehicles that would then be subject to rationing. By 1944 one needed to apply to the federal government in order to purchase one of the remaining 60,000 new automobiles. By 1949, four years after the end of the Second World War, NADA membership had soared from below 10,000 to nearly 35,000 individuals.

Despite seemingly prosperous times for NADA and automobile dealerships in general after the Second World War, dealers were slapped with additional taxes as a means of supporting the Korean War, specifically, a 7 percent excise tax on new cars. U.S. automobile dealers were hit again in the 1960s, when U.S. consumers were introduced to foreign-made vehicles from England, France, Germany, Italy, and Sweden.

In addition to NADA crises during times of war, members of the association also claim to struggle when various forms of legislation relating to the environment are mandated and also during oil embargoes. When the American International Automobile Dealers Association was founded in 1970, NADA claims to have foreseen difficulties because the public would have the "false perception" that NADA dealers sold only domestic automobiles. The Clean Air Act of 1970 was a second issue on NADA's plate. Leaders complained that this bill would contribute to the dramatic cutting of car and truck sales. Since the 1970s one of the central themes has been legislation that puts quotas on the number of new "gas guzzling" vehicles, as a means of controlling emissions.

In 1979 NADA officials lobbied Congress and emphasized dire financial conditions, in the hope that either Congress or President Jimmy Carter would adopt a plan that would increase car and truck sales. In response Carter increased the Small Business Administration loan guarantee fund on behalf of car and truck dealerships. In 1993, after 25 years as NADA's executive vice president, Frank McCarthy said that in the preceding quarter-century, "we've been through some challenges . . . two oil embargoes and one recession. . . . But people's love of the car—that's the strongest thing." This statement demonstrates not only NADA's status as a trade association but also its ideological beliefs as it relates to material objects, similar to the manner in which the National Rifle Association (NRA) reveres firearms.

ACTIVITIES: CURRENT AND FUTURE

NADA claims that it fully supports the use of safety measures, especially the use of seat belts and child safety seats. Although backing the use of passive restraints, such as airbags or automatic safety belts, NADA has expressed its interest in allowing car and truck buyers to decide on the use of these automobile occupant protection devices by providing on/off switches instead of on-demand activation. However, the association challenged the U.S. National Highway Traffic Safety Administration, which mandated the installation of dual airbags in all cars and trucks by 1998.

NADA lobbied Congress to urge legislation to pass an amendment that exempts teenagers under 18 years of age from being prohibited from driving a motor vehicle while on the job. Undoubtedly as a means to increase sales on cars and trucks, NADA supported H.R. 2327, which would allow young teens of 16 to 17 years of age to drive automobiles if they were engaged in part- or full-time employment. In opposition to NADA, the Department of Labor fined 59 new-car dealerships nearly $200,000 for violating child labor laws. These violations were in reference to teen employees working as lot attendants who had driven automobiles as part of their responsibilities at their place of employment. Under the Fair Labor Standards Act, minors are prohibited from driving motor vehicles while on the job; however, they may be exempt under certain conditions, for example, during an emergency. This law was changed, possibly with the influence of NADA, and in 1998 President Bill Clinton signed H.R. 2327, sponsored and introduced by Representatives Larry Combest (R-TX), Matthew Martinez (D-CA), and Gene Green (D-TX), which permits teenagers who are 17 years of age to perform a minimal amount of driving during work time. One stipulation, however, is that the employee must not drive over a 30-mile radius and must not be driving more than 20 percent of the time.

Another current lobbying activity in which NADA

is involved includes title branding legislation. Title branding refers to the indication on the automobile's title whether or not it had been "salvaged" or "junked." Legislation has been passed, and supported by NADA, that would require dealers to disclose information about a vehicle, like title branding, before it is sold. Trent Lott (R-MS), the House majority leader and key sponsor of the bill, vowed that he would try to urge Congress to pass this legislation in the 106th Congress, since it was not passed in the preceding Congress.

In addition to these efforts, NADA is one example of an interest group and PAC that may have federal impact on state policy-making. As a means of preventing certain states from following legislation of others, an interest group may lobby actively or passively in ensuring that certain legislation does not become enacted into law. For example, NADA moved quickly when California passed laws regarding vehicle emissions regulations and some northeastern states announced they would consider similar legislation. NADA held "passive" meetings at its headquarters in McLean, Virginia, to plan ways to dissuade other states from following in California's footsteps.

FINANCIAL FACTS

With the exception of the Association of Trial Lawyers of America (ATLA), NADA, with 1995–1996 contributions totaling $2,351,925, is the highest supporter in political elections among the interest groups discussed in this section. However, in stark contrast to ATLA, which has contributed nearly all of its political funds to the Democrats, records showing recent NADA financial contributions, particularly within the last decade, indicate that the association supports Republican Party candidates, both incumbents and challengers. Its contributions to political elections have been much higher than those of other PACs and interest groups. By the end of the 1988 elections NADA's political contributions totaled $1,202,420, approximately $730,500 of which was given to Republican candidates. By the end of the 1995–1996 election cycle, GOP candidates received an astonishing $1,912,925, while Democrats who were running for office received less than one-fourth that amount ($428,000).

DANIEL NESS

Bibliography

Anderson, Brian, and Burdett A. Loomis. "Taking Organization Seriously: The Structure of Interest Group Influence." In *Interest Group Politics,* 5th ed, edited by Allan J. Ciglar and Burdett A. Loomis. Washington, DC: Congressional Quarterly Press, 1998.

National Automobile Dealers Association: www.nada.org

Zuckerman, Edward, ed. *The Almanac of Federal PACs, 1998–1999.* Arlington, VA: Amward, 1998.

NATIONAL BEER WHOLESALERS ASSOCIATION

The National Beer Wholesalers Association (NBWA) is a trade organization with more than 1,800 member beer wholesale companies who distribute beer and other malt beverages to restaurants, convenience stores, drugstores, supermarkets, liquor shops and outlets, and other retail venues nationwide. Ronald A. Sarasin, a former member of the House of Representatives, is the NBWA's current president. The NBWA trade association and political action committee (PAC) headquarters is located in Alexandria, Virginia, a stone's throw from Washington, D.C., where it lobbies Congress on a number of issues, the most prominent of which involves excise taxes on malt beverages.

According to the NBWA, the association represents individuals who work for more than 2,900 licensed independent beer wholesalers who are affiliated with one or more of the 1,800 member beer wholesale companies. The beer industry is said to be a three-tier system: the beer wholesalers belong to the second tier, while the first tier is represented by the breweries, and the retailers are considered to be the third tier. This means that the wholesalers conduct their business as a go-between, acquiring beer and other malt beverages from the breweries and delivering and selling the merchandise to liquor and convenience stores, supermarkets, restaurants, and other retailers. This three-tier system eliminates direct contact between local or regional breweries with retail outlets for reasons that include preventing sole domination of one brand of beer, generating tax revenue, promoting moderate consumption of beer and other similar beverages, and challenging state and local jurisdictions over drinking laws that concern age limit and retail regulations regarding the sale of beverages. The NBWA also claims that, with the three tiers combined, the beer industry grosses annually approximately $175 billion and provides nearly $14.2 billion of its total revenue to local state and federal governments and $2.6 million for employees. (This last figure is erroneous, given that a single beer wholesale distributor company's annual direct payroll is slightly in excess of $1 million. A more accurate total payroll would be at least $1.95 billion for the 1,800 member companies.) Beer wholesale company owners' and operators' salaries vary greatly, and the data on owner earnings are inconsistent. The NBWA seems to keep the figure low—around the $100,000 mark. But more objective sources say that owners' personal incomes are anywhere from $75,000 to more than $1 million annually.

As described below, the NBWA, along with the National Federation of Independent Business was one of the single-most influential PACs that helped the Republican Party take control of the 104th Congress. Moreover, in the 1995–1996 election cycle, the NBWA contributed an astounding $1,324,992 to political elections, the third highest contributing PAC in this section on service interest groups—behind the Association of Trial Lawyers of America and the National Automobile Dealers Association (NADA)—more than four-fifths of which supported Republican candidates. After the NADA, the NBWA is the second largest contributor to the GOP. Also, the NBWA has the fourth largest trade association PAC, which contributed to 40 candidates, mostly GOP, in the 1994 congressional elections.

HISTORY

The NBWA was founded in 1938. In its early years the NBWA focused nearly all its attention on state and local governments and jurisdictions. This is because, after federal prohibition on alcoholic beverages was repealed, states themselves were given complete autonomy and responsibility for controlling the consumption of alcohol, authorizing age restrictions, and regulating its transportation between or within state boundaries. Central issues during this time included increasing taxes on beer and the raising of age limits on the consumption of alcohol. The NBWA's transition from local to federal lobbying efforts took place in the 1980s while Ronald Reagan was in office and Elizabeth Dole served as sec-

**National Beer Wholesalers Association
Political Action Committee Contributions**

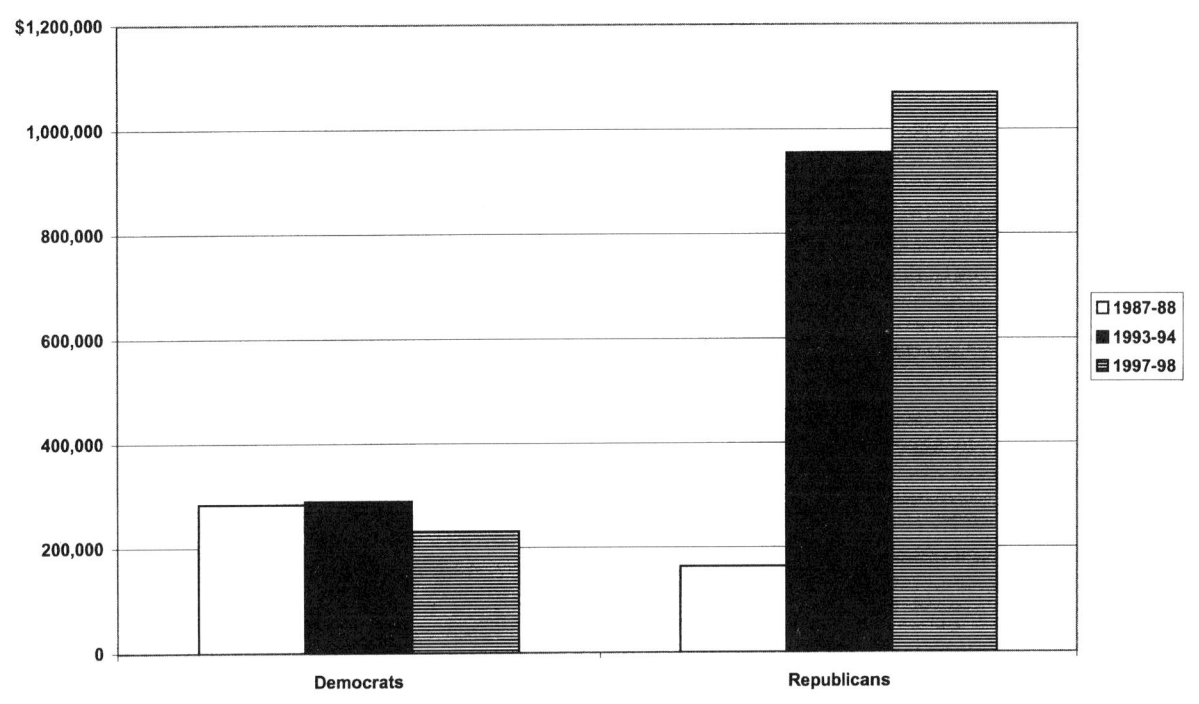

Data derived from official studies available from the Federal Election Commission, Washington, DC, 1987–1998.

retary of transportation. In this period federal authorities raised the mandatory drinking age from 18 to 21 in an attempt to curb the number of fatalities occurring on U.S. roadways. Then, in 1990 George Bush and the Democratic-controlled Congress doubled the tax on beer and other malt beverages. The NBWA's vice president of public affairs, David Rehr, a staunch supporter of the National Rifle Association, the Christian Coalition, and other interest groups supporting the GOP, claims that the 1990 tax increase on beer cost the industry 38,000 jobs and curbed beer purchases.

Since joining the NBWA in 1992, Rehr has encouraged NBWA brewers and wholesale company employees to challenge any bills or legislation that would lead to tax increases on beer. The first such occasion was in 1993, when the administration of Bill Clinton recommended a tax increase on beer as a means of reducing the national deficit. The NBWA's attacks on proponents of beer tax hikes and "anti-small-business" legislation have been widespread and were influential in favor of Republican candidates in subsequent election cycles. Despite its overwhelming backing of the GOP, the NBWA has supported some Democratic candidates, like Dick Gephardt of Missouri and Vic Fazio of California, whose congressional districts have large breweries.

ACTIVITIES: CURRENT AND FUTURE

Despite its relatively low membership of approximately 18,000—when compared with that of the NFIB and other similar interest groups with over a half a million members—perhaps one of the most significant factors of the NBWA's success is the association's ability to involve not only its members, who are wholesale distributor-owners and operators, but their employees as well. Since the Clinton election and the subsequent appointment of David Rehr as the association's vice president, the NBWA's agenda was clearly defined and outlined, in part, to generate member antipathy toward most congressional Democrats and opponents of small-business and beer wholesalers in general. The NBWA themes that have prevailed from earlier generations and still are on the plate to this very day include the support of a federal excise tax rollback on beer and malt beverage products and restrictions on beer and liquor advertising. Some of the more recent themes include opposition to recycling, workplace safety regulations mandated by the Occupational Safety and Health Administration, and support for prohibiting the sale of wine and beer by phone or mail or through the Internet. In total, there are approximately 25 items that the NBWA lobbyists bring to the floor when pressuring and attempting to sway Congress.

In numerous attempts throughout the years to curb federal regulations on alcoholic beverages, the NBWA has strongly supported measures relating to the rolling back of the federal excise tax. The NBWA argues that, although federal taxes had been imposed to help support the Civil War, current members of Congress who wish to enact legislation that would increase the tax on beer are those who would like to see a decrease in the amount of beer consumed in the United States. NBWA support of a tax rollback on beer is the direct result of the Omnibus Budget Reconciliation Act, legislation that Congress passed on January 1, 1991, which doubled the amount of federal tax from $9 to $18 for each 31-gallon barrel of beer—the equivalent of $1.30 per case of beer. The NBWA is currently supporting incumbent members of Congress and future candidates who will urge repeal of the Omnibus Act.

One of the central issues that has made headlines in recent years concerns the domination of beer and liquor wholesalers as they support regulations to prevent the selling of beer and wine over the Internet or by mail or phone. Beer wholesalers want to bar consumers from purchasing mostly wine and beer by mail, phone, or the Internet because this would allow consumers to bypass beer and liquor wholesalers and purchase alcoholic beverages from breweries, distillers, or retailers at cheaper rates. In demonstrating their power, beer wholesalers support members of Congress who advocate the "three-tier" system. The applicable bill (H.R. 2031), also known as the Scarborough Bill, was introduced by Representatives Joseph Scarborough (R-FL), James Sensenbrenner (R-WI), and Christopher Cannon (R-UT). The outcome is laws that essentially prohibit interstate sales of liquor and malt beverages in at least 30 states as well as a law enacted in five states that make it a felony to purchase cases of liquor—beer or wine—via mail, telephone, or the Internet. The NBWA has not yet come forth in directly supporting the Scarborough Bill. Nevertheless it is fairly certain that a number of its members have supported this measure.

FINANCIAL FACTS

During the 1987–1988 and 1989–1990 election cycles, Democratic candidates benefited from NBWA contributions, and much of this Democratic support was supposedly a consequence of several measures by the Republican executive branch to curb the consumption of alcohol by imposing federal taxes and raising the drinking age in all 50 states from 18 to 21. For example, by the 1988 elections, a little less than two-thirds of all NBWA contributions had gone to the Democrats ($282,752), while contributions to Republican candidates totaled $163,549. Support for the Democrats, however, would not last too much longer; by the time Clinton assumed office, financial contributions to GOP candidates were nearly double that given to the Democrats. And by the 1995–1996 election cycle, contributions to the GOP ($1,100,092) exceeded those given to Democratic candidates ($219,990) by nearly $1 million, or 83.5 percent of total congressional election contributions. Furthermore, the NBWA contributions for political elections nearly tripled within that period, from $446,301 in 1988 to $1,324,992 in the 1995–1996 election cycle.

DANIEL NESS

Bibliography

Biersack, Robert, and Paul S. Herrnson. "Introduction." In *After the Revolution: PACs, Lobbies, and the Republican Congress,* edited by Robert Biersack, Paul S. Herrnson, and Clyde Wilcox. Boston: Allyn & Bacon, 1999.

Drew, Elizabeth. *Whatever It Takes: The Real Struggle for Political Power in America.* New York: Viking, 1997.

National Beer Wholesalers Association: www.nbwa.org

Zuckerman, Edward, ed. *The Almanac of Federal PACs, 1998–1999.* Arlington, VA: Amward, 1998.

NATIONAL FEDERATION OF INDEPENDENT BUSINESS

The National Federation of Independent Business (NFIB) is a membership organization that represents more than 600,000 small-business owners. Research on political action committees (PACs) indicates that the NFIB, perhaps more than any other service interest group mentioned in this section, has been one of the key players, along with the National Rifle Association, the Christian Coalition, and the National Beer Wholesalers Association, in helping the Republican Party gain control of both the House and the Senate in the 1994 elections. The small-business enterprises represented by the NFIB range from single-person establishments to businesses with hundreds of employees. Altogether, there are over 7 million employees working for these small businesses, and the posted sales by these companies exceed $750 billion. The NFIB's national headquarters, along with its PAC, SAFE Trust, is located in Washington, D.C., where it plays a pivotal role as a conservative lobbying organization. In addition, the NFIB carries out its administrative tasks at its central office in Nashville, Tennessee, and maintains legislative centers in virtually every U.S. state capital.

Like most trade associations and corporation PACs, the NFIB's lobbying strategies are at times low-key, primarily working behind the scenes with Congress to encourage the passing of legislation that benefits the enterprises that their members own or operate—namely, small businesses. At other times, however, the NFIB has implemented additional strategies during election cycles—the 1993–1994 cycle in particular—as a means of enhancing the possibilities of the election of GOP candidates. During that time, and also in the more recent congressional elections, the NFIB mobilized its more than 600,000 members to work in collaboration with other Republican interest groups and members of Congress in a successful attempt to win GOP Senate and House seats.

The NFIB essentially employs two sets of strategies when lobbying Congress: it will either work surreptitiously, trying to convince members of Congress to support its current objectives and future agenda, or, as a membership organization, it will draw on its large membership to the fullest extent, asking members to contact their congressional leaders through toll-free numbers or the Internet as a means of carrying out the NFIB agenda. In terms of membership, the NFIB claims that 90 percent of its membership is made up of small-business owners and operators, generally having anywhere from one to 20 employees. However, this is not always the case: although large corporations are generally not associated with the NFIB, a large segment of its membership includes owners of companies that in some cases employ hundreds of workers. In fact, although it is a nonprofit business association representing the "Main Street" business, the NFIB employs 800 people and supposedly maintains an operating budget of over $70 million—hardly a "Main Street" business itself. The NFIB members pay dues on a sliding scale, ranging from $100 to $1,000, depending on their annual gross earnings.

HISTORY

Founded in 1943, the NFIB established itself quickly as a membership organization representing the interests of small-business owners and operators. Within the first two decades of its existence the NFIB developed connections within certain states by heading to particular state capitals and lobbying government officials. By the end of this period the NFIB's membership reached nearly 500,000 individuals, and it seemed to remain at that level for several years. Interestingly, however, the NFIB played a somewhat limited role in Washington politics; only within the last five years or so has it risen to a high level of prominence in terms of its overwhelming influence on GOP success in political elections.

The NFIB established its own PAC—the National

Federation of Independent Business/Save America's Free Enterprise (SAFE) Trust—in 1977 and contributed almost $10,000 to 54 candidates running for Congress. In 1982, the NFIB and its PAC, SAFE Trust, established its first five state PACs, and, although they were influential to some degree, they really did not gain much momentum and remained relatively innocuous for nearly a decade. By the 1993–1994 election cycle, however, the SAFE Trust war chest grew exponentially and surpassed $300,000 in contributions, which had been specifically earmarked for political candidates. During this period, from the late 1970s to the present time, NFIB membership grew by more than 100,000. In the 1996 elections the NFIB, along with the U.S. Chamber of Commerce, the National Association of Manufacturers, the National Restaurant Association, and the National Association of Wholesaler-Distributors, established The Coalition—Americans Working for Real Change, which served to counteract support by the AFL-CIO for Democratic candidates. During that election the coalition targeted 37 campaigns nationwide by using soft money to air television commercials in favor of Republican candidates.

ACTIVITIES: CURRENT AND FUTURE

Since its inception the NFIB has stressed the importance of small business in the United States, claiming that lawmakers have undermined the economic significance of "Main Street" businesses and, instead, concentrated on big business, Wall Street, and the global market. "Main Street," or "Mom and Pop" businesses, the NFIB claims, are the backbone of the nation's economy, reporting gross sales of close to three-quarters of $1 trillion. The NFIB also claims that small-business owners earn $40,000 on average.

Not surprisingly, the NFIB vehemently opposes any legislation that would require a tax increase for small businesses. The federation urges Congress to impose fewer business regulations, lower taxes, and adopt a "free-market approach to healthcare." To be sure, the Clinton healthcare plan that was up for consideration prior to the 1994 elections served as a catalyst for the NFIB; the federation's administration mobilized its members in an all-out campaign to kill the Clinton healthcare bill, arguing that it would be a damaging blow to small business. The measure was eventually defeated by Congress.

Like other business-related PACs and interest groups in this section, the NFIB strongly opposes increases in the minimum wage. Any increase, according to the NFIB leadership, would impose a burden on all small-business owners by forcing them to lay off so-called low-skill or first-time employees. Despite the NFIB's opposition to the minimum-wage bill, H.R. 3448, that raised the minimum hourly wage from $4.25 to $5.15, the rather large small-business community did receive some perks, including an amendment that provided over $10 billion in tax relief.

The NFIB's success is undoubtedly due to its grassroots communications network, which allows members to have easy access to its leaders and administrators. Furthermore, the federation claims to have over 1,000 members in each congressional district, and in any district small business is said to be the largest employer. The NFIB's networking efforts are successful due to the 4,000 to 5,000 activists throughout the country, who communicate to NFIB leaders through e-mail and faxes on behalf of the members. The NFIB also encourages its members to communicate with leaders through a toll-free number.

The 1996 race for a Senate seat in Colorado is an example of the NFIB's recent impact—through grassroots campaigning, the use of SAFE Trust contributions, and the group's internal communications—on the election of GOP congressional candidates who have won their contests by extremely narrow margins. In that election, Democrat Ted Strickland lost to the Republican and NFIB-backed candidate Wayne Allard, who had won an open seat in the House of Representatives in 1990. Allard beat Strickland by a 5 percent margin (51 to 46). To illustrate the federation's support of Allard, the NFIB sent members 10,709 foldouts—which are suitable for presentation in storefront windows—13,240 volunteer letters, and $9,500 in SAFE Trust contributions. Nearly $5,000 of that sum was an in-kind contribution, which promoted Allard's election through television commercials. Nearly 54 percent of Allard's contributions, approximately $200,000, was PAC money, and 5 percent of this total was SAFE Trust contributions. Moreover, the NFIB held two press conferences on Allard's behalf and attempted to gain momentum by arousing the anti-Democratic sentiment of small-business owners (and big-business owners, too) with a "Walk Down Main Street" event that included NFIB members. In addition, the NFIB played a pivotal role in electing Republican candidates in three other states—Arizona, Illinois, and Kentucky—who won by the extremely narrow margin of less than 1 percent.

The NFIB president, Jack Faris, sees the federation

having even a greater impact in politics than either of the two major political parties. Faris attracted the attention of some Clinton White House businessmen, like Erskine Bowles, as a means of counteracting Democratic efforts to court small business. Instead of 2,000 small-business owners and operators playing a role in the 1996 general elections, Faris predicts that, by the 2003–2004 election cycle, the NFIB will have the backing of 20,000 members actively contributing to the campaigns of GOP candidates.

FINANCIAL FACTS

Since its founding the NFIB has supported GOP candidates. Between 1987 and 1994 the NFIB's contributions to political elections never exceeded $317,000. When SAFE Trust was created, the NFIB contributed $9,688 to 54 congressional candidates, most of whom were Republicans. In the 1989–1990 election cycle, the NFIB contributed $282,067 of its $316,710 allocated for political contributions—almost 89 percent—to the GOP. Between 1987 and 1994, contributions to the Democrats remained extremely low, anywhere between 10 to 15 percent of all contributions. In the 1995–1996 election cycle, however, contributions skyrocketed to an astonishing $1,065,543. Moreover, in 1996 more than 25,000 members contributed in excess of $2 million to SAFE Trust, the federation's PAC, approximately $1.1 million of which went directly to finance GOP campaigns. In comparison, contributions of this type in 1994 amounted to $252,175, and there were allegedly few, if any, SAFE Trust contributions from members. Furthermore, Democratic contributions in the 1996 election year diminished even more; they received only 8 percent of all political contributions.

DANIEL NESS

Bibliography

Anderson, Brian, and Burdett A. Loomis. "Taking Organization Seriously: The Structure of Interest Group Influence." In *Interest Group Politics,* 5th ed., edited by Allan J. Cigler and Burdett A. Loomis. Washington, DC: Congressional Quarterly Press, 1998.

Drew, Elizabeth. *Whatever It Takes: The Real Struggle for Political Power in America.* New York: Viking, 1997.

National Federation of Independent Business: www.nfib.org

Shaiko, Ronald G., and Marc A. Wallace. "From Wall Street to Main Street: The National Federation of Independent Business and the New Republican Majority." In *After the Revolution: PACs, Lobbies, and the Republican Congress,* edited by Robert Biersack, Paul S. Herrnson, and Clyde Wilcox. Boston: Allyn & Bacon, 1999.

Zuckerman, Edward, ed. *The Almanac of Federal PACs, 1998–1999.* Arlington, VA: Amward, 1998.

NATIONAL FUNERAL DIRECTORS ASSOCIATION

The National Funeral Directors Association (NFDA) is the largest organization representing funeral directors, embalmers, and other individuals whose profession involves funeral or burial services. The NFDA's more than 15,000 members are mostly funeral directors and embalmers, and amount to about one-third of the total number of funeral directors nationwide. With nearly 22,000 funeral homes throughout the United States, there are currently almost 90,000 funeral home employees who are involved in other aspects of funeral home responsibilities, such as crematorium work, burial procedures and services, and mausoleum construction.

Like some of the other service PACs, or political action committees (the National Federation of Independent Business Free Enterprise PAC, in particular), the NFDA's PAC—the National Funeral Directors Association of the United States Inc. PAC (NFDA-PAC)—has been active in its efforts to lobby Congress to support funeral directors, most of whom are small-business owners or operators with anywhere from one or two to 10 employees. Despite its active presence in Washington politics, the NFDA is one of the few service interest groups whose headquarters is located outside the U.S. capital and its surrounding environs. Milwaukee and Brookfield, Wisconsin, have been the NFDA headquarters since its founding nearly 120 years ago. It currently employs a headquarters' staff of approximately 40 individuals. However, the NFDA maintains a government relations office in Washington, D.C., as a means of promoting its lobbying efforts. In addition to either promoting or blocking certain types of legislation, like federal tax increases, for example, the individuals elected to represent the NFDA seek to establish a "national identity" for funeral-related professions, form partnerships with individual state governing bodies, and increase the number of services for individual members.

HISTORY

Founded in 1882, the NFDA is the oldest interest group discussed in this section on service interest groups. At the time the NFDA was formed, several other institutions and professions, such as police groups and volunteer firefighters, changed from disparate entities that served only local urban or rural communities on an ephemeral basis to consolidated and, for the most part, bureaucratic systems that attempted to serve larger populations. These groups became systematized because a number of business leaders and the elite argued that police forces were need to quell disturbances and attempt to prevent the alleged increase in crime that they say could not be handled by individual watchmen alone. Similarly, funeral personnel were needed in greater numbers to handle funeral and burial services for a country whose population increased substantially during the late nineteenth century. This steady rise in the U.S. population, an increase in the number of individuals entering mortuary science programs, as well as minor fluctuations in the death rate are some reasons contributing to the NFDA's presence as a PAC in the special interest group community.

For the first 90 years of its existence the NFDA followed racist tactics, treating white and black clients differently. In fact, most of the NFDA's members only accommodated white families in bereavement, and it was not until 1973 that blacks received the same funeral services as did whites. In that year Wilbert Jean Oliver's federal lawsuit made it mandatory that funeral homes and funeral service enterprises nationwide provide equal services for all regardless of ethnic background.

**National Funeral Directors Association
Political Action Committee Contributions**

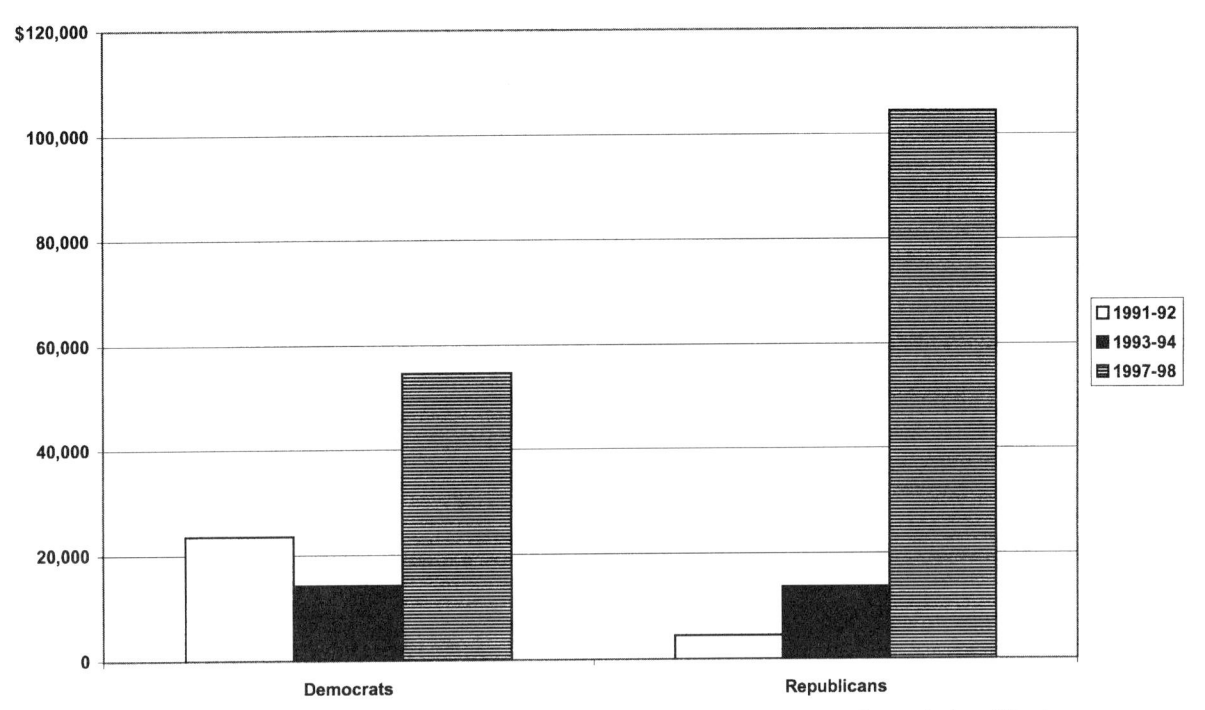

	Democrats	Republicans
1991-92	~24,000	~6,000
1993-94	~14,000	~15,000
1997-98	~55,000	~106,000

Data derived from official studies available from the Federal Election Commission, Washington, DC, 1991–1998.

Oliver was a civil rights activist who advocated for equal burial services for all races.

ACTIVITIES: CURRENT AND FUTURE

The NFDA's governing body is composed of three branches: a nine-member executive board; a policy board, whose members are delegates from each of the 50 states; and a house of delegates, serving as a legislative branch of the NFDA, whose officers are determined by the number of NFDA members in each state. Although the increase in population has kept the funeral home business occupied, the death rate has decreased to some degree since the 1960s, most likely as a result of new innovations in medical research. However, the NFDA's elected officials predict that the association will attract many more members in years to come, for they calculate that a much higher percentage of the U.S. population will be senior citizens by the year 2015.

According to NFDA statistics, nearly 85 percent of all funeral homes affiliated with the association are family-owned or -operated businesses. In addition, the association claims that approximately three-fourths of all NFDA member funeral homes are located in small cities or towns and villages located in rural regions. Given the overwhelming percentage of small, family-operated funeral homes, NFDA lobbyists monitor members of Congress whose legislative proposals may deeply impact the economy of small businesses. Some of the NFDA's key and current lobbying themes include the repeal of any amendments that favor increases in federal tax and opposition to government regulations concerning health and safety codes, the imposition of which would most likely require the hiring of additional employees.

The NFDA also has supported other trends in the industry in recent years. The association, for example, has seen an increase in the number of prepaid and planned funerals, as well as an increase in the number of after-care programs for bereaved family and friends of deceased individuals. Moreover, it accommodates people "with differing funeral customs" and those who are not accustomed to "traditional funeral" services. The association also claims an increase in the number of women and people of color who are active members or who are currently enrolled in mortuary science programs or in the process of obtaining directing or embalming licenses.

In terms of education, the NFDA allocates some of its funds for the purpose of providing scholarships for those wishing to enter the profession. However, as with other professions that require that the individual earn a license in order to enter practice, states differ dramatically in terms of the requirements needed for becoming an embalmer, funeral director, or any other type of profession involving funeral or burial services. In Nebraska, for example, one must earn a baccalaureate and take required courses in English, accounting, chemistry, biology, and psychology before being eligible for a license, while in the bordering state of Colorado, there are no current licensing requirements whatsoever. Approximately half the states, however, require the minimum of a high school diploma and two years of college, as well as some continuing education credits while in practice, and almost all of the states require that the license applicant assume an apprenticeship or internship either before or after a degree is earned. The NFDA's local or state agenda is to regulate more standard procedures in order for one to obtain directing or embalming licenses.

As a means of finding ways of increasing revenue, NFDA elected officials seek to provide a large array of products and services for its members. The association offers educational services, which inform new or veteran funeral directors and embalmers about current trends in prices (the national average cost of a funeral service is currently $4,600 to $5,000), competition with nearby homes, marketing tips, and cost-cutting ideas. Other membership services include a Funeral Service Credit Union, which makes available to members loans of up to $62,000; a Group Music License, which allows members to obtain copyright licenses at a one-third reduced rate; property and casualty insurance programs; health, dental, and disability insurance plans; retirement plans; and reduced admission to Disneyland or Disney World.

FINANCIAL FACTS

During the 1991–1992 election cycle, the NFDA's financial contributions totaled $28,000, but by the 1995–1996 election cycle their contributions dropped to $18,300. Moreover, they seem to favor the party that controls Congress at any given time. For instance, the NFDA favored Republican Party candidates in 1996 for the first time—the Republicans had gained control of both the House and Senate two years earlier. In the 1991–1992 election cycle, the NFDA contributed $23,500 to the Democrats, while GOP contributions amounted to only $4,500. Support for the Democrats in the 1995–1996 election cycle, however, dwindled considerably—they received only $3,000, a drop of more than $20,000 from the previous presidential election—while financial support for the Republicans soared to more than $15,000. By the 1997–1998 election cycle, NFDA contributions to Republicans far outweighed those to Democrats.

DANIEL NESS

Bibliography

Biersack, Robert, and Paul S. Herrnson. "Introduction." In *After the Revolution: PACs, Lobbies, and the Republican Congress,* edited by Robert Biersack, Paul S. Herrnson, and Clyde Wilcox. Boston: Allyn & Bacon, 1999.

National Funeral Directors Association: www.nfda.org

Zuckerman, Edward, ed. *The Almanac of Federal PACs, 1998–1999.* Arlington, VA: Amward, 1998.

NATIONAL RESTAURANT ASSOCIATION

The National Restaurant Association, whose membership exceeds 20,000 individuals representing over 100,000 food-service companies, is a major conservative political interest group and political action committee (PAC) in Washington, D.C. Members include fast-food enterprises; numerous restaurant chains; school, college, university, and hospital food services; cafeterias; military clubs; and numerous other companies involved in the consumption of food and beverages, away from home. (The National Restaurant Association's web site, however, claims that the organization has 30,000 members representing over 175,000 restaurants, chains, and food establishments. See www.restaurant.org.) Some of the PAC-sponsoring corporations or subsidiaries that are members of the National Restaurant Association include Burger King USA, Kentucky Fried Chicken, The Olive Garden, and Morisson's Hospitality Group. Their primary interest is to satisfy food company employers, restaurateurs, owners of cafeterias, and CEOs of major school, university, and hospital food corporations through encouraging tax breaks and monitoring Congress in order to keep the minimum wage low.

HISTORY

In 1919 the National Restaurant Association was formed after a group of restaurant owners had collaborated on an effort to mobilize a larger number of fellow restaurateurs throughout the country. Issues among restaurant and cafeteria owners in the early period were similar to those of other trade organizations—primarily those regarding tax hikes imposed on certain foods and beverages as well as increases in the minimum wage. Another National Restaurant Association concern promoted throughout its 80 years in existence, but not necessarily directly related to political lobbying, is the fostering of educational programs related to the food and hospitality industry. Each year the National Restaurant Association's educational programs allocate a certain portion of their revenue toward awards and scholarships relating to college programs in culinary arts and hospitality.

ACTIVITIES: CURRENT AND FUTURE

The National Restaurant Association was a crucial player in the 1996 elections. Given that the Republican Party shared similar interests and beliefs, such as a low minimum wage and tax breaks for both small and big business, the National Restaurant Association played a key role in helping the Republicans gain control of the 104th Congress. With a donation of $1 million in May 1996, the National Restaurant Association was the largest contributor to The Coalition—Americans Working for Real Change, an alliance of more than 30 business organizations that attempted to frustrate the campaign of the AFL-CIO, a labor federation, in assisting the Democrats' control of both houses of Congress. Other key conservative organizations that formed the coalition include the National Federation of Independent Business (NFIB), the U.S. Chamber of Commerce, the National Association of Manufacturers, and the National Association of Wholesaler-Distributors.

Changes in the minimum wage have also posed a great challenge for the National Restaurant Association lobbyists. In general, its spokespersons have always opposed minimum-wage increases and the withholding of tax from tip earnings. Because fast-food outlets are one of the several types of food-service businesses represented by the National Restaurant Association, the PAC's lobbyists have always been critical of any move to increase the minimum wage. According to the association, increasing the minimum wage may force restaurants and other food-service businesses to cut

**National Restaurant Association
Political Action Committee Contributions**

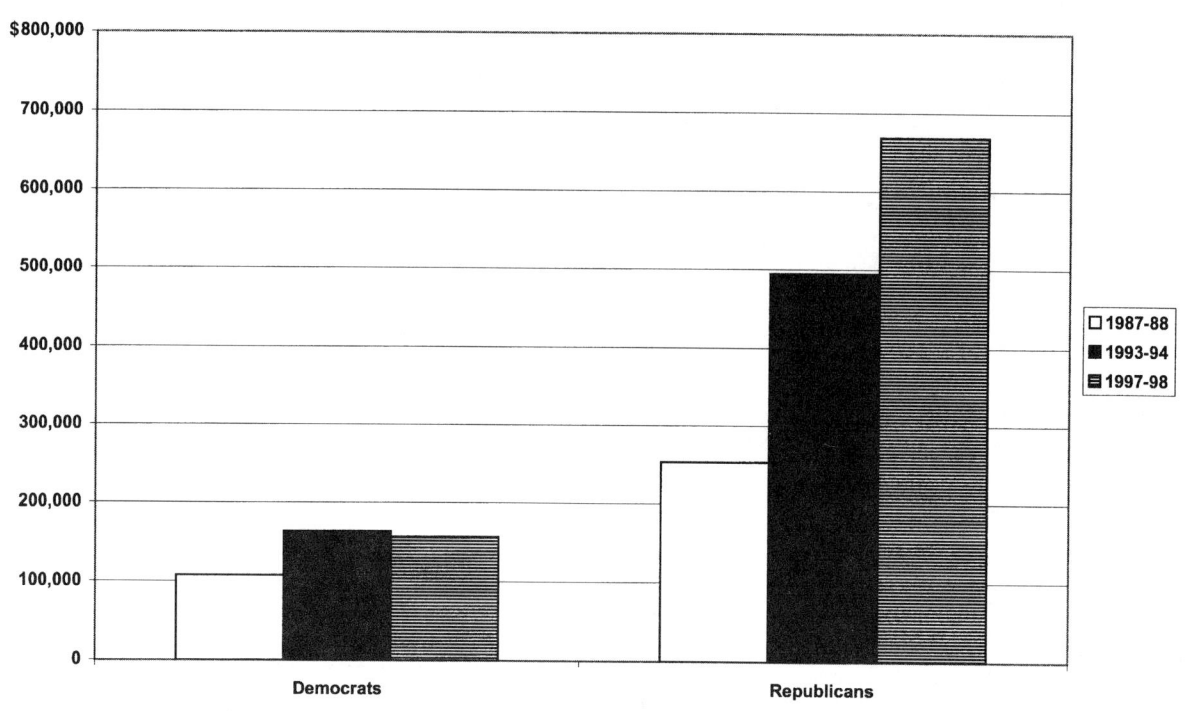

[Bar chart showing PAC contributions to Democrats and Republicans for 1987-88, 1993-94, and 1997-98. Democrats received approximately $105,000 (1987-88), $160,000 (1993-94), and $155,000 (1997-98). Republicans received approximately $250,000 (1987-88), $490,000 (1993-94), and $660,000 (1997-98).]

Data derived from official studies available from the Federal Election Commission, Washington, DC, 1987–1998.

entry-level jobs, thereby making it difficult for first-time and so-called low-skilled employees to enter the workforce. Furthermore, the National Restaurant Association favors full tax deductions for business-related meals. Its lobbyists argue that restrictions on such deductions burden business personnel (small-business people in particular), who presumably are able to make business transactions only during mealtimes. The recently passed Small Employer Tax Relief Act of 1999 will help National Restaurant Association advocates and GOP members as it increases tax-deductible meals from the present 50 percent deduction to 80 percent for small food businesses.

The National Restaurant Association opposes any legislation that would lower the Blood Alcohol Concentration (BAC) level. To illustrate, they are firmly against Senator Daniel Patrick Moynihan's (D-NY) effort to withhold highway safety funds from states that do not comply with the .08 BAC level. According to leaders of the association, a lower BAC threshold would lower alcohol consumption and thereby lower revenue from sales of alcoholic beverages in restaurants and other food-service establishments. While most states are currently holding the legal BAC standard at .10 percent, recent studies in alcohol-related accidents have shown that impairment in reaction time, tracking ability, concentration versus divided attention performance, information processing, vision, perception, and psychomotor performance can be significant at a BAC level of .05 percent, and, in some instances, may be apparent at a level of .02 percent.

The association is also against any laws that ban smoking in restaurants and cafeterias on a national level. As a PAC, the association opposed a 1998 Senate bill that would have prohibited smoking in fast-food establishments throughout the country. In the summer of that year the bill was not passed; whether the National Restaurant Association PAC was partially responsible is questionable.

The National Restaurant Association is opposed to any legislation that forces employers to offer employees mental health benefits in addition to accident or sickness insurance and to provide employee access to specialists like acupuncturists and homeopaths, and to legislation that makes employers liable in the event of medical malpractice. The association's leaders were pleased when the Senate passed the GOP version of healthcare reform and dismissed Senator Edward Kennedy's (D-MA) patient's bill of rights. They claim that Kennedy's plan would have forced businesses to provide the above-mentioned medical services.

In contrast, the association has voiced its opposition to the Family and Medical Leave Act of 1993—which grants individuals working for companies with 50 or more employees the opportunity to take 12 weeks of unpaid leave of absence for family or medical reasons—as well as any possible addition to the act. These additions would include companies with fewer than 50 employees, partially paid leave, as well as pension benefits while an individual is on leave.

Finally, other major concerns of the National Restaurant Association seem to be directly related to the possibility of lawsuits filed against food-service operators and restaurateurs. One such situation involves the Occupational Safety and Health Administration (OSHA) and its role in the ergonomics standard: ensuring that restaurant employers identify potential hazards or hazard areas so as to minimize employee injury or fatality. The National Restaurant Association supports the Workplace Preservation Act (H.R. 987), introduced by House member Roy Blunt (R-MO), which would force OSHA to hold its ruling so that Congress can be briefed on the results of an ergonomics study conducted by the National Academy of Sciences. Furthermore, in another scenario of possible lawsuits brought against the association's members, the National Restaurant Association firmly opposes the Copyright Damages Improvement Act, which forces restaurants and other similar businesses to obtain permission for every copyrighted musical work played. Failure for restaurants to do so carries stiff fines, and the National Restaurant Association claims that such penalties may cause small food businesses to go under.

FINANCIAL FACTS

The National Restaurant Association's contributions to political elections skyrocketed over 243 percent in the 10-year period from 1987 to 1996. It is important to note, however, that like those of the NFIB, the National Beer Wholesalers Association, the National Automobile Dealers Association, and a host of other conservative PACs, the National Restaurant Association's financial contributions to the GOP have been far greater than those given to Democrats. In the early part of this period GOP contributions were slightly more than those to the Democrats, or two-thirds of total contributions. Over this 10-year period, while National Restaurant Association contributions to the Democrats dropped slightly (from $107,500 to $100,050) contributions to the Republican Party increased nearly threefold, from $253,800 in 1987–1988 to $765,069 in 1996. In the 1995–1996 election cycle, for example, 88.5 percent of the National Restaurant Association's contributions went to GOP candidates for Congress, while in the previous election cycle, Democratic contributions amounted to $164,122, or 25 percent of the $658,844 total—still, however, favoring the GOP. Overwhelming GOP support does not seem surprising, given their strong ties to and their collaboration with the NFIB, the U.S. Chamber of Commerce, and nearly 30 other groups joining together to challenge the AFL-CIO campaign against a GOP Congress.

DANIEL NESS

Bibliography

Herrnson, Paul S. "Parties and Interest Groups in Postreform Congressional Elections." In *Interest Group Politics,* 5th ed., edited by Allan J. Cigler and Burdett A. Loomis. Washington, DC: Congressional Quarterly Press, 1998.

National Restaurant Association: www.restaurant.org

Shaiko, Ronald G., and Marc A. Wallace. "From Wall Street to Main Street: The National Federation of Independent Business and the New Republican Majority." In *After the Revolution: PACs, Lobbies, and the Republican Congress,* edited by Robert Biersack, Paul S. Herrnson, and Clyde Wilcox. Boston: Allyn & Bacon, 1999.

Zuckerman, Edward, ed. *The Almanac of Federal PACs, 1998–1999.* Arlington, VA: Amward, 1998.

PETROLEUM MARKETERS ASSOCIATION OF AMERICA

The Petroleum Marketers Association of America (PMAA) is a federation with a membership exceeding 10,000 individuals who are independent marketers, commissioned distributors, and retailers specializing in gasoline, heating, and diesel fuel. The PMAA has 43 state and regional chapters throughout the country. Approximately 50 percent of the gasoline, 60 percent of the diesel fuel, and 80 percent of the home heating oil consumed annually in the United States is sold by PMAA members. In addition, members of the PMAA supply gasoline to more than 16,000 stores nationwide; approximately 9,000 of them are convenience stores. The PMAA headquarters is located in Arlington, Virginia, and the PMAA political action committee (PAC) is an ardent lobbying group in Washington, D.C., which overwhelmingly supports Republican Party candidates running for office. The PMAA is sponsored by several multimillion-dollar corporations, including Mobil, Exxon, Shell, and such non-petroleum companies as Coors, R. J. Reynolds, and Hubbell Lighting Co.

Comparable to other trade interest groups—the National Beer Wholesalers Association (NBWA) is a good example—PMAA companies serve as a second tier in a three-tiered system, the first being the oil or petroleum refineries and the third being the retail stations, convenience stores, and outlets. As stated in its bylaws, the primary goal of the PMAA is to "preserve the private enterprise, risk reward system, to prevent undue economic concentration, to ensure a favorable competitive climate in petroleum distribution, and to encourage an adequate supply of petroleum products." PMAA's PAC, the Petroleum Marketers Association of America Small Businessmen's Committee, is also located in Arlington.

HISTORY

The federation was founded in 1909 as the Independent Petroleum Marketers Association (IPMA). Its first president, Thomas L. Hisgen, was a strong opponent of the Standard Oil Company, which he claimed was anticompetitive toward smaller petroleum and oil companies and suppliers. Hisgen openly expressed his views, especially during his run in 1908 as an Independent presidential candidate against Republican William Howard Taft, the twenty-seventh U.S. president, and William Jennings Bryan, who was running on the Democratic ticket. Despite Hisgen's ardent efforts to strengthen smaller petroleum companies, the IPMA did not last for more than two years. The breakup of the Standard Oil Company in 1911 and the subsequent creation of local and regional petroleum and oil marketing associations led to the collapse of the IPMA. It resurfaced in 1940 as the President's Council of Petroleum Marketers Associations and, after the Second World War, was modified and renamed again with the designation of the National Oil Jobbers Council. In 1984, more than 40 years after its revival, the organization was renamed the Petroleum Marketers Association of America.

ACTIVITIES: CURRENT AND FUTURE

Like the National Federation of Independent Business (NFIB), a federation whose constituents overlap in membership with other conservative federations (including the PMAA), the PMAA has benefited greatly from the GOP takeover of Congress. Similar to NFIB members, PMAA members are, for the most part, small-business or family-business owners who serve the petroleum and oil needs of their local communities and districts. These trade interest groups are also similar in the ways in which they lobby before Congress. Although the NFIB's membership far exceeds that of the PMAA, both organizations use insider and outsider methods as a means of lobbying. An insider method is one in which a particular interest group will make use of its PAC and lobby quietly before Congress. An outsider method, in contrast, is one in which a particular interest group will use its membership (and even employees of members—a tactic used by the NBWA) as a way of making its agendas and issues heard before Congress. Using the outsider approach, an interest group will make available toll-free telephone numbers and Internet access, so that members themselves can contact congressional leaders on behalf of the interest group. In numerous cases interest groups urge members to make frequent calls and "jam" phone lines to get their points across.

The PMAA is divided into six committees within each of its 43 regions. These committees are the Motor Fuels Committee, Heating Oil Fuels Committee, Lube Oil Committee, Member Services Committee, Legislative Affairs Committee, and Brand Chairman's Committee, all of which review the central issues within their region and make recommendations to the PMAA board of directors, the principal governing body of the organization. The PMAA board elects a 22-member executive committee, which then brings its lobbying issues to Washington.

The PMAA's lobbying tactics can be described as aggressive and, often, intolerant and discriminatory in terms of accusing others, particularly nonmembers or ethnic groups, of maintaining double standards. A case in point is the PMAA's opposition to what it calls Tax Treatment of Native Americans. PMAA leaders have accused Native American store owners and petroleum service proprietors of not remitting excise taxes on petroleum and petroleum products to the states in which they do business, and they are currently taking this issue up in Congress. But the PMAA is by no means innocent in its handling of legislation. PMAA leaders are attempting a counterattack through a grassroots effort in swaying Congress to believe that Native American owners are evading tax laws. Such stereotyping and accusations that lack evidence often lead to further unwarranted discrimination against Native Americans and their businesses.

The PMAA is also in competition with other power industries, such as natural gas, electricity, and nuclear power, and lobbies Congress to favor companies that provide oil heating. This overwhelming support for oil heat has been promulgated by the establishment of the National Oil Heat Research Alliance. Although the PMAA successfully brought the issue of the future of the oil industry to the congressional floor, the Senate did not pass any bills to support one particular form of heating over others.

PMAA leaders and lobbyists also get involved in areas entirely unrelated to petroleum and oil issues. For example, they have demonstrated their opposition to regulations enforced by the Food and Drug Administration (FDA) on the sale of tobacco products to minors by retailers and "legitimate business people." The PMAA and similar interest groups continue to flout FDA regulations that may prevent teen smoking by arguing that such regulations are directed to increase taxes rather than to curb tobacco use.

The association also expresses its antipathy toward the Occupational Safety and Health Administration (OSHA) and its regulations imposed on distributor or go-between companies. The PMAA strongly opposes any legislation that defends OSHA's mandate on penalties related to workers' injuries. Furthermore, the PMAA has struck down guidelines imposed by OSHA that require petroleum establishments to hire at least two clerks during night shifts. The PMAA's sentiment toward OSHA is similar to that of other interest groups, particularly those that represent distributors, middlemen companies, and small businesses.

FINANCIAL FACTS

Over the past decade the PMAA's contributions to elections increased by nearly $100,000, from $182,700 in the 1987–1988 election cycle to $275,888 in the 1995–1996 election cycle. While contributions to GOP candidates, both incumbents and challengers, always exceeded the amount contributed to Democrats running for office, the PMAA's contributions to the Democrats plummeted, especially after the Republicans gained control of the 104th Congress. The gap seemed to be closing in the 1991–1992 election cycle as contributions to Democratic candidates neared the $100,000 mark and contributions to candidates on the GOP ticket exceeded those contributed to Democrats by $60,000. In the 1995–1996 election cycle, GOP candidates received $239,188, while Democrats received only $35,000, or 13 percent of the PMAA's contributions.

DANIEL NESS

Bibliography

Biersack, Robert, and Paul S. Herrnson. "Introduction." In *After the Revolution: PACs, Lobbies, and the Republican Congress,* edited by Robert Biersack, Paul S. Herrnson, and Clyde Wilcox. Boston: Allyn & Bacon, 1999.

Petroleum Marketers Association of America: www.pmaa.org

Zuckerman, Edward, ed. *The Almanac of Federal PACs, 1998–1999*. Arlington, VA: Amward, 1998.

UNITED STATES CHAMBER OF COMMERCE

The United States Chamber of Commerce is the largest business association in the world. It is also one of the most prominent interest groups in the nation, representing some 3 million companies, 3,000 state and local chambers of commerce, 775 business associations, and 85 American chambers of commerce abroad. Since its creation in 1912, the association's main goal has been the promotion of business interests and free enterprise in the United States and around the world.

Today, the United States Chamber of Commerce remains an influential and complex umbrella organization with large resources available to help pursue its goals. It has lobbyists and policy experts working to advance legislation favorable to business; a litigation center representing the chamber and its members in court; a public policy think tank that develops research on current and prospective trends related to business interests; a grassroots network of 50,000 activists; a publication and media relations program; and a modern system of information available to members. The chamber also has an international division that monitors global commercial issues and promotes new opportunities for American products and services worldwide.

HISTORY

Whereas trade associations are made up of members from specific industries or sectors of society, chambers of commerce are recognized by geographic location and serve the interests of local business communities. The first chamber of commerce in the United States was organized in New York in 1768; by 1870, the number of state and local chambers had jumped to 40. Several of these groups joined the United States Chamber of Commerce when it was established in 1912.

The creation of a national chamber of commerce in the United States can be linked to the growth and expansion of American firms in the late nineteenth and early twentieth centuries. The widespread use of electric power, heavy machinery, and scientific management boosted production and gave rise to new industries and massive corporate enterprises. Trains and newly invented automobiles sped product distribution and helped create a large, national market. As commerce grew, business leaders sought new ways to articulate their interests and influence both government policy and public opinion.

During his presidency from 1909 to 1913, William Howard Taft urged minimum regulation of business and greater government cooperation with the private sector. He also urged formation of a national group that would represent the entire business sector and maintain regular communication with the government. People like Edward A. Filene, an entrepreneur who had introduced creative methods of retail distribution in Boston, Massachusetts, also saw the need for such an association and helped organize the United States Chamber of Commerce. Given the tremendous level of competition that the industrial boom caused during these years, the association's first activities concentrated on building consensus among entrepreneurs to standardize trade practices. These practices included drawing the line between lawful and unlawful activities, ethical and unethical dealings, and addressing such issues as the mislabeling and misrepresentation of the quantity and quality of goods and services. In 1924, the chamber published a general proposal on fair practices and profits, explicitly citing several principles that member groups had already accepted. Within the next few months, 270 business and trade associations ratified the chamber's proposal. This was an important step in the promotion of competitive stability and a cooperative business environment.

Throughout its history, the chamber has concentrated on legislation and government actions. It has analyzed thousands of bills and regulations, worked with congressional committees, and developed lobbying ac-

**U.S. Chamber of Commerce
Political Action Committee Contributions, 1997-1998**

Data derived from official studies available from the Federal Election Commission, Washington, DC, 1997–1998.

tivities to shape legislation favorable to business. The chamber has also held meetings, conferences, and special events to maintain communication and close relations with members of Congress and administration officials.

Global events and economic changes have prompted the United States Chamber of Commerce to advocate different policies at different times. In 1917, the upheavals caused by the First World War led the chamber to switch from opposing government intervention in the economy to supporting creation of the War Industries Board. This agency helped rationalize production and regulate industrial activity nationwide. During the Great Depression in the 1930s, the chamber backed the National Recovery Administration, a New Deal agency created to regulate trade practices and spur economic growth.

When the economy boomed after the Second World War, the United States Chamber of Commerce reverted to its original aims, advocating reduced government interference and little federal regulation of business. The organization's rhetoric took on a more ideological bent in the 1950s. Free enterprise, the chamber argued, provided a bulwark against communism and totalitarianism.

The organization expanded and soon branched into new fields. In the 1960s it created the National Chamber Foundation, a think tank devoted to funding research, educating the public, and promoting a favorable image of business. The National Chamber Litigation Center (NCLC) was established the following decade to challenge government agencies and oppose interest groups on cases involving environmental damage, product liability, class action matters, and contingency fees. The chamber also formed a political action committee (PAC) to back pro-business candidates. Today this PAC is one of the wealthiest, most influential PACs in the country.

The rise of the environmental movement in the 1960s had spurred the formation of many new interest groups, resulting in the enactment of numerous laws and regulations aimed at fighting pollution, protecting land and water, and improving the quality of life. Litigation exploded, often placing business on the defensive. The NCLC has fought many cases relating to environmental issues, consumer safety, and workplace conditions. In the 1980s the chamber began championing tort reform and initiatives designed to limit legal recourse on such suits. More recently, the chamber has argued that such suits force manufacturers to raise the price of goods and prevent them from introducing new products to the market.

The organization also sponsors the Grassroots Action Information Network (GAIN) to mobilize local, national, and international business groups around specific issues. Although the United States Chamber of Commerce has been in existence for almost a century, it has seldom joined forces with other groups. In 1973, the chamber issued a joint letter with the National Association of Manufacturers for the first time in its history. Such efforts will likely become more frequent. In the 1990s, the chamber formed alliances with other associations on such issues as healthcare, patients' rights, and potential Y2K computer liability suits.

ACTIVITIES: CURRENT AND FUTURE

The United States Chamber of Commerce has a staff of 1,200 and is headquartered in Washington, D.C. The chamber is governed by a board of directors composed of 65 corporate executives. The board normally follows recommendations of the staff but has considerable autonomy to make decisions.

The United States Chamber of Commerce has a broad base: approximately 96 percent of its members are small businesses with less than 100 employees. Large corporations, however, tend to dominate the group's positions and opinions. The chamber's most recent efforts include strengthening the organization as a vigorous force for economic growth in the United States and abroad; advocating entitlement reform and reduced government spending; fighting business tax increases and various healthcare regulations; and helping rebuild the country's transportation system and finding skilled workers.

The chamber will also continue lobbying for free trade at the international level, particularly among recently liberalized economic systems. Between 1996 and 1999, a dozen American chambers of commerce were established in former communist countries and republics of the former Soviet Union, including Bulgaria, Romania, Latvia, Azerbaijan, and Ukraine. The United States Chamber of Commerce also has several affiliated organizations fostering economic growth and democracy in more than 40 countries. These organizations support education, workforce preparation, and the interests of business.

The United States Chamber of Commerce publishes books, reports, newsletters, statistics, and electronic bulletins. It has a video production studio, a rich web site with information open to the public and areas restricted to members only, and a reference library with 10,000 volumes.

FINANCIAL FACTS

The United States Chamber of Commerce has a yearly budget of $70 million. According to the Center for Responsive Politics, the chamber's lobbying expenditures reached $17 million in 1998, up from $14.2 million in 1997.

MIRIAM JIMÉNEZ-HERNÁNDEZ

Bibliography

Donohue, Thomas. "American Business: The Next Agenda," in *Vital Speeches of the Day* (December 1, 1997).

Green, Mark, and Andrew Buchsbaum. "The Corporate Lobbies: Political Profiles of the Business Roundtable and the Chamber of Commerce," *Public Citizen* (February 1980).

Haefele, Edwin T. "Shifts in Business-Government Interactions," in Council of Trends and Perspectives, Chamber of Commerce of the United States, *Government Regulation of Business: Its Growth, Impact and Future*. Washington, DC: Chamber of Commerce of the United States, 1979.

Shaffer, Butler. *In Restraint of Trade. The Business Campaign Against Competition 1817–1938*. Lewisburg, PA: Bucknell University Press, 1997.

United States Chamber of Commerce: www.uschamber.com

Weidenbaum, Murray L. *Business, Government and the Public*. Englewood Cliffs, NJ: Prentice-Hall, 1977.

SECTION THREE
MEDIA, ENTERTAINMENT, AND INFORMATION

The information, media, and entertainment industries have advanced their interests in the national and state governments for over a century. Because the dissemination of information is essential to the proper functioning of a democracy, these industries have been endowed with a persuasive rationale on which to base their claims for preferential treatment. Legislators, well aware of the enormous power wielded by these industries over their own careers, have often responded favorably. Indeed, the government has facilitated the commercialization and profitability of these industries in numerous enactments, such as postal subsidies and exemptions from the minimum wage. In recent years, the ownership of the news and entertainment industries has become increasingly concentrated and entangled through mergers, which have been made possible by changes in national laws. As might be expected, these industries are represented primarily by well-financed trade associations. While these associations dominate the field, there are also watchdog groups that complain about the increasing concentration of ownership and competing groups that wish to retain noncommercial sources of information.

The current issue of the greatest concern to the information and entertainment industries is unquestionably copyright law, as technological developments, such as the Internet, have contributed to the potential for piracy—which, in turn, decreases profitability. These industries are seeking both legislative and technological solutions to this threat. Additionally, they have objected to governmental attempts at censorship and the restriction of tobacco and alcohol advertisements. In advancing their position on these issues, the industry's trade associations engage in traditional forms of lobbying, such as contacting legislators and contributing to campaigns. They focus their efforts not only on Congress, but also on those government agencies such as the Federal Communications Commission (FCC) and the Federal Trade Commission (FTC) that have jurisdiction over them. The groups that object to the power of this media lobby are more likely to employ outsider tactics, such as organizing and educating the public.

AREAS OF INTEREST

In the nineteenth century, the information industry utilized the medium of print. Given this fact, trade associations were primarily interested in retaining special, low-cost postal rates. Early in the twentieth century, advertising emerged as the major source of revenue for newspapers and other forms of media. As a result, the media's interest groups became advocates of this industry, as did the corporate world, opposing all restrictions on advertisements. As new technologies were introduced, such as radio broadcasting and film, the media's trade associations added to their interests. Broadcasters required regulation to avoid chaos on the airwaves and thus spearheaded the call for governmental action. With the use of these new technologies for entertainment purposes, the public and its representatives increasingly demanded censorship. The media's trade associations resisted these demands, preventing the censorship of films, and later, bans on offensive lyrics in recordings.

In the early years of the Depression, a reform movement calling for a noncommercial system of broadcasting coalesced. In response, the National Association of Broadcasters (NAB) fought to ensure that the landmark

Communications Act of 1934 protected the commercial system of broadcasting. This act established the FCC and consolidated the regulatory authority over all interstate and foreign communication by wire and radio. Henceforward, the commercial nature of the system was never questioned. At times, there were claims of "excessive commercialization," but the broadcast industry took it upon itself to resist any governmental regulations aimed at reducing commercialization, and it did so with success. Speaking in much softer tones than the trade associations, those representing the noncommercial world of information, such as educational institutions, have sought to obtain public funds for research and educational purposes without challenging the commercial nature of the system.

After the development of cable television and the rise in popularity of recorded music around mid-century, the trade associations' interest in copyright law intensified. Often, the various trade associations found themselves at odds over this issue. For example, the film industry desired copyright protection against the broadcasters' use of its products, while the broadcasters sought relief from the cable industry's interception of their signals. As users of recordings for entertainment purposes, hotels and casinos were not necessarily supportive of copyright protection at all. In addition to this issue, the entertainment industries, particularly hotels and casinos, have demonstrated a consistent interest in labor regulations, such as the minimum wage.

CURRENT CONTEXT

Over the past few decades, the information industry has become increasingly commercialized and entangled with the entertainment industry. Indeed, the United States has become an entertainment culture, with Hollywood the prime socializing agent for recent generations. Newscasts have adapted to this culture and are often designed to capture the interests of selected viewers, not to inform them. "Selected" viewers are those with money in a society characterized by a growing gap between the rich and poor. Because advertisers, which provide the major source of revenue for the information industry, are interested in speaking only to customers with disposable income, newspapers and news programmers seek to attract this type of audience and gear their stories accordingly.

Such a strategy fits perfectly with the interests of the media. In fact, the interests of the advertising and media industries are in harmony, as both are dominated by small numbers of corporate giants. Currently, there are approximately 10 vertically integrated conglomerates and between 30 and 40 large supporting corporations that define the global media industry. In each of the sectors, such as recording and movie production, oligopolies are present and make entry difficult. Competition among the members of the oligopolies is not fierce, as it has been softened by joint ventures and ties of cross-ownership. The trend toward concentration of ownership is expected to continue, given the profit incentives created by vertical integration and technological developments. A vertically integrated firm, exemplified best by Walt Disney, has ownership of both content, such as movies, and delivery mechanisms, such as television stations. Because of their ability to cross-sell products, these firms have a significant profit advantage over those not so integrated. For example, if a Disney movie fails at the box office but its Disney-owned recordings sell, the company can post a net gain. In comparison, an independent movie producer would depend solely on box-office revenues. This dynamic creates an incentive for more mergers. The digital revolution, which is erasing the distinction between forms of media, is also paving the way for further concentration of ownership. Ultimately, all forms of data, including music, will be produced and stored in interchangeable digital bits and will be instantaneously accessible. Already, cable and telephone companies have combined as their services have "converged," meaning one has the capability to perform the other's functions.

However, the consolidation of the information and entertainment industries could not have occurred without the government's acquiescence and support. Throughout the 1980s and 1990s, the government has adopted a deregulatory stance toward the communications industry, relaxing its limits on ownership restrictions. This trend culminated in the Telecommunications Act of 1996, which has been dubbed the "Magna Carta" for communications corporations. Replacing the 1934 Communications Act and eradicating many of the FCC's limits on ownership, this act deregulated the communications industry by removing barriers to consolidation. In so doing, it ensured that the profit motive would shape the structure of the communication system for years to come. Moreover, this trend in deregulation is not limited to the United States, but is global in scope.

Whereas the political context has been a friendly one for the commercial media, it has been a different story for noncommercial sources of information. Indeed, funding for higher education was cut significantly at both the national and state levels throughout the 1980s and early 1990s. When the Republicans took control of

Congress in 1995, the higher education community feared drastic cuts. As a result of the elimination of the federal deficit and other political developments, such cuts did not come to pass. However, federal funding for research, such as the National Endowment for the Humanities and for the Arts, was substantially reduced as was funding for public broadcasting systems.

TYPES OF ORGANIZATIONS

The commercial media are represented by trade associations, each of which extends membership only to those in a particular industry, such as book publishing, and perhaps to those who service or supply that industry. The trade associations reflect the ownership structure of their industries and thus tend to be dominated by the media conglomerates. While not nearly as powerful, there are also watchdog groups, which have individual members. Their mission is partly an educative one, as they attempt to uncover bias in reporting. The higher education community is represented by numerous groups that function somewhat like trade associations, limiting their membership to certain types of institutions and advocating on their behalf, and an umbrella organization, inclusive of both these associations and institutions.

With the exception of the Newspaper Association of America, the commercial media's trade associations have affiliated political action committees (PACs) formed to contribute funds to candidates. In addition, the nonprint trade associations, excluding the National Cable Television Association, make "soft-money" contributions to the political parties. Soft money consists of funds donated to parties that cannot be used to campaign for particular candidates, though the line between party advocacy and candidate promotion is virtually impossible to draw. Excluding the public watchdog groups, all of the associations pay substantial sums to outside lobbyists. The commercial groups were more generous to Republicans than to Democrats in the 1997–1998 election cycle. This bias developed in the aftermath of the Republican takeover of Congress and is indicative of the pragmatic orientation of trade associations. They contribute to advance their own interests, not ideological agendas, and are thus willing to work with those in power.

The various trade associations speak on behalf of powerful members, who contribute to campaigns and parties on an individual basis. For example, although the Motion Picture Association of America contributed $89,118 in PAC contributions in 1997–1998, its members' PACs donated more than $789,000. In this situation, the parts are greater and more powerful than the whole—not just in the aggregate, but in some cases, individually. Because the individual members have ownership interests in several sectors of the media industry, they might not always be speaking from the same perspective as the trade associations. However, the clout of trade associations is probably enhanced by the political participation and contributions of their members. The media's interest groups can also capitalize upon their prestige and connections in a way that few other lobbies can.

CURRENT ISSUES

In recent years, the powerful commercial lobby has been seeking to extend copyright protection into cyberspace by winning the ratification of, and enforcing legislation for, the World Intellectual Property Organization (WIPO) treaties. The WIPO treaties will facilitate the development of the Internet as a commercial medium. Groups representing the noncommercial sector, especially librarians, have raised concerns that copyright laws, in some forms, could limit access to information. The copyright issue is of monumental significance to the commercial media because it strikes at the heart of their revenue-generating potential. If an industry cannot control the sale of its product, then its profitability and thus future are in jeopardy.

Both the commercial and noncommercial media have been united in opposition to recent legislative efforts to censor information on the Internet. The commercial groups, which depend upon advertising as a major source of revenue, voice strong opposition to any restrictions on it, such as those on alcohol and tobacco. However, these groups can find themselves divided over this issue at times. For example, magazines benefit from the prohibition of tobacco ads on television. Because of the importance of their relationship with advertisers, though, the commercial groups are unlikely to support restrictions publicly even when they are in their interest. In light of the tobacco settlement talks, this issue remains on the agenda. Additionally, the print media have an interest in postal rates, while publishers and colleges monitor educational funding on a continual basis.

Public advocacy groups, such as Fairness and Accuracy in Reporting (FAIR), are concerned about the concentration of ownership in the media. The policies that govern the news and information industries have been formulated with little input from the public and virtually no concern for the needs of a democratic society. Because these issues have low priority, legislators have been happy to accommodate the demands of the trade associations. FAIR has thus sought to educate the public about these issues and, as a result, to mobilize public opinion. The commercial groups have been less likely to concentrate on public relations, but there are exceptions. The gambling industry, in particular, is currently working to transform its image so as to create a more favorable political climate.

TYPES OF ACTIVITIES

In pursuit of their interests, the information and entertainment industries engage in various forms of lobbying. Historically, the commercial media disagreed about the propriety of making financial contributions to campaigns. The broadcast industries supported this tactic well before the print industries, which still demonstrate some reluctance to donate to campaigns. Indeed, while all the trade associations tend to employ financial contributions as a lobbying strategy to some degree, the entertainment and broadcast industries continue to place more reliance on this strategy than the print industries. The umbrella organization for higher education, the American Council on Education (ACE), and the media watchdog groups do not make financial contributions to campaigns or parties.

Whether they rely heavily on financial contributions or not, all of the major trade associations employ "insider" tactics in their quest to influence public policy. Insider tactics refer to traditional forms of lobbying, which include contacting officials formally and informally, providing information and expertise to aid in the law-making process, and building coalitions with like-minded interests. Such tactics make sense when issues are not a priority and legislators are willing to accommodate the interested parties, as is the case with communications law. Of course, the commercial media have the capability to exercise a tremendous influence over public opinion. This power undoubtedly adds to the clout of the media's lobbyists, given the potential ramifications for politicians who challenge this interest. More subtly, the commercial media can utilize this power to ensure that pertinent legislation retains a low level of importance. The landmark Telecommunications Act of 1996, for example, was covered as a business story with little to no analysis of its effects on public discourse in the mainstream press.

In addition to lobbying Congress and utilizing the courts to advance their agenda, the media's trade associations, especially the NAB, have exerted considerable influence over the FCC. Established in 1934, the FCC has frequently capitulated to the demands of broadcasters. Its members, in fact, typically have management backgrounds in the broadcast industry. Because of their respective powers over foreign trade and advertising, the FTC and the Food and Drug Administration (FDA) have been the focus of the trade associations at times as well.

The public advocacy groups, and to a lesser extent, ACE are more inclined to invoke "outsider" tactics. Such tactics include protests, advertisements, and other educational activities designed to win public favor, which, in turn, is utilized to pressure lawmakers. While the trade associations do not attempt to organize the public via protest activities, they occasionally employ outsider tactics if they are in their interest. For example, the cable industry ran advertisements in 1992 to oppose a regulatory bill. The rare usage of outsider tactics by trade associations is a testament to the effectiveness of their "insider" game. More often than not, they are able to ensure that issues retain a low visibility and are resolved in their mutual interests.

In the future, the ownership structure of these industries might impact the role of the trade associations, as their most prominent members will increasingly be subsidiaries of larger media conglomerates. If the trends of convergence and industrial consolidation continue, the industry might rely more upon the lobbying efforts of individual competitors than it does now. However, trade associations might nonetheless be retained, as they have the advantage of speaking on behalf of a function that garners respect and is essential to democracy.

JULIE M. WALSH

Bibliography

Bagdikian, Ben. *The Media Monopoly*, 5th ed. Boston: Beacon Press, 1997.

Browne, William P. *Groups, Interests, and U.S. Public Policy*. Washington, DC: Georgetown University Press, 1998.

Center for Responsive Politics: www.crp.org

Cook, Timothy E. *Governing With the News: The News Media as a Political Institution*. Chicago: University of Chicago Press, 1998.

Fallows, James. *Breaking the News: How the Media Undermine American Democracy*. New York: Vintage Books, 1997.

Gais, Thomas. *Improper Influence: Campaign Finance Law, Political *Interest Groups, and the Problem of Equality*. Ann Arbor: University of Michigan Press, 1998.

Herman, Edward S., and Robert W. McChesney. *The Global Media: The New Missionaries of Corporate Capitalism*. Washington, DC: Cassell, 1997.

Maurer, Christine, Tara E. Sheets, and Ian A. Goodhall, eds. *Encyclopedia of Associations, Volume I, National Organizations of the U.S.* New York: Gale, 1998.

McChesney, Robert. *Corporate Media and the Threat to Democracy*. New York: Seven Stories, 1997.

Zuckerman, Edward, ed. and compiler. *The Almanac of Federal PACs, 1998–1999*. Arlington, VA: Amward, 1998.

ACCURACY IN MEDIA

Accuracy in Media (AIM), headquartered in Washington, D.C., acts as a watchdog of the news on behalf of conservative interests. Membership is available on an individual basis only. Currently, AIM boasts a membership of approximately 28,000. Given its ideological orientation, AIM is interested in exposing liberal bias in the news media. However, AIM goes well beyond criticism and analysis of news stories, offering conspiracy theories about political and other events, such as the suicide of Vincent Foster, a White House aide in the Clinton Administration. For this reason, critics often ridicule its name.

HISTORY

AIM was founded by Reed J. Irvine in 1969, the year in which Richard Nixon assumed the presidency. The conservative backlash against the domestic programs and rights established in the 1960s was in its burgeoning stages at this time. AIM has been clearly in the spirit of that reaction and has drawn its strength from the conservative movement in the United States. Its charges of liberal bias in the media aired in the mainstream press in the 1980s, when both public debate and policy turned rightward—developments that could be considered successes of AIM despite its limited responsibility for them.

AIM has adjusted to changing technological developments throughout its history, as it now maintains a web site and an electronic forum, AIMNet. The latter, established in 1990, enables subscribers (of which there are 200) to access news articles and phone numbers of media organizations. Users can and frequently do call these organizations to express their frustrations with the media. In part, AIM was energized by the election of Bill Clinton to the presidency in 1992, since he provided a target for AIM members. Clinton is often at the center of conspiracy theories about his aide Vincent Foster and about the TWA flight 800 crash off Long Island, New York, in 1996.

ACTIVITIES: CURRENT AND FUTURE

With a loyal membership and conservative funding, AIM will continue to highlight what it considers to be liberal bias in the media. As the media industry continues to become more concentrated in the hands of a few corporations, however, its charge of a liberal bias will most likely be supported by less and less evidence. Critics on the left accuse AIM's conservative supporters of fabricating a myth about a liberal media to distract the public from pondering the conservative biases of a corporate-owned media. If that charge is true, AIM will have more to do as the media's consolidation continues. Of course, many of the individual members of AIM undoubtedly perceive a liberal bias in the media. Scholars have observed that news organizations attempt to adopt centrist positions, particularly on social issues, to avoid alienating any portion of the upper-middle-class market. Determined to maximize revenue, news organizations need to retain this constituency in its entirety to attract advertisers at premium rates. However, to those on the extreme right, the adoption of centrist positions can appear liberal. As the search for global profits intensifies in the media industry, the incentive to avoid offending potential audiences will, if anything, become stronger. Hence, we can expect those on the right to patronize organizations such as AIM.

FINANCIAL FACTS

AIM has a budget of approximately $1.6 million and a staff of 13. Since annual dues are only $35, a substantial portion of AIM's funding is supplied by contributions from corporations and conservative foundations. Wealthy individuals have also made hefty donations, such as the conservative Richard Mellon Scaife, a right-wing founder of conservative movements and heir to the Mellon oil and banking family. In the late 1990s, Scaife endowed a professorship at Pepperdine University Law School for independent prosecutor Kenneth Starr. Given its mission, AIM does not have a political action committee, nor does it make soft-money contributions to either party. Indeed, the organization does not concern itself with lobbying the national or state governments and thus does not at all partake in the "insider" game familiar to trade associations. Instead, AIM seeks to increase public awareness of what it perceives as a liberal bias in the media. If AIM can persuade a significant percentage of the public about such a liberal bias, then it can exert pressure on media outlets to place more of a conservative spin on issues. The resultant change in coverage, in turn, would act to push public policy in a conservative direction.

To achieve these goals, AIM engages in a number of activities. It publishes a semimonthly newsletter, *AIM Report*, that exposes instances of bias. The newsletter has a circulation of 9,000 and does not accept advertisements. Additionally, its leaders write weekly columns, published in approximately 100 newspapers, and broadcasts a daily, three-minute radio commentary, *The Media Monitor*, for the same purpose. The program is broadcast on approximately 200 stations around the country. The organization sponsors speakers and produces and sells films and tapes, also to the end of demonstrating liberal bias in reporting. To publicize its agenda, AIM hosts three or four conferences a year. In October 1998, those attending AIM's conference discussed the crash of TWA flight 800 and the fate of government whistle-blowers. In all its activities, AIM seeks to perpetuate the idea of a "liberal media" by "educating" the public toward its point of view.

JULIE M. WALSH

Bibliography

Accuracy in Media: www.aim.org

Maurer, Christine, Tara E. Sheets, and Ian A. Goodhall, eds. *Encyclopedia of Associations, Volume I, National Organizations of the U.S.* New York: Gale, 1998.

Public Interest Profiles, 1996–1997. CQ Foundation for Public Affairs. Washington, DC: Congressional Quarterly, 1996.

AMERICAN COUNCIL ON EDUCATION

As centers of research and education, the colleges and universities of the United States play a vital role in the production of information and knowledge. Higher education is a $100 billion industry, with an estimated 14.3 million students attending over 3,600 colleges and universities. Although this industry is represented in Washington by over 200 associations, the six largest, known as the Big Six, garner the most attention and wield the most influence. One of these six, the American Council on Education (ACE), serves as an umbrella association for the higher education community. It represents all accredited colleges and universities, whether public or private, and other national and regional higher education associations, inclusive of the five major ones. The Career College Association, which represents for-profit or proprietary institutions of higher learning, belongs to the ACE as well, despite the fact that most of its members are not accredited and therefore not eligible for institutional membership. Because the ACE represents both institutions and associations, it can sometimes be torn between the role of an autonomous entity acting on behalf of its institutional membership and that of a facilitator attempting to forge a consensus among the many diverse groups that represent the higher education community. It tends to emphasize the latter role since the ACE is unchallenged in this function. As the unifying voice for higher education, the ACE has an interest in several issues of national policy, such as research grants, student aid, and affirmative action.

HISTORY

The ACE traces its origins to 1918, when eight educational associations formed the Emergency Council on Education in response to the drop in enrollments experienced during World War I. Later that year, when the war ended, the Council was given permanent status and its current name. At that time, its members decided that there would be a continuing need for a liaison between the federal government and higher education. However, there were very few federal issues of concern to the higher education community until World War II. Perhaps because of its sparse agenda, the ACE represented the interests of lower schools in the 1930s and 1940s. The close of World War II marked the beginnings of substantial federal involvement in higher education, as the G.I. Bill was passed and more federal dollars were directed at research. Fearful that the G.I. Bill would inundate colleges with unqualified students, the ACE initially opposed it. Soon, though, the ACE recognized the benefits of this and other pieces of federal legislation.

In the 1950s and 1960s, Washington insiders considered the ACE to be an ineffective lobby. Yet its shortcomings were of little consequence since prosperity and expansion in higher education marked these decades. In response to Russia's launch of the first artificial satellite, Sputnik 1, federal money was pumped into research. What is more, in 1965, Congress passed the Higher Education Act (HEA), which provided institutional funding and introduced federal grants, loans, and fellowships on an unprecedented scale. The ACE finally paid the price for its inept lobbying in 1972 when the HEA came up for reauthorization. In the amended legislation, Pell Grants, which are awarded to students directly, were introduced as substitutes for institutional funding, which the ACE and its members preferred. Because the ACE was blindsided by this issue and was coordinating the higher education community's efforts, it took most of the blame for the political failure of safeguarding institutional funding. Responding to the flood of criticism in the aftermath of this legislation, the ACE made enough improvements in its lobbying efforts to fare reasonably well in the 1980s. With threats of substantial cuts in funding for higher education at the federal and state levels, the ACE was mainly concerned with damage control. It prevented the elimination of federal programs for student aid and faculty research.

When the HEA was reauthorized in 1992, the ACE was not so fortunate and once again had to confront a failure. Concerned about high default rates in student loans and institutional abuses, Congress decided to strengthen the system of accreditation through the creation of state review boards, called "State Postsecondary Review for Entities" (SPREs). Colleges and universities were incensed, arguing that these were a threat to academic freedom. Obviously, such hostile legislation did not reflect favorably upon the lobbying effectiveness of the ACE. However, the ACE mobilized in response to this legislation, encouraging its members to voice their opposition and thereby keep the issue on the legislative agenda. As a result, Congress rescinded the funding for SPREs in 1996. This outcome was a significant triumph for the ACE. Indeed, the ACE had much to celebrate in the late 1990s. Despite the Republican takeover of Congress in 1995, there were increases in the funding for student financial aid in 1996 and 1997. In addition, the National Endowment for the Humanities and the National Endowment for the Arts, both of which provide funding for research, survived Republican plans to eliminate them, though their funding was drastically cut.

ACTIVITIES: CURRENT AND FUTURE

Despite its refusal to donate to candidates, the ACE is heavily involved in lobbying activities. The main focus of those activities is Congress, although the ACE represents higher education in front of federal agencies and the courts as well. Without contributing a dime, representatives of the ACE can still obtain access to congressional members because of the prestige of higher education, the number of schools and their resultant economic impact, and the geographical distribution of schools. Institutions of higher learning are found in every congressional district. Perhaps because of its privileged position, the ACE historically adopted a cautious approach to lobbying and utilized "insider" tactics. For example, lobbyists for the ACE would contact legislators on formal and informal bases, testify at congressional hearings, send letters and encourage others to do so, and otherwise attempt to shape legislation and regulations. When the Republicans captured a majority of congressional seats in 1994, however, the ACE employed additional tactics in its lobbying efforts that were more typical of nonprofit and "outsider" groups. Funding for higher education was gravely threatened at this time given the verbal assaults launched at it by Republican leaders. To make matters worse, the ACE and other higher education associations had much stronger alliances with the Democrats than the Republicans. As Constance Ewing Cook has documented in *Lobbying for Higher Education: How Colleges and Universities Influence Federal Policy*, the ACE began to engage in grassroots lobbying and to run advertisements in the media to build support for threatened programs and thereby to pressure Congress to retain them. Because of higher education's natural allies, such as faculty, students, and employees, grassroots tactics have the potential to be quite potent if fully exploited. Besides these tactics, which caused the cautious organization some fear, the ACE coalesced with other organizations on an ad hoc basis to strengthen its political voice. Given that these new tactics helped the ACE not only to reduce the damage inflicted by the Republican Congress in 1995–1996, but to extract gains, it continues to utilize them. The ACE is concerned that the presidential budget favors elementary and secondary over higher education. Obviously, it will lobby for more money and demand that greater attention be paid to higher education.

To help substantiate its positions and to serve as a resource for its members, the ACE has established a Center for Policy Analysis. The Center has embarked on projects that aid in the educative and organizational goals of the ACE. For example, the Center's Forum for Higher Education and Democracy has initiated a series of meetings entitled, "Listening to Communities." The stated purpose of these meetings is to explore the role of higher education in civic life and the ways for the community and institution to prepare students for the responsibilities of citizenship. However, they serve the dual purpose of including members of the local community in the educational endeavor and thus identifying them with the school. Such involvement would make members of the community more likely to rally in support of the school if it were under threat. To keep members abreast of its programs and pertinent legislative developments, the ACE also publishes a biweekly newsletter, *Higher Education and National Affairs,* and hosts conferences and meetings.

Although the higher education community has experienced failure in its lobbying efforts on more than one occasion in its history, it has not adjusted the organizational structure of its major lobbying associations. Indeed, the dominance of the Big Six and the role of the ACE as an umbrella organization have remained constant for decades. With no competitors, the ACE is likely to continue its roles of consensus builder and federal advocate for higher education. There will surely be strong incentive for the higher education community to represent itself effectively in Washington, given the growing significance of federal policy and funding in this area.

FINANCIAL FACTS

The ACE is a large organization, with approximately 175 employees and a budget of over $30 million. Its policies are established primarily by the association's leaders in conjunction with active college and university presidents, though all member institutions approve critical decisions. Because of its nonprofit tax status, the ACE is prohibited legally from making lobbying its principal activity. Yet the stakes in federal policy decisions are enormous for the higher education community since 15 percent of the total revenues of colleges and universities come in the form of federal dollars. Given these stakes, the ACE paid $171,066 to lobbyists in 1997. In total, the higher education community had lobbying expenditures of over $26 million in that year. The ACE does not have a political action committee (PAC) and therefore does not contribute to political candidates. Like print journalists, college educators have been hesitant to sacrifice their independence and tie their fortunes to particular candidates. Indeed, the higher education community was formerly reluctant to engage in lobbying of any kind. To be sure, there are some members of the ACE that have formed PACs. The ACE, which is a loose confederation of sovereign associations and members, has no control over the separate political strategies employed by its members.

JULIE M. WALSH

Bibliography

American Council on Education: www.ace.nche.edu

Center For Responsive Politics: www.crp.org

Cook, Constance Ewing. *Lobbying for Higher Education: How Colleges and Universities Influence Federal Policy.* Nashville, TN: Vanderbilt University Press, 1998.

King, Lauriston R. *The Washington Lobbyists for Higher Education.* Lexington, MA: Lexington Books, D.C. Heath, 1975.

Parsons, Michael P. *Power and Politics: Federal Higher Education Policy Making in the 1990s.* Albany: State University of New York Press, 1997.

ASSOCIATION OF AMERICAN PUBLISHERS

The Association of American Publishers (AAP), with offices in New York and Washington, D.C., is the trade association for publishers of books, journals, and other similar products. The U.S. book industry, which posted revenues of $21.3 billion in 1997, has by no means been exempt from the trend toward concentration of ownership in the media industry. Indeed, the industry is dominated by giants, such as Viacom, Hearst, and Time Warner, and has very few major independent publishers left. Not surprisingly, the AAP's membership consists increasingly of subsidiaries of these larger media conglomerates. The AAP has approximately 200 members, which are divided into full, associate, and affiliate categories. Full membership is limited to those with significant investments in an ongoing publishing business, while associate membership is available to nonprofit university presses and organizations. Those who service or supply the publishing industry are eligible for affiliate membership. As might be expected, the AAP seeks to expand the market for American books and other published works. To facilitate the health and growth of publishing, the AAP concerns itself with myriad issues, such as the protection of intellectual property, the defense of free speech and press, public funding for education and libraries, postal rates, and tax policies.

HISTORY

The AAP was founded in 1970 when the American Book Publishers Council and the American Educational Institute merged. In that year, the organization initially listed its interests as two postal reform bills, but later, as all legislation affecting the book publishing industry. The formation of this organization was a milestone for the industry, as it marked the first time that general and textbook publishers joined forces. Previously, the book publishing industry had been divided and inert. The industry was energized in the 1960s by the explosion in college enrollment and the influx of federal funds for schools and libraries in response to the superiority of the Russian space program. There were a series of mergers in the 1960s, as the once neglected industry became attractive to investors. It was at the close of this promising decade for publishers that the AAP was formed.

The AAP successfully defended the legality of yet another wave of mergers that swept the industry in the late 1970s. At that time, the Authors League and some members of Congress argued that these mergers were destroying the cultural commitment of publishing subsidiaries and reducing the potential earnings of authors. While the government investigated and even objected to some of the mergers, it did not create obstacles to further mergers in the publishing industry. As a result, another wave of mergers took place in the 1980s in which a number of foreign companies acquired American publishing houses.

The AAP has been successful in its campaign to strengthen copyright protection as well. Its most significant achievement came with the Copyright Act, which took effect in 1978 after years of debate among librarians, educators, authors, and publishers. In a gesture to librarians and educators, the law allowed for "fair use" of copyrighted material. However, this use was limited. To the relief of publishers, Congress proposed the establishment of legislation to ensure fair compensation to the owner of copyrighted material when copying exceeds fair use. Initially, fair use was defined narrowly to include the photocopying of a page for teaching or research purposes and the use of quotations in other published works. Although the definition of fair use has been subject to slight modification, the Copyright Act was a positive development for the industry. More recently, the AAP has been concerned with copyright problems posed by the Internet. It thus claimed another victory when President Bill Clinton signed the No Electronic Theft Act into law. This law closed a loophole in the Copyright Act that had prevented criminal prosecution for copyright infringement if there was no financial gain for the infringer. The AAP has achieved success in its legal fight against censorship on the Internet as well. For example, it was among the sponsors of a court case challenging a decency provision in a New York state law that was declared unconstitutional.

ACTIVITIES: CURRENT AND FUTURE

In its lobbying activities, the AAP undoubtedly benefits from the political clout of its member organizations. Indeed, the lobbyists of AAP members occasionally meet at the AAP's Washington office to discuss legislative strategies. The AAP is willing to form coalitions with other interest groups to advance its interests as well. Despite its own limited contributions to candidates, then, the AAP is nonetheless able to engage in the "insider" lobbying game. This approach is certainly evident in the choice of its current president, Patricia Schroeder, as she was a long-time member of Congress. The primary focus of the AAP's lobbying activities is protection of copyrighted material. More specifically, the AAP, together with other industries, seeks implementing legislation for the World Intellectual Property Organization (WIPO) treaties. The AAP is active in lobbying efforts to extend the terms of copyright protection and to stave off legislative efforts to protect online privacy rights. The copyright issue is critical to the AAP because of the increasing use of the Internet.

However, the AAP does not limit its lobbying activities to the matter of copyrights. It is active in its opposition to any attempts to censor information on the Internet. The AAP also supports selected forms of educational funding, such as "America Reads" legislation and the Reading Excellence Act, both of which provide support to develop reading skills. Because a large percentage of books are shipped and sold via the mail, the AAP is also active in its opposition to increases in postal rates. Like other trade associations, the AAP hosts an annual meeting, publishes a monthly journal, compiles data about the industry, and offers managerial and technological advice to members. Perhaps because of the nature of the industry's product, the AAP aims its educational activities at the general public as well. For example, it works to promote reading and literacy in the United States via the sponsorship of activities, such as "Get Caught Reading" Month aimed at those between the ages of 18 to 34. Obviously, increases in literacy and reading are to the benefit of the publishing industry.

Publishing companies are increasingly components of larger media corporations that have holdings in movies, newspapers, and television stations. This structural change in the industry might very well have ramifications for the AAP. The traditional allies of the AAP, such as librarians and educators, might be displaced by the new partners of its members, namely, entertainment conglomerates. As always, the AAP will continue to fight for copyright protection. Yet, aligned as it is with entertainment interests, the AAP might be less sympathetic to the concerns of librarians that a fee for each patron's use of an electronic book would be tantamount to charging patrons for browsing in the stacks. However it is finally resolved, the negotiation of a new arrangement with librarians over purchases in an electronic world is guaranteed a spot on the AAP's future agenda.

FINANCIAL FACTS

The AAP pursues these interests with a budget of $5 million and a combined professional and support staff of 38 individuals. The policies of AAP are set by its Board of Directors, which is composed of 20 individuals who are elected by full members for four-year terms. Like other trade associations, it has a political action committee (PAC). In the 1995–1996 election cycle, its PAC had receipts of $7,950 and expenditures of $6,954. Its political contributions for the past two election cycles were:

	Total	Democrat	%	Republican	%
1995–96	$6,550	2,450	37	4,100	63
1997–98	$ 750	250	33	500	67

In the 1993–1994 election cycle, the AAP had contributed almost twice as much money and had given over 75 percent of it to Democratic candidates. Its partisan distribution most likely changed in response to the Republican takeover of Congress, a development that demonstrates its pragmatic orientation. The relatively small dollar figures contributed in 1997–1998 might be indicative of the print industry's traditional reluctance to contribute to political campaigns, for the AAP paid $380,000 to lobbyists in 1997 alone.

JULIE M. WALSH

**Association of American Publishers
Political Action Committee Contributions**

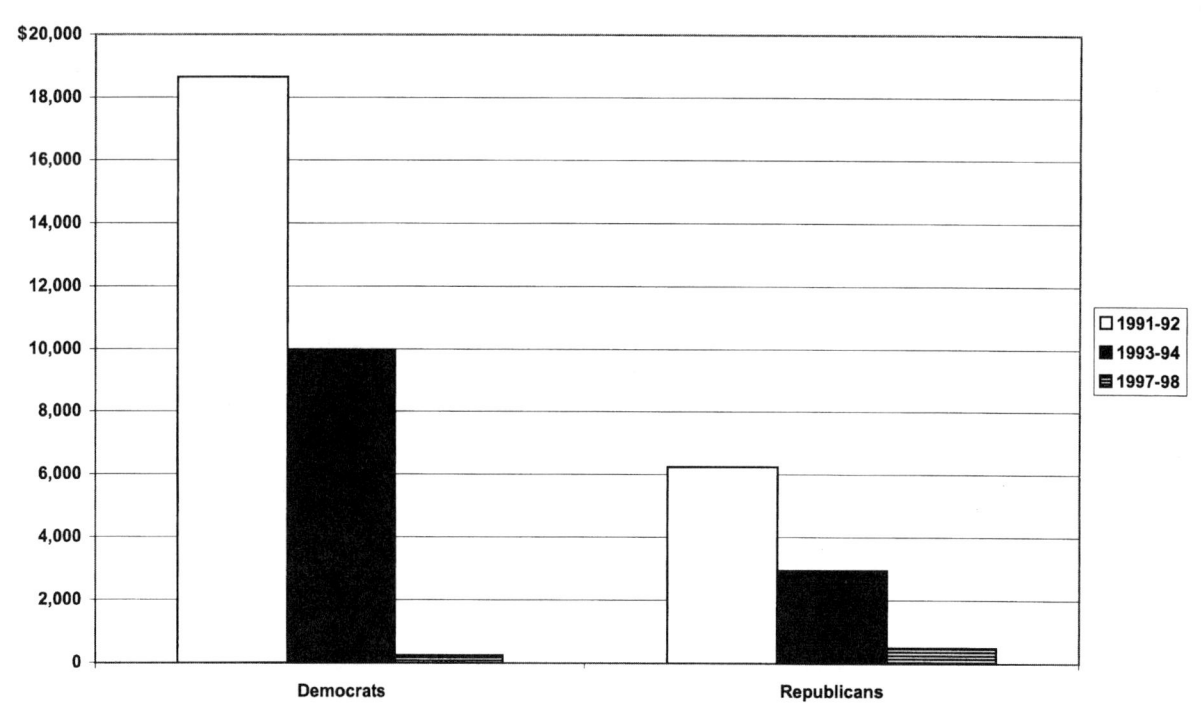

Data derived from official studies available from the Federal Election Commission, Washington, DC, 1991–1998.

Bibliography

Association of American Publishers: www.publishers.org

Center for Responsive Politics: www.crp.org

Dessauer, John P. *Book Publishing: What It Is, What It Does.* New York: R.R. Bowker, 1981.

Greco, Albert N. *The Book Publishing Industry.* Boston: Allyn and Bacon, 1997.

Kobrak, Fred, and Beth Luey, eds. *The Structure of International Publishing in the 1990s.* New Brunswick, NJ: Transaction, 1992.

FAIRNESS AND ACCURACY IN REPORTING

Fairness and Accuracy in Reporting (FAIR), based in New York City, is a watchdog organization that advocates media access for those constituencies in American society that do not have the wealth to purchase their own channels of communication. It has approximately 19,000 members, all of whom are individuals. With a special interest in media practices that ignore the public interest, peace, and minority viewpoints, FAIR seeks to expand the boundaries of public discourse by including more perspectives. It champions the rights of free speech and press contained in the First Amendment and thus does not aspire to prevent the public presentation of views opposed to its own. Because FAIR advocates the inclusion of alternative voices and criticizes the growing concentration of corporate power in the media, it is considered a liberal advocacy group.

HISTORY

FAIR was founded in 1986 by Jeff Cohen, who remains its director, and a few others. ABC and Capital Cities merged in 1985, and the decade saw an assault on all regulatory measures intended to police the communications industry for the sake of the public interest. For example, the Equal Time and Fairness Doctrines, which made the broadcasting of alternative perspectives more likely, were under attack and were revoked by the decade's end. The Federal Communications Commission, under the conservative leadership of Mark Fowler, relaxed ownership limits on media outlets in the 1980s as well, a development that paved the way for more mergers. Accuracy in Media, financed by conservative groups, was charging the media with liberalism and its accusations were receiving a hearing. Given this environment, Cohen saw the need for a media watchdog group that was concerned about corporate bias and the effects of the growing concentration in ownership of the media.

Since its inception, FAIR has published a number of articles and anthologies that have been well received. For example, the *Fair Reader: Press and Politics in the 1990s* and *The Best of Extra!* have been praised for the quality of their research and investigative reporting. FAIR has also had success in its public campaign to expose distortions and hatred on talk radio, particularly Rush Limbaugh's nationally syndicated show. Highlighting the falsity of Limbaugh's statements and the mainstream media's inattention to this fact, FAIR has received favorable coverage in the *Washington Post* and *Media Culture Review*.

ACTIVITIES: CURRENT AND FUTURE

FAIR dedicates itself to researching and exposing the exclusion of viewpoints and distortions in the mainstream press. To this end, the organization conducts extensive research focused on the output of the media and publishes its findings in several forums. Recent issues that have attracted the attention of FAIR include the commercialization of the Internet, the corporate takeover of public television, hatred and distortions on talk radio, and the growing concentration of the media industry in the wake of the Telecommunications Act of 1996. In the media's coverage of all of these issues, FAIR has documented an inattention to the general public's perspective and interests. The increasing concentration of the media and the surrender of public television are of the utmost concern to FAIR because they are perceived to be the root causes of conservative bias. However, FAIR is deeply committed to exposing racial, gender, and class biases in reporting, as evident in its establishment of women's, labor, and racism watch desks. These are specialized research and advocacy desks that work with activists and media professionals on these areas of bias.

FAIR publishes its findings six times a year in the form of a newsletter, *Extra!*. Because this publication criticizes corporations and their capacity to censor news via their leverage over advertising dollars, it does not accept this form of revenue. Additionally, its leaders host a weekly radio show, *Counterspin,* and write an op-ed column, *Media Beat,* to publicize the biases of the mainstream media. The former is broadcast on more than 100 stations, though most are college, community, or public in nature. FAIR's goal is to break the pattern of exclusion by entering into a dialogue with media programmers, reporters, and editors. In a sense, FAIR assumes that the exposure of bias will lead journalists to remedy the situation. FAIR publicly applauds hard-hitting journalism so as to reward those who take the risk to publish it. FAIR's conferences, which are organized around a particular theme, appear to be set up with the assumption that journalists will respond to both criticism and praise.

As a membership organization, FAIR also seeks to bring pressure on the media via activism. It provides its members access to a kit, which offers a step-by-step guide to personal involvement in media activism, and it publishes *Extra Update!,* which is geared toward activists, on a bimonthly basis. To further facilitate personal involvement, FAIR identifies and provides links to local media activist groups at its web site as well as information about national demonstrations. Additionally, the organization hosts an online discussion group for media activists and other interested parties. In so doing, FAIR adopts the techniques of "outsider" interest groups, which typically rely upon grassroots and educative strategies. In FAIR's case, its intended target is not only the government, but also the media.

FAIR's successes come with much hard work and effort in the forms of research and advocacy. As the media become increasingly concentrated and vertically integrated, FAIR will certainly have a plethora of examples of bias to unveil. In a sense, the government's acquiescence to the concentration of the media industry represents a failure for FAIR. It was unable to rally the public to protest the Telecommunications Act of 1996. In the future, FAIR—as has recently been the case—will have to focus on the root causes of bias and attempt to persuade the government to address them. This is, of course, a herculean task given the power wielded by the media lobby in Washington, not to mention its hold on public opinion. However, without action and legislation to change the structure of the media industry, FAIR will become a marginal group despite the fact that it represents the general public's interest. FAIR, of course, recognizes the need for and advocates structural reform of the media.

FINANCIAL FACTS

For the fiscal year ending in June 1998, FAIR had total revenues of $1,097,927, with the bulk of them coming from two sources. Direct public support in the form of grants accounted for 74 percent of total revenues, while subscriptions and sales of its publications comprised 23 percent. Expenses in fiscal 1998 totaled $820,647, with the greatest amounts spent on program services. FAIR employs a professional staff of approximately 10 people. Because FAIR exists to condemn the influence of wealth on the media and the government, it should not be surprising that it does not contribute to political candidates via PACs or soft money. FAIR is not engaged in lobbying activities and thus spends no money for that purpose either.

JULIE M. WALSH

Bibliography

Fairness and Accuracy in Reporting: www.fair.org

Maurer, Christine, Tara E. Sheets, and Ian Goodhall, eds. *Encyclopedia of Associations, Volume I, National Organizations of the U.S.* New York: Gale, 1998.

Public Interest Group Profiles, 1996–1997. CQ Foundation for Public Affairs. Washington, DC: Congressional Quarterly, 1996.

MAGAZINE PUBLISHERS OF AMERICA

With offices in both New York City and Washington, D.C., the Magazine Publishers of America (MPA) is the trade association for consumer magazines. The organization represents approximately 200 U.S.-based companies and 75 international companies. To be eligible for full membership, a company must publish at least four issues of a magazine annually. The magazine industry, like other sectors in communications, has grown increasingly concentrated, with approximately 160 magazines of 22,000 accounting for 85 percent of all revenues. Historically, the MPA has been the voice of the larger publishers, such as Hearst and Time Warner. However, a substantial portion of its members publish specialized magazines. The organization offers associate membership to about 90 companies that are providers of the industry. As an advocacy organization for magazine publishers, the MPA monitors state and national legislation affecting the industry, concerning such issues as postal rates, the deductibility of advertising costs, and copyright laws.

HISTORY

The MPA was founded in 1919, when the industry was poised for a post–World War I growth spurt. In the early years of the century, the reporting in magazines and newspapers began to diverge. While newspapers recounted events, magazines assimilated information and the perspective of the author. In the aftermath of World War I, the industry experienced a significant expansion fueled by a growth in advertising. Perhaps because of its increasing size and power, the industry became the object of governmental attention in the 1920s. The MPA was thus formed in time to combat governmental efforts at censorship and attempts to interfere with distribution. Throughout its long history, the MPA has changed its name several times. It began as the National Association of Periodical Publishers and was later the National Publishers Association, the National Association of Magazine Publishers, and the Magazine Publishers Association before assuming its current name in 1987.

Decades before the establishment of the MPA, in 1879, Congress authorized special low postal rates for mailings of magazines to subscribers. The preservation of these special or second-class rates and the prevention of gradual increases of them became one of the primary tasks of the MPA. Beginning as early as 1910, there were sporadic attempts to eliminate or to increase these special rates. Until contemporary times, the MPA has been successful in minimizing increases to these rates. For example, in the 1940s and again in the early 1960s, the MPA and its members convinced Congress that a substantial increase in these rates would eliminate all profits and signal the death knell of the industry. In other words, the reduced rates were still necessary to further the goal of the initial legislation in 1879, which was to ensure the dissemination of information. The tide turned against the MPA on this issue in 1988, as second-class rates increased 55 percent in the next seven years. In the early 1990s, the Postal Service granted a concession to the magazine industry via its policy of work-sharing. If publishers efficiently prepared and sorted their magazines, then there would be a corresponding reduction in postal rates. Unfortunately, many magazines with small circulations could not qualify for these reductions because their volume precluded them from meeting the efficiency standards of the Postal Service. In effect, this concession helped large-circulation magazines at the expense of small ones. Indeed, many small magazines have failed in recent years. Because the MPA's members are mainly large-circulation magazines, they were more than likely pleased with work-sharing. However, the MPA undoubtedly considers the astronomical increase in rates during these years a failure.

The MPA has had more success throughout its long history in challenging governmental efforts at censorship. For example, the Post Office's attempts to revoke the second-class mailing privileges of *Esquire* in 1943 and

Playboy in 1955 were challenged successfully in the courts. Because of its willingness to engage in some form of self-policing, the MPA has been able to prevent significant regulation of the industry's sales practices as well. As early as 1940, the MPA, in cooperation with others, established and maintained a Central Registry for the purposes of enforcing a code of sales practices acceptable to various Chambers of Commerce and Better Business Bureaus. Perhaps of greater significance than its legislative victories, the MPA has been instrumental in the industry's efforts to survive and flourish in the face of threats from radio and later, television broadcasting. Based on its extensive research, the MPA was able to market the concept of targeted audiences to advertisers and thus create a niche for the industry.

ACTIVITIES: CURRENT AND FUTURE

In its efforts to play the "insider game" of lobbying in Washington, the MPA is certainly not injured by its members' separate contributions. The MPA participates in formal and informal coalitions with other interest groups to bolster its influence as well. For example, the MPA is a founding member of the Ad Tax Coalition, which fights efforts to eliminate or reduce the business deduction for advertising costs and whose members include the National Association of Broadcasters, the Newspaper Association of America (NAA), and the American Association of Advertising Agencies. Demonstrative of the importance of advertising to the magazine industry, the MPA is also a founding member of the Freedom to Advertise Coalition, which opposes any restrictions on commercial speech. Additionally, the MPA belongs to the Media Coalition, which resists any encroachments upon editorial freedom, and the Mailers Council, whose goal is to reduce mailing costs.

As might be surmised by its membership in these coalitions, the MPA focuses its lobbying efforts mainly on postal issues, advertising regulations, and the protection of editorial freedom and intellectual property. Because the magazine industry is so dependent upon the U.S. Postal Service to deliver its products to subscribers in a timely and efficient manner, the MPA pays close attention to any legislation that affects postal rates and/or the organization of the Postal Service. The MPA was pleased with the Postal Rate Commission's recommendation to increase the average rate for magazines by 4.6 percent in 1998 because that sum was substantially below the rate of inflation since the last adjustment in 1995. While mailing costs are a substantial expense for magazine publishers, advertisements comprise a major portion of their revenue. As a result, the MPA has been active in its opposition to legislative restrictions on tobacco advertising. Recently, the MPA, teaming with the NAA, lobbied the Food and Drug Administration (FDA) to recognize the benefits of print advertising over that of television for prescription drugs. In August 1997, the FDA expanded the ability of prescription drug manufacturers to advertise on television and radio. In defense of its final product, the MPA has additionally lobbied against editorial restrictions of any kind, including those limited to the Internet.

The MPA, which is much more than a legislative advocate, aids in the professional development of its members and the industry by sponsoring numerous workshops and seminars. To ensure that its members are educated about developments in the industry, the MPA runs an Information Center and publishes a monthly newsletter. The MPA further advocates the interests of its members by engaging aggressively in advertising and consumer marketing. In response to complaints by the Federal Trade Commission about the aggressive tactics of subscription telemarketing agents, the MPA averted government regulation via a self-policing effort. The MPA works to advance the interests of its members in a myriad of other ways as well. What is more, its affiliate, the American Society of Magazine Editors, is also active in promoting the interests of the magazine industry.

Increasingly, large magazines are becoming holdings of conglomerates with additional ownership interests in newspapers, cable, and book publishing. This ongoing transformation in the structure of the communications industry will most likely affect the MPA's mission in the future. Because the Internet has implications for magazines, newspapers, and books, the protection of materials via copyright might feature more prominently on the MPA's agenda in the future. Indeed, electronic magazines are especially attractive to publishers in light of their ability to eliminate reliance on the Postal Service for delivery and all concerns about environmental issues. For the immediate future, however, postal rates and regulations on tobacco advertising promise to occupy the MPA's agenda.

FINANCIAL FACTS

The MPA has a staff of about 30 people and a budget of approximately $10.7 million. Like other trade associations, the MPA has a political action committee

**Magazine Publishers of America
Political Action Committee Contributions**

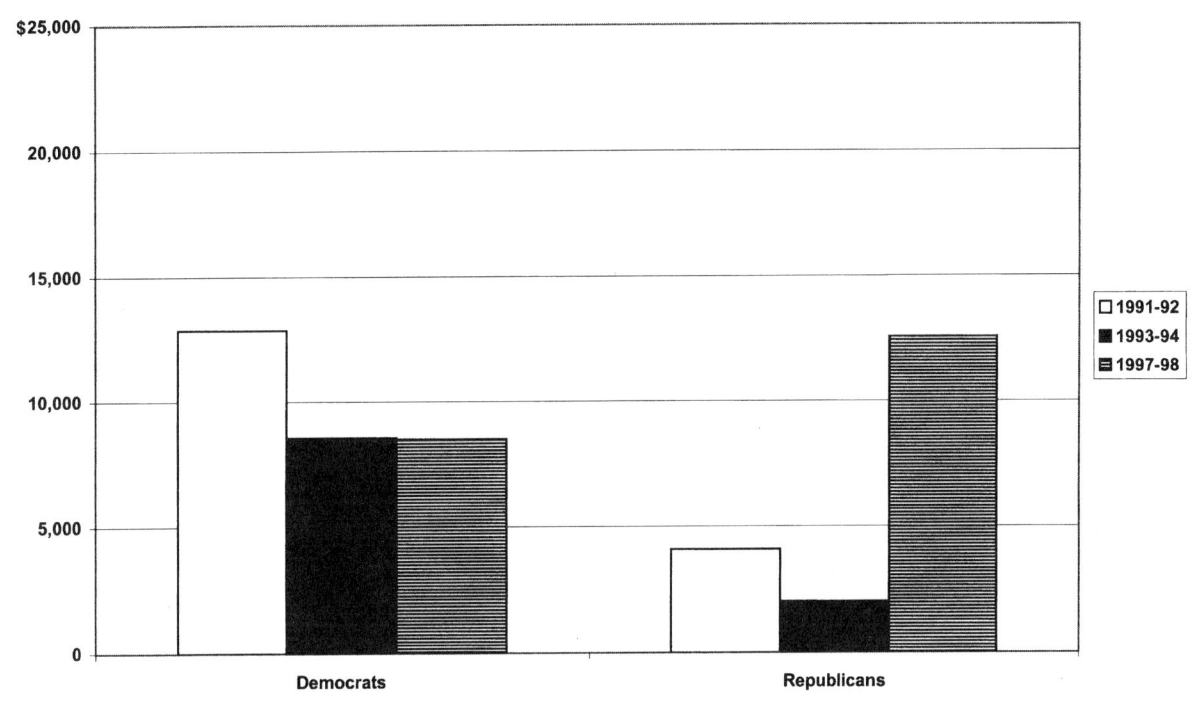

[Bar chart showing PAC contributions to Democrats and Republicans for three election cycles: 1991-92, 1993-94, and 1997-98. Democrats received approximately $13,000 in 1991-92, $8,500 in 1993-94, and $8,500 in 1997-98. Republicans received approximately $4,000 in 1991-92, $2,000 in 1993-94, and $13,000 in 1997-98.]

Data derived from official studies available from the Federal Election Commission, Washington, DC, 1991–1998.

(PAC) that contributes to candidates. In the 1995–1996 election cycle, its PAC had receipts of $17,500 and expenditures of $20,000. In the prior two election cycles, its political contributions were:

	Total	Democrat	%	Republican	%
1995–96	$15,750	2,750	17	13,000	83
1997–98	$21,000	8,500	40	12,500	60

This partisan distribution represented a stark break from the past two election cycles when the MPA gave over 75 percent of its contributions to Democrats. Clearly, the change coincided with the Republican takeover of Congress and is indicative of the MPA's pragmatic orientation. In the 1995–1996 election cycle, the MPA made soft-money contributions to the Democratic Party in the amount of $1,500 as well. Additionally, the MPA paid $420,000 to lobbyists in 1997. In this same year, the MPA spent a total of $1,708,900 on its government affairs office, an amount that represented 15 percent of its total expenditures. While the MPA devotes a considerable portion of its resources to government affairs, it does not contribute huge sums of money to politicians. In its restraint, it perhaps displays evidence of the print industry's traditional reluctance to donate to politicians. Yet, on the other hand, the most powerful members of the MPA contribute separately and heavily.

JULIE M. WALSH

Bibliography

Center for Responsive Politics: www.crp.org

Daly, Charles P., Patrick Henry, and Ellen Ryder. *The Magazine Publishing Industry*. Boston: Allyn and Bacon, 1997.

Magazine Publishers of America: www.magazine.org; and Annual Report of 1997.

Tebbell, John, and Mary Ellen Zuckerman. *The Magazine in America, 1741–1990*. New York: Oxford University Press, 1991.

Zuckerman, Edward, ed. and compiler. *The Almanac of Federal PACs, 1998–1999*. Arlington, VA: Amward, 1998.

MOTION PICTURE ASSOCIATION OF AMERICA

With headquarters in Washington, D.C., and offices in Los Angeles, the Motion Picture Association of America (MPAA) is the trade association for the nation's major motion picture and television production companies. Because the motion picture industry has an oligopolistic structure, the MPAA has only eight members. Communication and decision making can thus be done on an informal basis. It should be noted, however, that the MPAA itself is not small; it has 120 staff members. Yet, unlike other large trade associations, whose members can find themselves at odds with one another, the MPAA is often able to present a united front and, as a result, is a formidable power in Washington. The MPAA serves as an advocate for the motion picture, home video, and television industries in the legislative arena on issues such as copyright protection, antipiracy enforcement, and censorship. Since the movie industry is global in its reach, the MPAA has a related association, the Motion Picture Export Association (MPEA), which represents the industry abroad with nine offices on five continents. Jack Valenti serves as the president of both associations.

HISTORY

The MPAA traces its origins to 1922, when leaders of the emergent studios united to confront what was becoming a hostile environment for the film industry. By that year, no less than six state governments had adopted censorship regulations, in addition to various municipalities that had established boards of censorship. What was worse, several notable scandals had rocked Hollywood in the early 1920s. Worried that more states and perhaps even the national government would opt for censorship regulations, industry leaders formed a trade association and named Postmaster General Will Hays to lead it. Hays, who ran Harding's successful presidential campaign in 1920, had an outstanding reputation and was thus well-suited to the task of improving the industry's image. When initially formed in 1922, the industry's trade association was called the Motion Picture Producers and Distributors of America. It retained that name until 1945, when it became the MPAA. At that time, its foreign department, which had been responsible for lobbying efforts abroad, became a separate organization, the MPEA. The MPEA was organized as a legal cartel under the provisions of the Webb-Pomerene Export Trade Act of 1918.

In its early years, the MPAA aimed to improve the public image of the industry and stave off the threat of outright censorship. As it turned out, this goal became a long-term one for the organization and one at which it had much success. Initially, Hays established a public relations committee, which was to be a forum for religious and civic leaders to discuss means to improve the content of motion pictures. Given an outlet to express their views, these critics of the industry were appeased for the remainder of the 1920s. In the face of renewed criticism, the MPAA adopted a more rigorous form of censorship, the Hollywood Production Code, in 1930. When pressure mounted in 1934 for its enforcement and strengthening, the MPAA established the Production Code Administration and named Joseph Breen to lead it. This department would examine all scripts and pictures, and only those movies gaining its seal of approval could be shown in affiliated theaters. The establishment of this office was a significant triumph for the MPAA, as it enabled the industry to prevent a planned boycott by the Legion of Decency, which was a formidable Catholic organization that had the potential to affect the industry's bottom line. Of more significance, the Production Code Administration enabled the industry to avert the threat of government censorship.

The Production Code Administration began to lose its power in the late 1940s and 1950s. Several developments—one of which was a legal victory for the industry—contributed to its demise. In 1952, the Supreme Court extended the protections of the First

Amendment to film, signaling the death knell for censorship. Television and foreign films entered into competition with American film producers in this period as well. For marketing purposes, filmmakers now had incentives to produce movies that had material forbidden on television. As filmmakers followed their financial interests instead of the directives of the administration, the industry once again feared a public reaction and the possibility of government regulation. Under the leadership of Jack Valenti, the MPAA thus established the ratings system in 1968. Once again, the MPAA was successful in appeasing critics and thwarting censorship. The MPAA continues to fight efforts at regulation with much success. Because filmmakers provide much of the programming for television, the MPAA, under the leadership of Valenti, denied the need to curb violence on television in 1993. The MPAA ultimately lent its support to television ratings in 1996, with the caveat that it be done by the industry, not the government. The issue that provided the impetus for the birth of this trade association thus continues to have relevance despite a string of successes in this area.

Perhaps because of its rhetorical commitment to free speech, the MPAA's response to charges of communism by the House Committee on Un-American Activities was not its finest hour and was maybe even its greatest failure. Responding to congressional and public pressure, the MPAA, under the leadership of Eric Johnston, created the infamous black list, whereby those considered disloyal were denied employment in Hollywood. The black listing proceeded through 1951, 1952, and 1953. In this case, the industry clearly and unequivocally placed profits ahead of free speech. The early 1950s were, in fact, a time of economic uncertainty for the industry. In 1948, the landmark *Paramount* case had broken the industry's oligopolistic control of both theaters and producer-distributors. Prior to this case, the leaders of the industry cooperated to eliminate any independents within the industry by refusing to show their films. This vertically integrated oligopoly was attacked by the Justice Department as early as 1938. However, it was not until the *Paramount* case that the vertical oligopoly was broken, signaling a defeat for the industry.

The industry adjusted to the new legal environment quickly. After a brief boycott of television, the major studios learned to utilize the networks as a subsidiary market for licensing films. This arrangement led to some political confrontations in the 1970s when the networks began to produce their own feature films. The Federal Communications Commission instituted Prime-Time Access and Financial Interest and Syndication Rules in 1971, both of which were favorable to the film industry. Prime-Time Access rules placed a maximum on the number of hours that networks could run their own programming, thereby opening the market for studios. The Financial Interest and Syndication Rules removed the networks from the syndication industry and prohibited them from obtaining profit shares in the programming they obtained from independent suppliers. Instead of pursuing a legal challenge to these rules, the networks entered into consent decrees in the late 1970s that accommodated both the film and broadcast industries.

The MPAA has waged political battle with cable operators as well, as it objected to a 1976 law that allowed them to retransmit signals without cost. More recently, the MPAA found itself aligned with the cable industry when Congress passed the Cable Television Consumer Protection and Competition Act of 1992, which gave broadcasters the right to charge cable operators for the use of over-the-air signals, but neglected to require broadcasters to share those revenues with the film industry that creates the programs. Desiring a free market system in which each cable operator negotiates with program providers for retransmission rights, the MPAA was unable to block passage of even this objectionable bill. Thus, the MPAA has had a few setbacks. Yet on balance, the MPAA has been an extraordinarily effective voice for the industry. If the accomplishments of the MPEA were considered as well, the track record would be more impressive. Suffice it to say that the MPEA has been so successful in its foreign lobbying that it is at times referred to as the "little State Department." Because the members of the MPAA depend upon foreign revenue, the success of the MPEA is intricately related to that of the MPAA.

ACTIVITIES: CURRENT AND FUTURE

Such pragmatism is the mark of an association engaged in the "insider" lobbying game, as the MPAA is. The MPAA relies upon its connections and financial contributions to gain access to lawmakers. Enhancing the MPAA's clout, its eight members donate heavily to candidates on an individual basis. What is more, lawmakers recognize the significance of the film industry globally as an exporter of American ideology and products. Recently, the MPAA and its affiliated organization, the MPEA, have capitalized on this privileged position to express support for treaties protecting intellectual property, such as those of the World Intellectual Property Organization (WIPO). The industry remains poised to

**Motion Picture Association of America
Political Action Committee Contributions**

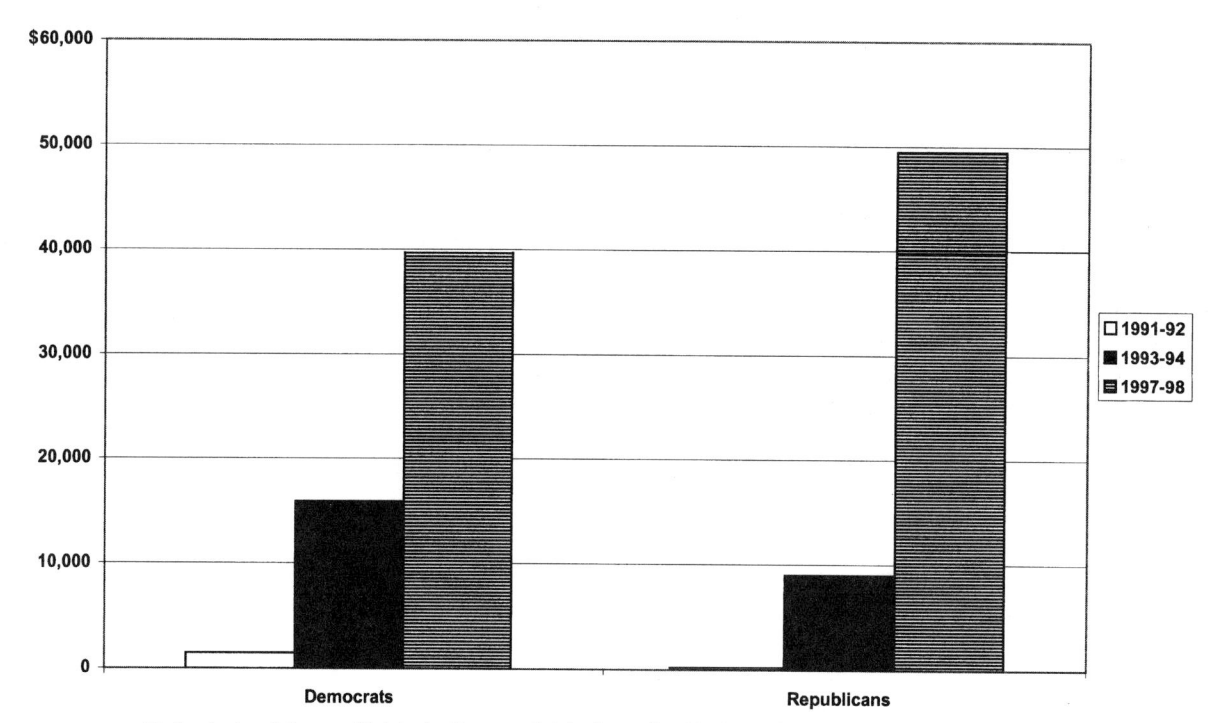

[Bar chart showing PAC contributions by party for 1991-92, 1993-94, and 1997-98. Democrats: ~$1,500 (1991-92), ~$16,000 (1993-94), ~$40,000 (1997-98). Republicans: ~$0 (1991-92), ~$8,500 (1993-94), ~$49,000 (1997-98).]

Data derived from official studies available from the Federal Election Commission, Washington, DC, 1991–1998.

guard against legislative efforts at censorship as well. Coming under fire for its violent and sordid fare in the wake of school shootings and controversy over studies about adolescent sexuality, the film industry has denounced studies that link violence in film and aggressive behavior. The MPAA has thus far had success in thwarting efforts to censor films.

The MPAA oversees the movie ratings system, as the symbols used by that system are federally registered certification marks of the MPAA. However, the Ratings Board is structured as an independent body so as to be immune from industry pressure, though its critics charge otherwise. The chairperson of the board is in fact selected by Valenti, the MPAA president. The ratings system is intended to stave off attempts at censorship and improve the public image of the industry. Closely related to its concerns about copyright protection, the MPAA directs an antipiracy program as well.

Looking ahead, the MPAA will become even more dependent on international markets, as the film industry is certainly not exempt from the trends of vertical integration and globalization that have swept the communications industry. Deferring to these trends, the FCC lifted Prime-Time Access and Financial Interest and Syndication Rules in the mid 1990s. The networks were thus able to act as gatekeepers, deciding what to air and at what price. Surely, this legal environment provides an advantage for those studios—such as Disney, that own an over-the-air outlet—and thus provides an impetus for vertical integration. Ten years ago, the MPAA's membership was comprised of independent American film studios, whereas now most of its members are under foreign ownership or are subsidiaries of larger corporations. The MPAA, like other trade associations in the communications industry, will have to adjust to a universe in which the interests of media outlets, such as broadcasters and cable operators, are increasingly one with their own.

FINANCIAL FACTS

As a legislative advocate for the industry, the MPAA spends a substantial amount of money on lobbying. In calendar year 1997, for example, the MPAA paid $600,000 to lobbyists. Like other associations, the MPAA also has its own political action committee

(PAC), which has shown steady increases in its contributions over the last few election cycles. In the 1991–1992 election cycle, the PAC had contributions of $1,500 compared to $89,118 in the 1997–1998 cycle. This increase is undoubtedly attributable to congressional consideration of the landmark Telecommunications Act of 1996 and forms of censorship, such as the V-chip. In the 1995–1996 election cycle, its PAC had receipts of $76,478 and expenditures of $80,608. In the prior two election cycles, its political contributions were:

	Total	Democrat	%	Republican	%
1995–96	$65,612	31,932	49	33,680	51
1997–98	$89,118	39,771	45	49,347	55

This partisan distribution represented a break from prior years, as the MPAA was formerly known for its Democratic bias. Once the Republicans took control of Congress in 1995, the MPAA adjusted to the new configuration of power and altered its giving habits. Continuing the new pattern, the MPAA also gave $4,000 in soft money to the Republicans in 1998.

JULIE M. WALSH

Bibliography

Balio, Tina, ed. *The American Film Industry*. Madison: University of Wisconsin Press, 1985.

Center for Responsive Politics: www.crp.org

Kindem, Gorham, ed. *The American Movie Industry: The Business of Motion Pictures*. Carbondale: Southern Illinois University Press, 1982.

Litman, Barry R. *The Motion Picture Mega-Industry*. Boston: Allyn and Bacon, 1998.

Motion Picture Association of America: www.mpaa.org

NATIONAL ASSOCIATION OF BROADCASTERS

Based in Washington, D.C., the National Association of Broadcasters (NAB) is perhaps the leading voice for the radio and television broadcasting industries. The association's 7,500 members consist primarily of radio and television stations licensed in the United States and its territories. Associate membership is offered to individuals and companies that offer products and services to the electronic media industries. While the NAB provides its members with information about market and industry trends, its primary mission is to monitor legislation and regulations at all governmental levels that could impact the broadcast industry.

HISTORY

The NAB traces its origins to 1922 when a group of radio station operators and radio receiver manufacturers joined together to pursue common interests. At the time, there was little government regulation over radio as well as a brewing battle over the allocation of spectrum. Under the leadership of its first president, Eugene McDonald, the NAB proposed and supported the formation of an independent commission to regulate the industry. Commercial broadcasters supported regulation because of the growing number of radio stations, which led to interference in the airwaves. In this first campaign, the NAB met with success: a temporary commission, the Federal Radio Commission, was established in 1927 and a permanent one, the Federal Communications Commission (FCC), in 1934. Throughout its long and quite successful history, the NAB has changed its name and has also absorbed other associations, namely, the Television Broadcasters Association (1951), the Daytime Broadcasters Association (1985), and the National Radio Broadcasters Association (1986). The organization itself was formerly called the National Association of Radio and Television Broadcasters.

The 1934 Communications Act was landmark legislation for the media industry, essentially defining the governmental role for years to come. Indeed, it remained the most significant law until the Telecommunications Act of 1996 and even since that, it has retained much relevance. Prior to the passage of this act, the issue of commercialism was on the table, with an organized broadcast reform movement tapping into public disdain for the increasing commercialization of radio. The debate over commercialization, to the extent that it occurred in 1934, focused on the Wagner-Hatfield amendment to the act. Calling for the revocation of broadcasting licenses within 90 days, the reallocation of 25 percent of all frequencies to nonprofit groups, and an allowance whereby nonprofit stations could sell air time to defray their expenses, this amendment would have been a major victory for the reformers or those seeking to limit commercialization. Needless to say, the broadcast industry and thus the NAB were opposed to the amendment since it would reduce commercial revenue by as much as 25 percent and extend the reach of regulation. The amendment was defeated with a recommendation that the newly created FCC study the issue, a clear victory for the NAB. From this point forward, organized opposition to commercialism was replaced with weaker voices complaining about "excessive" commercialization only.

Successful in its bids for a regulatory body and commercial structure, the NAB then adapted well to this framework. Perhaps its most significant victory came in 1963, when the NAB defeated the FCC's attempt to restrict commercial advertisements in the broadcast industry. At this time, the FCC proposed the adoption of rules that would require all broadcast stations to observe the limitations on advertising time as set forth in the NAB's radio and television codes. Despite the fact that the FCC was asking only that the industry adhere to its own standards, the industry, represented by the NAB, mounted a successful campaign to defeat the enforcement of any standards. The NAB focused its lobbying efforts on the House of Representatives, which ultimately passed an amendment that prevented the FCC from limiting advertising time. Gently reminding legislators that less profitable stations would not be able to fund local news, which would threaten their ability to send messages home, the NAB was able to convince congressional members to identify their interests with those of the broadcast industry. Although no action was taken on this bill in the Senate, the FCC got the message and refrained from making any general rules in this area. The episode was a clear victory for the NAB and a severe blow to the power and prestige of the FCC. When Congress passed the Public Broadcasting Act in 1967, which paved the way for public stations, it had the acquiescence of the NAB. By this time, commercial broadcasters had dropped resistance to a public system, based on the theory that it would do unprofitable cultural and public affairs programming, thereby relieving them of the responsibility. What is more, the NAB succeeded in persuading Congress to drop a sales tax on radios and televisions, which was originally going to provide the funding for the public system.

The NAB has additionally ensured that the interests of its members were served well by technological advances and the regulatory responses to them. For example, in 1962, the NAB was able to rebuff a major threat from UHF technology by lending its support to a legislative compromise that protected VHF interests as much as possible. Likewise, the NAB and the industry were successful in convincing the FCC to slow the expansion of cable in the 1960s and early 1970s. Court rulings in the late 1970s paved the way for cable's expansion and thus could be viewed as a defeat for the broadcast industry.

The NAB has waged and continues to mount successful bids to limit the regulatory reach of the FCC in substantive broadcasting as well. A major victory on this front came with the demise of the Fairness Doctrine in the late 1980s. This doctrine required broadcasters to present balanced views of controversial issues. The NAB charged that rules such as this and the Equal Time Provision, which required stations that granted or sold air time to any one political candidate to grant or sell others equal time, implied second-class status for broadcasters compared to print journalists, who had no such guidelines. After the FCC repealed these rules, the NAB lobbied Congress successfully to prevent their return in the form of legislation.

In the early 1990s, the NAB suffered a minor defeat when the Children's Television Act was passed. This law placed limits on advertising time and noted that broadcasters had a duty to meet children's educational and informational needs. However, the act provided only vague standards and failed to ban product-based programs, features that minimized the scope of this legislative loss to the industry. The NAB posted an unconditional victory in its effort to defeat a proposal for a Public Broadcasting Trust Fund in 1995. The fund would have been partially supported by a tax on commercial stations.

ACTIVITIES: CURRENT AND FUTURE

In light of the dollar sums involved, it is evident that the NAB is heavily involved in the "insider game" of lobbying. At one time, the NAB expressed reluctance about joining the political action committee (PAC) "game." Indeed, when the formation of a PAC was initially discussed in 1972, the Board of Directors would not allow the discussion to be recorded in the minutes. Given the current stakes of federal policy, the NAB is less circumspect about seeking access to lawmakers via contributions. Members of Congress may, in fact, be particularly susceptible to the pleas of the broadcast industry not only because of the substantial sums spent on lobbying, but also due to their reliance on broadcasters for exposure to their constituents. Typically, several members of Congress attend the NAB's annual convention in Washington, D.C. Although the FCC is specifically charged with the regulation of the broadcast industry, the NAB has long recognized the influence of Congress over that body and has waged successful lobbying campaigns to thwart regulations by focusing its efforts on Congress. That is not to say that the NAB does not lobby the FCC. To the contrary, the NAB exerts a considerable influence over both the FCC and Congress by providing information about proposed policies and technological developments. It further promotes ties with the FCC by inviting the committee's chairperson to speak at its annual convention.

In recent times, the NAB has had a host of issues on which to concentrate its lobbying efforts. For example, it has fought attempts to require that broadcasters provide free or discounted air time to political candidates and resisted legislative efforts to limit the tax deductibility of alcohol advertising. Additionally, the NAB has been a voice for the broadcast industry at a time when laws are being rewritten to accommodate technological changes. Exemplary of its efforts in these areas are its campaign to secure the spectrum that television broadcasters will need to make the transition to digital technology and its success in defeating both new spectrum user fees and the application of new performance rights

**National Association of Broadcasters
Political Action Committee Contributions**

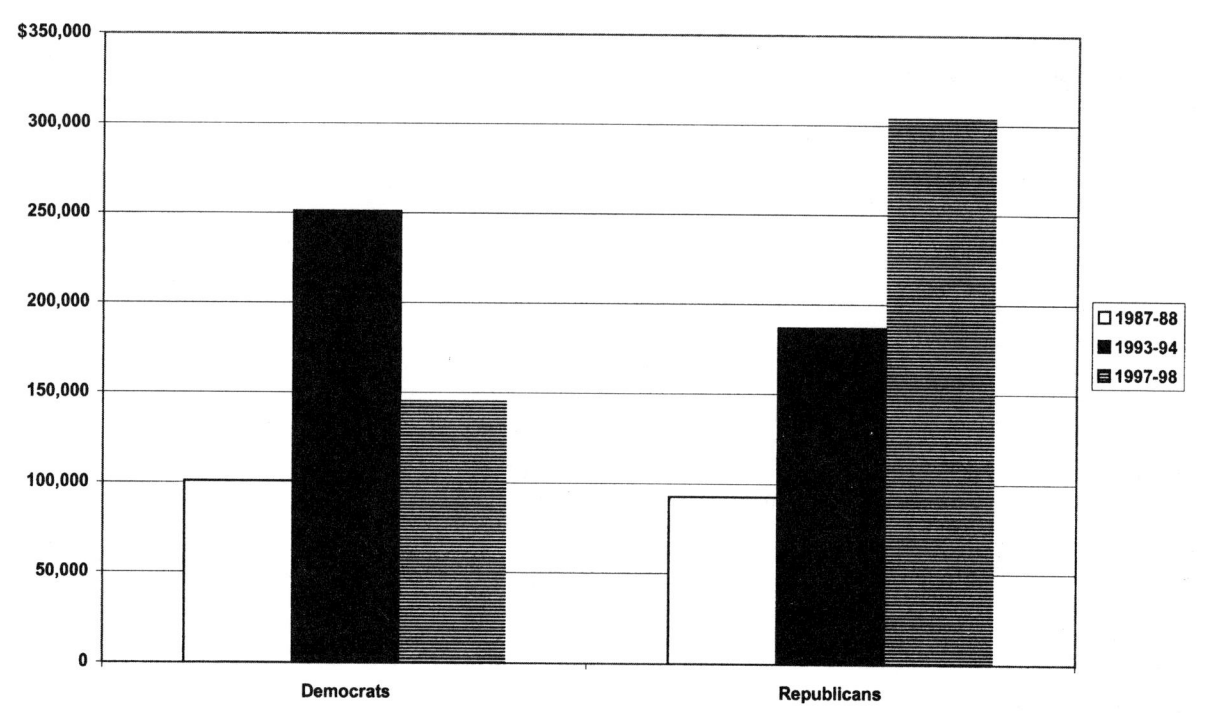

[Bar chart showing PAC contributions:
- Democrats: 1987-88 ≈ $100,000; 1993-94 ≈ $250,000; 1997-98 ≈ $145,000
- Republicans: 1987-88 ≈ $90,000; 1993-94 ≈ $185,000; 1997-98 ≈ $300,000]

Data derived from official studies available from the Federal Election Commission, Washington, DC, 1987–1998.

to radio stations. The association counts the 1996 Telecommunications Act and the 1992 Cable Act among its recent legislative victories. The 1992 act granted permission to broadcasters to charge cable operators for the retransmission of local signals, which had previously been grabbed out of the air for free. The 1996 act not only relaxed limits on the ownership of networks, but also guaranteed existing television broadcasters first opportunity to obtain spectrum for a new generation of digital broadcasts and extended the terms of radio and television licenses. In addition to its lobbying activities, the NAB assists members in meeting their public and community service requirements and engages in some educational activities.

In sum, the NAB has a long history of involvement in the legislative process and too many legislative achievements to chronicle here. It has been an extraordinarily effective voice for the industry. Indeed, one major threat to the future of the NAB has come as a result of its own success. As its membership increases, the NAB could find that its own members' interests might conflict. Some members, most significantly the Big Three networks, have already formed separate associations to represent their interests more specifically.

Despite the creation of more specialized interest groups, the NAB remains an authoritative voice for the broadcast industry, which has flourished in recent years. After dire predictions about the industry's inability to survive a world dominated by cable, the broadcast industry posted record profits in the mid 1990s. This medium retains its popularity partly because it alone can reach a mass audience at minimal cost per viewer, a very attractive feature for advertisers. If the industry remains profitable, its voice is sure to remain powerful. In the future, the NAB will closely monitor technological issues affecting television, such as spectrum allocation for digital television, and legislation impacting the ownership structure of the broader entertainment industry. As vertical integration continues to sweep this industry, the NAB will look to advance the financial interests of broadcasters.

FINANCIAL FACTS

The NAB employs a staff of approximately 165 people and has an operating budget of $27 million, numbers that clearly demonstrate its significance. Indeed, for the calendar year 1997, the NAB was ranked 45th in spending for outside lobbyists, with expenditures of $4,680,000. Its political action committee (PAC) had receipts of $739,226 and expenditures of $664,204 in the 1995–1996 election cycle. Its contributions in the last two election cycles were:

	Total	Democrat	%	Republican	%
1995–96	$430,910	122,750	28	308,160	72
1997–98	$450,103	145,560	32	304,543	68

The NAB's Republican bias was evident in its soft-money donations in 1997–1998 as well, since it gave $26,000 to that party and only $2,196 to the Democratic Party. However, this disparity should not be interpreted as an indication of an ideological agenda on the NAB's part. The NAB is pragmatic in its orientation, a fact that is best detected in its allocation of contributions in the 1993–1994 election cycle when Democrats controlled Congress. In that cycle, 57 percent of its $437,990 in contributions was given to Democrats, with the remainder donated to Republicans.

JULIE M. WALSH

Bibliography

Baughman, James L. *Television's Guardians: The FCC and the Politics of Programming, 1958–1967*. Knoxville: University of Tennessee Press, 1985.

Krasnow, Erwin G., and Lawrence D. Longley. *The Politics of Broadcast Regulation*, 2d ed. New York: St. Martin's Press, 1982.

Mackey, David. "The Development of the National Association of Broadcasters." *Journal of Broadcasting* I (1957): 305–325.

National Association of Broadcasters: www.nab.org

Walker, James, and Douglas Ferguson. *The Broadcast TV Industry*. Boston: Allyn and Bacon, 1998.

NATIONAL CABLE TELEVISION ASSOCIATION

The National Cable Television Association (NCTA), located in Washington, D.C., is the nation's largest cable trade association with approximately 3,075 members. Its membership consists primarily of cable systems, but also includes cable program networks and businesses that supply and service the industry. Indicative of its significance, the NCTA speaks on behalf of cable systems that serve more than 80 percent of the country's 64 million subscribers. While the mission of the NCTA is to advance the interests of the cable television industry before the national and state governments, it additionally provides its members with media services and research, publications, and scientific and technological assistance. The NCTA is guided by a board of directors, comprised of chief executive officers of its members' companies, and organized into working committees that address issues affecting the industry. It employs a staff of approximately 92 individuals.

HISTORY

The NCTA was founded in 1952, four years after the birth of cable television. It was formerly called the National Community Television Association. Cable television's birth resulted from a Federal Communications Commission (FCC) ruling that placed a freeze on the licensing of broadcast stations in 1948. Because of the freeze, many rural communities had no or very poor reception. Retailers of television sets in these areas erected "community antennas" on hilltops to receive broadcast signals and then retransmitted the signals through a cable that fed homes in the areas of poor reception. By 1950, the first pay-cable service was instituted. The FCC's freeze lasted until 1952 when it announced a new frequency allocation plan. It was in this year that the NCTA was formed, perhaps in recognition of the burgeoning industry's debt to federal regulation. The new allocation rules provided viewers with few options, a consequence that enabled cable to entice viewers with more choices in programming. Initially, the broadcast industry welcomed cable as a means to expand its market into rural areas. However, once the cable industry moved into cities solely to increase the number of stations available, it transformed itself from a partner of the broadcast industry to a competitor. Facing competition as formidable as the National Association of Broadcasters (NAB), it is not surprising that cable companies formed a trade association.

Indeed, the NAB immediately sought relief from the FCC. The cable industry was allowed to develop for about a decade—not because of the newly formed NCTA's clout, but because the FCC deemed the industry weak, engaged primarily in local retransmission. The cable industry had a slow start, as it took 15 years to connect the first million subscribers. As it began to grow more rapidly in the 1960s, the FCC responded to the concerns of broadcasters, not to the interests of the cable industry. In 1962, the FCC required cable carriers to demonstrate that they would provide only local signals. Much more detrimentally for the NCTA and cable industry, the FCC announced major restrictions on cable in 1966. Reversing its earlier declaration about a lack of jurisdiction over cable, the FCC required an effective halt to distant signal importation into the nation's top 100 markets. This freeze was a major defeat for the emergent cable industry, drastically reducing its rate of growth for the next decade.

Although the FCC lifted the ban in 1972, it simultaneously imposed very restrictive rules on the cable industry. Once again, the interests of broadcasters were elevated over those of the cable industry. Cable companies were required to carry all local broadcast signals, were restricted in the number of distant signals they could import, and were greatly limited in their ability to offer movies, sporting events, and syndicated programming. Fortunately for the cable industry, however, these rules had a very short life. Indeed, concerted efforts by the NCTA at all governmental levels led to a gradual relaxation of cable restrictions throughout the decade. Aided especially by favorable Supreme Court decisions, the industry was poised for a major growth surge by the end of the 1970s. For example, Home Box Office, launched in 1972 as the first subscription television service, challenged the most restrictive of the FCC's rules and was able to get them struck down as unconstitutional. In fact, by 1979, the Supreme Court had virtually eliminated the jurisdiction of the FCC over the cable industry with the exception of those matters affecting the use of broadcast spectrum.

Congress had also responded somewhat to the concerns of the NCTA in 1976 when drafting copyright reform legislation. To be sure, the law advanced the interests of the broadcast industry by requiring cable operators to pay royalties for the importation of distant signals. However, it additionally accorded cable systems a "compulsory copyright license," allowing them to retransmit broadcast signals without permission, and the law allowed for the retransmission of local signals without royalty payments. The NCTA, then, was beginning to achieve some recognition in Washington, as legislators were now acknowledging its concerns.

In 1984, the NCTA and the cable industry were able to claim their first unequivocal success on the legislative front when Congress passed the Cable Communications Policy Act. Considered in the wake of a long debate between the National League of Cities and the cable industry, the law favored the interests of the latter as it deregulated rates for all cable systems facing "effective competition" from regular broadcasting stations. This provision essentially relieved cable systems of municipal rate regulation and, accordingly, allowed for a surge in cable's growth. There were, to be sure, other provisions in the bill that were not in cable's interests, such as public and leased access provisions, both of which would negatively affect cable's profits. Yet because of lax enforcement and confusion over language, these provisions were weak in their overall impact.

These gains were reversed in 1992 when Congress moved to reregulate the cable industry with the passage of the Cable Television Consumer Protection and Competition Act. This law returned some of the power that local governments once possessed to regulate cable rates and mandated the FCC to set a standard rate for the most basic level of service offered by those cable operators that lack competition. What was worse in the NCTA's eyes, the law aimed to ensure cable's competitors, such as home satellite dishes, better access to cable-owned programming. This provision especially attracted the ire of the NCTA, which perceived it as dictating to whom and on what terms cable operators could sell programming. However, the NCTA focused its attack on a provision that allowed broadcasters to charge cable operators to retransmit local signals, effectively erasing a benefit of the 1976 law. Arguing that such a provision would boost, not lower, cable rates, the NCTA attempted to rally public support against the law. Despite political action committee (PAC) contributions of nearly $512,000, an amount greater than all other cable interests and the NAB, and a public relations blitz, the NCTA was unable to stop this act from becoming law. Indeed, the Democratic Congress overrode President George Bush's veto, for the first time in his presidency, to pass this act. Its passage marked a significant defeat for the NCTA and was exceptional in its reversal of a deregulatory trend in the communications industry.

The cable industry was given regulatory relief four years later with the passage of the historic Telecommunications Act, which deregulated rates for virtually all cable television packages. The law additionally enabled telephone companies to provide cable and video programming and generally relaxed barriers for consolidation within the telecommunications industry, inclusive of cable operators, phone companies, and broadcasters. To be sure, selected regulations pursuant to the 1992 law remained in place, but the NCTA could count the 1996 act as a success.

ACTIVITIES: CURRENT AND FUTURE

For the most part, the NCTA engages in the "insider game" of lobbying, contributing to campaigns, attending fund-raisers, and providing information to legislators. Its PAC targets contributions to those with committee jurisdiction over issues affecting the industry, a practice that denotes sophistication. Because cable television is subject to state and local jurisdiction in that its systems must be constructed on public streets, the NCTA pays attention to state legislators as well as congressional ones. The NCTA has also been willing to support its members in court cases challenging laws that disadvantage the cable industry in favor of broadcasters or others. On occasion, the NCTA and the cable industry additionally have tried their hands at what some label "astroturf" lobbying, which is an attempt to create the illusion of grassroots support for an issue. In 1992, for example, the NCTA sponsored an advertising campaign to encourage subscribers to contact

**National Cable Television Association
Political Action Committee Contributions**

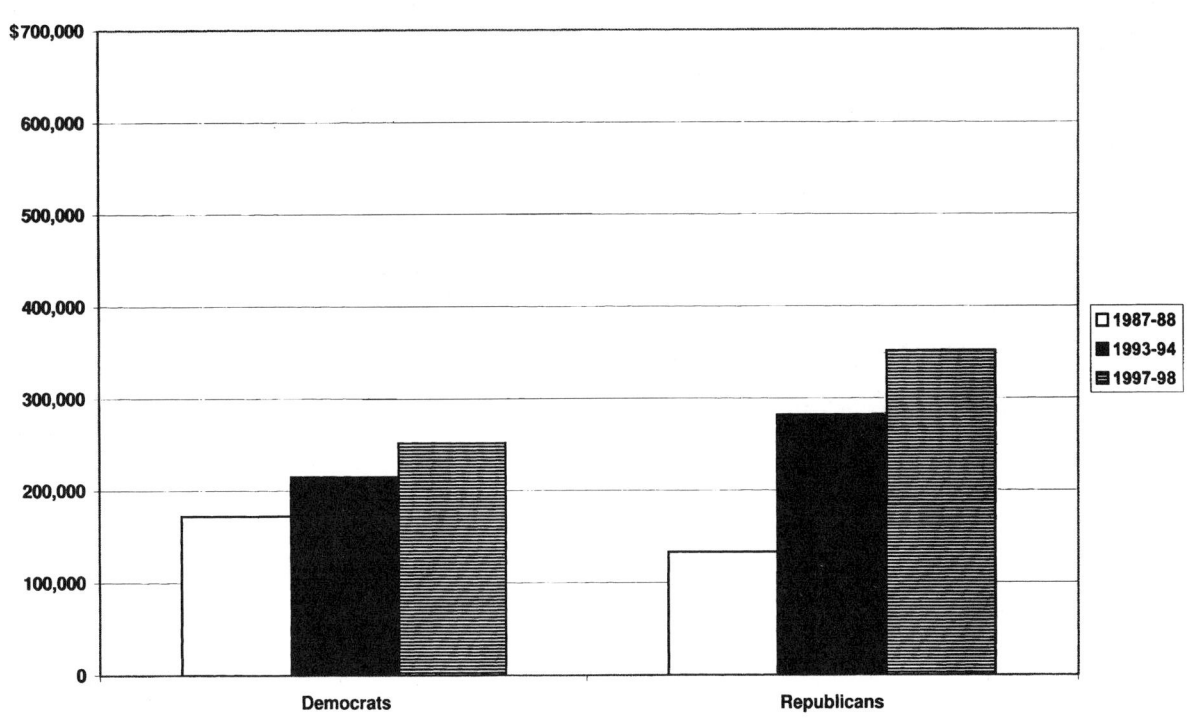

Data derived from official studies available from the Federal Election Commission, Washington, DC, 1987–1998.

Congress and express their disapproval of pending legislation. That tactic is rather unusual, though, as conflict about legislation affecting the industry typically has low importance. With the expiration of the FCC's authority to control cable markets on March 31, 1999, the NCTA will undoubtedly continue to fight against proposals in Congress to cap cable rates, increase competition, or reinstate the FCC's jurisdiction over the issue. Like other trade associations, the NCTA provides information about the industry and attempts to aid in its professional development as well.

The Telecommunications Act of 1996 together with developments in technology have worked to erode distinctions among media industries. The digital revolution, in particular, has eliminated technological barriers dividing media from telephony, and both from computers. Ultimately, all forms of data will be stored in interchangeable digital bits, which, when combined with satellite and fiber-optic communications networks, will become the basis for an information superhighway. Already, cable and telephone services have converged, as each is capable of offering the other's services. Given this technological reality and the opportunity in the law, cable and telephone companies have thus merged in several instances. These combined entities are in an excellent position to develop and sell Internet services to their existing customers. Although they will surely face competition in the Internet market, the power of those in the cable industry positions them well to emerge as competitors in other communications markets. The cable television industry has traversed from a collection of locally owned franchises to large multiple-system operators to combined telephone-cable operators. As one voice of this increasingly concentrated and powerful industry, the NCTA will monitor such issues as the Internet and potential restrictions over vertical integration in media markets. Its voice will be reinforced by the powerful lobbies representing the telephone industry.

FINANCIAL FACTS

Like many trade associations, the NCTA has established a political action committee (PAC). In the 1995–1996 election cycle, its PAC had receipts of $618,053 and expenditures of $641,640. Its political contributions in the past two election cycles were:

	Total	Democrat	%	Republican	%
1995–96	$547,346	174,870	32	372,476	68
1997–98	$602,968	249,388	41	353,580	59

Interestingly, the NCTA's PAC contributed greater amounts to the Democrats in the 1991–1992 election cycle and those preceding it, a pattern that exposes its pragmatic orientation since the Democrats were in power at that time. However, the PAC donated more to the Republicans than the Democrats in the 1993–1994 election cycle, before the Republicans had captured Congress. That switch might be explained by the NCTA's anger with legislation passed by the Democratic Congress in the 1991–1992 cycle in spite of its heavy spending. As with other powerful interest groups, PAC spending represents only one portion of the NCTA's lobbying budget. For example, in 1997, the NCTA spent $3,360,000 on lobbyists, placing it among the top 100 spenders of all those lobbying in Washington. Given these sums, the NCTA is clearly an important player in the policy-making process.

JULIE M. WALSH

Bibliography

Center for Responsive Politics: www.crp.org

Crandall, Robert W., and Harold Furchtgott-Roth. *Cable M Regulation or Competition?* Washington, DC: Brookings Institution, 1996.

Dolan, Edward V. *TV or CA TV? A Struggle for Power.* New York: National University Publications Associate Faculty Press, 1984.

National Cable Television Association: www.ncta.com

Parsons, Patrick, Robert Frieden, and Rob Frieden. *The Cable and Satellite Television Industries.* Boston: Allyn and Bacon, 1998.

NEWSPAPER ASSOCIATION OF AMERICA

Based in Vienna, Virginia, the Newspaper Association of America (NAA) is the major trade association for the $51 billion newspaper industry. It has over 1,500 members who together account for 87 percent of U.S. daily circulation. Although the NAA represents a significant number of independent newspapers, most of its members are part of national chains, such as Gannett and Knight-Ridder, and/or larger media conglomerates. Like the other sectors of the media industry, the newspaper business is increasingly under the control of media conglomerates. Indeed, newspapers suffer from a lack of competition on two fronts. Less than 2 percent of American cities now have more than one daily newspaper in competition and over 75 percent of these monopolistic dailies are owned by large chains. As an advocate of this concentrated industry, the NAA concerns itself with five major areas of interest—marketing, public policy, diversity, industry development, and newspaper operations. Representing the industry in Washington, the NAA attempts to foster a positive business environment for newspapers. More specifically, it focuses upon issues such as postal rates and reorganization, copyright protection of online materials, and tax issues, all of which affect the fortunes of the newspaper industry.

HISTORY

The NAA was formed in 1992 by the merger of seven associations, namely the American Newspaper Publishing Association (ANPA), the Newspaper Advertising Bureau, the Association of Newspaper Classified Advertising Managers, the International Circulation Managers Association, the International Newspapers Advertising and Marketing Executives, the Newspaper Advertising Co-op Network, and the Newspaper Research Council. Of these seven, the ANPA was the most significant voice on behalf of the industry prior to the merger. It was founded to advance the economic interests of newspapers in 1887, a time when the industry was concerned about the protection of postal subsidies, newsprint tariffs, and copyright and libel laws. Years before the creation of the ANPA, Congress granted a full postal subsidy to newspapers mailed to subscribers in the county where the paper was published. The ANPA successfully defended this subsidy in the face of periodic legislative threats until 1962, when it was finally repealed. Even then, the subsidy was phased out and thus not fully withdrawn until 1993.

Throughout its history, the ANPA was successful in winning special treatment from Congress in other areas as well. The ANPA asked for favorable treatment on the grounds that the industry's work was essential to the proper functioning of a democracy. The Supreme Court was not all that sympathetic to this argument, ruling in the 1940s that news organizations are not exempt from economic regulations that pertain to them as businesses. Beginning in 1939, Congress, on the other hand, relieved news deliverers from minimum wage, overtime, social security, and child labor laws. In addition, Congress provided tax exemptions for activities intended to increase circulation.

This tradition of exemption was continued with the passage of the Newspaper Preservation Act of 1970, which was supported by the ANPA. This act prevented antitrust actions against several newspapers that shared printing and advertising operations, but maintained separate editorial functions. While perhaps intended to assist newspapers in economic trouble, it contributed to the consolidation of the newspaper industry. When the energy crisis hit later in the decade, the newspaper industry succeeded again in winning favorable treatment. In the event of gas rationing, newspaper distribution would be classified as a priority, which would entitle newspapers to extra allotments at the normal price.

The ANPA also benefitted from the Freedom of Information Act and a string of Supreme Court decisions, such as *New York Times v. United States* (1971), or the Pentagon Papers case, that protected freedom of speech and the press. More recently, its successor, the NAA, has been able to obtain reductions in federal estate taxes and the protection of online databases, inclusive of classified advertisements. Despite the industry's historical reluctance to lobby, then, it has been very successful in furthering its interests in the legislative arena. Legislators are well aware of the power wielded over public opinion by newspapers across the country, and for this reason, are perhaps more inclined to respond to the subtle pleas of this lobby.

ACTIVITIES: CURRENT AND FUTURE

The NAA takes an "insider" approach to lobbying, joining coalitions with other organizations, filing amicus curiae, or "friend of the court," briefs on issues of concern, and interacting with legislators on informal and formal bases. It targets all levels of government in its lobbying efforts, but pays the greatest attention to the national government. It is in that arena that most of the high-stakes issues are decided. In recent years, the NAA has focused its lobbying efforts on postal reorganization, repeal of estate taxes that impact family-owned businesses, copyright protection for online products, and the relaxation or elimination of rules against cross-ownership of media, such as the one barring a newspaper from owning a broadcast television or radio station in the same market. The NAA was especially concerned with a proposal to allow the Postal Service to bypass the Postal Rate Commission in granting volume discounts and special rates to large mailers. Fearing that the Postal Service will grant favorable rates to advertising mailers and shift the expense to newspapers and others, the NAA is strongly opposed to the proposal. Estate taxes are of interest to the NAA because they have the potential to threaten local businesses, which are a major source of revenue for newspapers. With the rest of the media industry, the NAA advocates copyright protection to prevent piracy of materials from its databases. It, too, then is another voice in support of enforcing legislation for the World Intellectual Property Organization (WIPO) treaties.

Like other trade associations, the NAA provides information to its members about the industry, pertinent legislation, and technological developments via conferences and publications. To serve its members and advertisers, it operates an Information Resource Center as well. Because newspapers depend upon an educated citizenry, the NAA administers programs designed to promote literacy via newspapers. Focusing primarily on schools, the NAA operates a Newspaper in Education program, which encourages educators to use newspapers in every subject. It has recently instituted grants to provide funding for student newspapers as well. The NAA devotes the greatest amount of its energy to marketing efforts on behalf of the industry. Indeed, in 1997, marketing accounted for 37 percent of the NAA's total expenses. The association runs hundreds of programs, mainly directed at increasing advertising revenues for the industry. Via these programs and its promotion of readership and literacy, the NAA advocates the most fundamental interests of the industry.

Recently reorganized, the newspapers' major trade association, the NAA, is likely to continue in that role. Because of the concentration of ownership in newspapers, it is likely to favor the interests of the chains in the event that they conflict with independents. Like the other trade associations in the media industry, the convergence with other sectors, such as broadcasting, could ultimately challenge its role, or at the least affect its consideration of interests. In the meantime, the NAA will continue to focus on public policy issues, such as copyright protection and postal rates, that specifically impact newspapers.

FINANCIAL FACTS

The NAA is a financially strong organization, with a budget of $37.7 million in 1997 and a staff of approximately 200. Of its $36.1 million in expenses for that same year, the NAA allocated only 8.5 percent to its public policy division. Indicative of the traditional reluctance of the print industry to engage in lobbying activities, the NAA does not have a political action committee (PAC). However, it is actively engaged in lobbying. Of those in the printing and publishing industries, it spent the most on lobbyists in 1997, a sum of $1,362,048. Additionally, the NAA contributed $1,500 in soft money to the Democratic Party in 1995. As newspapers have become increasingly entangled with the broadcast media as a result of overlapping ownership interests, their trade associations have been more likely to participate in the lobbying process. With a history of government regulation by the Federal Communications Commission, the broadcast media have fewer qualms about involvement in the political process.

JULIE M. WALSH

Bibliography

Center for Responsive Politics: www.crp.org

Cook, Timothy E. *Governing With the News: The News Media as a Political Institution.* Chicago: University of Chicago Press, 1998.

Emery, Edwin. *History of the American Newspaper Publishers Association.* Minneapolis: University of Minnesota Press, 1950.

Keller, Bill. "How News Business Lobbyists Put Their Press on Congress . . . But With Mixed Feelings." *Congressional Quarterly* (August 2, 1980): 2176–2184.

Newspaper Association of America: www.naa.org; and Annual Report, 1997.

RECORDING INDUSTRY ASSOCIATION OF AMERICA

Based in Washington, D.C., the Recording Industry Association of America (RIAA) is the major trade association for the producers, manufacturers, and distributors of sound recordings. The recording industry is highly concentrated, with only six major players, namely Warner Music, Sony Music, PolyGram, BMG, EMI, and MCA. As the industry's voice, the RIAA is most often the mouthpiece of these companies, collectively known as the "Big Six." The RIAA's Board of Directors is composed of four representatives from each of the Big Six companies and seven representatives of independent companies. Despite the dominance of the Big Six in the industry, the RIAA boasts a membership of 250. Its members distribute approximately 90 percent of all legitimate sound recordings produced and sold in the United States. All of the RIAA's members are creators, manufacturers, or distributors of recordings, as membership is not open to those who service the industry or to individuals. The mission of the RIAA is to promote a business and legal climate that enhances the creative and financial vitality of its members. To fulfill its mission, the RIAA takes a special interest in persuading lawmakers to strengthen copyright protections and to avoid censorship.

HISTORY

In May 1952, the newly formed RIAA registered an expressed legislative interest in a bill to amend the U.S. code with respect to recording and performing rights in literary works. The Federal Communications Commission (FCC) lifted its freeze on broadcast licensing in this same year, which, in turn, would lead to more FM radio stations and thus a greater demand for musical recordings. African-American rhythm and blues began to attract a white, teenage market around 1952 as well. The RIAA, then, formed at a time of great promise for the industry. Originally called the Record Industry Association of America, the trade association changed to its current name in 1970.

For almost the first two decades of its existence, the RIAA had very little success on its primary issue, copyright protection. With the introduction of the eight-track tape player in the early 1960s, the volume of unauthorized tape sales, or piracy, began to explode. Despite strong appeals at the federal and state levels for antipiracy legislation, only eight states had passed such laws by 1971. In its early years, the RIAA simply did not have the clout of other trade associations in the communications industry, such as the National Association of Broadcasters (NAB), which, on behalf of radio stations, initially resisted copyright protection for recordings. The RIAA's first major success came in the early 1970s, when Congress finally extended copyright protection to the owners of sound recordings. In a concession to the NAB, radio broadcasters were relieved of paying any royalties to recording companies. Furthermore, the copyright was subject to the "First Sale Doctrine," which placed no restriction on the resale or rental of legitimately acquired copies. Despite these compromises, the recording industry was at last included under the umbrella of copyright protection when this law took effect in 1972.

From that point forward, the RIAA worked to strengthen and enforce its long-coveted copyright protection. Teaming with the Motion Picture Association of America (MPAA) in 1982, the RIAA convinced Congress to stiffen the criminal penalties for the piracy of recordings and motion pictures. In 1984, at the urging of the RIAA, Congress passed the Record Rental Amendment to the earlier Copyright Act. This amendment created an exception to the First Sale Doctrine to allow the owners of recording copyrights to prohibit the rental of phonograms. By this time, rentals posed a real threat to the recording industry, as customers could purchase a blank tape and a rental copy for considerably less money than an original.

Another area of concern for both the RIAA and the MPAA was home recordings. In its attempts to limit losses associated with home recordings, the RIAA has had less success. Congress passed the Audio Home Recording Act in 1992, which was the result of compromise among competing interests. Although the act exempts home taping from liability for copyright infringement, it levies a royalty on the sale of digital recording devices and blank digital media. From the RIAA's perspective, the act addressed the most likely source of future losses and provided some compensation for losses due to home taping. The RIAA scored another limited victory in 1995 when Congress passed the Digital Performance Right in Sound Recordings Act. This act serves mainly to protect against the pirating of digital copies over the Internet or via satellite, as it exempts broadcasters from its provisions. Of course, the RIAA counts the World Intellectual Property Organization (WIPO) treaties among its recent successes as well.

Although copyright protection has been the main focus of the RIAA's lobbying efforts in the past, it has also been concerned with censorship, antitrust, and other issues. Beginning in the late 1980s and continuing into the 1990s, the music industry has come under fire for lyrics deemed to be violent, profane, and misogynist. Congressional hearings were held in which groups, such as the Parents Music Resource Center, complained about the effects of these lyrics on children. To prevent government involvement in this area, the industry agreed to a system of self-regulation. Recordings with offensive lyrics would henceforward be identified by warning labels. The RIAA has successfully lobbied against state laws that would prohibit the sale to minors of recordings with these labels. To date, the industry has been successful in avoiding federal regulation in this area. Given the highly oligopolistic structure of the recording industry, the RIAA has been able to resist antitrust legislation as well.

ACTIVITIES: CURRENT AND FUTURE

Consistent with other trade associations, the RIAA opts for an "insider" approach to lobbying. It thus relies primarily upon its financial contributions and connections to gain access to lawmakers. However, because of the notoriety of musicians, the RIAA complements its insider strategies with public appeals by recording artists when their interests are one with its own. The RIAA has been instrumental in bringing artists to testify before Congress about its legislative priorities. No issue is of greater concern to the RIAA than copyright protection. Without copyrights, its major revenue stream would decline precipitously. For this reason, the RIAA has focused most of its current lobbying activities on winning the ratification of the WIPO treaties and on obtaining legislation to enforce their guarantees.

The RIAA has produced artists to speak against censorship of musical lyrics as well. In fact, the RIAA has waged political fights on the state level against the imposition of community standards of decency and restrictions on sales of offensive music to minors. In these cases, the RIAA has the cooperation of recording artists and relies on inside pressure and public advocacy to obtain results. The RIAA's interests are not always one with recording artists, however, as a debate over an amendment to a bankruptcy bill demonstrated in recent years. By donating to the political campaigns of legislators and providing information to Congress, the RIAA was able to win an exemption from a bankruptcy law to diminish the likelihood that musicians could use bankruptcy to escape their record contracts. In this instance, the RIAA employed a purely "insider" strategy with much success.

Many of the RIAA's nonlobbying activities are closely related to its primary concern, the protection of copyrights. For example, it has launched an educational campaign aimed at persuading young people, particularly college students, about the importance of respecting copyrights. The RIAA also supports the search for technological solutions to copyright concerns. To that end, the association hosted a technology forum in 1997. When necessary, the RIAA has litigated on behalf of its members to protect copyrights as well. Finally, the RIAA, in cooperation with the Federal Bureau of Investigation, has participated in an antipiracy campaign. Because of its concern with piracy, the RIAA opened a Miami office in August 1998. The office is to serve as a conduit between the RIAA and the U.S. Hispanic music industry, which has the highest rates of piracy. The RIAA is also known for its Gold and Platinum awards bestowed upon recordings that sell in excess of 500,000 and 1 million copies, respectively. Like other trade associations, the RIAA provides its members with information about consumers, the industry, and technical developments through its publications. Clearly, then, the RIAA acts to further the interests of its members on many fronts.

The RIAA faces the future with a new leader, Hilary Rosen, who took the reins of power from Jay Berman

**Recording Industry of America
Political Action Committee Contributions**

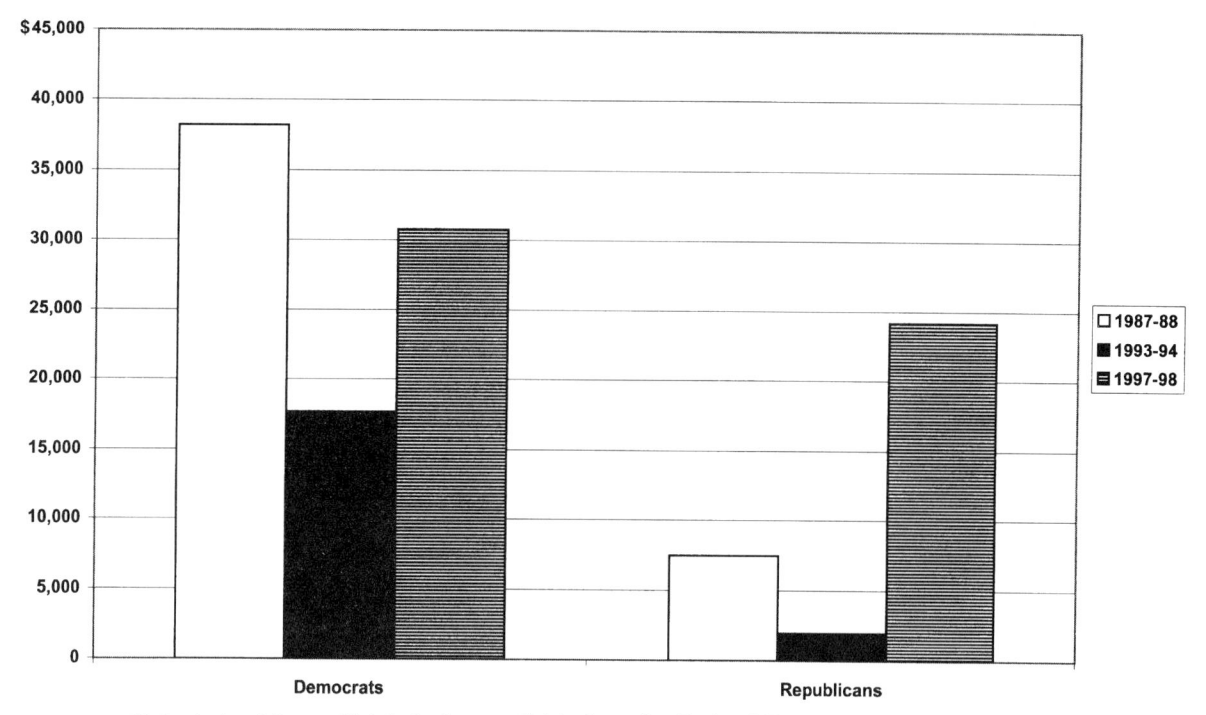

[Bar chart showing PAC contributions to Democrats and Republicans for election cycles 1987-88, 1993-94, and 1997-98. Democrats: ~$38,000 (1987-88), ~$17,500 (1993-94), ~$30,500 (1997-98). Republicans: ~$7,000 (1987-88), ~$1,500 (1993-94), ~$24,000 (1997-98).]

Data derived from official studies available from the Federal Election Commission, Washington, DC, 1987–1998.

in January 1998. Because recording artists can now create their own web sites and sell their products directly to consumers, the RIAA must face the challenge of obsolescence and emphasize the importance of the industry's role as a mediator between customers and artists. It has already begun to do so by reminding artists of the importance of traditional marketing. Of more pressing relevance, the RIAA will continue to confront the threat to copyright revenues posed by digital technology and the Internet. Digital technology makes it possible to translate all forms of expression, such as text, movies, and music, into a digital code that can be reproduced for global audiences and then copied by those audiences. To achieve technical solutions to the problem of digital piracy, the recording industry will need to cooperate with Internet service providers, the computer industry, and manufacturers of network equipment and computer software. Because recorded music is considered the most concentrated global media market, it is also ripe for further consolidation. As the structure of the communications industry continues to evolve, the RIAA, like all other trade associations in this industry, might have to adjust its mission and perhaps its organization.

FINANCIAL FACTS

Like other trade associations, the RIAA has established a political action committee (PAC) to donate to political candidates. In the 1995–1996 election cycle, its PAC had receipts of $117,125 and expenditures of $90,382. In the past two election cycles, its contributions were:

	Total	Democrat	%	Republican	%
1995–96	$73,839	47,839	65	26,000	35
1997–98	$55,002	30,802	56	24,200	44

The RIAA had been more skewed in its Democratic bias prior to 1995. For example, only 6 and 10 percent of its PAC contributions went to the Republicans in the 1991–1992 and 1993–1994 cycles, respectively. The RIAA dramatically increased its donations to Republicans in the election cycle immediately following their capture of Congress. As a trade association, the RIAA undoubtedly adopts a pragmatic philosophy and thereby contributes to those most likely to win office.

The RIAA does not limit its political spending to

PAC contributions. To the contrary, the RIAA paid $860,000 to lobbyists in 1997. What is more, the organization made soft-money contributions of $29,680 and $136,558 in the 1997–1998 and 1995–1996 election cycles. Interestingly, the RIAA gave more to Republicans than Democrats in the 1997–1998 election cycle, with contributions of $90,000 and $46,558, respectively. In 1995–1996, the RIAA contributed $19,680 to Democrats and $10,000 to Republicans. The dominant members of the RIAA also make hefty contributions to political candidates via their PACs and to the parties in the form of soft money. While such giving is independent of the RIAA, it certainly does not hurt its visibility and bargaining position in Washington. Over the past decade, in fact, the RIAA has gained more clout on Capitol Hill and it grew in size under the leadership of Jay Berman. It currently has a full-time staff of approximately 60 individuals.

JULIE M. WALSH

Bibliography

Center for Responsive Politics: www.crp.org

Fink, Michael. *Inside the Music Industry: Creativity, Process and Business*. New York: Schirmer Books, 1996.

Hull, Geoffrey. *The Recording Industry*. Boston: Allyn and Bacon, 1998.

Recording Industry Association of America: www.riaa.com; and Annual Reports.

Zuckerman, Edward, ed. and compiler. *The Almanac of Federal PACs, 1998–1999*. Arlington, VA: Amward, 1998.

SOFTWARE AND INFORMATION INDUSTRY ASSOCIATION

Headquartered in Washington, D.C., the Software and Information Industry Association (SIIA) represents the business interests of the computer software and digital content industries. It has more than 1,500 members, including Microsoft, which provides 80 percent of the operating software in the world. The SIIA, like the other trade associations in the media industry, is especially concerned with piracy and seeks legislative and technological solutions to this daunting problem. As a result, it takes a special interest in issues such as copyright protection and encryption. As an advocate for the computer industry, it also monitors tax laws, regulations of electronic commerce, and any other pertinent legislation.

HISTORY

In the past decade, associations representing the high-tech industries have been transformed from marginal into prominent players of the "insider" lobbying game. Consistent with an insider strategy, they seek formal and informal access to policy makers through campaign contributions and their ability to supply information. Currently, there are several bills pending in the U.S. Congress that would impact the software and digital content industries and thus have the SIIA's attention. The SIIA supports proposals that would prohibit the taxation of Internet commerce as well as those enforcing legislation for the World Intellectual Property Organization (WIPO) treaties so as to enhance copyright protection. Alternatively, the SIIA, desiring no controls on encrypted data, will most likely oppose a bill that requires that these data be accessible to law enforcement officials. U.S. software companies fear that restrictions on their ability to develop secure programs will enable foreign companies to challenge their dominance of the industry.

Given its recent formation, the SIIA has no record of accomplishments and failures. However, the Information Industry Association (IIA) was founded in 1968 to provide a forum for networking, education, and governmental advocacy on behalf of the creators and packagers of information content. Throughout its history, the IIA has been a strong advocate of removing restrictions on public information and thereby making it more accessible. The Software Publisher's Association (SPA) was established in 1984 to examine and research topics raised by the growth in software manufacturing. It ultimately became a public voice for the software industry, representing over 90 percent of it.

ACTIVITIES: CURRENT AND FUTURE

In the mid-to-late 1990s, as the computer industry became a much more visible presence in Washington, the SPA had much to celebrate in the legislative arena. For example, Congress granted a three-year moratorium on Internet taxation and extended the research and development tax credit, which benefits high-tech companies. In yet another tax break, the 1997 Budget Bill extended the Foreign Sales Corporation benefit, which provides a partial tax exemption to software companies for income earned from exports. The software industry has benefitted as well from the funding of new technologies, such as interactive educational software and computer networks, in the nation's classrooms. The SIIA will attempt to build upon these victories in the years ahead, undoubtedly maintaining a political presence in Washington and focusing upon such critical areas as copyright protection and the responsibilities of online service providers.

The SIIA will also continue the nonlobbying activities of the SPA and IIA. More specifically, it will host conferences, publish newsletters, conduct research about the industry, and sponsor educational programs. Indicative of the industry's concern about copyright protection, the SIIA will additionally sustain the antipiracy efforts of its predecessor bodies. The SPA operated an industry-wide campaign, supported by the Copyright Protection Fund, to stop software theft and to protect the legal rights of software holders.

FINANCIAL FACTS

The SIIA is a recent creation, formed by the merger of the Software Publishers Association (SPA) and the Information Industry Association (IIA) on January 1, 1999. The new organization is expected to have revenues in excess of $10 million and a staff of 50 professionals. Because the computer industry has experienced an explosive rate of growth over the past decade, it has attracted the attention of the government and been the subject of much legislation. The industry has responded by increasing its lobbying efforts and campaign donations quite dramatically. Indeed, the industry spent $7.3 million in political action committee (PAC), soft money, and individual contributions in 1995–1996, which represented a 52 percent increase over the 1991–1992 election cycle. In 1997, the SPA and IIA paid $600,000 and $505,511 to lobbyists, respectively. The SPA contributed $2,500 directly to campaigns in this same year, with 80 percent given to Democrats and the remainder to Republicans.

JULIE M. WALSH

Bibliography

Carney, Dan. "Software Firms Seek to End Ban on Exporting Encryption Codes." *Congressional Quarterly* (April 13, 1996): 985–987.

Center for Responsive Politics: www.crp.org

Mills, Mike. "Bill Advances to Nudge Industry to Get Schools Online." *Congressional Quarterly* (February 26, 1994): 469–470.

Shecter, Jennifer. "Connected: Political Superhighway Links Silicon Valley with Capitol Hill." *Capitol Eye* 5 (December 1998).

Software Publishers Association: www.spa.org; and Software and Information Industry Association: www.siia.net

SECTION FOUR
HEALTH AND MEDICAL

Healthcare-related organizations and interest groups in America include professional and business associations with economic and political interests that frequently intersect and diverge. Healthcare interest groups are comprised of three types of organizations: organizations that represent professional medical care practitioners; organizations concerned with finding cures for cancer, AIDS, and heart disease, and those suffering from diseases; and organizations that represent the healthcare industry, including health insurance companies, managed care companies, and hospitals and medical centers.

Interest groups that represent healthcare professionals, insurers, and philanthropic organizations are among the most influential in American politics. Typically these organizations have multimillion-dollar budgets; employ large staffs in Washington, D.C.; contribute millions to political action committees (PACs); and exert tremendous influence over Congress and federal government administrative agencies. Moreover, healthcare representative associations—unlike narrower interests—represent millions of American workers employed in the healthcare industry. And groups representing medical doctors, nurses, and other specialized healthcare personnel can call upon their members to lobby Congress and to vote in elections for candidates recommended by the associations.

THE POLITICAL INFLUENCE OF HEALTH INTERESTS

The American health insurance system emerged and evolved on an incremental basis, responding to periodic demands for more comprehensive coverage. The absence of a universal health insurance system guaranteed by the government is in part due to the historical opposition of the health lobby.

The United States does not guarantee cradle-to-grave healthcare as do other advanced industrial economies. In part this is due to the American pluralist political system, which allows private health interests to contribute political funds to candidates, lobby elected officials, and actively participate—and in some cases shape—policy debates. As a result, healthcare legislation in the United States has been enacted on an incremental basis in response to the specific concerns of health interests. The extension of guaranteed health insurance to the elderly and the poor in the 1960s through Medicare and Medicaid came in response to the failure of the private health insurance system to cover these groups—and in opposition to the American Medical Association (AMA) and the private health insurance industry. As a result of these programs, American health insurance is a hybrid system that is financed through the federal and state governments, private insurers, employers, and individuals who can afford coverage.

By contrast, Canada has a single-payer system financed through taxation that provides universal insurance coverage that is available to all citizens. The Canadian health insurance system—which is analogous to the American Medicare system—permits beneficiaries to choose between physicians who maintain private practices or enroll into managed care plans.

In the United States since the 1960s, the leading health interest groups have opposed increased demands for government-guaranteed coverage on the basis that national healthcare would interfere with the private system of health insurance or interfere with the pricing market and patient choice. Large private insurance companies, health management organizations, and private hospital corporations that have increased their influence over the American healthcare system place primary concern with profits. As a result, during the 1990s, advocates of healthcare reform argue that patient rights have declined, hospitals and nursing homes are understaffed, and doctors and other healthcare professionals have lost significant autonomy in medical decisions, leading to inadequate overall care.

SHORTFALL IN HEALTH INSURANCE COVERAGE

Since the 1940s, healthcare financing has been the primary and most enduring debate among interest groups representing healthcare practitioners, insurers, and philanthropic medical organizations. The United States healthcare system—unlike virtually all other advanced industrial countries with similar levels of economic development—combines private insurance coverage with a weak system of federal protections for older and impoverished Americans. Since the mid 1960s, Medicare has provided the primary health insurance for senior citizens. Medicaid, which grew in the 1970s and 1980s in response to rising demand for healthcare coverage among the poor who did not have private insurance through their jobs or otherwise could not afford private insurance, has provided health insurance for some of the poor; however, as eligibility criteria have been narrowed in the late 1990s, fewer Americans living in poverty have access to Medicaid. And proposed government cuts in Medicare and Medicaid coverage and the institution of managed healthcare have imperiled the programs' future ability to provide coverage to the elderly and the poor.

Most Americans receive health insurance coverage through their employers or purchase coverage through private health insurance plans. In 1997, the United States Department of Commerce estimated that over 44 million people, or more than 16 percent of the population, do not have any healthcare insurance coverage. Moreover, the number of Americans who do not have any health insurance has grown steadily over the last decade. Between 1996 and 1998, the number of Americans without health insurance grew by over 3 million.

Among the insured population in the United States, about 70.1 percent of Americans were covered by private health insurance. Most of this population received private insurance from employment-based plans. Although employment-based insurance has been the primary means to obtain insurance for most working Americans, only 15.5 percent of the poor received insurance from their employers. The poor were much more likely to receive health insurance from the government. Beneficiaries covered exclusively by government-based insurance—such as Medicare, Medicaid, and military healthcare—accounted for 24.8 percent of all Americans with health insurance.

Although the government provides health insurance to some of those without access to private health insurance, a disproportionate number of the poor were represented among the uninsured. According to the U.S. Department of Commerce, in 1997, nearly one-third of the poor had no health insurance. In addition to the 43.4 million uninsured Americans, another 45 million people are underinsured—considered to have inadequate health insurance that does not cover their medical needs. The underinsured in America typically do not have access to healthcare coverage for basic medical services through their employers.

RISING HEALTHCARE SPENDING AND MANAGED CARE

For the past few decades, the American health insurance system has been plagued with both high and rapidly rising costs and ironically the narrowing of medical choice. As a result, the United States has the highest per capita healthcare costs in the world. In 1992, healthcare expenses accounted for 13.6 percent of U.S. national income, a far higher percentage than the healthcare costs in Canada or European countries with similar levels of economic development and standards of living. Healthcare costs in the United States in 1992 rose to $3,503 per family or 18.2 percent of per capita income. By comparison, average healthcare expenditures in competing industrial countries ranged from $1,000 to $2,000 per family. It was this high cost structure—and the failure of health insurance to cover a significant share of Americans—which prompted government policy makers to pursue a new system in 1993–1994.

HEALTHCARE REFORM

In 1993–1994, proposals by the administration of President Bill Clinton to restructure healthcare financing in the United States and expand healthcare access to all Americans were met with fierce resistance from leading healthcare interests. Moreover, healthcare interest groups were actively engaged in lobbying and PAC activity to advance their narrower economic interests. The original effort to extend health insurance to all and to reduce healthcare costs was whittled down by healthcare lobbyists seeking to protect and advance the interests of their organizations and members. The health insurance industry rejected the proposal to extend universal health insurance coverage to all Americans and lobbied for the defeat of the plan. The Health Insurance Association of America (HIAA) and individual private health insurers engaged in a massive campaign to derail the Clinton administration's proposals to reduce costs and to broaden access. The particular interest of health groups in healthcare reform is starkly evident when viewing their PAC contributions to candidates for the U.S. Congress during the 1993–1994 election cycle. Almost without exception, health interests vastly increased political contributions during the debate, only to reduce contributions in subsequent election cycles.

The failure to achieve significant reform of the healthcare system in the mid 1990s has contributed to the declining access of healthcare coverage and a reduction in coverage among those Americans who already have health insurance. This sense of insecurity over healthcare coverage has remained a central issue for the body politic. As healthcare coverage declines, medical practitioners are demanding that health insurance provide greater coverage. Thus, at the close of the century, healthcare practitioner interests have promoted a patient's bill of rights that would expand coverage and increase third-party (health insurance company) reimbursements for patient care. Health insurance interests that do not see the need for healthcare reform have opposed the bill in principle and are seeking to dilute proposals that would reduce their profitability.

THE GROWTH OF MANAGED CARE

Managed care is a system that has emerged in the 1980s and has grown rapidly in the 1990s to become the primary form of healthcare delivery in the United States. Managed care is a system of healthcare delivery designed to contain the rapid growth in the cost of medical care coverage and, ostensibly, to improve the quality of service. The system is based on the belief that costs can be reduced through closely monitoring the use of healthcare by beneficiaries. The idea is that by preventing wasteful utilization of services, costs can be reined in. Managed care organizations require patients to receive authorization from their plans before obtaining specialized care or being hospitalized. Moreover, managed care plans have reduced the duration of covered hospital stays and closely monitor the use of specialized services.

The two primary forms of managed care are health maintenance organizations (HMOs) and preferred provider organizations (PPOs). In HMOs, beneficiaries select their primary doctor and usually pay small out-of-pocket expenses. Doctors, who are usually paid on salary or prepaid fee for each patient, are responsible for referrals. HMOs do not pay for the cost of medical care outside the plan. PPOs typically operate like HMO plans, but the doctor is usually paid on a reduced fee-for-service basis. Beneficiaries are usually covered when obtaining care outside the network—usually at higher cost to the consumer.

The advantage of managed care plans is that they typically cost less than standard health insurance plans because they hold down the costs of healthcare by controlling large segments of the patient market, which the plans use to reduce doctor and hospital fees. Critics charge, however, that the cost savings are usually a result of the denial or elimination of coverage. As a result, while managed care plans are championed by the health insurance industry and government cost-cutters, they have come under severe attack by physicians, healthcare practitioners, and increasingly beneficiaries who are uneasy over their reduced coverage.

The rapid growth of managed care in the 1990s to cover the majority of healthcare beneficiaries in the United States has significantly curtailed third-party insurance reimbursements for medical care, contributing to rising competition among healthcare providers for available funding. Associations representing doctors, medical practitioners, and healthcare institutions have actively contributed to congressional campaigns and lobbied key committee members and federal and state healthcare administrative agencies to advance the interests of their members and organizations. Thus, the AMA and other organizations representing healthcare practitioners are among the most vociferous critics of managed care, lobbying Congress and the Healthcare Financing Administration to mandate the expansion of coverage. In June 1999, the AMA, long opposed to unionization, approved the formation of a doctors' union as a means to expand the leverage of physicians in negotiation with the managed healthcare companies on reimbursements, salaries, and services. The AMA unionization plan was initiated because many doctors have joined labor unions in response to managed care.

The HIAA and the Blue Cross and Blue Shield Association (BCBS) are two leading interest associations representing the health insurance industry. The HIAA represents the economic interests of private health insurance companies and managed care organizations. The organization promotes managed health care, the importance of the private healthcare system, supports the extension of health insurance to all segments of society, and seeks to reduce regulations governing the industry. The BCBS also supports the extension of managed healthcare and seeks to expand managed care coverage to Medicare and Medicaid services.

TYPES OF ORGANIZATIONS

This section analyzes nine leading healthcare professional societies representing the interests of medical and health practitioners of all kinds. The AMA, representing physicians, is the leading healthcare association in the United States and is perennially rated by members of Congress and leading experts as one of the five most influential interest groups in Washington. The section also includes profiles of four branches of specialized medicine and medical practitioners. The American Academy of Ophthalmology (AAOP), which represents eye doctors, for example, has gained prominence representing the interests of specialized medical doctors with particular group concerns. The AAOP has been lobbying Congress and administrative agencies to increase reimbursements for eye treatments. The AAOP is also engaged in defending the profession of ophthalmology from encroachment by optometrists who are seeking to gain regulatory approval to perform specialized eye treatment procedures. Although ophthalmologists have exclusive license to practice laser surgery in most states, in several states regulations do not prevent optometrists from performing the procedure. Both at the federal level and at the state level, the AAOP has sought to prevent optometrists from performing laser surgery. On the other hand, the American Optometric Association has sought to expand public and private medical reimbursements for services provided by optometrists. Another prominent interest group, doctors specializing in anesthesiology, have also sought to advance their economic and professional interests; their organization, the American Society of Anesthesiologists (ASA), is responsible for accrediting programs, providing ongoing training for practitioners, and promoting the specialization.

New medical practitioner societies have emerged to reflect the changing nature of the medical field. In the late 1960s, the American College of Emergency Physicians (ACEP) emerged to standardize and accredit physicians who specialize in emergency medicine. As a result of the ACEP's activities, emergency medicine has become recognized as an established branch of medicine. The growth of managed care in the 1990s has brought new challenges to the field of emergency medicine. Government and third-party-provider efforts to curtail emergency room visits through managed care have spurred the organization to devote greater energy to lobbying government officials to defend emergency medicine from cutbacks.

The American Psychiatric Association (APA) and the American Society of Anesthesiologists represent two other medical specialties. In addition to accrediting training programs and providing continuing education for practicing physicians, the two organizations seek to advance the interest of the professions through PAC contributions and lobbying Congress and administrative agencies. Like other branches of medicine, psychiatrists and anesthesiologists are faced with reduced medical reimbursements and limitations on their services imposed by managed care. Psychiatrists advance the idea that mental health should be treated as a disease equivalent with physical health. Thus, the APA believes that persons suffering from mental health disabilities should receive the same equity in coverage as other branches of medicine. The APA also lobbies against the growing tendency to incarcerate youthful criminal offenders and supports increased funds for mental health services.

NONPHYSICIAN INTEREST GROUPS

The health interests section also includes representatives of healthcare practitioners who are not physicians—the American Nurses Association (ANA) and the American Occupational Therapy Association (AOTA). Both organizations are the accrediting bodies that oversee specialized educational programs for students in each field and provide continuing education for practitioners. The ANA and AOTA are the leading organizations of nurses and occupational therapists. They both engage in campaign contributions, lobby Congress and government agencies, promote the professions in the public arena, and defend the professions in hospitals and other healthcare facilities. More than two dozen ANA branches are labor unions that represent nurses and engage in collective bargaining with management. Both the ANA and AOTA are concerned with the effect of managed care and changes in healthcare financing on the future of their respective professions.

The American Dietetic Association—representing

professional nutritionists—actively contributes to political campaign committees and lobbies Congress and federal government authorities to promote nutritional health in the United States. The organization has promoted accurate food labeling as a means to help consumers discern the nutritional attributes of all food products. In addition, the organization has actively lobbied the government to mandate the inclusion of nutritional services as a component of public and private managed healthcare plans.

The American Chiropractic Association (ACA) seeks to advance chiropractic care as a distinct field of medicine independent of the American Medical Association. Doctors of chiropractic medicine manipulate the musculoskeletal structure, which functions to advance the healing process. The ACA seeks to persuade public and private health insurance providers to include and expand chiropractic services as an essential part of medical care.

PHILANTHROPIC ORGANIZATIONS

Healthcare interests active in Washington, D.C., also include philanthropic organizations that seek to cure serious diseases and ease the conditions of persons suffering from illnesses. As nonprofit organizations that seek private donations, philanthropic health interests are forbidden from engaging in political campaign contributions. Three of the most active organizations are the American Cancer Society (ACS), the American Heart Association (AHA), and the American Federation for AIDS Research (AmFAR). The organizations provide public education on prevention, fund research for cures, and assist those who suffer from the diseases. The organizations also lobby the federal government to increase funding for research and services for those afflicted with the diseases.

HOSPITALS AND NURSING HOMES

Two interest groups in this section are organized to advance the interests of medical care institutions. The American Hospital Association (AHA), the national organization that represents hospitals and medical institutions, seeks to promote hospitals as an integral part of healthcare services. The organization tries to ensure that third-party medical care providers adequately reimburse hospitals for their services. The American Healthcare Association (AHCA) represents the nursing home industry, which provides long-term chronic care for elderly and infirm patients who are unable to live independently.

The healthcare interests in this section provide a composite of the influence of healthcare practitioners and providers, health insurance companies, and philanthropic organizations in the American political system. As managed care continues to expand in America, the health interests are finding themselves increasingly at odds over the future of the American healthcare financing system.

IMMANUEL NESS

Bibliography

Aaron, Henry, and William B. Schwartz. *The Painful Prescription: Rationing Health Care.* Washington, DC: Brookings Institution, 1984.

Bennefield, Robert L. "Health Insurance Coverage: 1997." Report P60-202 in *Current Population Reports.* Washington, DC: U.S. Department of Commerce. September 1998.

Center for Responsive Politics web site: www.crp.org

Cunningham, Robert M. *The Blues: A History of the Blue Cross Blue Shield System.* De Kalb: Northern Illinois University Press, 1997.

Jonas, Steven. *An Introduction to the U.S. Health Care System.* 4th ed. New York: Springer, 1997.

Law, Sylvia A. *Blue Cross: What Went Wrong?* New Haven: Yale University Press, 1974.

Navarro, Vicente. *The Politics of Health Policy: The U.S. Reforms, 1980–1994.* Oxford: Blackwell, 1994.

Peterson, Mark A. *Healthy Markets? The New Competition in Medical Care.* Durham: Duke University Press, 1998.

Rassell, Edith. "Health Care Reform." In *Reclaiming Prosperity: A Blueprint for Progressive Economic Reform.* Ed. Todd Schafer and Jeff Faux. Armonk, NY: M.E. Sharpe, 1992.

Starr, Paul. *The Social Transformation of American Medicine.* New York: Basic Books, 1982.

Stevens, Rosemary. *In Sickness and in Wealth: American Hospitals in the Twentieth Century.* New York: Basic Books, 1989.

Wolinksy, Howard, and Tom Brune. *The Serpent and the Staff: The Unhealthy Politics of the American Medical Association.* New York: Tarcher/Putnam, 1994.

Zelman, Walter A., and Robert A. Berenson. *The Managed Care Blues and How to Cure Them.* Washington, DC: Georgetown University Press, 1998.

Zuckerman, Edward, ed. *The Almanac of Federal PACs, 1998–99.* Arlington, VA: Amward, 1998.

AMERICAN ACADEMY OF OPHTHALMOLOGY

The American Academy of Ophthalmology (AAOP) is a professional association representing about 22,000 ophthalmologists in the United States and Canada. In addition, the organization represents more than 5,000 international ophthalmologists. Members of the organization are physicians and surgeons who specialize in ophthalmology, a branch of medicine that studies the structure, functions, and diseases of the eye. Doctors of ophthalmology conduct eye examinations, prescribe corrective lenses, administer medicine, and perform surgery on the eyes. The organization's primary mission is to promote the need for vision and eye care treatment in the United States.

The AAOP, headquartered in San Francisco, is directed by a board of trustees that is responsible for formulating policies and manages the ongoing operations of the organization. The organization also receives reports from the executive, nominating, planning, insurance, and bylaws and rules committees.

The organization provides medical education and certification programs for ophthalmologists and is a major source of ophthalmic education for ophthalmology residents and medical students, other eye care professionals, and other physicians. Like so many other medical practitioners in recent years, ophthalmologists have become increasingly concerned with the growing power of managed care programs to dictate reimbursements for medical services and the reduction of access to needed eye care services for patients. The AAOP maintains a foundation that provides resources on the history and current activities of the profession, available to both members and the public, and supports ophthalmic research. In addition, the organization provides financial support to impoverished persons over 65 years of age or under four years of age for the treatment of vision problems.

HISTORY

The origins of the AAOP can be traced to 1896 with the founding of the American Academy of Ophthalmology and Otolaryngology (AAOO). Otolaryngologists are more generalized practitioners who treat the ear, nose, and throat. In the 1970s, as the two professions grew more distinct, sentiment increased among both professions to establish independent organizations representing the interests of ophthalmologists and otolaryngologists. In 1979, the AAOO was formally divided into two academies. The primary objective of the AAOP has been to provide programs, products, and services for ophthalmologists. The AAOP, which claims to represent more than 90 percent of all practicing ophthalmologists in the United States, is interested in defending and promoting the professional and economic interests of doctors of ophthalmology. This objective is advanced through engaging in educational and political activities that support increased public access to professional services and treatment of the eyes. The AAOP is active in upgrading member skills through providing clinical education and information on new techniques, medical equipment, and recent developments in the field. This education is provided through organizational publications.

ACTIVITIES: CURRENT AND FUTURE

A major concern of the organization is that an increasing number of optometrists are performing procedures typically performed by ophthalmologists. The AAOP has stressed the distinction between ophthalmologists, optometrists, and opticians. Ophthalmologists, according

**American Academy of Ophthalmology
Political Action Committee Contributions**

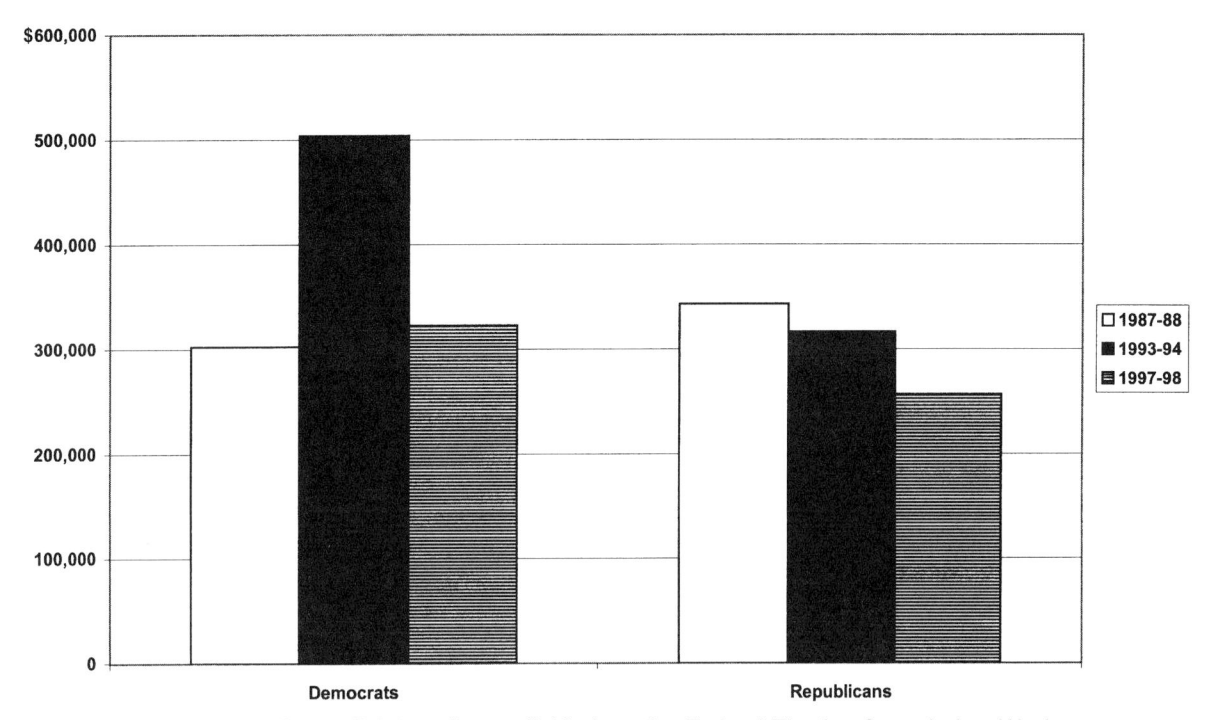

Data derived from official studies available from the Federal Election Commission, Washington, DC, 1987–1998.

to the AAOP, are medical eye doctors who are trained and licensed to perform surgical procedures on patients and in the treatment of diseases and injuries to the eye. Ophthalmologists typically receive more than 13 years of medical training, including medical education, training, and experience.

Optometrists, according to the AAOP, are educated in four-year medical training programs to exclusively treat vision problems and to prescribe corrective glasses, lenses, and eye exercises. In most states, optometrists are barred from performing surgical procedures; however, a growing number are performing photorefractive keratectomy (PRK), a corrective procedure that does not involve conventional surgical procedures. PRK, or laser surgery is becoming more common as a corrective procedure for improving vision. The AAOP has sought to maintain and increase laws that bar optometrists from performing PRK procedures. Opticians, according to the AAOP, are technicians responsible for making and verifying lenses, frames, and other corrective optical devices.

The AAOP provides public information on environmental hazards and risks that might contribute to the impairment of an individual's vision. The organization recommends practices for avoiding these potential risks and improvements in general eye care. In particular, the organization recommends preventive activities, such as using eyewear to protect your eyes from the sun and other hazards and refraining from sporting activities and games that place eyes in potential contact with dangerous objects.

The AAOP opposes efforts to limit ophthalmic services by Medicare and private health insurance plans. The organization lobbies to increase eye care treatment services and to maintain and expand medical reimbursements for the treatment for glaucoma. The AAOP believes that the insufficiency of Medicare reimbursement payments for eye treatment services of senior citizens is reducing the ability of ophthalmologists to perform needed eye treatment on patients. The organization lobbies Congress and executive branch officials to maintain and improve Medicare and private health insurance coverage for ophthalmic treatment. The organization believes that budget cuts in ophthalmic services threaten the professional integrity and economic interests of doctors. There is great concern that the growth of managed care interferes with the need for quality ophthalmic care since decision making is taken away from the doctor and is made by managed healthcare companies.

The AAOP has formed coalitions with leading scientific and philanthropic foundations to promote eye care education and the need for expanding access to eye treatment. In particular, the organization is a prime sponsor of such awareness programs as Glaucoma Awareness Month (January), Sports Eye Safety Month (April), and National Diabetes Month (November).

FINANCIAL FACTS

The AAOP's Advocacy and Ophthalmic Relations Division attempts to influence federal and state healthcare policy. The organization is responsible for providing professional testimony and specialized information to state legislators, healthcare regulatory bodies, health insurance companies, and other healthcare professionals.

The AAOP is one of the few organizations to have reduced its political action committee (PAC) contributions between the 1987–1988 and 1997–1998 election cycles, although it remains one of the largest healthcare contributors to federal candidates. The organization's PAC contributions declined 10.3 percent over the 12-year period, from $646,000 to $579,663. Its contributions in 1997–1998 were more than $240,000 less than in the 1999–1994 election cycle, when the AAOP was actively engaged in the debate over the future of healthcare financing. Like most other PACs, the AAOP's contribution pattern reflects the shift in control of Congress to the Republicans in 1995. Nevertheless, in the 1997–1998 election cycle, the AAOP still contributed 55.7 percent of its PAC money to Democratic candidates.

IMMANUEL NESS AND JAMES CIMENT

Bibliography

American Academy of Ophthalmology: www.eyenet.org
Center for Responsive Politics: www.crp.org
Zuckerman, Edward, ed. *The Almanac of Federal PACs, 1998–99.* Arlington, VA: Amward, 1998.

AMERICAN CANCER SOCIETY

The American Cancer Society (ACS) is the nation's largest nonprofit organization dedicated to the prevention, treatment, and cure of cancers of all types. The ACS includes a national office, 57 regional divisions, and over 3,400 local units or chapters. The national headquarters in Atlanta is responsible for overall strategic planning and the administration of research and education at the national level. Divisions and units are responsible for education at the state and local level, respectively.

The ACS has recently begun to institute a major transformation of its organizational structure. This includes merging state offices to save money and increase efficiency by sharing resources. This, says the organization's president Charles McDonald, will allow more of those resources to be focused on community cancer control. Eventually, the organization hopes to reduce the number of divisions to just 17. All of this is being done to achieve the goal of reducing cancer incidence and mortality by up to 50 percent over the next 15 years.

Reorganization plans aside, the society continues to focus significant resources on research, awarding hundreds of grants in the fields of cancer prevention, education, diagnoses, treatments, and cures every year. In the 1997–1998 fiscal year alone, the ACS awarded 485 grants, professorships, postdoctoral fellowships, and institutional and research opportunity grants—spending some $84.3 million in the process.

HISTORY

The ACS began in 1917, when 15 prominent physicians and business leaders met in New York City and organized the American Society for the Control of Cancer (ASCC). The mission of these founders was partly medical and partly social. They hoped, among other things, to remove the stigma attached to the disease and make it a permissible topic of public discussion. This, the founders believed, was the first step in combating a disease that at the time claimed nearly 75,000 American lives annually. Articles were written for popular magazines and professional journals, and a monthly bulletin was sent out to thousands of healthcare professionals, including doctors, public health officials, and hospital administrators.

In 1936, the ASCC launched the Women's Field Army, as it came to be called, to "wage war on cancer." Styled after the Salvation Army—with uniforms and ranks—the army set itself the mission of raising money to fund cancer research and educating the public on the disease. Within the three years, the army had increased the number of persons dedicated to the control of cancer in the United States from 15,000 to 150,000.

Reflecting a renewed dedication to improving public health in the wake of World War II, the ASCC reorganized itself as the American Cancer Society in 1945. A year later, the new ACS had raised over $4 million, one-fourth of which went to establish and fund the society's research program. Soon dozens and then hundreds of research grants were offered to researchers around the country. In the years since, the society has committed nearly $2 billion to research, funding 28 Nobel Prize winners in the process.

ACTIVITIES: CURRENT AND FUTURE

The single most important political issue that the American Cancer Society has had to grapple with in recent years has been tobacco legislation. The ACS was, of course, one of the earliest organizations to warn about the dangers of tobacco smoke and its role in the development of pulmonary and other cancers. The ACS has actively backed legislation that would hold tobacco companies liable for the diseases and deaths their products cause, and it supported the 1998 agreement reached by the tobacco companies and some 40 state attorneys general in which the tobacco companies agreed to set up a fund to make restitution to the states for the cost of treating health victims of smoking. This settlement was criticized by many as allowing the tobacco companies off the hook legally, since it essentially prevented the initiation of any new suits. The ACS, while also critical of this aspect of the deal, believed that the settlement was probably the best that could be hoped for short of a continuing and costly legal campaign.

In addition, the society has been vigorous in its attempts to persuade the federal government to ban all advertising of tobacco products or, at the very least, regulate them heavily so that advertisements are not geared toward children. This emphasis on fighting tobacco advertising also has a long tradition with the society. In the 1960s and 1970s, the ACS heavily pushed for warnings on cigarette packs and cigarette advertising. The ACS also supported Senate efforts—notably one by Senator John McCain of Arizona—to impose heavy taxes of up to $1 or more per pack on cigarettes, in order to prevent young people from smoking. The bill would have also imposed penalties on the industry if smoking by teenagers did not decline sharply.

On a research-related issue, the ACS recently withdrew its sponsorship of the Patients' Cure, a group dedicated to publicizing the medical benefits of stem-cell research. (Stem cells are contained in embryos and serve as the origin, or stem, of all other types of cells that come to form a living being.) Anti-abortion groups and the Roman Catholic Church have been strongly opposed to stem-cell research—and have promised political retaliation against any politician who supports it—because the research can involve the use of tissue from aborted embryos. Initially, the ACS came out in strong support of stem-cell use as a critical research tool in the fight against cancer but, under pressure from the above-noted groups, dropped its support for fear that it would suffer a loss of donations.

The ACS's decision has been heavily criticized by scientists and others interested in stem-cell research. They say that the society has become too oriented toward fund-raising and dares not risk offending any group that threatens its cash flow. Others offer broader criticisms. Many persons in the fields of nutrition and alternative medicine say that the society is far too focused on finding cures rather than on basic nutritional and lifestyle measures that could cut the incidence of the disease sharply and for far less money. They say that the society absorbs too much in the way of government money and voluntary donations—money that could go much farther on low-tech alternatives. Environmental groups also criticize the ACS for not doing more in the way of lobbying and public advocacy to expose environmental factors that lead to cancer, especially those involving corporate polluters. These critics say that the ACS's reticence is due to the fact that it receives millions of dollars in corporate donations annually.

FINANCIAL FACTS

While the ACS lobbies effectively on behalf of researchers and institutions involved in the fight against cancer, it maintains no political action committee (PAC) and does not donate to the campaign funds of candidates for public office. It has, however, donated small sums of so-called soft money to the coffers of the national Republican Party, as well as several state Republican parties.

The ACS is a very wealthy institution. Its total assets in 1998 stood at over $800 million. In that same year it took in roughly $677 million in donations and grants and spent roughly $570 million on administration costs and grants for research.

JAMES CIMENT

Bibliography

Bennett, James T. *CancerScam: Diversion of Federal Cancer Funds to Politics.* New Brunswick, NJ: Transaction, 1998.

Ross, Walter Stanford. *Crusade: The Official History of the American Cancer Society.* New York: Arbor House, 1987.

Stout, David. "The Tobacco Bill: The Senator; Though His Bill Is Dead, McCain May Be Enlivened." *New York Times,* June 18, 1998, p. 24.

Wade, Nicholas. "Cancer Society Quits Group on Cell Research." *New York Times,* July 29, 1999, p. 18.

AMERICAN CHIROPRACTIC ASSOCIATION

The American Chiropractic Association (ACA) is the largest interest group that represents practitioners of chiropractic medicine. Chiropractic is a therapeutic system developed in the late nineteenth century that treats pain and illness triggered by the decline of nerve functions. Doctors of chiropractic treat patients by manipulating and adjusting the spinal column, thus stimulating the musculoskeletal, neurological, and vascular systems of the body. Today, the practice is typically performed on persons who suffer from lower back pain. The American Chiropractic Association represents some 22,000 licensed chiropractic practitioners in the field.

According to the ACA, chiropractic is a philosophy, art, and science that is a legitimate branch of the "healing arts." Chiropractic practitioners consider the human body as an integrated organism and emphasize the physiological and biochemical aspects of the human body. In particular, the ACA defines the practice of chiropractic therapy as the "adjustment and manipulation of the articulations and adjacent tissues of the human body, particularly the spinal column."

The exclusion of medication and surgical procedures and the emphasis on the relationship between pain and treatment through adjusting and manipulating the spinal column are the defining differences between chiropractic and other branches of medicine and healthcare. Chiropractors emphasize the importance of healthy living through improving the patient's physiological, biochemical, and environmental conditions. The ACA's primary mission is to preserve, protect, improve, and promote the practice and to advance the professional and economic interests of chiropractic doctors. The organization seeks to advance the public appreciation of the profession through organizing members.

The organization's primary objectives are to maintain chiropractic as a separate and distinct health profession, to maintain and advance the philosophical principles and medical practices of chiropractic care, and to protect the professional interests of members of the association. The ACA believes that chiropractic doctors offer a unique health service that other doctors are unable to perform through other techniques and services.

The organization, headquartered in Arlington, Virginia, is directed by a board of governors, an executive committee, state delegates, councils, and commissions. To gain a doctorate in chiropractic, students are trained at accredited chiropractic colleges, which require four years of academic training and clinical experience.

HISTORY

The origins of chiropractic healthcare can be traced to ancient China. According to the ACA, the ancient Chinese practiced an early form of chiropractic some 4,700 years ago. According to the ACA, chiropractic gets its name from the Greek words "cheir" and "pratkkos," which together mean "done by hand." However, chiropractic has only been used in the West for about 100 years. In 1895, Daniel David Palmer of Davenport, Iowa, performed an adjustment on the spine of a hearing-impaired janitor who subsequently reported his hearing to have improved. The spinal manipulation technique subsequently became known as the Palmer Method.

During the twentieth century, chiropractic has struggled for stature and recognition as a legitimate profession. The ACA was founded in 1930 to standardize the education and training of chiropractic doctors and to promote the practice of chiropractic as a distinct form of healthcare. As the understanding of the physiology and biochemistry of the human body has advanced, the chiropractic field has also advanced to understand the spinal column's critical role in interfering with nerve function.

Over the years, the ACA has succeeded in promoting the importance of the field of chiropractic care among public and private healthcare providers. The

**American Chiropractic Association
Political Action Committee Contributions**

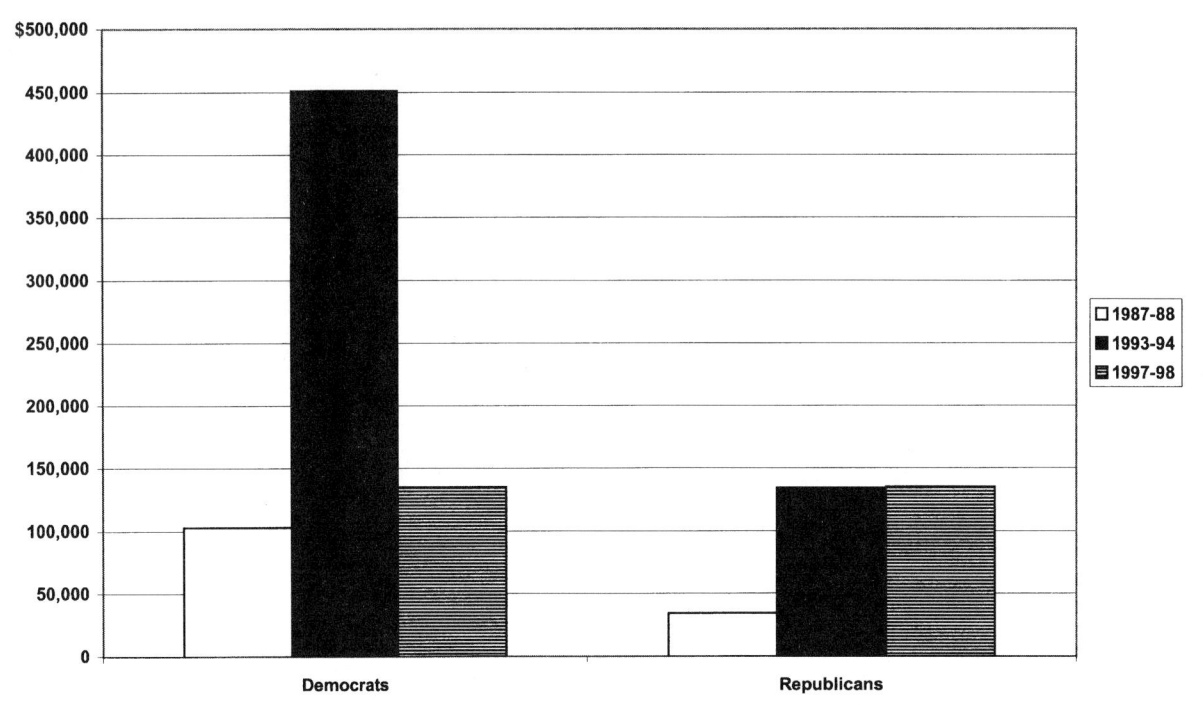

Data derived from official studies available from the Federal Election Commission, Washington, DC, 1987–1998.

profession has sustained a lot of criticism from mainstream health providers, including a boycott by the American Medical Association. A focal point of criticism has been insufficient training; however, the ACA emphasizes that chiropractors complete a minimum of six and an average of seven years of college and postgraduate study for their degree, including classroom, laboratory, and clinical experience. The organization notes that chiropractors receive some of the same coursework as medical doctors.

Today, the practice of chiropractic is licensed in all 50 states. A 1994 study found there to be an estimated 50,000 chiropractors in the United States. The ACA projects that with the aging of the population and the growth in awareness of the benefits of chiropractic care the number of chiropractors will double by the year 2010. In 1998, the *Annals of Internal Medicine* found that 80 percent of Americans with health insurance had plans that included chiropractic services. In part, the extensive growth in healthcare coverage for chiropractic care reflects the expansion in demand for health plans that cover the service. According to a recent study, about 46 percent of patients suffering lower back pain received care from doctors of chiropractic and about one out of five persons between the ages of 55 and 64 have used a chiropractor.

ACTIVITIES: CURRENT AND FUTURE

A primary concern of the ACA has been to establish the legitimacy of chiropractic treatment and medicine as an accepted medical specialization for the treatment of patients and to rebut efforts by the established medical profession to discredit the field. The ACA has sought to promote chiropractic as an accepted medical practice through research, public relations, media attention, and lobbying political officials. One motivation for the ACA's promotion of chiropractic as an acceptable form of medical care is to ensure that medical reimbursement coverage by private and public health benefit plans continues and expands.

The ACA's Department of Government Relations is responsible for directing the organization's political agenda. The department lobbies and delivers testimony to Congress to develop Medicare utilization guidelines that promote the use of chiropractic. The organization is seeking to eliminate Medicare's requirement that an x-ray be taken before chiropractic can be performed. Many chiropractors do not have x-ray facilities, because they believe that they can detect skeletal joint dislocation through direct spinal manipulation. By eliminating the x-ray requirement, more chiropractors can gain Medicare reimbursements for their services. To establish provisions that allow reimbursements for chiropractic care, the organization has lobbied members of Congress and has directly presented information to the Healthcare Financing Administration.

FINANCIAL FACTS

The ACA contributes money to federal politicians to further the professional and economic interests of its members. The organization is vitally concerned with maintaining and expanding Medicare and private health plan coverage for its services. In the last decade, the ACA has vastly expanded political action committee (PAC) contributions to members of Congress. Between the 1987–1988 and 1997–1998 election cycles, the ACA's PAC contributions to congressional candidates nearly doubled to $270,427. In the 1993–1994 election cycle—a period when the future of healthcare financing and coverage was under debate—the ACA increased its political contributions to $585,628, more than double the organization's contributions in the 1997–1998 election cycle. Between the 1993–1994 and 1997–1998 election cycles, the ACA's pattern of PAC contributions has shifted away from the Democratic Party. In 1993–1994, 77 percent of the organization's PAC contributions went to Democrats. After Republicans gained control of the House of Representatives, the ACA sharply reduced contributions to Democratic candidates. In the 1997–1998 cycle, the organization split its political contributions among candidates in the two major parties.

IMMANUEL NESS

Bibliography

American Chiropractic Association: www.amerchiro.org

Center for Responsive Politics: www.crp.org

Starr, Paul. *The Social Transformation of American Medicine.* New York: Basic Books, 1982.

Stevens, Rosemary. *In Sickness and in Wealth: American Hospitals in the Twentieth Century.* New York: Basic Books, 1989.

Zuckerman, Edward, ed. *The Almanac of Federal PACs, 1998–99.* Arlington, VA: Amward, 1998.

AMERICAN COLLEGE OF EMERGENCY PHYSICIANS

The American College of Emergency Physicians (ACEP), based in Washington, D.C., is a national organization representing the interests and concerns of emergency physicians. The organization, which represents nearly 20,000 emergency physicians in the United States and Canada, is primarily interested in increasing government and public support for emergency medical care and promoting the interests of emergency physicians. According to the ACEP, emergency care is a fundamental individual right that should be available to all people. A major concern of the organization is to promote and advance emergency medicine as a distinct medical field that requires education, research, and accreditation for physicians who specialize in it. Therefore, the organization believes that emergency physicians with specialized credentials should play a leading role in the planning, organization, and practice of emergency medicine. To further the interests of emergency physicians, the ACEP closely follows the rapidly changing health insurance and regulatory trends and develops policy positions and strategies to advocate on behalf of members in the profession.

The ACEP's monthly professional journal, *Annals of Emergency Medicine,* publishes original research, clinical reports, case studies, practice methods, techniques, and opinions in the field of emergency medicine. The organization also publishes *ACEP News*, which appears 11 times a year to provide regular news affecting the profession. The organization also holds an annual convention for members.

The ACEP is governed by a national council of at least 200 members drawn from the organization's 53 chartered chapters that represent members at the organization's annual meeting. The council is responsible—under the leadership and guidance of the ACEP's board of directors—for setting policy directives for the organization. Each year, the council democratically elects the ACEP's leadership, including the speaker and vice speaker of the council, the board of directors, secretary-treasurer, vice president, and president elect.

HISTORY

In 1968, physicians who were concerned with addressing the growing need for medical treatment standards, and professionally trained specialists in emergency care founded the ACEP. The ACEP's emergence and expansion as an organization has corresponded with the growth of hospital emergency rooms, in response to federal mandates for greater access to emergency care. Prior to the organization's formation, there were no established standards for emergency room treatment and care. The major goal of the ACEP in its first decade was to improve the education and specialized training of emergency physicians and accrediting "emergency medicine" as a legitimate medical specialty—a goal that was achieved in 1979. Since 1980, emergency physicians have been required to pass specialized examinations to be licensed to practice in the field. Moreover, emergency physicians are required to complete 150 hours of training every three years to maintain their license to practice emergency medicine. To meet the requirement for continued education and training, the ACEP offers specialized clinical and practice management courses in emergency medicine. In addition, through the Emergency Medicine Foundation, founded in 1973, the organization also provides grants for emergency medicine education and research.

ACTIVITIES: CURRENT AND FUTURE

The organization considers that the growth of managed healthcare and rigorous restrictions on healthcare fi-

**American College of Emergency Physicians
Political Action Committee Contributions**

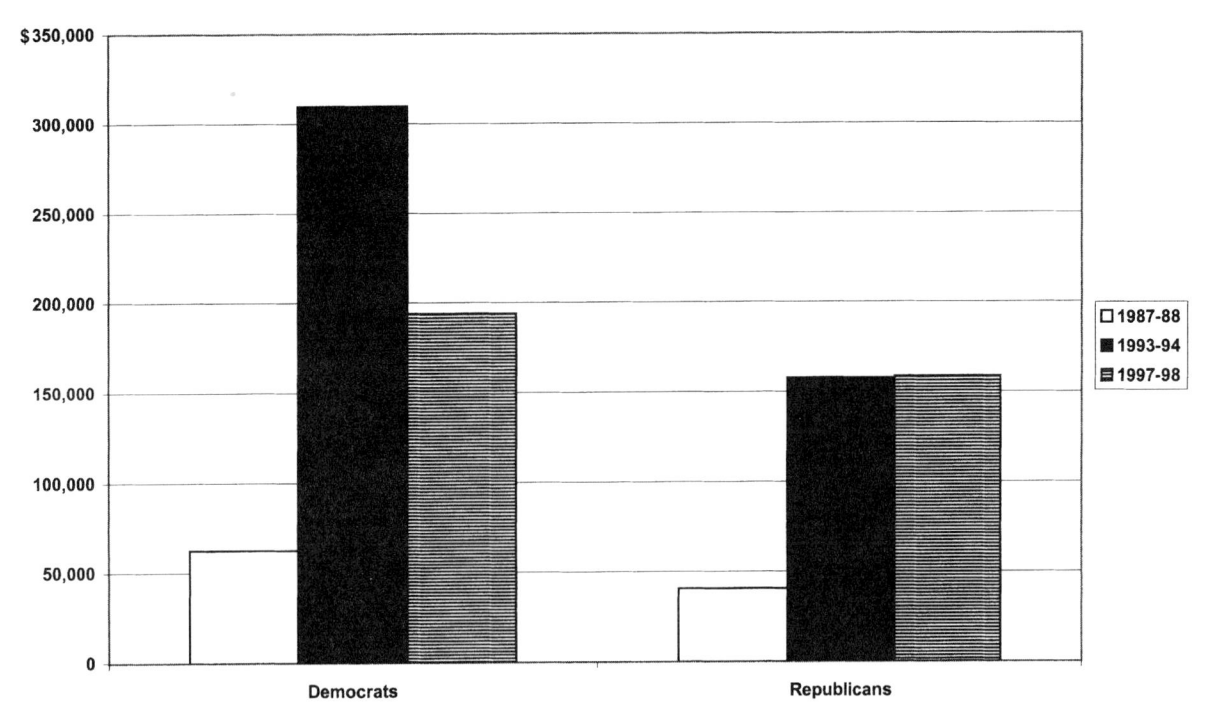

Data derived from official studies available from the Federal Election Commission, Washington, DC, 1987–1998.

nancing by third-party health insurers potentially threatens necessary funding for the continuation of quality emergency medicine in the nation's hospitals and medical facilities. The organization also opposes other government limitations on emergency healthcare coverage. The organization does not believe that emergency medical care should be jeopardized by reduced medical funding and thinks that emergency physicians should be responsible for medical decisions, rather than bureaucrats who administer managed care plans. In its attempt to promote the ethical practice of emergency medicine, the ACEP lobbies the government to maintain standards for third-party financing of emergency procedures.

To support physicians in advancing the practice of emergency medicine, the ACEP promotes changes and guidelines that improve the practice environment. The organization seeks to provide support for emergency training programs and to educate the public about the importance of emergency medicine. To advance the organization's policy agenda on a federal level, the ACEP has developed a comprehensive and well-funded advocacy program in Washington, D.C.

The organization is actively involved in public health education, injury prevention, and safety measures that prevent health emergencies; to this end, it releases periodic reports to physicians, the press, and other organizations. For example, the ACEP recently issued a report on automobile safety precautions. Due to the large number of Americans who suffer injuries or die in automobile accidents, the organization seeks to promote safe driving and automobile use among the public. One recent concern is the safe use of airbags, which have been found to pose a serious danger to young children when airbags are activated in accidents. In addition, the organization also recommends motorists to always use automobile safety belts.

FINANCIAL FACTS

The ACEP's Public Affairs Committee operates in Washington, D.C., to provide public information and to lobby Congress and appeal to federal government executive departments and agencies on behalf of the profession. The organization is a leading political campaign contributor for congressional candidates. Between the 1987–1988 and 1997–1998 election cycles, the organization's political contributions have expanded more than three times, from $105,875 to $352,675, reflecting the overall growth of political action committee (PAC) contributions in the healthcare field. In the 1993–1994 election cycle, contributions swelled to $468,650 due to the ACEP's concern with defending the interests of emergency medicine in the healthcare reform debate. Although the organization continues to contribute a majority of its PAC contributions to Democrats, following the emergence of a Republican majority in the House of Representatives in 1995, the ACEP has begun to reduce contributions to Democratic candidates; between the 1993–1994 election cycle and the 1997–1998 election cycle, the ACEP's political campaign contributions to Republicans have increased from 34 percent of its total contributions to 45 percent.

IMMANUEL NESS AND JAMES CIMENT

Bibliography

American College of Emergency Physicians: www.accp.org

Center for Responsive Politics web site: www.crp.org.

Navarro, Vicente. *The Politics of Health Policy: The U.S. Reforms, 1980–1994.* Oxford: Blackwell, 1994.

Stevens, Rosemary. *In Sickness and in Wealth: American Hospitals in the Twentieth Century.* New York: Basic Books, 1989.

Zuckerman, Edward, ed. *The Almanac of Federal PACs, 1998–99.* Arlington, VA: Amward, 1998.

AMERICAN DIETETIC ASSOCIATION

With over 70,000 members—including dieticians, food service managers, educators, nutrition researchers, and other professionals in the field of nutrition sciences and services—the American Dietetic Association (ADA) is America's largest professional association in the field of nutrition and diet.

According to ADA spokespersons and literature, the organization is dedicated to enforcing professional standards in the field of nutrition and dietetics, promoting a healthier diet for all Americans, working with government to ensure rigorous enforcement of regulations concerning diet and nutrition, and working with the private sector—including food manufacturers, manufacturers of food, nutritional, and dietary supplements; food wholesalers and retailers; and restaurateurs—to assure that Americans get proper nutrition and to ensure that all advertised dietary claims made by industry are honest and accurate. And, of course, the ADA vigorously protects and promotes the interests of its own members; for example, it works to ensure that the services of dieticians, nutritionists, and other dietary professionals are included in all government and private-sector health insurance programs. The organization also serves to bring the latest information on dietetic and nutritional breakthroughs to its members. To that end, it publishes the *Journal of the American Dietetic Association* (*JADA*), which contains studies on the latest research in the field of dietetic and nutritional sciences. Most of these articles are geared to scholars and professionals.

Aside from working with government and industry, the ADA also maintains a strong public outreach program concerning dietary and nutrition issues. In 1990, the organization founded the National Center for Nutrition and Dietetics (NCND). A public education center, the NCND offers information on nutrition, diet, and other health issues through a variety of programs and services, including programs for schools and senior centers. The NCND maintains a Nutrition InfoCenter and Consumer Nutrition Hotline, which provides information on diet and nutrition as well referrals for ADA members in the caller's area. More recently, the ADA established a presence on the World Wide Web. Its web site (www.eatright.org) offers constantly updated information on the organization and on dietary issues for professionals as well as providing dietary and nutritional tips for the public.

HISTORY

The origins of the ADA go back to 1899, when a number of members of the American Home Economics Association (AHEA) formed a subgroup that specialized in dietetics. In 1917, this subgroup decided to break with the AHEA to form the ADA, in order to help parents and food providers make healthier food choices for themselves, their families, and their customers. At the same time, the organization was also founded to help promote the idea of dietary and nutritional research as a legitimate science and dieticians and nutritionists as serious practitioners worthy of the public's respect. Indeed, the founding of the ADA occurred during the Progressive Era, a time when many professionals in health and other fields were attempting to establish their credentials through the creation of professional organizations. The Progressive Era was also a time of burgeoning public concern over the content of their diets. Just 11 years earlier, Upton Sinclair had published his best-selling exposé of the meatpacking industry—*The Jungle*—which helped push the federal government to establish the Food and Drug Administration to protect Americans from tainted food and dangerous drugs.

More recently, the ADA has attempted to update its mission with a five-year plan, culminating in the year 2000, called "Creating the Future." According to the ADA, the plan has three components: to seek federal and private-sector insurance reimbursements for nutritional services, to make sure its members continue to

**American Dietetic Association
Political Action Committee Contributions**

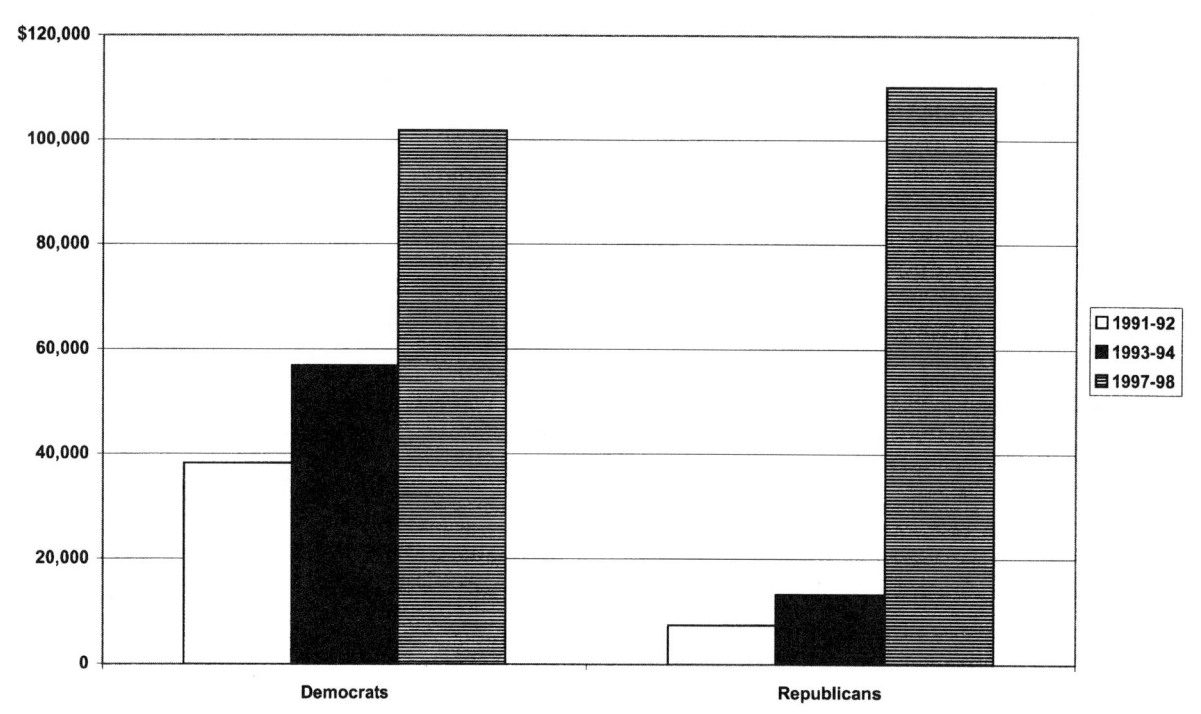

□ 1991-92
■ 1993-94
☰ 1997-98

Data derived from official studies available from the Federal Election Commission, Washington, DC, 1987–1998.

play an important role in a rapidly changing health and health maintenance environment, and to promote their message that ADA members are the nation's most important sources of nutritional and dietary information, guidance, and services.

ACTIVITIES: CURRENT AND FUTURE

Perhaps the most important legislative issue confronting the ADA and its members in the year 2000 and following years is Medicare and Medicaid reform. (Medicare is the federal program that provides medical care for the elderly and the disabled; Medicaid is a federal program—largely state adminstered—that provides medical care for the poor.) Specifically, the ADA wants to ensure that nutrition services are adequately covered under Medicare, and the organization has persuaded over 200 members of Congress to back the Medicare Medical Nutrition Therapy Act. (Medical nutrition therapy refers to a comprehensive dietary and nutrition program administered by a registered dietician or other nutrition professional.)

In particular, the ADA wants to ensure that outpatient nutritional services are covered since more and more Medicare and private-sector coverage is emphasizing outpatient treatment as a way to fight rising medical costs. As ADA president Ann Gallagher noted, "The evidence is overwhelming that medical nutrition therapy will both save money and improve the quality of care for Medicare beneficiaries." And ADA lobbyists point out that studies show that the costs of extending Medicare coverage to include outpatient nutritional services are vastly offset by the savings in other forms of treatment later. A study in *JADA* cites potential savings of $370 million over six years between 1998 and 2004, if medical nutrition therapy was included under Medicare. Currently, reimbursement for nutritional services is arbitrary and uncertain under both Medicare and private insurers. The ADA hopes that inclusion under Medicare will help push private insurers into offering reimbursements to nutrition professionals.

On a related issue, the ADA is also trying to ensure that nutritional services are covered by Medicaid. But with increasingly more of Medicaid's administration being transferred to the states, this means a lobbying effort in 50 different political arenas. To help meet the challenge, the national ADA is offering assistance and shifting resources to state affiliates. Also, at the state level, the ADA is working with the last 11 states that have not established licensing credentials for dieticians and nutritionists to do so.

While Medicare, Medicaid, and licensing issues are of most direct concern to ADA members, the organization is also lobbying for more general public health issues. Specifically, the ADA is trying to persuade the federal government to update its dietary guidelines, currently known as Recommended Daily Allowances (RDAs). The ADA would like to see the government utilize a system of Dietary Reference Intakes (DRIs). Replacing the one-dimensional RDAs, the new system would include measures of adequate intake, estimated average requirement, tolerable upper intake level, as well as something equivalent to the old RDAs.

According to the ADA, the RDAs are fine for the average layperson and will continue in some new guise on all labels, but they have come to serve a number of health and scientific roles for which they are inadequate. The new DRIs will provide different kinds of information suitable to both laypersons and professionals.

On a more controversial nutritional issue, the ADA supports irradiation of food in principle, but insists that it be labeled and that labels not be misleading. (Irradiation is a method of food preservation that, as its name implies, involves subjecting perishable food items to doses of radiation. While the food processing industry says irradiation is entirely safe and does not leave any radiation in food, opponents—including many organic food activists—say that irradiation drains food of important nutriments. In addition, environmentalists worry about radiation leakages from equipment used to irradiate food.) On the issue of labeling irradiated food, the ADA comes out in opposition to food processing interests. Most recently, the ADA found itself in opposition to the Food Marketing Institute over the latter's "Free of E. Coli" label for irradiated meat products. The ADA says that irradiation does not guarantee meats will be free of E. coli, since they can become contaminated between the time the meat is irradiated and the time it is served by or to the consumer.

FINANCIAL FACTS

Until the last election cycle, the ADA had been a modest, but growing, contributor of campaign funds to congressional and presidential candidates from both parties. In the 1987–1988 election cycle—which included both presidential and congressional elections—the ADA donated $30,250 to candidates from both parties. By the 1993–1994 election cycle—which was for Congress only—the ADA was giving $70,300 to both parties. But in the 1997–1998 election cycle—again, a congressional election only—the ADA gave $212,118, over seven times more than 10 years earlier. At the same time, the proportions given to Democrats and Republicans have shifted, with increasing amounts of money going to the latter. For example, in the 1993–1994 election cycle, $57,100—or fully 81 percent—of the ADA's donations went to Democratic candidates. But four years later, $101,300—or just 44 percent—went to Democrats.

JAMES CIMENT AND IMMANUEL NESS

Bibliography

"ADA Plans for Flurry of State Legislative Action in 1990–2000." *Journal of the American Dietetic Association* 99, no. 2 (February 1999): 162.

Cassell, Jo Anne. *Carry the Flame: The History of the American Dietetic Association.* Chicago: The American Dietetic Association, 1990.

Coulston, Ann M. "Shaping Health Policy, Influencing Policy Makers." *Journal of the American Dietetic Association* 99, no. 3 (March 1999): 276.

Erickson-Weerts, Sally. "Past, Present, and Future Perspectives of Dietetics Practice." *Journal of the American Dietetic Association* 99, no. 3 (March 1999): 291.

"Food Industry Agrees to Use Radura Logo for Irradiated Meat." *Food Labeling News,* May 5, 1999.

Kennedy, Rachael. "New Dietary Standards Supplement Daily Guides." *Cox News Service,* July 27, 1999.

"Medical Reimbursement for Nutrition Help." *PR Newswire,* July 28, 1999.

"Save Dollars and Lives, Says American Dietetic Association." *PR Newswire,* March 18, 1999.

AMERICAN FEDERATION FOR AIDS RESEARCH

As the leading nonprofit organization dedicated to promoting research on AIDS (acquired immunodeficiency syndrome) and HIV (human immunodeficiency virus), the American Federation for AIDS Research (AmFAR) lobbies vigorously to get more federal funding for research for the prevention, treatment, and possible cure for AIDS. The organization also claims that its advocacy mission is to promote "sound AIDS-related public policy." Many of the most important and respected AIDS researchers and public health experts are represented on AmFAR's board and its advisory committees.

As AmFAR's president Arthur J. Amman expressed it, the federation is "a powerful advocate for sound, national AIDS-related public policies, appropriate increases in federal appropriations, and protection of the rights of people with HIV/AIDS." Amman adds that as a public advocacy group, AmFAR works with other national organizations, employing "a variety of strategies to accomplish its objectives, including testifying before congressional committees, meeting and working with key legislators and policy-makers, expressing opinions and policy positions publicly, and gaining the support of the scientific community on policy issues."

Aside from lobbying the federal government for more AIDS research money, the federation also offers funding of its own for AIDS research. Over the past 15 years, AmFAR has disbursed more than $155 million—mostly in the form of grants—to over 1,750 research teams working nationally and internationally toward improved prevention, diagnosis, treatment, and potential vaccines and cures for HIV/AIDS.

Arguing that the AIDS crisis with its tens of thousands of dying sufferers warranted unorthodox measures, AmFAR pioneered and continues to be active in the promotion of its Community-Based Clinical Trials (CBCT) program, which utilizes experimental HIV/AIDS treatment facilities in community settings, so that research and treatment can proceed hand in hand. Overall, more than 35,000 persons have participated in the CBCT program, and according to AmFAR, the program has led to numerous breakthroughs in drug therapies for people living with AIDS/HIV.

AmFAR is also very active in the educational arena and has sponsored scientific conferences on the latest developments in AIDS therapies, training seminars for healthcare practitioners in the treatment of people with AIDS/HIV, classes for people with AIDS/HIV on methods to control their disease and change their lifestyle to improve their survival odds, and forums for the general public to dispel common myths and fears about AIDS/HIV and people living with AIDS/HIV.

HISTORY

AmFAR was founded in 1985, as the incidence of AIDS infection and mortality reached epidemic proportions among the nation's gay and intravenous-drug-user populations. In 1988, it pioneered a new form of community-based medical research, eventually establishing 24 community-based research centers throughout the country. According to AmFAR, community-based research—with more than $30 million of AmFAR funding—has led to the approval by the Food and Drug Administration (FDA) of three compounds for the prevention and treatment of several AIDS-related illnesses. Over the years, the organization claims, these community-based sites have become self-sufficient research centers, capable of winning grants from the government and industry.

ACTIVITIES: CURRENT AND FUTURE

Over the past few years, AmFAR has focused its public policy program on three key issues: increasing funding for the National Institutes of Health AIDS/HIV research programs, revising the FDA's approval process for AIDS/HIV drugs and drug therapies, and lifting the ban on federal funding of needle exchange programs.

In 1999, AmFAR lobbied Congress to increase funding for the National Institutes of Health (NIH) by 15 percent for the coming fiscal year. Pointing out that the disease has not disappeared and that tens of thousands of new cases occur in the United States each year, AmFAR argues that AIDS "research must be a part of a broad, well-funded overall research effort conducted by the NIH." Moreover, say AmFAR lobbyists, ongoing research has led to enormous breakthroughs toward the prevention, diagnosis, treatment, and even cure of HIV/AIDS and HIV/AIDS-related diseases; increased funding will only speed up the process and lead, perhaps, to a cure in the not-too-distant future.

AmFAR has also been active in pressuring the administration of President Bill Clinton to drop the current ban on federal funding for needle exchange programs. These programs offer intravenous drug users a safe and secure place to exchange used needles for clean ones. Numerous officials in the Clinton administration, including Barry McCaffrey (the so-called drug czar who oversees federal drug policy), opposed lifting such a ban, saying that it would encourage intravenous drug use and would send the wrong message to the nation's young people—that is, that the federal government condones intravenous drug abuse. But AmFAR and other advocates point out that sharing needles is among the prime causes of HIV transmission in the United States today, accounting for nearly one-half of all AIDS cases.

In addition, AmFAR is strongly opposed to currently considered legislation in the House of Representatives that would threaten local and state needle exchange programs. Indeed, in 1998, over AmFAR objections, Congress banned all needle exchange programs in Washington, D.C. As Amman declared in testimony before a House Committee on Health and Human Services, "Scientific research shows that needle exchange programs reduce HIV infections, do not lead to increased drug use, and are cost effective."

AmFAR has also encouraged reforms in the FDA's drug approval process, arguing that drugs for life-threatening diseases need to be given different priority than drugs for routine or treatable illnesses. AmFAR has insisted that such drugs require different risk-benefit calculations and should be approved much more quickly than other drugs. Among the measures that AmFAR would like to see the FDA adopt are preapproval access to experimental drugs that show reasonable safety and promise of efficacy, encouragement to manufacturers to provide early access to promising therapies, relaxation of the approval process for new uses of drugs that are currently on the market, the assurance that pharmaceutical applications to the federal government to market new drugs include data for all populations that are likely to use such drugs, including women, racial minorities, older Americans, or children. Overall, AmFAR says the FDA should maintain its current vigorous approach to drug approval, but add a certain flexibility in the area of drugs needed for potentially fatal diseases such as HIV/AIDS.

On a related issue of drug development, AmFAR has been increasing its criticism of a Clinton administration policy that threatens sanctions against countries that allegedly violate U.S. and international law by producing generic versions of drugs that hold U.S. patents. Specifically, AmFAR has denounced the administration for threatening to impose stiff sanctions against metal imports from South Africa in retaliation for that country's threat to license local companies to produce HIV/AIDS drugs that are currently under patents held by major American pharmaceutical companies. By producing these drugs generically, South Africa can lower the price of the treatments to a level that more people in its AIDS-ravaged population can afford. Drug companies and the Clinton administration argue that this will set an unfortunate precedent that will undermine patents and reduce the willingness of drug companies to invest in expensive and necessary research. According to AmFAR, this is not only an immoral position but a misleading one, since most funding into drug research is paid for by the federal government, universities, and foundations.

FINANCIAL FACTS

While the AmFAR lobbies effectively on behalf of researchers and institutions involved in the fight against HIV/AIDS, it maintains no political action committee (PAC) and does not donate to the campaign funds of candidates for public office. AmFAR spends approximately $10 million financing research into the diagnosis, treatment, and cure of HIV/AIDS and HIV/AIDS-related diseases.

JAMES CIMENT AND IMMANUEL NESS

Bibliography

House Appropriations Committee. Prepared Statement of Allan Rosenfield, M.D., Dean, Columbia University, Joseph L. Mailman School of Public Health. *Federal News Service,* April 15, 1999.

House Committee on Health and Human Services. Testimony of Arthur J. Amman, President of the American Foundation for AIDS Research. February 3, 1998.

Pugh, Clifford. "Activist Says AIDS Battle Far from Over." *Houston Chronicle,* March 11, 1999, p. 1.

AMERICAN HEALTHCARE ASSOCIATION

The American Healthcare Association (AHCA) is the trade organizaion representing the long-term healthcare industry, more popularly known as the nursing home industry. A federation of 50 state organizations, the AHCA includes nearly 12,000 member groups, including nonprofit and for-profit assisted living facilities, nursing facilities, and sub-acute care providers. This represents just over 70 percent of the nearly 17,000 such institutions across the country. Altogether, AHCA member groups care for more than 1 million elderly and disabled individuals in the United States.

The AHCA sees its mission as representing the long-term care community to the nation at large—to government, business leaders, and the general public. While the association maintains a major presence as a lobbying group in the nation's state capitals (all nursing home facilities and administrators are licensed by state regulatory agencies) and Washington, D.C., it is also involved in research into the industry and its needs, as well as education for the public, for nursing home patients, and nursing home staff and administrators. With nursing home abuses in the media of late and with the industry under increasing public and government scrutiny, the AHCA say it has expanded its efforts to improve professionalism and ethical behavior among all who provide long-term care (LTC).

HISTORY

The history of nursing homes in the United States goes back to the turn of the century, when many such facilities grew out of more informal boarding houses for the elderly and disabled. By the 1920s, the health departments of various states began to develop licensing programs for such facilities.

In 1945, a group of nine nursing facility administrators met in Indianapolis to discuss the possibility of establishing a national organization for their industry. At this meeting, they decided to hold a larger conference for nursing home administrators throughout the Midwest. Two such conferences were held in 1948 and 1949, and the latter meeting—held in Toledo, Ohio—led to the formation of the American Association of Nursing Homes (AANH).

At that meeting, the organizers of the AANH laid out the tenets of their association, tenets which the AHCA maintains are still at the heart of the organization's mission: "to improve the standards of service and administration of member nursing homes; to secure and merit public and official recognition and approval of the work of nursing homes; and to adopt and promote programs of education, legislation, better understanding, and mutual cooperation.

In November 1952, the AANH began publishing its journal for the trade, the *American Association of Nursing Homes Journal*. In 1975, the AANH changed the name of its organization to the American Healthcare Association, to reflect the many changes in the nursing home industry and the many different kinds of long-term care facilities the association represented.

ACTIVITIES: CURRENT AND FUTURE

Arguably, the most important issue that the American Healthcare Association is currently addressing—and will continue to address into the foreseeable future—is Medicare reform. Indeed, the AHCA has recently established the ad hoc "Coalition to Fix Medicare Now." The coalition lobbies the federal government to increase the value of Medicare payments that go to nursing homes and other long-term care facilities. Among the other members of the coalition are the Occupational Therapy Association and the National Association for the Support of Long-Term Care. The coalition is also planning a major public relations effort aimed at building grassroots support to include long-term care coverage under Medicare. According to a study conducted by the MetLife Insurance Corporation, long-term care issues cost employers $29 billion annually in time and productivity lost. Indeed, two out of three persons of the baby boom generation told pollsters that they are not prepared to deal with the costs connected with their own long-term care coverage. Annual costs of a nursing home stay currently average $41,000 annually and are expected to climb to about $100,000 in the next 30 years.

The administration of President Bill Clinton has recently proposed in its year 2000 budget a provision that would allow federal workers and their families to buy long-term care as part of their benefits package. The AHCA supports this Clinton initiative, but would also like to see it expanded. Long-term care is covered by Medicaid but not by Medicare. According to the association, most Americans are not aware that long-term care is not covered by Medicare and that people have to be reduced to poverty—at which point they are eligible to receive Medicaid (the federal government's healthcare plan for the poor)—before they can get government support for their long-term care. While the AHCA is not certain whether it supports placing long-term care within the package of Medicare benefits, it does support tax credits for long-term care.

On a related issue, the AHCA is urging both Congress and the Clinton administration to address healthcare issues as they consider long-term Social Security reform. As AHCA President Paul Willging noted before Congress in 1998, "How we pay for the long-term healthcare bills of our nation's retirees is the critical issue that sits on the doorstep of . . . Congress as the baby boom generation ages." According to the AHCA, only 25 percent of the baby boom generation can afford private nursing facility care and only 1 percent has purchased long-term healthcare insurance. The AHCA says it would like to see any Social Security reform take into account the costs of LTC.

Meanwhile, on more immediate issues, the AHCA has been less than enamored with a recent "antidumping" bill that President Clinton signed into law. The bill makes it illegal for nursing homes to evict Medicaid patients. While the law does not apply to homes that do not participate in Medicaid, it requires such homes to warn incoming residents that once their assets run out and they become eligible for Medicaid they may be forced to leave. In an effort to protect its already tarnished public image, the AHCA half-heartedly endorsed the legislation but warned that it would lead to more nursing homes opting out of Medicaid, since the program offered inadequate payments for LTC.

Part of that tarnished image has come from a series of fraud and abuse cases within the LTC industry that have recently come to light and have prompted Congress to consider two separate antifraud bills and the Department of Health and Human Services to consider a new set of False Claims Act guidelines. While the AHCA has supported the legislation, it does not want to pay for investigations called for by the currently comtemplated laws and would like to see any new guidelines or legislation cover all healthcare providers, including hospitals and health maintenance organizations.

Meanwhile, a General Accounting Office (GAO) report has come out criticizing both state and federal regulators for their slow response to complaints against nursing homes and other LTC providers. But the AHCA says the GAO and Congress are making too big a deal of this. As an association spokesperson declared, government inspectors often focus their attention on "technical violations posing no jeopardy to residents." The AHCA also complains that regulators are too adversarial and prefer to expose negligent homes rather than work with them to address the complaints. Still, the AHCA says it supports many of the recommendations in the report, but says that there are too many catchall categories in the regulations. For example, it notes that a lot of minor technical violations are catalogued under the heading "severe deficiencies." Saying that the system is broken, the AHCA would like to see regulations that address specific problems with specific solutions, so that LTC providers can bring themselves up to code.

A statement issued by the AHCA declared: "the current federal inspection system has all the trademarks of a bureaucratic government program out of control. Inspectors are prohibited from working with facilities to solve problems. Although they are not doctors themselves, inspectors have penalized facilities for following the orders and treatment plans of physicians." The AHCA complains that inspectors have closed down facilities for technical violations without consulting residents and families. The AHCA says it wants to set up a more collaborative relationship with government regulators. Given the many stories of abuse that have come out of nursing homes in recent years, critics of the industry say that a softer regulatory approach is precisely what LTC patients do not need.

FINANCIAL FACTS

The AHCA has been a massive donor of campaign funds to candidates of both parties in recent years. Moreover, the overall amounts of contributions have risen steadily since the late 1980s. In the 1987–1988 election cycle—which included campaigns for both Congress and the presidency—the AHCA donated a total of $253,528 to candidates. In the 1993–1994 election cycle—a congressional election only (normally a time when donations fall off somewhat)—the amounts given by the AHCA to both parties increased substantially to $475,080, a rise of 187 percent. In the 1997–1998 election cycle, the amount had increased to $722,580, an increase of 152 percent. Generally, the AHCA has donated somewhat more to Democrats than to Republicans. In the 1987–1988 election cycle, Democratic candidates for Congress and the presidency received $155,564, or 60 percent of the total donated by the AHCA. In the 1993–1994 election cycle, the AHCA gave $305,030 to Democrats, or 64 percent of the total. However, in the 1997–1998 election cycle, the Republicans had the edge, receiving $383,767—or 53 percent—of the funds donated by the AHCA.

JAMES CIMENT AND IMMANUEL NESS

Bibliography

Gardner, Jonathan. "Nursing Home Skirmish: Battle over Cost-Based Reimbursements Splits Industry." *Modern Healthcare,* October 26, 1998.

Gemignani, Janet. "Weighing in on LTC Insurance; Long-term Care." *Business and Health,* May 1, 1999.

Gubrium, Jaber F. *Living and Dying at Murray Manor.* Charlottesville: University Press of Virginia, 1997.

Hallan, Kristen. "Government Looks at Nursing Home Fraud." *Modern Healthcare,* February 22, 1999.

Jennings, Marian, ed. *Financing Long-Term Care.* Frederick, MD: Aspen, 1991.

"Lobbying: AHA to Spend $2 Million for Budget Relief." *Health Line,* August 6, 1999.

"Long-Term Care: A Call for Inclusion in Social Security Debate." *Health Line,* November 20, 1998.

"Long-Term Care: AHCA Calls for Reforms." *Health Line,* March 24, 1999.

"Medicare Reform: New Benefits Suggested." *Health Line,* September 9, 1998.

"Nursing Homes: Clinton Signs Antidumping Bill." *Health Line,* March 26, 1999.

"Nursing Homes: GAO Criticizes Complaint Response." *Health Line,* March 23, 1999.

AMERICAN HEART ASSOCIATION

With 4.2 million paying members—known as "volunteers"—the American Heart Association (AHA) is the largest organization in the United States dedicated to fighting cardiovascular diseases and strokes. These related illnesses are the number-one killer of Americans and cause 1 million deaths annually.

A not-for-profit organization that receives the bulk of its funding from private and corporate sponsors—as well as the dues of its millions of members—the association emphasizes public and professional education, lobbying private insurance providers and governmental bodies charged with the nation's healthcare, and research into the diagnosis, treatment, and cure of cardiovascular disease, strokes, and other related diseases.

Headquartered in Dallas, Texas, the AHA maintains a large lobbying group in Washington, D.C. AHA lobbyists in Washington—in conjunction with the AHA's 15 affiliates around the country—coordinate and implement a national program for legislative and regulatory change. Much of this advocacy work involves lobbying for increased federal funding for public education and scientific research. The AHA makes a special point of coordinating its advocacy work in Washington with other interested organizations, including other health associations, insurers, healthcare professional groups, and hospital associations. Each fall the AHA creates an agenda for public policy that is used to guide the activities of its Office of Communications and Advocacy and to serve as a guide for state, local, and community-based advocacy efforts.

In recent years, the AHA Delegate Assembly—the main policy-making group within the organization—has taken on the goal of reducing the risk and incidence of coronary heart disease and stroke by 25 percent by the year 2008. In addition, the AHA is working to double federal funding for heart disease research at the National Institutes of Health by 2004. In addition, it is working to increase funding for the Department of Veterans Affairs—which conducts extensive research on cardiovascular disease and strokes—and the Agency for Healthcare Policy Research. According to the association, its public policy agenda falls into four main categories: research, health promotion and disease prevention, quality and availability of care, and charitable organizations.

To better promote public and professional education, improve medical techniques, and further research in the field, the AHA maintains a number of scientific councils dedicated to different aspects of heart disease and stroke, such as arteriosclerosis, thrombosis, and vascular biology; cardiopulmonary and critical care; cardiovascular nursing; cardiothoracic and vascular surgery; clinical cardiology; high blood pressure research; stroke; basic science; cardiovascular disease in the young; cardiovascular radiology; circulation; epidemiology and prevention; and kidney complications in cardiovascular diseases. Members on these various councils include physicians, researchers, and university, medical school, and hospital administrators.

HISTORY

Founded in 1924 by six New York City cardiologists, the AHA was initially for physicians and scientists only. In 1948, however, it opened its membership to nonmedical volunteers, in the hopes that these members could help raise the nation's consciousness about heart disease. Noting that there was little medical science could do in the way of treatment at the time, it was hoped that by furthering public education the organization could cut down on the incidence of cardiovascular disease and strokes.

In 1956, the AHA issued its first warnings about the dangers of smoking and its effect on heart disease, followed the next year by the first public warnings about the role of dietary fat in the promotion of cardiovascular ailments. From the 1960s through the 1980s, AHA members helped fund scientific research that led to major advances in surgical treatment, including coronary artery bypass operations, heart transplants, artificial hearts, and internal defibrillators. In recent years, the AHA has funded research into clot-busting drugs and gene therapy. Clot-busting drugs, which lessen the damage of heart attacks, were first administered in the early 1990s.

ACTIVITIES: CURRENT AND FUTURE

Arguably the single most important and immediate issue facing the AHA is federal tobacco legislation. Having been one of the first major organizations to warn the public about the dangers of smoking, the AHA has, in recent years, focused its efforts on using federal legislation and the courts to reduce the incidence of smoking in the United States. Over the past few years, the AHA has come out in favor of higher taxes on cigarettes, increased legal liability for tobacco companies facing lawsuits by individuals seeking damages and states seeking settlements to cover the healthcare costs they incur because of smoking, and stricter limits on tobacco advertising, particulary advertising that is directed at children and adolescents.

Among the current measures, the AHA supports significant price increases on tobacco products through taxation; the prohibition on tobacco marketing and advertising, particularly advertisements and promotions that target women, children, and minorities; bans on smoking in public places; "significant, meaningful penalties" on the tobacco industry for failure to reach targets for reduction of tobacco use among youth; full Food and Drug Administration (FDA) authority over the manufacture, sale, distribution, labeling, and promotion of tobacco; significant funding for public health programs, including smoking cessation, counteradvertising, and state and local initiatives; funding for international tobacco control initiatives that prohibit U.S. government activities that would facilitate marketing tobacco products overseas; and an end to all government financial support for the growth, promotion, and marketing of tobacco, while supporting the creation of programs to assist farmers and tobacco-growing regions in developing economic alternatives to tobacco.

Citing diet as the second most important preventable cause of heart disease after smoking, the AHA has asked the FDA to prohibit food manufacturing companies from making health claims for their foods unless the claims originate from the "acceptable authoritative statement of a scientific body and that they be based on significant scientific agreement." In particular, the AHA pushed for a number of rules set forth by the FDA in June 1999 that prohibit the use of health claims made by food manufacturers regarding vitamins A, C, and E; beta-carotene; B-complex vitamins; garlic; omega-3 fatty acids; calcium (on bone density); vitamin K (on proper blood clotting and bone health); chromium (on glucose intolerance); and zinc (on wound healing).

As a major funder of scientific research, the AHA has argued in favor of rational use and humane treatment of laboratory animals in cardiovascular research and opposes legislation and regulations that would reduce medically necessary cardiovascular disease and stroke research or limitations that would substantially increase cost.

FINANCIAL FACTS

While the AHA lobbies effectively on behalf of researchers and institutions involved in the fight against cardiovascular disease and strokes, it maintains no political action committee (PAC) and does not donate to the campaign funds of candidates for public office.

At the same time, the AHA is an organization that collects and disburses large amounts of money for governmental advocacy, as well as research and public education. In the 1997–1998 fiscal years, for example, the AHA had a record-setting income of $429.6 million. During that same period, it spent $127 million on research, $92.3 million on public health education, $43.1 million on professional education, $49.5 million on community outreach and education, and another $81.3 million on administrative overhead and fund-raising.

JAMES CIMENT AND IMMANUEL NESS

Bibliography

"Cereal and Bread Manufacturers Allowed 'Healthy' Advertisements by FDA." *Food & Drink Weekly,* July 12, 1999.

"FDA Asked for Labeling Health Claim for Lowfat Dairy Products." *BP Report,* August 12, 1998.

"Health Associations, Consumer Group Support FDA Rules Prohibiting Food Health Claims." *Food Labeling News,* September 23, 1998.

"Health Groups Hoping to Fire Up Another Tobacco Debate." *National Journal's CongressDaily,* September 23, 1998.

"Heart Disease Treatment Is Gaining More Ground than Prevention." *Health Letter on the CDC,* October 12, 1998.

"Of Capitol Hill War Rooms, Holy and Otherwise." *National Journal's CongressDaily,* June 10, 1998.

AMERICAN HOSPITAL ASSOCIATION

The American Hospital Associaton (AHA) is the national trade association for all forms of hospitals in the United States. In addition, the AHA represents healthcare networks and hospital administrators. Altogether, the association—with its main headquarters in Chicago and its lobbying arm in Washington, D.C.—represents nearly 5,000 hospitals and other healthcare-providing institutions, a total of some 40,000 hospital administrators.

A primary activity of the AHA is advocacy. The association maintains a powerful voice in Washington that works to ensure the needs and wants of its member hospitals are represented both in Congress and in the various regulatory agencies of the executive branch, including the Department of Health and Human Services, the Department of Veterans Affairs, the National Institutes of Health, and the Centers for Disease Control.

In 1987, the association underwent a major transformation intended to meet the changing needs of the healthcare industry, as health maintenance organizations (HMOs) began coming to the fore as the primary providers of health insurance to vast numbers of Americans. During the 1987 transformation, most of the AHA's standing councils were eliminated, replaced by ad hoc committees that could more rapidly respond to developments in health policy. At the same time, the smaller and more manageable board of trustees took over—replacing the larger and more unwieldy House of Delegates—as the administrative body with the power to make final approvals or rejections of AHA policy.

HISTORY

The predecessor organization to the American Hospital Association—the Association of Hospital Superintendants—was founded by nine Cleveland, Ohio, hospital administrators in 1899. The original organization was intended to provide a forum for administrators to share ideas on how hospitals should be run. At first, it excluded anyone below the level of chief administrator. Within seven years, however, the exclusivity was relaxed and all hospital administrators and supervisors were allowed to join. At the same time, in 1906, the name was officially changed to its current American Hospital Association. In 1918, a new form of membership—for institutions—was inaugurated.

For its first few decades of existence, the AHA largely confined itself to the exchange of information among members on such subjects as hospital administration, hospital economics, hospital maintenance and upkeep, and hospital inspection. In 1937, the AHA started its Hospital Service Plan Commission, now better known as Blue Cross. The AHA severed all ties with Blue Cross, however, in 1972. Beginning in 1951, the AHA began to push for a federal health program for the elderly, which culminated in the 1965 establishment of the Medicare program.

ACTIVITIES: CURRENT AND FUTURE

As the major lobbying group for America's hospitals, the AHA is deeply involved in the debate over Medicare reform. Specifically, AHA lobbyists continue to work in Congress to prevent steep cuts in Medicare that were proposed by Republicans in their five-year balanced federal budget plan announced in 1997. In late 1999, the legislation proposed by Republican lawmakers would supposedly produce some $115 billion in savings over five years. While Republicans say the cuts are necessary to save Medicare, the AHA argues that budget surpluses now render such cuts unnecessary, if they ever

**American Hospital Association
Political Action Committee Contributions**

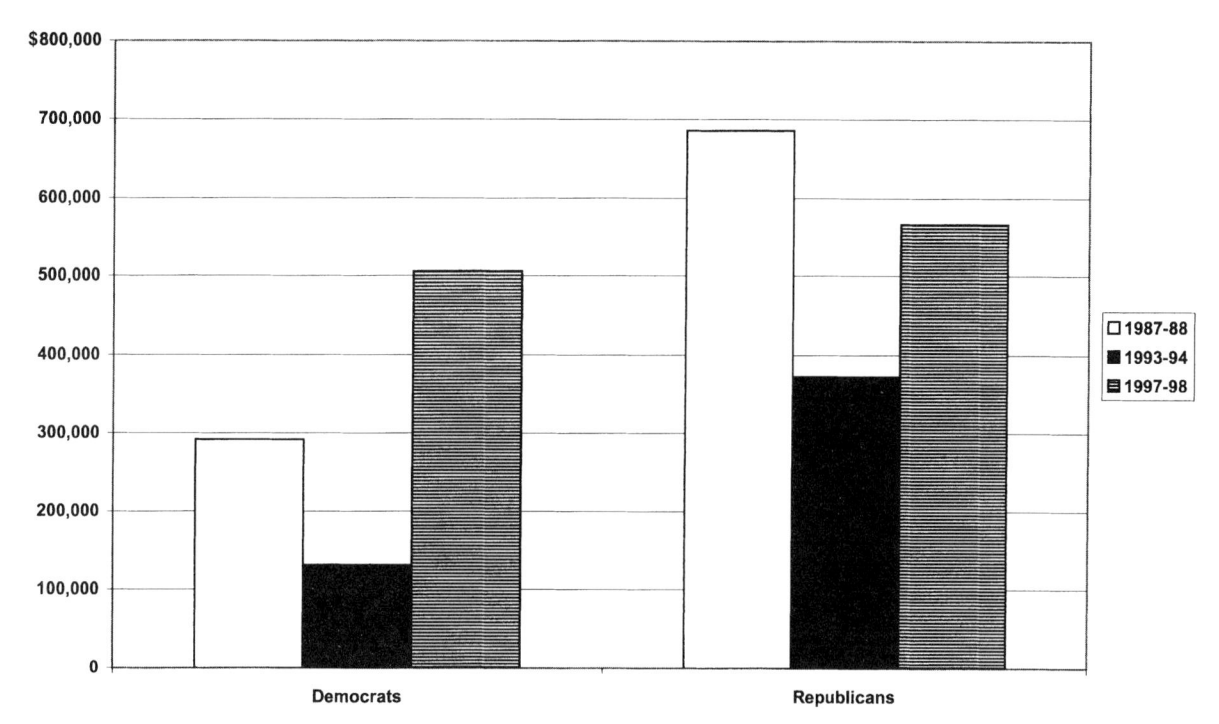

□ 1987-88
■ 1993-94
☰ 1997-98

Data derived from official studies available from the Federal Election Commission, Washington, DC, 1987–1998.

were necessary. Moreover, the AHA says such cuts would seriously jeopardize healthcare for the elderly.

At the same time, the AHA is trying to persuade the federal government to ease its fight against Medicare fraud. Citing recent raids on several hospitals that produced little or no evidence of billing fraud, the AHA says that the efforts by investigators from the Department of Health and Human Services (HHS)—which administers the Medicare program—have gone too far. The AHA says it would prefer that HHS investigators move quietly on corrupt hospitals, rather than conducting high-profile raids that tarnish the reputations of honest hospitals as well as dishonest ones and jeopardize the health of elderly patients at the hospitals under investigation. The AHA tried and failed to get a bill passed in 1998 that would have limited the government's right to use the False Claims Act in punishing cases of Medicare fraud. Rather than going through Congress, the AHA is lobbying the HHS and the Department of Justice to establish more careful limits on the extent and means of investigations into and punishment of Medicare fraud by hospital billing departments.

On a related issue, the AHA has fought against a rule change made by the Joint Commission on Accreditation of Healthcare Organizations that effectively ends the "courtesy call," which offered hospitals 24- to 48-hours notice of spot investigations. Some 80 percent of American hospitals are accredited by the commission. And while hospitals accept such accreditation voluntarily, they cannot be reimbursed by Medicare unless they are. Under pressure from consumer rights activists and the HHS, the commission agreed to drop the prior notification custom.

The so-called patient's bill of rights is another controversial issue in Washington, D.C., that the AHA finds itself involved in. The bill of rights proposed by the administration of President Bill Clinton, while it contains many elements, includes a protocol for healthcare customers to appeal insurance company decisions to deny certain procedures or to sue them for damages. The AHA not only vows to fight this Democratic bill, it has also lobbied against a Republican-sponsored bill that passed the Senate in the summer of 1999, which also allowed for an appeals process but essentially put the procedures under the control of the health insurers themselves.

Like the Health Insurance Association of America— the trade group of healthcare insurers—the AHA says that the issue of denied services is best left to the market, since customers have a choice of plans and can therefore opt for companies with lower premiums and fewer covered services or companies with higher premiums and a more extensive list of covered services. Advocates of the bill of rights say this does not help someone who needs a denied procedure immediately since most insurers will not take on someone with an existing condition that requires immediate care.

Another recent complaint that many consumer rights groups—as well as civil libertarians and healthcare professional associations—have with health insurers and health providers such as hospitals is the lack of privacy concerning medical records. Indeed, with the growth of electronic databases and electronic data transfer, it has become increasingly easy for medical records to be sent to various institutions, as well as increasingly likely that they may fall into the hands of the wrong people, such as employers who would like to avoid taking on workers with existing medical conditions or financial lenders who risk losing money if their customers die from an existing medical condition. The AHA believes that hospitals and health insurance providers need to have access to as much information as possible in order to increase the cost-effectiveness of their services. Moreover, both claim that there are adequate privacy protections and that when personal records are sent all information that identifies an individual is encoded.

Another issue of concern to the AHA is doctor unionization. In 1999, members of the American Medical Association (AMA) voted to allow private doctors to unionize. The rationale was that, in a changing healthcare environment in which HMOs set most prices for most doctor services, medical practitioners need a collective voice to negotiate on their behalf. But under the nation's antitrust legislation, private practitioners are prohibited from organizing. (Doctors who are on salary with hospitals or other institutions are allowed to unionize under current law.) Thus, the AMA and other doctor groups have been lobbying the government to make an exemption for them. The AHA has come out vigorously in opposition to such an exemption, saying it would increase healthcare costs dramatically and thereby jeopardize patient care.

FINANCIAL FACTS

The AHA is one of the largest donators of campaign contributions in Washington, D.C. Over the past five election cycles—since 1987–1988—it has consistently given hundreds of thousands of dollars to candidates. In the 1987–1988 election cycle, the AHA gave a total of $1,025,196 to Republican and Democratic candidates for Congress and the presidency. In the 1993–1994 election cycle—which was for Congress only and thus normally a period of smaller overall donations—the total figure given to Republican and Democratic candidates was $432,727. By the 1997–1998 cycle the amount had climbed back up to $1,072,868. Despite these fluctuations, the proportion of money given to the two major parties has remained relatively consistent, with about two-thirds going to Republicans and one-third going to Democrats.

JAMES CIMENT AND IMMANUEL NESS

Bibliography

"Concern Over Medical Confidentiality." *Marketletter,* August 2, 1999.

Correa, Tracy. "Hospitals Lose Prior Warning of Review." *Fresno Bee,* August 17, 1999.

Cunningham, Robert. *The Blues: A History of the Blue Cross and Blue Shield System.* De Kalb: Northern Illinois University Press, 1997.

Hallam, Kristen. "AHA Uses Hospital Raid in Lobbying Efforts." *Modern Healthcare,* May 24, 1999, p. 3.

———. "Hospital Groups Fight Doc Antitrust Relief." *Modern Healthcare,* June 28, 1999.

"Lobbying: AHA to Spend $2 Million for Budget Relief." *Health Line,* August 6, 1999.

Miller, Susan R. "Hospital Execs Exhorted to Lobby Congress." *Broward Daily Business Review,* July 30, 1999.

Noguchi, Yuki. "Ex-BJC Head Takes the Helm at American Hospital Association." *St. Louis Post-Dispatch,* February 1, 1999.

Zitner, Aaron. "Report Assails Medicare Cuts; Hospitals Say Reductions Were Deeper than Intended." *Boston Globe,* May 18, 1999.

AMERICAN MEDICAL ASSOCIATION

The American Medical Association (AMA) is the most prominent professional association for physicians in the United States, representing nearly 300,000 physicians who practice all types of medicine. The national organization is one of the largest and most influential interest groups in the nation in terms of political contributions to members of Congress and political influence over the federal government's agencies. Through its 50 state branches, the organization also exercises significant influence over state and local decisions that relate to medical practices. The AMA operates as both a gatekeeper defining and regulating entry into the medical profession and a defender of the interests of physicians who are members of the association.

The AMA seeks to retain and expand its position as the most prominent voice for physicians, and more broadly, the medical profession. Although the AMA's stated mission is "to promote the art and science of medicine and the betterment of public health," the organization also seeks to advance the position of physicians in the healthcare field. By the early twenty-first century, the AMA had succeeded in maintaining and expanding physicians' leading position in the healthcare workplace. However, the growth of managed care as the primary form of medical insurance has shifted a significant share of physicians' oversight over medical decisions to health insurance companies. In the last decade, the effort to regain medical supervision over medical decisions has become the leading political goal of the organization.

The AMA is controlled by a democratically elected board of directors that is responsible for operations and carrying out members' policy goals. The organization is responsible for evaluating and accrediting medical schools and residency programs in the United States. Moreover, the AMA is also responsible for accrediting continuing physician education programs. The organization publishes the *Journal of the American Medical Association* and other specialized books and software on medical care.

HISTORY

The AMA was founded in 1847 by Nathan Smith Davis to improve and standardize medical education and training. Davis, a New York physician, and other medical doctors believed that few American physicians had basic training in medicine, particularly physicians practicing in the rural regions of the United States. By improving the standards of professional medical education and medical care, the AMA believed that public health could be vastly improved. Moreover, due to the scarcity of established medical institutions in the United States, many doctors studied medicine in Europe.

In its formative years, the AMA was a relatively small society of physicians with little influence, but in the late nineteenth century and early twentieth century the organization became more prominent, in part due to the greater recognition of the need to train doctors in the United States. The organization also gained standing as a proponent of public health and medical research to identify the causes of disease in the major cities and throughout the country.

Federal government efforts in the 1960s to extend healthcare coverage to Americans were initially opposed by the AMA, including Medicare and Medicaid because of its belief that such programs would regulate physician medical fees. The organization also strongly opposed any form of national health insurance that would guarantee medical coverage to all Americans. In place of Medicare, the AMA favored a program known as Eldercare, which would cover only the elderly poor and indigent. However, after Congress enacted Medicare, the AMA became one of its primary proponents. Government and corporate efforts to rein in healthcare spending in the 1980s and 1990s through the introduction of managed care have severely reduced physician fees and autonomy. Today, the AMA considers managed care to be a major impediment to providing quality healthcare to all Americans. The organization now sup-

**American Medical Association
Political Action Committee Contributions**

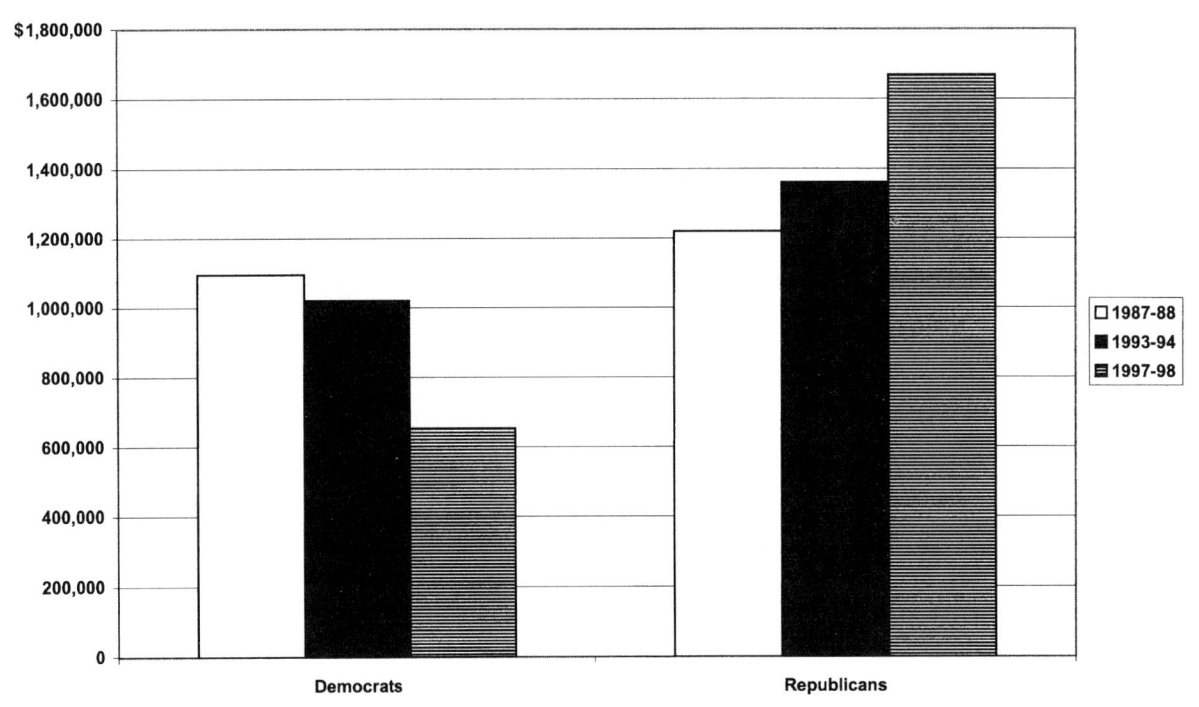

[Bar chart showing PAC contributions with legend: □ 1987-88, ■ 1993-94, ≡ 1997-98. Democrats: approximately $1,100,000 (1987-88), $1,025,000 (1993-94), $660,000 (1997-98). Republicans: approximately $1,225,000 (1987-88), $1,370,000 (1993-94), $1,680,000 (1997-98).]

Data derived from official studies available from the Federal Election Commission, Washington, DC, 1987–1998.

ports efforts to establish a patient's bill of rights that would improve coverage and potentially increase access to healthcare. The unprecedented June 1999 vote to support the formation of a national union to bargain on behalf of doctors with health insurance companies reflects the weakening power of the AMA to influence public policy on managed care.

ACTIVITIES: CURRENT AND FUTURE

At the forefront of the AMA's current agenda is the effort to increase the quality of healthcare and patient access through limiting the power of health insurance companies to oversee medical decisions and determine access. The AMA believes that the current direction of healthcare financing is not working for patients and is constraining the economic ability of doctors to practice medicine. The organization claims that reimbursement by third-party insurers generally is inadequate to cover the necessary services for patients. The growth of managed care tends to shift medical decision making from doctors and physicians to health insurance companies who tend to evaluate the need for medical services on the basis of financial determinations of managed care bureaucrats rather than the medical need of patients.

In public testimony, the AMA strongly supports the introduction of patients' rights legislation that would increase access to healthcare and reduce the ability of managed care providers to deny health coverage. Although the AMA has supported the extension of a patient's rights bill, it has opposed congressional bills in the late 1990s that tinkered at the edges of the system rather than fundamentally reforming healthcare. In the summer of 1999, the AMA argued that patients' rights legislation passed by the U.S. Senate did not improve patient access to necessary healthcare but instead included provisions that greatly protected health insurance companies.

The AMA believes that the managed care companies should be liable in the case of unjust denial of healthcare services. According to the AMA, managed care companies should not prevent patients from going to the nearest emergency room and should not impede patients who are in need of emergency care from using healthcare services that are out of their plans. According to the AMA, if managed care companies prevail in the ongoing healthcare debate, "ambulance drivers and paramedics will be forced to make life or death decisions while the insurance company contemplates what it is willing to pay for."

In June 1999, Thomas R. Reardon, president of the AMA, argued that the Republican-controlled 106th Congress passed legislation that permitted "insurance companies to impose arbitrary, narrow definitions of what's medically necessary when they determine patient healthcare needs." Echoing the sentiment of the AMA, Reardon added that "insurance companies will be free to decide if care is necessary [based] on what's good for their profits rather than what's good for patients."

Since 1994, the AMA has actively supported passage of healthcare reform legislation to improve patient access to medical services that have been eroded by managed care. In particular, the organization has been actively fighting for a patient's bill of rights that "could protect patients from the abuses of managed care." The AMA believes that such legislation must include four essential elements: the independent and fair external appeal of health plan decisions, the ability to hold health plans accountable when their decisions harm patients, the right to have physicians decide what treatment is medically necessary, and the guarantee that patient rights apply to all Americans. The AMA believes that the issue of patient access to healthcare will continue to remain a top priority for the organization and its members in the years to come.

In the long term, the AMA believes that health insurance reform is necessary. It has proposed changes in the federal tax code that would transfer employer-based health plans to individually owned health insurance. The organization believes that such a program would preserve the patient-physician relationship and potentially lead to new changes that would extend health coverage to the uninsured.

Since 1994, the organization's campaign for passage of a patient's bill of rights has included campaign contributions to sympathetic congressional candidates, lobbying key members of Congress, radio and newspaper media campaigns, and public appearances by AMA leaders. The organization believes that though the American public strongly supports such legislation to improve access to healthcare, members of the Senate and House of Representatives have been swayed by the interests of the health insurance industry. By the summer of 1999, the AMA had failed to win passage of what it believed was an adequate patient's bill of rights.

Another key health policy issue on the AMA agenda is to strengthen the ability of doctors to bargain with managed care plans. Currently, self-employed physicians have little power to improve the terms of health reimbursements with insurance companies. In response to significant pressure, the AMA came out in support of doctors' strengthening their bargaining power by collectively negotiating with health plans.

The AMA supports Medicare reform to maintain the long-term solvency of the program. However, the organization believes that current efforts by the government to impose huge financial penalties for fraud and abuse is unfair to physicians who may have inadvertently made billing errors. In the 1990s, changes in healthcare financing and the emergence of managed healthcare as the dominant form of health insurance has eroded the ability of doctors to defend the profession. Increasingly, physicians are finding that medical decisions are being usurped by managed healthcare insurance companies that define the parameters of allowable healthcare. This decline in physician authority has contributed to calls for radical changes to regain control over decision making and payments. In the late 1990s, rather than negotiate as individuals with healthcare providers, a growing number of physicians have supported efforts to negotiate on a collective basis with healthcare providers and insurers.

In June 1999, the growing support of unionization among doctors prompted the 494-member AMA House of Delegates to vote in favor of the formation of its own national labor union of doctors. The AMA believes that a national physicians union is necessary to give doctors who are under severe financial and workload pressure greater negotiating power with managed care companies. The organization maintains that the new national union will not be a traditional labor union because doctors will be prohibited from striking or jeopardizing patient care. According to the AMA, the new union will only apply to doctors who are employees of HMOs or managed care companies until Congress gives self-employed doctors collective bargaining rights.

The AMA also disseminates information on public health, personal healthcare, and prevention, and is issuing new guidelines on proper personal healthcare and treatment. The AMA continues its antismoking campaign, which began in 1972, that educates the public on the health risks of cigarette smoking. In addition, the organization is actively engaged in medical ethics issues.

FINANCIAL FACTS

Since the early twentieth century, the AMA has been lobbying Congress and administrative agencies. AM-

PAC (American Medical Association Political Action Committee), the organization's political action committee (PAC), is among the most prominent in the nation. It is a leading contributor to members of Congress and is perennially rated by members of Congress as one of the most powerful lobbies in Washington, D.C. However, unlike other lobbies that have increased their contributions in recent years, since the 1987–1988 election cycle, AMPAC has continued to contribute about $2.3 million. Traditionally, AMPAC has directed a larger share of its campaign contributions to Republican candidates. Even when Democrats controlled the House of Representatives, the AMA directed a majority of its campaign contributions to Republicans. In the 1997–1998 election cycle, Republican candidates received 72 percent of AMPAC's $2.3 million in contributions. In recent years, public policy organizations have disclosed that the AMA has paid for the cost of trips of members of Congress to attend conventions and fact-finding missions.

IMMANUEL NESS

Bibliography

American Medical Association: www.ama-assn.org

Center for Responsive Politics: www.crp.org

Johnson, James A., and Walter J. Jones. *The American Medical Association and Organized Medicine: A Commentary and Annotated Bibliography.* New York: Garland, 1993.

Marks, Geoffrey, and William K. Beatty. *The Story of Medicine in America.* New York: Charles Scribner's Sons, 1973.

Navarro, Vicente. *The Politics of Health Policy: The U.S. Reforms, 1980–1994.* Oxford: Blackwell, 1994.

Wolinsky, Howard, and Tom Brune. *The Serpent and the Staff: The Unhealthy Politics of the American Medical Association.* New York: Tarcher/Putnam, 1994.

Zuckerman, Edward, ed. *The Almanac of Federal PACs, 1998–99.* Arlington, VA: Amward, 1998.

AMERICAN NURSES ASSOCIATION

The American Nurses Association (ANA) is the national organization that represents the professional and economic interests of nurses. The organization's stated mission is to improve the health standards and the availability of healthcare services. The ANA believes that high health standards can be advanced in the profession through encouraging professional development and improving the economic conditions of nurses.

The organization represents nurse administrators and clinical practitioners employed in medical institutions, community agencies, and educational and research organizations. The ANA believes that nurses have a distinct set of professional and economic interests that are frequently independent of doctors and other health professionals. The organization seeks to promote these interests through public education and lobbying politicians and government officials. The ANA's primary goal is to promote policy positions that advance the ability of nurses to provide healthcare. According to the organization, these positions include engendering high standards of nursing practice and improving the economic condition of nurses. The ANA lobbies members of Congress and regulatory agencies on healthcare issues important to nurses and their patients. The organization regularly seeks to help advance the public image of nurses and to draw attention to the importance of the nursing profession in the administration of medical care.

The ANA is led by a 16-member board of directors that is elected by the organization's membership. The board of directors is primarily responsible for framing the policy agenda of the organization. The ANA is one of the nation's largest professional organizations that engages in a broad range of activities. The organization operates the American Nurses Credentializing Center, which establishes standards for credentializing nurses. In addition, the ANA offers a range of activities, services, and products to its members. The ANA holds conventions on a biennial basis, publishes the *American Journal of Nursing,* and provides continuing education programs.

HISTORY

The ANA was founded in 1874 to set standards of education and practice for the nursing profession. Prior to the organization's founding, no standardized system of nursing education and accreditation was in place in the United States. Initially, the organization's primary objective was to promote and engender a formalized system of professional training for American nurses. Over the last century, the ANA has expanded rapidly and gained in stature as the leading voice of the nursing profession. By the late 1990s, the ANA had grown to represent the interests of 2.2 million registered nurses organized in 53 state and territorial associations.

Headquartered in Washington, D.C., the ANA has over 180,000 members. The Washington headquarters also serves as the national center of operations for 25 labor unions that represent nurses on a regional basis. These engage in collective bargaining and negotiate contracts on behalf of nurses with medical centers, hospitals, and other healthcare management organizations. In recent years, the ANA has been actively involved in political debates on the future of medical care. The organization considers the growth of managed care and other cost-cutting programs to be potentially detrimental to the health and safety needs of patients and nurses.

ACTIVITIES: CURRENT AND FUTURE

A leading policy effort of the ANA is to restructure the healthcare system to improve the delivery of primary care on a community basis and to defend and improve the quality of the healthcare workplace environment. The ANA seeks to advance the economic and professional stature of registered nurses and advanced practice nurses in administering basic and primary healthcare. To advance the professional development of nurses, the ANA solicits federal funding for education and training programs.

The ANA has been an active participant in the national debate over the future of healthcare in America. In particular, the organization is concerned with the changes in government and private healthcare insurance systems that have in recent years narrowed and restricted medical care services to patients by reducing reimbursements for medical care procedures. An ongoing legislative priority for the organization is to provide Medicare reimbursements for all nurse practitioners and clinical nurses. The ANA is concerned with the effect of managed healthcare on the quality of patient care. In particular it is troubled that the reduction of nurse staffing levels has had a harmful effect on the quality of patient care.

The ANA considers the improvement of the healthcare of patients to be one of its most important objectives. To improve the delivery of healthcare, the ANA closely monitors how the changing healthcare environment affects the care of patients. For example, the organization has established an advisory board to study and report on how scientific and medical advancements influence the ethical standards in nursing and the medical profession more generally.

Although the ANA has endorsed the passage of the Patient Safety Bill—an act introduced in Congress that would require hospitals to provide information on how medical staffing levels influence patient medical outcomes—it has opposed efforts by the health insurance industry to insert provisions in the bill that erode patient access to healthcare.

Other interests of the association include enhancing the role of registered nurses in the delivery of basic and primary healthcare, gaining federal funding for the education and training of nurses, and improving the economic and working conditions of nurses. Maintaining and enhancing workplace safety for nurses is one of the ANA's primary areas of concern; the key workplace safety issues are maintaining appropriate staffing levels, promoting safety, and ensuring that health hazards are minimized. According to the ANA, nurses constantly are faced with occupational hazards and dangers from needles and exposure to toxic substances and medical wastes and risk back injuries and developing latex allergies. The ANA has produced information brochures and conducted national videoconferences to educate nurses on avoiding workplace hazards. On a legislative level, the ANA is actively educating and lobbying members of Congress to support a proposed Healthcare Worker Protection Act, which would mandate the expansion of workplace safety protections for nurses and other medical practitioners.

In addition to workplace safety, the ANA is also committed to promoting and advancing economic security for nurses—including benefits, pensions, and collective bargaining. The organization is active in researching the latest strategies and tactics on labor-management relations. The ANA maintains a labor and workplace division that provides data and assistance to nurses and state nursing associations on collective bargaining, contract negotiations, economic restructuring, and personnel issues.

The ANA and its state affiliates lobby federal and state governments to advance the condition of nurses. The organization's government affairs division lobbies Congress and members of the executive departments and testifies before congressional committees on issues that concern nursing. The primary goals are to educate Congress on the nursing profession's positions and to provide data for the development of congressional bills. The government affairs staff also assists federal government agencies on the implementation of laws affecting nurses. The organization's legislative priorities include passing a patient's bill of rights, and advancing patients' access to medical care.

As an active supporter of a comprehensive patient's bill of rights, the ANA opposes efforts by the U.S. Congress to water down the bill's provisions that protect from retaliation by hospital management nurses who advocate for their patients. In addition, the organization opposes efforts that would exempt healthcare plans that are not regulated by federal law—leaving more than 100 million beneficiaries unprotected—and efforts to weaken the patient appeals process.

The ANA is a staunch advocate for the continuation of federal funding for Community Nursing Organizations (CNOs)—health programs operated by nurses that serve Medicare beneficiaries in home and community settings. Funding for the CNO programs, authorized in 1987, will be terminated January 1, 2000, if no additional funding is authorized by Congress. CNO demonstration projects are operated at sites in Minnesota, Illinois, Arizona, and New York State. In addition to these legislative programs, the ANA supports increased access to women's healthcare services, improved third-party reimbursements to nurses, funding for nursing education and training programs, and support for Medicare and Social Security.

The organization also supports and trains nurses who are seeking state and federal elective office and mobilizes members and their families to work and vote for candidates selected by the association. The ANA provides testimony from the nursing perspective before leading government bodies, including the U.S. Department of Health and Human Services, the Department of Labor, the National Institutes of Health, and other U.S. government agencies. In addition, the ANA has worked with the United Nations, the World Health Organization, and other international nongovernmental organizations.

FINANCIAL FACTS

Campaign contributions to congressional candidates are funneled through the American Nurses Association Political Action Committee (ANA-PAC), which according to the ANA, is the third-largest healthcare political action committee (PAC) in the nation. ANA-PAC has raised more than $1 million from nurses in three consecutive election cycles between 1993 and 1998. ANA-PAC's objective is to endorse and contribute to candidates from both parties that support the legislative policy agenda of the organization. ANA-PAC is funded through member donations.

IMMANUEL NESS

Bibliography

American Nurses Association: www.nursingworld.org

Zuckerman, Edward, ed. *The Almanac of Federal PACs, 1998–99*. Arlington, VA: Amward, 1998.

AMERICAN OCCUPATIONAL THERAPY ASSOCIATION

The American Occupational Therapy Association (AOTA) is the leading national association that represents and seeks to advance the professional and economic interests of occupational therapy practitioners, assistants, and students. Occupational therapy is a professional medical field that assists individuals to recover from illnesses or injuries or to cope with developmental disabilities, or changes that may occur through aging. Occupational therapists assist individuals to regain and maintain a productive and fulfilling life through restoring and maintaining physical abilities that they have lost or never developed. According to the AOTA, the primary goal of occupational therapists is to help patients who are impaired by physical and mental problems that hinder their ability to function in their homes, schools, or workplaces.

The AOTA's 60,000 members are registered occupational therapists, certified occupational therapy assistants, and occupational therapy students. The organization's mission is to maintain the professional environment for its members and to advance and defend the continued viability and importance of the profession. The primary activities of the AOTA are to serve the interests of members, to educate the public about the importance of the profession of occupational therapy, and to support and extend access to occupational therapy services through government and third-party health insurance providers. In the 1990s, the AOTA sought to expand its relationship with state and local occupational therapy organizations. Thus, the AOTA closely advises state occupational therapy associations to promote and advance standards in occupational therapy practice with state health departments, regulatory bodies, and other healthcare policy-making organizations that govern the field. Particular attention has been devoted to states that do not have adequate licensing and regulatory guidelines for occupational therapists.

The organization, based in Bethesda, Maryland, is actively involved in educating therapists, assistants, students, and other interested parties. The organization disseminates practice guidelines detailing accepted regulations for the practice of occupational therapy. The practice guidelines are widely distributed to healthcare practitioners, health insurers and managed care organizations, and healthcare policy-makers.

HISTORY

The origins of the AOTA date back to 1917, when the organization was founded in Washington, D.C., as the National Society for the Promotion of Occupational Therapy. Four years later, the organization changed its name to the American Occupational Therapy Association. Initially, the primary concern of the national society was to investigate and promote the development of productive occupations for disabled persons. In addition, the organization sought to promote partnership and collaboration among occupational therapy societies across the nation.

Shortly after its founding, the organization was encouraged by hospital administrators and interested physicians in the field to establish a national register of occupational therapists to identify qualified practitioners and to prevent unqualified individuals from practicing in the field. To achieve the goal of establishing a national register, the organization established standards for training occupational therapists. By 1923, the AOTA used its standards for the first time to accredit qualified educational programs engaged in training occupational therapists. Over the next decade, professional occupational therapy standards were developed and institutionalized. By 1935, the AOTA's standards and guidelines for occupational therapy education—officially known as "Essentials of an Acceptable School of Occupational Therapy"—were adopted by the American Medical Association (AMA) for the training of registered occupational therapists. This collaborative relationship with the AMA continued in the decades to come. By 1958, the AOTA developed standards and guidelines for the approval of training for occupational therapy assistants.

**American Occupational Therapy Association
Political Action Committee Contributions**

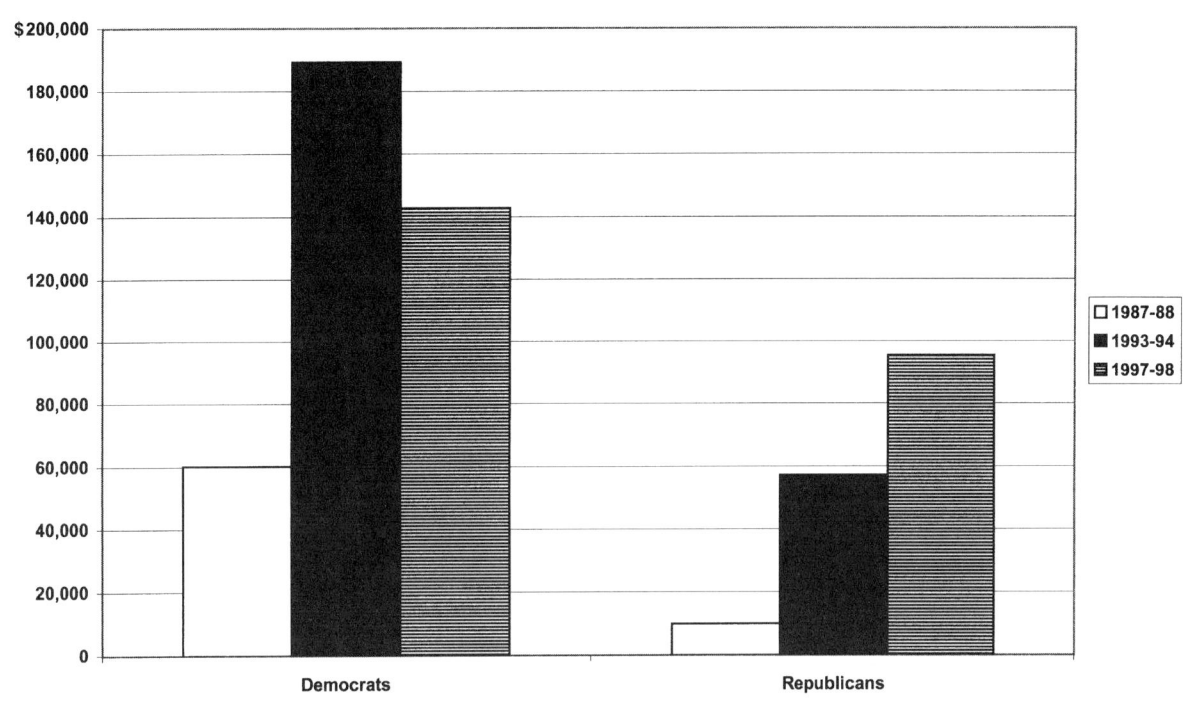

- 1987-88
- 1993-94
- 1997-98

Data derived from official studies available from the Federal Election Commission, Washington, DC, 1987–1998.

Over the next 40 years, the AOTA's accreditation guidelines for occupational therapists and occupational therapy assistants have been accepted by leading organizations, including the Council on Postsecondary Education, an agency that accredits higher education training programs. By 1994, the United States Department of Education (USDE) recognized the AOTA Accreditation Council for Occupational Therapy Education (ACOTE) as the official accrediting agency for occupational therapy professional training programs. The USDE approval is necessary before an educational institution such as the ACOTE can participate in federal funding programs. The ACOTE is now responsible for monitoring nearly 200 occupational therapy and occupational therapy assistant training programs.

ACTIVITIES: CURRENT AND FUTURE

To promote the importance of occupational therapy services, the AOTA is actively engaged in educating the public. The AOTA regularly contributes to newspaper columns about the importance of occupational therapy in rehabilitation for persons who have arthritis, visual perception losses, carpal tunnel syndrome, and depression. The organization seeks to draw public attention to occupational therapy's importance to mental health. According to the AOTA, occupational therapists screen patients for depression and other psychological conditions. To emphasize the profession's important role, AOTA president Karen Jacobs observed: "Whether it is a school child referred for handwriting problems, or an older personal being treated for a stroke, the occupational therapist is on the front lines of helping to identify underlying health issues that may be affecting the individual's well-being." The association provides education through national and regional conferences and continuing education courses and workshops held at state and local levels. In addition, the organization provides specialized training in pediatrics and neurorehabilitation.

Occupational therapy services for rehabilitation is increasingly in demand as the baby boom generation ages and the demographic profile of the American population grows older. According to the AOTA, the population over 60 years of age is expected to grow from

17 percent in the late 1990s to 25 percent by the year 2020. As a result of the growth in demand, according to the Bureau of Labor Statistics, occupational therapy is one of the fastest growing professions. By the late 1990s, while the number of occupational therapists expanded to meet the rising demand, there continued to be a shortage of occupational therapists in the United States. Despite the shortage, dramatic changes in medical care payments during the 1990s placed considerable strain on the capability of occupational therapists to survive and grow financially. According to the AOTA, the introduction and expansion of managed health care, which closely monitors and limits access to occupational therapy services, potentially undermines the prosperity and future growth of the profession. The AOTA is troubled with federal and private health insurance restrictions that have been placed on occupational therapy services.

The rising demand for occupational therapy services, coupled with declining health insurance coverage for services, is a leading concern of the organization. In 1999, the AOTA supported legislation in Congress aimed at restoring Medicare benefits that had been reduced—specifically, restrictions placed on occupational therapy services—in the Balanced Budget Act of 1997. According to Jeanette Bair, executive director of the AOTA, the $1,500 cap on occupational therapy services imposed by the act severely impedes full recovery for patients.

The AOTA is equally troubled that the proliferation of health maintenance organizations and the spiraling growth of private managed care has given too much power to investors and owners who are concerned with profitability at the expense of reducing critically needed occupational therapy services. Between 1985 and 1998, the percentage of Americans enrolled in HMOs had increased from 26 percent to 62 percent, contributing to the reduction in occupational therapy and other needed healthcare treatment and services.

The credentialing of occupational therapists has been one of the organization's most important issues in the last decade. In 1999, the AOTA considered extending the requirements for registered occupational therapists to include a postbaccalaureate degree.

FINANCIAL FACTS

The AOTA is an active contributor of political action committee (PAC) funds to Democratic and Republican candidates in the U.S. Congress. Two trends can be observed in the activity of the American Occupational Therapy Political Action Committee (AOTPAC): the spiraling in political contributions and the moderation of funds given to Democrats. AOTPAC funds are directed to congressional representatives who support the organization's interests and to legislators sitting on key committees in Congress that address issues related to healthcare. Moreover, AOTPAC has vastly increased its PAC activity in recent decades. Contributions to congressional candidates have grown from $70,311 in the 1987–1988 election cycle to $238,445 in the 1997–1998 election cycle. The AOTPAC's political contributions reflect the pragmatic needs of the organization. In the 1987–1988 election cycle—when Democrats controlled the House of Representatives—about 86 percent of AOTPAC's contributions went to Democrats. By the 1997–1998 election cycle, the organization's contributions to Democrats accounted for 60 percent of all AOTPAC money—reflecting the Republicans' control of the House beginning in 1995. In addition to funding political candidates, AOTA also encourages its members to vote for candidates who support its agenda and influential members of committees who are expected to continue to exert influence on key issues to the association.

IMMANUEL NESS

Bibliography

American Occupational Therapy Association. "AOTA President Attends White House Center for Conference on Mental Health." *News Release,* June 14, 1999.

Johansson, Cynthia. "Quality of Care versus Profits in HMOs." *O.T. Week* 13, no. 28 (July 22, 1999): i, iv.

Steib, Paula A. "Assessing the Changes in Health Care." *O.T. Week* 12, no. 42 (October 15, 1998): 10.

Zuckerman, Edward, ed. *The Almanac of Federal PACs, 1998–99.* Arlington, VA: Amward, 1998.

AMERICAN PSYCHIATRIC ASSOCIATION

With some 40,500 members—largely in the United States, but also from around the world—the American Psychiatric Association (APA) is the largest association dedicated to furthering the interests of professional psychiatrists and the psychiatry profession. The APA is an educational, research, and advocacy group dedicated to maintaining standards within the profession and advocating policies—both within the government and the private sector—that serve psychiatrists and their patients.

According to its own literature, the APA is dedicated to the following objectives: "to improve the treatment, rehabilitation, and care of the mentally ill, the mentally retarded, and the emotionally disturbed; to promote research, professional education in psychiatry and allied fields, and the prevention of psychiatric disabilities; to advance the standards of all psychiatric services and facilities; to foster the cooperation of all who are concerned with the medical, psychological, social, and legal aspects of mental health and illness; to make psychiatric knowledge available to other practitioners of medicine, to scientists in other fields of knowledge, and to the public; to promote the best interests of patients and those actually or potentially making use of mental health services; and to advocate for its members."

The APA is governed by several bodies including a board of trustees, an assembly, and the joint reference committee. While these bodies set the overall policy and position of the APA, the organization's day-to-day affairs are carried out by constitutional committees, topic councils, and commissions. The 11 councils are responsible for the following areas: addiction psychiatry; aging; children, adolescents, and their families; economic affairs; internal organization; international affairs; medical education and career development; national affairs; psychiatric services; psychiatry and law; and research.

HISTORY

The APA was founded in 1844 and, among its first activities, published the world's first professional journal concerned with mental illness. First titled the *American Journal of Insanity,* the journal's name was later changed to its current *American Journal of Psychiatry*. Over the years, the APA has grown in size and influence and came to publish the *Diagnostic Statistical Manual of Mental Disorders*. Now in its fourth edition, the manual—usually referred to as the DSM—has been called the "bible" of the profession in that it provides clinicians with precise definitions of all mental disorders. Over the years, numerous new illnesses have been added, while a few controversial ones—such as homosexuality—have been dropped.

ACTIVITIES: CURRENT AND FUTURE

Several forces have come together in recent years that have had an enormous impact on the APA and the psychiatric profession generally. These forces have included scientific advances such as the remarkable proliferation of psychopharmaceutical drugs and social change, including the growing public acceptance of mental illness as a legitimate and unstigmatized health problem. In economics, the biggest impact has been the emergence of health maintenance organizations (HMOs) and their cost-cutting health measures. In addition, science and economy have come together, as healthcare insurers have come to emphasize psychopharmaceuticals as a cost-effective alternative to long-term traditional psychiatric treatment. This has led to the growing spread of therapists. With less formal education and lower fees,

**American Psychiatric Association
Political Action Committee Contributions**

Data derived from official studies available from the Federal Election Commission, Washington, DC, 1987–1998.

therapists offer a lower-cost alternative to traditional psychiatry.

The spread of HMOs and the increasing numbers of persons seeking psychiatric and psychological treatment have led to a growing problem regarding the financing of mental health treatment. The APA has declared itself in full support of the so-called patient's bill of rights, an initiative of the administration of President Bill Clinton that would guarantee HMO customers the right to sue their health insurance company if the latter refuses to pay for medically necessary treatment. Since mental health treatment—and particularly expensive and long-running therapy—is often not covered, this issue is of particular importance to the APA and its members. According to statements issued by the APA, a proper patient's bill of rights would include such features "as reasonable and clearly defined appeals procedures and peer-level utilization review standards."

At the same time, the APA has been lobbying vigorously to assure full parity for mental illness treatment (including substance abuse treatments) in HMO healthcare plans. Working with various members of Congress, APA lobbyists have tried to get bills introduced that would eliminate discriminatory copayments and deductibles for mental health patients (mental health patients usually pay higher copayments and deductibles than patients with physical ailments). In addition, the APA would like rules that prevent strict limits on the number of visits with or dollar amount a patient can spend on a therapist whose services are covered by an HMO plan.

Also connected to the rise of HMOs is the issue of medical record privacy. As experts in the field of healthcare point out, HMOs—in their efforts to cut costs—have sought ever-greater amounts of information about clients and prospective clients. While health insurers say the privacy of this information is highly protected and is used simply to study trends in healthcare provision so that insurers can utilize their resources more effectively, critics say the proliferation of records, new electronic means to transfer records, and the HMOs' desire to seek out all the information it can on patients has led to a dangerous situation in which such records could fall into the wrong hands. Specifically, they worry that medical records made public could be used by employers who want to avoid taking on the costly healthcare needs of potential employees or lenders who do not want to loan money to people who might die before they can pay it back.

Needless to say, as the largest organization of mental healthcare providers, the APA is extremely sensitive to the issue of privacy and has lobbied hard to prevent a national patient identifier system. In addition, the APA has sought to prevent the "routine use" of private medical records in Medicare fraud cases. Still, says the APA, the battle to protect patients' medical records is far from over. The association is currently fighting off a Republican initiative that the APA believes would give healthcare insurers a "wide latitude in disclosing patients' medical records to financial services companies," which "would overturn the principle of patient consent for disclosure of medical records to third parties."

FINANCIAL FACTS

The APA has donated modest amounts to political campaigns compared to many associations of healthcare professionals over the past five election cycles, and the total given to candidates has remained roughly the same over these same years. In the 1987–1988 election cycle—which included both presidential and congressional campaigns—the APA gave a total of $95,405. In 1993–1994—which was a congressional election only and therefore should have seen donations drop—the organization donated roughly the same amount, $94,295. By the 1997–1998 election cycle—again, only a congressional campaign season—the APA gave $85,486. Similarly, the proportions given to the two major parties has remain largely unchanged over the past six election cycles. In the 1987–1988 election cycle, for instance, Democrats received $71,830, or roughly 72 percent of the total; in 1993–1994, Democrats received $72,595, or 76 percent; and in 1997–1998, they received $61,976, or 72 percent.

JAMES CIMENT AND IMMANUEL NESS

Bibliography

Barton, Walter E. *The History and Influence of the American Psychiatric Association.* Washington, DC: American Psychiatric Press, 1987.

Clements, Colleen. "It's a Mistake to Make Patient Privilege Eternal." *Medical Post,* September 22, 1998.

"Doctors Say Privacy Protections Lacking in House Bill." *AIDS Policy and Law,* August 6, 1999.

"Mental Health: Clinton Wants Parity for Federal Employees." *Health Line,* May 25, 1999.

"Mental Health Showdown." *Courier-Journal* (Louisville, KY), June 22, 1999.

Wallerstein, Robert S. *Lay Analysis: Life Inside the Controversy.* Hillsdale, NJ: Analytic Press, 1998.

"White House Announces Labor Department Outreach to Inform Consumers About Mental Health Benefits." *U.S. Newswire,* June 7, 1999.

AMERICAN SOCIETY OF ANESTHESIOLOGISTS

Representing the interests of professional anesthesiologists, the American Society of Anesthesiologists (ASA) is an educational, research, and advocacy group dedicated to maintaining standards within the profession and advocating policies—both within the government and the private sector—that serve anesthesiologists, the science and practice of anesthesiology, and patients who undergo anesthesia. (Anesthesiologists administer a variety of drugs—orally, by injection, and through the airways—that render the individual unconscious—and thus insensitive to pain—while maintaining vital functions such as breathing, heart rate, and blood pressure during surgery. In addition, anesthesiologists are often involved in postoperative care, providing pain-killing drugs and other treatment, as well as in monitoring life functions during this critical recovery period.)

The ASA includes approximately 35,000 members who must be licensed doctors of medicine (MDs) or osteopathy who have also successfully completed a training program in anesthesiology certified by the Accreditation Council for Graduate Medical Education or the American Osteopathic Association.

Headquartered in Park Ridge, Illinois, and with a lobbying office in Washington, D.C., the ASA is governed by its House of Delegates, consisting of ASA officers, regional directors, past presidents of the organization, the editor-in-chief of the ASA's journal *Anesthesiology,* as well as the chairpersons of the organization's more important committees, including education and residency, and clinical care, among others. In addition to the House of Delegates, the ASA also has a board of directors, which supervises the business and publication affairs of the organization. The ASA also manages the Wood Library-Museum of Anesthesiology, which is located at its headquarters in Park Ridge.

The organization sponsors a number of education programs for its members. It holds an annual meeting, where anesthesiologists are introduced to the latest research, procedures, and products related to the profession. Seminars at the annual meetings and elsewhere contribute to the continuing education of anesthesiologists. In addition, the ASA offers its Self-Education and Evaluation Program, which allows practicing anesthesiologists to gain an objective measure of their own continuing education and skills. Finally, the ASA acts as the secretariat of the American Board of Anesthesiology. Together, the society and the board prepare and administer the examination taken by some 5,000 anesthesiology program residents throughout North America.

HISTORY

The first direct predecessor organization to the American Society of Anesthesiologists was founded by nine Long Island, New York, physicians in 1905. It was founded both to improve and advance the research and practice of anesthesiology and to improve the quality of care experienced by patients undergoing surgery. Within five or so years, the group had expanded to some two dozen members and had named itself the New York Society of Anesthetists. With the inclusion of members from various parts of the country, the organization was chartered as the American Society of Anesthetists in 1935 and, 10 years later, the name was changed to the American Society of Anesthesiologists. In 1947, the society moved its headquarters from New York to Chicago and then, in 1960, to the Chicago suburb of Park Ridge.

ACTIVITIES: CURRENT AND FUTURE

Like other professional associations in the field of medicine, the ASA is trying to cope with the rapid changes being experienced in healthcare in recent years. Spe-

**American Society of Anesthesiologists
Political Action Committee Contributions**

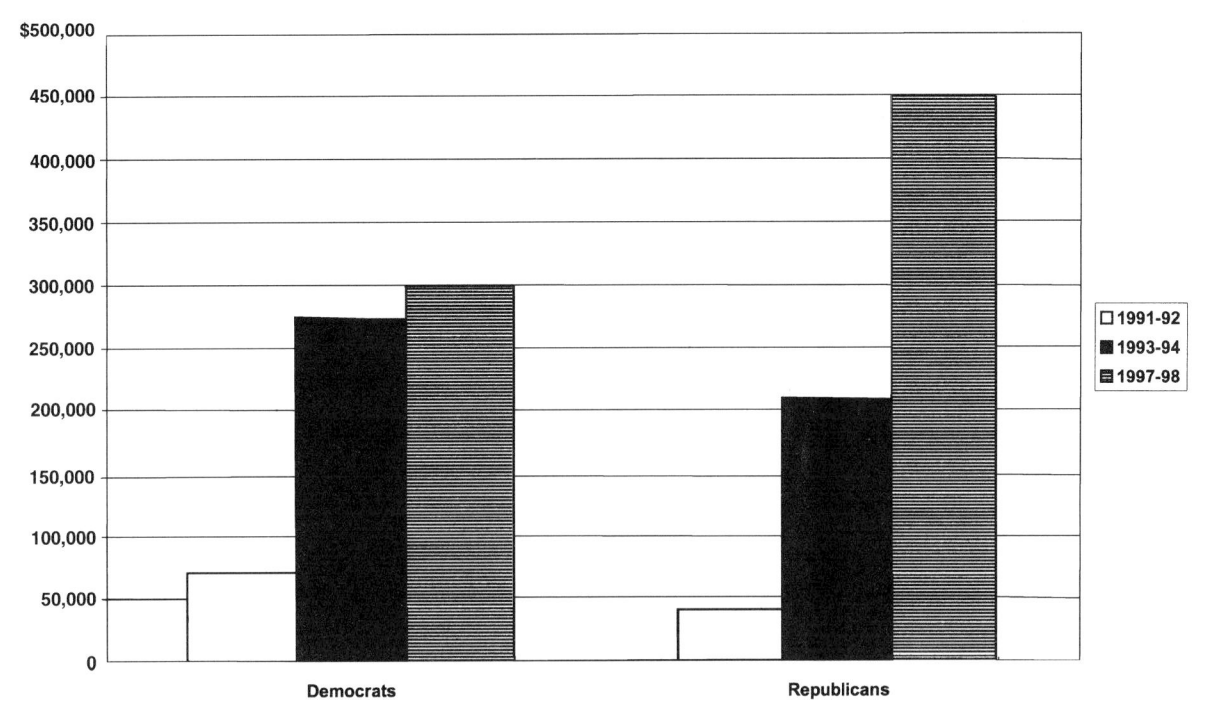

	Democrats	Republicans
1991-92	~70,000	~40,000
1993-94	~275,000	~210,000
1997-98	~300,000	~450,000

Data derived from official studies available from the Federal Election Commission, Washington, DC, 1987–1998.

cifically, the ASA is battling both with health maintenance organizations (HMOs) and the federal government, as the latter two attempt to cut costs in the provision of healthcare to customers and beneficiaries. Among the most critical of showdowns between the ASA and the federal government is an attempt by the Department of Health and Human Services (HHS) to allow for the replacement of regular licensed anesthesiologists (who are MDs) with nurse anesthetists for more routine types of surgery. At issue, specifically, is a recent proposal by the HHS's Healthcare Financing Administration (HCFA) to allow hospitals to decide if a nurse can be used to administer anesthetics to Medicaid and Medicare patients without a doctor's supervision. (Medicare and Medicaid are federal government programs offering health care to the elderly/disabled and poor, respectively.)

The cost saving, says the HCFA, could be substantial, as anesthesiologists earn on average nearly three times as much as nurse anesthetists ($218,000 versus $85,000 annually). While anesthesiologists argue that the rule change would endanger the lives of patients, nurse anesthetist organizations say that it would not jeopardize healthcare in major hospitals and could actually improve the healthcare service in small and rural hospitals, which often do not have an anesthesiologist on staff. Thus far, ASA-supported legislation to block the rule change has been stuck in Congress, although recent proposals to support more scientific studies about the implications of the rule change are being discussed. Meanwhile, nurse anesthetists are trying to introduce a bill that would require the HCFA to finalize the rule change by April 2000.

On a related issue, the ASA has recently been caught up in the controversy over limiting Medicaid coverage to women in childbirth. Following a series of revelations that hospitals—under the urging of Medicaid—were denying epidurals (lower-spine painkillers) to women undergoing difficult birthings, the ASA came out strongly on the side of some of its members who administered epidurals despite hospital and Medicaid policy. In several cases reported in New York and California, hospitals were demanding that women on Medicaid pay for epidurals in cash and in advance of surgery. The ASA is urging the federal government to look into state Medicaid programs (Medicaid, though partially federally funded, is largely administered by the states) that deny such procedures and to stop this practice.

Regarding HMOs, the ASA is trying to halt the spreading practice of in-office surgery. In recent years, the health insurance companies have vigorously attempted to remove many small and routine surgical operations from costly hospital settings to less expensive doctors' offices. The shift obviously undermines the need for hospital-based anesthesiologists and jeopardizes the incomes of many ASA members. At the same time, however, ASA president John Neeld says that the organization is "concerned about possible hazards in an office-spaced practice where you don't have the resources of a hospital when an emergency arises." Neeld says the organization may pursue efforts in Washington to limit the growth of in-office surgery through federal regulation.

Finally, on issues that are not directly related to the well-being of its members, the ASA has come down strongly on a recent, highly controversial sociomedical issue: assisted suicide. Since assisted suicide usually involves the administration of painkilling drugs along with the fatal ones, the ASA has felt a need to speak out against the practice. Along with the American Medical Association, the ASA has said that providing assistance in suicide is incompatible with the role of the physician, which—particularly in the case of anesthesiologists—should be the immediate alleviation of pain and suffering only.

FINANCIAL FACTS

Like other major associations of medical professionals, the ASA is a major donor of funds to the campaigns of congressional and presidential candidates. In the 1997–1998 election cycle alone, the ASA gave $751,529 to congressional candidates of both parties. This is a significant increase over previous election cycles. In 1991–1992—an election cycle that included races for both Congress and the presidency—the ASA gave just $112,450. At the same time, the ASA has varied over the years in its giving pattern to candidates from the two major parties. In the 1993–1994 congressional election cycle, the organization gave $275,000—or 57 percent—to Democrats. In the 1997–1998 election cycle, however, the ASA donated $467,804—or 61 percent—to Republican candidates.

JAMES CIMENT AND IMMANUEL NESS

Bibliography

"Decent Pain Control Not a Frill." *Omaha World-Herald,* March 12, 1999.

Paire, Jennifer Rampey. "Anesthesiologist Zeroes in on Safety of Patients." *Atlanta Business Chronicle,* January 15, 1999.

Zeller, Shawn. "Clamps, Sutures, and Big, Big Bucks." *The National Journal,* March 20, 1999.

BLUE CROSS AND BLUE SHIELD ASSOCIATION

The Blue Cross and Blue Shield Association (BCBSA) is the trade organization and lobbying group representing the Blue Cross and Blue Shield organization of health insurance providers. Blue Cross and Blue Shield (hereinafter referred to as "Blue Cross") is the oldest and largest health insurance organization in the United States. But Blue Cross—technically, a nonprofit organization—is not a monolithic entity. Instead, it consists of 52 independent, locally operated companies that are called "member plans" or "blue plans." These plans are located in all 50 states, the District of Columbia, and Puerto Rico.

Blue Cross companies offer health insurance to individuals, groups, small businesses, and large employers. Blue Cross provides both traditional health insurance programs—in which patients select their own physicians—and newer health maintenance organization (HMO) plans. These latter provide predetermined lists of doctors covered by the plans and are usually offered at somewhat lower rates than traditional, choice-oriented healthcare plans. Altogether, approximately one in four Americans—roughly 73 million individuals—is covered by one of Blue Cross's member plans.

The BCBSA provides a number of services to the various Blue Cross plans around the country. These services include technical support, business strategy planning, and financial consulting. In addition, the BCBSA acts to coordinate the policies of the various plans and to share technical and other resources among them. In Washington, D.C., the BCBSA serves as the member plans' voice in government. The BCBSA lobbies Congress on bills that concern the Blue Cross plans and contributes donations to candidates who are perceived as supportive of the policy position of Blue Cross member plans.

HISTORY

The origins of Blue Cross and Blue Shield go back to 1929 when an official at Baylor University in Dallas introduced a plan to guarantee schoolteachers 21 days of hospital care in an emergency situation. The fee for this service was $6 a year. Soon other groups of employees in the Dallas area joined the plan, and thus, modern health insurance provision was inaugurated. The idea quickly caught the nation's attention, and similar plans were started elsewhere in the country. Meanwhile, the blue shield symbol emerged in the Pacific Northwest, where employers—particularly in the hazardous timber industry—began paying for their employees' visits to the doctor. Arrangements were then made with certain physicians to compensate them at a predetermined rate for specific services offered to the employee-patient. In 1917, a Tacoma plan became the first to adopt the blue shield symbol.

With the Great Depression and New Deal of the 1930s—and particularly in the light of the establishment of Social Security—many doctors and hospitals feared that medicine would soon be socialized. To counteract such a move by the government, they spread the idea of health insurance plans, like that adopted in Dallas.

The Blue Cross name originated in 1933, when a Minnesota plan adopted the blue cross symbol, no doubt imitating the famous red cross that symbolized universal access to emergency healthcare, food, and shelter. Soon other health insurance plans around the country adopted it, and in 1939, the American Hospital Association adopted the symbol for all plans meeting the guidelines it had set. In 1960, the Blue Cross Association was established, which offered far more centralized leadership and guidance to the local member plans.

The Blue Cross and Blue Shield Association was created as a result of the merger between the two existing

**Blue Cross and Blue Shield Association
Political Action Committee Contributions**

Data derived from official studies available from the Federal Election Commission, Washington, DC, 1987–1998.

trade organizations that represented Blue Cross and Blue Shield in Washington, that is, the Blue Cross Association and the National Association of Blue Shield Plans, respectively.

ACTIVITIES: CURRENT AND FUTURE

Among the most controversial topics facing the Blue Cross and Blue Shield Association in recent years concerns the so-called patient's bill of rights, prompted by the meteoric growth of HMOs over the past decade or so. HMOs are different than traditional healthcare insurance companies in that they require patients to visit only those general practitioners and specialists registered with the company. To cut costs, HMOs have added a number of restrictions to the services they offer to pay for. First, before visiting a specialist, patients are required to obtain a recommendation from a general practitioner. Second, HMOs set specific payment schedules for both physicians on their list of providers as well as physicians who are not included in their plans. Many physicians complain that the HMOs do not provide adequate compensation for the services they provide. This has led to calls—by the American Medical Association (AMA) and others—for a doctors' union to fight the rates set by HMOs. But most complaints have come from customers who protest the denial of services by HMOs or, more specifically, the denial of payments for necessary services. Numerous cases have emerged in the media of HMO customers being denied important and life-saving operations.

Faced with these growing complaints, both congressional Republicans and the administration of President Bill Clinton have proposed a patient's bill of rights. In July 1999, the Republicans in the Senate were able to push through their own version, providing billions of dollars in tax breaks for health insurance customers and an appeals process for patients denied specific treatments, though the latter would have been administered by committees paid for by the health insurance companies. Clinton and congressional Democrats wanted much more, including a far more independent complaint hearing board. In addition, the Democrats wanted a more rigorous set of protections for patient privacy.

The BCBSA said that the Republican measure was

far more acceptable than proposed Democratic ones, and it remains opposed to any federal role in the complaint process against health insurance companies. According to the BCBSA, "[The] private market is better equipped to handle the challenges facing the healthcare industry than the government." Essentially, the BCBSA argues that people will purchase their policies from companies that provide a wider range of services or purchase policies with a narrower range if it means lower health insurance premiums.

On privacy, the BCBSA maintains that there are adequate protections for individual customers but that various health insurance companies need access to records in order to cut costs and provide better service. Public interest groups disagree, arguing that health insurance companies want this information in order to avoid customers who may require lots of medical care. In addition, civil liberties groups fear that looser controls of patients' records may lead to information falling into the wrong hands, such as employers who may not want to be burdened with employees with special healthcare needs.

On Medicare reform, the BCBSA says it applauds the Clinton administration's efforts to ensure its financial health into the near and long-term future. In order to do this, the BCBSA advocates more private insurance involvement in Medicare, specifically the shifting of more Medicare patients to HMOs. At the same time, however, the BCBSA stands opposed to the so-called Medigap measure advocated by the Clinton administration and congressional Democrats. Medigap would allow for the inclusion of most prescription drugs in Medicare programs. Since Medicare pays insurance companies for covering patients, this means a potential added expense to the insurance companies. The BCBSA argues that adding prescription drugs to Medicare could cause annual premiums to rise by as much as $1,200 and if shifted to the government could jeopardize efforts to ensure the future financial viability of the Medicare program.

On the issue of individuals without health insurance—now believed to be more than one in seven Americans—the BCBSA says it supports the Clinton administration's effort to use some of the budget surplus to extend coverage, especially to children. But the BCBSA insists that this not be done as a federal program or as an extension of existing programs that provide healthcare for the poor—such as Medicaid. Instead, the organization believes that the best way to extend insurance coverage is by providing tax credits to small firms for their low-wage workers which would allow them to purchase health insurance on their own, providing tax deductibility for insurance premiums to the self-employed and others without employer-sponsored coverage, and giving states federal funds to support community-based health coverage programs.

As noted above, there has been a growing move among doctors to unionize in order to fight the power of HMOs and to make sure that payments for services offered by doctors to their patients are adequately reimbursed. Currently, less than 10 percent of the nation's 680,000 doctors—that is, those who are employed directly by hospitals as salaried employees—are allowed to form unions and negotiate directly with employers. Federal antitrust laws prohibit doctors in independent practice from collective bargaining. Current efforts in Congress to lift such antitrust restrictions are strongly opposed by the BCBSA, which says that such measures confuse patient protection with protectionism for doctors. The organization also argues that such a move could cost consumers as much as $80 billion annually in additional healthcare costs. However, doctor organizations such as the AMA argue that—faced with the overwhelming power of the HMOs to set unfairly low fees—independent practitioners are independent in name only and deserve to be exempted from antitrust legislation.

On a related matter, the BCBSA is pushing for more use of so-called hospitalists. These are doctors permanently on staff at hospitals who take over from a patient's regular physician once the patient has entered the hospital. While doctors' organizations and patients' rights groups argue that this jeopardizes the patient's healthcare, the BCBSA says it will not and adds that it could save customers billions in premiums, since it will make hospital care far more cost-effective since doctors will be able to see more patients in an efficient manner. The AMA opposes the plan because it sacrifices personalized doctor–patient relationships.

FINANCIAL FACTS

The BCBSA is a moderate to large contributor to congressional and presidential campaigns, although its giving pales in comparison to those of corporate and professional association donors. Still, over the past decade's election cycles, the BCBSA has increased its donations significantly. In the 1987–1988 election cycle—which included both presidential and congressional campaigns—the BCBSA gave a total of $133,617. In the 1997–1998 election cycle—which included congressional campaigns only—the organization donated some $347,114. At the same time, the ratio given to the two major parties has changed dramatically. The Democrats received $96,358—or 71 percent—in the 1987–1988 election cycle. In the 1997–1998 election cycle, however, Democrats received just 32 percent of the BCBSA's donations, even though total donations given to Democrats had increased somewhat to $111,300.

JAMES CIMENT AND IMMANUEL NESS

Bibliography

"BCBSA Says 'Private Market Best Equipped to Handle Challenges Facing Health Care Industry Not Government.'" *PR Newswire,* July 15, 1999.

"BCBSA Urges Politicians to 'Seize the Day' and Use Newly Projected Budget Surplus to Fund Initiatives for Uninsured." *PR Newswire,* June 29, 1999.

"Blues Caution Medicare Reform Requires Responsible Action Not Political Gamesmanship; Choices of Health Plans Must Be Preserved." *PR Newswire,* June 29, 1999.

Cunningham, Robert. *The Blues: A History of the Blue Cross and Blue Shield System.* De Kalb: Northern Illinois University Press, 1997.

"Insurers Fight Change in Antitrust Laws." *BestWire,* June 22, 1999.

"Medigap Mandates Threaten to Price Seniors Out of the Market." *BestWire,* May 17, 1999.

"Physician Groups Challenge Mandatory Hospitalist Programs." *Medicine and Health,* May 3, 1999.

SECTION FIVE
AGRICULTURE

There are more than 175 agricultural interest groups actively involved in national politics in the United States today. These groups represent the growers, processors, and distributors of a wide variety of agricultural products. Prior to the 1970s, agricultural policy was made in relative isolation by the congressional agriculture committees, the Department of Agriculture, and relevant interest groups. More recently, a wide variety of interests have affected policymaking in this area.

AREA OF INTEREST

Great changes have occurred in American agriculture. At the beginning of the twentieth century, 42 percent of Americans lived on farms. By century's end, only 1.6 percent of Americans will still live there. American agriculture produces more commodities than ever, is an essential source of food and fiber, and a major earner of foreign exchange. However, fewer and fewer Americans every year are able to earn their living directly from the soil.

A much larger segment of the American workforce is involved indirectly in the production, processing, and distribution of food. When absolutely everyone who is involved in this process is counted, the total comes to just less than 19 percent of the American workforce. Eighty-two percent of these jobs, however, are located in metropolitan areas.

Between 20 percent and 25 percent of all lobbyists employed in Washington, D.C., represent interest groups that are somehow involved in the food production process. Interest groups represent all stages of the production process. Producer groups constitute only about one-fifth of all the active interest groups. Processors, agribusiness, intermediaries, middlemen, suppliers, and, more recently, agriculturally oriented public interest groups, constitute the vast majority of all groups.

TYPES OF ORGANIZATIONS

The strictly agricultural groups can be divided into general purpose and commodity groups. The general purpose groups are the oldest and largest farm organizations. The general purpose groups try to represent all farmers and ranchers in the industry. The Grange, the American Farm Bureau Federation (commonly called the Farm Bureau), the National Farmers Union, and the National Farmers Organization are the established general purpose organizations. The American Agriculture Movement, although a much newer and more militant organization, also tried to organize itself as a general purpose organization. Membership fees for these groups are quite modest, and individual farmers often belong to more than one organization.

The general purpose groups provide a wide range of services to their members. The Farm Bureau and National Farmers Union provide insurance. The National Farmers Organization acts as a bargaining agent. The Grange is now a social fraternity.

The commodity groups are organized to represent large-scale farmers and ranchers who produce a single product, such as wheat or corn. These groups reflect the increasing specialization of agriculture. They are often funded by marketing checkoffs, which are fees charged on a per-unit basis at the time of sale. Although some of these checkoffs were originally voluntary, special legislation usually requires their payment today. Some commodity groups, such as the wheat, corn, and soybean producers, represent only growers. Others, such as the National Cotton Council, represent processors as well.

A somewhat different group of food-related interest groups also exist. Food processors, such as the National Dairy Food Association, represent firms that are located farther along in the production process. These firms take raw materials that have been raised by others and turn them into food products. In addition, a number of corporations, such as Cargill, Archer Daniels Midland, and Monsanto, also play a direct and important role in agricultural politics. Cargill is the major American grain trader. Archer Daniels Midland makes a wide variety of products from corn and soybeans. Monsanto is a chemical company that produces both agrichemicals and genetically altered seeds.

AGRICULTURAL POLITICS

The politics of agriculture is changing. From the 1930s to the 1970s, agriculture policy was largely self-contained. The policy subsystem was composed of the agriculture committees in the U.S. Congress, the Agriculture Department, and the traditional agricultural interest groups. The decline in farm population that followed the Second World War, however, made it impossible for rural representatives to prevail on their own. Consequently, a series of grand compromises was made with urban representatives. The first involved a *quid pro quo*, in which farm state representatives voted in favor of the Food Stamp program in return for urban support for agricultural subsidies. The second involved the merging of environmental and agricultural concerns with the creation of the Conservation Reserve.

Agricultural politics is highly regional. The biological requirements for favorable soil and weather conditions combined with the economies of scale available to larger processors concentrate the production of different commodities in a limited number of geographic locations. The wheat, corn, and cotton belts are relatively large, while more specialized crops have much more restricted geographic bases.

The geographic concentration of agricultural producers helps them to obtain special attention from congressional representatives; however, the decline in the number of farmers and ranchers has weakened even this relationship. In 1940, 51 percent of U.S. House of Representatives members represented districts with 20 percent or more of their populations living on farms. By 1990, there were no House members who represented this kind of district. In 1940, 88 percent of United States senators represented states with 10 percent or more of their populations living on farms. By 1990, fewer than 8 percent of senators represented this kind of state. On the other hand, 13 percent of the House and 26 percent of the Senate members represent districts or states with rural majorities who are presumably more sympathetic to agricultural problems.

The political importance of agriculture is also enhanced by the propensity of agricultural groups to change political allegiances. Since the 1950s, changes in rural voting patterns have had a major impact on control of Congress. The current, extremely close partisan division in Congress has enhanced the ability of organized agriculture to obtain concessions.

The public has a largely positive view of agriculture, a view that has been of great advantage to agricultural interest groups. Like all myths, the notion of the independent farmer living in harmony with nature and supporting his family and society through honest labor has some truth to it. Most people's view of rural America is, however, more likely to be based on the romanticized memories of our parents and grandparents rather than upon current realities. Some of those current realities, such as genetic engineering, factory farming, and corporate ownership, strike a particularly dissonant chord. As agricultural experience fades even further from societal memory and more discordant notes are sounded, public support for agricultural programs will inevitably erode.

POLICY PROCESS

The policy-making process encourages the formation of a large number of interest groups. Each commodity has had slightly different legal provisions that affect it. Consequently, producers form separate organizations to monitor a very narrow range of special provisions. In addition, since the 1930s, agricultural policy has been subject to continuous revision. Farm bills were enacted periodically, usually every five years, until the 1996 Farm Bill, which extended the time period to seven years. The 1996 Farm Bill was supposed to be a permanent change, but amendments to the law ensure that, if it lapses, policy will return to the much more expensive 1938 permanent farm legislation.

RECURRING ISSUES

Historically, agricultural policy has had three major concerns. Initially it began as an attempt to maintain farmers' incomes, then quickly evolved into an effort to cope with surplus production, and more recently has dealt with environmental and consumer concerns.

For a variety of reasons, farmers and ranchers have found it difficult to maintain their incomes. As societies develop, the consumption of agricultural goods rises more slowly than income does. Changes in the weather and the impossibility of controlling production lead to greater fluctuations in the price of agricultural as opposed to industrial products. Although the large number of farmers and ranchers ensures competition among producers, these producers are at a disadvantage because their suppliers, processors, marketers, and lenders all belong to increasingly concentrated industries.

During the 1930s, the Roosevelt administration developed a number of programs designed to stabilize agricultural prices and incomes. These programs involved both credit subsidies and price supports. The government also created programs that were designed to stabilize prices by holding commodities off the market until prices rose. To protect incomes, farmers were allowed to obtain loans from the Commodity Credit Corporation, using their crops as collateral. If the price rose above the loan rate, the farmers could sell their crops and pocket the difference. If prices stayed below the loan rate, the farmers could surrender the crops in lieu of repaying the loan. Originally, this system applied to field crops that could be stored for significant lengths of time—specifically, corn, wheat, rice, peanuts, tobacco, cotton, feed grains, and honey. After 1948, subsidies were used to support dairy products as well. Later still, a system of target prices allowed farmers to receive deficiency payments if the market price fell below the national average cost of production—a figure that was usually higher than the loan rate. The levels at which loan rates, subsidies, and target prices are set have a major influence on producers' incomes.

Improvements in agricultural technology have led to the accumulation of large surpluses in both the United States and Europe, and, although many of the world's poor are hungry, they lack the income necessary to buy commodities on the world market. Consequently, the demand for agricultural commodities is often insufficient to consume all the items offered for sale. In addition, the American system of price supports and the European system of subsidies, by paying more than the theoretical market price for commodities, also encourage overproduction. Several techniques have been used to deal with surpluses. At various times, the United States has withdrawn land from production, aggressively promoted exports, and subsidized food purchases by the domestic and foreign poor. There are several methods for withdrawing land from production. Acreage limitations can be included as a requirement for participating in loan and subsidy programs. Production can be legally limited by allotment systems. Farmers can be paid to withdraw environmentally sensitive land from production through such programs as the Soil Bank during the 1950s or, as they have done more recently, with the Conservation Reserve.

Since the nineteenth century, the United States has been a major agricultural exporter. One-third of all farm land in cultivation is growing commodities for export. Consequently, it is vital to maintain foreign markets. Agricultural groups uniformly oppose the imposition of political and economic embargoes. The government has also used aggressive salesmanship and, on occasion, bonuses paid in surplus commodities to enhance exports.

While serving humanitarian ends, domestic and foreign food subsidy programs also increase the market for agricultural commodities. The school lunch program was one of the first such efforts to increase food consumption. In addition, the Food Stamp program, although primarily a domestic welfare program, also resulted in a small increase in consumption. More notably, the federal government's PL. 480 program has transferred large amounts of surplus farm commodities to underdeveloped countries that lack the ability to purchase these items on the open market.

Environmental and consumer concerns are increasingly important. Farmers and ranchers control 44 percent (cropland and pasture) of the land area in the United States. They are responsible for producing food for human consumption. Their production techniques increasingly make use of biotechnology and genetic engineering. A large number of environmental concerns affect the way farmers and ranchers manage their land. Concerns over soil erosion, wetlands protection, farmland protection, and water pollution all have a major impact on the way agricultural land is used. Food safety issues are raised by the use of pesticides, antibiotic treatment of livestock, the use of growth hormones, and factory farming techniques. Finally, ethical, practical, and safety concerns are raised by cloning, genetic engineering, and the development of transgenic species.

1996 FARM BILL

Concerned about the budget deficit and worried that the expiration of the 1990 Farm Bill would result in a return to more expensive 1938 legislation, Congress passed a new seven-year farm bill in 1996. This bill reversed many of the policies that had been in effect since the 1930s and moved agricultural policy closer to the marketplace. The bill ended limitations on production and replaced many subsidies with a declining system of deficiency payments that were supposed to phase out after seven years. Peanut and sugar price support programs were reduced, but not eliminated. Commodity loans were continued, but at a reduced level for most crops. Dairy price supports were also phased out, but regional marketing orders were retained as a way of regulating prices. Finally, the Conservation Reserve was also continued.

The 1996 bill was passed at a time of relatively high agricultural prices. It was supported by the Republican leadership in Congress, with the strong support of Representative Pat Roberts of Kansas. Agribusiness and midwestern corn and soybean farmers were also supportive of the legislation. Cotton, peanut, and western wheat farmers were generally opposed. Democrats, particularly farm-state Democrats, were not happy with the bill but went along after the Food Stamp and Conservation Reserve programs were continued. A number of urban and suburban Democrats, however, abandoned their previous position of supporting subsidies as part of a quid pro quo for food stamps. President Bill Clinton, although critical of the bill for eliminating an important farm safety net, signed it into law.

The collapse of foreign export markets in Asia and Russia has undermined many of the justifications used to support the 1996 Farm Bill. Prices will be extremely low at precisely the moment when subsidies are finally phased out—all of which sets the stage for a new round of farm legislation in 2003.

AGRICULTURAL POLITICAL ACTION COMMITTEES (PACs)

Agriculture, as an economic sector, is a significant source of campaign contributions. During the 1997–1998 election cycle, this sector gave $15 million to candidates for public office. This figure is half of what was given in the previous, 1995–1996, cycle. Campaign contributions from agriculture rank well behind the leading financial, insurance, and real estate sectors, which gave $35 million in the 1998 cycle. Agriculture, however, gave more than defense ($5.8 million), communications and electronics ($11.9 million), energy and natural resources ($14.8 million), transportation ($14.3 million), and construction ($8.3 million).

Within agriculture, large contributions are made by the noncrop-producing agricultural service ($2.9 million) and food processing ($2.8 million) sectors. The tobacco industry usually makes substantial ($2.3 million) contributions. Among the tobacco interests, Philip Morris was by far the largest contributor ($794,533) in 1998. The dairy industry is also a major donor ($1.3 million). Dairy contributions came from a number of producer and processor cooperatives. Contributions from crop producers and basic processors were also substantial ($3.3 million). This is, however, a diverse group. Sugar producers are among the largest contributors ($1.3 million) in this category. The forestry and forest products industry is the most Republican (83 percent) portion of the agricultural contributors, whereas the crop producers and basic processing group is the least Republican (52 percent) portion of the industry.

AGRICULTURE COMMITTEES

The Senate Agriculture, Nutrition, and Forestry Committee and the House Agriculture Committee are responsible for writing agricultural legislation. The Senate Agriculture, Nutrition, and Forestry Committee has 18 members who serve on four subcommittees. The House Agriculture Committee has 51 members who serve on five subcommittees. In general, the majority of the members of both the House and Senate committees represent the agricultural states of the South and Midwest.

The patterns of campaign contributions given to members of the two committees are very different. Agricultural interest groups are only one, and not even a very important one at that, of several sources of funds for members of the Senate Agriculture, Nutrition, and Forestry Committee. On the other hand, agricultural interest groups are a major (first or second most important) source of funds for members of the House Agriculture Committee.

Congressional reforms in the 1970s increased the autonomy and importance of congressional subcommittees. These changes contributed to the increasing importance of commodity groups in subsequent agricultural politics. The commodity groups, however, were unable to agree on farm legislation in the 1980s. Interest groups at that time were frequently described as occupying policy niches in a new, more decentralized, decision-making process.

AGENCIES

Agricultural interest groups have a close working relationship with the United States Department of Agriculture, its related organizations, and the land grant universities. The Agriculture Department was created in 1862 as a result of Republican efforts to mobilize support for the Lincoln administration and to address the needs of farmers in rural America. The addition of new responsibilities, which occurred as a consequence of the New Deal, quadrupled the size of the department. With 98,000 employees, the United States Department of Agriculture (USDA) is the fifth-largest civilian agency. Its budget of $63 billion, most of which is spent on food programs, constitutes 3.7 percent of the federal budget.

Founded in 1933 and incorporated in 1948, the Commodity Credit Corporation (CCC), a wholly owned government corporation, is contained within the Agriculture Department. The secretary of agriculture is the chairman of the board of the CCC. Among other things, the CCC helps to moderate fluctuating agricultural prices by buying commodities when their prices are low and selling them when prices rise. The Commodity Credit Corporation is authorized to borrow up to $30 billion from the treasury and private lenders.

Land grant universities—universities that were dedicated to the teaching of the agricultural and mechanical sciences—were created as a result of the Morrill Act of 1862. They became centers of agricultural research late in the nineteenth century and developed particularly close ties to rural communities. These universities developed outreach programs (known as extension programs) that were designed to serve citizens of their states who still lived on farms. In 1914, these programs were given federal support and direction by the Smith-Lever Act, which created the Cooperative Extension Service.

The Agriculture Department not only cooperates with agricultural interest groups, but also has promoted the creation of some of those interest groups, such as the Farm Bureau. The relationship between interest groups and the Agriculture Department varies by program. The Extension Service and CCC originally had particularly close ties to the Farm Bureau. The relationship is also affected by political party control over the department. Historically, the Farm Bureau has had more influence during Republican administrations and the National Farmers Union has had more influence during Democratic administrations.

The Cooperative Extension Service responds to both state and federal mandates. The land grant universities, which are state-supported institutions, administer the Cooperative Extension programs in their states. Consequently, state legislatures can, within certain federal guidelines, also regulate their operations—a fact that is important because the relative influence of agricultural interest varies considerably by state.

CONSEQUENCES OF INTEREST GROUP ACTIVITIES

When evaluating the effects of interest group activity, one must examine the impact of that activity on the individuals who are represented by those groups and the impact on society as a whole. Agricultural interest groups have been most active when they represented producers who feared lower-cost foreign imports (sugar), who were socially reprehensible (tobacco), or who required government assistance to overcome foreign trade barriers (wheat). Agricultural interest groups have been most effective in only the first two circumstances. Import restrictions on sugar and cotton have been retained. The tobacco companies have also managed to delay societal retribution and modify proposed tobacco settlements. Efforts to gain access to foreign markets, however, have been less successful.

Moreover, agricultural interest groups have not been able to save the family farm. The number of farmers has declined precipitously since the 1930s. While the economies of scale are very modest in agriculture, large farms have a greater volume of production that can be used to support income. All farmers, both large and small, are more productive, but agricultural income has not kept pace with urban income. Consequently, many small farmers left agriculture for higher-paying city jobs, and only a tiny fraction of the previous number of families continued to earn their living from agriculture. Agricultural products have also declined in value in both absolute and relative terms.

One reason agricultural interest groups and the government programs that they support have not been able to reverse the decline in the number of farms is the way those benefits are paid. Only 15 percent of farmers received more than 70 percent of all the benefits, and only 32 percent of all farmers grew program crops that were eligible for direct government support.

Consumers in the United States spend a relatively small amount of their income, 13 percent, on food. While some government programs—sugar, milk, and cotton—keep prices above a level that would result in a completely open market, the impact on relative food prices is small because of the greater comparative prosperity of the nonfarm economy.

Taxpayers in the United States pay the costs of agricultural policies through direct and indirect payments to farmers. The changes made in farm programs in the 1996 Farm Bill reduced those payments. These reductions occurred in response to demands by politically powerful fiscal conservatives to reduce the federal budget deficit. Farmers without price supports and government subsidies must now compete directly with larger, corporate-owned farms, and this competition may threaten their survival.

ANDREW D. MCNITT

Bibliography

Albrecht, Don, and Steve Murdock. *The Sociology of U.S. Agriculture.* Ames: Iowa State University Press, 1990.

Blanpied, Nancy A., ed. *Farm Policy, The Politics of Soil, Surpluses, and Subsidies.* Washington, DC: Congressional Quarterly, 1984.

Block, William J. *The Separation of the Farm Bureau and the Extension Service.* Urbana: University of Illinois Press, 1960.

Browne, William P. *Private Interests, Public Policy, and American Agriculture.* Lawrence: University of Kansas Press, 1988.

Browne, William P., and Allan Cigler. *U.S. Agricultural Groups.* Westport, CT: Greenwood Publishing Group, 1990.

Browne, William P., Jerry R. Skees, Louis E. Swanson, Paul B. Thompson, and Laurian J. Unnevehr. *Sacred Cows and Hot Potatoes: Agrarian Myths in Agricultural Policy.* Boulder, CO: Westview Press, 1992.

Greenblatt, Alan. "Farmers Have Whip Hand in Drive for Control of House." *Congressional Quarterly Weekly,* August 15, 1998.

Heinz, John. "Political Impasse in Farm Support Legislation." In *Interest Group Politics in America,* edited by Robert Salisbury. New York: Harper and Row, 1970.

Herring, Pendleton. *Group Representation Before Congress.* New York: Russell and Russell, 1929.

Kurian, George T. *A Historical Guide to the U.S. Government.* New York: Oxford University Press, 1998.

Makinson, Larry, and Joshua Goldstein. *Open Secrets: The Encyclopedia of Congressional Money and Politics.* Washington, DC: Congressional Quarterly, 1992–1996.

Rapp, David. *How the U.S. Got into Agriculture and Why it Can't Get Out.* Washington, DC: Congressional Quarterly, 1988.

AMERICAN FARM BUREAU FEDERATION

The American Farm Bureau Federation (commonly referred to as the Farm Bureau) is both the largest and most important of the general interest agricultural groups. The Farm Bureau's general headquarters is in Park Ridge, Illinois, and it also maintains an office in Washington, D.C. Although the Farm Bureau represents a broad range of agricultural producers in all 50 states and Puerto Rico, its traditional base of support has been in the Midwest and South. It is usually described as an organization that represents prosperous corn and cotton farmers in those regions.

The Farm Bureau claims to represent 4.7 million families. This figure, however, vastly exceeds the 2.1 million farms that the census bureau reported in 1991—using an extremely loose definition of a farm as any agricultural property that sold over $1,000 worth of commodities per year. Consequently, a large proportion of Farm Bureau members are obviously not directly involved in agricultural production. Membership roles include a large number of other rural residents as well as insurance subscribers who have purchased insurance from the Farm Bureau's insurance companies.

The Farm Bureau takes positions on a wide variety of issues. Although it originally supported the New Deal farm programs, the Farm Bureau broke with the national government over the Roosevelt administration's policy of increased agricultural production during the Second World War. Since that time, the Farm Bureau has, at least at the national level, preferred greater reliance on free-market solutions. State farm bureaus, however, are free to disagree with—and in fact do on occasion disagree with—national policies. One of the outstanding examples of this diversity of opinion is the Wisconsin Farm Bureau's disagreement with the National Farm Bureau over the question of dairy price supports.

HISTORY

The American Farm Bureau Federation was founded in Chicago in 1920. The national organization is a federation of state and local organizations. The land grant colleges, through their extension services in cooperation with the United States Department of Agriculture, helped to create the Farm Bureau. The Farm Bureau tended to attract the more prosperous farmers, who were interested in sponsoring agents. Rather than work through existing farm organizations, the Cooperative Extension Service promoted the creation of entirely new county agricultural groups, which sometimes included other rural professionals and business leaders as members in order to meet the minimum size requirements to get a county agent. In order to qualify for a county agent, a community had to have a local farmers organization that would agree to sponsor the program. These county organizations then formed state farm bureaus, which in turn founded the national federation. The Farm Bureau experienced rapid initial growth, peaking in 1921 at 466,000, but was hurt by the agricultural depression of the twenties, which reduced its membership to a low of 163,000 in 1933. The Farm Bureau managed to recover after endorsing the New Deal agricultural programs. Again, the Cooperative Extension Service helped the Farm Bureau recover by providing vital explanations of new government programs that became available under the Agricultural Adjustment Act to members of the local farm bureaus. Before the Second World War, the National Grange, which represented farmers in the northeast and Pacific Northwest, with 639,000 members as late as 1939, was much larger than the Farm Bureau. It was only after the Second World War that the Farm Bureau became the dominant general-purpose agricultural interest group.

The Farm Bureau was periodically criticized by other farm organizations for its close ties to the extension service. Members of the National Farmers Union and, on occasion, the Grange criticized the extension service for allegedly discriminating against their members. Of particular concern was the relationship between the Farm Bureau and the extension service in 15 states where state farm bureaus made direct financial contributions to the extension program, as well as the actions of some county agents who actively recruited Farm Bureau members. Although the Farm Bureau won most of the legislative and court battles that resulted from this conflict, the leadership of the Farm Bureau eventually decided that legal separation would not damage the Farm Bureau and instead would remove a source of continuing criticism. Consequently, legal separation was implemented with the Farm Bureau's acquiescence on a state-by-state basis during the 1950s. By 1960, institutional—but not informal—links between the Farm Bureau and the extension service were largely dissolved.

The Farm Bureau's ability to dominate agricultural policy making eroded in the 1960s and 1970s as a result of the rise in commodity organizations. The commodity groups specialized in representing the interests of only those farmers who produced a single crop. Although they did not replace the Farm Bureau, and in fact often had members in common, the commodity groups collectively exercised increasing influence over the policy process. The 1996 Farm Bill has also created problems for the Farm Bureau. The bill's reduction of support payments and production controls is a source of internal dissension. A number of local farm bureaus have broken with the national organization over support for the bill.

ACTIVITIES: CURRENT AND FUTURE

The national, state, and local farm bureaus take positions on a wide range of agricultural and national political issues. They are interested in a broad spectrum of public policies that affect rural America. Although the national organization does not have a political action committee, state and local farm bureaus frequently make political contributions. The Farm Bureau's endorsement is actively sought by politicians in a number of states—even politicians who do not receive the Farm Bureau's endorsement are compelled to appear at Farm Bureau forums.

The Farm Bureau is politically conservative and, since the 1950s, has been closely identified with the Republican Party. It has frequently taken positions hostile to organized labor. In the 1940s, it helped to kill the Farm Security Administration, a program designed to help tenant farmers acquire title to their own land. In recent years, it has generally opposed extension of minimum wage and labor laws to agricultural workers.

The Farm Bureau is more than a political interest group. Its strength and longevity are a result of the wide range of services it provides to members. Originally, the close tie between the Farm Bureau and the Cooperative Extension Service gave Farm Bureau members access to a wealth of information on new developments in scientific agriculture. The Farm Bureau provides training in commodity marketing for members, who also qualify for a wide range of consumer discounts. One of the most attractive features of the Farm Bureau is its insurance business. Even individuals who have significant differences with the Farm Bureau often belong because of the comprehensive insurance coverage. All individuals who purchase Farm Bureau insurance are considered to be members of the organization.

There is every reason to believe that the Farm Bureau will continue to be the major, general-purpose, agricultural organization. The wide range of economic benefits it provides to members, its close association with the largest, most successful agricultural producers, and its ability to expand membership to rural residents not directly engaged in agriculture all point to its continued organizational influence. Its role as the major representative of agricultural interests, however, will not be unchallenged. The growing importance of commodity organizations, the increasing disparity in the number of individuals involved in processing (as opposed to producing) agricultural commodities, and the increasing importance of nontraditional environmental and consumer groups in agricultural policy-making will all complicate the Farm Bureau's future.

FINANCIAL FACTS

The American Farm Bureau Federation does not have a national political action committee (PAC). Many—but not all—state federations, however, have their own PACs. In 1998, 11 state Farm Bureau PACs and the six regional Missouri Farm Bureau PACs gave a total of $296,545 to 109 congressional candidates. This means that the Farm Bureau organizations are, in combination, by far the largest political contributor of all the general farm organizations. The relative sizes of contributions vary considerably by state. The smallest contributor, the Arizona Farm Bureau, gave $224 during the 1998 cycle, whereas the largest contributor, the Texas Farm Bureau, gave $77,050.

The Farm Bureau's state federations generally give only to their local congressional candidates. Most funds go to candidates for the House, and the Republican candidates receive 74 percent of all contributions. Democratic candidates receive significant contributions only from farm bureaus located in certain southern states and two of the six midwestern states.

ANDREW D. MCNITT

Bibliography

American Farm Bureau Federation (The Farm Bureau): www.fb.com

Browne, William P., and Alan J. Cigler. *U.S. Agricultural Groups*. Westport, CT: Greenwood Publishing Group, 1990.

AMERICAN AGRICULTURE MOVEMENT

Growing out of the "tractorcade" protests for farm aid in the 1970s, the American Agriculture Movement (AAM) became an effective advocate for agricultural interests during the 1980s. The American Agriculture Movement is a general farm organization that represents small farmers and ranchers. Although its formal membership is small, it has had a considerably greater influence on the agricultural community because of the large number of AAM sympathizers in other organizations, including the relatively conservative Farm Bureau.

Most of the members of the American Agriculture Movement are from the southern plains, Nebraska, South Dakota, the corn belt, and the deep south. The organization maintains an office in Washington, D.C., and has acquired considerable skill in lobbying Congress. Members testified at hearings on farm bills in 1981, 1985, 1990, and 1996.

HISTORY

In 1977, the American Agriculture Movement was founded in Colorado by farmers and ranchers who suffered from low prices, high interest rates, and the declining value of farmland. Most of the members of the American Agriculture Movement were younger farmers and ranchers who operated their own enterprises.

The leadership of the American Agriculture Movement was particularly adept at attracting media coverage. "Tractorcades" and carefully staged protests increased public awareness of the organization. Dissatisfaction with President Jimmy Carter's agricultural policies led the American Agriculture Movement to support presidential candidate Ronald Reagan in the 1980 national election. Reagan's even greater support for free-market agricultural policies, however, proved a great disappointment to the organization.

Like many social movements that came before it, the American Agriculture Movement split into mainstream and fundamentalist groups in 1983. The National AAM followed the path of formal institutionalization and became a traditional interest group. Grassroots AAM, however, remained a collection of militant local activists who increasingly adhered to a political ideology that can best be characterized as a mixture of left-wing and right-wing conspiracy theories. National AAM continues to operate with some difficulties, whereas grassroots AAM has largely faded from the scene.

ACTIVITIES: CURRENT AND FUTURE

The American Agriculture Movement has five goals: 100 percent parity, that is, equality in commodity prices; food reserves at 100 percent; farmer boards involved in policy making at all levels; requiring imports to enter the country at 100 percent parity; and a long-range plan for agriculture. Although several of these goals are probably unobtainable, the organization is currently working for many that are more achievable. Specifically, the AAM favors legislation requiring imported commodities to be labeled with the country of origin; it is concerned about tax advantages given to foreign owners of American farmland and it would like to see the reform of inheritance taxes.

The American Agriculture Movement opposed the 1996 Farm Bill. The organization is skeptical of the Clinton administration's commitment to agriculture and has called for Secretary of Agriculture Dan Glickman's resignation. Although the AAM has declined in size, the organization maintains a web site and has just held a convention to commemorate the 20th anniversary of the original "tractorcade." It has also worked to establish ties to environmental, labor, and urban groups.

The American Agriculture Movement's future is difficult to predict. It had a progressively harder time raising money during the 1980s. The organization was caught in a strategic paradox. Militant tactics had been deemphasized because they alienated policy makers. However, those same militant tactics were the major recruiting tool for the organization. Without militant action, the AAM was just another interest group, and, as another interest group, the AAM did not offer the economic benefits that other older groups offered their members. Moreover, the collapse of agricultural prices again in the late nineties created an opportunity for a more militant agricultural organization. The American Agriculture Movement may be able to take advantage of this new situation.

FINANCIAL FACTS

The American Agriculture Movement established a political action committee, AAM-PAC, in the early 1980s. At one time, this PAC had assets of over $220,000, which made it one of the most prosperous of the general-purpose agricultural groups. Fund raising, however, declined precipitously during the 1984 election cycle. Between 1984 and 1988, contributions to candidates declined from $27,525 to $17,072. The requirements for endorsing candidates also proved to be particularly divisive. The PAC was dissolved in the 1990s. During its brief existence, the American Agriculture Movement's PAC gave significantly more contributions to Democratic candidates than to Republican candidates.

ANDREW D. McNITT

Bibliography

Browne, William P., and Alan J. Cigler. *U.S. Agricultural Groups.* Westport, CT: Greenwood Publishing Group, 1990.

Mooney, Patrick, and Theo J. Majka. *Farmers' and Farm Workers' Movements.* New York: Twayne Publishers, 1995.

AMERICAN MEAT INSTITUTE

With headquarters in Arlington, Virginia, the American Meat Institute (AMI) represents the meat and poultry industry to the federal government, the media, and the public. Although the organization concentrates on lobbying against further regulation of the industry, it also focuses on issues involving international trade. Current areas of focus for the AMI include food safety, meat irradiation, free trade, user fees for inspections, and labeling laws.

There are currently about 1,060 AMI members, with three levels of membership. The first level, general membership, which consists of about 47 percent of the total, is available to any North American company dealing with packing or processing animal proteins. Dues at this level are based on the number of employees. The second level, supplier membership, which makes up about 28 percent of the total, is open to any company that supplies goods, equipment, or services to animal protein packers and processors. At this level, dues are based on annual sales, and range from $750 to $10,000 per year. The third level, associate membership, which consists of about 25 percent of the total, is available to any company involved in the meat or poultry industry exclusive of the first two membership options. Dues for associate membership are $1,000 per year.

Member benefits include an annual member directory, a domestic and international trade referral service, insurance coverage, membership on specialized committees, management conferences, and discounted services, such as long-distance service, overnight shipping, and the like. The AMI also provides members with information about proposed regulations and policy changes through legislative monitoring and alerts.

HISTORY

The AMI, originally named the American Meat Packers Association, was founded in 1906, when federal meat inspection laws were first passed. In response to the 1907 Federal Meat Inspection Act, the group sought to aid companies in complying with the new federal regulations as well as to fight further regulation by Congress. The AMI changed its name in 1919 to the Institute of American Meat Packers, and adopted its current name in 1940. The AMI merged with the National Independent Meat Packers Association in 1982. The organization grew again in 1990, when it began managing the U.S. Hide, Skin, and Leather Association, and, in 1991, as the AMI began allowing poultry processors to join as full members.

ACTIVITIES: CURRENT AND FUTURE

The AMI has a regular lobbying presence in Washington, D.C. Indeed, in the late 1970s, the group moved its headquarters from Chicago, the traditional center of the meatpacking industry, to Arlington, Virginia, just outside of Washington, D.C., where the group could have a greater effect on federal policy making. In 1997, the AMI employed five in-house lobbyists, and spent $120,000 on lobbying efforts.

The AMI takes a traditional "insider" approach to lobbying Congress and executive agencies. Testimony at congressional committee and executive agency hearings, published statements sent to lawmakers, and meetings with lawmakers are the typical lobbying strategies used by the group. Briefings between AMI members and lawmakers are held on a regular basis. In some cases, the AMI provides lawmakers with educational trips to learn more about the meat and poultry industry. Also, a Government Affairs Conference is held in the spring of odd-numbered years. All members are invited to Washington, D.C., for this conference to discuss federal issues related to the industry. During this conference, the AMI coordinates face-to-face meetings between members and their representatives.

The AMI is also involved in campaign finance. Its political action committee supports industry-friendly candidates for federal office, typically Republican candidates. Furthermore, the Political Education Committee funds projects designed to support the meat and poultry industry in Washington. Finally, the AMI has occasionally engaged in more indirect lobbying, through letter-writing campaigns by members protesting or supporting legislative or regulatory actions.

The AMI has increasingly become involved in international trade issues. In 1997, it hired a senior official from the Office of the U.S. Trade Representative to lobby on trade issues. The AMI also established an International Trade Committee to focus on trade issues and the removal of trade barriers. It has actively testified before House and Senate committees, as well as the Office of the U.S. Trade Representative, against trade barriers. The weekly *Trade Alert Newsletter* keeps members up to date on domestic and international trade issues.

The AMI is also heavily involved in the regulatory politics of meat and poultry production. It has regular meetings with a number of regulatory agencies, including the Department of Agriculture, Department of Commerce, Department of Justice, Environmental Protection Agency, Food and Drug Administration, and Occupational Safety and Health Administration. The AMI's *Regulatory Action Alerts* provides members with faxed announcements of regulatory changes. Also, the organization's staff helps members in dealing with regulatory problems, often representing them in disputes with the United States Department of Agriculture (USDA).

Besides lobbying activities, the AMI is active in educating members about issues concerning the meat and poultry industry. AMI members also have access to several educational products offered by the organization. One important topic is Hazard Analysis and Critical Control Points (HACCP), which is a new food-safety inspection system. The AMI offers a training program in HACCP in several locations throughout the country every year, and offers company-specific training programs as well. Information kits are available to members, covering a wide range of topics, including animal welfare, food safety, irradiation, worker safety, and consumer trends. In addition, the AMI helps members deal with public relations. It provides members with *Communication Alerts*, informing them of breaking news-media stories that could affect the industry. Outlines of press releases and statements are made available to members, as well as crisis-management assistance. Public relations and crisis-management handbooks are published by the AMI to further aid members in dealing with the media and public opinion. Finally, it offers members access to a generic advertising campaign, which can be customized to individual companies.

Although Congress and state governments have passed increasingly stringent laws dealing with food safety and production, the AMI has been successful in shaping government policy to minimize the costs of regulation for producers. For instance, it has successfully fought proposed bans on the food preservative sodium nitrate in food products. The AMI has also strongly supported greater self-regulation by the industry, such as HACCP, and less government regulation. In the area of international trade, the AMI has fought for greater competition with the European meat industry, especially in terms of regulations.

Although the AMI has generally been successful in removing trade barriers and minimizing federal and state regulations, it faces several strong challengers. Many consumer groups, environmental groups, and labor unions oppose the AMI in the area of regulation. These groups have not always succeeded in fighting the AMI, but they do pose a threat. As the media make the public more aware of dangers associated with meat and poultry production, it is likely that the U.S. government will enact stronger regulations. For instances, if cases of E coli and salmonella increase and are reported by the media, the public will probably demand stronger regulation. Similarly, media reporting of the "mad cow disease" threat in the mid 1990s resulted in the USDA's taking a closer look at the livestock feeding practices of the meat and poultry industry.

Despite these potential threats, the AMI will probably continue to expand in the area of international trade. From 1991 to 1995, U.S. exports of red meat products increased from nearly $2.9 billion to over $4.5 billion. Similarly, U.S. exports of poultry products increased from $680 million to over $2 billion. Such significant increases in only four years suggest that the AMI's focus on free trade has been successful and will continue to grow. Furthermore, it appears that the AMI has dealt with public relations problems, such as the "mad cow disease" threat, quite well. The USDA's decision to move toward more self-regulation, through HACCP, reflects some confidence that the industry can

**American Meat Institute
Political Action Committee Contributions**

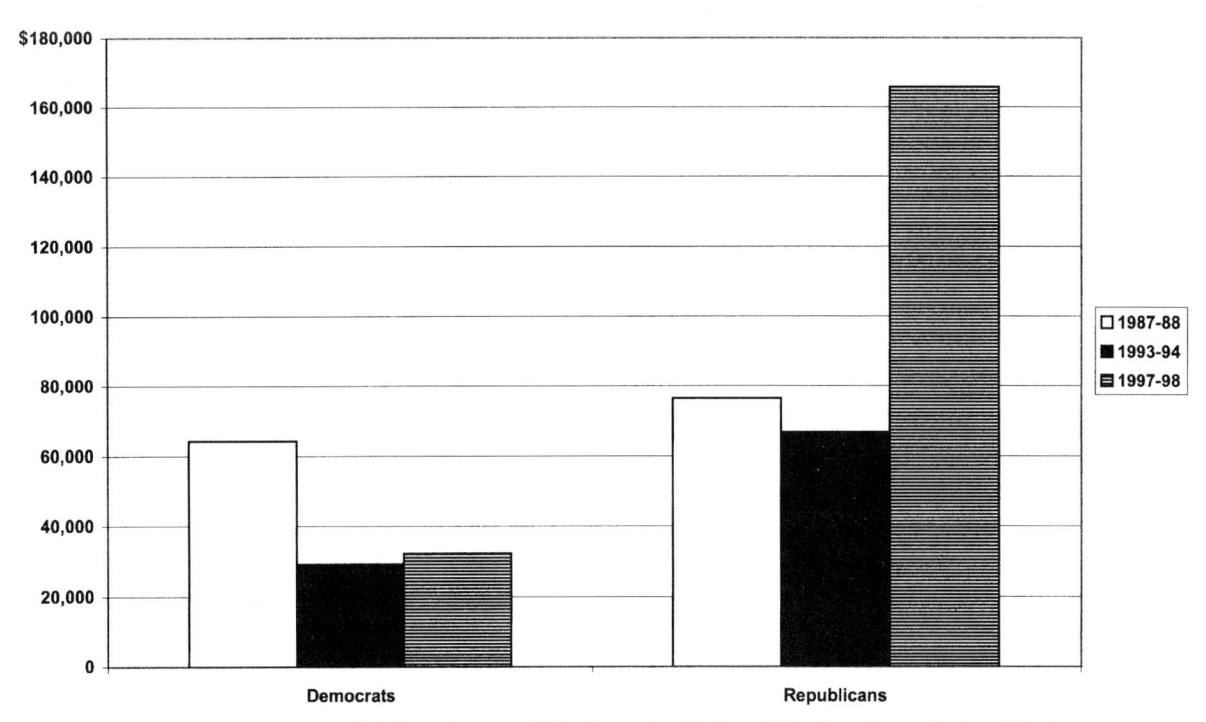

[Bar chart showing PAC contributions to Democrats and Republicans for 1987-88, 1993-94, and 1997-98. Democrats received approximately $65,000 (1987-88), $30,000 (1993-94), and $32,000 (1997-98). Republicans received approximately $77,000 (1987-88), $68,000 (1993-94), and $167,000 (1997-98).]

Data derived from official studies available from the Federal Election Commission, Washington, DC, 1987–1998.

set its own approach in regulating production. The AMI should continue to be a powerful lobby for the meat and poultry industry.

FINANCIAL FACTS

In 1998, the AMI's receipts totaled $132,383, and its expenditures came to $187,950. Whereas it makes campaign contributions to both major political parties, it has increasingly favored the Republican Party. In particular, Republican dominance in Congress since 1994 has caused a significant shift in contributions, away from Democratic candidates and toward Republican candidates.

ANDREW D. McNITT

Bibliography

American Meat Institute: www.meatami.org

Browne, William P., and Alan J. Cigler. *U.S. Agricultural Groups*. Westport, CT: Greenwood Publishing Group, 1990.

Center for Responsive Politics: www.crp.org

Federal Election Commission: www.fec.gov

AMERICAN SUGARBEET GROWERS ASSOCIATION

The American Sugarbeet Growers Association is a commodity group, representing 12,000 sugar beet growers who live in 13 western and midwestern states. The American Sugarbeet Growers Association was founded in 1975 after the 1974 expiration of the Sugar Act. The American Sugarbeet Growers replaced the earlier National Federation of Beet Growers, which dated back to the 1950s. The association belongs to the sugar alliance that unites sugar beet, cane sugar, and corn producers with sugar millers and corn sweetener producers—most notably, the Archer Daniels Midland Corporation. The American Sugarbeet Growers Association is, in spite of its small size, politically active. Its staff is located in Washington, D.C., and employs two full-time lobbyists. In 1996, sugar beet growers received cash receipts of $1 billion for the sale of their commodity.

HISTORY

One of the first acts of the United States government was to impose an import duty on sugar in the 1790s as part of Secretary of the Treasury Alexander Hamilton's efforts to balance the budget. Although this early tariff was primarily aimed at raising revenue, it began a long history of government intervention in the sugar market. In 1890, the government shifted its policy from revenue enhancement to promotion of the domestic sugar industry. From 1934 to 1974, a series of sugar acts divided the American market between domestic and foreign producers—each of whom was assigned a separate import quota. The effect of this controlled market was to raise U.S. sugar prices significantly above world prices. The failure to reauthorize the Sugar Act in 1975 resulted in a brief experience with an open market, until low prices led to renewed legislative protection in 1977.

The politics of sugar became more interesting in the 1980s as industries that used sugar as a component in food processing sought changes in the system of price supports and import restrictions. The sugar industry was able to resist their challengers in 1985, but had to accept some changes in the 1996 Farm Bill.

The future of the American Sugarbeet Growers Association depends on its ties to the producers of other sweeteners. Although domestic sugar producers, both cane and beet, achieve relatively high yields per acre, their costs of production are higher than those of foreign producers of cane sugar. The above-market U.S. price also creates room for the corn sweetener industry, which would not have its current price advantages if it had to compete with sugar at the world price. In combination, all of these groups have significantly greater access to political power and so far have been successful in maintaining significant protections. For sugar beet growers, the costs of failing to control the policy-making process would be great; they are the most vulnerable of domestic producers. Sugar beets earn a great deal more per acre than any other substitute crop, and the average price of sugar produced from sugar beets is slightly higher than that for domestic cane sugar.

ACTIVITIES: CURRENT AND FUTURE

The American Sugarbeet Growers Association's activities are largely channeled through the Sugar Alliance. Most of the information about the organization's policy preferences and political positions is found on the Sugar Alliance's home page rather than the Sugarbeet Growers' web site. This organization is concerned primarily with adjusting to the changes in the sugar market that are the result of NAFTA, GATT, and the 1996 Farm Bill. Although none of these initiatives will produce a worldwide free market in sugar, all will increase the level of competition. NAFTA will, over a long period of time, eventually create a common North American

**American Sugarbeet Growers Association
Political Action Committee Contributions**

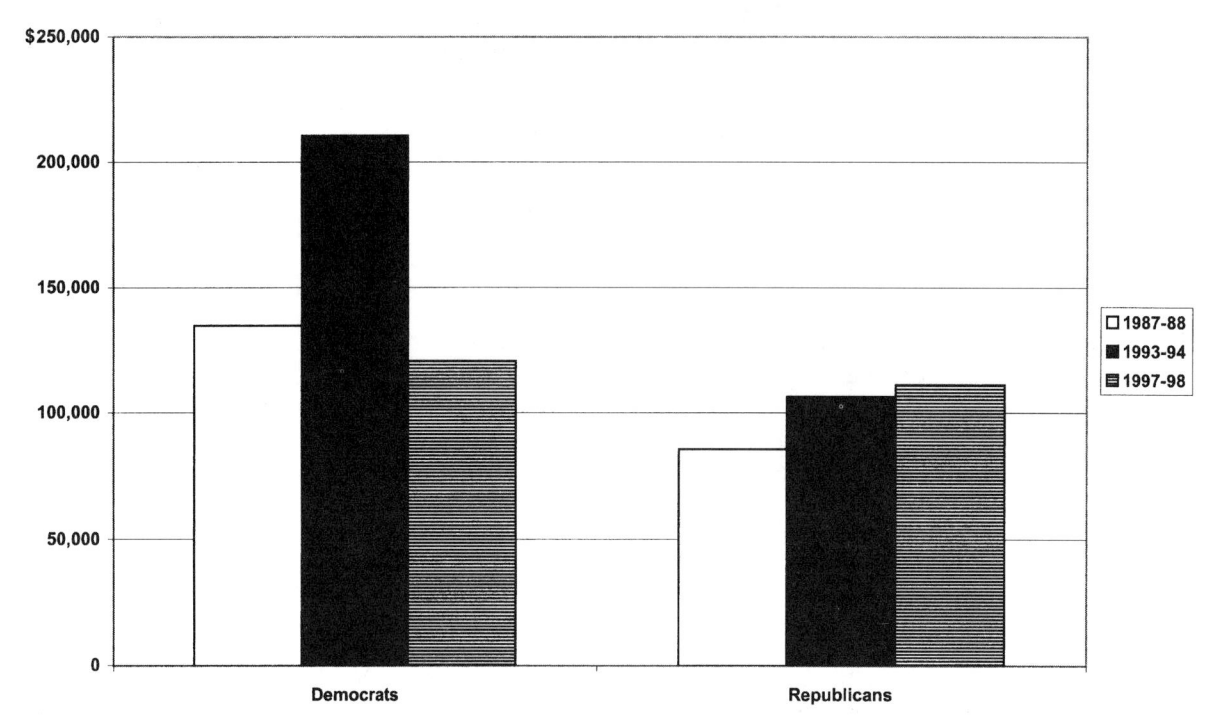

[Bar chart showing PAC contributions to Democrats and Republicans for election cycles 1987-88, 1993-94, and 1997-98. Democrats received approximately $135,000 (1987-88), $210,000 (1993-94), and $120,000 (1997-98). Republicans received approximately $85,000 (1987-88), $105,000 (1993-94), and $110,000 (1997-98).]

Data derived from official studies available from the Federal Election Commission, Washington, DC, 1987–1998.

sugar market. This market, however, will be protected from the world market by a common tariff structure. GATT tries to make agricultural policy less rigid by requiring a shift from the use of import quotas to tariffs, and for a reduction in export subsidies. The 1996 Farm Bill eliminated marketing allotments for domestic producers, made crop loans less financially attractive, and allowed for higher sugar imports.

FINANCIAL FACTS

The American Sugarbeet Growers Association and the other representatives of the sugar industry are major political donors. They give a lot of money to a large number of representatives on a regular basis. Since 1988, the Sugarbeet Growers have given between $220,000 and $327,000 per election cycle to candidates for Congress.

The largest donation came during the run-up to the 1996 Farm Bill. Total donations were $327,057 for 1990, $311,707 for 1992, $317,140 for 1994, and $304,667 for 1996. After the passage of the Farm Bill, donations dropped back to $231,985 for the 1998 election cycle. The sugar beet growers give money to both political parties. When the Democrats were the majority party in Congress prior to 1994, the Sugarbeet Growers gave them between 59 percent to 68 percent of their contributions. After the Democrats lost their majority in 1994, the pattern of donations changed. The sugar beet association's contributions to Democrats dropped to 50 percent for the 1996 cycle and 52 percent for the 1998 cycle.

The American Sugarbeet Growers Association gives almost all—89 percent to 94 percent—of its money to incumbents. The association also gives more—69 percent to 78 percent—of its money to House as opposed to Senate members. This, however, does not mean that the Senate is ignored. There are more than four times as many House members as there are senators, but, because only one-third of senators run for election in any one cycle, they actually receive greater per capita donations than representatives do. Of the 535 members of the House and Senate, between 250 and 293 receive political action committee (PAC) contributions from the American Sugarbeet Growers Association during each electoral cycle.

ANDREW D. McNITT

Bibliography

American Sugarbeet Growers Association: members.aol.com/asga/policy.htm

Browne, William P. *Private Interests, Public Policy, and American Agriculture.* Lawrence: University of Kansas Press, 1988.

Browne, William P., and Alan J. Cigler. *U.S. Agricultural Groups.* Westport, CT: Greenwood Publishing Group, 1990.

Ives, Ralph, and John Hurley. *United States Sugar Policy: An Analysis.* U.S. Department of Commerce, 1988.

Makinson, Larry, and Joshua Goldstein. *Open Secrets: The Encyclopedia of Congressional Money and Politics.* Washington, DC: Congressional Quarterly, 1992–1996.

INTERNATIONAL DAIRY FOODS ASSOCIATION

The International Dairy Foods Association is a federation of three other industry groups: the Milk Industry Foundation, the National Cheese Institute, and the International Ice Cream Association. The association represents the processors and sellers of milk, but not the dairy farmers. The organization has over 800 member companies. It represents companies that handle 85 percent of fluid milk, 80 percent of cheese, and 85 percent of ice cream produced in the United States. The organization believes that it can substantially increase the sale of milk products by lowering prices and consequently has consistently opposed the federal system of price supports and dairy compacts. The association is headquartered in Washington, D.C.

HISTORY

Milk is heavy and spoils quickly. Consequently, dairies and dairy farms traditionally were located close to their markets. There is also substantial seasonal variation in milk production, which results in significantly more milk being available in the spring than in the fall. Therefore, the seasonal surplus has to be turned into products that have a longer shelf life. Improvements in transportation, refrigeration, and productivity have led to a general concentration of the industry. The number of dairy farms, dairies, and dairy cows have all decreased rapidly, without any reduction in the amount of milk products produced.

Although organizational names were changed several times, the component groups that make up the International Dairy Foods Association were formed at the turn of the century. The National Ice Cream Manufacturers was founded in 1900; the Milk Industry Foundation was founded in 1908; and the Cheese Institute was formed in 1925. After a substantial period of close cooperation, the three organizations formed the International Dairy Foods Association in 1990.

As a processor-based organization, it has taken positions consistent with the economic interests of its members. It is noted for opposing both dairy price supports and the sugar program. Hence, it provides one of the few examples of truly countervailing pressure in the agricultural interest group system. In general political terms, the International Dairy Foods Association is a typical business organization.

ACTIVITIES: CURRENT AND FUTURE

The International Dairy Foods Association is currently involved in a campaign against dairy compacts—regional associations, established by law, that set the price of milk above the national minimum price. The Northeast Dairy Compact was scheduled to terminate in April 1999; however, legislation was introduced to extend its life. The International Dairy Foods Association opposed this legislation because of the fear that other regions will establish their own dairy compacts. This puts the association at odds with dairy farmers. Consumer and taxpayer groups also oppose the continuation of the Northeast Dairy Compact because it results in higher prices for consumers, leads to the overproduction of milk, and creates problems for the federal government in disposing of surplus milk products. The International Dairy Foods Association is also interested in promoting foreign trade. Its strategy for dealing with the changing economic environment is to become more efficient and price-competitive in the hopes of attracting additional sales.

The International Dairy Foods Association has a fundamental conflict of interest with dairy farmers and sugar refiners that will not go away. The International Dairy Foods Association has succeeded in uniting milk, cheese, and ice cream processors. Its positions attract consumer and executive branch support, and are closer

**International Dairy Foods Association
Political Action Committee Contributions**

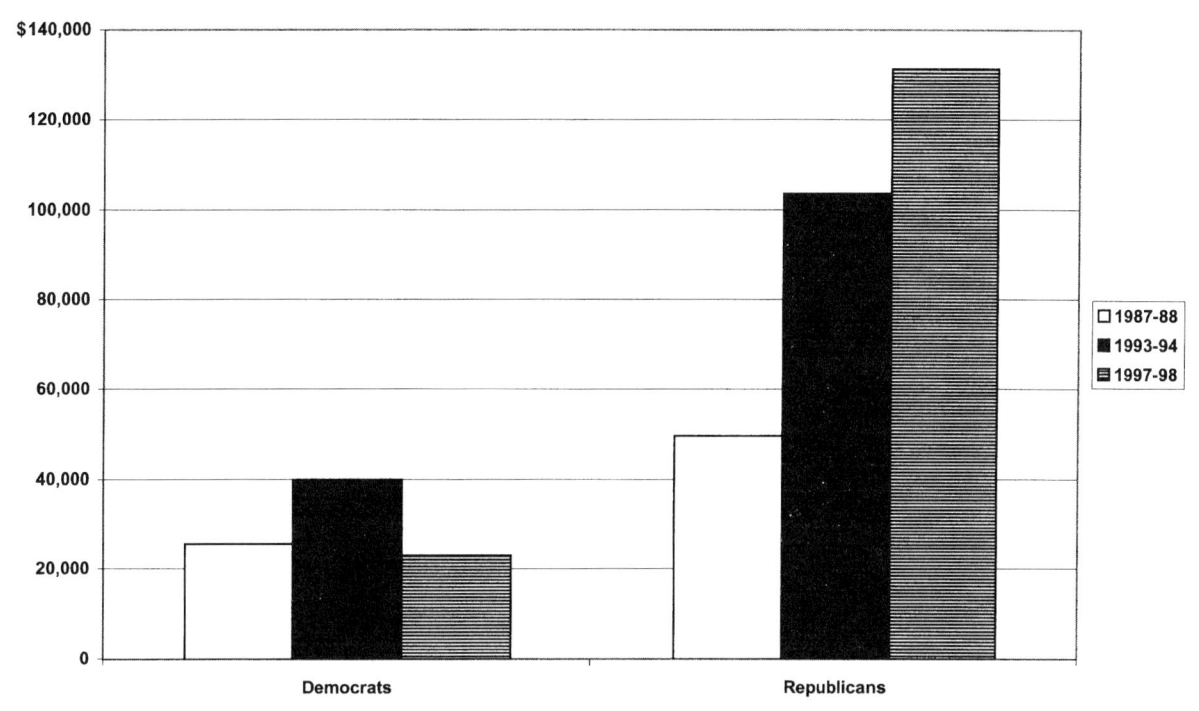

Data derived from official studies available from the Federal Election Commission, Washington, DC, 1987–1998.

to free-market ideals than those of their opponents. The problem facing the International Dairy Foods Association is that it is easier to defend old policies than to create new ones. Also, although the International Dairy Foods Association is a large interest group, the combined resources of dairy farmers and sugar producers are considerably larger.

The International Dairy Foods Association has had some success in reducing milk and sugar subsidies. If we have in fact changed from a time of government deficits to a new era of surpluses, then much of the pressure to reduce agricultural subsidies will decline. New fights are likely to erupt as milk and sugar producers seek to return to the more protective era. The International Dairy Foods Association will be best equipped to counter those demands if the U.S. government is under a market-oriented Republican administration.

FINANCIAL FACTS

The dairy foods industry accounts for $65 billion, and there are a number of dairy-related political action committees (PACs). The International Dairy Foods Association is the third largest PAC. It ranks behind Mid American Dairymen and the Associated Milk Producers, both of which represent dairy farmers.

The International Dairy Foods Association contributed $152,413 to 127 congressional candidates in the 1998 election cycle. This figure is significantly higher than the 1986 contribution of $64,000 to 55 congressional candidates and reflects a pattern of steadily increasing campaign contributions.

The International Dairy Foods Association political activities are consistent with its role as a business organization. The International Dairy Foods Association has always supported more Republican candidates than Democratic ones. Even when the Democrats controlled Congress, the association consistently gave two-thirds or more of its funds to the Republican Party. The association's contributions to the Republican Party became even larger after the Democrats lost control of Congress in 1994. In the 1993–1994 election cycle, Republicans received just over 70 percent of all contributions from the International Dairy Foods Association. By 1998, 85 percent of the group's contributions went to Republican candidates.

ANDREW D. MCNITT

Bibliography

Browne, William P., and Alan J. Cigler. *U.S. Agricultural Groups*. New York: Greenwood Press, 1990.

Federal Election Commission: www.fec.gov

International Dairy Foods Association home page, 1999: www.idfa.org

Makinson, Larry, and Joshua Goldstein. *Open Secrets: The Encyclopedia of Congressional Money and Politics*. Washington, DC: Congressional Quarterly, 1992–1996.

Shepherd, Geoffrey S., and Gene A. Futrell. *Marketing Farm Products*. Ames: Iowa State University Press, 1982.

NATIONAL ASSOCIATION OF WHEAT GROWERS

Founded in 1950, the National Association of Wheat Growers is a commodity organization that represents farmers who produce about 85 percent of wheat grown in the United States. The organization is composed of 22 state associations, most of which are located west of the Mississippi River. The association has played an important role in the formation of agricultural policy and is relatively more active than the other grain-based commodity organizations. The National Association of Wheat Growers is headquartered in Washington, D.C.

HISTORY

In 1950, Senator Clifford Hope of Kansas helped to form the National Association of Wheat Growers by encouraging the merger of existing state associations. Founded as the National Wheat Association, the organization grew rapidly during the 1960s, and, by the 1970s, it had become one of the more influential commodity groups in Washington. In the 1980s, it set up its official political action committee (PAC), Wheat PAC.

Wheat is the third most valuable grain crop grown in the United States and the most important grain crop that is exported. Between 70 percent and 80 percent of the wheat grown in the United States is winter wheat. Although wheat can be grown in most agricultural regions, its ability to tolerate harsh conditions has resulted generally in its growth in the drier, less fertile regions of the country. Consequently, wheat farmers are often interested in maintaining government support programs because they lack the ability to produce other commodities at competitive prices.

The association's position on international trade is affected by the structure of the world market. Canada and Australia have national marketing boards that sell their wheat abroad, and the European Economic Community subsidizes its exports. Consequently, the National Association of Wheat Growers wants a vigorous U.S. program to counter the government assistance received by its foreign competitors.

ACTIVITIES: CURRENT AND FUTURE

The National Association of Wheat Growers is critical of current farm policies. It argues for more generous loan rates and high support levels for producers. The association takes a strongly internationalist position on trade. It favors fast-track legislation, export promotions, and P.L.480 food-aid programs that subsidize commodity exports to underdeveloped countries. The organization also strongly opposes trade embargoes that currently bar U.S. grain sale to 11 percent of the world market. This opposition includes specific requests that the federal government reconsider trade policies toward both Iraq and Cuba.

The National Association of Wheat Growers takes the usual agricultural position on environmental programs. It favors reasonable environmental protection, but with the usual caution that regulations should be based on good scientific evidence and should take the legitimate interests of landowners into consideration.

The National Assocation of Wheat Growers also favors changes in the tax laws that would help owner-operators who sell grain in a highly variable market. Specifically, it favors a return to income averaging and further reductions in inheritance taxes. The continuing importance of wheat in international trade ensures a role for the National Association of Wheat Growers. However, the role will involve confronting a number of challenges. Although American wheat growers are competitive, their access to foreign markets is limited. The European Community stopped importing and became a net exporter of wheat in the 1980s. Poor economic conditions in Asia and the former Soviet Union in the late 1990s undermined the world export market. Mergers among grain dealers, banks, and farm suppliers continue to squeeze producers. Furthermore, wheat farmers are particularly disadvantaged by the lack of alternate crops and off-farm employment in the wheat-growing West.

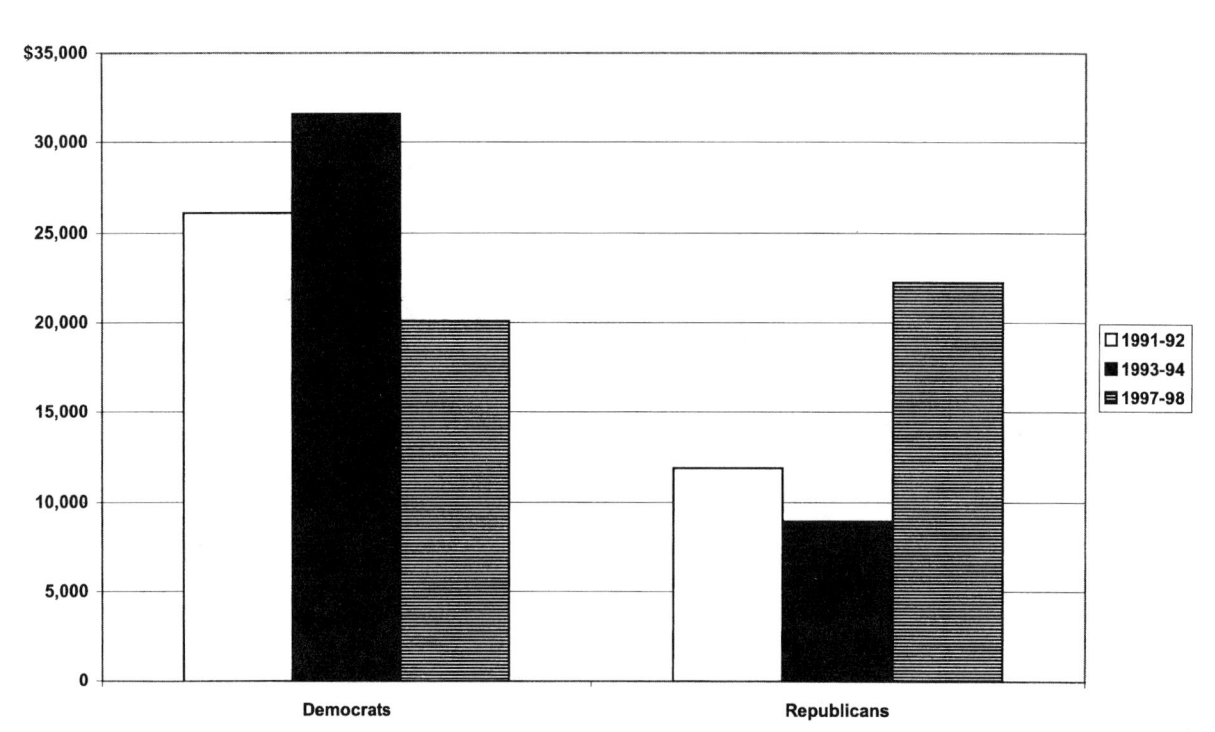

**National Association of Wheat Growers
Political Action Committee Contributions**

Data derived from official studies available from the Federal Election Commission, Washington, DC, 1987–1998.

FINANCIAL FACTS

In 1996, farm receipts from the sale of wheat totaled $9.9 billion. The National Association of Wheat Growers has, since 1986, contributed between $33,000 and $42,000 per election cycle to congressional candidates. Although the $42,350 contribution made in 1998 was the largest contribution to date, the overall pattern of giving is actually one of great stability. Contributions typically fluctuate around $40,000 per cycle and usually go to incumbents from wheat-growing states, although the association has occasionally given as much as 30 percent of its contributions to nonincumbents.

The National Association of Wheat Growers follows a regionally concentrated strategy. Its contributions are largely made to members of Congress from the wheat belt. The number of candidates to whom the association gives has fallen over time from a high of 64 in 1986 to a low of 32 in 1998. The pattern of contributions was affected by the 1994 shift from Democratic to Republican control of Congress. Before 1996, the National Association of Wheat Growers not only favored Democratic candidates, but was actually slowly increasing its level of support for that party. In 1986, 62 percent of all contributions went to Democratic candidates. By 1994, this figure rose to 77 percent of all contributions. In 1996, after the Republicans gained control of Congress, the association gave only 37 percent of its contributions to the Democratic Party. The situation, however, evened out a little by 1998 when, after the Democratic Party managed to reduce the Republican majority in Congress, the wheat growers contributed 47 percent of their funds to the Democrats.

ANDREW D. McNITT

Bibliography

Browne, William P., and Alan J. Cigler. *U.S. Agricultural Groups*. Westport, CT: Greenwood Publishing Group, 1990.

Butler, Nick. *The International Grain Trade: Problems and Prospects*. New York: St. Martin's Press, 1986.

Makinson, Larry, and Joshua Goldstein. *Open Secrets: The Encyclopedia of Congressional Money and Politics*. Washington, DC: Congressional Quarterly, 1992–1996.

National Association of Wheat Growers: www.wheatworld.org

NATIONAL CATTLEMEN'S BEEF ASSOCIATION

The National Cattlemen's Beef Association (NCBA) serves as a marketing organization and trade association for U.S. cattle ranchers. The NCBA's headquarters is in Greenwood Village, Colorado. The NCBA focuses on representing the interests of ranchers to state and federal policy makers, the media, and consumers.

Approximately 40,000 individuals belong to the NCBA, which also represents 46 state cattle associations and 27 national breed associations. Altogether, the NCBA represents approximately 230,000 people associated with the cattle ranching industry. Besides policy representation, member benefits include a monthly magazine, *National Cattlemen*; a weekly newsletter, *Beef Business Bulletin*; and access to members-only material on the NCBA web site.

A 1995 survey of over 1,000 NCBA members asked respondents to rank the most important priorities for cattle producers and the beef industry. The respondents provided the following ranking:

1. Implement a meat-inspection system based on science; eliminate inequities between red meat and poultry.
2. Educate youth to perceive beef as healthful and producers as good stewards of land and animals.
3. Reform the Endangered Species Act to protect property rights and private stewardship of resources.
4. Develop scientific information to emphasize beef's healthfulness and reverse inaccurate diet and/or health statements.
5. Pass property-rights legislation and remain involved in property-rights litigation.
6. Position cattle producers as conscientious stewards of the environment who care about beef safety and quality.
7. Support line-item veto legislation and a constitutional amendment requiring a balanced budget.
8. Expand beef exports and achieve measurable objectives in terms of increased shipments to specific countries and regions.
9. Work in alliances with national health organizations to show consumers that beef is a valuable part of healthful diets.
10. Seek legislation to reduce impact of estate taxes.

As the results of this survey illustrate, NCBA members have a wide range of current policy interests, including environmental policy, property rights, taxes, and consumer relations.

HISTORY

The NCBA can trace its development to the 1880s, when the National Cattle and Horse Growers Association met in St. Louis to lobby the government concerning grazing rights. In 1898, the first permanent cattle rancher association was formed, the American National Livestock Association, focusing primarily on government regulation of the livestock industry and opposing beef imports. During the 1920s and 1930s, this organization expanded its areas of interest to include trade, cattle prices, disease control, and to fighting New Deal programs. In the 1950s, the American National Livestock Association changed its name to the American National Cattlemen's Association and focused its attention on opposing government price supports for beef.

Although the American National Livestock Association was successful at keeping beef imports low and tariffs high, the livestock industry suffered serious setbacks in the early 1970s due to the weak economy combined with a beef boycott and a beef price freeze in 1973.

Recognizing the need for a greater public relations focus, the organization changed its name again in 1977, to the National Cattlemen's Association, focusing on trade, food safety, taxes, grazing rights, and consumer relations. In 1996, the National Cattlemen's Association

**National Cattlemen's Beef Association
Political Action Committee Contributions**

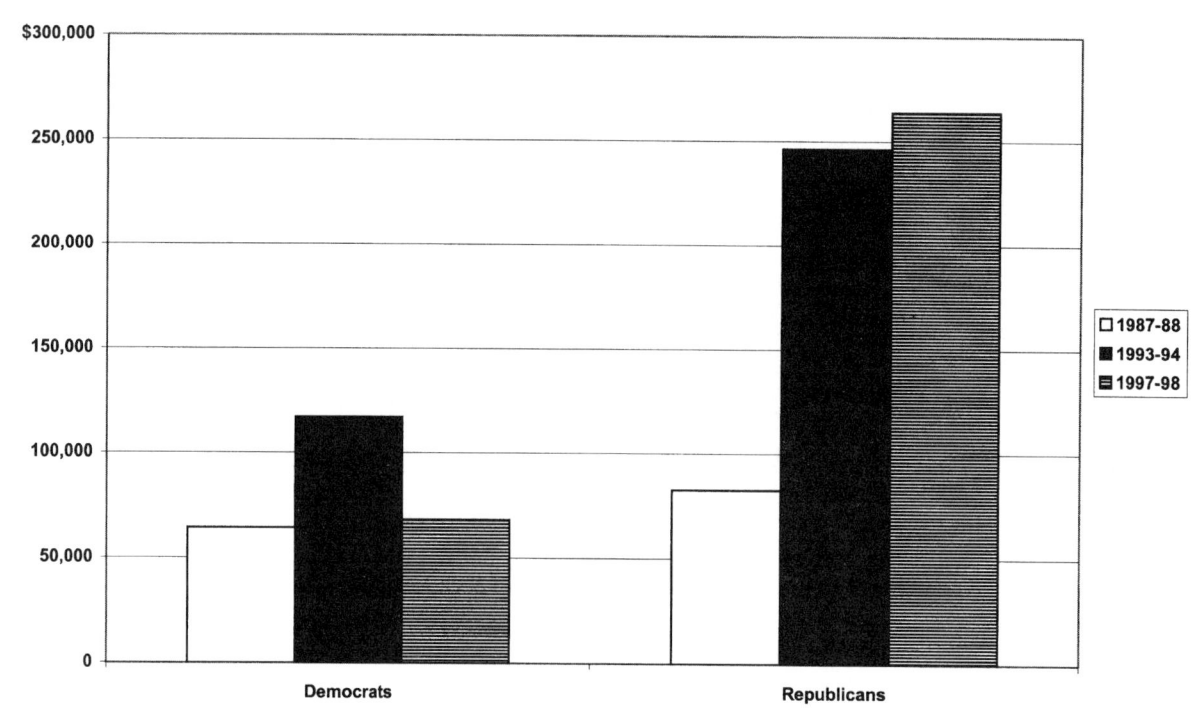

[Bar chart showing PAC contributions to Democrats and Republicans for 1987-88, 1993-94, and 1997-98. Democrats received approximately $65,000 (1987-88), $117,000 (1993-94), and $68,000 (1997-98). Republicans received approximately $80,000 (1987-88), $245,000 (1993-94), and $262,000 (1997-98).]

Data derived from official studies available from the Federal Election Commission, Washington, DC, 1987–1998.

merged with the National Live Stock and Meat Board/Beef Industry Council and changed its name to the National Cattlemen's Beef Association. Through this merger, the traditional lobbying efforts of the National Cattlemen's Association were integrated with the beef checkoff activities of beef product promotion and research.

ACTIVITIES: CURRENT AND FUTURE

Although the NCBA's primary headquarters is located in Colorado, in the center of the cattle ranching industry, the group still regularly lobbies in Washington, D.C., where its policy office is located. Its total reported lobbying expenditures for 1997 were $400,000. Two outside lobbying firms were hired during 1997, and seven in-house lobbyists were employed by the NCBA. These lobbyists focused on a variety of issues, ranging from taxes, banking and trade, to agriculture, natural resources, and the food industry.

Recent examples of lobbying activities include meetings with the Department of Agriculture (concerning a food-aid package to Russia containing beef) and meetings with the U.S. Trade Representative (concerning Japanese beef tariffs). The NCBA is also active in a case in which Mexico is accusing U.S. beef producers of dumping beef (selling below cost) on the Mexican market. In the early 1990s, the NCBA successfully opposed an increase in grazing fees for public lands. Fees for grazing on public lands are about one-fifth the cost of fees for grazing on private lands. Environmentalists argue that overgrazing, due to the low prices, is resulting in severe overuse, erosion, and water shortages. Efforts to increase these fees have continually been blocked by a bipartisan group of western legislators, supported by such groups as the NCBA.

When Bill Clinton was elected president in 1992, he promised to increase the fees, responding to the demands of environmental groups. However, he and Interior Department Secretary Bruce Babbitt were unsuccessful in making any significant changes to the fee structure. Ultimately, the president announced in 1994, after Republicans won majorities in the House and Senate, that the issue would be left up to Congress.

Like other business-oriented interest groups, the

NCBA takes a traditional "insider" approach to lobbying, through contacting policy makers, testifying at hearings, and providing research to the legislature as well as executive agencies. The NCBA is also active in campaigning for candidates for federal office. Its political action committee (PAC), founded in 1971, contributes to candidates who are pro beef, typically Republicans. The PAC also provides voter "scorecards" of state congressional delegations to NCBA members and affiliates. These scorecards show the vote of all legislators on issues of interest to the NCBA.

In addition to its lobbying activities, the NCBA is also active in product marketing. Its Chicago office focuses on advertising, human nutrition research, and new product development. For instance, its beef checkoff division provides industry promotion through such advertising campaigns as "Beef, It's What's For Dinner."

The NCBA gained media notoriety in 1997 and 1998, when it supported a group of Texas cattle ranchers who sued television talk-show host Oprah Winfrey. The NCBA and the Texas ranchers argued that a 1996 Winfrey program, exploring whether "mad cow disease" posed a threat to the U.S. beef supply, had caused a drop in cattle prices and cost the industry millions of dollars. The Texas ranchers sued Winfrey under the False Disparagement of Perishable Food Products Act of 1995, a law protecting agricultural products from libelous remarks. The ranchers also argued that Winfrey should be held liable for spreading alarmist and false information about beef. The ranchers were unable to prove either that beef fell under the jurisdiction of this law, as a "perishable food," or that Winfrey's program had "knowingly" made false statements. The court ruled in favor of Winfrey, although the ranchers have promised to appeal the ruling. While the NCBA and the Texas ranchers were not successful in this case, many argue that the case provided some positive publicity for the group, particularly among conservatives who generally support the U.S. beef industry. Furthermore, laws such as the False Disparagement of Perishable Food Products Act may discourage criticism or investigation of the industry, and many people may not have the money to defend themselves against litigation as well as Winfrey did.

The NCBA has suffered some setbacks throughout its history. Government regulations continue to restrict the industry. Published research suggests that the consumption of red meat produces negative health effects. Food safety threats, like "mad cow disease," result in negative publicity for the beef industry. Furthermore, environmental concerns over grazing rights and natural resources continue to jeopardize the NCBA's goals. Nonetheless, the NCBA continues to be a formidable lobbying group in representing the beef industry.

It is unlikely that any of these problems will disappear for the NCBA. However, it also appears that the NCBA can successfully deal with these problems, despite occasional setbacks. Even the general negative publicity from the Oprah Winfrey trial can be seen as a limited success for the NCBA, as it gained them more support from conservatives. Indeed, while the NCBA's source of financial support stems from the cattle ranching industry, it also has policy support from many conservative states' rights and property rights activists. Its broad appeal will likely gain more support, particularly at the state level. Furthermore, the recent merger in 1996 that resulted in the NCBA provides the organization with greater cohesion and focus, providing an opportunity for an even stronger lobbying presence in the federal and state governments.

FINANCIAL FACTS

In 1998, the NCBA's receipts amounted to $215,914, and its expenditures amounted to $217,723. Until the 1994 election, when Republicans took control of Congress, the NCBA typically gave to both parties, although it favored the Republican Party slightly. However, since the 1994 election, the NCBA has strongly favored the Republican Party in campaign contributions. Over the 1990s, the organization increased substantially its contributions to Republican candidates. In 1990, 62 percent of the group's $215,384 contributions went to Republicans. By 1998, 80 percent of the NCBA's $327,000 in contributions was directed to Republican candidates.

MELINDA MUELLER

Bibliography

Browne, William P., and Alan J. Cigler. *U.S. Agricultural Groups.* Westport, CT: Greenwood Publishing Group, 1990.

Center for Responsive Politics: www.crp.org

Federal Election Commission: www.fec.gov

National Cattlemen's Beef Association: www.beef.org

Wolpe, Bruce C., and Bertram J. Levine. "Grazing Rights." In *Lobbying Congress: How the System Works,* 2d ed. Washington, DC: Congressional Quarterly, 1996.

NATIONAL CHICKEN COUNCIL

The National Chicken Council (NCC) was founded in 1954 as the National Broiler Council, and it operated under that name until January 1, 1999. The name of the association was changed to the current National Chicken Council in an attempt to clear up consumer confusion about the organization's mission. The council represents integrated broiler producer-processors and the companies that produce, process, and market chickens. Member companies of the National Chicken Council account for more than 95 percent of the chickens sold in the United States, and allied membership is open to companies that supply services and equipment to the integrated broiler industry. NCC programs include government relations, promotion and marketing, and public relations. The council publishes its weekly newsletter, *The NCC Washington Report,* and it holds conferences and seminars for industry members. Since 1965, the National Chicken Council has been headquartered in Washington, D.C.

HISTORY

The National Chicken Council was founded in 1954 to address the critical economic problems facing the broiler industry. Its founding president, Jesse Jewell, was a pioneer in the modern broiler industry, and he was instrumental in bringing together the chicken producers and processors for the first time in this umbrella trade organization. The original purposes of the National Chicken Council were product promotion, market development, and consumer education. Over time, however, the realization quickly grew that many of the industry's primary issues involving inspection, packaging, sanitation, health, and worker safety had to be addressed in the political arena.

Chicken promotion and consumer education are still important roles for the council. This is indicated by the council's extensive contacts with food editors, sponsorship of chicken-cooking contests, and dissemination of recipes, publication of consumer leaflets, videos, and other point-of-sale materials.

ACTIVITIES: CURRENT AND FUTURE

The National Chicken Council staff keeps members informed on legislative and regulatory developments, communicates the views and concerns of the industry to government officials, and works to improve the direction and outcome of government programs and regulations that have an impact on the broiler industry. During 1997 and 1998, the council was in active opposition to the attempt to amend the 1967 Agricultural Fair Practices Act to allow associations of farmers to bargain collectively over contracts in their dealing with chicken food processors. The council helped orchestrate an intense campaign against changes in contract procedures with broiler growers, and it was able to deliver nearly 1,800 letters to the United States Department of Agriculture (USDA) protesting changes in the rules.

In conformity with other U.S. agricultural interest groups, the National Chicken Council is strongly supportive of free trade, particularly assistance to keep the Asian markets open during the current economic crisis. The NCC is also strongly opposed to foreign import restrictions on U.S. chicken exports, and it is working with the U.S. trade representatives to resist such impediments to the export of chicken meat.

In general, the political agenda of the National Chicken Council is heavily weighted toward domestic issues and the promotion of chicken consumption in the United States. The council closely monitors the regulatory initiatives of the Environmental Protection Agency and the USDA, and it has expressed its concern about recent regulatory proposals to impose additional environmental regulations on the industry. The council

**National Chicken Council
Political Action Committee Contributions**

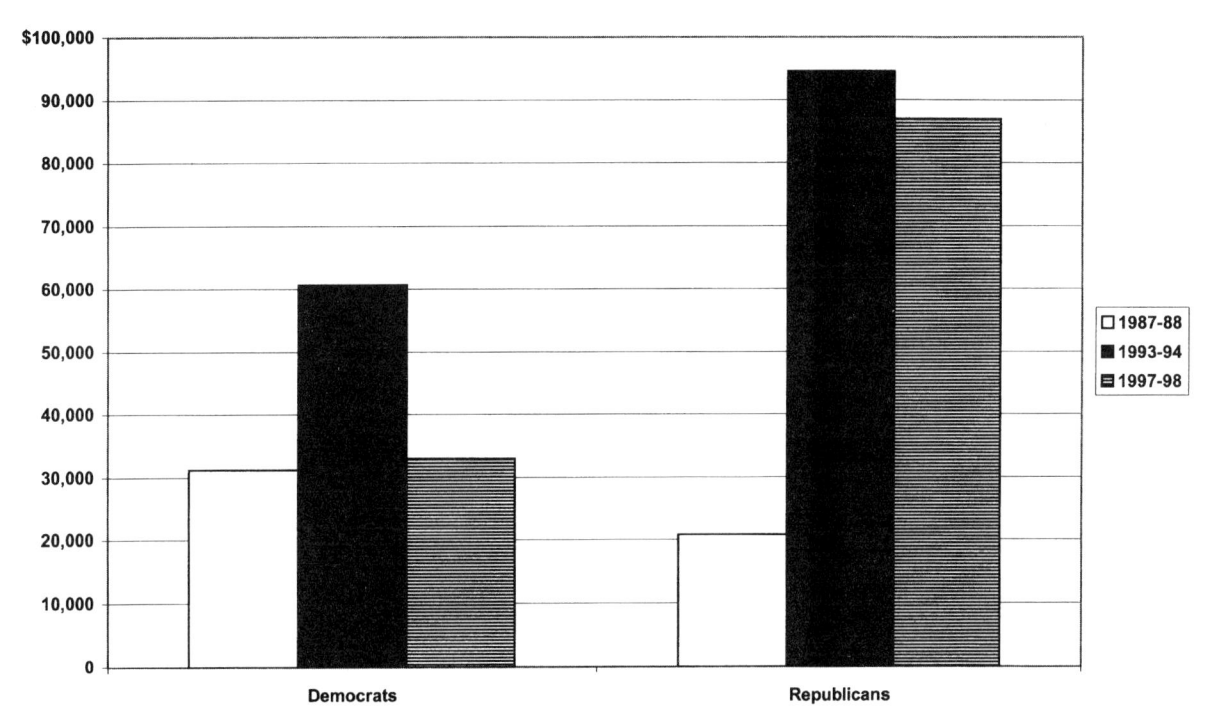

[Bar chart showing PAC contributions to Democrats and Republicans for years 1987-88, 1993-94, and 1997-98. Democrats: ~$31,000 (1987-88), ~$61,000 (1993-94), ~$33,000 (1997-98). Republicans: ~$21,000 (1987-88), ~$95,000 (1993-94), ~$87,000 (1997-98).]

Data derived from official studies available from the Federal Election Commission, Washington, DC, 1987–1998.

has been proactive in advancing the voluntary acceptance of health, safety, and sanitary conditions in the chicken processing industry.

From the perspectives of the chicken producers and processors, the relatively low price of chicken, the wide availability of the meat achieved through rapid technological innovation, and the broad consumer adoption of chicken as a healthy food product suggest that there is a strong and positive future for the council. The recognition of chicken as a virtually globally acceptable meat for consumption, and the industry's capacity to export competitively frozen chicken products to Asia, Islamic countries, and the European markets has tremendous potential for growth and a rosy future for the industry.

There are some political risks for the council, particularly as a result of the resumption of conflict with chicken farmers over the fairness of current contracting arrangements with chicken food processors. The council also needs to be vigilant and respond quickly to potential scandals involving safety issues with workers or health concerns from the potential of E. coli and salmonella contamination in the chicken processing and distribution system. A final concern is the heightened concentration and market consolidation that may generate political opposition and attempts to impose market regulation on the industry.

FINANCIAL FACTS

The average American currently buys more than 74 pounds of chicken every year and purchased approximately $35 billion worth of chicken meat in 1998. Approximately 40 percent of the National Chicken Council's budget is used to promote the use of chicken and to maintain a positive image of the industry, but the NCC's primary purpose is to represent the interests of the broiler industry in Washington.

In real dollars, the National Chicken Council has decreased its political action committee (PAC) contributions from $144,650 in 1989–1990 to $120,000 in 1997–1998. Associated firms, however, have independent PACs, so that the cumulative impact of the broiler industry in political campaigns has not declined significantly over time. In 1989–1990, the council contributed to 145 candidates, of which all but five were incumbents. In this period, 51 percent of PAC funds went to Democrats. Of the $120,000 contributed by the NCC PAC in 1997–1998, $87,000 (73 percent) went to Republican candidates and $78,000 (65 percent) helped fund House campaigns, particularly for candidates with districts in the southeastern United States, where the poultry industry is most heavily concentrated. Altogether, 21 incumbent senators received contributions ranging between $1,000 to $4,000, and 66 House candidates received contributions ranging between $500 to $3,500.

JAMES SEROKA

Bibliography

Browne, William P., and Alan J. Cigler. *U.S. Agricultural Groups*. Westport, CT: Greenwood Publishing Group, 1990.

Center for Responsive Politics. Open Secrets home page: www.opensecrets.org

Makinson, Larry. *Open Secrets: The Encyclopedia of Congressional Money and Politics*. Washington, DC: Congressional Quarterly, 1990.

National Chicken Council: www.eatchicken.com

NATIONAL COTTON COUNCIL OF AMERICA

Founded in 1938, the National Cotton Council of America is a commodity organization representing all aspects of production. Growers, ginners, warehousers, merchants, crushers, cooperatives, and manufacturers are all included. The cotton industry directly employees some 340,000 people in 17 states. Although traditionally based in the southeast, the industry moved west during the twentieth century, when increasing amounts of cotton were grown in Texas, Arizona, and California.

The National Cotton Council of America does not distinguish between family and corporate farmers. It represents the interests of both growers and processors. Consequently, it is concerned primarily with promoting the use of cotton. The National Cotton Council of America is headquartered in Memphis, Tennessee. The not-for-profit Cotton Foundation was established by the Cotton Council to allow groups that could not belong to the Cotton Council to help support education and research.

HISTORY

The National Cotton Council of America was founded as a result of the very low cotton prices of the late 1930s. Historically, the National Cotton Council of America was a major supporter and beneficiary of the New Deal price support system. After the Second World War, cotton producers often allied themselves with peanut and rice growers to regularly support the legislative reauthorization of agricultural subsidies.

Cotton producers have had to confront a number of serious challenges during the latter half of the twentieth century. For example, in the tire industry, fiberglass and rayon cord replaced the more expensive cotton reinforcing cord used in rubber tires; likewise, in the clothing industy, cheaper synthetics replaced cotton. In addition, foreign competitors were able to produce cotton more cheaply than American producers. In response, the industry reduced its labor costs through mechanization and turned to the government for protection.

The late-twentieth-century trend toward greater reliance on the market, however, also affected the cotton industry. Although some small steps were taken as early as the 1960s to increase competitiveness, more extensive efforts were required. In 1991, additional changes were made in government programs to improve the competitiveness of American cotton. The success of these initiatives was mixed. While American consumers are using more cotton, foreign consumers are still shifting to synthetics. Also, the economic problems of Asia, Brazil, and Russia depressed international demand. Furthermore, China went from being a large importer of cotton before 1998 to becoming an exporter after that date, producing cotton more cheaply than cotton producers in the United States, which severely reduced America's competitiveness. Consequently, the gap between U.S. and foreign prices has not been closed.

ACTIVITIES: CURRENT AND FUTURE

The National Cotton Council of America is concerned with maintaining the profitability of American cotton producers in a complicated global environment. Inasmuch as American cotton currently costs more than imported cotton, a three-step program was instituted in 1991 to make American cotton more competitive. The first step gave the secretary of agriculture greater authority to set benchmark prices closer to world levels. The second step provided subsidy payments to U.S. exporters and domestic users of cotton to improve competitiveness and to make up some of the difference between U.S. and foreign prices. The third step allowed for an increase in imports of cotton to the United States as a way of lowering U.S. cotton prices. Currently, the

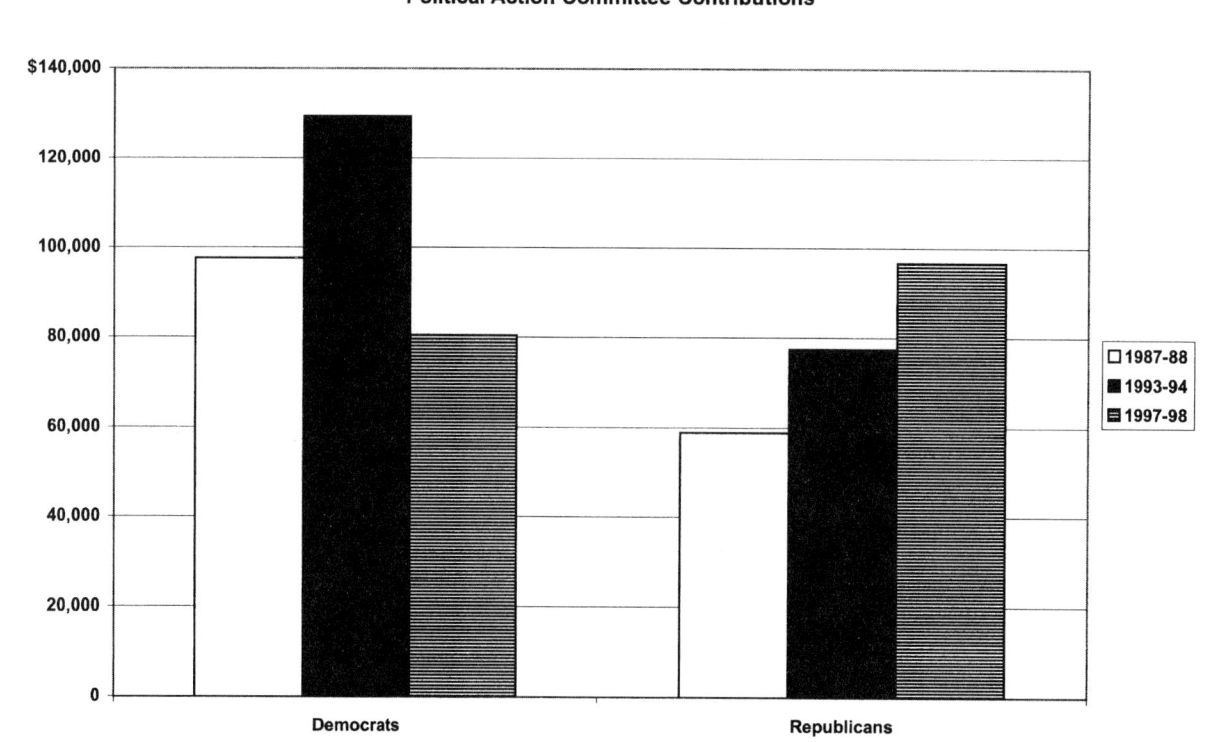

**National Cotton Council
Political Action Committee Contributions**

[Bar chart showing PAC contributions to Democrats and Republicans for 1987-88, 1993-94, and 1997-98. Democrats: ~$97,000 (1987-88), ~$130,000 (1993-94), ~$80,000 (1997-98). Republicans: ~$58,000 (1987-88), ~$77,000 (1993-94), ~$96,000 (1997-98).]

Data derived from official studies available from the Federal Election Commission, Washington, DC, 1987–1998.

Cotton Council is concerned about restoring funding for step-two payments. The collapse of agricultural prices in the late 1990s caused these funds to be exhausted more rapidly than expected, and the Cotton Council is now working on a legislative remedy.

The National Cotton Council of America is also concerned with a wide variety of environmental and worker safety issues. Cotton requires extensive use of chemical fertilizers and insecticides in its production; consequently there is a great deal of concern over the regulation of these items. In addition, safety questions arise because of problems associated with workers breathing in cotton dust during the manufacturing process. Rather than oppose these regulations outright, the Cotton Council instead concerns itself about their extent and stringency. The National Cotton Council of America also supports the use of genetically altered strains of cotton in the hope that they will allow growers to reduce their use of insecticides.

Export earnings are necessary if the American cotton industry is to remain healthy. The only way to ensure export earning is to make American cotton competitive with foreign cotton and man-made fibers. The even lower prices currently available for alternate crops probably ensures the continued worldwide overproduction of cotton. Although the eventual recovery of foreign economies would help, this change is unlikely to entirely resolve the underlying competitive disadvantage.

From a political point of view, the National Cotton Council of America will also have to cope with a changing environment here as well. If the federal government continues to run a budget surplus, the pressure for further reductions in agricultural subsidies, including cotton subsidies, is likely to decline. At the same time, the shift of southern representatives in Congress from the Democratic to the Republican Party may complicate matters for the cotton industry. In the past, the cotton-growing districts were represented by Democratic politicians more sympathetic to direct intervention in the agricultural market. At present, however, cotton districts are represented by Republicans who have a strong ideological commitment to the free market. If the Republican Party is unwilling to make an exception in its economic policy for cotton, then the cotton industry will have to be even more adept at forming coalitions with other agricultural groups.

FINANCIAL FACTS

In 1984, the Cotton Council gave $100,575 to 170 congressional candidates. Over time, the council increased the amount of contributions, which were particularly high during the run-up to the 1996 Farm Bill. In dollar terms, the greatest amount of money was given in 1994, when the council contributed $206,822 to 165 candidates. Since then, contributions have fallen. The council contributions totaled $159,226 in the 1995–1996 election cycle and $177,291 in the 1997–1998 cycle.

The Cotton Council gives money to both parties, but it gives more money to the majority party. When the Democratic Party held a majority of seats in Congress, Democratic candidates received from 50 to 62 percent of all contributions. In 1996, after the Democrats lost their majority, the council gave only 34 percent of all contributions for that cycle to Democratic candidates and slightly more, 46 percent, for the 1998 cycle. The Cotton Council also favors incumbents, who receive over 95 percent of all contributions, and House members, who receive between 60 percent to 77 percent of all contributions.

ANDREW D. MCNITT

Bibliography

Browne, William P., and Alan J. Cigler. *U.S. Agricultural Groups*. Westport, CT: Greenwood Publishing Group, 1990.

Makinson, Larry, and Joshua Goldstein. *Open Secrets: The Encyclopedia of Congressional Money and Politics*. Washington, DC: Congressional Quarterly, 1992–1996.

National Cotton Council. Cotton's Three Step Competitiveness Plan: www.econcentral.org/reports/3stepplan.httm

National Cotton Council: www.cotton.org

Shepherd, Geoffrey S., and Gene A. Futrell. *Marketing Farm Products*. Ames: Iowa State University Press, 1982.

NATIONAL COUNCIL OF FARMER COOPERATIVES

The National Council of Farmer Cooperatives was created by a 1990 merger of the American Institute of Cooperation, originally founded in 1925, with the National Cooperative Council, originally founded in 1929. These organizations were created as educational and political representatives of agricultural cooperatives, and the newly combined organization continues to perform those functions today.

The formation of agricultural cooperatives was promoted by the passage of the Capper-Volstead Act in 1922, which freed cooperatives from the threat of antitrust prosecutions. Because of the wide range of activities with which the National Council of Farmer Cooperative deals, it is sometimes classified as a general-purpose agricultural group. The organization is a federation of 110 major marketing, purchasing, and credit cooperatives. Banks affiliated with the Farm Credit system are also eligible for membership. The combined membership of all of these organizations totals some 2 million individuals.

HISTORY

Farm cooperatives were promoted by the Grange and the National Farmers Union, beginning in the 1890s, as a way to undercut the role of middlemen in agriculture. Initially, the cooperative movement had its greatest success in organizing the dairy industry. Hard times in the 1920s increased farmers' reliance on cooperatives, several of which were legally harassed by antitrust actions. The Capper-Volstead Act of 1922 exempted cooperatives from antitrust prosecutions and promoted their formation. Cooperatives became an integral and accepted part of farm life. Collectively, marketing cooperatives account for about one-third of sales, and farm supply cooperatives account for about 20 percent of all sales. In spite of their origin, today's farm cooperatives function more like businesses than instruments for social cooperation.

The National Council of Farmer Cooperatives has historically has been aligned with the American Farm Bureau Federation on agricultural questions. Its membership increased rapidly in the 1920s, and for a brief period it was the largest of farm organizations. In national politics, however, the National Council of Farmer Cooperatives has been more supportive of Democratic congressional candidates, although a number of Republicans are also supported.

ACTIVITIES: CURRENT AND FUTURE

The National Council of Farmer Cooperatives is noted for its relatively low-key approach to public policy questions. It has extensive educational programs and maintains a legal office that specializes in the problems of the farm cooperative. The National Council of Farmer Cooperatives is currently concerned with the way government regulations affect cooperatives' internal structure, tax liabilities, and stock regulations. It supports provisions that are designed to promote trade, including fast-track authority for the president and funding for the International Monetary Fund. The National Council of Farmer Cooperatives also participates in symbolic environmental programs such as Earth Day, but opposes the Global Warming Treaty.

While farm cooperatives may increasingly be operating like businesses in the economic sphere, until recently they have behaved very differently in the political sphere. The contribution pattern of the National Association of Farmer Cooperatives suggests closer alignment with the Democratic Party than is common for other business organizations. Even the post-1994 swing to the Republican Party was moderate when compared to other agricultural organizations. The swing in fact

**National Council of Farmer Cooperatives
Political Action Committee Contributions**

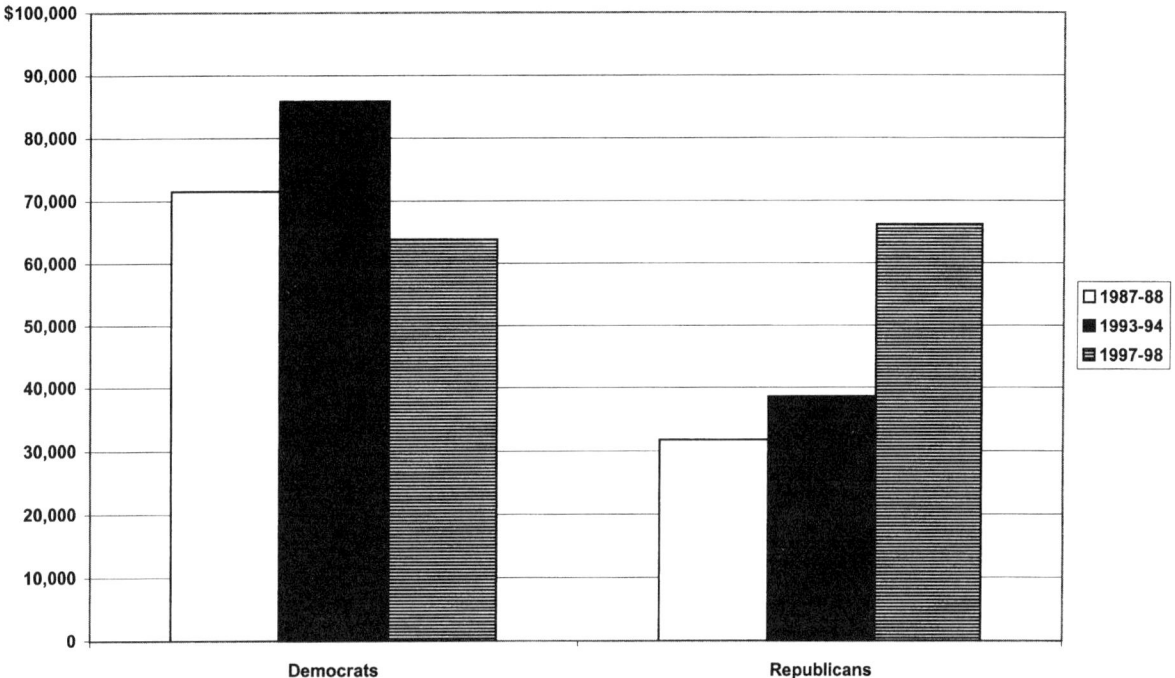

Data derived from official studies available from the Federal Election Commission, Washington, DC, 1987–1998.

was so moderate as to suggest that a return to a Democratic majority would be quickly followed by a return to a Democratic advantage in campaign contributions.

FINANCIAL FACTS

Since 1990, the National Council of Farmer Cooperatives has given between $120,000 to $130,000 each election cycle to congressional candidates. Over time there has been a tendency to give more money to fewer candidates. The council gave $126,000 to 181 candidates in 1990, but gave to progressively fewer candidates in each succeeding election cycle until 1998, when it gave $130,161 to 121 candidates.

The National Council of Farmer Cooperatives has historically supported more Democratic candidates. Democratic candidates received 69 percent of all money contributed in 1988, and relative support for Democratic candidates gradually increased through 1994 to 71 percent. The Democratic loss of control of Congress in 1994 changed the council's pattern of giving; however, rather than switching to the Republican Party, the Council became more bipartisan in its approach. Democrats received 47 percent of all contributions in the 1996 cycle and 49 percent of all contributions for the 1998 cycle.

The council gives to midwestern and southern candidates. It gives most of its money (87 percent) to incumbents. It also gives more (69 percent to 74 percent) to House as opposed to Senate candidates.

ANDREW D. McNITT

Bibliography

Browne, William P. and Alan J. Cigler. *U.S. Agricultural Groups*. New York: Greenwood Press, 1990.

Makinson, Larry, and Joshua Goldstein. *Open Secrets: The Encyclopedia of Congressional Money and Politics*. Washington, DC: Congressional Quarterly, 1992–1996.

National Council of Farmer Cooperatives, 1998: www.ncfc.org

Zeigler, Harmon. *Interest Groups in American Society*. Englewood Cliffs, NJ: Prentice-Hall, 1964.

NATIONAL FARMERS ORGANIZATION

Founded in 1955, the National Farmers Organization (NFO) is a general farm organization that acts as a bargaining agent for its members. The NFO has explicitly adopted a collective bargaining model and advocates actions designed to withhold agricultural products from the market as a way of increasing prices. Membership figures are difficult to obtain because the NFO keeps these secret for strategic reasons; however, estimates vary from a 1956 claim by the NFO's president of 180,000 members to a 1980 academic estimate of 40,000. The fluctuating size of other agricultural organizations and the large decline in the number of farmers since the 1950s lends some credibility to both figures. The National Farmers Organization's headquarters is in Ames, Iowa, and most of its members are from the upper midwest.

The NFO often acts as an ally of the National Farmers Union (NFU). Both organizations are more willing to support agricultural subsidies and restrictions on production than is the American Farm Bureau Federation. In national politics, the National Farmers Organization, while not as liberal as the National Farmers Union, is also closely associated with the Democratic Party.

HISTORY

The National Farmers Organization was founded in 1955 in response to a decline in agricultural prices. Under the leadership of Oren Lee Staley, the NFO first organized farmers in southern Iowa and northern Missouri. The NFO went on to organize grain and dairy farmers in the other midwestern states. The NFO first began to experiment with limited holding actions in 1959. Although often criticized in the press, these holding actions proved sufficiently effective in raising prices to attract new members.

When the NFO applied holding actions to perishable dairy products, opposition from dairy processors and scattered violence associated with these actions attracted government attention. The federal government launched a number of unsuccessful antitrust actions directed against the NFO. For its part, the NFO responded by filing its own equally inconclusive antitrust actions challenging the marketing practices of dairy processors. In time, the NFO even managed to get on President Richard Nixon's enemies list. The Securities and Exchange Commission also brought charges against the NFO in 1973 for loan irregularities.

More damaging than government harassment, however, was the increase in grain prices that resulted from the Nixon administration's grain sales to the Soviet Union. These sales resulted in high prices that came at a time when many farmers had long-term grain contracts negotiated for them by the NFO at lower rates. Under economic pressure, a number of farmers defaulted on these contracts, creating severe financial problems for the NFO.

In the late eighties, the NFO shifted its focus away from public confrontation. The organization experienced considerable success in collective bargaining for milk and livestock. Although it lent informal support to the American Agriculture Movement's protests in the 1980s, its formal efforts were directed toward more traditional political activities.

ACTIVITIES: CURRENT AND FUTURE

The National Farmers Organization currently operates grain, dairy, and livestock marketing programs. It is also experimenting with a farmer-owned grain bank that would help to manage fluctuating grain prices by holding a portion of the grain crop in storage until the market prices rise to a predetermined level. Like the NFU, the NFO supports family farms and is critical of corporate farming. The NFO, however, has also been critical of cooperatives—many of which are owned by other agricultural organizations. Not only has the NFO been on the opposite side of the fence when negotiating contracts with the cooperatives, but it has also argued that these cooperatives no longer respond to their members' interests.

The NFO survives because it occupies a special niche in the agricultural industry. Its role as a bargaining agent for a number of agricultural commodities provides it with a sufficient basis for continued survival. Its activities as a general-purpose interest group, however, are less unusual. Like the other general-purpose interest groups, its importance in policy making is challenged by the increasing role played by commodity groups. Like all producer-based organizations, the NFO is weakened by the continuing reduction in the number of producers. Like its ally, the NFU, the NFO has close ties to the Democratic Party; this means that its influence will vary depending on which party controls the White House and Congress. However, even when the Democrats are in charge, the NFO is the smaller of the two Democratically oriented interest groups.

FINANCIAL FACTS

The National Farmers Organization maintained a small political action committee (PAC), NFO-GRIP, in the late 1980s and early 1990s. From 1986 through 1992, the NFO gave from $31,000 to $34,000 per election cycle. The NFO consistently gave in excess of 80 percent of all of its funds to Democratic candidates. The pattern of contributions was one of giving small contributions to from 63 to 73 candidates per cycle, most of whom were House members and incumbents.

In the early 1990s the NFO, because of cash-flow problems, decided that it was no longer cost-effective to maintain its PAC. The organization continues to be interested in agricultural policy, but has returned to a letter-writing strategy. In addition, the NFO is able to work with the NFU, which still maintains a PAC. Given the long history of cooperation between the NFO and the NFU, this constitutes a relatively painless strategy.

ANDREW D. MCNITT

Bibliography

Browne, William P., and Alan J. Cigler. *U.S. Agricultural Groups*. Westport, CT: Greenwood Publishing Group, 1990.

Makinson, Larry, and Joshua Goldstein. *Open Secrets: The Encyclopedia of Congressional Money and Politics*. Washington, DC: Congressional Quarterly, 1992–1996.

Mooney, Patrick, and Theo J. Majka. *Farmers' and Farm Workers' Movements*. New York: Twayne, 1995.

National Farmers Organization: www.nfo.org

NATIONAL FARMERS UNION

Founded in 1902, the National Farmers Union (NFU) is the second-most important general farm organization in the United States. With 300,000 members, it is considerably smaller than the American Farm Bureau Federation; however, only family farmers and ranchers can belong to the National Farmers Union. The Farmers Union is a distinctly regional organization. Headquartered in Denver, its membership is concentrated in the Great Plains. It is particularly strong in Minnesota, North and South Dakota, Colorado, Kansas, and Nebraska. Its members are often involved in wheat production and dairying. It is the most politically liberal of the general farm organizations, has ties to organized labor, and usually aligns itself with the Democratic Party in national politics. The fundamental purpose of the National Farmers Union is to act as an advocate for the small farmer and rancher. As such, it often finds itself opposing the interests of corporate farmers. The Farmers Union usually supports higher subsidy payments, limitations on production, and, at least in theory, 100 percent parity payments (equality in payments for commodities)—all of which are designed to raise farm income.

The National Farmers Union also runs a wide range of cooperative enterprises, most of which are headquartered in Minneapolis and St. Paul. These enterprises include farm supply and marketing cooperatives. Like the larger Farm Bureau, the National Farmers Union also provides a wide range of insurance benefits to its members through the National Farmers Union Insurance Company.

HISTORY

Hard times for farmers at the end of the nineteenth century led to an agrarian revolt that produced the People's, or Populist, Party. The Farmers Alliance was the major agricultural organization that backed this revolt. Early in the twentieth century, former members of the alliance, meeting in Point, Texas, founded the National Farmers Union. Isaac Gresham, a tenant farmer and newspaperman, was their first leader.

Before the First World War, the Farmers Union grew rapidly. Originally the NFU was particularly strong in the South, but as time passed its membership shifted to the upper midwest. There, the NFU helped to organize a number of cooperatives and supported the Nonpartisan League in the Dakotas.

During the 1920s, the Farmers Union cooperated with the more conservative Farm Bloc, an alliance of agricultural groups that lobbied Congress. At the same time, it participated in efforts to form a progressive bloc that had ties to organized labor. Subsequently, in 1924, the Farmers Union supported Robert La Follette's third-party bid for the presidency.

During the 1930s, the Farmers Union supported New Deal agricultural policies, but tried unsuccessfully to get the cost of production built into support formulas. The Farmers Union was particularly close to the Farm Security Administration, which administered a number of programs designed to aid low-income producers and consumers. The eventual elimination of this agency as a result of pressure from the American Farm Bureau Federation was a blow to the Farmers Union.

Internal conflicts reduced the effectiveness of the Farmers Union during the 1930s. Conflicts involved controversies over the support by some Farmers Union leaders for the ideological, fascist-sympathizing priest, Father Charles Coughlin, and the radical Farmers Holiday Movement. The election of James Patton in 1940 resolved most of these controversies and helped to change the Farmers Union into a decidedly Democratic, but at the same time more typical, interest group.

During the 1940s and 1950s, the relationship between the Farmers Union and the Department of Agriculture varied, depending on a number of circumstances. In the early 1940s, President Franklin Roosevelt's administration used the National Farmers

**National Farmers Union
Political Action Committee Contributions**

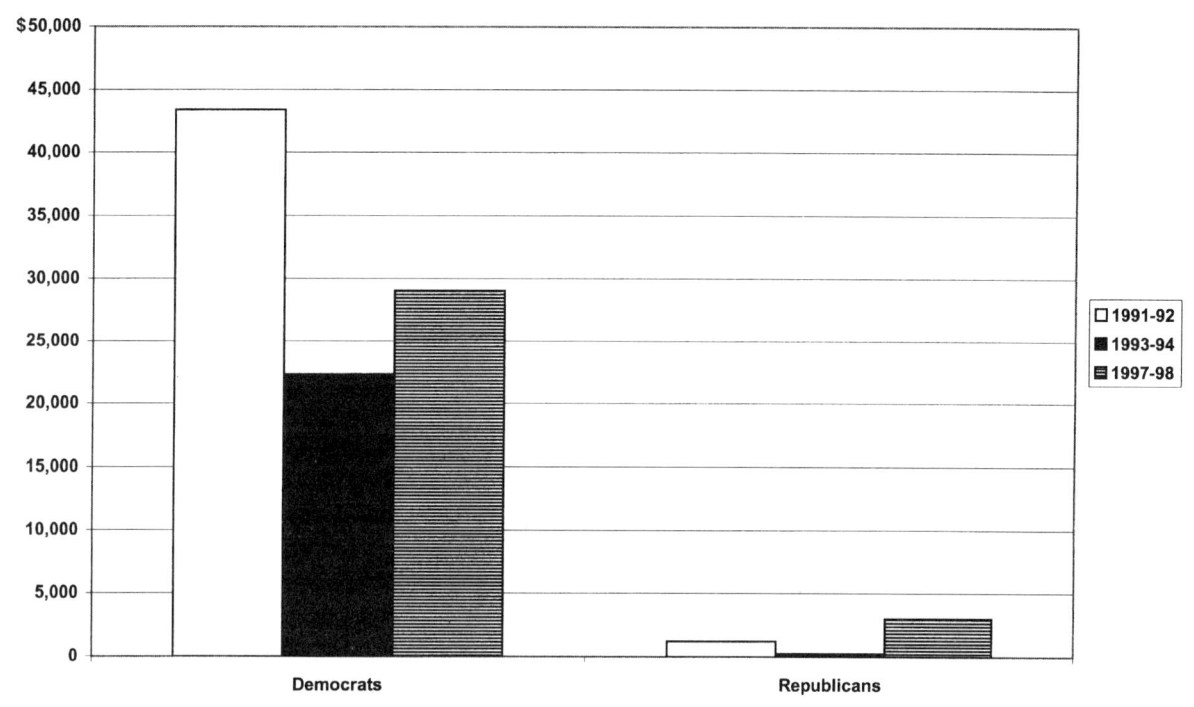

Data derived from official studies available from the Federal Election Commission, Washington, DC, 1991–1998.

Union as a counterbalance to the increasingly Republican Farm Bureau. The National Farmers Union continued to have a close working relationship with the Department of Agriculture during the Truman administration, but became much less influential during Eisenhower's term in office.

The NFU's influence rebounded during President John Kennedy's and President Lyndon Johnson's administrations. Secretary Orville Freeman appointed a number of officials who had close ties to the NFU. The NFU was also generally supportive of Freeman's proposals for production controls. During President Ronald Reagan's administration, the National Farmers Union worked with other farm groups in a successful effort to defeat administration attempts to reduce subsidies and increase reliance on the free market.

ACTIVITIES: CURRENT AND FUTURE

The National Farmers Union favors federal farm commodity marketing programs that are tailored to support independent family farmers. Consistent with this goal, the National Farmers Union often advocates caps and other restrictions on government agricultural programs designed to steer benefits to smaller producers and ensure that those benefits go directly to the cultivators rather than owners of property. During the late 1990s, the National Farmers Unions response to extremely low agricultural prices was to support President Bill Clinton's call for restoration of the farm safety net. It has been alarmed by the trend toward corporate concentration in both agricultural supply and marketing industries. The National Farmers Union has also expressed concern about the scheduled drop in dairy support prices, which are being phased in as a result of the 1996 Farm Bill.

The National Farmers Union does not limit itself simply to agricultural issues. It supports graduated income taxes, increases in corporate tax rates, minimum wage legislation, and price controls—all positions which are consistent with its political support of liberal Democratic politicians.

With the elimination of the National Farm Organization's political action committee (PAC) in the 1990s, the National Farmers Union is now the most active of the Democratically oriented farm groups. In theory, the NFU should do well when the Democrats control both Congress and the presidency. When the Democrats and Republicans split control of the government, the best the NFU can do is to try to block policies that it opposes.

Today's political climate makes even this negative strategy difficult. The current hostility toward government-based solutions, which have been picked up by Democrats as well as Republicans, isolates the NFU. Agribusiness and the commodity groups have become more important in the policy process. The NFU badly needs to cultivate urban and suburban interests, but this is becoming harder to do every year.

FINANCIAL FACTS

The NFU's contribution pattern is similar to that of a labor union. The organization consistently gives Democratic candidates over 90 percent of its funds. Incumbents receive more money than nonincumbents, but the NFU takes more electoral risks than other agricultural interest groups. In some years, as much as 36 percent of all contributions go to nonincumbents.

The National Farmers Union is a relatively small PAC. Total contributions fluctuate over time. In 1986, the union gave $5,000 to 22 candidates. By 1992, the NFU was able to give considerably more money, $49,875, to 112 candidates, but total contributions fell dramatically in 1994 to $22,500 to 64 candidates. Most recently in 1998, the NFU was able to push its contribution level back up to $32,300, which it gave to 74 candidates.

ANDREW D. McNITT

Bibliography

Browne, William P., and Alan J. Cigler. *U.S. Agricultural Groups*. Westport, CT: Greenwood Publishing Group, 1990.

Hadwiger, Don. *Federal Wheat Commodity Programs*. Ames: Iowa State University Press, 1970.

Makinson, Larry, and Joshua Goldstein. *Open Secrets: The Encyclopedia of Congressional Money and Politics*. Washington, DC: Congressional Quarterly, 1992–1996.

Mooney, Patrick, and Theo Majka. *Farmers' and Farm Workers' Movements*. New York: Twayne, 1995.

National Farmers Union: www.nfu.org

NATIONAL GRANGE

Founded in 1867, the National Grange is the oldest general-purpose agricultural interest group in the United States. It was originally organized as an agricultural fraternal order, with offices and rituals patterned after the Order of Freemasons. During the late nineteenth century, the Grange was, for several years, the major vehicle for agrarian protest. At the end of the nineteenth century, as its base of support shifted from the Midwest and South to New England and the East, it became both more conservative and politically less active. During the early twentieth century, it was one of the largest, general-purpose farm organizations. In fact, it was not until after the Second World War that the American Farm Bureau Federation surpassed the National Grange in size.

The Grange currently has 300,000 members in 37 states. The national headquarters is located in Washington, D.C. Although the Grange takes positions on a wide range of issues, it is neither a particularly partisan nor an aggressive organization. At the present time, the leaders of the organization are prohibited from directly engaging in electoral politics, and the organization does not have a political action committee (PAC). However, every year the Grange publishes and distributes an extensive list of its positions on current issues. Grange members are then urged to write to their members of Congress requesting their support for these positions.

HISTORY

The Grange was founded in 1867, during the agricultural recession that followed the Civil War. The founders of the Grange, Oliver Hudson Kelley and William Saunders, worked for the Department of Agriculture. Although Kelley and Saunders originally conceived of the Grange as an educational and social organization, it began to grow rapidly when it took a more political stance. The early antimonopoly positions taken by the Grange and its support for railroad regulation resulted in increased membership. By 1875, the Grange had 858,050 members, located mostly in the Midwest and the South.

In an attempt to undermine the role of middlemen in agriculture, the Grange went on to develop a broad range of cooperative enterprises, including insurance companies and even some manufacturing enterprises. The financial failure of these enterprises in the 1880s hurt a number of Grange members who had invested in them. These financial problems, combined with the inability to find new political issues following the passage of the Interstate Commerce Act (which regulated railroad rates) resulted in a rapid decline in membership.

After 1890, the Grange rebuilt itself by de-emphasizing partisan politics, stressing its social activities, and shifting its base of operations first to the northeastern and then eventually to the northwestern states as well. The rebuilt Grange was well organized, but not nearly as political.

Its influence on politics in the more urbanized eastern states was limited because of the relatively smaller role played by agriculture in these states. Also, its new members, who were more likely to be involved in general farming and less likely to produce commodities (large crops of a single variety), were less radicalized because they had more stable incomes than its earlier southern and midwestern members.

During the 1920s and 1930s, the Grange was able to maintain its membership, but because of its internal organization it was a much-less-active proponent of farm relief than the American Farm Bureau Federation. As a consequence, the Farm Bureau surpassed the Grange in size after the Second World War. Although occasionally critical of the Farm Bureau's relationship with the Cooperative Extension Service, the Grange largely allied itself with the Farm Bureau during the 1950s. Cooperation between the two groups during this period was facilitated by the growing number of individuals who belonged to both organizations.

The decline of the Grange since the 1950s is largely

the result of two factors. First, it lost membership to other more aggressive organizations, specifically the Farm Bureau and the National Farmers Union; second, the continuing consolidation and reduction in number of farms in the United States after the Second World War was particularly rapid in those geographic areas where the Grange had most of its supporters.

ACTIVITIES: CURRENT AND FUTURE

The social and fraternal aspects of the Grange are of primary importance. The Grange, however, is in contact with the Department of Agriculture, and the representatives of the Grange occasionally make important contributions to the policy-making process. Unlike other agricultural organizations, the Grange is interested in a broader range of issues that affect the quality of rural life. Currently, the Grange is concerned with improving rural schools, increasing Medicare reimbursements for rural providers, ensuring access of rural residents to the Internet, and improving the rural road system.

The positions taken by the Grange on agricultural policies are moderately conservative. The Grange is often—but not always—allied with the Farm Bureau on subsidy and set-aside issues. Officially, the Grange "favors the elimination of direct government farm programs." In addition, the Grange supports fast-track authority for trade agreements, the elimination of estate and capital gains taxes, the formation of regional dairy compacts, deregulation of electric utilities in the states, and continued support for the tobacco growers. On environmental questions, the Grange supports farmland preservation, as long as farmers' property rights are protected, and the reauthorization of the Endangered Species Act, again, as long as farmers are protected from "undue" regulation.

Although it would be foolish to predict disaster for an organization that has been in existence for more than 130 years, the Grange is clearly not what it used to be. On the positive side, the Grange is concerned with quality-of-life issues that are ignored by other agricultural interest groups, and it practices a style of interest-group politics that is ethically beyond reproach. On the negative side, social functions of the Grange have become less important as modern technology has reduced the relative isolation of rural residents. The Grange is also much more directly affected by the decline in agriculture than are its competitors.

FINANCIAL FACTS

The National Grange does not have a political action committee (PAC) and does not make campaign contributions. They have an extensive issue-development process that, after much consultation, produces a position statement that is distributed to Congress. Grange members are then urged to contact their legislators in support of these goals. The Grange has a legislative affairs office with three employees in Washington, D.C., which lobbies national and state politicians. Currently, the Washington office spends about $40,000 a year on lobbying expenses. The National Grange develops an agenda through extensive consultation with members, who also engage in direct lobbying of representatives.

ANDREW D. McNITT

Bibliography

Block, William J. *The Separation of the Farm Bureau and the Extension Service.* Urbana: University of Illinois Press, 1960.

Browne, William P., and Alan J. Cigler. *U.S. Agricultural Groups.* Westport, CT: Greenwood Publishing Group, 1990.

National Grange. Welcome to National Grange of the Order of Patrons of Husbandry: nationalgrange.org

Zeigler, Harmon. *Interest Groups in American Society.* Englewood Cliffs, NJ: Prentice-Hall, 1964.

NATIONAL PORK PRODUCERS COUNCIL

Founded in the mid 1950s as the National Swine Growers Council, the National Pork Producers Council is a commodity group that represents 85,000 pork producers in 44 states. The organization is a federation of state associations. It is funded by a legislatively mandated checkoff, or fee, that is paid to pork producers each time they market a hog. In 1996, cash receipts from the marketing of hogs totaled $12.6 billion. The organization represents the interests of both large and small producers. The national headquarters is in Des Moines, Iowa, and a legislative office is maintained in Washington, D.C.

HISTORY

Traditionally, hogs have been produced by farmers who also raised the required feed grains. Consequently, much of the commercial production is centered in the midwestern corn belt, although North Carolina has recently become an important producer. The development of the ability to raise hogs in containments has led to a rapid decline in the number of producers, but not in the number of hogs produced.

The reduction in the number of producers has been further influenced by the arrival of the "mega" hog farms that raise hogs in very large containment facilities. These large producers have located next to large packing plants, which has resulted in the closing of a number of smaller packers who used to serve a more geographically diverse clientele. This, in turn, further disadvantages small producers, many of whom have stopped producing hogs because of the increasing distances that small producers must ship to market.

Pork producers have been challenged by the collapse of pork prices in 1998. Pork prices normally follow a four-year cycle of boom and bust. This time, the cycle was particularly severe because of the collapse of foreign markets and the overproduction of pork that followed the rapid entry of mega hog farms into the market. Pork producers, like other livestock producers, have traditionally not been directly subsidized by the federal government. As a consequence, the National Pork Producers Council, although one of the largest commodity organizations, was relatively inactive at the national level.

Changing methods of production have created new challenges for the organization. The development of mega hog farms has also resulted in increased environmental concerns. Since some form of increased regulation is inevitable, the National Pork Producers Council and its state affiliates have become more active at both the state and national levels.

ACTIVITIES: CURRENT AND FUTURE

The National Pork Producers Council provides members with a number of useful services. It promotes pork consumption, distributes useful information about production techniques, and monitors legislation that affects the industry. It has developed ties with the Pork Industry Congressional Caucus, a group of 28 Democrats and 40 Republicans who are "pork industry friends."

The National Pork Producers Council takes positions on a broad range of issues. It favors trade policies that will facilitate the export of pork products. It is willing to accept some environmental regulations as long as those regulations are based on scientific evidence and do not constitute an "undue burden" on producers. The council also favors freedom-to-farm legislation as a way of protecting producers from nuisance suits arising out of disputes over unpleasant odors. It is interested in ensuring consumer confidence in the safety of pork products. Consequently, it supports food safety legislation. In particular, the council is interested in ensuring that

**National Pork Producers Council
Political Action Committee Contributions**

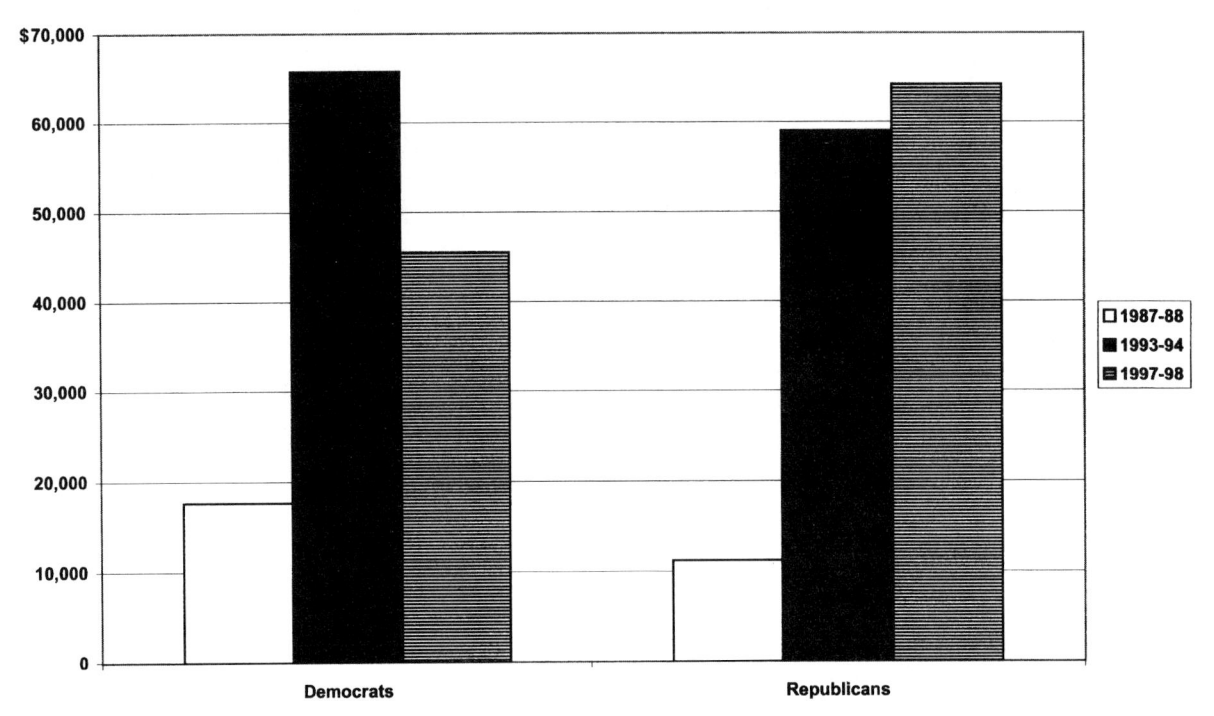

[Bar chart showing PAC contributions to Democrats and Republicans for 1987-88, 1993-94, and 1997-98]

Data derived from official studies available from the Federal Election Commission, Washington, DC, 1987–1998.

poultry products meet the same sanitary standards as pork, beef, and lamb. Positions on tax policies, such as favoring deductibility of health insurance and income averaging, are designed to help independent producers.

The trend toward a smaller number of larger producers in the industry is likely to continue. The largest producers have the economic resources necessary to weather the current collapse of pork prices, and are, in fact, to some extent protected from the price fluctuations by long-term contracts with wholesalers.

As the industry relies more on large-scale production techniques it will come into political conflict with other interests concerning environmental regulations. Rural as well as urban residents have called for stricter regulations of large pork producers. Policy makers at the national level have even proposed treating the largest producers as industrial rather than agricultural firms. Pork producers have expressed a willingness to accept some regulations, but are concerned about both how restrictive and how stable that legislation will be—concerns shared by other kinds of livestock producers who are also increasingly reliant on large-scale containment production techniques.

FINANCIAL FACTS

The National Pork Producers Council began making campaign contributions in 1988, when it gave $28,400 to 65 congressional candidates. The council increased its activities in the early 1990s. Total contributions peaked at $124,858, which was given to 145 candidates in 1994 during the run-up to the 1996 Farm Bill. Total contributions then fell back in 1996 and 1998 to approximately $110,000 per election cycle. Seventy-five candidates received contributions from the National Pork Producers Council in 1998.

The National Pork Producers Council gives money to both parties. In 1988, the council gave 61 percent of its contributions to Democratic candidates. Since then there has been a steady decline in support for the Democratic Party, which predated that party's 1994 loss of a majority. Support for Democrats, in fact, dwindled to 41 percent by 1998. The National Pork Producers

Council gives money to candidates from the pork-producing midwestern and southern states. The council also disproportionately rewards incumbents, who receive in excess of 85 percent of all contributions.

ANDREW D. MCNITT

Bibliography

Browne, William P., and Alan J. Cigler. *U.S. Agricultural Groups*. Westport, CT: Greenwood Publishing Group, 1990.

Makinson, Larry, and Joshua Goldstein. *Open Secrets: The Encyclopedia of Congressional Money and Politics*. Washington, DC: Congressional Quarterly, 1992–1996.

National Pork Producers Council. General Issues: www.nppc.org

National Pork Producers Council. Pork Issues Handbook: www.nppc.org

Shepherd, Geoffrey S., and Gene A. Futrell. *Marketing Farm Products*. Ames: Iowa State University Press, 1982.

ORGANIC TRADE ASSOCIATION

*I*n 1985, representatives of several smaller organic businesses and farming groups established the Organic Food Production Association of North America. Now known as the Organic Trade Association, this group is an industry-based, political organization that represents growers, retailers, brokers, distributors, and suppliers of organic agricultural products. The Organic Trade Association has 950 mostly business members. The association promotes the use of organic products and represents the political interests of the organic industry. The organization is headquartered in Greenfield, Massachusetts.

HISTORY

After the Second World War, American agriculture became increasingly dependent on the chemical industry. At the same time, the trend toward specialization of production and integrated distribution networks also reduced the number of farmers who sold a wide variety of agricultural products in local markets. The organic agriculture movement is a reaction to these changes.

The organic movement has a strong, well-developed ideology. Its value system emphasizes the use of appropriate technology and living in harmony with nature. Scholars have identified two major trends in organic agriculture. The first trend consists of producers and consumers who practice a strictly organic form of agriculture. The second consists of ecologically oriented producers who use both organic and standard farming practices.

The organic movement has members in all parts of the country. The National Organic Council has a large number of members on the east and west coasts, but there are also strong organic advocates in Wisconsin, Missouri, Kansas, Nebraska, and Texas. Organic farmers produce a broad range of crops. In addition to fruits and vegetables, organic producers of poultry and even cotton have had some success in the marketplace.

Practitioners of organic agriculture are suspicious of the Cooperative Extension Service, which they view as primarily responsive to the interests of large-scale agriculture. Consequently, organic agriculture has tended to rely upon alternative sources of information. The Rodale Press and the Rodale Institute have been particularly influential.

The United States Department of Agriculture (USDA) has shown some interest in organic methods of production. The extent of commitment to the organic industry has varied. After initial studies indicated that organic agriculture was economically and agriculturally viable, the organic industry was attacked by the chemical industry, which dismissed organic agriculturalists as "hobby farmers." This attack was followed by a decline in official interest. The continued growth of the organic industry and the willingness of consumers to pay a premium for organic produce, however, has led to a revival of government interest that has centered on the question of certification.

ACTIVITIES: CURRENT AND FUTURE

The Organic Trade Association supports the Organic Food Production Act of 1990. This act created a national Organic Standards Board to advise the USDA on the establishment of national certification standards. The first draft of the USDA certification rules was criticized for inclusion of a number of nonorganic practices. A second draft, designed to respond to some of these earlier criticisms, is currently under review.

The future of organic agriculture is relatively bright. It offers a survival strategy for small farmers who need to both reduce the cost of inputs and increase the price that can be charged for produce. Marketing difficulties have led organic producers to develop their own marketing outlets, with extensive use being made of farmers markets and food cooperatives.

The development of the Organic Trade Association is part of this movement. It is similar to other commodity groups in structure although it is not funded through a commodity checkoff program.

Officially sanctioned commodities groups collect a fee on each unit of product sold, which is used for research and marketing. Although officially not used for political purposes, they help to create a stable financial base for an organization that can then collect other funds for political contributions. Furthermore, commodity checkoff money can be used for public information. For the most part, commodity checkoffs are not voluntary. They are legislatively mandated. Still, votes are held to authorize the checkoff.

The association has just entered the political arena. While it is a small organization with limited resources, it is operating in an environment in which there is a substantial amount of public support for its ideals. Consequently, the Organic Trade Association has a greater potential to be influential than might be first assumed.

Organic agriculture is here to stay; the question now is how large a niche in the food system it will occupy.

FINANCIAL FACTS

The Organic Trade Association does not have a national political action committee (PAC). However, it employs a part-time lobbyist in Washington, D.C. In 1997, the total value of organic products sold in the United States was $4 billion. The sales of organic items have been growing rapidly, increasing by 20 percent per year for the last nine years.

ANDREW D. McNITT

Bibliography

Organic Trade Association: www.ota.com

Youngberg, Garth. "Alternative Agriculturalists: Ideology, Politics and Prospects." In Don Hadwiger and William Browne, eds., *The New Politics of Food*. Lexington, MA: Lexington Books, 1978.

UNITED EGG ASSOCIATION

The United Egg Association (UEA) is actively involved in working with the United Egg Producers and other agricultural interests to promote the egg industry, enhance the quality of egg production, and stimulate exports of egg industry products. The United Egg Producers provides management for this alliance. The association is headquartered in Atlanta, Georgia, and it maintains a government relations office in Washington, D.C.

HISTORY

The UEA is an alliance of three separate trade associations that are involved with processing, packaging, and providing other services to the egg industry. These organizations are the UEA Further Processors, the UEA Allied, and the UEA Producer/Packer. The UEA Further Processors was organized in 1984 as a trade association representing processors of eggs into egg products and manufacturers of liquid, dried, and frozen egg products. This trade group has a membership of approximately 35 firms. The UEA Allied, which was organized in January 1995 as a trade association, represents companies or individuals engaged in providing products, services, consulting, and information services to the egg industry but do not produce eggs or engage in the processing of eggs into egg products. Approximately 40 firms are members of this division. The UEA Producer/Packer, with approximately 10 members, was organized in September 1995 as a trade association to represent companies or individuals in the northeastern states that pack or produce eggs, but which do not qualify for membership in a Capper-Volstead Cooperative. The 1922 Capper-Volstead Act gave agricultural producers the right to market their products in interstate and foreign commerce.

ACTIVITIES: CURRENT AND FUTURE

The UEA works closely with other agricultural interest groups to promote the egg industry, as well as "informed and reasonable" government regulation in the industry. As is the case for nearly all agricultural interest groups, the United Egg Association advocates an open trade policy, particularly in support of the International Monetary Fund's assistance to the Asian markets, and the exemption of agricultural products from U.S. economic sanctions legislation.

The UEA supports appropriate environmental procedures and regulations and has been a participant with the U.S. Department of Agriculture (USDA) and the Environmental Protection Agency (EPA) in their food manufacturing coalition to improve environmental quality and productivity in the food manufacturing industry. The UEA and United Egg Producers jointly hold an annual legislative conference in the spring in Washington, D.C. It maintains a Washington office that closely monitors proposed legislation on Capitol Hill, as well as the regulatory activities of the USDA, the EPA, and the Department of Commerce.

Members of the association are informed about market, regulatory, and legislative issues through the biweekly newsletter, *United Voices*. Partly as a result of its selective membership size, the UEA tends to ally itself with other agricultural and commercial organizations in areas of joint interest, particularly with respect to international trade, rather than to act independently on a broad range of issues on the legislative scene.

The incredible productivity of the U.S. egg industry suggests that there will be a prominent role for the UEA, with particular emphasis on its efforts to expand to foreign markets. The industry's achievements in being proactive with respect to food safety, nutritional education, concern for animal welfare, and its capacity to police itself have given the association a

**United Egg Association
Political Action Committee Contributions**

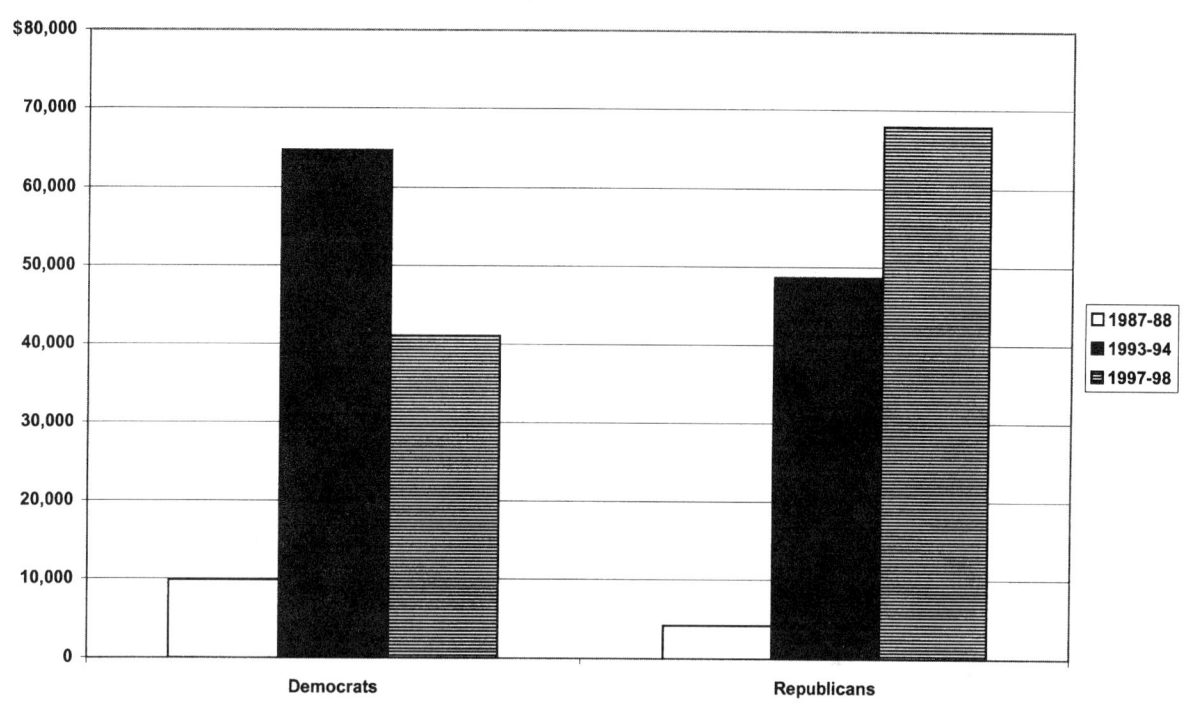

□ 1987-88
■ 1993-94
▤ 1997-98

Data derived from official studies available from the Federal Election Commission, Washington, DC, 1987–1998.

broader influence than its membership size would suggest.

FINANCIAL FACTS

The fact that the UEA is not involved in the direct production of eggs makes it difficult to accurately establish the association's impact upon the total U.S. economy. In 1997–1998, association contributions to congressional candidates through its political action committee, EggPAC, totaled $109,000. This sum is a considerable increase from the 1989–1990 total of $28,250. EggPAC, which includes both the UEA and the United Egg Producers, set a goal of raising $75,000 during 1999, of which the UEA's share is $10,000. EggPAC contributions usually go to incumbents and members of relevant agricultural committees.

Overall, the partisan pattern of contributions was heavily affected by the 1994 shift to Republican control of Congress. In 1989–1990, incumbents received 100 percent of the EggPAC funds, of which Democrats garnered 53 percent. In 1997–1998, Republicans received 62 percent of the total contributions. As expected, EggPAC's interest is higher in the larger and more numerous committees in the House of Representatives, whose members received 80 percent of allocated EggPAC funds. In 1997–1998, 73 candidates received contributions—16 Senate candidates and 57 House candidates. The size of the contributions ranged generally from $500 to $2,000. Two House members, however, received significantly larger contributions totaling $10,000 each. In 1989–1990, only 36 candidates received political action committee allocations from the UEA.

JAMES SEROKA

Bibliography

Center for Responsive Politics. Open Secrets Home Page, 1999: www.opensecrets.org/pacs/

Gregory, Gene, ed. *United Voices*. Newsletter. 1999.

Makinson, Larry. *Open Secrets: The Encyclopedia of Congressional Money and Politics*. Washington, D.C.: Congressional Quarterly. 1990.

United Egg homepage 1999: www.unitedegg.org

SECTION SIX
ENVIRONMENT

The environment is the backdrop of virtually every area of human endeavor and activity. Yet, certain activities are more central to the topic of environmental concerns than others. The needs and use of natural resources in the more intensive resource extraction industries, such as mining, logging, and timber usage, are areas of concern in the environmental arena. The impact of huge population concentrations, particularly in terms of water and air pollution, creates environmental stress. Finally the impact of the activities of humans on other species, both directly through harvesting for use and indirectly through destruction of habitats, generate disputes.

The interest groups that operate in the environmental arena vary in their stances toward the public policy process and the institutions and individuals in it. Some are deeply involved in direct lobbying and negotiating, while others are very suspicious of all traditional sources of power and wealth and view those who compromise on environmental issues as the enemy. Some environmental groups predate the modern environmental movement by many years, while others have been organized since the first Earth Day, in 1970. Few environmental groups are or have political action committees (PACs). Most are officially nonpartisan. All of the groups depend on membership for their financing, but some also depend on contributions from foundations and others provide services and products that help pay their costs.

The most sweeping current concern of the environmental movement is global warming. The claim that increases in carbon dioxide are warming the earth's atmosphere is cited by environmentalists as a reason to regulate carbon dioxide emissions and for the need to protect forests to counteract emissions. The new field of genetic engineering has generated issues concerning possible harm from the introduction of hybrid plants and animals into the environment. Urban sprawl—the spread of urban and suburban development over wider and wider areas of surrounding countryside—has recently received increased attention. Environmentalists argue that this trend threatens to destroy important ecosystems.

The target of much of the activity of environmental groups includes such agencies as the Environmental Protection Agency (EPA) and the Interior Department, as would be expected. But the Commerce Department, U.S. Army Corps of Engineers, and many other agencies are also lobbied because of the effects of their activities on the environment and their ability to regulate private activity.

AREAS OF INTEREST

In the aftermath of the great depression and the Second World War, Americans were interested in economic growth and the enjoyment of material prosperity. The growing use of chemicals, the expansion of cities and suburbs, the explosion in the number of automobiles, the construction of many miles of new roads, and numerous other activities that cause environmental stress were undertaken at an accelerated pace. Moreover, the development of nuclear weapons demonstrated mankind's power to destroy, and the warnings of environmental dangers by authors such as Rachel Carson, Fairfield Osborn, and Paul Erlich affected the public. Events in the 1960s eroded the public's faith in government, industry, and science, preparing the way for a shift in attitudes and beliefs. The year 1969 proved pivotal and marks the beginning of the modern environmental movement. An oil spill in Santa Barbara gained national publicity and symbolized the destruction of natural beauty and precious resources by pollution. Eleven tons of salmon were seized in Wisconsin and Minnesota because they contained excessive concentrations of the pesticide DDT, demonstrating the threat to public health by chemical pollution. In Cleveland, an oil slick on a section of the Cuyahoga River briefly burned, symbolizing a degree of pollution so severe that a river could catch fire. The first Earth Day in April 1970 proved a dramatic success. The participation and publicity were so great that they propelled the environmental movement into a prominent place in the public's consciousness. In the wake of that Earth Day, traditional conservation groups gained influence, an entire new generation of groups formed, and old environmental laws were strengthened, while new ones were passed. The Clean Air Act was toughened in 1970 with regulation of many more pollutants. The EPA was also established in 1970, and environmental-impact statements were required by the same law. The Clean Water Act was passed in 1972, and others, such as the 1973 Endangered Species Act, followed.

Successful social movements generate reactions, and the environmental movement soon caused a backlash. In the late 1970s, conservatives, along with managers and workers in affected industries, formed a loose coalition calles the "wise use" movement. The energy shortages and economic crises of the decade eroded some support for further gains. When Ronald Reagan was elected president in 1980 this antienvironmental movement gained a powerful ally who took steps to curb or roll back environmental regulation. However, President Reagan was only partly successful. With his election, a group of the largest environmental organizations formed the Group of Ten to coordinate a response to Reagan's policies. By the 1980s, most Americans were broadly supportive of environmental values, and Reagan was not able to undo many environmental regulations then in place.

The 1990s were a time of mixed results for the environmental movement. The decade began with the attempt by President George Bush's administration to balance economic concerns with environmental issues—typically coming out on the side of business interests. President Bill Clinton's administration offered more promise, but its focus on developing a strong economy often led to compromises over environmental policy. When Republicans gained control of Congress in the 1994 elections, the environmental movement was put on the defensive, protecting old gains rather than seeking new ones. Membership in environmental groups also experienced ups and downs during this period. The 1980s were a boom time for environmental groups, as sympathetic citizens were frightened by the Reagan administration, but the economic downturn of the early 1990s and the election of a Democratic administration slowed, and even reversed, membership growth. The environmental movement approaches the next decade in a strong, but uncertain, position.

Current Social Context

Most surveys show the public strongly supports environmental values. The news media are also generally supportive of environmentalism. Schools include in their curriculums units and exercises designed to teach environmental lessons to children. Many communities, businesses, and institutions now routinely have recycling programs. Environmentalism is part of a broader concern for maximizing the health and safety of society that has become part of American culture in the post–Second World War era. Yet, other elements of the culture work against environmentalism. Americans remain very materialistic. Environmentalists still run into resistance when they propose major changes in lifestyles that would interfere with the enjoyment of the material abundance of the culture. Trends such as urban sprawl—a target of concern among environmentalists—are testimonies to the desire of Americans for "the good life." Many Westerners find the restrictions proposed and enforced by environmentalism to be harmful to a consumer-oriented way of life. Business interests—and the adherents of capitalism who support them—feel that environmentalism harms the free market system without providing sufficient benefits.

Current Economic Context

The American economy of the mid-to-late 1990s has enjoyed a long run of prosperity. Businesses can better afford to implement environmentally sound innovations in products and production processes, and workers are more secure in their jobs and feel less of a threat from environmental regulations. Consumers do not find the cost increases or inconveniences created by some environmental regulations especially burdensome. The budget surpluses enjoyed by the federal government reduce pressures to cut back on programs and personnel.

At the same time, other trends are working against environmentalists. American consumption is running at record rates, and some specific trends are reversing gains of the past. Urban sprawl is accelerated by a heated economy. The love affair of American drivers with sport utility vehicles, and the rapidly increasing number of miles driven, are expanding fuel consumption, vehicle production, and pollution.

In the international economy, the desire to increase development has pushed environmental concerns to the background in many countries and led to environmentally unsound policies by international development agencies. Trade agreements frequently permit multinational corporations to avoid pollution restrictions on production facilities. Environmental groups are increasingly attempting to reverse powerful negative trends and forces that are generated by the understandable desire of those in less-developed economies for a better life.

Current Political Context

Environmentalists were often on the defensive in the 1990s. Early in the decade, recession and a Republican administration that was not committed to environmental values forced environmentalists to depend heavily on the Democratic Congress to preserve the laws and regulations that were in place, and gains were out of the question. President Clinton's victory in the 1992 election offered hope for a reversal of the trend, but he was concerned with economic development and was on the defensive himself after his first two years in office. When Republicans gained control of Congress in 1994, accompanied by a "Contract with America" that promised to drastically reduce federal regulation, the threat to environmentalism reached a peak. Republicans stalled further progress in environmental regulation, but they did not succeed in their more ambitious goals. The House passed many of the changes called for in the Contract, but the Senate often refused to go along or watered down the changes. The American public was not as hostile to environmental values as the Republican leadership or the House Republican rank and file.

As the decade wound down, the trends were mixed. Environmentalists continue to find their lobbying efforts and fund-raising ability overmatched by big business. In addition, the wise use movement has demonstrated a capacity for organizing and bringing pressure on government officials that weakens the environmentalists' one-time near-monopoly on public action.

TYPES OF ORGANIZATIONS

The 1990s were a decade of relatively slow growth for environmental groups. The explosion of membership that followed the election of President Ronald Reagan, with his perceived threat to environmental values, was followed by a period of anxiety and lowered enthusiasm. The trend of growth during times of heightened danger, and stagnation when signals are less clear, is common for public interest groups.

The environmental movement can be divided into mainstream and radical wings. Mainstream groups negotiate with politicians, bureaucrats, and even leaders of interests to which they are opposed. These groups are pragmatic and moderate. Some mainstream groups, such as the Audubon Society, the Sierra Club, the National Wildlife Federation, and the Izaak Walton League, were formed earlier in the twentieth century, with a narrow perspective to achieve very specific goals. The Sierra Club was founded to preserve the Sierra Nevada mountains. The National Wildlife Federation was founded by sportsmen who wanted to protect wildlife habitats in order to enjoy hunting, as well as to promote preservationist values. The Izaak Walton League was formed to protect fish and wildlife habitats for fishing and hunting. These organizations have broadened their focuses over the years and now emphasize environmental values and political ends. However, they still depend on interest in their original goals to maintain their membership.

The groups in the radical wing are products of the modern environmental movement. They are hostile to established authority of any sort. They believe that success for the environmental movement requires a complete change in lifestyles. Rather than compromising with authority, these groups wish to defeat it. Their tactics involve confrontation, civil disobedience, and, for the most extreme, violence against property. Such organizations as Greenpeace, Friends of the Earth, and the Rainforest Action Network depend heavily on an activist, committed membership. They often consist of several small local groups linked through an umbrella organization.

Groups in the environmental movement must depend primarily on membership dues, contributions, and institutional support. Within this pattern there is great variability. The National Wildlife Federation has a series of very successful publications that help it raise funds and membership. Many of the groups depend, at least in part, on foundation grants. The trend in the 1990s has been for groups to reduce such dependence because of the perception it creates of reliance on important interests and because of the instability of such support. The League of Conservation Voters is the only political action committee (PAC) among the environmental groups, though the Sierra Club has an affiliated PAC.

CURRENT ISSUES

Legislation

The 1990s were an era of trying to hold ground, rather than expanding power, for environmental groups. The groups found themselves fighting for increased funding for existing programs. There were certain issues that led to calls for legislation, including proposals for U.S. participation in international environmental treaties, funding for less-developed nations to help them develop without destroying their environments, and restrictions in trade agreements to protect the environment. Urban sprawl and genetically engineered plants and animals are two recent areas of concern that might generate new legislation.

On the other hand, environmentalists find themselves fighting with new approaches against proposals to weaken environmental regulations. One such type of approach, proposed by the property rights wing of the antienvironment movement, has been trying to weaken regulations through takings legislation in the states and at the national level. Takings legislation is designed to block the ability of regulators charged with enforcing environmental laws from requiring that owners of private property comply with the regulations.

Regulations

There is great variety in how environmental groups approach regulation. The Environmental Defense Fund is noted for proposing free-market solutions to regulatory issues, whereas many groups reject such solutions for more traditional restrictions. The movement lost a battle to change the law on grazing and mining rights on federal land when western senators blocked changes proposed by Secretary of the Interior Bruce Babbitt. Other areas of regulation, including those affecting logging, wetlands, and many other areas, have been given attention by environmental groups.

Government Policy

Trade policies, particularly those that involve the exploitation of natural resources or threaten to weaken the enforcement of environmental laws, are a subject of activity by environmental groups. These groups have also lobbied the government to support strong regulations in international treaties on whaling, fishing, control of carbon dioxide emissions, and other environmental concerns.

TYPES OF ACTIVITIES

The basic approach of the environmental movement became part of mainstream American values in the 1970s, and the movement succeeded in many of its policy goals. The consequence was that mainstream groups found they had to switch from policy development to policy oversight and protection. This change required more political sophistication, inside tactics, and a more stable organizational structure. These changes have been reflected in the activities of the mainstream groups.

Lobbying

The League of Conservation Voters (LCV), which is a PAC supported by several environmental groups, has raised and spent several million dollars to support and oppose candidates since its formation in 1970. The Sierra Club Political Committee is the PAC affiliated with that organization. Although this PAC has not been as active as the LCV, it has provided significant contributions to candidates, mostly Democrats. These PACs are exceptions to the rule that environmental groups stay out of electoral politics in order to retain their tax status.

The environment is an area of public policy that demands a command of information and scientific evidence if a group is to have credibility. Environmental groups include scientific experts on their staffs who can produce reports that back up testimony, direct conversations, and influence the shaping and critiquing of legislation. Many interest groups also use letter and e-mail campaigns generated by communications with their members to affect legislative outcomes. The effectiveness of such campaigns is always open to question, but they allow members to participate and keep a mechanism in place that can prove extremely effective under certain circumstances.

Agencies

The relationships between government agencies and environmental groups range from confrontation to infiltration. This range can be illustrated by the fact that James Watt, President Reagan's secretary of the interior, made a career out of fighting the staff of his own department on behalf of industry clients, while Bruce Babbitt, President Clinton's secretary of the interior, is a past president of the LCV. Environmental groups keep close watch on the implementation of environmental laws by executive branch agencies, provide comment on proposed regulations, and attempt to generate mail and participation at hearings by members of their groups. They have also used regulations to achieve ulterior ends. One example of this tactic was the use of the fact that the spotted owl was on the Endangered Species List to slow or stop logging in old-growth forests in the West.

Litigation

The Environmental Defense Fund was formed to litigate environmental issues. Other mainline groups have taken advantage of provisions in environmental laws passed by Congress that permit private groups to sue agencies they believe are not properly enforcing legislation. Environmental groups have also supported agencies when they have been sued by antienvironmental interests. A loss in one recent case involved a decision by a Federal District Court that the EPA had overstepped its authority when it wrote regulations incorporating new air pollution standards. The case is bound to be appealed, and supportive environmental groups will, no doubt, file *amicus curiae* (friend of the court) briefs in the case.

Coalition Building

Mainline environmental groups regularly engage in building coalitions among themselves and with other groups. To enhance the efficiency of these coalitions, the groups develop specialties in which they take the lead. For example, the Sierra Club tends to take the lead on oil pollution issues, while the Environmental Defense Fund is the lead group on air pollution, and the Audubon Society on wildlife issues.

Activities Aimed at the Public

Communication with members and the public is an important part of the activities of any membership group. Most, if not all, environmental groups maintain a web page and some sort of e-mail communications network today. These sites are used to educate, organize, sell products, take surveys, encourage the sending of correspondence to public officials, and recruit members. The groups that depend most heavily on activists use their web sites for organizing and mobilizing their members.

More traditional methods of educating the public, such as journal and book publication, are also common among environmental groups. Those groups that are long established are particularly likely to have magazines with wide circulation. Some groups use techniques that depend upon their specialization, such as summer camps sponsored by the Audubon Society that are used to educate the participants in the values of the organization.

The radical groups depend heavily on their members. These groups organize protests and demonstrations. The strategy of such groups that has achieved perhaps the most publicity is the use of the ship *Rainbow Warrior* by Greenpeace to interfere with whaling, nuclear testing, and the shipping of old-growth lumber. The most radical groups, denounced by others, use destruction of property, such as putting sand in the gas tanks of logging trucks, to achieve their ends.

CONCLUSION

The environmental movement is now a permanent part of the political and social landscape of America. Many of the groups in the movement have survived for long periods of time, and recent events suggest that environmental values are deeply embedded in American culture. However, this does not mean the environmentalists win every battle. Environmentalism is an issue so broad and deep that it is the basis for the creation of political parties in some democracies.

FRANK CODISPOTI

Bibliography

Bosso, Christopher J. "Adaption and Change in the Environmental Movement." In *Interest Group Politics*, 3d ed., edited by Allan J. Cigler and Burdett A. Loomis. Washington, DC: Congressional Quarterly, 1991.

———. "The Color of Money: Environmental Groups and the Pathologies of Fund Raising." In *Interest Group Politics*, 4th ed., edited by Allan J. Cigler and Burdett A. Loomis. Washington, DC: Congressional Quarterly, 1995.

Cooper, Mary H. "Environmental Movement at 25." *CQ Researcher* 5, no. 12: 275–295.

Gottlieb, Robert. *Forcing the Spring: The Transformation of the American Environmental Movement*. Washington, DC: Island Press, 1993.

Helvarg, David. *The War Against the Greens: The "Wise Use" Movement, the New Right, and Anti-Environmental Violence*. San Francisco: Sierra Club Books, 1994.

Hrebenar, Ronald J. *Interest Group Politics in America*. Armonk, NY: M.E. Sharpe, 1997.

Kamieniecki, Sheldon, George A. Gonzalez, and Robert O.

Vos, eds. *Flashpoints in Environmental Policy Making: Controversies in Achieving Sustainability.* Albany: State University of New York Press, 1997.

Kline, Benjamin. *First Along the River: A Brief History of the U.S. Environmental Movement.* San Francisco: Acada Books, 1997.

Lacey, Michael J., ed. *Government and Environmental Politics: Essays on Historical Developments Since World War Two.* Washington, DC: Woodrow Wilson Center Press and the Johns Hopkins University Press, 1991.

List, Peter C., ed. *Radical Environmentalism: Philosophy and Tactics.* Belmont, CA: Wadsworth, 1993.

Pepper, David. *Modern Environmentalism: An Introduction.* New York: Routledge, 1996.

Switzer, Jacqueline Vaughn. *Green Backlash: The History and Politics of the Environmental Opposition in the United States.* Boulder, CO: Lynne Rienner, 1997.

Vig, Norman J., and Michael E. Kraft, eds. *Environmental Policy in the 1990s: Toward a New Agenda,* 2d ed. Washington, DC: Congressional Quarterly, 1994.

ENVIRONMENTAL DEFENSE FUND

The Environmental Defense Fund (EDF) is a 300,000-member organization that focuses on issues dealing with toxic chemicals, wetlands, water quality, and power generation. The EDF—founded in 1967 and headquartered in New York City—utilizes various strategies to achieve its ends, including lobbying, litigation, and publicity via press reports and the Internet. It also conducts extensive research aimed at both analyzing environmental problems and developing scientific solutions to them. Considered a mainstream and even conservative environmental group by some—especially in comparison to direct-action organizations like Greenpeace and Friends of the Earth—the EDF has come to increasingly support free-market solutions to environmental problems in recent years.

HISTORY

The founding date of the EDF in 1967 is often used to mark the beginning of the transformation of the conservation movement into the present-day environmental movement. In 1966, Victor Yannacone Jr., an attorney who lived on Long Island, New York, brought suit to stop the Suffolk County Mosquito Control Commission from using the pesticide DDT for mosquito control. Yannacone received voluntary help from a group of concerned biologists. When he and his colleagues presented their case against DDT in court, the judge ordered an injunction against its use. This incident demonstrated that the courts could be used as a public forum for environmental issues. Yannacone and his associates incorporated as the Environmental Defense Fund on October 6, 1967, and began a series of cases against the use of DDT. In 1972 a permanent, nationwide ban against DDT was established, which was one of the EDF's biggest victories.

Yannacone left the EDF within a year or two, after which the organization approached the Ford Foundation for funding in order to hire a permanent legal staff. The foundation was reluctant to fund such an effort, but eventually was persuaded by the success of another environmental group that used litigation as a strategy. This allowed the EDF to launch a membership drive and to hire more staff.

The subsequent history of the EDF has involved expanding its original focus and methods. Along with the campaign against DDT, early EDF efforts included lobbying for airborne lead standards in California in 1971, establishing national maximum limits on airborne levels of asbestos, mercury, and beryllium, and other efforts over the years to reduce airborne pollutants, toxic materials used on clothing, and water contaminants. In addition, the EDF has pushed for cleaner energy sources, including the elimination of lead from gasoline.

A secondary effort that resulted from the original DDT issue was the protection of wildlife habitats, as it was discovered that the chemical also had adverse effects on animals. In one of its earliest efforts, the EDF worked on getting all hunted whales onto the endangered species list. In 1977, the group lobbied for eliminating the use of tuna fishing nets in order to reduce the number of dolphins drowning as a result of being caught in the nets. The EDF was part of an effort in 1995 that led to the reintroduction of gray wolves to their natural range in Wyoming and Idaho. Other such efforts have also been part of the EDF's activities.

In most of these efforts, the EDF formed coalitions with other environmental groups. However, the group has been successful in using its own unique strategy with increased frequency. This strategy involves a pragmatic approach to environmental issues that includes working with business. Unlike some other environmental groups, the EDF is not afraid to be seen as friendly to business. In 1990, the EDF and McDonald's created a joint task force that resulted in McDonald's ceasing the use of foam hamburger boxes, along with other steps to cut waste. In 1993, the group joined with six large paper companies to examine paper purchasing practices. In 1998, the Alliance for Environmental Innovation, of which the EDF is part, and the United Parcel Service developed reusable express envelopes. The EDF has also demonstrated its pragmatic approach by advocating market solutions to a number of environmental issues over the years.

At the same time, the group's scientific expertise has grown. The EDF has been able to write laws and file lawsuits on behalf of its interests on many issues by using a battery of scientists and the research they produce to bolster its position. The group has also depended on its economists to make arguments concerning the efficiency of environmentally friendly manufacturing and business practices.

The EDF used a Ford Foundation grant to sustain its development early on and it continues to depend on institutional support for part of its funds. However, the group's membership has grown over the years. In 1970, the organization had 11,000 members. By 1980, its membership had grown to 46,000 and by 1990, it had 150,000 members. During the 1990s, membership in the EDF doubled to 300,000. Over the years, regional offices have opened in Colorado, California, Texas, and other states. The EDF, like most interest groups, recognized the importance of national government in environmental policy-making, and therefore opened an office in Washington, D.C., early in its existence, in 1970.

The EDF is a pragmatic, mainstream environmental organization that would seem to be well-positioned to have a strong role in environmental issues in the future. Its major weakness may be its dependence on institutional support. Around 30 percent of its annual funding is institutional; such funding is always subject to changing priorities and trends. In addition, the EDF has constantly expanded its interests. The use of legal strategy for environmental groups has grown more difficult as the judiciary has been populated with conservative judges, but it has become more essential as the list of laws to be protected has increased and become more complex. While it is possible that the reach of the group could exceed its grasp as it continues to broaden its interests, there is currently no sign that this is happening.

ACTIVITIES: CURRENT AND FUTURE

The EDF began as an organization that used litigation to influence outcomes. As a natural outgrowth, the group took an interest in the passage, expansion, and renewal of environmental laws. The organization began as a group committed to litigating suits against corporate polluters; however, its focus has diversified over the years. While it still uses litigation as one of its strategies, the EDF is now a full-service organization that lobbies Congress and state legislatures. In recent years, the EDF has developed a network of grassroots lobbying strategies. By using the Internet and other methods of communication, the group mobilizes its membership to influence legislative outcomes, referendums, and administrative decisions.

The EDF pursues a strategy of developing solutions to environmental problems that use free-market incentives when possible. The organization is more likely than other groups to seek cooperation, rather than confrontation, with businesses and private property owners. For example, the EDF has proposed a modification to the application of the Endangered Species Act that encourages private land owners to set aside habitats on their land by allowing the land owner to later modify the land, if they so desire. This reduces the incentive for private landholders to eliminate a habitat before it is declared protected so they will not lose control of their property.

The EDF has a staff of 170, including 75 scientists and lawyers. These experts are organized into teams that work on various issues such as air quality, toxic wastes, and energy issues. The teams develop solutions to problems that are pragmatic, and therfore have the promise of gaining acceptance from industry and other affected individuals. A number of these efforts involve cooperative efforts with businesses and political entities. For example, negotiations and collaboration between EDF experts and the McDonald's professional staff resulted in a plan for McDonald's to cut waste. The EDF and the Pew Charitable Trusts have created the Alliance for Environmental Innovation to create model manufacturing and business practices for businesses to adopt. In addition, the EDF is part of the Partnership for Regulatory Innovation and Sustainable Manufacturing (PRISM), which has developed a model alternative regulatory system for vehicle manufacturing. The group is also part of the Paper Task Force, a group of paper buyers and sellers trying to purchase more environmentally preferable paper.

As with many environmental groups, there is an emphasis on public education as an element of the activities of the organization. However, the EDF also depends heavily on its own expertise. The group uses its professional credentials to promote knowledge and distribute information designed to make people more aware of environmental hazards. For example, the EDF web site currently includes interactive features that allow an individual to determine the major sources of pollution in his or her community. Another interactive page allows users to determine the sources of electric power generation in their communities. Other pages on the site present information on global warming. The EDF also developed an environmental sustainability kit, which includes resources and information that can be used by local leaders, presidents, and businesses to make their communities more environmentally sustainable. The EDF does not seek a hostile relationship with businesses or political leaders; instead, it encourages cooperation with and among such entities.

FINANCIAL FACTS

The EDF is registered by the Internal Revenue Service as a non-profit organization. The organization does not make political action committee (PAC) contributions to the campaigns of government officials. In 1998, the organization had total receipts of $27.8 million. About half a percent of the organization's revenues are derived from membership and contributions, 29 percent from foundation grants, and 4 percent from government grants. Program services accounted for 78 percent of the organization's $24 million budget; fund raising accounted for 13 percent; membership maintenance accounted for 5 percent; and administration accounted for 4 percent.

FRANK CODISPOTI

Bibliography
Environmental Defense Fund: www.edf.org

FRIENDS OF THE EARTH

Friends of the Earth endorses a radical environmentalism that opposes technological growth as dangerous for an already overtaxed ecological system. Friends of the Earth has always been an organization that takes a position opposed to all of the traditional sources of political and economic power. As an outgrowth of this position, Friends of the Earth depends on grassroots organizing and action. This stance leads the organization and its 35,000 members to be wary of any activity that can be portrayed as compromise. Friends of the Earth would rather put pressure from outside on government and business in order to change their actions. Opposition to technological change and economic development is a key element of its focus in these efforts. Friends of the Earth joined with Taxpayers for Common Sense and the Public Interest Research Group five years ago in a campaign to oppose federally funded projects that they believed were wasteful, beneficial to the wealthy and powerful at the expense of the average citizen, and harmful to the environment. The campaign targets numerous developmental projects and subsidy programs. It is typical of Friends of the Earth's approach in that it is a sweeping, comprehensive proposal that puts Friends of the Earth and its allies in opposition to many important industries, federal agencies, and state and local governments.

Friends of the Earth also maintains efforts on its own to block government projects. It publicly opposed the Tennessee–Tombigbee Waterway, a $2 billion channel built by the Army Corps of Engineers, which provides a shortcut for barges carrying coal from fields in Tennessee to the port of Mobile, Alabama. The group also opposed U.S. government support for the building of a pipeline through the Amazon forest, and lists 50 road construction projects it believes are particular threats to the environment.

HISTORY

The history of Friends of the Earth is one of conflict, division, and struggle. It was formed in 1969 by David Brower, after he left his post as executive director of the Sierra Club. Brower was an advocate of grassroots activism and a believer in deep ecology, a radical ideological viewpoint that is based on the claim that humans are part of nature and need to learn to live with nature, and not attempt to control it. He was less interested in the insider game of lobbying and bargaining with public officials and businesses, for fear that his organization would abandon its principles for the sake of compromise. Brower does not generally trust authority. The approach he favors requires expansive campaigns, but Brower eschews fund-raising activities for support for fear of limiting the organization's freedom. When Brower came into conflict with the more pragmatic elements of the Sierra Club and lost a key vote of the board, he left the organization and formed Friends of the Earth.

Brower put the headquarters of Friends of the Earth in San Francisco. He believed in keeping the national office as far away from Washington, D.C., as possible and the insider game of politics. From its inception, Friends of the Earth struggled for funds and direction. In 1970, the organization reported having 6,000 members. Brower wanted the organization to take an international approach and to identify with Third World countries and peoples. At the same time, Friends of the Earth had a large professional staff that was more oriented toward policy research and development and legislative advocacy. The tension between the staff orientation and the goals set by Brower was never really resolved, and the Washington professional staff left Friends of the Earth in 1972 and formed the Environmental Policy Institute.

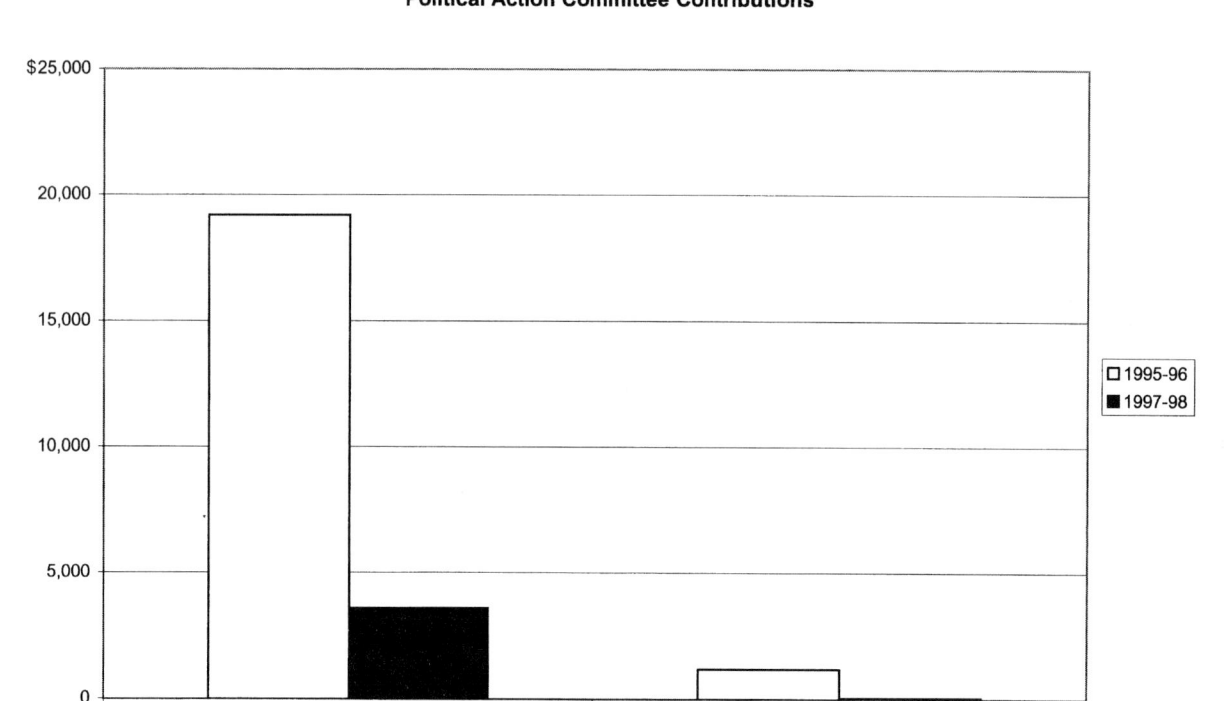

**Friends of the Earth
Political Action Committee Contributions**

[Bar chart showing PAC contributions. Democrats: 1995-96 approximately $19,000; 1997-98 approximately $3,500. Republicans: 1995-96 approximately $1,000; 1997-98 near $0. Legend: □ 1995-96, ■ 1997-98.]

Data derived from official studies available from the Federal Election Commission, Washington, DC, 1995–1998.

Friends of the Earth also spawned another organization, the League of Conservation Voters. The creation of the league did not arise out of conflict within Friends of the Earth, but was the result of an idea by Marion Edey, a congressional staff aide, for an electoral arm for the environmental movement. Edey was referred to Brower by Lloyd Tuppling, a lobbyist for the Sierra Club. Brower gave Edey space in the Washington offices of Friends of the Earth. From that beginning the league was built into an independent organization that continues to operate today.

During the 1970s, Friends of the Earth tried to develop new themes, create new coalitions, and take on new environmental issues in an effort to overcome its problems. It managed to gain publicity for its fight against nuclear energy when Ralph Nader endorsed the group's efforts, symbolized by his appearance as the main speaker at a press conference announcing the intention of Friends of the Earth to file a lawsuit against the Nuclear Regulatory Commission. The organization used its internal publication, *Not Man Apart,* to transmit its agenda and encourage activism among its members. Friends of the Earth also developed a more international focus for its activities, creating autonomous chapters in other countries.

Friends of the Earth continued to suffer from internal divisions, between its radical stance and its professional lobbying structure, into the 1980s. The battles came to a head in 1984 in a bitter internal struggle that caused Brower to leave. By that time, the membership of the organization stood at 30,000. After that final schism, Friends of the Earth underwent a series of mergers. In 1989 it merged with the group it had spawned in 1972, the Environmental Policy Institute. In 1990, Friends of the Earth also merged with the Oceanic Society. This helped to push the membership of the Friends of the Earth, which had dropped to 9,000 in five years, to 50,000 by 1992.

Friends of the Earth spent the 1990s recovering from the internal conflicts of the previous years. During that time it had to reduce its debt while its membership remained stable. It has continued to develop its international focus and its stance as a group that favors a shift in the basic assumptions of economic development. Friends of the Earth also continues its promotion of local activism, including a project aimed at molding the future of Washington, D.C.

ACTIVITIES: CURRENT AND FUTURE

While Friends of the Earth occasionally joins other groups in lobbying Congress, it usually relies heavily on encouraging citizen activity, rather than playing an insider game of lobbying and negotiation. This approach fits with the outsider and purist ideology of the group. Friends of the Earth provides information for local groups on how to engage in grassroots organizing, to identify issues and projects, and to carry out public actions against government and private projects perceived as environmentally dangerous. The tactics suggested by the group for such organizations are those that put pressure on opponents, while strengthening the organization. The instructions from Friends of the Earth also suggest that the tactics used by a group should be aimed at the news media so as to spread the group's message to the broader public.

Friends of the Earth's educational approach suggests the desire of the group to stimulate grassroots activity. Friends of the Earth publishes a newsletter entitled *Close to Home,* which contains reports on the actions of local and state activists and gives its readers information on contacts, web sites, and training opportunities. This is in addition to the *Friends of the Earth Newsmagazine,* which goes to members and combines information on issues with recommendations for action by local groups.

Friends of the Earth also encourages activism in other ways. In 1998, Friends of the Earth created the Road Warrior award. This award recognizes successful efforts to block the building or expansion of roads that would facilitate industrial or residential expansion that the group believes would be environmentally harmful, or whose construction would be environmentally destructive. The recipient of the award is chosen by a panel with representatives from other environmental groups, but it is clearly a project of Friends of the Earth.

Opposition to Policies of International Financial Institutions

Friends of the Earth has a more international focus than many environmental groups. The organization has targeted the World Bank, the International Monetary Fund (IMF), and the World Trade Organization (WTO) for policies it believes are environmentally dangerous. Friends of the Earth has run public relations campaigns, joined in lobbying campaigns, and stimulated grassroots actions against projects, funding, and trade agreements that it evaluated as damaging to the environment. The basic goal of Friends of the Earth is to scale back traditional development and economic activities to the greatest extent possible and replace them with activities that are less dependent on modern technology, extensive energy requirements, or land development. Friends of the Earth portrays itself as fighting for the health, welfare, and rights of the weak and poor over the wealthy and powerful. The organization was one of a large number of groups in the United States and in other countries that opposed a proposed multilateral agreement on investment that the groups said would have allowed corporations to bypass national and local environmental regulations. Friends of the Earth also worked for the creation of an inspection panel at the World Bank to review development projects for their environmental impact and for their effects on local populations. The organization is a strong critic of the policies of the IMF, which it accuses of weakening environmental protection in developing countries and sacrificing the health and welfare of indigenous populations. Friends of the Earth accuses the IMF of following policies that are claimed to be necessary for the health of the free enterprise system but which benefit multilateral corporations most. The Friends of the Earth has also targeted the activities of specific corporations in the developing world by organizing and participating in campaigns against them. In an attempt to affect the national and international economy more generally, the Friends of the Earth has an educational program designed to encourage investors to force their pension plan administrators to invest in an environmentally "responsible" manner.

The Washington, D.C., Project

The *D.C. Environmental Agenda 99* project is one involving Friends of the Earth that reflects its philosophy and activities. Thirteen local and national organizations are involved in developing and promoting a series of goals for the government of Washington, D.C., relating to parks, rivers, trash and garbage control, transportation, and economic development. The theme of the proposals is to shape the city in ways that are consistent with the environmental vision of the member organizations.

Friends of the Earth gives the report of this initiative more coverage on its web site than other national organizations named as members of the coalition, suggesting that Friends of the Earth commits more energy to this project.

FINANCIAL FACTS

In 1998, Friends of the Earth had total receipts of $3 million. The two leading sources of receipts were foundations, members, and gifts. Foundation support accounted for about 72 percent of the organization's contributions, whereas members and gifts accounted for about 24 percent of the organization's contributions. In 1998, Friends of the Earth had a budget of $3.4 million. About 76 percent of the organization's budget was devoted to programs.

FRANK CODISPOTI

Bibliography

Friends of the Earth: www.foe.org

GREENPEACE

Greenpeace, with its 500,000 members in the United States, is an organization of deep-ecology activists; these are activists that believe that humans are a part of nature, and should therefore not attempt to control it. Members focus their activities on controlling toxic materials, stopping overfishing of the oceans, preserving forests, and meeting threats to the world's climate. Although this entry focuses on Greenpeace in the United States, the organization is part of a much larger international one that has offices in 27 countries and 5 million members worldwide. Greenpeace divides its concerns among four general areas: the earth's climate, primarily global warming; the protection of old-growth (or mature) forests; threats to the oceans; and the production, use, and disposal of toxic substances.

HISTORY

The early history of Greenpeace set the stage for the subsequent philosophy and activities of the organization. In 1969, three members of the British Columbia chapter of the Sierra Club, James Bohlen, Irving Stowe, and Paul Cote, became discouraged over the Sierra Club's failure to protest the testing of nuclear weapons. The men started the *Don't Make a Wave* committee, named in reference to concerns that underground tests at Amchitka Island might create tidal waves or contribute to seismic activity. Inspired by Quaker-sponsored ships that had protested nuclear tests by sailing into the test zones, the committee members decided to sail a ship into the Amchitka test zone. It took two years for them to obtain a ship and captain, and their voyage never reached its destination, but the experience was a publicity success. They had been given good wishes by the Canadian prime minister. The group was inspired to try again. Their first ship had been stopped by the U.S. Coast Guard, so they tried again with another ship. That ship was forced back from its attempts several times by high winds and was 700 miles from Amchitka when the nuclear test was conducted. Each ship had been renamed the *Greenpeace*, and the name became the name of the group.

The tactic of disrupting actions that the group found objectionable was applied to whaling and the killing of Newfoundland seal pups. In 1975, Greenpeace began to focus on the Russian and Japanese whaling fleets. The organization confronted a Soviet whaling fleet while debates were going on at a meeting of the International Whaling Commission. A Greenpeace vessel managed to successfully place itself between a ship of the Soviet whaling fleet and its intended targets. Eventually the Soviet ship left the area and Greenpeace considered itself successful.

The group also sailed to Newfoundland and tried to interfere with the killing of seal pups. That expedition was dramatic, but less successful. The Royal Canadian Mounted Police assisted the seal fleets and stopped the Greenpeace operation. The group has used various methods of interfering with actions of those they oppose and of dramatizing their position. Greenpeace has climbed smokestacks, interfered with ships, and engaged in other confrontational actions.

The philosophy of Greenpeace was outlined in 1976 in terms of three "laws of ecology." These statements claim that all forms of life are interdependent. The consequence of this principle is that the destruction of any species can have catastrophic effects for many others, including humans. The second "law" is that the stability of an ecosystem depends on its diversity. The implication of this is that activities that reduce the diversity of an environment, such as the clear-cutting of a diverse stand of trees and replacing it with all trees of one type, creates a system that is more susceptible to being completely destroyed by a single disease or pest. Finally, Greenpeace argues that all resources are finite, and the use of resources by humans must be limited. Greenpeace places little faith in technological solutions to scarcity.

By 1977, Greenpeace was a very active organization, but the type of internal bickering that is common to highly committed organizations and the use of the "Greenpeace" name by numerous unaffiliated groups threatened to cause the collapse of the organization. The Canadian, U.S., and European groups agreed to form an umbrella organization headquartered in Amsterdam. Greenpeace also undertook an aggressive direct-mail campaign and even mounted a door-to-door campaign. At about the same time, the organization rejected proposals for a violent campaign. Paul Watson, the leader of those who wanted such a campaign, and his followers were forced to leave Greenpeace and formed the Sea Shepherd Conservation Society.

The aggressive direct-mail campaign and concerns among supporters of the environmental movement about conservative political victories led to a dramatic growth in membership. By the early 1990s, Greenpeace had a membership of around 2 million. However, the costs of direct-mail campaigns and the instability of the membership created by the process prompted the leadership of Greenpeace to reduce its efforts. This led to a drop in membership during the last decade. Greenpeace remains an activist organization with a militant, but nonviolent, approach.

ACTIVITIES: CURRENT AND FUTURE

Greenpeace has relied a great deal on direct action, including many acts of civil disobedience, rather than lobbying. As with many of the deep-ecology groups, Greenpeace tends to be suspicious of close working relationships with those in the political system. However, the organization watches the legislative process in Washington and across the country and routinely exhorts its members to send letters, e-mail messages, and faxes to legislators. Greenpeace's web site contains numerous such suggestions. Recently, Greenpeace has increased its lobbying activities, including extensive lobbying in the European Union nations as they consider continent-wide environmental rules.

Direct Action

While the international Greenpeace has recently increased its lobbying in the European Union as the latter considers environmental rules, the organization is best known for its direct-action approach to political activity. Greenpeace routinely mounts demonstrations, marches, and other acts of civil disobedience in support of its causes. On September 22, 1998, climbers from Greenpeace placed a banner opposing old-growth forest products on a tower overlooking Niagara Falls. Other members of the group climbed on the anchor chain and other parts of a whaling vessel in Japan to delay its departure from port. In October 1998, Greenpeace's ship, the *Rainbow Warrior,* confronted a freighter bringing lumber from old-growth forests to Long Beach, California. Through several hours of activity, the group attempted to prevent the unloading of the lumber. Another confrontation took place when other members of Greenpeace interrupted a meeting of wood producers. All of these actions demonstrate the multiple aims of Greenpeace's activities—stopping or slowing activities the group perceives as damaging to the environment, bringing attention to an issue, and gaining publicity for Greenpeace. Additionally, these actions become a recruiting tool for individuals who are likely to be attracted by passion for the cause or the sense of adventure involved in these types of actions. Greenpeace even involved children in its actions when it sponsored a gathering of youth in Canada to protest the clear-cutting of old-growth forests. The children had painted posters that were hung in the forest.

Educational Activities

Greenpeace engages in the writing and publishing of numerous reports and fact sheets to support its positions, to inform local activists, and to use in conjunction with its media events. The organization lists 14 publications on its web site concerning the earth's climate and what the organization considers to be potential solutions to the problems it identifies. A similar set of publications exists on forests, toxic chemicals, nuclear energy, and oceans. Greenpeace has also written several publications taking a strong stance against genetic alteration of crops. Greenpeace serves as a source of information for local activist groups. For example, its information on waste water has helped such groups in opposing waste sites.

Greenpeace remains a well-known environmental organization that has successfully adopted an international pattern of organization and activity. The organization recently noted that it had spent 25 years fighting whaling practices. It is perhaps significant that as of this date, Greenpeace has said nothing on its web site about the gray whale kill by members of the Makah tribe in May 1999. The hunt places two of the environmental movement's values, opposition to whaling and protection of indigenous peoples and their ways of life, in conflict. Such conflicts may become more common as the scope of the environmental movement and groups such as Greenpeace continue to expand.

FINANCIAL FACTS

The American wing of Greenpeace had a 1998 annual budget of $37 million. Globally, the organization has an annual budget of $130 million. Individual donations and contributions are the organization's primary source of revenue. Other sources of revenue are derived from membership fees. Historically, the organization had devoted a significant share of its resources to local organizing. Much of the organization's expenses are devoted to public information campaigns. However, because of instability in membership and the high cost of direct-mail campaigns in recent years, the organization's revenues have become less predictable.

FRANK CODISPOTI

Bibliography

Greenpeace. "Declaration of Interdependence, 1976." In *Radical Environmentalism: Philosophy and Tactics,* ed. Peter C. List. Belmont, CA: Wadsworth, 1993.

Greenpeace: www.greenpeaceuse.org

Hunter, Bob. "Taking on the Goliaths of Doom." In *Radical Environmentalism: Philosophy and Tactics,* ed. Peter C. List. Belmont, CA: Wadsworth, 1993.

IZAAK WALTON LEAGUE

The Izaak Walton League is an organization of hunters, fishers, and other outdoor enthusiasts. The Izaak Walton League—with 50,000 members and based in suburban Washington, D.C.—states that its mission is "to conserve, maintain, protect and restore the soil, forest, water and other natural resources of the United States and other lands; to promote means and opportunities for the education of the public with respect to such resources and their enjoyment and wholesome utilization."

The Izaak Walton League has 370 chapters in 32 states. It also has divisions, used to coordinate the efforts of chapters, in 21 states. Members may join one of the chapters or they may become members-at-large. The latter memberships are for those who do not live near a chapter or who want to support the efforts of the national organization. Many of the nonlobbying activities of the league are carried out through the local and state organizations.

HISTORY

The Izaak Walton League was formed on January 14, 1922, by 54 sportsmen who met in Chicago to discuss the deteriorating nature of America's top fishing streams. The organization was named after a seventeenth-century English fishing enthusiast who wrote *The Compleat Angler* in 1653. The organization named Will Dilg, the organizer of its initial meeting, as its first president. In August 1922, the league published the first edition of its magazine, the *Izaak Walton League Monthly* (later renamed *Outdoor America*). In April 1923, the league held its first national convention.

The league's first campaigns represented its founding purpose. It called for the creation of a 300-mile-long Mississippi River national preserve to protect all bottomlands from drainage between Lake Pepin, Minnesota, and Rock Island, Illinois. Proposals for legislation and policy involving water, and later wetlands, would continue to be a priority of the league throughout its history. The league also began campaigns concerning wildlife. It endorsed or sponsored legislation to have states and the federal government purchase wildlife refuges, including legislation to help provide methods of funding for such purchases. A third early area of interest for the league was outdoor recreation. League delegates attended the first national Outdoor Recreation conference in May 1924. The league supported initial legislation to levy an excise tax on sporting arms and ammunition to pay for wildlife projects. The league has continued to develop programs on hunter safety and outdoor ethics, as well as policies for multiple use of public lands.

The Izaak Walton League grew to over 100,000 members in 3,000 local chapters by 1928. Most of this membership was in the midwest. But the organization was riddled with internal strife over the balance between the interests of hunters and fishers, and those who wanted to provide more complete wilderness protection. The fight divided many local chapters from the national organization and led to the forced resignation of Will Dilg. It also led Jay "Ding" Darling, a well-known political cartoonist and member of the league, to form the National Wildlife Federation in 1936. During this time, the league took a stand in opposition to conservation when it opposed plumage restrictions supported by the Audubon Society, an organization with which the league had usually agreed. The Audubon Society supported strict regulations to protect birds, while the league wanted less restrictive laws to allow fishers to continue to have access to certain feathers for use on lures. This issue illustrates the importance of hunters and fishers to the league. Through the years the league's membership slipped to around 50,000, but has remained relatively stable. Even during the 1970s and 1980s, when many conservation and environmental groups grew significantly, league membership changed little.

The league has expanded its focus over the years to

reflect a changing understanding of the threats to the wilderness. In 1936, the league began its first attempts to create conservation programs for the public schools in order to teach sustainability. This general issue took on more force with the league in the 1960s and 1970s as resource consumption and energy efficiency became important national issues. The league began to develop policies concerning soil issues, such as the use of pesticides, grazing, rangeland use, and agricultural runoff. Air pollution became a focus in the 1960s as the relationship between such pollution and the enjoyment of the outdoors, as well as the destruction of forests and pollution of streams and lakes from acid rain, became known. Today the league is interested in such issues as greenhouse gases and climate change, which would have seemed far removed from its earlier interests.

To fund its operations, the league has depended on contributions from individuals, nonprofit organizations, and businesses. At times this dependence on business contributions has caused more ardent environmentalists to call into question the league's commitment to environmental values, but the league continues to solicit contributions. Over half of its funding in recent years has come from institutions.

ACTIVITIES: CURRENT AND FUTURE

The Izaak Walton League monitors the actions of Congress and administrative agencies. The league conducts activities on its own and in cooperation with other conservation groups. The primary activity of league representatives is to provide testimony and information supporting league positions. Its positions are officially determined at the league's annual convention through a formal resolutions process. Each year members, chapters, and divisions draft resolutions addressing conservation issues they want to have adopted. Those formally adopted become official policy and, together with that body of policy developed in the past, provide guidance to league staff and officers. Draft resolutions can be submitted to the league president. A separate resolution committee, consisting of the chairperson from a set of resource committees, makes the final recommendations on resolutions before they are presented to convention delegates for a vote. This screening process gives the leadership a great deal of power in the choice of policies.

The league presents information on government activity to its chapter leaders through its *Conservation Newsletter*. There is also an issues-update feature on the league's web site that provides the current status of federal legislation and regulatory decisions.

One of the league's current legislative efforts is assuring funding for conservation programs. The league is supporting bills providing full funding for several programs. The executive director of the league has given testimony before the House of Representatives Resources Committee. The league has also posted a draft letter supporting the funding bills on its web site that can be sent to representatives and senators. The league has also prepared a special report criticizing the states for depending too much on fees from hunters and fishers for funding conservation programs and not funding them from state treasuries. This report can be used in legislative attempts to increase state and federal funding. The federal programs the league supports would create incentives for states to provide matching funds for conservation programs.

The league produces several publications that allow it to communicate with its members, to provide a benefit to membership, and to contribute to its education programs. *Outdoor America* is a quarterly magazine that has been published since the founding of the league in 1922. The magazine contains stories about current conservation issues involving everything from air and water resources to endangered species, energy efficiency, outdoor recreation, and public lands and wildlife management. The magazine also reports on natural resource legislation and developments in Congress, and has a "shooters page," covering news and developments of particular interest to hunters, shooters, and shooting range operators. In 1974, the league began publishing *League Leader*, a newsletter that comes out five times a year and is designed to inform the league's volunteer leaders about the organization's national award programs, the annual convention, league conservation programs, and ways to build successful volunteer organizations. Some of the league's programs publish their own newsletters.

Major Education and Advocacy Programs

The league has programs attempting to affect several subjects. Save Our Streams (SOS) is a grassroots program that was begun in 1969. It includes a feature called "Stream Doctor," which provides videos and publications that teach people how to determine the quality of streams and diagnose what is wrong with them. Another feature helps in the study of macroinvertebrates in streams. The SOS program was expanded in 1966 to include the study of wetlands. A publication produced for members by this program is designed to help in education and grassroots advocacy.

The Sustainability Education project was formed in 1996. According to information on the league's web site, its goal is to help bring human population growth, economic development, and natural resource consumption into balance with the limits of nature for the benefit of current and future generations. This program is designed to study sustainability issues; to identify how these issues affect environmental stewardship, social justice, economic security, and civic democracy; to develop educational materials that provide people with the information they need to recognize and address local, regional, and national sustainability; and to support grassroots action on these issues. Among several program publications, one set, *The Conservation Issues Forum* series, provides instructions and information for local groups to develop sustainability programs. *The Sustainability Newsletter* is a bimonthly publication by the project.

A program that reflects the interest in outdoor use that was the basis for the formation of the Izaak Walton League is the Outdoor Ethics program. This program, which began in 1996, is designed to develop a set of ethics for hunters, fishers, and boaters. The program works with government agencies and outdoor industries. The program has published educational materials, developed a hunter education project, engaged in research projects, and sponsored conferences. A newsletter is planned for the program.

A recent effort of the league is the Virginia Clean Air Now campaign, developed in cooperation with the Southern Environmental Law Center. The goal of the campaign is to educate the public on the effects of coal-burning power plants on air pollution, and to clean up such plants. The pollution from such plants is affecting outdoor recreation and sightseeing areas.

The Izaak Walton League is a stable group whose growth and development is limited by its appeal to outdoor enthusiasts. The modern environmental movement is dominated by those who emphasize environmental issues. The league is finding ways to expand its areas of concern to cover more environmental issues, and it is forming alliances with other environmental groups. The success of the league and the direction it takes will depend upon these trends.

FINANCIAL FACTS

Although data for receipts are not available for 1998, the organization's income is primarily derived from membership dues, and foundation and institution support. Membership dues account for about 40 percent of revenue while foundation and institutional support account for about 56 percent. With a 1998 budget of $2 million, the Izaak Walton League has a significantly smaller budget than other environmental interest groups.

FRANK CODISPOTI

Bibliography

Izaak Walton League: www.iwla.org

LEAGUE OF CONSERVATION VOTERS

The League of Conservation Voters (LCV) was founded in 1970 by environmental activists and organizations to serve as the environmental movement's electoral and lobbying arm in Washington. As a political action committee (PAC), the league—with its 60,000 members—is not subject to the lobbying and electoral restrictions placed on most of the nonpartisan environmental organizations. In other words, the league can and does give financial contributions to specific candidates and parties, generally to the Democrats. It is probably best known for its pioneering "environmental scorecard," which lists the environmental votes of members of Congress.

HISTORY

In 1970, Marion Edey, a congressional staff aid, conceived of the idea of an electoral arm for the environmental movement. She suggested her idea to Lloyd Tuppling, who was a lobbyist for the Sierra Club. Tuppling suggested that Edey speak to David Brower, leader of the new organization, Friends of the Earth (FOE). Brower agreed to help Edey form a group and gave her space in FOE's offices. Edey started to raise funds, recruit a staff, and plan a campaign. In its first two major efforts, the LCV helped to defeat George Fallon, the chair of the House Public Works Committee in 1970, and Wayne Aspinal, chair of the House Interior and Insular Affairs Committee in 1972. These two unexpected victories over powerful members of Congress gave the league early credibility. In 1974, 13 of 17 candidates that the LCV endorsed won their races. With these successes, the league was able to establish its credentials as an effective organization.

By the late 1970s the LCV was being overwhelmed in its ability to raise money by the explosion of PACs that followed the revisions of the Federal Campaign Finance law. The organization began to depend more on its ranking of members of Congress and other less-expensive tactics to maintain its ability to compete with the wealthier and more powerful PACs. Over the next 10 years, the league established itself as the lead election arm of the mainstream environmental movement. In order to achieve this success, the league had to stake out a moderate stance among environmental groups. By targeting supporters and opponents among members of Congress, the organization committed itself to negotiation and compromise. The LCV cannot take a radical stance and hope to be effective.

In the 1990s, the LCV steadily expanded its funds and membership. Its membership has doubled in the last seven years. The organization has taken advantage of communications changes and has shown signs of adopting the strategy of increasing its independent advertising in election campaigns. The use of independent advertising is a tactic that has expanded rapidly in the last two election cycles among interest groups.

ACTIVITIES: CURRENT AND FUTURE

Legislative Activities

The LCV manages an extensive campaign of political information designed to affect decisions in Congress, to inform their members and sympathizers about the results of votes in Congress relevant to environmental issues, and to identify allies and opponents among the members of Congress. The strategies employed to achieve these goals by the LCV make extensive use of the most recent communications technologies. The LCV sent 10 letters to members of the House of Representatives in 1998 and 17 letters to the members of the Senate, and it posts the letters on its web site. It also provides a link to the e-mail address of every member of Congress so that anyone visiting the site can send a letter of his or her own.

**League of Conservation Voters
Political Action Committee Contributions**

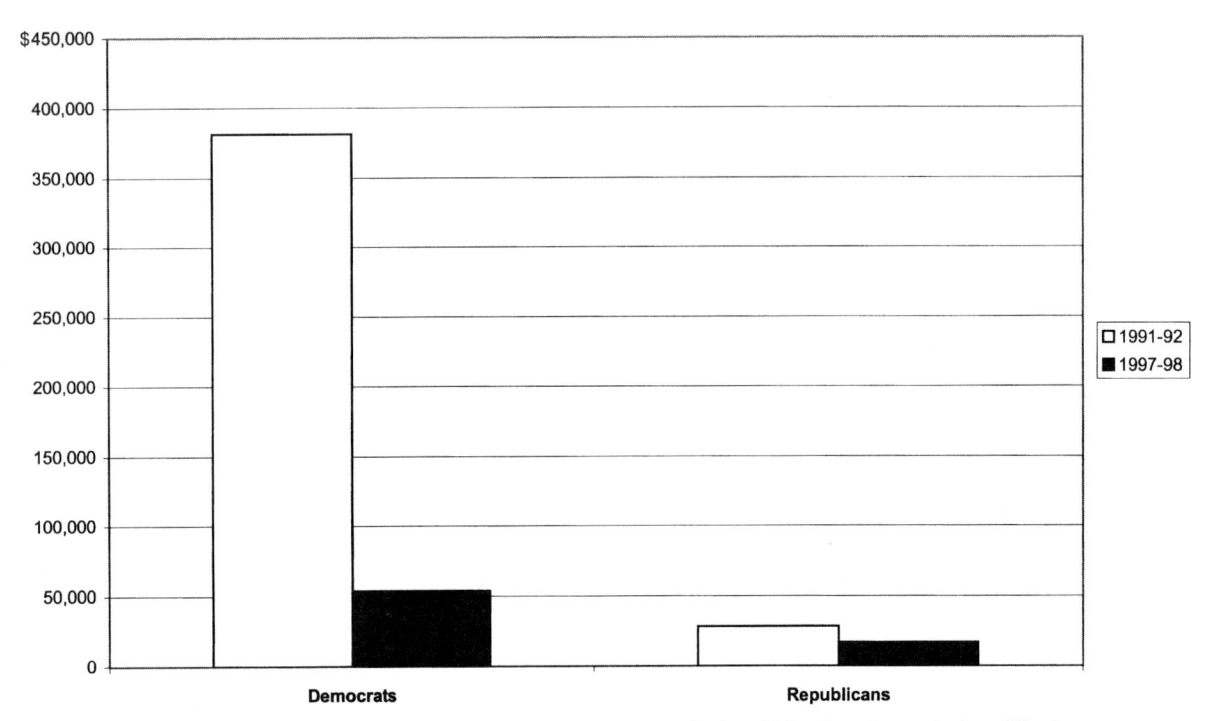

[Bar chart showing contributions: Democrats 1991-92 approximately $380,000, 1997-98 approximately $55,000; Republicans 1991-92 approximately $30,000, 1997-98 approximately $20,000]

Data derived from official studies available from the Federal Election Commission, Washington, DC, 1991–1998.

The letters are also an opportunity to educate the site visitor. Moreover, the LCV also provides a service that allows subscribers to receive updated information on activities in Congress via e-mail. This service sends an e-mail message to subscribers with results of votes in Congress within 24 to 48 hours of when the votes take place.

The Environmental Scorecard

One of the best-known weapons used by the LCV is the national environmental scorecard. The idea of generating a "score" for members of Congress based on how often they vote on the side favored by a group and how frequently members vote on the opposite side goes back to 1919, when it was used by the National Farmers Union. Today, numerous groups use this technique. The LCV develops its ratings using a list of key environmental votes developed by 30 environmental groups. The rankings for the members of Congress are now available on the organization's web site. This technique provides a handy method for summarizing the records of members and identifying allies and opponents. The information can then be used in channeling money and informing voters in election campaigns. In 1996, the LCV took over the publication and use of the Dirty Dozen campaign. This strategy refines the use of the scorecard by identifying 12 members of Congress who have low rankings on the environmental scorecard in a particular Congress and who are considered vulnerable in the following election. A public relations campaign is used to maximize coverage in their own districts of the fact that members have been named to the list. The announcements are timed to come during the election campaign. The LCV uses the list to solicit donations. It also recruits volunteers to work against members of Congress on the list and runs independent attack advertisements against them. By selecting vulnerable members, the LCV can encourage contributions, claim victories, and add to their reputation for being able to defeat those they oppose. The opposite side of the Dirty Dozen is the Earthlist, which is a list of the candidates the group believes can win election or reelection and are strong supporters of the LCV positions. The league also endorses other candidates. In 1996, for example, the LCV endorsed 97 congressional candidates.

The choice of votes on which to base the league's rankings reflects political needs for compromise and inclusiveness, the need to motivate potential voters, and the desire to reward friends and punish opponents. In each of the last three Congresses, a range of issues was represented in the votes. In 1998, for example, the scorecard was created by experts from 30 different environmental organizations. The creation of a "balanced ticket" of issues widens the number of environmental groups that have a stake in the scorecard and in publicizing it, and creates interest for more potential environment voters. The number of votes used is usually kept at around 13 in each chamber, though as few as eight votes and as many as 18 have been used in recent elections. The LCV also spreads the votes among those measures they favor and those they oppose, although they tend to count more votes that they oppose. This tendency does not seem to be related to Republican control of Congress, since the LCV used more votes it opposed in both the House and Senate in the 104th Congress, when the Democrats still controlled both houses of Congress. Although it is hard to be sure, the group may also try to take into account pet projects of friendly members of Congress and not use votes that might be opposed by too many of their strong supporters. Finally, the LCV includes information in its scorecard on proposals that have not come to a vote but on which the group has a strong interest.

The 2000 election could be a critical one for many environmental groups, especially one that focuses so much on electoral politics as the LCV. The Republican majority in the House of Representatives is very small, creating the opportunity to take control from the party that has been less sympathetic to environmentalism; for Democrats to recapture the Senate is not out of the question. But none of these outcomes is certain, and the power of the environmental movement will be at stake. Even a victory is not an unmitigated positive outcome. Many social movements, both conservative and liberal, have found that victories create unwarranted complacency among their supporters and can reduce, rather than increase, giving and activism. But defeat could be even worse. It is possible that opponents of the environmental movement could control both houses of Congress and the presidency for the first time since the modern environmental movement began. Such an outcome would provide a monumental challenge to the LCV, with its emphasis on electoral strategies and moderate politics.

FINANCIAL FACTS

In 1998, the League of Conservation Voters had a budget of $2.6 million. The League of Conservation Voters Action Fund, which is the group's PAC, raises and gives money to influence the outcomes of elections. Between 1990 and 1998, the Action Fund raised $1,759,000, endorsed 627 candidates, gave $806,000 to candidates on its Earthlist, and spent $1,500,000 to defeat members of the Dirty Dozen. Its total spending placed the Action Fund 54th among PACs during this period. In addition to raising and spending money through the Action Fund, the LCV provides in-kind help to candidates it supports in the form of volunteer workers from its own organization and those of the environmental groups that sponsor the league. The LCV also has used independent expenditures on behalf of some candidates and in opposition to others.

FRANK CODISPOTI

Bibliography
League of Conservation Voters: www.lcv.org

NATIONAL AUDUBON SOCIETY

Named after pioneer American ornithologist John Jay Audubon, the National Audubon Society focuses on the study and protection of all species of birds, the protection of endangered species, and the preservation of wilderness habitats for birds and other wildlife. The National Audubon Society currently has about 550,000 members in some 508 chapters, largely in the United States but increasingly in countries throughout the Western Hemisphere. The society—headquartered in Washington, D.C.—employs a 25-member government relations staff as its principal lobbying arm. The National Audubon Society has a very powerful combination of incentives with which to attract members. Amateur ornithology has been a widespread hobby across the nation for many years. Studying birds is more than a hobby for many people; it is a way of life. No organization is identified more with ornithology than the National Audubon Society. Thousands of bird lovers join the National Audubon Society to engage in the hobby, learn more about it, and meet others with similar interests. The National Audubon Society sponsors trips, organizes outings, and recognizes individuals and chapters that gather information on birds and bird migration.

HISTORY

It took two attempts to create the National Audubon Society and sustain its long-term existence. George Bird Grinnell, a paleontologist and editor of *Field and Stream* magazine, proposed the formation of a society for the protection of birds in the pages of his magazine in 1886. Unfortunately, the response was so overwhelming that Grinnell had to give up the project in 1888 after publishing two volumes of *The Audubon Magazine*. Eight years later, in February 1896, Harriet Hemenway called together a small group of individuals to form a society for the protection of birds. Thus was born the Massachusetts Audubon Society; this time the organization survived.

From its creation, the National Audubon Society was concerned with political issues. The society's first battles were fought over the use of bird plumage in women's hats. The extensive killing of birds for this purpose threatened the existence of herons and other birds. The efforts of the group helped to pass state and federal laws protecting birds and bird sanctuaries. The society began to acquire its own sanctuaries and today manages a series of them.

The first Audubon societies were state organizations. When Frank Chapman, an ornithologist with the American Museum of Natural History, began publishing *Bird Lore* magazine, he created an organizing vehicle for the societies. Chapman sponsored the first Christmas bird count in 1910, which became an annual event for birders and a major activity of the National Audubon Society. In 1905, the state societies formed the National Association of Audubon Societies. The society continued to work for laws protecting habitats and pushed for the creation of the National Wildlife Refuge system during its early years.

During the period from 1905 through the 1930s, the society created educational programs for children and adults, including leaflet campaigns and summer camps for youngsters. In the 1930s the society began sponsoring scientific research to help in its efforts. The society also purchased the magazine *Bird Lore* and changed its name to *Audubon Magazine*. All these efforts strengthened the organization's ability to meet its political goals.

In the 1940s, the society underwent significant organizational changes. In 1940, the name of the organization was changed to the National Audubon Society. The network of local chapters that is the backbone of the organization was begun in 1944. This network has grown to 512 chapters across the United States and in other countries.

The National Audubon Society was at the forefront of the modern environmental movement that exploded in the 1960s and 1970s. The society expanded its membership and activities throughout this period. Its membership, which was 32,000 in 1960, grew to 120,000 by 1970, and to 500,000 by 1985. Since then, membership growth has slowed. In 1969, the society opened an office in Washington, D.C., and has expanded its lobbying efforts dramatically since that time.

The National Audubon Society has had a long-standing interest in issues concerning wildlife habitat, including humankind's destruction of those habitats. With the 1962 publication by Rachel Carson of *Silent Spring*, which tells of the effects of the use of the pesticide DDT, the society expanded its efforts to protect habitats and prohibit the use of harmful chemicals in them.

ACTIVITIES: PRESENT AND FUTURE

The National Audubon Society has a 25-member government relations staff, which acts as its main lobbying arm. It conducts lobbying activities on a variety of issues. The common thread connecting the society's actions is the protection of endangered species and their habitats. The society is engaged in lobbying activities involving several subjects in the 106th Congress. It supports the Better Bonds proposal by President Bill Clinton. This proposal would leverage $700 million in federal tax credits to provide $9.5 billion to purchase open space for bird habitats in the next five years. The society is also working for legislation to increase the size of the Alaska Arctic National Wildlife Refuge. The organization is lobbying for strong reauthorization of the Endangered Species Act. It is working for full funding for President Clinton's Clean Water Action plan. Another of the society's goals is full funding for the Conservation Reserve program and the Wetland Reserve program. It is also co-sponsoring the Neotropical Migratory Bird Habitat Enhancement Act to increase protection for migratory birds. This is not a complete list of the legislation that the society is working for or opposing, but it illustrates the range and quantity of their activities.

The National Audubon Society is constantly developing new ways to use the power of its numbers. Recently, the society began a "Sister Chapter" program. This program links chapters that are fighting government decisions, but do not have a friendly and powerful member of Congress from their district, with sister chapters that do have powerful members and are willing to lobby for the sister chapter. This is a way to take advantage of the size and geographic coverage of the society's membership.

As a natural outgrowth of their interest in birds, the members of the National Audubon Society have a deep concern for bird habitats. As they study bird populations, members discover patterns of population decline and extinction that would obviously be of concern to them. It comes as no surprise, therefore, that the chapters have worked to protect 173 wetlands consisting of 400,000 acres of land since 1990. The society also maintains dozens of wildlife sanctuaries.

The National Audubon Society runs a wide variety of educational programs. Ten of the society's sanctuaries run educational programs. In addition, the Audubon Expedition Institute prepares college and graduate students for environmental careers. The society also has teacher aids, films, and programs for grade-school children, in addition to *Audubon Magazine* and other materials put out by the society for its members and the public.

The National Audubon Society organizes letter-writing campaigns, writes legislation, conducts and publishes research, and sponsors a web site as functions of its advocacy of environmental causes. The web site presents updates on current activities of interest to the society in Congress and the states. It also gives the e-mail addresses of the members of Congress for members to use in contacting their representatives.

In the early years of the 1990s, the National Audubon Society hoped to grow to 1 million members. It has not achieved that goal. The organization continues to be an innovative member of the mainline environmental movement. It sponsors internships, runs many educational programs, lobbies for legislation, and engages in a wide variety of activities. While the society has a broad scope of activities, it continues to focus generally on issues that involve wildlife and its habitat. Its recently released strategic plan calls for more action on the conservation of birds and other wildlife and their habitats. The society should continue to be a major player on environmental issues in the foreseeable future.

FINANCIAL FACTS

The National Audubon Society is registered by the Internal Revenue Service as a non-profit organization. As such, the organization does not make political action committee (PAC) contributions to the campaigns of government officials. In 1998, the organization had total receipts of more than $72.2 million, of which 48 percent were derived from contributions and bequests, 15 percent from earned income and royalties, 14 percent from membership dues, and 19 percent from the sale of investments. In the same year the organization had total expenses in excess of $49.3 million, of which program services accounted for 70 percent, membership expenses 22 percent, and management expenses eight percent of the total budget.

FRANK CODISPOTI

Bibliography

Graham, Frank. *The Audubon Ark: A History of the National Audubon Society*. New York: Alfred A. Knopf, 1990.

National Audubon Society: www.audubon.org

NATIONAL WILDLIFE FEDERATION

With its 4.4 million members, the National Wildlife Federation (NWF) is the largest environmental organization in the country. The federation states as its mission, "to educate, inspire, and assist individuals and organizations of diverse cultures to conserve wildlife and other resources and to protect the Earth's environment in order to achieve a peaceful, equitable, sustainable future." The NWF views humans as stewards of the wilderness. The federation's slogan is "People and nature. Our future is in the balance." The federation seeks the proper balance between humans and nature; it does not seek to reduce the position of humans to equality or even subservience to nature.

HISTORY

The NWF, the inspiration of political cartoonist Jay "Ding" Darling, was first organized at a conference in Washington, D.C., in February 1936. Darling saw the need for a conservation association that was committed to the preservation of wildlife and their habitats and was politically active. The organization was dominated by sportsmen and focused on issues such as clean water, wilderness protection and expansion, wildlife research, and restrictions on trapping of fur-bearing animals. The federation was made up of state conservation organizations affiliated with the national organization. The NWF enjoyed one of its early victories with the passage of a federal excise tax on firearms that provided federal matching funds to states for the acquisition, restoration, and maintenance of habitat for the management of wildlife and for research concerning wildlife management. A National Wildlife Week was established by proclamation of President Franklin Roosevelt in 1938.

For the next two decades the NWF struggled first to survive and then to establish its place in the conservation movement. In 1962, publication of *National Wildlife* began. By 1968, circulation reached 340,000, far larger than competing magazines. This is one example of the ability of the NWF to produce marketable products that boost revenues and membership and have propelled the NWF into a large, successful organization.

The group has had its problems. When the federation supported the banning of lead shot in favor of steel shot in shotgun shells in 1976, it was opposed by many hunters, led by the National Rifle Association (NRA). This emotional battle led to many members of the NRA distancing themselves from the NWF. On the other side of the political spectrum, the NWF has come under fire for having representatives of private companies with interests in environmental issues on their board. This practice has raised the suspicions of the new wave of environmental groups that grew out of the environmental movement of the 1960s and 1970s.

In the early 1990s, membership in the NWF stagnated, as was the case with many environmental and conservation groups. This trend may have reversed itself in the last years of the decade, as Congress has been dominated by members more hostile to environmental values.

ACTIVITIES: CURRENT AND FUTURE

The NWF maintains a lobbying staff to work on Capitol Hill and engages in other lobbying activities in its various areas of interest. The president of the NWF testified before the House Resources Committee in March 1999 concerning funding for conservation proposals. Other officials of the NWF have testified before committees concerning the protection of wetlands. The federation has also lobbied extensively on issues of mining, grazing, and the protection of national forests. These issues all come under the heading of "stewardship" for the NWF. Given its stance on the relationship between humans and nature, it comes as no surprise that the federation expends a great deal of resources on the issues named. Two major efforts come under this heading. The NWF has mounted a vigorous campaign against takings legislation. Takings legislation is designed to block the ability of regulators charged with enforcing environmental laws from requiring that owners of private property comply with the regulations. There are two types of such legislation. Compensation bills would require the government to compensate landowners for any loss of value to their property that arose from restrictions on its use. Assessment bills would require that proposed regulations include an assessment of how much such regulation would cost all potentially affected land owners. Takings bills have been proposed at the state and national levels, and the NWF vigorously opposes them. The protection afforded private property owners against public action to protect the environment contradicts the idea of public stewardship of the land promoted by the NWF. The organization has lobbied Congress, gathered numerous examples of how anti-takings legislation would have wide-ranging negative effects, and even collected statements from religious organizations opposed to these bills. The last effort fits into the religious underpinnings of the public stewardship theory. The NWF has also lobbied to change allowable grazing and mining on public lands, renewal of the Clean Water Act, and on other issues.

The NWF has weighed in on issues of international trade and development legislation. The federation has lobbied Congress and written the federal government arguing for stronger protection of environmental standards in fast-track trade legislation. The organization has also lobbied heavily with the federal government and foreign governments to include environmental protection in the North American Free Trade Agreement.

Another major effort that reflects the NWF's belief in public stewardship is its proposed Teaming with Wildlife legislation. The federation has written legislation that would charge an excise tax on hunting and fishing equipment. The funds would be used for conservation, recreation, and education efforts for endangered species that are not hunted or fished.

Administrative Lobbying

The federation does not limit its lobbying efforts to Congress. The organization maintains a close watch on the implementation of legislation in its areas of interest. The NWF supports its monitoring of program implementation through a series of natural resource centers. These offices are designed to monitor the decisions and practices of regional offices of federal executive branch agencies to see that they are enforcing environmental legislation. The centers are staffed with lawyers, scientists, and resource specialists who can take action and organize local members for public action when they believe the laws are not being properly enforced.

The NWF has been a vocal and active opponent of the Army Corps of Engineers' Nationwide Permit program for land development. The corps is charged with regulating the dredging and filling of wetlands under the Clean Water Act. The NWF has argued that some of these permits, particularly Nationwide Permit 26 (NWP 26), violate the Clean Water Act by allowing too much destruction of wetlands. The organization has written the corps, published the dates and places of "open-comment" meetings of the corps and encouraged their members to attend and oppose the permits, and encouraged a letter-writing campaign to the White House opposing the permits. The corps has agreed to phase out NWP 26, but the NWF opposes the proposed replacements as even worse.

The NWF has also written a report criticizing the payment of repeated claims for flooding by the Federal Emergency Management Agency's (FEMA) National Flood Insurance program. The federation argues that a few properties located in floodplains account for a disproportionate share of insurance payments and FEMA should be requiring that these properties be bought out and the land reserved for floodplains. The NWF has issued press releases on the properties that they believe should not be insured in each state.

The NWF pursues a litigation strategy. It has filed suits, joined suits, or filed *amicus curiae* (friend of the court) briefs in federal and state courts in regard to such issues as the reintroduction of wolves into Yellowstone National Park, the Army Corps of Engineers' plan to build dams on the lower Snake River in Oregon, the failure of the Environmental Protection Agency to enforce regulations regarding the Great Lakes, and numerous other issues.

Grassroots Activism

The NWF is not a direct-action organization. It encourages its members to participate in political appeals to officials through channels provided within the political system, such as writing letters or making statements at open-comment hearings. The federation promotes local activism through programs that will increase preservation, recycling, and awareness, rather than putting pressure on public officials or private parties through demonstrations or protests. One program provides guidance and encouragement for the development of environmentally sound practices on college campuses. In addition, for 25 years, the NWF has run its Backyard Wildlife Habitat program, which teaches participants how to provide an environment for wildlife in their backyards. It is part of a broader effort by the federation to develop compatibility between urban and suburban settings and wildlife, and to educate the public about wildlife habitats and the need to preserve and create them. This goal fits in with the NWF's broader philosophy of human stewardship of the wild. The federation also runs a variety of other programs designed to create an educated and aware citizenry that values the wilderness and wildlife and wishes to preserve them.

The NWF has numerous publications. Five deserve special notice for their popularity and relevance for conservation education and promotion. *National Wildlife* is the primary publication of the NWF. It has over 500,000 subscribers. It is sent to members with their $15 membership fee. *International Wildlife* is similar to *National Wildlife,* but it has an international focus and a smaller number of subscribers. Both of these magazines are noted for their wildlife photography. For those who are more serious about taking part in political activity, the federation sends *EnviroAction* to those who request it. It is a monthly publication that follows environmental legislation and the annual rankings of members of Congress compiled by the NWF. Those on the list also receive e-mail with information on important upcoming votes in Congress and how to send messages to his or her representative or senator. The final two publications of note from the NWF are *Ranger Rick* and *Your Big Backyard.* The former is aimed at children who are ages seven and up and is distributed to over 1 million children. It mixes education with entertainment. *Your Big Backyard* is aimed at children between the ages of three and six. All of these publications contribute to the large membership of the federation, because the subscribers to the various publications are counted among the members. The NWF produces films for the theater, television, and I-Max theaters. These films are aimed at young and adult audiences and help to get the federation's message to a much wider public.

The NWF is a large, established organization with a definite niche in the environmental movement. It successfully balances the pressures from more radical environmental groups, particularly animal-rights activists, with its traditional stance as an organization that sees humans as stewards of nature, rather than just another part of it.

FINANCIAL FACTS

The NWF had an operating budget in 1998 of $100 million. As one of the largest organizations in the country, the federation generates a significant share of its revenue from membership fees and product marketing. The operating budget is utilized for membership outreach and development, legislative and administrative lobbying, program monitoring, and public education.

FRANK CODISPOTI

Bibliography

Allen, Thomas B. *Guardian of the Wild: The Story of the National Wildlife Federation, 1936–1986.* Bloomington: Indiana University Press, 1987.

National Wildlife Federation: www.nwf.org

RAINFOREST ACTION NETWORK

According to the organization's mission statement, "the Rainforest Action Network [RAN] works to protect the Earth's rainforests and support the rights of their inhabitants through education, grassroots organizing, and non-violent direct action." The RAN, with its 25,000 members, is a direct-action organization. Its ideology and program are based on a strong distrust of power and wealth. The organization operates on the premise that it is necessary to organize those who do not have power to put pressure on elites in order to obtain modification of undesirable elite behavior. The organization's tactics involve confrontation, publicity, and nonviolent civil disobedience.

HISTORY

The RAN is a relatively young group. It was formed in 1985 by activist Randall Hayes as a militant direct action group and has remained true to its founding. David Brower, another well-known environmental activist, has served on the RAN's board of directors from its beginning. The organization began by sponsoring an international rainforest conference that brought together delegates from 35 organizations. Since then, the meeting has become an annual event held in August and called the Rainforest Action Group chautauqua.

The RAN survived its first few years on foundation grants, but built its membership to 10,000 within 19 months of its creation. The RAN's first reported successful campaign was in 1987 against Burger King. After a boycott against it, the fast-food chain canceled $35 million in contracts for beef from South America that came from cattle raised on land in cleared rainforests. The RAN claimed credit for the change in Burger King policy. In 1988, the RAN absorbed another group, People of the Earth.

During its early years, the RAN depended heavily on foundation support for its funding, but by 1992, it was getting 70 percent of its funds from member dues. However, the RAN still lists numerous foundation grants among its sources of income. The membership of the RAN has fluctuated during its existence. By the middle of the 1990s, the group's membership had climbed to 35,000, but more recently it has declined to 25,000.

ACTIVITIES: CURRENT AND FUTURE

The RAN's structure is based on grassroots organizing. The RAN maintains a network of over 175 Rainforest Action Groups (RAGs). The RAGs are small local groups of activists that join the network after creation as independent organizations. The groups are affiliated with the RAN and receive support and publicity from the RAN, but are not directed by it. The groups are connected to each other and to other rainforest groups through the RAN, which provides them with its "action alerts," containing information on an action by a government or corporation. Included in the alerts are names of officials to contact, with e-mail addresses and recommended messages. RAGs also receive *World Rainforest Report,* which is published four times a year. This report contains stories on actions by RAGs, information on campaigns by the RAN, editorials from the executive director of the RAN, and reports of actions by governments and corporations. The RAN also provides other occasional information to the groups.

The RAN provides advice for RAGs on operations and tactics. The group maintains a page on its web site that reports news on actions taken by RAGs and presents news from RAG offices. This page lists names, addresses, phone numbers, and mission statements of new RAGs. Another page announces upcoming events. A third page gives inspirational updates on current campaigns run by the RAN and provides advice on how to organize and operate, such as how to make use of the news media. The final page lists web sites maintained by RAGs. Recently, the RAG director began a new program designed to make more efficient use of the talents of the RAN members. The program involves collecting information from potential volunteers who have skills that might be useful to a RAG and who would be willing to provide advice to a RAG if asked. The information is kept on file and a RAG in need of specific assistance is put in touch with a member with the proper skills.

The RAN operates a series of grants for RAGs. One grant program is for any group, as long as it has been in existence for at least six months. A second program is limited to RAGs working on the continent of Africa. A third program provides services and experts offering financial and administrative advice. The RAN provides direct encouragement and advice to individuals on its web site on actions to take, from boycotting products and corporations to learning more about various issues. The RAN also maintains a clearinghouse for information on rainforests. The RAN claims to have filled over 30,000 requests for information from teachers and students in a recent year.

DIRECT-ACTION CAMPAIGNS

Protection of Indigenous Peoples

The RAN's strategy is to attack both the supply and demand for wood from old-growth forests. The organization champions the cause of native groups that inhabit tropical forests on the grounds that such groups live within the forests and do not threaten them. Such advocacy also fits with the political ideology of the RAN, which favors those who do not have power. One such program involves native groups in Brazil. The RAN has supported the claims of indigenous tribes to 200 million acres of rainforest lands. The organization also supported a letter-writing campaign to the World Bank as well as a movement by groups in Brazil to oppose a project that they argued threatened the Nambikwara people. The RAN recently urged its members to send letters of support to the president of Ecuador for his decision to protect certain national parks because they would preserve the ancestral lands of several tribes, as well as preserving old-growth forests. Finally, in Brazil, the RAN supported a successful effort to get recognition by the Brazilian government of the land rights of the Panara people.

In addition to the efforts in Brazil, the RAN opposed a Shell Oil gas project in Peru partly because it threatened several indigenous populations. A similar argument, although not involving tribal peoples, is the opposition of the RAN to projects by Mitsubishi Corporation in Myanmar. The RAN publicized the oppression by the Myanmar government of its own people and accused Mitsubishi of exploiting it for its own benefit.

Opposition to Supply from Old-Growth Forests

The RAN has worked with local interest groups to find methods of stopping illegal and predatory logging practices in Brazil. It tries to put pressure on the government for stricter enforcement of logging legislation and endorses the development of alternative economic uses of Brazilian rainforests. The organization argues that rubber tapping, fishing, and the production of nuts, fruits, medicinal plants, and fibers provide means for the indigenous people to make a living from the forest without destroying it.

The RAN has also opposed the development of several major highways in northern Brazil and the nations bordering it. These roads are designed to connect major cities across the regions with Pacific ports and the Amazon. They would make oil production and lumber production cheaper and easier. The roads are part of a series of trade agreements among the countries on the paths of the proposed highways. The RAN opposes the roads because of the destruction of forest habitats involved in building them, the increased economic exploitation of the rainforests they will encourage, and the disruption of lands that are home to indigenous tribes in the region.

Attempts to Reduce Demand for Old-Growth Forest Products

Two of the RAN's campaigns illustrate its attempt to reduce the demand for old-growth forest products. RAGs have been involved in efforts to convince local governments to reduce the use of such products. The organizations, along with other environmentalists, have been successful in getting some local governments to stop using rainforest wood to build boardwalks in Wildwood, New Jersey. They also convinced the Philadelphia Bridges department and Long Beach, California, to eliminate the use of rainforest products. In addition, the RAN has convinced certain retail chains to eliminate rainforest products in their buildings and other products.

The largest campaign of this sort is currently going on and is aimed at Home Depot, the world's largest retailer of products that come from old-growth forests. The RAN argues that there are alternatives to many of the products produced from old-growth timber. It admits, however, that other steps, such as conservation, will be necessary to achieve the goal of eliminating the use of old-growth lumber. In the meantime, the RAN is trying to put pressure on Home Depot through a public action campaign to reduce or stop its purchase of products made from old-growth timber. On March 17, 1999, RAGs in several cities demonstrated at Home Depot stores. Demonstrators picketed, made announcements on the store intercom system, chained themselves to displays of materials made from old-growth lumber, spoke to customers about the problem, and unfurled banners from the roofs of the stores calling on Home Depot to stop using old-growth products. The campaign had been planned and coordinated through the RAN, with the RAGs given instructions on materials to make, actions to take, and methods of assuring press coverage. The actions led to stories in some newspapers and on some news web sites.

All of the RAN's techniques can be seen in its campaign against Mitsubishi, a large Japanese firm that has been a target for its financing of a government-sponsored gas pipeline project in Myanmar that cut across a tropical rainforest. The firm was also accused of providing financial backing for lumber operations in Canada and for the purchase of containers (wood crates and boxes) made out of lumber from mature forests and other products by its car division. The RAN demonstrated at car dealerships, in addition to other actions. In 1998, the RAN reached an agreement with Mitsubishi Motors U.S.A. to phase out the use of rainforest-produced products.

The RAN continues to promote its deep-ecology views; that is, that humans should not attempt to control nature. Its recent accomplishment in its efforts against Mitsubishi is the type of occasional success that is necessary for a group that feeds on the energy and passion of its members. But the RAN suffers from the type of high turnover and potential for fatigue that all such groups must deal with. Unlike the groups that have nonpolitical activities to build membership and raise funds, a group such as the RAN always faces an uncertain future.

Financial Facts

In 1998, the RAN had a rather modest budget of $2.1 million. The organization devotes the bulk of its budget to membership outreach, publications, grassroots organizing, direct action, public information, and education programs.

FRANK CODISPOTI

Bibliography

Rainforest Action League: www.ran.org

Rainforest Action Network, 221 Pine Street, Suite 500, San Francisco, CA 94104.

SIERRA CLUB

Often called the "granddaddy" of environmental organizations, the Sierra Club, founded by renowned naturalist John Muir in 1892, is a member-supported, nonprofit interest group that promotes conservation of the natural environment by influencing public policy decisions on a wide variety of issues, most importantly the protection of public lands. Indeed, key leaders of the Sierra Club have gone on to form other environmental organizations such as Friends of the Earth and the League of Conservation Voters. The Sierra Club currently has 550,000 members, with chapters in all 50 states.

HISTORY

In spring 1892, famed naturalist John Muir and magazine editor Robert Underwood Johnson decided to form a club to preserve the Sierra Nevada mountains. Muir and Johnson were joined by geologist Joseph Le Conte and a group of college professors and students from San Francisco who wanted to form an alpine club. The club had 182 charter members. Muir was elected president of the Sierra Club and remained president until he died in 1914.

The Sierra Club was immediately embroiled in political battles, making it one of the earliest political interest groups in the United States. The club's first fight was over an 1890 law that had ceded the Yosemite land grant to California for protection as a park. For 10 years, the Sierra Club fought to repeal this law. In 1903, John Muir hiked Yosemite with President Teddy Roosevelt. Two years later, the California legislature ceded Yosemite Valley and Mariposa Grove to the federal government. The Sierra Club would become embroiled in one more battle over the land in the Sierra Nevada mountains, and it would lose.

San Francisco spent many years looking for a more abundant and reliable source of water and settled on the idea of damming the Hetch Hetchy Valley, a valley like Yosemite and within the boundaries of the park as it was laid out in 1890. The proposal split the Sierra Club. Many naturalists, led by Muir, opposed the idea, while others, including some board members from San Francisco, believed that the reservoir was necessary. The club conducted a referendum among its members, who voted overwhelmingly to oppose the dam. The vote established a tradition of consulting the membership that became a permanent part of the Sierra Club's operating methods. The club fought against the Hetch Hetchy proposal for several years, but finally lost the battle in 1913 when President Woodrow Wilson signed a bill to build the dam. John Muir died one year later and the Sierra Club entered a period of limited political activity. The Hetch Hetchy issue was not forgotten, however, and today the Sierra Club is fighting to eliminate the Hetch Hetchy reservoir on the grounds that it is no longer necessary.

The Quiet Years

During the period from 1920 through the 1940s, the Sierra Club engaged in a moderate amount of political activity. The club opposed the building of a dam in Yellowstone National Park and supported legislation to create Kings Canyon National Park, which passed in 1940. The club opposed the building of hydroelectric dams in Kings Canyon during the 1940s. But, for the most part, the Sierra Club engaged in conducting outdoor activities, such as camping trips. These trips did, however, have a political dimension. John Muir believed that taking people into the wilderness and letting them experience its beauties and pleasures would turn campers into preservationists. The membership of the Sierra Club throughout this period remained exclusively in California; there were still no chapters outside of that state.

The Transformation of the Sierra Club

In 1950, the membership of the Sierra Club was at 7,000, mostly in California. That year the Atlantic chapter, which encompasses 18 eastern states and the District of Columbia, became the first chapter outside of California. A more significant development took place in 1952, when the club hired David Brower as its first executive director. Brower was a friend of photographer Ansel Adams, a committed activist, and had a background of working for the University of California Press. Brower brought these characteristics to his position, and they helped, as well as hurt, the Sierra Club. Brower's skills were demonstrated when he led the club in its fight against the building of a dam within Dinosaur National Monument at the intersection of the Green and Yampa rivers on the Colorado–Utah border. Brower got Alfred Knopf to publish *This Is Dinosaur,* a beautiful photographic work on the monument, and used it as a tool for conservation lobbyists in fighting the dam. In 1955, Congress eliminated plans for the dam from the Colorado River project. The Sierra Club gained a visibility from its role in the fight, and by 1960, membership in the organization increased to 15,000. Another development at this time that affected the development of political activism in the Sierra Club was the Biennial Wilderness conference. The Sierra Club began cosponsoring the conferences, along with the Wilderness Society, in 1949. This conference became a major force in wilderness campaigns. In 1964, joint efforts led to the Wilderness Act.

Brower expanded his publishing efforts, creating a series of lavish coffee table books that brought attention to the Sierra Club but lost money. Brower also brought the attention of the Internal Revenue Service to the club when he published full-page advertisements in the *New York Times* and the *Washington Post* opposing the building of two dams in the Grand Canyon. An investigation that threatened the club with the loss of its tax-exempt status for engaging in political activity led to a drop-off in contributions. At the same time, however, memberships increased from 57,000 in 1967 to 75,000 by 1969.

The budgetary problems caused by Brower's actions contributed to strains between Brower and the professional staff, on the one hand, and between the board and volunteer activists, on the other. The strains were made worse by Brower's desire for a powerful professional staff, which was contrary to the Sierra Club's practice of giving a great deal of authority to its volunteer board and giving voice to club members. The differences came to a head over the board's decision not to oppose the construction by Pacific Gas and Electric of a nuclear power plant at Diablo Canyon, which is located at Nippomo Dunes on the California coast, south of San Luis Obispo. Brower believed that the club should oppose all nuclear power plants, and he spoke out against Diablo Canyon, despite the board's position. In 1969, Brower supporters ran for five open positions on the board as the ABC (active-bold-constructive) slate. They were opposed by the CMC (concerned members for conservation) slate. The bylaws of the Sierra Club allowed canvassing, and both slates advertised in Sierra Club publications. The ABC slate was defeated and Brower resigned from his position. He left the Sierra Club to form Friends of the Earth.

The 1950s and 1960s brought fundamental change to the Sierra Club. It grew into a large organization. More importantly, it became national, although one-third of its members still came from California. Finally, the Sierra Club had been transformed into a very active organization whose goals were mostly political in nature. In the 1970s, the Sierra Club continued to expand its political role and capabilities. In 1976, the Sierra Club Committee on Political Education (SCCOPE) was formed. Membership in the Sierra Club expanded through most of the period, reaching a peak of 650,000 on its 100th anniversary in 1992. In recent years, however, the membership has dipped to its current level of 550,000.

ACTIVITIES: CURRENT AND FUTURE

The Sierra Club has a highly sophisticated lobbying operation centered in its office in Washington, D.C. The office has an average of nine full-time lobbyists who are trained and skilled professionals. They can call on a membership that includes a large number of experts in the various substantive areas of interest to the group, as well as members trained in law. This gives the club the ability to be knowledgeable and persuasive. This expertise is also used in direct lobbying by members. The Sierra Club's professional staff is skilled and willing to bargain and build coalitions. Staff members also enjoy a great deal of autonomy from the Sierra Club headquarters, which is across the country in San Francisco. The lobbyists are not without direction, but they have a great deal of day-to-day freedom.

In addition to the Washington staff, the Sierra Club maintains a staff of field representatives whose respon-

**Sierra Club
Political Action Committee Contributions**

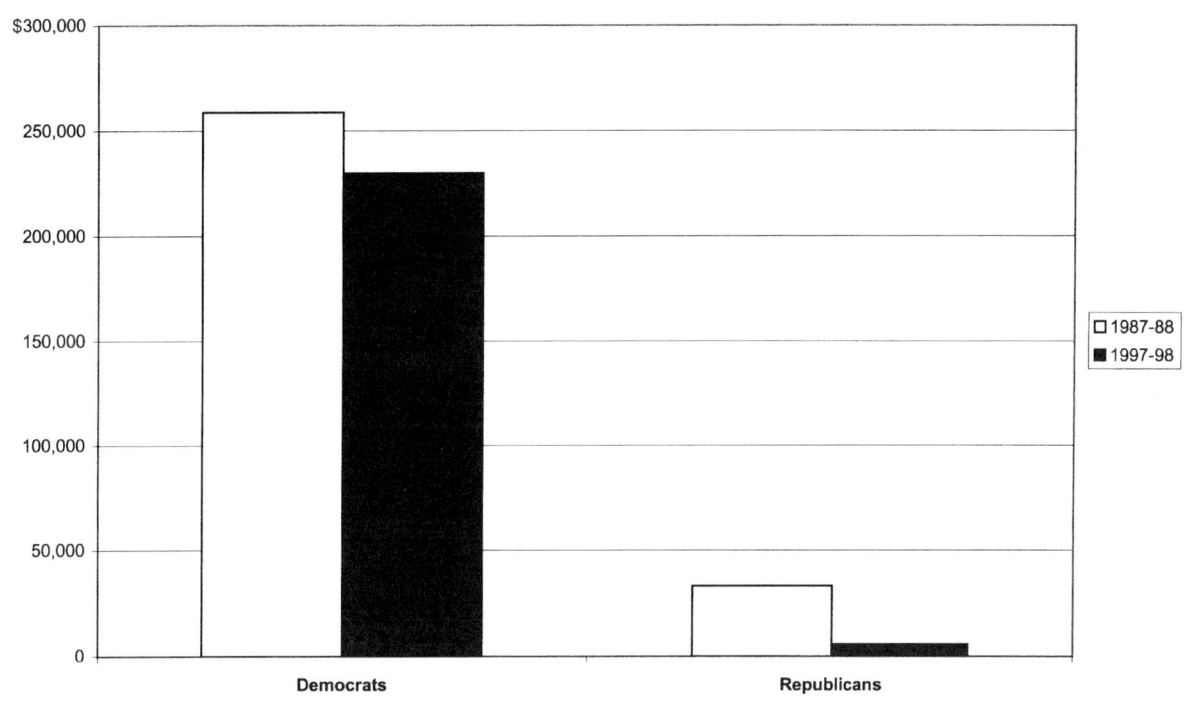

Data derived from official studies available from the Federal Election Commission, Washington, DC, 1987–1998.

sibility is to know the important political actors in their congressional districts. These representatives are professional lobbyists and are called upon regularly to attempt to influence Congress. They are an important part of the Sierra Club lobbying operation.

As an organization, the Sierra Club does not directly engage in litigation, but it maintains a close relationship with the independent Sierra Club Legal Defense Fund (SCLDF). The SCLDF and the Sierra Club develop agreement on which cases to litigate. The SCLDF often is involved in the legal process before cases come to court, when a regulatory agency is making decisions. The staff must be able to negotiate as well as litigate. The SCLDF works on cases involving a variety of regulatory legislation, including the Clean Air Act, Clean Water Act, and the protection of public lands.

Electoral Activity

The Sierra Club Political Committee (SCPC), formerly known as the Sierra Club Committee on Political Education, is the political action committee (PAC) of the Sierra Club. The SCPC is composed of 10 members who work with the chapters to identify candidates to support. The final decisions on disbursement are with the SCPC. The SCPC is nonpartisan and backs candidates from either party who support its agenda, but most of its money goes to the Democrats. In the 1997–1998 election cycle, the SCPC gave $228,950 to Democratic candidates and only $5,708 to Republicans. In addition, SCPC money went to several state Democratic committees.

The Sierra Club publishes a wide variety of books, magazines, and pamphlets. Its flagship publication is *Sierra,* a glossy magazine sent to members. *The Planet* is more directly aimed at activists. Free to all Sierra Club members, it contains articles on activities, election news, and suggestions and instructions on activities. The club also maintains a series of information networks and newsgroups on its web site.

The Sierra Club has established itself as a nationwide environmental organization. It is also an outdoor recreation organization. Whether the club can continue to blend these two interests is a question it will continue to face. A second question that might face the organization is how it will build an orientation toward the wild within an urban society. As previously discussed, the first major battle lost by Sierra was over the building of a reservoir to support urban development. Many of the club's battles have involved attempts to keep urban growth from destroying the wild. Its most recent such target is urban sprawl. This is a large, complex issue with the potential to create a great deal of stress among the Sierra Club's members.

FINANCIAL FACTS

During the 1980s and 1990s, SCCOPE raised and spent increasing amounts of money on campaigns. In 1972, SCCOPE spent $107,000 in cash and gave $124,000 in in-kind payments to candidates and organizations. The amount increased steadily, and by 1998 contributions had increased to $441,208. In 1996, the name of the organization was changed to the Sierra Club Political Committee. In 1998, the Sierra Club organization, as a whole, had a budget of $43 million.

FRANK CODISPOTI

Bibliography

Mundo, Philip A. "The Sierra Club," in *Interest Groups: Cases and Characteristics,* ed. Chicago: Nelson-Hall, 1992.

Public Disclosure Inc.: www.tray.com/fecinfo; maintained by Public Disclosure Inc., Suite 1198, 50 F Street NW, Washington, DC 20001.

Sierra Club: www.sierraclub.org

WISE USE MOVEMENT

The "wise use" movement is a general term for a large, diverse, loose coalition of groups that represent a variety of individuals and business interests who oppose the environmental movement. The term *wise use* is taken from a motto originated by conservationist Gifford Pinchot in 1907. Although they have adopted the term, the leaders of the Center for the Defense of Free Enterprise (CFDFE) make it clear on their web site that they do not do so out of reverence for Pinchot. The major umbrella organizations of the movement are the CFDFE, the Alliance for America, the Blue Ribbon Coalition, and the Western States Public Lands Coalition. The CFDFE is the source of much of the ideological grounding of the movement. The Alliance for America is a broad coalition of small, mostly local groups. The Blue Ribbon Coalition represents people who enjoy and support outdoor recreation. The Western States Public Lands Coalition represents the mining industry. Many other individuals and groups are associated with the wise use movement. Because it is a loose coalition of groups with no official membership, estimates vary. Actual membership may be around 100,000.

HISTORY

Social movements that achieve a great deal of success tend to generate an organized opposition. The environmental movement is no exception. The wise use movement began to emerge by 1976 in response to environmental laws and regulations. At that time, the restrictions being put into place on public land use were being felt in the West. Loggers were the first to believe that their livelihoods were being threatened by restrictions on logging in old-growth forests. In 1976, the Associated California Loggers organized two protests in opposition to a proposed logging buffer zone around Redwood National Park. The first protest involved 100 logging trucks that blocked the Golden Gate Bridge at morning rush hour. The second protest involved two dozen logging trucks that were joined by 300 timber workers in Washington, D.C., to protest the logging ban. At around the same time, in separate actions, property owners in Yosemite National Park protested the government landholding policies in and near national parks. These types of protests and organizing continued in opposition to government policies and the seeming indifference of the administration of President Jimmy Carter to the loggers' and western landowners' interests. Miners and those involved in grazing on public land, who were already upset with the new policies, joined the movement.

In the early 1980s, Ron Arnold joined Alan Gottlieb as leaders of the Center for the Defense of Free Enterprise. Arnold and Gottlieb established themselves as the most articulate and savvy leaders of the wise use movement. They provided an ideological basis for the movement through the principles they have articulated with their communications expertise. Arnold and Gottlieb adopted a confrontational style that generated a great deal of attention and attracted new members. Arnold and Gottlieb also activated their opponents with their inflammatory language that minimized the need for environmental protection.

The movement spawned many groups, most of which were small and local. However, large established interests, such as industrial trade groups, also participated. The movement gained strength from loggers, miners, the cattle industry, and communities that depended on them, which faced hard times in the 1980s. These groups might have suffered during those years without government environmental regulations, but those regulations, and the environmental movement seen as responsible for them, provided a convenient target for frustrations.

Two events of the later 1980s and early 1990s can be seen as important for the movement. The first was the successful defeat of a Yellowstone vision document in 1991. The vision project was a plan to coordinate management of the 11-million-acre Yellowstone ecosystem. The project called for improving federal coordination of the land in the ecosystem. The wise use movement, in turn, organized against this coordinated land management vision. The successful defeat of the plan demonstrated the mixed nature of the movement. Trade groups of the logging, mining, and cattle industries sent out letters to workers and their families attacking the plan and its potential effects on jobs. Other groups associated with the wise use movement contacted their members, and all groups affiliated organized rallies and packed the hearing halls when the National Parks Service held hearings on the proposal. Eventually, the vision document was replaced with a much shorter, less sweeping version. Although some environmentalists would later claim that the defeat of the vision statement was the work of President George Bush's administration and powerful industrial interests, they admitted they had been out-organized.

The second event that brought the wise use movement publicity and encouraged organization was the designation of the spotted owl as an endangered species. That designation threatened to close huge areas of the western forests to logging. The spotted owl became a symbol for the claim that animals were being protected at the expense of humans. Even some environmental groups saw the spotted owl controversy as a no-win situation for the environmental movement. This controversy became a national issue, unlike the Yellowstone vision document, and thus helped the wise use cause.

ACTIVITIES: CURRENT AND FUTURE

The activities of the wise use movement are many and varied, reflecting the diverse nature of the groups that comprise it. Perhaps the best summary of a set of beliefs that would cover most or all of the groups is provided on the CFDFE web site. It lists five principles as beliefs of the movement: first, that humans, like all organisms, must use natural resources to survive; second, that the earth and its inhabitants are tough and resilient, not fragile and delicate; third, that we learn about the world only through trial and error; fourth, that our limitless imaginations can break through natural limits to make earthly goods and carrying capacity virtually limitless; and finally, that reworking of the earth by humans is revolutionary, problematic, and ultimately benevolent.

One should add to the list a strong belief in individualism as the most basic value of society, and belief in the free enterprise system as an expression of that value. The last two principles help explain the wise use movement's hostility to almost any restrictions on private behavior or business activity by government. The wise use movement engages in a wide variety of legislative techniques and strategies. The more affluent members can lobby Congress extensively, including testifying before Congress and engaging in personal lobbying. The many local, grassroots organizations associated with the movement use mail campaigns, demonstrations, and other forms of communications with members of Congress on important issues. When congressional hearings on public land use are held in the western states, they can be the site of demonstrations, rallies, and emotional testimony. The movement has a reputation for being able to rapidly mount massive letter, fax, and e-mail campaigns in support of its positions. One major campaign by a grassroots group that is part of the movement was the lobbying effort by the California Desert Coalition (CDC) to oppose the California Desert Protection Act. The group testified before Congress, gave members of Congress tours of the area covered in the proposed legislation, and explained their view of the effects of the law. The CDC fought the legislation for eight years before it was finally passed in 1994.

Wise use members and groups do not limit their lobbying to Congress. They have engaged in many activities to affect the decisions of administrative agencies, particularly those involved in land use. An example of the ability of the movement to engage in such activities was the generation of over 5,600 letters opposing any restrictions on industry activity on a plan for the expansion of the Yellowstone National Park ecosystem.

Education

The wise use movement has an extensive public relations and educational network. Ron Arnold and Alan Gottlieb maintain the Center for the Defense of Free Enterprise and run a publishing and distribution operation from its base. This operation publishes what it calls "battle books." Authors are selected to write books that analyze problems from their perspective on free enterprise and what they see as attacks on it. The books define a problem and propose actions that readers can take to solve the problem. They have covered such topics as regulation, private property rights, and taxation. They are distributed widely among members of the movement and provide information and arguments that can be used to support wise use positions.

The CFDFE also produces a newspaper column that is sent to over 400 newspapers in the United States. The group has a broadcasting network as well. In addition to these CFDFE efforts, other wise use groups produce literature and reports, and the Outdoor Channel, available to cable-television owners, presents a wise use point of view on outdoor issues and activities. Finally, the wise use movement has mounted public relations campaigns to counter negative press coverage and to attack its opponents. The wise use movement has used public relations opportunities to attempt to discredit the environmental movement. It portrays environmentalists as elitists and pagans who love nature more than they care about what happens to average people.

In recent years, the wise use movement has seen its momentum slowed. The expectation that the Republican Congress would roll back many of the environmental laws that the movement opposed did not materialize. The wise use movement may have overestimated its strength and popularity. Many Americans express support for environmental positions that the wise use movement opposes. At the same time, the movement has had successes. Attempts to change mining and grazing regulations were defeated by the Senate. Takings legislation, which is designed to block the ability of regulators from requiring that owners of private property comply with environmental laws, is supported by the property rights wing of the movement at the state and national levels. Perhaps most significantly, a federal court recently ruled that the Environmental Protection Agency did not have the authority to create new regulations under authority granted by Congress. If that decision holds up, it could severely weaken many environmental regulations.

FINANCIAL FACTS

The wise use movement has no official budget.

FRANK CODISPOTI

Bibliography

Center for the Defense of Free Enterprise: www.eskimo.com/~Erarnold/index.html

Helvarg, David. *The War Against the Greens: The "Wise-Use" Movement, the New Right, and Anti-Environmental Violence.* San Francisco: Sierra Club Books, 1994.

Switzer, Jacqueline Vaughn. *Green Backlash: The History and Politics of Environmental Opposition in the United States.* Boulder, CO: Lynne Rienner, 1997.

SECTION SEVEN
INDUSTRY, CONSTRUCTION, AND TRANSPORT

The interest groups discussed here are business associations that represent four major industries: manufacturing, utilities, transport, and construction. All but one of these groups are trade associations, which represent companies within one industry, however broadly or narrowly defined. The exception is the National Association of Manufacturers (NAM), which is considered a national "umbrella" organization that represents businesses in a wide range of industries.

There are more than 10,000 business associations in the United States, including local, state, regional, national, and international groups, with budgets totaling more than $20 billion. Half of the national and international associations have annual revenues that exceed $1 million. All the associations covered here are at least national in scope, and several have international members and affiliates as well. Nationally, the median membership of business associations is 315, but most of the groups here have many more members.

HISTORY

Each of the industry associations discussed in this section is unique, but they all developed in much the same way. The history of trade groups in the United States begins in the eighteenth century: The first recorded American trade association was founded in Philadelphia by house carpenters (house builders) in 1724, and the Boston Society for Encouraging Trade and Commerce was established in 1761. Gradually, many local and regional organizations were founded; a few of today's national trade associations have their roots in these earlier organizations.

Trade associations at the end of the nineteenth and the beginning of the twentieth century were notorious for attempting to fix prices and control markets, acting essentially as trusts and monopolies in their industries. (A *trust* is a combination of firms that agree to work together to set prices or reduce competition; a *monopoly* is a single organization that controls an entire industry in a particular market area.) In acting to protect the interests of their members and with very little government regulation to stop them, trade associations controlled numerous industries to a degree that would be surprising today.

Eventually the federal government stepped in, passing legislation to limit the formation of trusts and monopolies. Watershed legislation included the Interstate Commerce Act of 1887, the Sherman Antitrust Act of 1890, and the Clayton Antitrust Act of 1914. Decades of political and legal repercussions of these acts drove trade associations to shift their focus from controlling prices and restricting competition and toward working with local, state, and national authorities to influence economic and regulatory policies affecting their industries. The associations also began to focus on providing services to their member companies such as organizing conferences, seminars, and trade shows; compiling industry statistics; and creating ways for members to exchange information. These services are still an important part of the activities of business and trade associations.

CURRENT CONTEXTS

Business and trade associations today are among the most powerful organizations in the United States. They exert considerable political influence through political action committees (PACs), which lobby legislators to act in ways favorable to their industries. For the associations discussed here, much of the lobbying effort and contributions have been directed at Republican political candidates and legislators because they are often seen as more "pro-business" than Democrats. During the 1997–1998 election cycle, for instance, the Air Transport Association of America PAC contributed $26,000 to candidates and parties, $20,750 (80 percent) to Republicans and $5,250 (20 percent) to Democrats. These percentages roughly parallel the 71.7 percent to Republicans and 28.3 percent to Democrats that the air transport industry contributed as a whole.

PAC lobbyists also keep a close watch on regulatory, judicial, and other agencies, always seeking to represent their industries and businesses in the best possible light and to encourage activities that will benefit their member companies. For some associations that represent a single industry, such as the American Textile Manufacturers Institute, the goals and aims of the members are clear and rarely contradictory; for others, such as the National Association of Manufacturers, which represents a broad spectrum of industries, the goals are necessarily more general and less narrowly defined.

CURRENT ISSUES AND ACTIVITIES

Manufacturing

Manufacturing groups discussed here are the American Furniture Manufacturers Association (AFMA), the American Textile Manufacturers Institute (ATMI), the Chemical Manufacturers Association (CMA), the Distilled Spirits Council of the United States (DISCUS), the National Association of Manufacturers (NAM), the Pharmaceutical Research and Manufacturers of America (PhRMA), the Printing Industries of America (PIA), the Semiconductor Industry Association (SIA), and the Technology Network (TechNet). The American Forest and Paper Association (AF&PA) and the National Mining Association (NMA) represent suppliers of raw materials for manufacturing. Some of the primary concerns of associations representing manufacturing in the late twentieth century revolved around trade issues, regulatory issues, and taxes.

Many of the concerns of the manufacturing groups center on issues of international trade, particularly the protection of American manufacturing interests in a global economy. In the 1990s, these groups focused much of their lobbying efforts on political and economic trade measures such as the North American Free Trade Agreement (NAFTA) and the General Agreement on Tariffs and Trade (GATT). One of the most influential associations in the formulation and implementation of these agreements was the National Association of Manufacturers. In 1991, for instance, NAM sponsored an international conference that furthered GATT negotiations. It was also influential in the negotiations preceding passage of NAFTA and in the debate over granting China "most favored nation" trading status.

Other issues of concern to these groups as a whole include the regulations of the Occupational Safety and Health Administration (OSHA), the Environmental Protection Agency (EPA), and other Federal agencies. Generally, these associations tend to act as watchdogs, working to protect their member companies from what they see as overregulation by the government. Efforts to reduce government intervention in their business take many forms, depending on the specific concerns and needs of each industry. The Chemical Manufacturers Association, for example, is working for revision of the regulations of and additional laws that followed the Emergency Planning and Community Right-to-Know Act of 1986, such as the Toxics Release Inventory (TRI) Phase 3, initiated by the EPA, because it requires manufacturers to release proprietary information (trade secrets) to the public and to competitors.

Taxes are another major concern of manufacturing associations. The Distilled Spirits Council of the United States, for instance, lobbies against increasing taxes on whiskey and other liquors, and the Printing Industries of America (PIA) supports repeal of the Alternative Minimum Tax (AMT) because of its impact on small printing businesses. The PIA also supports capital gains tax reduction, repeal of estate taxes, and replacing the current tax code with a flat tax.

Utilities

The utility groups to be discussed include the Edison Electric Institute (EEI) and the Nuclear Energy Institute (NEI). Utility organizations all support deregulation of their industry, a process that accelerated during the 1990s. All utilities are concerned that an atmosphere of free and fair competition continues to exist in a newly deregulated marketplace. The EEI, for instance, is working to influence the nature of competition in the new climate of deregulation. The organization says that it wants to ensure that all competitors are treated equally and that consumers will benefit from the competition. It is also concerned, however, about "stranded costs"—the costs to electricity providers of the move from being regulated to being unregulated—and it has worked to get Congress to recognize these costs as legitimate and recoverable.

The nuclear power industry has also had to respond to the era of deregulation, and the NEI has taken the lead in this area. In particular, it seeks to ensure that nuclear energy plants are not placed at a competitive disadvantage by deregulation.

Transport

Transport organizations covered here are the Aerospace Industries Association (AIA), the Air Transport Association (ATA), and the American Trucking Association.

The Air Transport Association was a major player during most of the twentieth century in coordinating the activities of airlines and regulatory agencies, and it continued in this role in the 1990s. The ATA has several programs that serve its members and the public, including the Airline Clearing House, the Airline Inventory Redistribution Systems (AIRS), the Industry Audit Program, the Universal Air Travel Plan, the Civil Reserve Air Fleet, and the Airline Scheduling Committees. Its main concerns are operations and safety, passenger and cargo services, and legislation affecting the air transport industry.

The American Trucking Associations works to protect the interests of its many member trucking companies. It focuses on advocating fewer taxes and fewer government regulations. It also sought during the 1990s to eliminate weight–distance taxes, reduce estate taxes, prevent tolls on interstate highways, promote "cost-effective and sound environmental policies," eliminate the Single State Registration System, and reform hours of service for truckers.

Construction

Construction organizations included here are Associated Builders and Contractors (ABC) and the National Association of Home Builders (NAHB). Like many other associations, these organizations devote much of their effort to monitoring and seeking to influence governmental regulatory bodies such as OSHA and the EPA because these agencies have the largest impact on regulating the construction industry as a whole.

Environmental concerns are an important focus of this industry. As an example, the National Association of Home Builders publishes informational "Fact Sheets" on environmental topics, and it sponsored the National Green Building Conference in 1999, the first conference devoted to "environmentally friendly home building practices."

SUMMARY

Since the first trade associations were established in America in the eighteenth century, they have grown into powerful organizations that represent the interests of their industries both externally (seeking to influence public, economic, and governmental policy) and internally (working to provide their members with information and support). The industries represented by these associations are varied, but they all have one goal: supporting the needs of their member companies. As the twenty-first century unfolds, this support will most likely include the continuation of monitoring the global marketplace, responding to the impact of technology on business, and transforming the relationship between government and private industry.

VIVIAN WAGNER

Bibliography

Baumgartner, Frank R. *Basic Interests: The Importance of Groups in Politics and in Political Science.* Princeton, NJ: Princeton University Press, 1998.

Biersack, Robert. *After the Revolution: PACs, Lobbies, and the Republican Congress.* Boston: Allyn Bacon, 1999.

Browne, William Paul. *Groups, Interests, and U.S. Public Policy.* Washington, DC: Georgetown University Press, 1998.

Hrebenar, Ronald J. *Interest Group Politics in America,* 3d ed. Armonk, NY: M. E. Sharpe, 1997.

Kollman, Ken. *Outside Lobbying: Public Opinion and Interest Group Strategies.* Princeton, NJ: Princeton University Press, 1998.

Mack, Charles S. *Business, Politics, and the Practice of Government Relations.* Westport, CT: Quorum, 1997.

———. *The Executive's Handbook of Trade and Business Associations: How They Work and How to Make Them Work Effectively for You.* New York: Quorum Books, 1991.

Rozell, Mark. *Interest Groups in American Campaigns: The New Face of Electioneering.* Washington, DC: CQ Press, 1999.

Silverstein, Ken. *Washington on $10 Million a Day: How Lobbyists Plunder the Nation.* Monroe, ME: Common Courage Press, 1998.

West, Darrell M. *The Sound of Money: How Political Interests Get What They Want.* New York: W. W. Norton, 1999.

Wilson, James Q. *Political Organizations.* Princeton, NJ: Princeton University Press, 1995.

Wolpe, Bruce C. *Lobbying Congress: How the System Works.* Washington, DC: Congressional Quarterly, 1996.

Zuckerman, Edward, ed. *The Almanac of Federal PACs, 1998–1999.* Arlington, VA: Amward, 1998.

AEROSPACE INDUSTRIES ASSOCIATION

The Aerospace Industries Association (AIA) represents the nation's leading manufacturers of aircraft, spacecraft, and related products and technologies. AIA members include manufacturers of commercial, military, and business airplanes, helicopters, aircraft engines, missiles, spacecraft, and related components. Activities of the AIA include lobbying Congress on aerospace issues, research and technology development, public relations, and relations with federal agencies.

Headquartered in Washington, D.C., AIA departments and divisions include communications; public relations; membership; policy and planning; compensation practices and labor issues; legislative affairs; research; international issues; environmental, safety, and health; government; procurement and finance; technical operations; engineering management; national aerospace standards; product support; manufacturing and material management; quality assurance; and supplier management. In addition, the AIA includes divisions that handle issues connected with various aspects of the aerospace industry, including civil aircraft, commercial aircraft, and military-related products and technologies.

The membership of the AIA includes all of the largest U.S. aerospace companies, as well as many smaller ones and numerous subcontractors to the big aerospace firms. Some of the better-known members of the organization are Allied Signal, Boeing, General Dynamics, General Electric, Gulfstream, Honeywell, Hughes Electronics, Hughes Space and Communications, IT&T Industries, Defense and Electronics, Litton Industries, Lockheed Martin, Northrop Grumman, Raytheon Company, and United Technologies.

Among the services to the industry that the AIA plans to provide in the coming years is establishing a framework to streamline the working relationship between prime contractors and their suppliers. This effort is needed, says the AIA, because of the end of the Cold War, the drop in defense spending, and the shrinking role of the Pentagon. "When one customer is the bulk of the sales, their policies become the standard," explained AIA president John Douglass. With commercial sales now dominating the industry, it is more difficult for suppliers to satisfy conflicting requirements of different customers.

HISTORY

The predecessor to the Aerospace Industries Association—the Aircraft Manufacturers' Association (AMA)—was founded in 1917 and was originally concerned with technical issues, public relations, and business issues facing the industry. Following U.S. entry into the First World War—and the subsequent realization of the importance of aircraft to modern warfare—the AMA was recruited by the government to help convert civilian production to military needs.

The AIA itself was founded in 1919 and was first known as the Aeronautical Chamber of Commerce of America (ACCA). Its initial membership of 100 aerospace pioneers—both individuals and companies, including Orville Wright and Glen Curtiss—pledged "to foster, advance, promulgate and promote aeronautics" and "do every act and thing which may be necessary and proper for the advancement" of American aircraft development.

During the Second World War, the ACCA all but ceased to function, as government-industry councils took up the burden of focusing the industry on military production. After the war, the ACCA came back to life and underwent a major reorganization, becoming a more traditional trade organization and focusing on the industry's trade and commercial interests. It also changed its name to the Aircraft Industries Association of America (AIAA). In 1959, reflecting developments in the arena of air and space technologies, it again changed its name, to the Aerospace Industries Association.

ACTIVITIES: CURRENT AND FUTURE

Although Defense Department contracts now make up just 20 percent of the business of its members, the Aerospace Industries Association continues to push for increased defense purchasing. Specific projects, however, are usually promoted by the companies that will compete for the orders. The AIA also lobbies for government research and development money in both Defense Department and National Aeronautics and Space Administration (NASA) budgets. A recent plan advocated by the AIA calls for a $70 billion increase in government aerospace research and development contracts. The AIA says that new and ongoing operations—such as the 1999 air war in Kosovo—should not detract from research and development spending. Failure to increase research and development spending, the AIA argues, will jeopardize both U.S. military superiority and the American aerospace industry's ability to compete in the international marketplace.

At the same time, the AIA recognizes that international customers are an increasingly important source of business for the American aerospace industry. Some 40 percent of aerospace products produced by AIA members have been sold overseas in recent years. However, the government limits the export of the most advanced technologies developed by the American aerospace industry. The AIA would like to see major amendments to the current rules to allow fewer restrictions.

According to AIA president Douglass, Congress needs "to draft an Export Administration Act that is geared for the next century." Among the aspects of such an act that the AIA seeks are rules that allow U.S. firms to sell products to all available markets. Unilateral controls—barring exports to all countries—should always be written as temporary measures, until more specific multilateral controls can be developed. Companies should be able to continue exporting a product they have already sold abroad, even if new sales are prohibited to a particular country. All restrictions should have time limits written into them, and economic sanctions should be of limited duration and end automatically unless they are renewed.

Critics argue that exporting sophisticated technologies creates a vicious circle that benefits only the aerospace industry. That is, America has set itself the goal of being one generation ahead of the rest of the world in terms of new military technologies. Thus, if the latest generation is sold, the United States has to put research and development funds into the coffers of aerospace companies to develop new military technologies. In addition, critics point out that the purpose of existing restrictions is to limit sales of military technology to countries that have opposed the United States in the recent past, or that have violated international attitudes toward human rights. In addition to the moral considerations of dealing with human rights violators, critics say that sales of military technology to such countries threatens U.S. security.

Frustrated by 11 failures since 1994 to pass a new export act, the AIA has recently begun lobbying Congress to create a public–private entity to oversee export licensing. According to the AIA, this would spare the Defense and State Departments the burden of checking thousands of export licenses and also would allow these agencies to focus on the most sensitive technologies. The AIA also pushes U.S. trade officials to work on behalf of American aerospace companies in resolving trade disputes. In this arena, a recent case involves a European Union (EU) ban on so-called hushkits—or re-fit packages for aircraft designed before new and tighter EU noise restrictions were written. The EU claims that the hushkits do not meet the noise restrictions, but the AIA says the EU's decision is really another way to protect the European aerospace industry by banning U.S. aircraft. Under the EU rules, only the latest Airbus Industrie aircraft meet the standards.

FINANCIAL FACTS

Although it represents defense and aerospace manufacturers that individually and collectively give enormous sums to the campaign coffers of congressional and presidential candidates of both parties, the Aerospace Industries Association itself does not have a political action committee and does not donate sums either to political parties in the form of soft-money contributions or to candidates in the form of regular hard-money contributions.

JAMES CIMENT AND VIVIAN WAGNER

Bibliography

Bilstein, Roger E. *The American Aerospace Industry: From Workshop to Global Enterprise.* New York: Prentice-Hall, 1996.

"Industry Leaders Lobby for United States Space Leadership." *Space Business News,* May 26, 1999, vol. 17, no. 11.

Pattillo, Donald M. *Pushing the Envelope: The American Aircraft Industry.* Ann Arbor: University of Michigan Press, 1998.

AIR TRANSPORT ASSOCIATION

The Air Transport Association (ATA) was the first—and is still the only—organization that represents the major U.S. airline carriers. It represents 22 U.S. airline companies and three foreign carriers, which together make up 95 percent of the country's passenger and cargo airline industry. According to the ATA's Articles of Association, airlines qualify as members if they are common carriers in air transportation of passengers or operate a minimum of 20 million revenue ton-miles (RTMs) annually. They must also operate for at least one year prior to their application for ATA membership and have a valid operating certificate as described by Section 604 of the Federal Aviation Act.

ATA divisions and departments mirror the divisions within the airline industry. Some of the important departments and divisions of the ATA deal with operations and safety, engineering, maintenance, airport operations, air traffic management, cargo, electronic data interchange, federal and state government affairs, international affairs, legal affairs, passenger and public relations, and security.

The ATA helps its members, it says, by promoting "the safety, cost effectiveness, and technological advancement of operations; advocating common industry positions before state and local governments; conducting designated industry-wide programs; and assuring governmental . . . understanding of all aspects of air transport."

The U.S. members of the ATA include Alaska Airlines, Aloha Airlines, America West Airlines, American Airlines, American Trans Air, Continental Airlines, Delta Air Lines, DHL Airways, Emery Worldwide, Evergreen International Airlines, Federal Express, Hawaiian Airlines, KIWI International Air Lines, Midwest Express Airlines, Northwest Airlines, Polar Air Cargo, Reeve Aleutian Airways, Southwest Airlines, Trans World Airlines, United Airlines, United Parcel Service, and US Airways. Foreign members include Air Canada, Canadian Airlines International, and KLM–Royal Dutch Airlines.

The ATA, through its Industry Services Department, also actively supports and administers programs that serve its members and the traveling public. Some of these industry-wide programs include the Airline Clearing House, the Airline Inventory Redistribution Systems, the Industry Audit Program, the Universal Air Travel Plan, the Civil Reserve Air Fleet, and the Airline Scheduling Committees.

Much of the work done by the ATA is done by its committees and councils. These are organized as follows:

The Law Council focuses on legal matters of concern to the industry, government rules and procedures, international trade, tourism, aviation policy, equal opportunity employment, affirmative action, and personnel matters, and includes the Litigation Committee, the International Affairs Committee, the Facilitation Committee, and the Human Resources Committee.

The Government and Public Affairs Council focuses on legislation and governmental issues at the local, state, and federal levels and includes the Federal Affairs Committee, the Public Affairs Committee, and the Public Relations Committee.

The Operations Council focuses on safety and efficiency within the industry and includes the Air Traffic Control Committee, the Airports Committee, the Airspace Systems Implementation Committee, the Aviation Safety Committee, the Flight Systems Integration Committee, the Meteorological Committee, the Security Committee, the Training Committee, the Cabin Operations Panel, the Communications Panel, and the Medical Panel.

The Engineering, Maintenance and Materiel Council develops standards, procedures, and positions regarding airworthiness, engineering and maintenance, aircraft performance, environment and industrial health, and digital data standards. It also represents these positions to regulatory, governmental, and industry groups. It is divided into the Airworthiness and Engineering Committee, the Maintenance Engineering Committee, the Materiel Management Committee, the Environmental Committee, and the Technical Information and Communications Committee.

The Air Cargo Council handles concerns relating to cargo, such as mail transportation, air freight services, and the shipment of dangerous goods. It is divided into the Dangerous Goods Board, the Cargo Services Development Committee, and the Airlines Postal Advisory Committee.

Finally, the Passenger Council works on issues that affect airline passengers, such as fares, reservations, ticketing, baggage, and other services. It is divided into the Baggage Committee, the Reservations Committee, the Passenger Processing Committee, the ATA/IATA Reservations Interline Message Procedures Board, the Passenger Data Interchange Standards Board, and the Industry Fares and Rules Exchange Standards Board.

HISTORY

The ATA was founded by representatives of a group of airlines who met in Chicago on January 5, 1936. The founding members described their goal as follows:

> ... to promote and develop the business of transporting persons, goods and mail by aircraft between fixed termini, on regular schedules and through special service, to the end that the best interests of the public and the members of the Association be served, ... [and] to promote aviation safety in general.

During the course of its history, the ATA has addressed air traffic control, all-weather operations, advanced navigational aids, the development of a collision-avoidance system, and antihijacking measures. The ATA received the Collier Trophy for its "high record of safety" in 1939, and in 1941 received a second Collier award for "pioneering world-wide air transportation vital to immediate defense and ultimate victory."

The ATA has been known for working with its members for the national good in times of war and national emergency. In 1936, with the Army Air Corps and the Army War College, it began to formulate plans to mobilize its members in the event of war. Later, in conjunction with the Department of Defense, the ATA formed the Civil Reserve Fleet and the War Air Service Program.

The ATA helped in formulating the Civil Aeronautics Act, which established the Civil Aeronautics Authority. This board later became the Civil Aeronautics Board (CAB), which was responsible for safety, technical, and economic regulation of air carrier operations. The ATA also helped to develop the Federal Aviation Act of 1958, which transferred responsibility for safety and technical regulations from the CAB to the Federal Aviation Administration and the National Transportation Safety Board. The ATA was also heavily involved in the formation of the Aviation Trust Fund. After the Second World War, the ATA worked with the U.S. Post Office to promote air mail and international parcel post.

Some of the programs developed by the ATA include the Universal Air Travel Plan, electronic reservation systems, improved methods of ticketing and baggage handling, and mechanized cargo loading. In the 1940s, its member airlines, via ATA's Air Traffic Conference, established the travel agency information and reservations program that is still used universally. The Airlines Reporting Corporation now administers this program, which provides a unified national ticketing service for airline passengers.

ACTIVITIES: CURRENT AND FUTURE

Three main areas of concern for the ATA are operations and safety, passenger and cargo services, and legislation. The ATA says that it desires "to promote safety by coordinating industry and government safety programs" and to serve as "a focal point for industry efforts to standardize practices and enhance the efficiency of the air transport system." Its concerns also include the design and construction of airports and passenger terminal boarding spaces.

The lobbying efforts of the ATA are conducted by its Office of Government Affairs, which focuses on tracking the actions of Congress and various transportation-related committees, the Department of Transportation, and the Federal Aviation Administration. The Office of Government Affairs presents the interests of the association to Congress, the executive branch, and state and local governments; it also gathers information, presents testimony, and provides information about the industry to legislators.

Over the past few years, the ATA has been involved in a number of critical issues facing the airline industry. Perhaps the most important legislative item is the so-

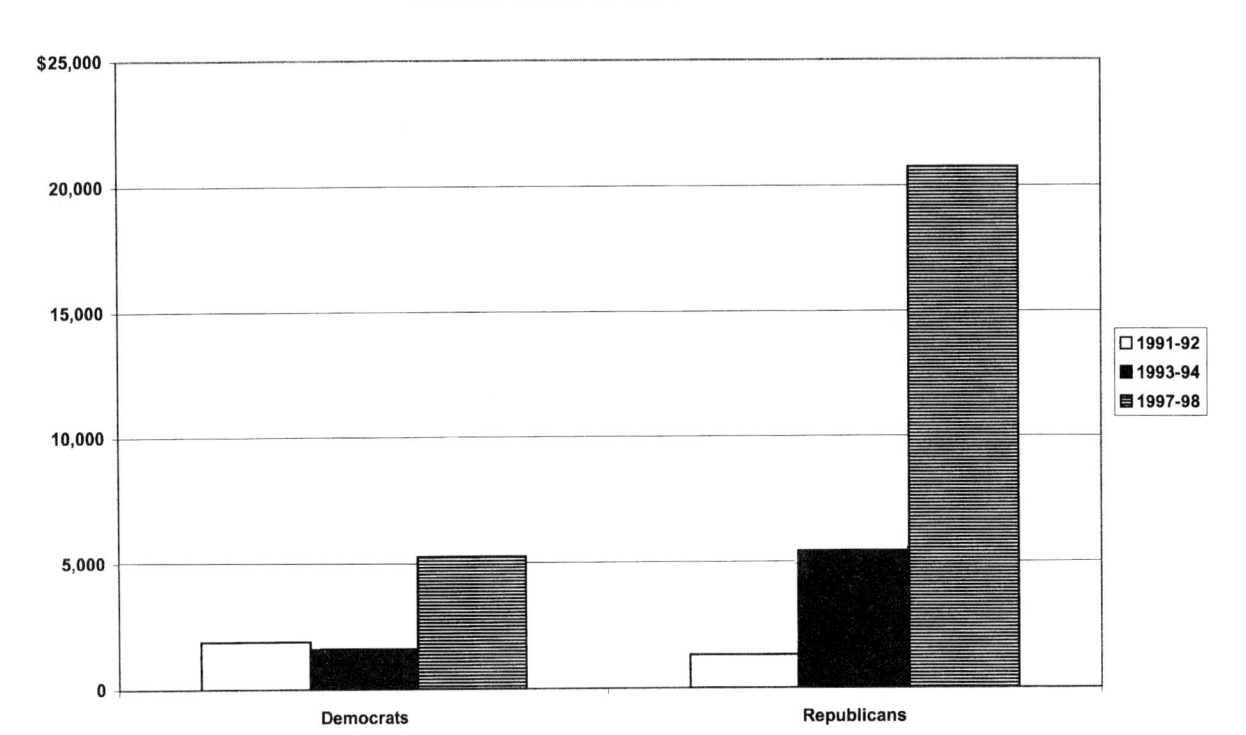

**Air Transport Association
Political Action Committee Contributions**

Data derived from official studies available from the Federal Election Commission, Washington, DC, 1991–1998.

called passenger rights bill, proposed federal legislation currently being contemplated by Congress that would guarantee passengers the right to on-time travel and would regulate the wide variation in ticket prices, whereby some passengers pay many times more than others for the same kind of seat on the same flight. The ATA vehemently opposes such legislation, saying that it would cost the airlines too much and would hamper their ability to fill planes to capacity. Instead, the organization suggests a voluntary industry program that it calls "the customer service plan."

As far as the growing number of delayed flights is concerned, the ATA supports its member airlines and says that many of the delays supposedly blamed on the airlines, are actually the fault of air traffic controllers. Thus, to blunt public anger and thwart passenger rights legislation, the organization is asking that the Department of Transportation change the method of measuring delays, so that it more accurately reflects the responsibility of air traffic controllers.

In the arena of labor rights, the ATA is fighting several measures that would affect pilots. The organization opposes new federal regulations that would require more rest time for pilots between flights.

Finally, the ATA actively opposes federal moves to regulate or prevent airline mergers. The organization says that, given the competitiveness of the airline industry, antitrust suits are dangerous. Moreover, it has tried to block federal legislation requiring more intense inspection of foreign carriers that have merged with American ones.

FINANCIAL FACTS

The ATA has an annual operating budget of approximately $27 million. During the 1997–1998 election cycle, the Air Transport Association of America political action committee (PAC) gave a total of $26,000 in contributions to candidates and political parties, $5,250 to Democrats and $20,750 to Republicans. In the 1993–1994 election cycle, the organization donated $6,909 to congressional candidates, including $1,386 to Democrats and $5,523 to Republicans. As these numbers indicate, the ATA tends to give about four times as much to Republicans as to Democrats. Moreover, there was roughly a fourfold increase between the election cycles of 1993–1994 and 1997–1998, both of which involved congressional candidates only.

JAMES CIMENT AND VIVIAN WAGNER

Bibliography

"ATA Calls for U.S. to Disclose ATC Delays." *ATC Market Report,* August 5, 1999, vol. 8, no. 16, p. 8.

"ATA Customer Service Plan Draws Monitors from Congress, DOT." *Aviation Daily,* June 18, 1999, vol. 336, no. 56, p. 1.

Belden, Tom. "Congress Seems Eager to Address Complaints About Airlines." *Philadelphia Inquirer,* March 14, 1999.

Kjelgaard, Chris. "ATA Protests DOT's Huge Proposed Fee Hikes." *Air Transport Intelligence,* March 23, 1999.

———. "DOT Wants to Widen Safety Audit Net to Foreign Airlines." *Air Transport Intelligence,* August 5, 1999.

———. "FAA to Attack Growing US Flight Delay Problem." *Air Transport Intelligence,* August 13, 1999.

"Report Says Congress Should Act to Increase Airline Competition." *Airline Financial News,* August 16, 1999, vol. 14, no. 32.

"Reveals Wide Divergence of Opinion on Pilot Fatigue." *Air Safety Week,* August 9, 1999, vol, 13, no. 32.

AMERICAN FOREST AND PAPER ASSOCIATION

The American Forest and Paper Association (AF&PA) describes itself as "the national trade association of the forest, paper, and wood products industry, representing member companies engaged in growing, harvesting, and processing wood and wood fiber, manufacturing pulp, paper, and paperboard products from both virgin and recycled fiber, and producing engineered and traditional wood products. AF&PA represents a segment of industry which accounts for over 8 percent of the total U.S. manufacturing output." It has 450 member companies across the United States, and it is active as both a trade organization and a lobbying association, with lobbying efforts at the federal and state levels.

Members of AF&PA include Boise Cascade, Champion International, Georgia-Pacific, International Paper, Mead, Plum Creek Timber, Procter & Gamble, Riverwood International, Stone Container, Union Camp, Westvaco, Weyerhaeuser, and Willamette Industries. Divisions of AF&PA include the American Wood Council; Containerboard and Kraft Paper; Forest Resources; and Paperboard, Paper, and Pulp.

HISTORY

The AF&PA was formed in 1992 as the result of a merger of the National Forest Products Association, the American Forest Council, and the American Paper Institute. In late 1995, the organization underwent a major restructuring, largely in response to numerous companies dropping out of the organization, complaining about high dues. Fort Howard withdrew in 1994 and Scott Paper in 1995. Moving away from a traditional loose organization of semiautonomous departments—each with its own budget and concerned with different aspects of the industry—the organization centralized its budgeting and consolidated its industrial components into two large units, one for paper goods and one for forest resources. At the time, an AF&PA spokesperson said the reorganization would significantly lower operating costs and therefore membership dues.

ACTIVITIES: CURRENT AND FUTURE

The two most important issues that the AF&PA addresses in its lobbying efforts are trade and environmental legislation, which are often linked. The AF&PA is on record as supporting what it calls a "forest management" approach—that is, one that continues to support forestry on government-owned lands. It seeks to define itself as being balanced between supporting environmental concerns and defending the financial and political interests of the industry. The AF&PA has spoken out for the Estate Tax Rate Reduction Act (HR-8) and against the Clinton administration's moratorium on forest road construction. It has also supported passage of the Ocean Shipping Reform Act, which lowered freight rates, and the Tucker Shuffle Relief Act for property rights. It helped to defeat a bill calling for new responsibilities under the previously passed Superfund legislation and worked to narrow the scope of an Environmental Protection Agency initiative on high production volume chemicals. It also promoted an amendment to the Clean Air Act to permit the continued use of methyl bromide, a poisonous gas used by the industry.

General issues that have concerned AF&PA lobbyists recently have included agriculture; the budget and appropriations; clean air and water; nuclear energy; environmental issues and the Superfund; health issues; labor, antitrust, and workplace issues; natural resources; real estate; land use and conservation; railroads, taxation, and the Internal Revenue code; domestic and foreign trade; and trucking and shipping.

In lobbying for domestic timber interests, the AF&PA has worked to increase U.S. access to the Japanese housing market and to protect U.S. exports of pallets, saw lumber, veneer, and plywood to Mexico. It also has been working to support growth opportunities via the proposed International Building Code and in other arenas. On trade issues generally, the AF&PA wants the government to press for lower tariffs around the world on forest and paper products, a position that is opposed by environmental groups who argue that lower prices would encourage more consumption of wood and paper products, leading to more logging and more destruction of forest habitats worldwide. The AF&PA, however, says that lower tariffs would probably increase consumption by no more than 3 or 4 percent.

Still, the AF&PA maintains that environmental concerns and recycling remain high on its list of priorities. As AF&PA president W. Henson Moore said in the organization's 1998 Annual Report, "This year, AF&PA introduced a three-to-five-year, 'inside-the-beltway' performance-based media campaign designed to position our industry as responsible, trustworthy stewards of the environment." The AF&PA has tried to counteract the antienvironmental image of the forest products industry by supporting programs and initiatives to benefit the environment. For instance, in 1998 it started the Sustainable Forestry Initiative (SFI) program, which chairman Rick R. Holley says, demonstrates "a commitment to future generations to ensure they will have the abundant forest and diverse wildlife we enjoy today while providing the forest and paper products that enrich our lives." The SFI program is based on the integration of responsible environmental policy and sound business practices. It includes voluntary SFI Verification Principles and Procedures and Qualification Criteria, which industry members can use to evaluate measure their environmental practices.

The AF&PA also supports the Agenda 2020 Sustainable Forestry Request by funding projects in four different research fields: biotechnology, basic physiology, soil productivity, and sensing. It has funded 21 projects in collaboration with federal agencies, universities, national laboratories, and industry. It also sponsors the annual Wildlife Stewardship Awards, which recognize outstanding wildlife stewardship on industrial forestlands, and it supports a national program called Project Learning Tree, which focuses on engaging students and teachers in environmental issues.

The AF&PA says that its recycling goal is to see 50 percent of paper recovered for recycling and reuse by the year 2000. To support recycling, it sponsors the Paper Recycling Awards, which, as of 1999, were in their 10th year. This program honors the best paper recycling programs in America. At the same time, however, the organization has argued strongly—both in Washington and in the nation's press—that the United States needs to ease up on its harshly restrictive environmental laws, which raise the costs of U.S. wood products and make them noncompetitive in the world market. In particular, the AF&PA would like to see restrictions on the harvesting of timber on public lands substantially lifted.

In addition, the organization has opposed strong enforcement of the Endangered Species Act. Faced with continuing lawsuits that prevent timber cutting in the name of protecting such species, the AF&PA has been pushing Congress to enact legislation that would compensate owners of private timberlands for losses incurred when they are forced to stop cutting to protect endangered species. Again, environmental groups are opposed to such initiatives, arguing instead for laws that would provide incentives to protect endangered species.

Other issues of concern to the AF&PA include mortgage and housing finance bills, U.S. Agriculture Department authorization and appropriation bills, the management of federal lands, measures meant to protect wilderness, U.S. Forest Service operations and budget, and federal timber sale contracts.

FINANCIAL FACTS

During the 1997–1998 election cycle, the AF&PA political action committee (PAC, formerly the Forest Industries PAC—FIPAC) received $112,731 and spent $124,231. The latter figure includes $118,207 in contributions to candidates and political parties, $106,407 to Republicans and $11,800 to Democrats. During a previous congressional election cycle—1993–1994—the group donated $62,328, $40,212 to Republicans and $22,116 to Democrats. In the 1995–1996 presidential election cycle, the AF&PA donated $133,800 to congressional and presidential campaigns, all but $11,000 going to Republicans. This overwhelming bias in favor of Republicans, experts say, reflects the fact that Democrats are often seen as more likely to sacrifice the interests of the forestry industry in favor of the environment.

JAMES CIMENT AND VIVIAN WAGNER

**American Forest and Paper Association
Political Action Committee Contributions**

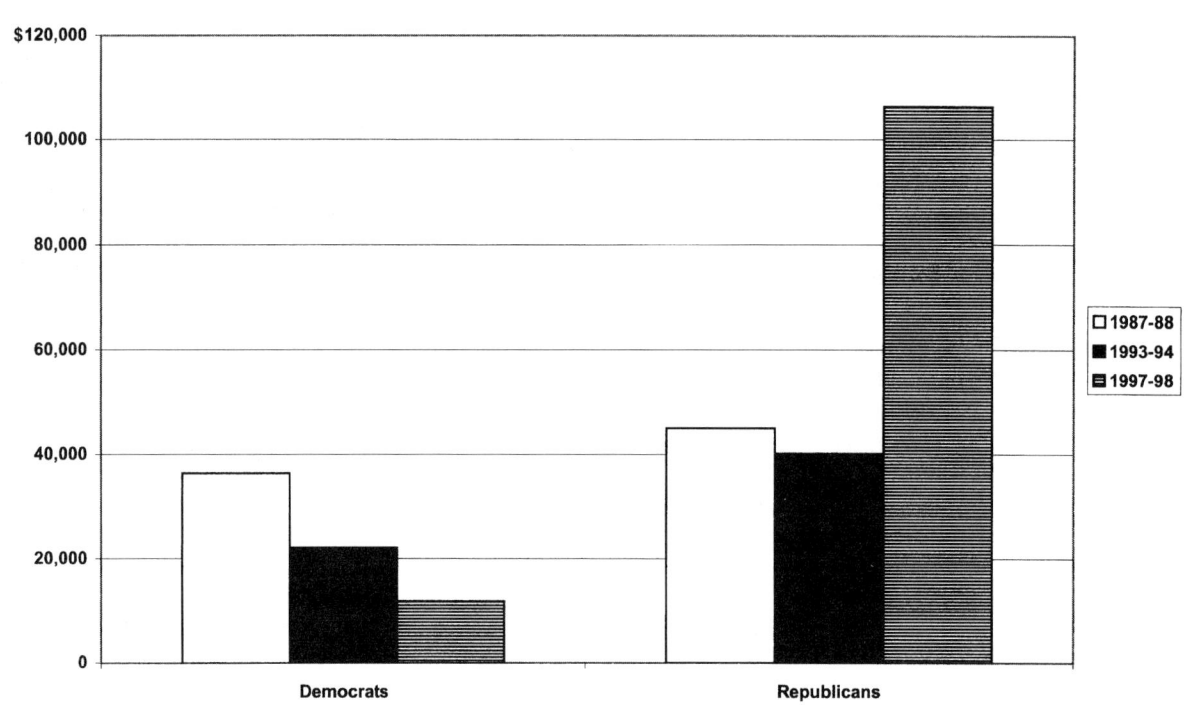

[Bar chart showing PAC contributions. Democrats: 1987-88 ≈ $36,000; 1993-94 ≈ $22,000; 1997-98 ≈ $12,000. Republicans: 1987-88 ≈ $45,000; 1993-94 ≈ $40,000; 1997-98 ≈ $106,000.]

Data derived from official studies available from the Federal Election Commission, Washington, DC, 1987–1998.

Bibliography

"Budget: Forest, Oil Interests Lobby for Tax Measures." *Greenwire,* July 16, 1999.

Dekker-Robertson, Donna L., and William J. Libby. "American Forest Policy—Global Ethics Tradeoffs." *BioScience,* vol. 48, no. 6 (June 1998), p. 471.

Hogan, Dave. "Expected Attempt to Revise Endangered Species Law Sparks Debate. *The Oregonian,* December 28, 1998.

"Interview: Industry Seeks Less Enviro Impact—API Prez." *Greenwire,* December 5, 1997.

Moore, W. Henson. "Elimination of Tariff Barriers a Must for Health of the Industry." *Pulp & Paper,* vol. 72, no. 5 (May 1998), p. 144.

Sonner, Scott. "Campaign Gifts Said to Help Timber Industry Keep Road Funds." *The Associated Press,* December 16, 1997.

"Timber Industry: Trade Group Prez Criticizes US Laws." *Greenwire,* March 8, 1999.

U.S. Environmental Protection Agency. *Profile of the Pulp and Paper Industry.* Washington, DC: Office of Compliance, Office of Enforcement and Compliance Assurance, U.S. Environmental Protection Agency, 1995.

AMERICAN FURNITURE MANUFACTURERS ASSOCIATION

The American Furniture Manufacturers Association (AFMA), the largest trade association for furniture manufacturers in the United States, represents 336 member manufacturers across the country. The association says that it is interested in the expansion of the furniture industry and improving the profitability of American furniture producers.

In addition to attending to the needs of the furniture industry and its members, the AFMA encourages communication and networking among manufacturers; aids in developing efficient management practices within the industry, promotes its members' legislative and regulatory interests, and sponsors technical, statistical, and research programs.

The AFMA's headquarters are located in High Point, North Carolina, and it also maintains a lobbying office in Washington, D.C., where there is a full-time staff devoted to lobbying Congress and other political groups on behalf of AFMA member companies. Reflecting the industry's varied concerns, the AFMA is divided into the following professional divisions: Finance, Human Resources/Safety, Manufacturing, Used Equipment, Fabric Remnants, Marketing, the Summer and Casual Furniture Manufacturers Association, Suppliers, and Transportation and Logistics. Each of these divisions is relatively independent, and some of them have their own board of directors.

The Finance division is composed of executives from AFMA member companies who have a particular interest in finance. It sponsors several meetings and events, including an annual information meeting, an annual financial management seminar, an economic forecast conference, and specialty seminars for financial management personnel. Among the publications the Finance division regularly sends to its members are the *Sales Planning Guide,* the *Survey of Current Business,* and the *Quarterly Economic Forecast.*

The Human Resources/Safety division, according to the AFMA, addresses labor management practice and issues that effect the ability of furniture companies to remain competitive with foreign producers. This division provides human resources personnel in member companies with up-to-date information about the latest laws, standards, rulings, compliance procedures, and organized labor activities that affect the furniture manufacturing industry. It also produces surveys, information kits, educational programs, newsletters, an award program, and an annual Human Resources/Safety expo.

The manufacturing division provides its members with the latest information about techniques and developments within furniture manufacturing. It sponsors regular semiannual meetings and technical seminars for its members and operates the Advisory Committee on the Environment.

The Used Equipment and Fabric Remnants divisions makes it possible for members to search databases to locate and purchase used equipment and fabric remnants from fellow members.

The Marketing division keeps the marketing personnel within the industry abreast of changes in the marketing field through meetings, seminars, committees, publications, and surveys.

The Summer and Casual Furniture Manufacturers Association is an organization operating within the larger organization of the AFMA. Founded in 1959 to promote the interests of manufacturers in this field, it provides its members with legislative and regulatory updates and information about management techniques and sponsors research programs.

The Suppliers division has its own board of directors, committee structure, and membership directory. It provides its supplier members with statistical information, legislative news, and other benefits.

Like other professional organizations in the manufacturing industry, the AFMA supports external lobbying activities and internal professional development.

HISTORY

The AFMA was founded in 1984 when the Southern Furniture Manufacturers Association (SFMA) merged with the National Association of Furniture Manufacturers (NAFM). As most of the positions in the AFMA would be held by SFMA officials, some members of the NAFM feared that the SFMA would dominate the new organization. However, the merger went ahead, as most members of both organizations recognized the need to have the industry speak with one voice. It was also decided that the new organization would include associate members, such as fabric mills and suppliers, as well as regular members like furniture manufacturing companies.

ACTIVITIES: CURRENT AND FUTURE

The AFMA maintains a high profile in Washington, D.C., where its staff seeks to advance the interests of the industry with Congress and regulatory agencies. The AFMA represents manufactures' concerns before Congress, the administration, the Consumer Product Safety Commission, the Environmental Protection Agency (EPA), the Federal Trade Commission, the International Trade Commission, the Occupational Safety and Health Administration, and the Office of the U.S. Trade Representative.

The AFMA also sponsors the Furniture Political Action Committee (FurnPAC), which according to its literature promotes itself as supporting "private enterprise candidates seeking election to the United States Senate and House of Representatives." A board of directors representing small, medium, and large furniture manufacturing companies—all members of the AFMA—runs the bipartisan FurnPAC.

On the state level, AFMA works on issues such as taxes, business practices, and environmental concerns. In addition to sharing in the lobbying and legislative efforts of the AFMA, the professional divisions within the organization all address their particular concerns, issues, and activities.

In the early 1990s, the organization worked with the EPA on regulating the use of volatile coatings in the manufacture of furniture. The EPA has insisted that furniture manufacturers reduce factory emissions, particularly those hazardous air pollutants caused by the use of various coating materials. While the EPA has suggested stronger regulations, the AFMA has asked that furniture companies be permitted to emit a certain amount of hazardous air pollutants. Those who emitted less than allowed amounts of pollutants could then sell their pollution credits to other manufacturers who did not meet the requirements.

By 1999, however, the AFMA was asking the North Carolina government to exempt some 85 furniture companies from state rules designed to protect people from the highly toxic air pollutants resulting from the use of volatile coating materials. These exemptions would save the industry some $850,000 in compliance costs. Environmental organizations vehemently oppose the exemptions. "We're seeing this as a piecemeal approach to eliminating the state health-based (air) standards," said Janet Zeller of the Blue Ridge Environmental Defense League. The state had turned down a request for wider exemptions in 1998, but may be willing to permit limited exemptions this time.

FINANCIAL FACTS

During the 1997–1998 election cycle, FurnPAC received $212,005 in receipts and spent $198,252. The latter figure includes $158,750 in contributions to candidates and parties—$21,000 to Democrats and $137,750 to Republicans. During the previous Congress-only election cycle of 1993–1994, FurnPAC gave $140,950 to candidate campaigns, with all but $15,000 going to Republications. Similarly, there was a strong bias in favor of Republicans in the 1995–1996 presidential election cycle, when the organization gave $126,200 to Republican presidential and congressional candidates, but only $11,500 to Democrats.

JAMES CIMENT AND VIVIAN WAGNER

Bibliography

Downs, Buck, et al. *National Trade and Professional Associations of the United States.* Washington, DC: Congressional Quarterly, 1998.

Henderson, Bruce. "Furniture Firms Want to Exempt 85 Carolina Factories from Clean-Air Rules." *Charlotte Observor,* May 8, 1999.

Hrebenar, Ronald J. *Interest Group Politics in America,* 3d ed. Armonk, NY: M. E. Sharpe, 1997.

Mack, Charles S. *Business, Politics and the Practice of Government Relations.* Westport, CT: Quorum Books, 1997.

AMERICAN TEXTILE MANUFACTURERS INSTITUTE

The American Textile Manufacturers Institute (ATMI), which is the national trade association for the United States textile industry, represents spinners, weavers, tufters, knitters, and finishers of textile products. The ATMI's membership represents about 80 percent of the U.S. textile manufacturing industry in more than 30 states. According to the ATMI, there are approximately 6,000 textile manufacturing units in the United States.

In addition to serving the internal interests of its members as a professional trade organization, ATMI represents the industry to the legislative and administrative branches of the government and to the news media. As it says about itself in its literature, "ATMI's activities encompass government relations, international trade, product and administrative services, communications and economic information."

ATMI also helped to organize the American Textile Foundation, which operates solely for charitable and educational purposes, as defined by Section (c) (3) of the Internal Revenue code of 1986. The foundation promotes and sponsors educational and research activities related to textile manufacturing, develops programs aimed at improving workplace safety, and fosters other activities that contribute to the fulfillment of its mission of assisting the American manufacturing industry.

HISTORY

The ATMI is the result of several mergers. The first merger came in 1949, when the American Cotton Manufacturers Association merged its largely southern membership with the largely northern membership of the Cotton Textile Institute. The resulting new association was named the American Textile Manufacturers Institute.

In 1958, ATMI merged with the National Federation of Textiles, bringing under its umbrella the silk-textile and man-made-fiber industries. Other trade groups that merged with ATMI were the Association of Finishers of Textile Fabrics in 1965, the National Association of Wool Manufacturers in 1971, and the Thread Institute in 1989.

ACTIVITIES: CURRENT AND FUTURE

Given the intensely competitive nature of the worldwide textile business, the ATMI has focused much of its lobbying efforts in Washington on trade issues. These include pushing antidumping action that would prevent the export of textiles by Asian exporters to the American market below production cost, pressing for action against the transshipping of textiles (that is, shipping textiles produced in a country that has met its quota of textile exports to the United States via another country that has not); free-trade pacts with textile-producing countries in the Caribbean and Africa that allow producers to export low-cost textile products or the American market; and the inclusion of extraterritorial dispute-resolution panels in future trade agreements.

On the dumping issue, the ATMI has frequently asked that the U.S. government look into charges that foreign countries are dumping textiles into the United States below cost to guarantee employment at home and to maintain a stronger position in the U.S. market. The problem, says the organization, has become particularly acute since the collapse of East Asian economies in 1997. Citing government statistics, the ATMI says that man-made fiber fabric imports increased 50 percent between 1997 and 1998, while prices of these imports declined by as much as 45 percent. "We're looking at the various products to see where there may have been dumping, to what extent, and see if we have enough evidence to present to the government," said Doug Bulcao, ATMI director of government relations, in 1998.

**American Textile Manufacturers Institute
Political Action Committee Contributions**

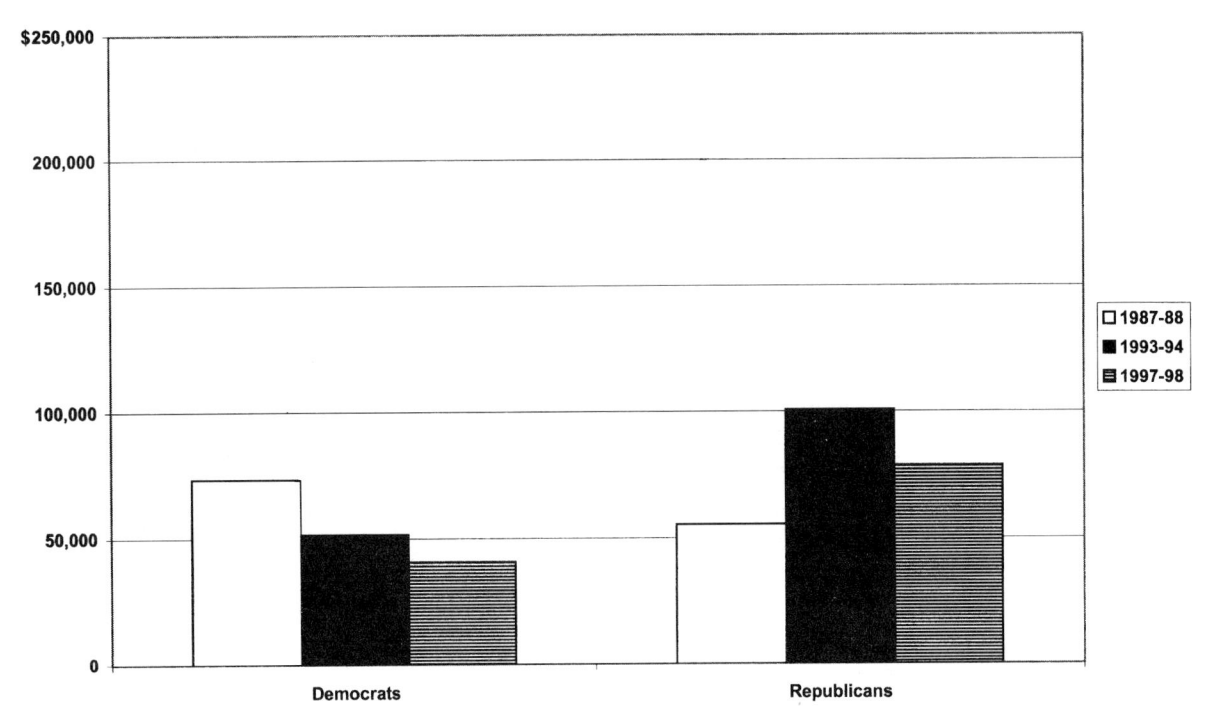

Bar chart showing PAC contributions to Democrats and Republicans for 1987-88, 1993-94, and 1997-98. Democrats: ~$73,000 (1987-88), ~$52,000 (1993-94), ~$42,000 (1997-98). Republicans: ~$57,000 (1987-88), ~$102,000 (1993-94), ~$80,000 (1997-98).

Data derived from official studies available from the Federal Election Commission, Washington, DC, 1987–1998.

Citing China as the worst abuser of transshipment practices, the ATMI has asked that the government push for standard labeling practices on all textiles imported to the United States. The organization says that a great many textiles produced in China are shipped via Hong Kong and Macao and are labeled as products of these two places. Moreover, the ATMI would like the government to be more vigilant in its anti-transshipping investigations.

And while the ATMI has expressed limited support for including Caribbean nations under the North American Free Trade Agreement (NAFTA), the organization says it would like to see Caribbean nations receive access to the American market for their apparel exports—similar to the access that Mexico has under NAFTA—but only so long as the apparel contains U.S.-made yarns and fabrics. At the same time, however, the ATMI has expressed concern about the Clinton initiative that would allow African countries to export textiles to the United States tariff free. Similarly, the organization would like to ensure that any future trade pact—including any with sub-Saharan Africa—would not include extraterritorial dispute-resolution panels. That is to say, the ATMI does not want panels with non-U.S. members to decide what constitutes a breach of the treaty, especially as far as dumping and transshipping are concerned.

The ATMI opposes unfair trade practices and has denounced sweatshops. It is also concerned with the effect of low-cost Asian imports, and it continues to monitor the effect of NAFTA on the textile industry. Since it supports American manufacturers, the association is always on guard to protect the interests of American companies producing textiles within American borders, and it lobbies for positions that support the domestic industry.

In a code of conduct adopted by the ATMI board of directors on September 24, 1996, the ATMI says that "we strongly oppose and find repugnant any human rights violation including the exploitation of children, prison labor, discrimination based on race, gender, age, national or ethnic origin or religion. . . . We urge all companies that manufacture, import, distribute or sell textile products here and abroad to do all they can to protect the rights of their employees."

Recently the ATMI has focused on environmental concerns within the industry. It created the Encouraging Environmental Excellence (E3) program in 1992 to address these concerns. ATMI representatives contend that "the program's main purpose is to challenge U.S. textile companies to strengthen their commitment to the environment by going beyond simply complying with environmental laws. E3 encourages U.S. textile companies to get out in front of regulations and set standards for other industries to follow."

To qualify for E3 membership, a company must go beyond compliance with environmental laws and governmental regulations: it must also adopt 10 guidelines, developed by the ATMI to solidify its commitment to environmental concerns. After qualifying for membership, a company can display the E3 logo on its products and elsewhere in its marketing and trade-show participation. In response to the E3 program, the Environmental Protection Agency has said that the ATMI is among the most proactive trade associations on pollution prevention in the United States.

FINANCIAL FACTS

During the 1997–1998 election cycle, the ATMI Committee for Good Government contributed $119,000 to the campaigns of congressional candidates, of which $78,500 went to Republicans and $40,500 went to Democrats. In the election cycle of 1993–1994, the committee gave $152,650 to candidate campaigns, with $100,100 going to Republicans and $52,550 going to Democrats. This roughly two-to-one bias in favor of Republicans is reflected in the amount of campaign contributions going to the two parties' presidential and congressional candidates in the 1995–1996 election cycle. In those years, the committee contributed $112,500 to Republicans and $50,000 to Democrats.

JAMES CIMENT AND VIVIAN WAGNER

Bibliography

"ATMI Eyeing Anti-Dump Move on Asia." *WWD,* February 24, 1999, p. 25.

Clune, Ray. "Fabric Makers Get New Tool for Complying with EPA Regs." *Daily News Record,* November 4, 1998, p. 9.

Green, Paula L. "US Presses to Keep China Textile Quotas." *Journal of Commerce,* April 16, 1999, p. 3A.

———. "Textiles Group Appeals Ruling on Transshipments; Court Has Turned Down the Case Against Limited Two Times So Far." *Journal of Commerce,* June 10, 1998, p. 3A.

———. "Importers May Yet Be Hemmed in by Whistle-Blower Law." *Journal of Commerce,* January 22, 1998, p. 1A.

Hall, Kevin G. "Trade Groups Want End to NAFTA Dispute Panels." *Journal of Commerce,* January 29, 1998, p. 3A.

Lawrence, Richard. "Weaving and Bobbing in Lobby Land." *Journal of Commerce,* April 19, 1999, p. 9A.

Morrissey, James A. "ATMI Says Bill Poses Threat to U.S. Jobs." *Textile World,* March 1, 1999, vol. 149, no. 3, p. 18.

———. "Congress Eyes Issues Impacting Textiles." *Textile World,* January 1998, vol. 148, no. 1, p. 64.

Owens, Jennifer. "Lobbyists Ready for Reruns in January." *WWD,* November 3, 1998, p. 19.

"Trade Issues Dominate ATMI History." *Textile World,* May 1999.

AMERICAN TRUCKING ASSOCIATIONS

The American Trucking Associations (ATA), a federation of trucking associations, represents 50 state associations and 13 affiliated national conferences. It is also a trade association representing 4,500 trucking companies across the United States.

The ATA's membership is open to companies at all levels of the trucking industry, including motor carriers, private carriers, large or small companies, equipment suppliers, and service providers.

According to its mission statement, the ATA strives "to serve and represent the interests of the trucking industry with one united voice; to positively influence Federal and State governmental actions; to advance the trucking industry's image, efficiency, competitiveness, and profitability; to provide educational programs and industry research; to promote highway and driving safety; and to strive for a healthy business environment."

Some of the nonlobbying educational and advocacy programs of the ATA include America's Road Team, National Truck Driver Appreciation Week, Highway Watch, and "How to Drive" press conferences. These programs are intended to increase public appreciation for the industry. The ATA publishes "Truckline," a three-times-weekly fax featuring brief industry updates, statistical publications, a web site with information for its members and the public, and special announcements of events affecting the trucking industry.

The ATA has established national conferences and gatherings to address different issues within the trucking and transportation industry, including the following: American Movers Conference; Film, Air and Package Carriers Conference; Interstate Carriers Conference; Munitions Carriers Conference; National Automobile Transporters Association; National Tank Truck Carriers; Oil Field Haulers Association; Regional and Distribution Carriers Conference; Regular Common Carrier Conference; and Specialized Carriers & Rigging Association.

HISTORY

The ATA was formed by a number of trucking organizations in 1933. In the early years of the Great Depression, the association brought together various state and national trucking federations as a means of coping with economic troubles and of preparing for a toughening regulatory environment anticipated in the incoming Franklin Roosevelt administration. Indeed, just two years after the ATA was founded, Congress passed the Motor Carrier Act of 1935, which effectively placed the trucking industry under the regulatory control of the Interstate Commerce Commission. Many experts agree that in the years since, the ATA and the trucking industry have exercised enormous influence over the ICC.

ACTIVITIES: CURRENT AND FUTURE

The ATA in general advocates fewer taxes on and less governmental regulations of the trucking industry. The ATA's literature informs prospective members that the organization will "save you from undue tax burdens and cut regulatory red tape . . . prevent government interference in your business . . . put money back in your pocket where it belongs." The ATA works closely with Congress and regulatory agencies, in order to improve the profitability of the trucking industry.

The critical issues the ATA focuses on include emissions and pollution, accidents and truck safety, cross-border trucking issues, highway tolls, and highway crime. On the issue of emissions, the trucking industry is facing more intense scrutiny in recent years from regulatory agencies like the Environmental Protection Agency (EPA), especially as emissions of other vehicles on the road—such as automobiles and light trucks—

become increasingly cleaner. Currently, diesel trucks and buses produce 26 percent of the nitrogen oxides and 70 percent of urban soot in the air.

Officially, the ATA says that it has never been opposed to strengthening heavy-duty diesel standards. However, the organization points out that locomotives, construction vehicles, and other diesel machines are regulated even less closely than motor carriers. Moreover, the ATA points out that only 2.5 percent of the vehicles on the road are diesel powered. While it has no objection to increasing the cleanliness of emissions of new vehicles, it is concerned that because diesel vehicles have a longer life on the road than most gasoline-powered vehicles, retroactive regulations may be too costly for truckers operating on marginal budgets.

Indeed, the ATA has even tried to stop the EPA from instituting sweeping regulatory changes of any kind. In 1999, the U.S. Circuit Court of Appeals in Washington ruled on behalf of the ATA that changes in the enforcement of the Clean Air Act were so sweeping that they actually constituted making legal changes, a power reserved to Congress.

On the issue of trucking and highway safety, the ATA also affirms that it is in agreement with the government—in this case, the Department of Transportation—that trucking accidents occur too frequently and should be reduced by 50 percent over the next few years. But consumer watchdog groups like Public Citizen say that the ATA is not being entirely honest in its publicly professed dedication to lowering trucking accident rates. Indeed, Public Citizen says that the Department of Transportation's increasingly weak enforcement of trucking safety is due to the fact that the department has become "a tool of the motor carrier industry." Public Citizen says that industry oversight should be moved to the Highway Traffic Safety Administration, a move the ATA opposes. "We disagree with anyone who tries to disparage the safety record of professional truck drivers," the ATA has declared. The organization also notes that the move to more "just-in-time delivery" has helped the economy but put economic pressure on truck drivers to make deadlines. In 1999, the ATA offered a proposal to shift responsibility for the safety and roadworthiness of intermodal transport containers and chassis (that is, those containers that have become commonplace in the past decade that are transferred directly from ships to trucks) from the truckers to the owners of the equipment or the shipping-terminal operators, a proposal that was strongly opposed by the American Association of Port Authorities.

Similarly, the ATA backs congressional moves to raise the legal limits on truck weight and size, arguing that larger and heavier trucks actually increase safety since they reduce the overall number of trucks on the road. Consumer groups like Public Citizen vehemently oppose these changes.

Concerning the issue of cross-border trucking, the ATA has sought to eliminate restrictions on the use of Mexican trucks and to ease the strictness of safety inspections required of these trucks at the U.S.-Mexican border. The organization says that NAFTA's trucking provisions must require all foreign carriers operating in the United States to abide by U.S. standards and regulations. Moreover, the long safety delays at the border mean that "trucking companies continue to operate in an inefficient transportation system—even as we face increasing levels of trade flows." Public interest groups oppose easing any such restrictions and safety inspections. In addition, the ATA says that it would like to see an end to the Immigration and Naturalization Service's policy of checking the papers of foreign nationals as they leave the United States to make sure that they have not overstayed their visas. The ATA opposes this practice because it creates enormous delays at the border that can cost truckers time, money, and cargo, especially if the latter contains perishable goods.

On the issue of crime, the ATA supports the 1999 Cargo Theft Deterrent Act currently awaiting review in the Senate. Provisions of the bill require a minimum three-year prison sentence for persons convicted of cargo theft; allocate $3 million annually to the Interstate Theft Union for investigation, prosecution, and prevention of cargo theft; allocate an additional $5 million for state and local cargo-theft task forces; and allow motor carriers more extensives access to employees' criminal records.

FINANCIAL FACTS

Over the past six election cycles—going back to the late 1980s—the ATA has given significant amounts of money to the campaigns of presidential and congressional candidates. Indeed, between the 1987–1988 and the 1997–1998 election cycles, this amount has steadily increased from $284,372 to $419,196, a remarkable increase given the fact that 1987–1988 was a presidential election cycle—which normally sees higher levels of campaign donations—and the 1997–98 was a Congress-only election cycle. Perhaps most unusual in the ATA's donation pattern has been the enormous fluctuations in donations to Democratic and Republican candidates.

**American Trucking Associations
Political Action Committee Contributions**

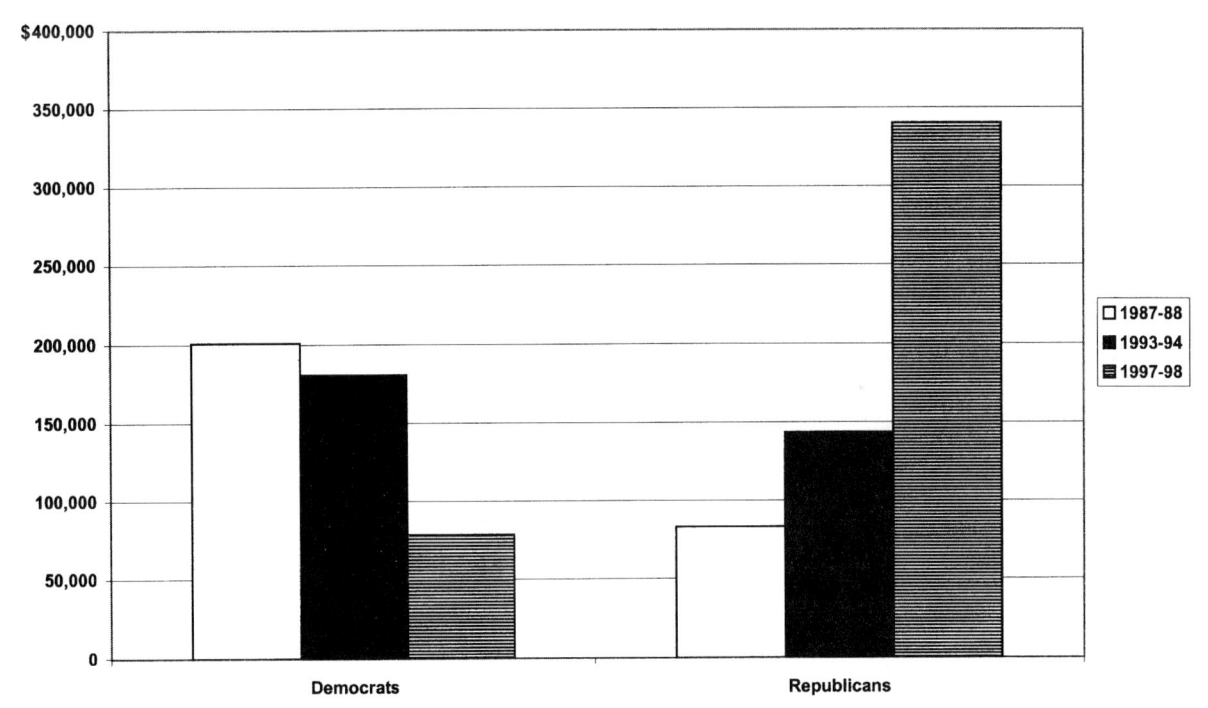

Data derived from official studies available from the Federal Election Commission, Washington, DC, 1987–1998.

Normally, lobbying groups tend to be consistent in giving more to one party than to another. The ATA donated roughly 70 percent to Democrats in the 1987–1988 election cycle, but only about 20 percent in the 1997–1998 election cycle.

JAMES CIMENT AND VIVIAN WAGNER

Bibliography

Davis, Mary. "Overreaction on Global Warming Could Prove Costly for Trucking." *Modern Bulk Transporter,* May 1998.

Hall, Kevin G. "Border Proviso Remains in Limbo." *Journal of Commerce,* October 14, 1998, p. 3A.

———. "Customs Agrees to Revisit Border Diversion Plan." *Journal of Commerce,* February 26, 1998, p. 1A.

Kochiesen, Carol. "Court Reins In EPA in Clean Air Suit." *Nation's Cities Weekly,* May 24, 1999, vol. 22, no. 21, p. 9.

Mottley, Robert. "Rigged? Jury Settlement Has Insurers Crying Foul. ATA Proposal Would Steer Truckers Clear Of Liability." *American Shipper,* June 1, 1999, vol. 41, no. 6, p. 46.

Robyn, Dorothy L. *Braking the Special Interests: Trucking Deregulation and the Politics of Policy Reform.* Chicago: University of Chicago Press, 1987.

"RSPA, Truckers Debate Merits of En Route Hazmat Inspections." *Transport News,* November 1, 1997, vol. 18, no. 16.

"TCA President Calls for United Lobbying Efforts." *Modern Bulk Transporter,* July 1999.

Watson, Rip. "House Bill Proposes Putting Heftier Trucks on Nation's Highways." *Journal of Commerce,* May 7, 1999, Friday, p. 1A.

———. "Lobby Blasts Federal Regulations." *Journal of Commerce,* June 7, 1999, p. 17.

———. "Ports Blast Proposal to Blame Terminals." *Journal of Commerce,* August 5, 1999, p. 14.

———. "TA Supports DOT on Safety, Emissions." *Journal of Commerce,* June 24, 1999, p. 14.

ASSOCIATED BUILDERS AND CONTRACTORS

Associated Builders and Contractors (ABC) is a national trade association representing subcontractors, material suppliers, and related firms in the construction industry. It represents more than 20,000 "merit-shop," or nonunion, construction and construction-related firms. At the base of the structure of ABC are 83 local chapters throughout the United States. The association maintains its headquarters in Arlington, Virginia, where it lobbies Congress, monitors Washington activity for its members with its *Government Affairs Update* and *Regulatory Update*, and represents the construction industry before the Department of Labor, the Occupational Safety and Health Administration (OSHA), and the Environmental Protection Agency. ABC's committees include Budget and Finance, Business Development, By-laws and Policy, Contract Documents, Craft Training, Insurance, Legal Rights and Strategy, Legislative, Management Education, Pension, Political Action, and Safety.

ABC, through its political action committee (PAC) and the PAC's subgroup, Contractors for Free Enterprise, is a strong supporter of merit-shop principles. In 1989 it created the Construction Legal Rights Foundation (CLRF), which helps its members in legal cases, and it also operates the Contractors Referral Service, which, it says, is the leading source for America's construction users to identify the best merit-shop firms.

Within its industry the association is active on issues concerning safety, training, and education. Through its chapters it supports a school-to-work program, which seeks to interest children in construction careers. It is also affiliated with the National Center for Construction Education and Research. Its primary publication is *ABC Today,* a semimonthly magazine aimed at merit-shop contractors.

HISTORY

In 1950 Associated Builders and Contractors was founded as an interest group representing six contractors in the Baltimore area. Over the past 50 years, the organization has grown dramatically, appealing to thousands of construction firms and contractors who stand opposed to closed-shop, unionized construction sites. Indeed, it is this position, says the organization, that has made ABC the fastest-growing construction trade association in the country. According to ABC, open-shop contractors today perform over 70 percent of all construction nationwide and its membership includes over one-third of the top 400 construction companies in the United States.

ACTIVITIES: CURRENT AND FUTURE

Associated Builders and Contractors has made a name for itself in Washington as one of the strongest anti-union advocates of any manufacturing interest group and a firm opponent of government regulation of the construction industry. In 1999, ABC launched a major offensive against what it called federal blacklisting rules, which had been proposed by the Clinton administration and backed by presidential candidate and Vice President Albert Gore. Specifically, these rules would bar from receiving a government contract any firm that had a history of violating labor, environmental, or tax laws and regulations. ABC president David Bush says that the proposal is "one more tool that unscrupulous unions will use to attack merit shop [better known as open-shop] contractors." According to the organiza-

**Associated Builders and Contractors
Political Action Committee Contributions**

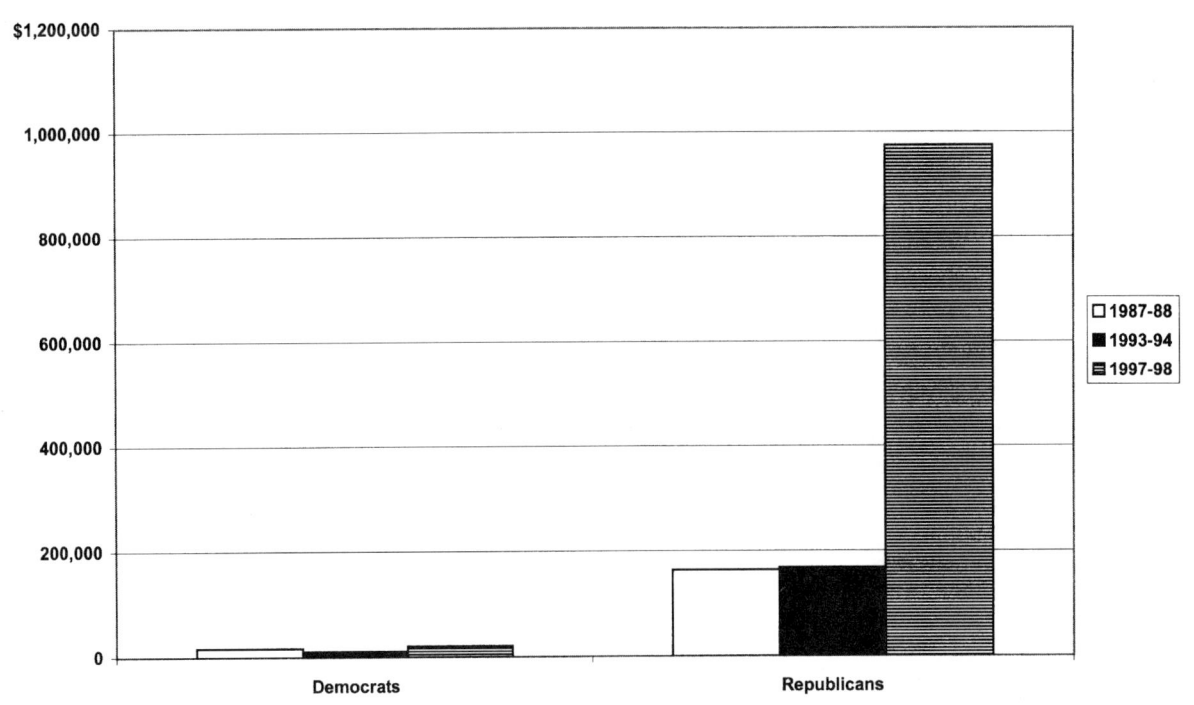

[Bar chart showing PAC contributions to Democrats and Republicans for years 1987-88, 1993-94, and 1997-98. Democrats received minimal contributions (near $0) in all three periods. Republicans received approximately $175,000 in 1987-88, $175,000 in 1993-94, and approximately $985,000 in 1997-98.]

Data derived from official studies available from the Federal Election Commission, Washington, DC, 1987–1998.

tion, labor unions often file frivolous charges against nonunion construction firms in order to drive up their costs and make them less competitive. With a federal blacklist of such firms in operation, unions, the organization says, would be more encouraged to file such frivolous suits as a way to punish their open-shop opponents.

At the same time, ABC has been an active opponent of so-called project labor agreements, or PLAs. Under a PLA, a government agency that puts out bids for construction contracts can require that a company—even an open-shop company—must operate as a union shop for the duration of the project. ABC and other antiunion organizations won a significant victory in 1998 when a Boston area judge—in a case involving a school-renovation project—ruled that PLAs need not apply to small or medium construction projects. Until the ruling, PLAs were quite common on small- and medium-sized government construction sites throughout the United States.

Similarly, ABC has pushed for congressional legislation that would allow entry-level "helpers" on federal construction projects. Helpers—unskilled or semi-skilled, generally nonunion workers—are widely used on private-sector construction projects. Citing the need for more entry-level positions, ABC says this practice should be extended to the government contracting sector of the industry. Unions generally have opposed the move, saying that it undermines union membership.

Finally, on regulations, ABC has been actively seeking to diminish the extent of OSHA rules on construction projects. Specifically, ABC wants OSHA to ease the record-keeping requirements for contractors on small- and medium-sized construction projects, saying that it places an inordinate paperwork burden on the generally smaller companies that work on such projects. But Knut Ringen, director of the Center to Protect Workers Rights, says continuing the record-keeping requirements is essential for both employers and workers. "One reason we're seeing declines in injury rates is because employers' reporting behaviors have changed," he says. "They're avoiding reporting injuries to save on workers' compensation costs."

FINANCIAL FACTS

Given its strong support for open-shop, antiunion hiring practices, it is not surprising that Associated

Builders and Contractors eschewed giving donations to the more pro-labor Democratic Party. Indeed, the amount of money given to Democrats has remained a tiny fraction of that given Republicans for the past half-dozen election cycles since 1987–1988, even as the organization's overall amount given to political campaigns has grown dramatically over that same time period. For example, in 1987–1988, ABC gave $163,726 to political candidates for president and Congress, with over 90 percent going to Republicans. Ten years later, in the 1997–1998 election cycle, ABC gave congressional candidates a total of $966,117, representing an increase of almost 600 percent. However, the $21,000 given to Democrats in the latter cycle represented only 2 percent of the amount given to Republican candidates.

JAMES CIMENT AND VIVIAN WAGNER

Bibliography

"ABC Pans Clinton's Plan for the Project Labor Agreements." *Engineering News-Record,* May 3, 1999, vol. 242, no. 17, p. 9.

"Industry Fears Bureaucratic Pinch of Proposed Record-Keeping Rule." *Occupational Health and Safety Letter,* September 29, 1997, vol. 27, no. 20.

Lewis, Diane. "Judge Overturns Labor Agreement; Says Nonunion Workers Entitled to Work on Project." *Boston Globe,* April 2, 1998, p. C1.

Semien, John. "Builders' Group, Contractor Sue Over Set-Asides for Minorities." *Commercial Appeal* (Memphis, TN), January 6, 1999, p. B2.

Winston, Sherie. "Rules Rile Contractor Groups." *Engineering News-Record,* July 19, 1999, vol. 243, no. 3, p. 10.

Winston, Sherie, and Jeff Barber. "Labor: Court Upholds Suspension of Helper Rules." *Engineering News-Record,* August 18, 1997, vol. 239, no. 7, p. 7.

BUSINESS ROUNDTABLE

The Business Roundtable (BRT) is an association of the chief executive officers (CEOs) of many of the largest corporations in the United States, including those in the manufacturing, extractive, transportation, communications, banking, insurance, and retailing sectors. Membership in the organization is by invitation only. And while the CEOs play a major role in BRT, their companies are the actual members; the CEOs are, technically speaking, merely their companies' representatives.

BRT is headed by a chairman, who serves for a year, although most serve for two consecutive terms. There are also two to four co-chairmen. Much of the analysis and policy-formulating work of BRT is conducted by task forces. These include Corporate Governance, Education, Environment, Federal Budget, Government Regulation, Health and Retirement, Human Resources, International Trade and Investment, Taxation, Tort Policy, and Construction Cost Effectiveness (the only industry-specific task force in BRT). The task forces—which often include experts drawn from industry and academe—and their chairmen draft position papers and use them in their advocacy efforts, which include testifying before Congress, working with scholars, and influencing public opinion through public relations and advertising. In general, the task forces focus on general policy principles, rather than on immediate and specific legislation.

For the most part, BRT focuses its analysis and lobbying efforts on major issues that affect business, including governmental fiscal and regulatory policy, environmental matters, international trade, and tort reform. While the organization is less well-known to the public than the U.S. Chamber of Commerce and other business advocacy organizations, experts say it is among the most powerful lobbying groups in Washington—a role it has achieved through the influence of its member companies' representatives. Overall, the CEOs who serve on BRT run companies that employ over 10 million people in the United States and millions more overseas. In addition, the member companies of BRT spend over $100 million dollars annually lobbying Congress. BRT is headquartered in Washington, D.C., and every June its member companies' representatives hold a meeting to establish overall policy goals for the association.

HISTORY

BRT came into being in 1972, the result of a merger of three existing business organizations. These included the March Group, a group of CEOs who had been meeting informally to discuss public policy issues; the Construction Users Anti-Inflation Roundtable, an organization of businesspersons in the construction industry who were dedicated to fighting the rising costs of construction; and the Labor Law Study Committee, an organization of executives in the field of labor relations who were dedicated to containing the power of unions and establishing more managerial control over the workplace. Some of the key figures behind the formation of BRT included the CEOs of Alcoa, General Electric, and U.S. Steel (now USX).

The Business Roundtable has been cited as one of the key policy-formulating interest groups that helped elect Ronald Reagan president in 1980 and pushed for pro-corporate and pro-wealthy tax breaks during the first years of his administration. Indeed, BRT is seen as one of the key groups behind the rise of the conservative, pro-business climate of the 1980s and the Republican takeover of Congress in 1994.

ACTIVITIES: CURRENT AND FUTURE

As noted above, BRT has focused its efforts largely on the most important public policy issues. These break down roughly into the following categories: government regulation of the environment, working conditions, and corporate bookkeeping; overall government fiscal policy (currently focusing on the debate over Social Security reform); international trade; tort reform; and healthcare reform.

On issues of international trade, BRT has supported the North American Free Trade Agreement and further liberalization of U.S. commercial policy. It has also favored expansion of global agreements like the one that created the World Trade Organization to include more nations, such as China. BRT argues that since the United States is the world's largest exporter, it must be the world's leading proponent of free trade.

Some critics have accused BRT of being antienvironment. They point to the group's opposition to the 1997 Kyoto Protocol, an international agreement to limit the emission of carbon gases. The emission of carbon compounds—largely by industry and transportation—is seen by most scientists as the main culprit in the trend toward global warming. BRT's main objection to the Kyoto Protocol is economic. According to the association, the agreement requires the major industrialized countries—especially the United States—to take on the bulk of the reductions, a task that would hamper American economic growth and make the country less competitive in the world market, particularly against less industrialized countries that are not required to lower their emissions as much. And while BRT acknowledges that the protocol includes market-based incentives for carbon gas reduction, it believes that these do not go far enough. The association wants the U.S. government to oppose the protocol until it can demonstrate that the required reductions will not harm economic growth.

On the domestic front, perhaps the most critical issue BRT addressed in the late 1990s was healthcare reform. The association opposed the Dingell-Norwood bill, commonly known as the Patient's Bill of Rights, because it would have given healthcare consumers the right to sue their health insurance providers for denial of essential services. BRT argues that this would lead to costly, frivolous litigation, raise insurance rates, and force consumers to lose their plans. The association also claims it would subject employers to undue liabilities. Proponents of the bill dispute this charge, arguing that employers who hire third-party insurance companies and health maintenance organizations to provide healthcare will remain immune to such suits. Texas, they point out, enacted a patient's bill of rights more than a year ago, and workers have brought very few suits against health insurance providers and virtually none involving employers.

On government fiscal policy, BRT has leaned heavily behind Republican lawmakers in Congress, advocating "spending restraint by keeping to the discretionary spending limits enacted in 1997." BRT strongly supports keeping Social Security off-budget surpluses separate—rather than using these surpluses to pay for domestic spending—and privatizing at least part of the Social Security system. Calling the current budget process flawed by an "inherent bias toward higher taxes and higher spending," BRT backs reductions in the capital gains tax and corporate tax rates. Many Democrats have denounced these proposals as "budget-busters." Consumer and labor groups say they would largely benefit the wealthy, while requiring vast cuts in domestic social spending.

Of more immediate concern to BRT members is regulatory reform. For several years, the association has promoted numerous bills with the same objective: lessening the regulatory impact on business. Specifically, the association wants regulations to be based on "science-based risk assessments" and cost-benefit analyses. The association also says it supports "open[ing] the rulemaking process by soliciting public participation." A bill to that effect, the 1999 Regulatory Right-to-Know Act, has been heavily pushed by BRT.

Critics charge that risk assessments and cost-benefit analyses are skewed in industry's favor, because they often gloss over large social and environmental costs, while focusing on the narrowest view of the impact of regulatory easing. They also dismiss corporate-sponsored "public participation" as "astroturf-root organizing" because it allows for Washington insiders to artificially mimic genuine grassroots organizing and unduly influence regulators and legislators.

BRT has also been pushing for tort reform—or a tightening of federal restrictions on the scope of litigation brought against corporations by consumers, workers, and the general public—and limits on the size of jury awards given to plaintiffs when corporations are found liable for civil damages. BRT argues that such limits are necessary to avoid costly settlements that unfairly penalize companies that were trying to act in good faith. Such settlements, the association claims, raise insurance rates, add to the costs of goods, and undermine economic growth. Critics counter that large punitive judgments, which tort reform aims to reduce, are the only way to keep corporations from making faulty products, damaging the environment, and relying on cost-benefit analyses that justify such actions.

FINANCIAL FACTS

Although it represents businesses that give enormous sums to congressional and presidential candidates of both parties, the Business Roundtable itself does not have a political action committee and does not donate sums either to political parties in the form of soft-money contributions or to candidates in the form of regular hard money contributions. However, it has been a very active force in Washington with one of the largest lobbying budgets of any organization. BRT spent $9.4 million on lobbying in 1997 and $11.6 million in 1998.

JAMES CIMENT

Bibliography

Deann, Christinat. "Taxing Dreams." *CFO, The Magazine for Senior Financial Executives,* June 1, 1999, vol. 15, no. 6, p. 27.

Mack, Charles S. *Business, Politics, and the Practice of Government Relations.* Westport, CT: Quorum, 1997.

McGregor, Deborah. "Business to Renew Attack on Healthcare Reforms." *Financial Times,* June 23, 1999.

Miller, William. "New Initiative Aims to Unify Business' Political Efforts." Industry Week, Aug. 16, 1999.

Przybyla, Heidi. "Commerce Gets Its Road Show Together." *Journal of Commerce,* April 19, 1999.

Silverstein, Ken. *Washington on $10 Million a Day: How Lobbyists Plunder the Nation.* Monroe, ME: Common Courage Press, 1998.

Wechsler, Jill. "Senate GOP Pushes Through Patient Rights Bill." *Managed Healthcare,* vol. 9, no. 8 (August 1999).

West, Darrell. *The Sound of Money: How Political Interests Get What They Want.* New York: W.W. Norton, 1999.

CHEMICAL MANUFACTURERS ASSOCIATION

The Chemical Manufacturers Association (CMA) serves as the association for the chemical industry's legislative, regulatory, and legal concerns on the international, national and state levels. It has some 200 members and partners and "more than 2,000 scientists and engineers, [and] health, safety and environmental managers from CMA's member companies, who participate in CMA committees and task groups. Thousands more participate in activities to implement industry programs." The CMA acts as an advocate on issues of concern to the chemical manufacturing industry by meeting with government policy makers on the federal and state level, working with regulators, supporting grassroots programs, sponsoring meetings with legislators, forming coalitions with other industry leaders, and litigating on the industry's behalf.

HISTORY

The Chemical Manufacturers Association was founded in 1872 as the Manufacturing Chemists Association. It is one of the oldest trade associations in the United States. Some of its member companies have belonged to the organization for over one hundred years. In 1993, the CMA launched its anniversary awards to honor the companies that had been members for 50, 75, and 100 years. Other awards granted by the organization include its safety citations. Begun in 1951 and named for former CMA head Lammot du Pont, the safety awards are given to companies that work more than 20 million exposure hours annually without a serious health or safety mishap. In 1999, the CMA began a major restructuring campaign for the coming century. According to president Frederick Webber, the CMA simplified the organizational structure by reducing a number of levels of bureaucracy. This was done to focus on the group's key activities and to increase productivity.

ACTIVITIES: CURRENT AND FUTURE

Because of the thicket of laws and regulations covering this highly important but potentially environmentally dangerous business, the Chemical Manufacturers Association focuses much of its lobbying efforts on regulatory change and reduction. Specifically, it tries to convince government to ease the costs and difficulties of complying with current regulations and tries to influence the writing of future regulations to make them more industry-friendly. These regulations concern both environmental and worker-safety issues. In addition, the CMA attempts to influence laws that deal with the interaction between the public and the chemical industry, specifically in the realm of right-to-know laws and in the area of class action suits. The CMA is heavily involved in trying to influence trade issues, and has recently become engaged in the ongoing debate over electricity deregulation. As a major consumer of electricity, the chemical industry stands to make or lose a great deal of money, depending on the course this deregulation takes. In 1999, the CMA and the Environmental Protection Agency (EPA) published the results of a unique three-year collaborative project—the EPA/CMA Root Cause Analysis Pilot Project—that surveyed two dozen chemical companies involved in civil, judicial, or administrative enforcement actions to find out why they failed to comply and to discover ways to improve performance. The study found that unclear environmental regulations and a lack of compliance assistance by the government were at least partially to blame.

The CMA has backed congressional legislation that would require government agencies to calculate and disclose the costs of various regulations. Under the so-called Regulatory-Right-To-Know bill, the president would be required to submit to Congress an annual report—compiled by various executive department agencies—enumerating the total annual costs and benefits of federal regulatory programs. While the CMA sees this as a cost-effective measure, the bill is strongly opposed by environmental groups, which say that such reports would siphon resources away from drafting and enforcing needed regulation.

In the workplace, the CMA, along with representatives of the petroleum industry, are seeking to speed up OSHA revisions of permissible exposure limits for hundreds of industrial chemicals. As far as the relationship between the public and the chemical industry is concerned, the CMA has been asking congressional leaders to get the EPA to delay a requirement that chemical plants submit "worst case scenario" disaster information on the Internet. Under the Clean Air Act of 1990, the industry is required to inform the public about some 66,000 toxic chemicals. But this requirement has been delayed over the years, partly because of CMA lobbying. The organization insists that such information would be an aid to terrorists. But the U.S. Public Interest Research Group, a consumer advocacy organization, says terrorism is not the issue. The chemical industry, the group says, is worried that disclosure could lead to increased protests and lawsuits.

Indeed, lawsuits—and particularly class action lawsuits—are another target of CMA lobbying. Arguing that there are "serious abuses in the class action process," the CMA strongly supports legislation pending in Congress that would shift more such cases to the federal courts, which are generally friendlier to industry than state courts.

On the electricity deregulation issue, the CMA is pushing strongly for more states to deregulate the electrical utility industry. Experts say the chemical industry will save some 20 percent of electricity costs if competitive market forces are allowed to come into play because, as some of the biggest users of electricity, chemical companies will be able to bargain for the best rates.

FINANCIAL FACTS

By the standards of industry, the Chemical Manufacturers Association remains a relatively modest donor of funds to congressional and presidential campaigns. In the 1997–1998 election cycle, the CMA political action committee (PAC) contributed $125,199. Of this amount, $96,370 (77 percent) went to Republican campaigns and $28,829 (23 percent) went to Democratic campaigns. The total figures represent a substantial increase over those of previous election cycles. In the 1995–1996 presidential and congressional election cycle—presidential elections are usually times when donations go up significantly—the total amount donated by the CMA was just $65,638, of which Republicans received $54,638 (83 percent). These figures represent a major increase over those for the 1991–1992 presidential and congressional election cycle, when the CMA gave just $26,250 overall.

JAMES CIMENT AND VIVIAN WAGNER

Bibliography

"CMA Endorses Legislation to Reform Class Action Lawsuits." *Chemical Market Reporter,* May 24, 1999, vol. 255, no. 21, p. 25.

"Committee Endorses CMA-Backed Cost-Benefit Analysis Legislation." *Chemical Market Reporter,* May 31, 1999, vol. 255, no. 22, p. 4.

Fagin, Dan. *Toxic Deception: How the Chemical Industry Manipulates Science, Bends the Law, and Endangers Your Health.* Monroe, ME: Common Courage Press, 1999.

Hess, Glenn. "Administration's Utility Proposal Receives Guarded Support from CMA." *Chemical Market Reporter,* April 26, 1999, vol. 255, no. 17.

———. "CMA Cautions EPA on Its Internet Data Plan." *Chemical Market Reporter,* September 21, 1998, p. 5.

———. "CMA Tentatively Endorses Restrictions on Access to Worst-Case Scenario Data." *Chemical Market Reporter,* May 31, 1999, vol. 255, no. 22, p. 1.

———. "CMA-EPA Study Assesses Reasons Why Companies Fail to Comply with Gov't Environmental Guidelines." *Chemical Market Reporter,* July 19, 1999, vol. 256, no. 3, p. 28.

———. "Trade Groups Call for Revisions to OSHA'S PELs; Occupational Safety and Health Administration's Permissible Exposure Limits." *Chemical Market Reporter,* January 18, 1999, vol. 255, no. 3, p. 40.

Knee, Richard. "U.S. Health Group Plans Chem Lobby Effort." *Chemical News and Intelligence,* June 4, 1999.

Ulbrecht, Jaromir J., ed. *Competitiveness of the U.S. Chemical Industry in International Markets.* New York: American Institute of Chemical Engineers, 1990.

Usdin, Steve. "U.S. House Passes Regs Accountability Bill." *Chemical News and Intelligence,* July 27, 1999.

DISTILLED SPIRITS COUNCIL OF THE UNITED STATES

The Distilled Spirits Council of the United States (DISCUS) is the national trade association representing the producers, marketers, and distributors of distilled spirits products sold in the United States. With its 24 members it comprises more than 90 percent of this nation's distillers. DISCUS claims that the distilled spirits industry directly and indirectly employs 1,390,000 people, producing $25 billion in U.S. wages and $89 billion in economic activity.

HISTORY

DISCUS was founded in its current form in 1973, following the merger of the Distilled Spirits Institute, founded in 1933 after the end of Prohibition; the Bourbon Institute, founded in 1958; and Licensed Beverage Industries, founded in 1946. The new organization soon absorbed the Tax Council–Alcoholic Beverage Industries group. Over the years DISCUS has been involved in most major developments in the alcohol industry but has often been forced to fight a rearguard action in a declining market for distilled beverages and in an increasingly hostile anti–alcohol political and cultural environment.

ACTIVITIES: CURRENT AND FUTURE

Much of DISCUS's lobbying effort has focused on taxes—working on both the federal and state level to lessen existing excise taxes and prevent increases. As it has said in a statement on the issue of taxes, "recent history has shown that higher distilled spirits taxes result in less government revenue, because the taxes are so high already that they have reached the point of diminishing returns. Despite two tax increases totaling 29 percent since 1985, distilled spirits tax revenues are lower today than they were in 1980." Other statistics DISCUS refers to in support of its position include the fact that in 1991, after the Federal Excise Tax was raised 8 percent, federal revenue from distilled spirits taxes fell by $89 million. The organization also argues that raising liquor taxes does not deter alcohol abuse, but instead limits availability (through increased cost) to those who are not alcohol abusers. In response to the argument that the distilled spirits industry should pay the "social cost" of problem drinking through increased taxes, DISCUS emphasizes that this cost should be balanced against presumed health benefits of moderate drinking and that "all relevant information about beverage alcohol products—reported risks and benefits alike—should be taken into account in order that tax policy is both fair and nondiscriminatory."

On the issue of Blood Alcohol Content (BAC) levels, DISCUS says it "neither supports nor opposes any particular BAC level." It says that "this is a state issue and should be decided by each state." It does support improved data collection on BAC levels and traffic accidents and "mandatory BAC tests in fatal accidents and also mandatory testing for all substances, so that the relative role of alcohol versus illegal drugs could be determined." And while the organization has come to accept warning labels on alcohol, it has fought recent moves to make those warnings more explicit. It successfully lobbied against a 1996 congressional bill that called for a rotating series of six different warning labels on all alcoholic beverage containers.

In recent years questions involving the advertising of alcohol have arisen for DISCUS. Faced with a Federal Trade Commission report in early 1999 that found beer companies to be advertising in ways that promote underage drinking, DISCUS has argued that the federal government should not get involved in decision making about the content of private advertising. Some of the controversy over alcohol advertising, however, has been self-created. In 1996 DISCUS announced that the in-

**Distilled Spirits Council
Political Action Committee Contributions**

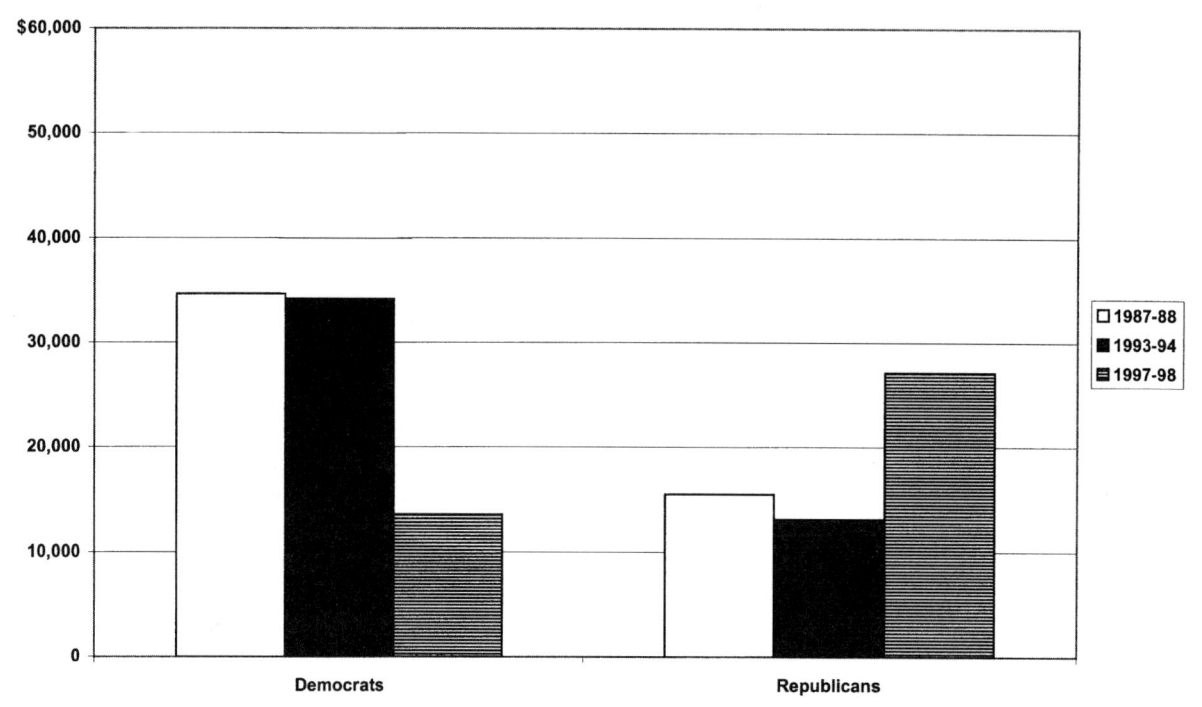

Data derived from official studies available from the Federal Election Commission, Washington, DC, 1987–1998.

dustry was dropping its self-imposed ban on radio and TV ads that had been in effect for 60 years. The move was denounced by both President Bill Clinton and a number of congressional leaders. While Clinton insisted that the industry should maintain its voluntary ban, some congressional leaders talked of enacting a law to the same end, much like the quarter-century-old ban on television and radio advertising of tobacco products. DISCUS maintains that it is unfair to allow broadcast advertising for beer but not distilled spirits, given the fact that a typical 12-ounce beer contains the same amount of alcohol—that is, roughly 1.5 ounces—as a typical 4-ounce mixed drink.

On other issues DISCUS tries to present the industry as a responsible group of corporate citizens. For example, on environmentalism, DISCUS says that it "is committed to voluntary cooperation with government and a proactive stance on environmental issues." It supports comprehensive recycling programs and has supported finding alternatives to heavy-metal packaging for liquor containers.

To protect itself in an increasingly hostile anti-alcohol environment, DISCUS is also heavily involved in various public education campaigns, printing brochures and other materials for use by the media, educators, and the general public. Some of the topics of these materials have included alcohol abuse, consumption figures, industry trends, and excise taxes. However, many critics say that these public interest advertisements, which run on cable TV and radio, are really efforts to promote liquor drinking.

FINANCIAL FACTS

The Distilled Spirits Council's political action committee (PAC)—DISPAC—has donated moderate sums to political campaigns over the past 12 years. In 1987–1988 it contributed $50,178 to congressional and presidential candidates, including $34,663 to Democrats and $15,515 to Republicans. During the 1993–1994 Congress-only election cycle it donated $45,633—once again to candidates of both parties, with the majority of the funds being contributed to Democrats. However, in the 1997–1998 election cycle, given the growing Democratic willingness to back higher taxes on alcohol, DISPAC gave more to Republicans for the first time in many election cycles. Of its $40,626 in campaign contributions, fully $27,134, or roughly two-thirds, went to Republican congressional campaign coffers.

JAMES CIMENT AND VIVIAN WAGNER

Bibliography

Bang, Hae-Kyong. "Analyzing the Impact of the Liquor Industry's Lifting of the Ban on Broadcast Advertising." *Journal of Public Policy & Marketing,* vol. 17, no. 1 (Spring 1998): 132.

Farhi, Paul. "An Ounce or Two of Suspicion; Distillers' TV Spot Has Critics Questioning Industry's Motives." *Washington Post,* July 28, 1998, p. E01.

"Liquor Industry Public Education Commercial Questioned." *Associated Press,* July 29, 1998.

Stern, Christopher. "Booze on Back Burner at FCC." *Daily Variety,* February 2, 1998.

Tong, Kathryn. "Exporters Pour on the Spirits Globally." *Journal of Commerce,* August 4, 1998, p. 13A.

EDISON ELECTRIC INSTITUTE

The Edison Electric Institute (EEI) is a national association representing 190 U.S. shareholder-owned electric companies. Together EEI member companies generate and distribute over 75 percent of the country's electricity and serve over 90 percent of the customers of the shareholder-owned segment of the electric industry and about 70 percent of all electric customers in the country. The EEI also has international affiliates, who provide electricity worldwide, and associates, who provide services to the electric industry.

The EEI represents its members in legislative and public forums and to the government at both the state and federal levels. It also provides a means of exchanging information about the industry among its members.

HISTORY

The EEI was organized in 1933, replacing the older National Electric Light Association (NELA), which voted to become the EEI at its annual convention of that year in Atlantic City. The decision grew out of the fact that the old NELA was seen as largely discredited, since it had been so unwilling to work with the government on spreading electricity to rural districts and other sections where power generation was not as profitable as in more populous areas. Indeed, there was a great fear as Franklin Roosevelt came to office that the government might seek to nationalize American utilities. Accepting the inevitability of utility regulation, the EEI has consistently tried to limit the extent of that regulation as much as possible, even as it has faced periodic threats of government takeover, most recently during the energy crises of the 1970s.

ACTIVITIES: CURRENT AND FUTURE

Many of the issues of concern to the EEI revolve around the topic of the increasing deregulation of, and resulting increased competition within, the electricity industry. The EEI is active in determining the nature of competition in the new climate of deregulation, with electricity providers given a chance at fair competition with one another. It wants to ensure universal electricity service is available to all consumers and to prevent cost-shifting from companies to consumers, and it supports the implementation and continuation of social and environmental programs along with the new climate of deregulation. In general the EEI says that it wants to make certain that all competitors are treated equally and that consumers will benefit from the competition. In particular it is concerned with controlling cross-subsidization in electrical utility regulation, and it maintains a close watch on the consolidation of the electric-power concerns.

In terms of deregulation in general, "stranded costs"—the costs electricity providers incur in the shift from being regulated to being deregulated—are a key issue of concern to the EEI. It supports viewing these costs of transition to competition and deregulation as legitimate, recoverable costs. In other words it endorses the idea of stranded cost recovery and is seeking ways to minimize the impact of the transition on electricity providers. In general it does not support cost-shifting from large companies to residential customers or small businesses, and it also does not believe that utility shareholders should be penalized for the shift. The primary source of cost recovery, therefore, is the government, and the EEI continues to support governmental relief from these stranded costs in order to maintain effective competition and avoid what it sees as cost-shifting.

Regarding the Public Utility Holding Company Act

**Edison Electric Institute
Political Action Committee Contributions**

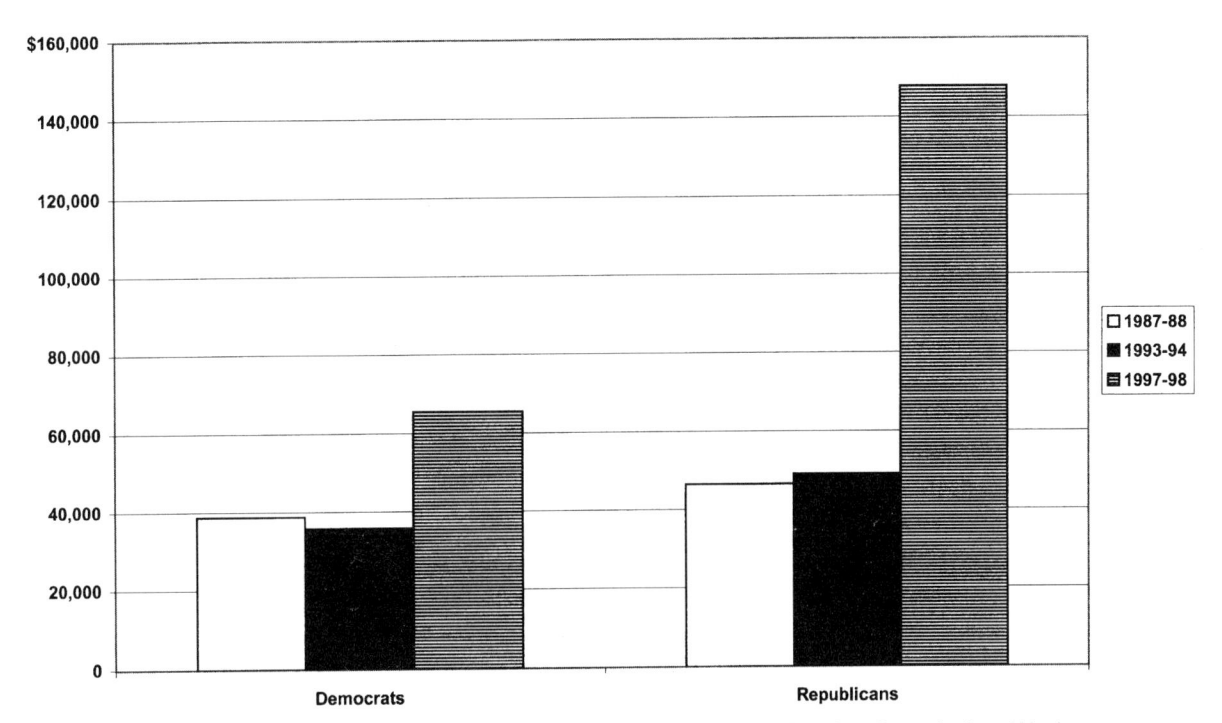

Data derived from official studies available from the Federal Election Commission, Washington, DC, 1987–1998.

of 1935, the EEI is against the restrictions that it imposes on registered holding companies and subsidiaries, preventing them, the EEI argues, from responding quickly to consumer needs and from competing effectively in the modern marketplace. It sees the act as a barrier to efficient competition and thus supports legislation to repeal the act.

Still, the EEI has made it clear that it does not want to see the deregulation process controlled too extensively by the government. In 1993 it funded a policy paper on that process by the Progress and Freedom Foundation. In the paper the foundation warned that Congress still wanted to intervene in the electricity marketplace and that the industry should be wary of "regulatory wolves in free market clothing." The paper offered twelve criteria to measure whether Congress was truly acting to deregulate the electric industry in a way that utilities could live with. The criteria included whether the federal government would let the states have control over the deregulation process, whether it would truly remove federal agencies from regulation of the industry, whether it would continue to force utilities to produce a certain percentage of their power from renewable resources, whether it would get out of the electricity-generating business by selling the Tennessee Valley Authority, whether it would end favoritism to municipality-owned and cooperatively owned utilities over privately owned ones, and whether the bill would end the government's right to make fuel-use decisions favoring renewable resources or would allow the market to make those decisions. This last element is particularly important because the industry does not want to see itself penalized for burning cheaper, but more pollution-causing, coal at its power plants.

Another key area of lobbying interest for the EEI is taxes. Specifically, the EEI has strongly backed provisions of a 1999 Republican-sponsored tax-cut bill that would facilitate utility mergers. One provision of the bill would make sure that the tax-preferred status of nuclear cleanup funds be passed along to the new purchasers of existing nuclear power plants. In addition the EEI is pushing to get the so-called double taxation clause removed when an American-owned utility buys a foreign one.

Finally, the EEI has been backing a bill introduced in Congress in 1999 that would help streamline the relicensing of existing hydropower projects. "The future contribution of hydroelectricity to the nation's energy portfolio must not be taken for granted," said EEI president Thomas Kuhn. "Unless steps are taken to reduce burdensome relicensing requirements, we can expect the steady erosion of our hydro resources seen over the past decade to continue, if not worsen, well into the future."

FINANCIAL FACTS

The EEI's Political Action Committee (PAC)—POWERPAC—has given moderate sums of money to the political campaigns of both presidential and congressional candidates. Until the election cycle of 1997–1998 POWERPAC had consistently contributed between $80,000 and $90,000 collectively to Republican and Democratic candidates. In general, however, POWERPAC tended to favor Republican candidates, although not by margins as great as those of other industrial PACs. In 1987–1988, for instance, it gave $85,300, with $46,500 (55 percent) going to Republican presidential and congressional candidates and $38,800 (45 percent) going to Democrats. Similarly, in 1993–1994, POWERPAC gave 58 percent of its $84,750 in donations to Republicans and 42 percent to Democrats.

But in the 1997–1998 cycle things changed dramatically, both in the total contributed and the proportions that went to the two parties' candidates. In this election cycle POWERPAC gave $213,472 in contributions to congressional candidates, with $147,967 (69 percent) going to Republicans, and $65,505 (31 percent) destined for the coffers of Democratic candidates. This change reflects the increasingly politicized nature of electric-power generation as the move toward deregulation of the industry picks up momentum. Republicans are seen as favoring a faster and less government-monitored deregulation process, positions with which EEI tends to agree.

JAMES CIMENT AND VIVIAN WAGNER

Bibliography

"Beware of Regulatory Wolves in Free Market Clothing, Progress and Freedom Foundation Warns." *Foster Electric Report,* August 4, 1999, report no. 171, p. 32.

"Bill Targets 'Double Tax' on U.S. Utilities Overseas." *Electric Utility Week,* June 28, 1999, p. 13.

Chambers, Ann. *Power Branding.* Tulsa, OK: Pennwell, 1998.

"Commentary: Comments on Clinton Electric Bill." *The Electricity Daily,* April 19, 1999, vol. 12, no. 74.

"Consumer Group Challenges EEI Ads." *The Electricity Daily,* August 11, 1999, vol. 13, no. 29.

"Dams: Power Industry Forms Lobbying Group." *Greenwire,* June 1, 1999.

"Deregulation: Lobbyists Swarm the Capitol." *National Journal's Daily Energy Briefing,* March 11, 1999.

"EEI: Most Like Their Home Utilities, Are Suspicious of Federal Deregulation." *The Energy Daily,* August 3, 1999.

"Energy Advocates Among Top Five Lobbyists." *Power Generation Technology & Markets,* December 11, 1998, vol. 19, no. 48.

Kwoka, John E. *Power Structure: Ownership, Integration, and Competition in the U.S. Electricity Industry.* Boston: Kluwer Academic, 1996.

Smeloff, Ed. *Reinventing Electric Utilities: Competition, Citizen Action, and Clean Power.* Washington, DC: Island Press, 1997.

Sullivan, Kevin. "Lobbyists Turn Up the Heat at Global Warming Forum; Industry Makes Its Case Against Proposed Treaty." *Washington Post,* December 4, 1997, p. A1.

"Utilities Backed New House Speaker with Hefty Campaign Contributions." *The Energy Report,* January 11, 1999, vol. 27, no. 2.

NATIONAL ASSOCIATION OF HOME BUILDERS

The National Association of Home Builders (NAHB) is a trade association representing 850 state and local builders associations, with a total of 195,000 members across the country. The NAHB's members include both home builders and remodelers, as well as people working in fields related to the housing industry.

Headquarters of the NAHB are in Washington, D.C., where it maintains a staff of more than 300. Calling itself "The Voice of America's Housing Industry," the NAHB says that its mission is "to enhance the climate for housing and the building industry, and to promote policies that will keep housing a national priority. Chief among [the] NAHB's goals is providing and expanding opportunities for all consumers to have safe, decent, and affordable housing." The NAHB's efforts include lobbying, research, analysis, and public relations on behalf of its members and the housing industry. It is also affiliated with two centers it sponsors: the NAHB National Research Center, Inc., which is devoted to research within the industry, and the Home Builders Institute, which develops educational and job-training programs. The association works with federal agencies to represent its industry in the formation of regulations regarding mortgage finance, codes, energy, and the environment.

The divisions of the NAHB are devoted to analyzing policy issues, representing the industry to the public, monitoring and improving the housing finance system, analyzing and forecasting economic and consumer trends, educating and training, and disseminating information to its members. The NAHB hosts an annual convention and exposition called the International Builders' Show.

The primary political action committee (PAC) of the NAHB is called the Build PAC of the National Association of Home Builders. Other affiliated PACs include the Colorado Association of Home Builders PAC, the Home Builders Association of Central Arizona PAC, and the Home Builders Association of Louisville PAC.

In addition to its lobbying efforts, NAHB is committed to the education of its membership. Recently, for instance, the NAHB has devoted itself to educating its members about the revised building codes and accessibility requirements of the Fair Housing Act. As NAHB president Charles Ruma stated, "[the] NAHB supports the Fair Housing Act and encourages members to comply with the accessibility provisions of the law." To this end it held training sessions across the country for its members.

The NAHB has also been committed to increasing environmental awareness within the industry. It publishes a series of informational fact sheets on topics related to environmentalism, and in 1999 it sponsored the National Green Building Conference—the first conference devoted to "environmentally friendly home building practices."

HISTORY

The NAHB was founded in 1942, at a time of enormous housing shortages caused by wartime defense industry relocation. At that time, home-building companies around the United States felt that their expanding industry needed a single voice in Washington to maintain private control over the home building industry at a time when the federal government was getting involved in all aspects of private industry. In addition the founders of the NAHB were looking to the future, trying to prepare the member companies for what it hoped would be—and what would turn out to be—a rapidly expanding market for inexpensive housing in the postwar era. To that end the organization backed various measures to promote first-home buying by returning GIs. Over the years the organization has backed most government initiatives that help finance mortgages. Thus, the NAHB has been both an advocate of government involvement in financing of home buying, while at the same time trying to ward off any interference in the

**National Association of Home Builders
Political Action Committee Contributions**

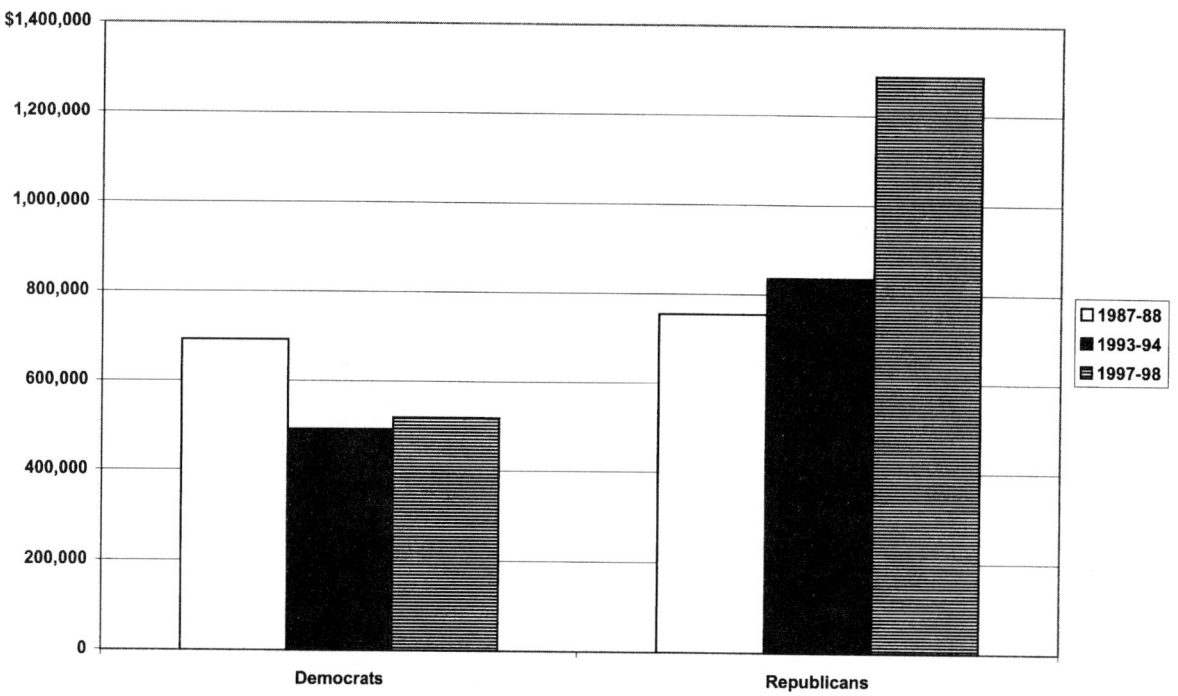

[Bar chart showing PAC contributions in dollars to Democrats and Republicans for three election cycles: 1987-88, 1993-94, and 1997-98. Democrats received approximately $690,000 (1987-88), $490,000 (1993-94), and $510,000 (1997-98). Republicans received approximately $740,000 (1987-88), $820,000 (1993-94), and $1,270,000 (1997-98).]

Data derived from official studies available from the Federal Election Commission, Washington, DC, 1987–1998.

industry itself. In 1981 the association joined with the rival National Association of Home Manufacturers. Six years later it absorbed the much smaller, but growing, North American Log Homes Council.

ACTIVITIES: CURRENT AND FUTURE

According to the NAHB, 15 percent of legislation introduced in Congress has a direct impact on the housing construction industry. The lobbying work of the NAHB focuses on issues affecting the industry, such as labor policy, mortgage-interest tax deductions, mortgage financing, and environmental issues. To that end the NAHB releases an annual agenda, written by its president, outlining its principles, activities, and goals; the 1999 edition is called "Preserving the American Dream: NAHB Agenda for 1999."

As part of its long-standing tradition of supporting government initiatives to make home buying more affordable for moderate-income persons, the NAHB has strongly backed the Department of Housing and Urban Development's newly proposed efforts to expand its Fannie Mae and Freddie Mac programs for subsidizing mortgage costs. In the summer of 1999 Charles Ruma announced a joint effort by the NAHB, the Clinton administration, and the U.S. Conference of Mayors to construct 1 million new homes in the inner cities and close-in suburbs over the next 10 years. "This is a significant step forward and should contribute greatly to the common goal embraced by government, housing finance organizations and NAHB and the building industry generally to expand home ownership to an even greater percentage of American households," Ruma said. The NAHB has also joined forces with Fannie Mae to encourage the development of more environmentally friendly housing. This includes housing that would be both more energy-efficient and closer to existing mass-transit lines. By building near such lines, the NAHB says, new home owners will use less energy to commute and will cause less pollution getting to and from work.

Still, all the talk of a greener home-building industry is not being advocated for purely altruistic reasons, say outside experts on the industry. Indeed, as the presidential candidacy of Democrat Al Gore shows, the subject of suburban sprawl is likely to become an increasingly contentious political issue in coming years. The NAHB has made it clear that it stands against antidevelopment measures at the local, state, or federal level—even to the extent of opposing any kind of incentives to prevent suburban sprawl.

To bolster its position, the NAHB conducted a survey in 1999 that found that most Americans still want to live in single-family homes in the suburbs and expected to continue driving to work alone, though they supported measures to halt suburban sprawl and increase public transportation. The NAHB advocates construction of more urban housing and more multi-dwelling units as well as more traditional housing. "It takes generations to change attitudes," says the secretary and vice president of the NAHB, Gary Garcyznski. "The one thing you never want to drop is choice."

The NAHB is also opposed to legislation for the protection of farmland and wetlands that are threatened by new home construction and suburban sprawl. According to Ruma, farm acreage is actually on the rise. As for wetlands, the organization argues that there are already adequate laws on the books, an argument that environmental organizations say is a misreading of the facts and the law.

FINANCIAL FACTS

The electoral arm of the NAHB—also known as Build PAC—has been a major contributor to the campaign coffers of presidential and congressional candidates of both the Democratic and Republican parties. However, over the past six election cycles there has been a general trend toward supporting Republicans over Democrats. Thus, in the 1987–1988 congressional and presidential election cycle, Build PAC gave $1,448,560 in contributions, with $755,885 (52 percent) going to Republican candidates and $692,675 (48 percent) going to Democrats. By the 1993–1994 Congress-only election cycle, fully $836,000 (63 percent) of its more than $1.3 million in total contributions went to Republican candidates, while just $491,799 (37 percent) went to Democrats. In the 1997–1998 Congress-only election cycle, the trend continued: Build PAC gave $1,807,240 to candidates of both parties, with $1,289,250 (71 percent) going to Republicans, and $517,990 (29 percent) going to Democrats.

JAMES CIMENT AND VIVIAN WAGNER

Bibliography

Anason, Dean. "The Lobbyists: 'One Helluva Fight' Over Thrift Charter." *The American Banker,* March 10, 1999, p. 2.

"Big Housing Guns Blast Ginnie Bill." *The Mortgage Marketplace,* March 29, 1999, vol. 22, no. 13, p. 1.

Brown, Steve. "Local-Growth Regulations, Labor Shortages Concern Home Builders." *The Dallas Morning News,* January 18, 1999.

Cleary, Mike. "Survey Finds Home Buyers Oppose Sprawl but Prefer Suburbs." *The Washington Times,* May 12, 1999.

"Congress Considers Family-Friendly Climate Change Bill; Alliance to Save Energy, Homes Coalition Urge Congress to Pass Home Energy Tax Credit." *PR Newswire,* June 23, 1999.

"Fannie and NAHB Strike Partnership." *National Mortgage News,* June 21, 1999.

"Fannie Mae Plays Political Cards with the Best of Them." *National Mortgage News,* May 10, 1999.

"Financing Product Tied to Green Building Criteria with Builders and Lenders." *PR Newswire,* June 10, 1999.

Hicks, Darryl. "Industry PACs Donate $10.8 Million." *National Mortgage News,* February 15, 1999.

"Home Builders Support Proposed Affordable Housing Goals." *PR Newswire,* July 29, 1999.

Ichniowski, Tom, and Sherie Winston. "Tax-Cut Bills Could Be Vehicles for Construction Breaks." *Engineering News-Record,* February 22, 1999, vol. 242, no. 8, p. 11.

McManus, Reed. "Taking It to the Streets; Al Gore's Plan to Battle Urban Sprawl." *Sierra,* May 1, 1999, vol. 84, no. 3, p. 22.

NATIONAL ASSOCIATION OF MANUFACTURERS

The National Association of Manufacturers (NAM) is a restricted national umbrella organization representing the U.S. manufacturing industry. It has 14,000 member companies throughout the country.

NAM says that its mission is "to enhance the competitiveness of manufacturers and improve living standards for working Americans by shaping a legislative and regulatory environment conducive to U.S. economic growth, and to increase understanding among policymakers, the media and the general public about the importance of manufacturing to America's economic strength." NAM has its headquarters in Washington, D.C., its national division office in Greenbelt, Maryland, its field headquarters in Arlington Heights, Illinois, and nine regional offices in cities across the country.

HISTORY

NAM was founded in January 1895 by a group of businessmen in Cincinnati, Ohio. It came into being during the 1890s depression, when struggling businesses were striving to find new markets for their products outside the United States.

The members of that original convention came up with these goals: "Retention and supply of home markets with U.S. products and extension of foreign trade; development of reciprocal trade relations between the U.S. and foreign governments; rehabilitation of the U.S. Merchant Marine; construction of a canal in Central America; and improvement and extension of U.S. waterways." At the first annual convention in Chicago in January 1896, the organization adopted the title National Association of Manufacturers of the United States of America. Although in its first incarnation NAM was an association of groups, it quickly evolved into an association for individual manufacturers.

Throughout its history it has been active in educational, advocacy, professional, and lobbying efforts. In the first two decades of its existence, it promoted trade overseas, and established education and advocacy programs on employee relations, intellectual property, vocational education, workplace safety, and fiscal responsibility. In 1917 it established the National Industrial Council and the National Safety Council.

During the 1930s and 1940s NAM was heavily involved in defense efforts. Before the Second World War started it formed the Committee on National Defense and Industrial Mobilization and during the war worked with the federal government to coordinate wartime production in plants throughout the country.

From the 1950s to the 1980s the association was involved in developing its public relations through new electronic media, advocating for labor legislation, documenting alleged union abuses of power, pressing for trade expansion, reforming the civil rights practices of its member companies, and providing training for undereducated workers. In 1974 NAM moved its headquarters from New York to Washington, D.C.

ACTIVITIES: CURRENT AND FUTURE

NAM lobbies Congress on almost every conceivable issue that might affect U.S. manufacturing interests, although much of its work involves trade issues, the environment, labor, and the legal climate. As far as trade is concerned, much of NAM's lobbying activity has focused on global economics and exports. Its position is that exports are vital to the livelihood of the U.S. manufacturing industry. In 1991 NAM helped the General Agreement on Tariffs and Trade negotiations along by sponsoring an international conference. It was also a major player in formulating the North American Free Trade Agreement and getting approval for China's "most favored nation" status. It still continues to push for fast-track legislation, whereby Congress would restrict itself to an up-or-down vote on any trade bill negotiated by the White House, rather than approving or rejecting specific provisions. On the environment NAM lobbied Congress diligently in 1998 and 1999 to pass legislation that would give industries credits for early action to reduce greenhouse gas emissions, retroactive to 1991. While critics argue that industry would receive an unfair windfall for things they had already done, NAM says that such a credit plan would provide an incentive for industry support for greenhouse legislation.

As for labor issues, NAM has been a consistent opponent of stronger rules governing workplace safety. In 1999 the organization lobbied hard against a proposed Occupational Safety and Health Administration ruling that would make all employers establish workplace safety and health programs. "If the ultimate goal is to make workplaces safer, OSHA should encourage employers' innovative and effective approaches to safety instead of imposing a one-size-fits-all standard," says Jennifer Krese, director of employment policy for NAM. But worker advocacy groups say that such rules are necessary precisely because many NAM members have not developed a safe and healthy working environment.

On legal issues, NAM has gone on record as seeking legislation that would limit large jury awards against industry, especially in the case of class action suits. It is pushing for congressional legislation—the so-called Interstate Class Action Jurisdiction Act—that would force more of these class action suits into federal courts. There, NAM hopes, it will be more difficult for plaintiffs and plaintiff attorneys to win such cases or even get them heard, since federal courts make it more difficult to press class action suits. "Litigation in federal court is the best way to end frivolous class action lawsuits because it will stop plaintiff lawyers from shopping for favorable forums," said Lawrence Fineran, assistant vice president for regulatory policy for NAM. Public interest groups argue that frivolous class action suits are adequately dismissed in state court and that legitimate class action lawsuits are the only way to keep industry honest.

Finally, aside from individual issues, NAM seeks to create a more business-friendly environment in Congress. In the early 1990s, for instance, it established an educational and research affiliate called the Manufacturing Institute, after research showed that "policymakers, congressional staff and others had an antiquated view of American industry and insufficient knowledge upon which to base sound policy choices." The Manufacturing Institute sends monthly mailings to Congress, performs research into trade and manufacturing policies and procedures, conducts public opinion polls, and produces books and CD-ROMs as educational and informational tools. It has also established the Center for Workforce Success, which among other things awards excellent workers within the manufacturing industry.

In addition, as part of its educational and advocacy effort NAM sponsors an annual National Manufacturing Week Expo in Chicago, as well as a Mexican Manufacturing Week. It has also formed the Small and Medium Manufacturers Initiative, which among other things distributes a monthly publication called *Just in Time,* and has been behind the creation of the President's Council on Small Manufacturers Action Committee.

FINANCIAL FACTS

Although it represents manufacturers that individually and collectively give enormous sums to the campaign coffers of congressional and presidential candidates of both parties, NAM itself does not have a political action committee (PAC) and does not donate sums either to political parties in the form of soft-money contributions or to candidates in the form of regular hard-money contributions. Overall the organization operates on a budget of roughly $20 million, much of it going for a variety of industry-supporting services, as well as for lobbying efforts.

JAMES CIMENT AND VIVIAN WAGNER

Bibliography

Baker, Gerard. "Big Labour, Big Fightback: Leaders of Trade Unions in the U.S. Believe They Have Started to Reverse a Generation of Decline." *Financial Times* (London), September 29, 1997, p. 19.

Bellinger, Robert, and George Leopold. "Industry Lauds H-1B Vote; Vows to Aid U.S. Education." *TechWeb News,* October 23, 1998.

Berlau, John. "Does Rule 'Blacklist' Business?" *Investor's Business Daily,* June 18, 1999, National Issue, p. A1.

Crow, Patrick. "EPA's Agenda." *The Oil and Gas Journal,* December 7, 1998, vol. 96, no. 49, p. 48.

Dunne, Nancy. "Washington Resumes Annual Battle over Trade." *Financial Times* (London), July 22, 1998, p. 4.

Karey, Gerald. "EPA Plots Appeal of Court Verdict on Ozone, Soot Regulations." *Platt's Oilgram News,* May 18, 1999, vol. 77, no. 94, p. 1.

"Litigation Reform Moves In House." *New Technology Week,* July 27, 1998, vol. 12, no. 30.

Love, Alice Ann. "Campaigns Under Way to Influence Social Security Debate." *Associated Press,* March 10, 1999.

MacMillan, Robert. "Lobbyists Fan the Senate's Y2K Flames." *Newsbytes,* June 8, 1999.

Pope, Carl. "Slugs and Dinosaurs: Why Some Industries Drag Their Feet." *Sierra,* September 19, 1997, vol. 82, no. 5, p. 14.

Porstner, Donna. "Manufacturers Spin Off Lobby for Taking Social Security Private." *The Washington Times,* July 21, 1998.

"Proposed OSHA Rule Deemed 'Unworkable'; Occupational Safety and Health Administration Rule Requiring Workplace Safety and Health Programs in All Companies." *Chemical Market Reporter,* August 2, 1999, vol. 256, no. 5, p. 24.

Przybyla, Heidi. "Business Groups to Lobby for China Deal." *Journal of Commerce,* March 30, 1999, p. 2A.

Salant, Jonathan. "Businesses, Trial Lawyers Square Off over Y2K." *Associated Press,* April 24, 1999.

Sidler, Stephen. "U.S. Manufacturers Call for Tax Cut as Fed Holds Interest Rates." *Financial Times* (London), December 23, 1998, p. 14.

Sissell, Kara. "Court Strikes Down OSHA Compliance Program." *Chemical Week,* April 21, 1999, p. 12.

Steelman, Aaron. "Are Trade Sanctions Worth It?" *Investor's Business Daily,* September 23, 1998, National Issue, p. A1.

Zuckerman, Amy. "Manufacturers Group Official Spending More Time Helping Members Cope with Standards." *Journal of Commerce,* October 15, 1997, p. 14C.

NATIONAL MINING ASSOCIATION

The National Mining Association (NMA) is the trade association representing the mining industry in the United States, with 550 coal and mining extraction companies as its members. It says that its membership includes "coal, metal and mineral hardrock mining operators, mineral processors, bulk transporters, mining equipment manufacturers, financial and engineering firms, and other businesses related to the mining industry."

Its headquarters are in Washington, D.C., and it has local offices in 42 states. The administration of the association is divided into the following offices: Office of the President, Administration and Finance, Government Affairs, Legal and Regulatory Affairs, Manufacturers and Services Division, Policy Analysis, Public and Constituent Relations, and Special Programs and Affiliates.

HISTORY

The NMA came into being in 1995 as the result of a merger between the National Coal Association, which was founded in 1917, and the American Mining Congress, which was founded in 1897. These two organizations were among the oldest trade groups in the United States. The merger of the two was effected to help further the interests of the mining industry as a whole, especially in the face of increasing environmentalist pressure. While the old National Coal Association's political action committee (PAC) would continue to operate, the NMA would organize a new PAC to represent the interests of the nonferrous mining industry.

ACTIVITIES: CURRENT AND FUTURE

The lobbying efforts of the NMA are led by its two PACs, CoalPAC and MinePAC. These groups, together with the NMA, are advocates for the mining industry. Much of their recent focus has been on counteracting the move to curtail mining on the grounds of environmental concerns. The NMA has worked against the Kyoto Protocol on Global Warming portions of the Clean Air Act, and new EPA regulator proposals, as well as environmentalist attempts to ban mountaintop mining.

Since it represents the industry and not the workers, it remains at a distance from the union representing miners—the United Mine Workers of America—though in a recent statement the NMA president and CEO Richard L. Lawson said, "The National Mining Association supports the United Mine Workers of America in its endeavors to draw public, political and media focus to issues that require greater attention, including overzealous environmental policies that threaten the very existence of the nation's coal industry."

About the political climate facing mining in the 1990s, the NMA says that "few, if any, industries can surpass mining for the quantity, diversity and complexity of issues faced in the legislative and regulatory arena of Washington, D.C. In the nation's capital during 1997, the industry once again confronted an almost daunting array of challenges, whose sources can ultimately be traced to groups and individuals dedicated to precluding mining activity in the United States."

Its response, it says, has been to react "with a focused but comprehensive government and regulatory affairs effort, aimed not only at immediate response to specific activities in Congress and the regulatory agencies, but also at the longer term goal of educating target audiences that 'everything begins with mining.'"

Specifically, the NMA has focused its lobbying attention in recent years on several key issues affecting the industry, most of which have to do with environmental regulations. It has backed Senate moves to block an Interior Department decision to limit a single five-acre mill site for each lode claim on public lands, preferring instead to have more access to land. NMA lobbyists have also been active in the ongoing struggle over mine noise

**National Mining Association
Political Action Committee Contributions**

Data derived from official studies available from the Federal Election Commission, Washington, DC, 1987–1998.

regulations. In addition, the organization has been challenging the Environmental Protection Agency's (EPA) authority to regulate carbon dioxide emissions. Citing an NMA-sponsored legal study, organization president Richard Lawson said, "There is no authority in the Clean Air Act (CAA) for EPA to regulate carbon dioxide, and the sections of the CAA cited by EPA's general counsel are not 'potentially applicable to carbon dioxide.'"

Finally, the NMA has been fighting the Office of Surface Mining's (OSM) recent decision on new ownership and control rules in the coal mining industry. These rules, enforced under the OSM's application violator system, can be used to prevent coal operators with past environmental and labor violations from getting new permits until and unless those old violations have been settled.

FINANCIAL FACTS

While the NMA is in the process of developing a PAC to provide contributions to congressional and presidential candidates from the nonferrous mining industry, the coal industry PAC—or CoalPAC—has been a longtime participant in the political process. Indeed, CoalPAC has seen its contributions to candidates climb over 60 percent between the 1987–1988 and 1997–1998 election cycles. In the former it gave $101,750 to presidential and congressional candidates, while in the latter it donated $164,575 to congressional candidates only.

Reflecting the fact that Republicans are less active in the push for expanded environmental regulations, CoalPAC has given the majority of its donations to candidates from that party, especially in the last few years. In the 1987–1988 election cycle, for instance, CoalPAC gave $55,100 (54 percent of its contributions) to Republicans. Ten years later, in the 1997–1998 cycle, CoalPAC gave $148,075 (90 percent of its donations) to Republican congressional candidates.

JAMES CIMENT AND VIVIAN WAGNER

Bibliography

Bourge, Christian. "Battle Lines Drawn on Mine Noise Proposals." *American Metal Market,* May 31, 1999, vol. 107, no. 104, p. 6.

"Coal Challenges EPA on CO2 Authority." *The Electronic Daily,* October 30, 1998, vol. 11, no. 85.

"Coal Industry Airs Views at Global Warming Hearing." *Coal Week,* June 29, 1998.

Kertes, Noella. "Mining Joins R&D Initiative." *American Metal Market,* October 13, 1997, vol. 105, no. 198, p. 4.

———. "NMA Alleges Assault by Federal Agencies." *American Metal Market,* April 10, 1998, vol. 106, no. 68, p. 2.

———. "NMA Urges Speed-Up of Environmental Process." *American Metal Market,* March 24, 1998, vol. 106, no. 55, p. 8.

"Latest Air Standards Push Limits of Clean Air Act, Mining Chief Says." *Alaska Journal of Commerce,* August 18, 1997, vol. 21, no. 33, p. 12.

Lobsenz, George. "Utilities, Coal Groups Float NOx Control Proposal." *The Energy Daily,* February 3, 1998.

Sanda, Arthur. "NMA Becoming a Force in Washington." *Coal Age,* September 1997, p. 37.

NUCLEAR ENERGY INSTITUTE

The Nuclear Energy Institute (NEI) is an organization representing approximately 300 members, both in the United States and throughout the world, involved in various aspects of the nuclear energy industry. Its headquarters are located in Washington, D.C. A 60-member board of directors, which includes representatives from a cross-section of the industry, governs the institute. A 15-member executive committee oversees its business and policy affairs.

Members of the NEI include, it says, "companies that operate nuclear energy plants in the U.S. and abroad, nuclear plant designers, architect and engineering firms, nuclear fuel suppliers, radiopharmaceutical manufacturers, law firms, consulting firms, labor unions, universities and research laboratories." The NEI claims that its members "share a commitment to maintain nuclear energy as an option for the U.S. and the world—now and in the years to come."

HISTORY

The NEI was created in 1994 as the result of a merger of the American Nuclear Energy Council, the industry's congressional lobby; the Nuclear Management and Resources Council, the industry's representative before the Nuclear Regulatory Commission (NRC); the U.S. Council for Energy Awareness, the industry's public relations arm; and the nuclear power division of the Edison Electric Institute (EEI), which dealt with such technical issues as high- and low-level radioactive waste, advanced reactor development, and the extension of operating licenses on existing plants. While the merger did not change any of these activities, industry leaders believed that, faced with ongoing environmental challenges, they needed a single organizational voice to represent and further the interests of the nuclear power–generating industry.

ACTIVITIES: CURRENT AND FUTURE

As the main interest group for what is arguably the most regulated and scrutinized industry in the United States, the NEI lobbies vigorously both to shape and reduce regulations issued by the NRC and other government agencies. Among its recent priorities, the NEI has filed petitions with the NRC to "risk-inform" the regulations governing commercial reactors. As one industry monitor explained, "risk-informing the regulations means that the definition of key terms in the regulations, such as the term safety-related, would be redefined to include only equipment and procedures which statistical analysis or probabilistic risk data, tempered by experience and judgment, show are important to safety." The effect of such a change, says an industry observer, "could be the most sweeping and dramatic changes to NRC regulation since its inception." Critics say it would be highly risky and would provide a financial windfall to the industry. Indeed, by some of the industry's own predictions, such a change in the regulations would cut 10 to 15 percent off the cost of running a nuclear power plant.

Similarly, the NEI has been an active proponent of the Clinton administration's efforts to deregulate the utility industry. But the NEI has made it clear that it does not want nuclear power plants to suffer in the transition to a deregulated utility industry. It says amendments to the 1954 Atomic Energy Act and the tax code are needed to protect the nuclear sector of the nation's electricity-producing industry. Concerning the former, it wants provisions of the Atomic Energy Act that ban foreign ownership of nuclear power plants and that require antitrust reviews during proceedings for plant license transfers to be dropped. The NEI would also like legislation that allows the industry to charge consumers a fee for the decommissioning of nuclear power plants, closed either because of age or environmental concerns.

**Nuclear Energy Institute
Political Action Committee Contributions**

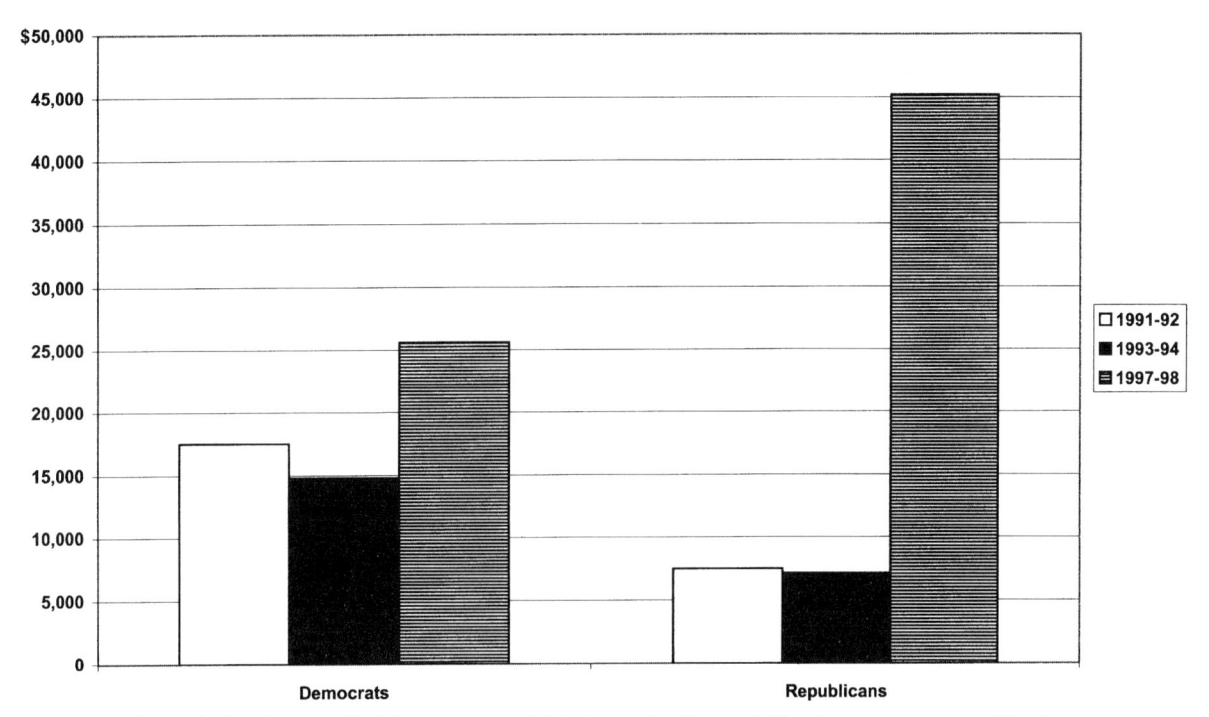

[Bar chart showing PAC contributions to Democrats and Republicans for election cycles 1991-92, 1993-94, and 1997-98. Democrats: ~$17,500 (1991-92), ~$15,000 (1993-94), ~$25,750 (1997-98). Republicans: ~$7,500 (1991-92), ~$7,500 (1993-94), ~$45,500 (1997-98).]

Data derived from official studies available from the Federal Election Commission, Washington, DC, 1991–1998.

As recent decommissionings indicate, these costs can be enormous, and a number of consumer and public interest groups strongly oppose such fees.

Along with decommissioning, the most contentious environmental issue facing the nuclear industry is waste. In terms of specific legislation reviewed by the NEI, it supports reforms in the federal management of used nuclear fuel that would ensure federal acceptance of used fuel and consolidate waste at over 100 commercial nuclear power plants in 40 states. The NEI has also been pushing the federal government to increase funding and speed up construction of the national nuclear waste storage facility at Yucca Mountain, Nevada. Geologic studies of the site—indicating recent tectonic activity and water seepage—have led environmental groups to seek further study of the site as a safe receptacle for the nation's nuclear waste or to end the project altogether.

The NEI has also been following state legislation regarding the shipment and transportation of nuclear fuel and waste through states. It supports some of this legislation insofar as it prepares states to deal with interstate transportation issues. It is against other legislation, however, since, as it says, it creates "procedural roadblocks to make shipments difficult, if not impossible."

FINANCIAL FACTS

By the standards of the manufacturing sector generally, the NEI's political action committee (PAC) has contributed modest amounts to presidential and congressional candidates of both major political parties, though the total have risen somewhat dramatically in the past decade. While the NEI gave $25,053 to presidential and congressional candidates in the 1991–1992 election cycle, that figure had risen to $70,819 by the 1997–1998 election cycle. The increase is even more dramatic because the latter cycle involved a Congress-only election, typically a cycle in which donations go down. Over the same years the proportion of campaign contributions going to Republican candidates has increased significantly. While just $7,505 (30 percent) went to Republican congressional and presidential candidates in the 1991–1992 election cycle, fully $45,195 (64 percent) went to Republican congressional candidates in the 1997–1998 election cycle.

JAMES CIMENT AND VIVIAN WAGNER

Bibliography

Airozo, Dave. "NEIPAC Pre-Election Spending Adds $14,000 to Contributions." *Nucleonics Week,* January 7, 1999, vol. 40, no. 1, p. 13.

———. "Nuclear Industry Election Giving Creates a Tangled Trail of PACs." *Nucleonics Week,* August 20, 1998, vol. 39, no. 34, p. 1.

Barber, Wayne. "Nader Group Attacks NEI Ads with 'Greenwashing' Claim to FTC." *Nucleonics Week,* June 10, 1999, vol. 40, no. 23, p. 15.

Cohn, Steve. *Too Cheap to Meter: An Economic and Philosophical Analysis of the Nuclear Dream.* Albany: State University of New York Press, 1997.

Holm, Erik. "NEI Calls for Overhaul of NRC Enforcement Policy." *The Energy Daily,* July 6, 1998.

Jasper, James. *Nuclear Politics: Energy and the State in the United States, Sweden, and France.* Princeton, NJ: Princeton University Press, 1990.

Kauzlarich, David. *Crimes of the American Nuclear State: At Home and Abroad.* Boston: Northeastern University Press, 1998.

MacMillan, Robert. "Some Nuclear Plants Still Not Y2K-Compliant." *Newsbytes,* July 7, 1999.

Ryan, Margaret L. "Actions Favoring NEI Raising Fairness Questions in Industry." *Inside N.R.C.,* May 24, 1999, vol. 21, no. 11, p. 1.

Weil, Jenny. "NEI Calls for Legislative Fixes to Help Industry Be Competitive." *Inside N.R.C.,* December 21, 1998, vol. 20, no. 26, p. 13.

PHARMACEUTICAL RESEARCH AND MANUFACTURERS OF AMERICA

The Pharmaceutical Research and Manufacturers of America (PhRMA) is a trade organization that represents approximately 100 U.S. companies that are primarily involved in pharmaceutical research and manufacturing. In its literature the PhRMA claims that the organization's mission involves "discovering, developing and bringing to market medicines that improve our health and quality of life—as well as reduce the overall cost of health care."

The PhRMA is divided into several committees: an executive committee that provides overall policy and runs the day-to-day operations of the organization, a nomination and compensation committee that deals with new membership and dues scheduling, a finance committee with oversight on budgets, an alliance committee that attempts to establish connections with other interest groups working in the fields related to pharmaceutical research and manufacturing, a communications committee responsible for press relations and outreach to the public, a Food and Drug Administration (FDA) committee that focuses on the relationship between the PhRMA and the federal regulatory agency most involved in the pharmaceutical industry, and an international committee that maintains relationships with other pharmaceutical groups and companies around the world. The organization also runs a philanthropic foundation that, in the PhRMA's words, "is dedicated to enhancing public health through biomedical technology and pharmaceutical scientific research."

Headquartered in Washington, D.C., the PhRMA also maintains offices in Albany, New York; Sacramento, California; and Minneapolis, Minnesota. All three states are homes to major pharmaceutical industries. In addition, the PhRMA has two international offices: in Brussels, home to most of the agencies of the European Union, and in Tokyo.

ACTIVITIES: CURRENT AND FUTURE

At the top of the current issue agenda for the PhRMA is the Clinton administration's plan to offer new prescription coverage to all 39 million elderly and disabled Medicare beneficiaries. The PhRMA does not oppose such an initiative but is strongly against the attempt to impose price controls on the industry as part of the move to include pharmaceuticals under Medicare. According to the PhRMA, price caps would result in less money being spent on research into drugs that can aid the elderly. "Profits attract investment," PhRMA president Alan Holmer, is on record as saying, noting that investments pay for research into new drugs. If companies can't make enough money from selling drugs to the elderly, they'll cease developing new ones.

Lawmakers who want to add the drug benefit to Medicare say the pharmaceutical industry is trying to terrify the elderly through an extensive newspaper advertising campaign—and thereby pressure Congress. "What you have here is an extremely greedy and profitable industry that is ripping off the American people big time and using its profits to put extraordinary pressure on Congress, through campaign contributions to both parties, not to move forward to protect American consumers," says Independent Vermont Representative Bernard Sanders.

On a connected issue the PhRMA is working actively to block Medicaid drug restrictions, specifically an initiative by some states' Medicaid agencies that demand "prior authorization" of drugs. (Medicaid, as opposed to Medicare, is a federal program, administered through the states, which provides medical care for the poor.) According to the PhRMA, the "newest and most effective drugs"—and the most expensive—often are on the "prior authorization" list of drugs issued by state Medicaid agencies.

Because all of the products researched and manufactured by its member companies must meet the approval of the Federal Drug Administration (FDA), the PhRMA has actively lobbied Congress to make that approval process easier and faster. According to most observers of the industry, PhRMA lobbying was critical in the passage of the 1997 Food and Drug Administration Modernization Act (FDAMA), which was designed to bring new medications onto the market faster, supposedly without lowering safety standards. But according to PhRMA officials, the FDA has been slow in implementing the changes called for in the law, particularly in the area of providing incentives for research and testing of drugs for children. The agency has also been slow, says the PhRMA, in speeding up the dissemination of scientific and healthcare information concerning new pharmaceuticals to doctors and other healthcare providers.

"In enacting FDAMA Congress did more than just streamline the drug discovery, development and approval process," says PhRMA president Holmer. "It also helped create an environment that encourages research that will result in more new cures and therapies to help those with unmet medical needs." Public interest groups and consumer activists, however, say that the recent spate of incidents in which medications were removed from the market due to health concerns reflects a policy of speeded-up new drug approvals.

Disagreeing with such criticism, the PhRMA is going one step further, lobbying for new fast-track approaches to meeting post-approval requirements. The PhRMA would like to fast-track drugs that have the potential to address "unmet medicinal needs," especially if the "product . . . shows the potential to provide some meaningful therapeutic benefit to patients over existing treatments."

On a different research issue the PhRMA has been actively lobbying Congress not to prohibit cloning technologies that could prevent potential cures from being developed. The PhRMA says that bans on cloning are unnecessary because unethical cloning practices are already prohibited by the FDA.

Finally, on advertising and marketing, the PhRMA has been asking Congress to stop the FDA from issuing new rules on the dissemination of off-label information for marketing drugs. (Off-label information dissemination refers to any advertisement in the press or on broadcast media that provides information to health providers or consumers about a prescription drug.) According to the PhRMA, the FDA "is confusing promotion and dissemination [of information]" and misreading what Congress wrote into the law, taking its regulatory function further than lawmakers intended as far as controlling drug advertising is concerned.

FINANCIAL FACTS

The PhRMA has been a modest contributor to congressional and presidential campaigns in the 1990s, at least by the standards of manufacturers. In each of the three election cycles from 1993–1994 to 1997–1998 the PhRMA has donated approximately $40,000 to candidates of both the Democratic and Republican parties. The peak cycle was 1995–1996—a presidential as well as congressional election—when the PhRMA gave $43,152. Over the years the amount given to Democratic candidates has declined while the amount given to Republicans has risen. For example, in the 1993–1994 election cycle Democrats received $19,306 (52 percent) of a total of $36,993 donated to both parties. By 1997–1998 Republicans were receiving the majority of campaign funds from the PhRMA, $24,367 (64 percent) out of a total of $38,167 donated to all candidates.

JAMES CIMENT AND VIVIAN WAGNER

Bibliography

Bastra, Lisa. *Searching for the Magic Bullets: Orphan Drugs, Consumer Activism, and the Pharmaceutical Development.* New York: Pharmaceutical Products Press, 1994.

Danzon, Patricia. *Pharmaceutical Price Regulation: National Policy Versus Global Interests.* Washington, DC: American Enterprise Institute Press, 1997.

Dickinson, James G. "Off-Label Uses: Tiny Concession Splits Industry; Pharmaceutical Industry." *Medical Marketing & Media,* November 1997, vol. 32, no. 11, p. 12.

Drake, Donald. *Making Medicine, Making Money.* Kansas City, MO: Andrews and McNeel, 1993.

Fincham, Jack, and Albert Wertheimer, eds. *Pharmacy and the U.S. Health Care System.* New York: Pharmaceutical Products Press, 1998.

Hess, Glenn. "PhRMA Takes a Wait-and-See Approach to a Medicare Prescription Drug Plan." *Chemical Market Reporter,* July 5, 1999, vol. 256, no. 1, p. 1.

Schweitzer, Stuart. *Pharmaceutical Economics and Policy.* New York: Oxford University Press, 1997.

Wechsler, Jill. "FDA Faces 'Modernization'; FDA to Reform Following Congress Approval of Its Modernization Act of 1997." *BioPharm,* January 1998, p. 10.

Whitmore, Elaine. *Product Development Planning for Health Care Products Deregulated by the FDA.* Milwaukee: ASQC Quality Press, 1997.

PRINTING INDUSTRIES OF AMERICA

Printing Industries of America, Inc. (PIA) is the largest trade association representing the graphic arts industry. Its headquarters are in Alexandria, Virginia.

PIA represents over 14,000 member companies, which belong to the association via 30 regional affiliate organizations in the United States, by joining the Canadian Printing Industries Association or—in the case of international, non–North American companies—by joining directly. Its members include commercial printers, graphic arts firms, equipment manufacturers, and suppliers. PIA says that its mission is to promote "programs, services, and an environment that help its members operate profitably."

In addition to its primary association, PIA sponsors groups that focus on specialized concerns and fields within the industry. These include the Graphic Communications Association, Web Offset Association, Web Printing Association, Graphic Arts Marketing Information Service, International Thermographers Association, Label Printing Industries of America, and Binding Industries of America. It also recently announced a consolidation with the Graphic Arts Technical Foundation. In addition to advocating for its member companies in the realm of governmental and legislative affairs, PIA also sponsors and organizes research, management education, and technological information for its members.

HISTORY

PIA, one of the oldest trade organizations in the country, was founded in 1887. Originally consisting of 22 printing associations in Chicago, it was formed to fight union requests for a nine-hour workday for printing industry workers. At the organizing convention the members passed two strong resolutions on the labor question: the first read that the organization would "henceforth not tolerate control of their employees by any Trades' Union, to the exclusion of workmen who are not members of such unions"; the second said "that in the event of any office connected with this organization being compelled to meet a strike, we individually bind ourselves to render them all the moral and material aid within our power." In the years since, PIA has developed two divisions to deal with labor issues. The Graphic Arts Employers of America works with printing companies that have union shops, while the Master Printers of America serves open-shop, or nonunion, printing companies. The latter division was founded in 1945. Labor relations continue to play an important role in the activities of PIA, with the two labor divisions receiving nearly 50 percent of the dues collected from PIA affiliates.

ACTIVITIES: CURRENT AND FUTURE

Some of the general issues of concern for PIA lobbyists include taxes, labor/job safety, environmental issues, healthcare, copyright concerns, and free trade. On the tax front, PIA supports the repeal or reform of the Alternative Minimum Tax (AMT), because of its impact on small printing businesses. It wants it to be eliminated so "the industry can again realize the full value of their adjustable and tax preferences without penalty." PIA supports recent legislation calling for capital gain, tax relief, and the total repeal of estate taxes. PIA also favors abolishing the tax code and replacing it with a flat tax. This latter position was formed in direct response to a survey of PIA members in 1998 that revealed that 87 percent of its members supported abolishing the tax code—41 percent in favor of a flat tax and 40 percent in favor of some combination of a flat tax and a sales tax.

PIA is actively involved in following legislation af-

**Printing Industries of America
Political Action Committee Contributions**

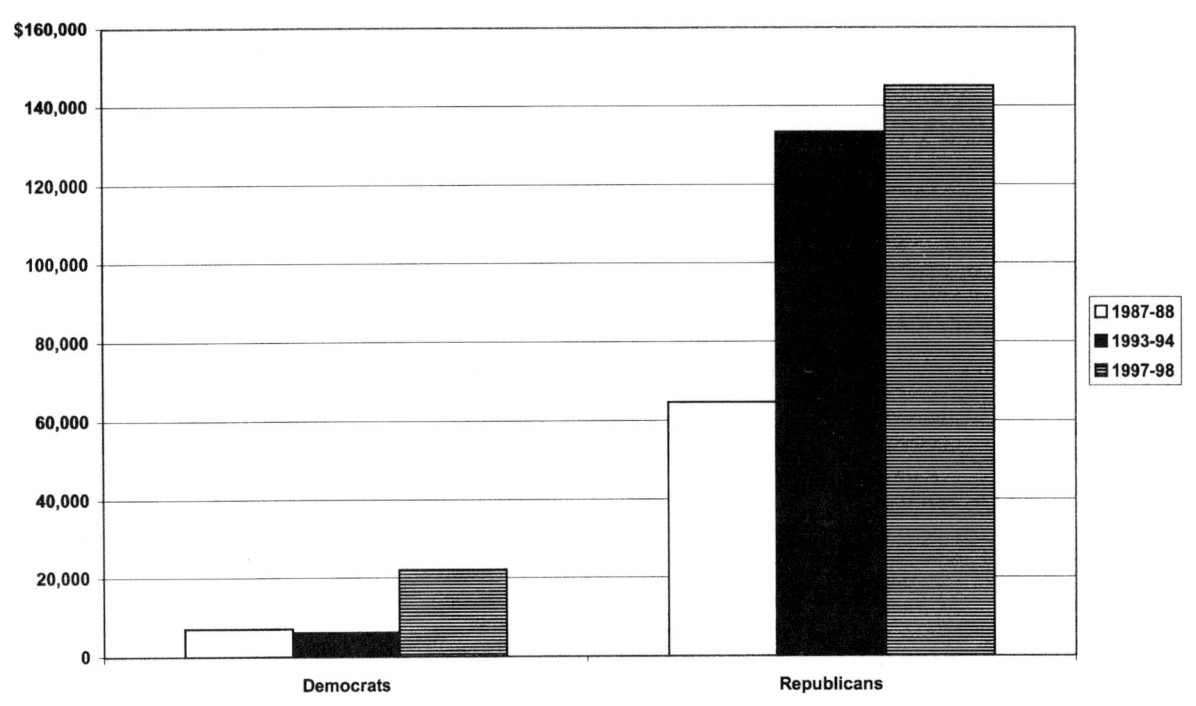

[Bar chart showing PAC contributions to Democrats and Republicans for election cycles 1987-88, 1993-94, and 1997-98. Democrats received approximately $7,000 (1987-88), $6,000 (1993-94), and $22,000 (1997-98). Republicans received approximately $65,000 (1987-88), $135,000 (1993-94), and $145,000 (1997-98).]

Data derived from official studies available from the Federal Election Commission, Washington, DC, 1987–1998.

fecting the health and safety of printing industry workers. One recent ruling by the Occupational Safety and Health Administration, which would require employers to have written safety and health programs, was not supported by PIA because the association prefers voluntary programs aimed at the needs of specific industries. PIA is not supportive of general safety rules. Thus, it says it will oppose the new rule and will lobby Capitol Hill to block its implementation. On the copyright front PIA is supportive of the Digital Millennium Copyright Act of 1998, which manages and protects Internet copyrights.

FINANCIAL FACTS

PIA's political action committee (PAC)—PRINT-PAC—has been a major contributor of campaign funds to congressional and presidential candidates over the past 10 years. Indeed, overall contributions to candidates' campaigns have climbed from $71,733 in the 1987–1988 election cycle to $166,100 in the 1997–1998 cycle. This increase is even more significant in light of the fact that 1987–1988 was a cycle that involved both a presidential and congressional election—which generally brings in more donations—while 1997–1998 was a Congress-only election cycle.

At the same time, PRINTPAC has given the majority of its campaign donations to Republican candidates for president and Congress. In 1987–1988 PIA gave $64,623 (90 percent) of its donations to Republicans. Ten years later it gave just below 90 percent to Republican candidates.

An interesting aspect about PRINTPAC's donation strategy has been its traditional focus on nonincumbent candidates. Over the years it has led the business community in the support of such candidates for the House and Senate. Typically, it has supported 90 to 100 House candidates and 20 to 25 Senate candidates. Recently, however, PRINTPAC has announced that its strategy is changing. Beginning in the 1995–1996 election cycle and continuing through today, PIA says it will be focusing its support more narrowly, on only about 20 to 25 House members, in order, it says, to build close relationships with a few key legislators who can themselves develop a better understanding and knowledge of the needs of the printing industry.

JAMES CIMENT AND VIVIAN WAGNER

Bibliography

Cross, Lisa. "Tax Reform Promises Printers a Break; Effects of the 1997 Tax Bill on the Printing Industry." *Graphic Arts Monthly,* September 1997, vol. 69, no. 9, p. 79.

Environmental Protection Agency. *Profile of the Printing Industry.* Washington: Office of Enforcement and Compliance Assurance, U.S. Environmental Protection Agency, 1995.

Foster, Andrea. "House Passes MSDS Bill." *Chemical Week,* August 12, 1998.

"Printing Industry Supports Moratorium on EPA's National Air Quality Standards; Printing Industry Representatives Deliver Letters Which Oppose the New National Ambient Air Quality Standards." *Printing News East,* December 8, 1997, p. 6.

Simonsis, Yolanda. "Is There a Kinder and Gentler OSHA?" *Paper, Film & Foil Converter,* November 1998, vol. 72, no. 11, p. 6.

SEMICONDUCTOR INDUSTRY ASSOCIATION

The Semiconductor Industry Association (SIA) is the primary trade organization representing the computer chip industry, and is based in San Jose, California. Its 70 member companies are responsible for 90 percent of U.S. semiconductor production, including the manufacturer of integrated circuits, microprocessors, and discrete components. Altogether, the semiconductor industry employs more than 260,000 people in the United States.

The SIA says that its mission is "to provide leadership for U.S. chip manufacturers on the critical issues of trade, technology, environmental protection and worker safety and health." The stated goals of the SIA are as follows: to achieve "free and open markets world wide, maintain U.S. leadership in technology, drive state-of-the-art programs to protect the environment and provide safe working conditions, and to maintain our top ranking in worldwide market share."

The committees of the SIA include Communications, Environmental, Facilities and Building Standards, Law, Occupational Health, Technology, Trade and Public Policy, and Trade Statistics. In addition to its governmental relations and lobbying efforts, the SIA maintains statistics for the semiconductor industry. It is also affiliated with the Semiconductor Research Corporation and SEMATECH, both of which are research organizations.

HISTORY

The SIA was founded in 1977 by five businessmen in the field of microelectronics: Robert Noyce of Intel Corporation, Wilfred Corrigan of LSI Logic Corporation, Charles Sporck of National Semiconductor Corporation, W. J. Sanders III of Advanced Micro Devices, Inc., and John Welty of Motorola, Inc. It was founded largely as a way to focus the industry's attention on environmental issues. Over the years it has become more of a traditional trade association, lobbying the federal government on issues of concern to American semiconductor manufacturers. Because of the highly competitive global nature of the semiconductor business, the SIA has become much more focused on trade issues over the past two decades.

In 1982 the SIA formed the Semiconductor Research Corporation, which had two goals: sponsoring initiatives to provide the qualified technical personnel that the industry needs, and developing long-range technological research strategies for the industry. Five years later the SIA established an independently operated corporation called SEMATECH, with the objective of conducting technology development. At the same time, the SIA created the Semiconductor Technology Roadmap (STR). Utilizing technical contributors from industry, academe, and government, the STR was designed to coordinate the activities of the two research arms of the SIA and to develop better working relations with government and universities.

ACTIVITIES: CURRENT AND FUTURE

Trade is a key issue for the SIA. Indeed, there is a continuing tension within the semiconductor industry between competition and cooperation among the U.S. and the global semiconductor industries, and the SIA's work with the STR and other initiatives is aimed at easing this tension. The SIA has predicted that the United States will be the largest market for semiconductors over the next four years, and it currently represents about one-third of worldwide chip revenues. But the Asia-Pacific, non-Japan market will most likely emerge as the second-largest worldwide chip market, after it gets over the Asian economic crisis. And Europe will be a key player in the semiconductor market as well. The SIA forecast that global semiconductor sales would rise 12.1 percent during 1999, making it the first year of double-digit growth since 1995. Chip sales worldwide were expected to reach $140.8 billion during 1999 and rise 15.4 percent to $162.5 billion in 2000. Much of the growth of the market worldwide has been fueled by the phenomenal growth of the Internet, which does not appear to be slowing and will remain a major factor in SIA strategies.

In general the SIA supports free trade and has lobbied the Clinton administration to push for an end to trade barriers during upcoming World Trade Organization (WTO) negotiations. In particular, it wants U.S. trade officials to get China to adopt new, more open trade arrangements on semiconductors. Darryl Hatano, the SIA's vice president of international affairs, recently told Congress that member companies of the SIA are struggling with curbs on direct sales to foreign customers—often hampered by U.S. national security issues—as well as with various "buy national" campaigns in countries with state-owned enterprises.

At the same time, the SIA is asking that U.S. trade negotiators not agree to South Korean and Japanese government attempts to weaken antidumping procedures with the WTO. Dumping involves the selling of semiconductors at below-cost prices in order to protect national industries and local jobs. Both the Korean and Japanese governments insist that companies in their countries do not engage in dumping practices.

Other matters of concern to the industry are immigration and Y2K problems. The SIA would like to have the United States modify its immigration regulations to allow an influx of high-tech workers. A strong economy, a lack of properly trained domestic workers, and Y2K pressures have led to a desperate shortage of high-skilled workers. Unions are opposed to these changes, saying that the industry should train more American workers rather than seek out high-skilled foreign workers who are willing to work for less. On the Y2K question the semiconductor industry pushed hard for legislation that would limit the liability of industry for damages caused by the so-called millennium bug. The Year 2000 Readiness and Responsibility Act and the Year 2000 Fairness and Responsibility Act encourage businesses to address Y2K issues by protecting those who mobilize prompt, good-faith efforts to make applications millennium-proof. The SIA, along with the semiconductor industry as a whole, boasts of strong support for environmental measures. And, indeed, it has worked with the World Semiconductor Council to come up with the goal of reducing emissions of perfluorocompounds (PFCs) to 10 percent below 1995 levels by the year 2010.

Other public policy priorities of the SIA for 1999 include supporting a reformed version of the International Monetary Fund (IMF) financial assistance package for Asia and working with the U.S. High-Tech Industry Coalition on China. Its technology priorities include ensuring a U.S.-based semiconductor capability, ensuring manufacturing excellence through cooperation, maintaining high standards for semiconductor research within the United States, and supporting tax depreciation reform. In addition the SIA would like to see more tax relief for companies with heavy research and development costs.

FINANCIAL FACTS

Although it represents manufacturers that individually and collectively give enormous sums to the campaign coffers of congressional and presidential candidates of both parties, the SIA itself does not have a political action committee (PAC) and does not donate sums either to political parties in the form of soft-money contributions or to candidates in the form of regular hard-money contributions. The annual budget of the SIA is approximately $4.4 million.

JAMES CIMENT AND VIVIAN WAGNER

Bibliography

Angel, David P. *Restructuring for Innovation: The Remaking of the U.S. Semiconductor Industry.* New York: Guilford, 1994.

Haavind, Robert. "Is the Roadmap Losing Its Effectiveness? Semiconductor Industry Association's Technology Roadmap." *Solid State Technology,* February 1, 1999, vol. 42, no. 2, p. 12.

MacMillan, Robert. "Govt Helps Create Chip Fund." *Newsbytes,* December 10, 1998.

Niccolai, James. "Chip Industry Distances Itself from Y2K Issue. *InfoWorld Electric,* December 4, 1998.

Quinlan, Tom. "Chip Industry, U.S. Government Commit to Research Effort." *San Jose Mercury News,* December 10, 1998.

Robertson, Jack. "SIA Praises Clinton's Trade Extension for China." *Electronic Buyers' News,* June 4, 1999.

———. "SIA to Congress: Scrap Trade Barriers." *Electronic Buyers' News,* August 9, 1999.

———. "SIA Warns Congress About Anti-Dumping." *Electronic Buyers' News,* August 5, 1999.

Semiconductor Industry Association. *Status Report & Industry Directory.* Cupertino, CA: The Association, 1997–98.

TECHNOLOGY NETWORK

The Technology Network (TechNet) is a national political organization representing over 140 high-technology industry leaders, with members ranging from the CEOs of a variety of small and large corporations to capital firms, investment banks, and law firms. Its headquarters are in Palo Alto, California.

TechNet says that it was formed "to help build bipartisan support for policies aimed at strengthening American leadership of the New Economy . . . [and that it has] experienced significant success in facilitating dialogues between business leaders and policy makers, educating lawmakers of the value about specific, tech-related legislation and broadening its membership." It is the first group devoted to helping high-tech industry executives establish working relationships with the nation's political leaders.

TechNet seeks to spread its influence through meeting with leading politicians, advocating public issues that will help to grow the New Economy—shorthand for an economy led by technology stocks and companies—form alliances with other technology organizations and leaders, and give financial support to political candidates. The technology industry as a whole has until recently been more focused on its own research agendas than on politics but, with the emergence of TechNet, this will likely change. Though in its infancy in 1999, TechNet is poised to become a major player in the political arena in the years to come.

HISTORY

TechNet was founded in July 1997 as the first industry-wide organization representing the interests of a variety of technology businesses, manufacturers, and researchers. The organization came about as many members of the computer and Internet industry realized that they had no real, unified voice in Washington that would speak to the interests of the burgeoning high-tech industry. Those who study the high-tech world of software development and the Internet say that with an industry largely composed of young entrepreneurs with little interest in politics and a strong penchant for free market values, it took a number of years for the realization to sink in that such a voice was needed in Washington. The formation of TechNet, say many experts on Washington interest groups, reflects the growing power of the Internet and software industries in the United States and their realization that they must work with government—particularly on trade and software piracy issues—if they want to maintain their global dominance.

ACTIVITIES: CURRENT AND FUTURE

During 1998 TechNet successfully promoted the Uniform National Standards for Securities Litigation, which makes it more difficult for investors to file class action securities fraud suits against public companies. Its support for this legislation took the form of leading a coalition of industry leaders that ultimately achieved wide bipartisan support for the bill in Congress. TechNet has also supported legislation to raise the cap on H-1B visas for skilled workers, assisting Republican Senator Spencer Abraham of Michigan and other legislators to work up a compromise bill for what had seemed doomed legislation. It also threw its energies and power behind the Charter Public Schools Legislation in California. TechNet helped to get legislation passed that will expand the number of charter schools in the state and give parents more control over their children's schools. The group plans to continue such involvement in social and educational issues. TechNet's first year was also spent building relationships between high-ranking technology executives and politicians, and this work will most likely be a primary focus in future years as well. As of

1999 it claimed to have facilitated 120 meetings with top political leaders, including President Bill Clinton, Vice-President Al Gore, Senate Majority Leader Trent Lott, Senate Minority Leader Tom Daschle, and a variety of congressional and state politicians.

TechNet says that its 1999 policy goals include strengthening the research and development agenda in the United States and achieving a permanent research and development tax credit. Protecting and increasing federal research funds is a primary part of the general research and development goal, since these funds have been behind much of the most progressive work within the technological fields. TechNet sees the future of the United States as tied to such federal support, particularly since American (and increasingly global) markets are fueled by technology stocks and the innovation that lies behind them. TechNet also seeks to protect employee ownership incentives for high-tech companies, supporting the maintenance of existing employee stock option accounting standards and seeking to prevent what it sees as unnecessary changes by the Financial Accounting Standards Board (FASB). Other issues of concern for TechNet, on which it is working with its own members and other industry associations, include encryption and Y2K compliance standards for technology companies.

TechNet represents a large percentage of the technology companies responsible for much of the general market growth of the last decade of the twentieth century, and its political and other goals will be rooted in a desire to see this unprecedented growth continue. It will most likely seek influence in the 2000 presidential race, particularly to make candidates aware of the global economic issues affecting the technology markets.

FINANCIAL FACTS

Because the Technology Network is such a new trade organization, it only began to contribute to the campaigns of candidates for federal office during the 1997–1998 Congress-only election cycle. Thus far, its donations remain modest by the standards of the manufacturing sector. In the 1997–1998 election cycle the TechNet political action committee (PAC) gave a total of $42,191 in contributions to congressional candidates and parties, with $13,034 (31 percent) going to Democrats and $29,157 (69 percent) going to Republicans.

JAMES CIMENT AND VIVIAN WAGNER

Bibliography

Birdis, Ted. "Congress Agrees on New High-Tech Laws." *Associated Press,* October 16, 1998.

"Campaign Funding: Gore Goes to the Source." *InformationWeek,* April 12, 1999.

Borland, John. "High-Tech Checkbooks Open for Campaign Season." *TechWeek News,* September 16, 1998.

Mosquera, Mary. "Congress Commits to Long-Term R&D Tax Credit." *TechWeb News,* August 2, 1999.

Reddy, Tarun. "Computing Bill Emphasizes Basic R&D Funding." *Federal Technology Report,* June 3, 1999, p. 3.